Rural Transformation and Newfoundland and Labrador Diaspora

TRANSGRESSIONS: CULTURAL STUDIES AND EDUCATION

Cultural studies provides an analytical toolbox for both making sense of educational practice and extending the insights of educational professionals into their labors. In this context *Transgressions: Cultural Studies and Education* provides a collection of books in the domain that specify this assertion. Crafted for an audience of teachers, teacher educators, scholars and students of cultural studies and others interested in cultural studies and pedagogy, the series documents both the possibilities of and the controversies surrounding the intersection of cultural studies and education. The editors and the authors of this series do not assume that the interaction of cultural studies and education devalues other types of knowledge and analytical forms. Rather the intersection of these knowledge disciplines offers a rejuvenating, optimistic, and positive perspective on education and educational institutions. Some might describe its contribution as democratic, emancipatory, and transformative. The editors and authors maintain that cultural studies helps free educators from sterile, monolithic analyses that have for too long undermined efforts to think of educational practices by providing other words, new languages, and fresh metaphors. Operating in an interdisciplinary cosmos, Transgressions: Cultural Studies and Education is dedicated to exploring the ways cultural studies enhances the study and practice of education. With this in mind the series focuses in a non-exclusive way on popular culture as well as other dimensions of cultural studies including social theory, social justice and positionality, cultural dimensions of technological innovation, new media and media literacy, new forms of oppression emerging in an electronic hyperreality, and postcolonial global concerns. With these concerns in mind cultural studies scholars often argue that the realm of popular culture is the most powerful educational force in contemporary culture. Indeed, in the twenty-first century this pedagogical dynamic is sweeping through the entire world. Educators, they believe, must understand these emerging realities in order to gain an important voice in the pedagogical conversation.

Without an understanding of cultural pedagogy's (education that takes place outside of formal schooling) role in the shaping of individual identity–youth identity in particular–the role educators play in the lives of their students will continue to fade. Why do so many of our students feel that life is incomprehensible and devoid of meaning? What does it mean, teachers wonder, when young people are unable to describe their moods, their affective affiliation to the society around them? Meanings provided young people by mainstream institutions often do little to help them deal with their affective complexity, their difficulty negotiating the rift between meaning and affect. School knowledge and educational expectations seem as anachronistic as a ditto machine, not that learning ways of rational thought and making sense of the world are unimportant.

But school knowledge and educational expectations often have little to offer students about making sense of the way they feel, the way their affective lives are shaped. In no way do we argue that analysis of the production of youth in an electronic mediated world demands some "touchy-feely" educational superficiality. What is needed in this context is a rigorous analysis of the interrelationship between pedagogy, popular culture, meaning making, and youth subjectivity. In an era marked by youth depression, violence, and suicide such insights become extremely important, even life saving. Pessimism about the future is the common sense of many contemporary youth with its concomitant feeling that no one can make a difference.

If affective production can be shaped to reflect these perspectives, then it can be reshaped to lay the groundwork for optimism, passionate commitment, and transformative educational and political activity. In these ways cultural studies adds a dimension to the work of education unfilled by any other sub-discipline. This is what Transgressions: Cultural Studies and Education seeks to produce—literature on these issues that makes a difference. It seeks to publish studies that help those who work with young people, those individuals involved in the disciplines that study children and youth, and young people themselves improve their lives in these bizarre times.

Rural Transformation and Newfoundland and Labrador Diaspora

Grandparents, Grandparenting, Community and School Relations

Edited by;

Amarjit Singh
Memorial University, St. John's, NL Canada

and

Mike Devine
Memorial University, St. John's, NL Canada

SENSE PUBLISHERS
ROTTERDAM/BOSTON/TAIPEI

A C.I.P. record for this book is available from the Library of Congress.

ISBN: 978-94-6209-300-3 (paperback)
ISBN: 978-94-6209-301-0 (hardback)
ISBN: 978-94-6209-302-7 (e-book)

Published by: Sense Publishers,
P.O. Box 21858,
3001 AW Rotterdam,
The Netherlands
https://www.sensepublishers.com/

Printed on acid-free paper

TABLE OF CONTENTS

**From Feeling of Cultural Loss to Nostalgia to Agency (Praxis)
For Sustaining Home and Place**

DR. CLAR DOYLE

PREFACE

The Loneliness of the Long-Distance Family

We have always had a vague sense of the power and the place of grandparents in our lives, family and community. The chapter titles in this telling text spell out for us the wide-ranging scope of that power and place of grandparents.

This book is based on the premise that significant knowledge resides in the local, and in the focused reflection on the local context. When this local reflection and experience is placed in a wider educational perspective valuable intellectual insights are gained and personal information becomes instructive for the wider community. The local becomes global.

This book offers a platform not only to look in on the lives of vital grandparents but paints, in broad strokes, a mural of coming, changing, as well as challenging cultural and social settings. In what the astute editors, Amarjit Singh and Michael Devine, call "small nuanced studies" we find telling narratives of generational connections in the face of changing and challenging odds. The editors write about the "changing patterns of communities" and in the very presentation of the grandparents, who often possess well-honed voices, reinforce the notion that knowledge is local and governed by context. Singh and Devine are very aware of the direct link to and importance of this contextualized production of knowledge. While this linkage can be seen as linear it, in time, becomes embedded in the fabric of our thinking and living. In other words, the voices shared here help produce culture and society. It is, then, part of a moving entity.

This book does a great service to the concept of *diaspora,* as well as to the changing nature of that concept. We often associate diaspora with the image of hordes of people moving from one land to another in quaint ships, seldom to return to the homeland. The fact that we now live in a jet-hopping, tweet-frenzy world does not lessen the pain of dislocation. The voices and stories in this book attest to that. These voices and stories also show that our views of grandparents are changing: their roles are changing. This book elevates the status of grandparents by positioning them as vital members of a complex and challenging society where their skills, gifts, and sheer presence are most formative. In the book Singh and Devine have given opportunities for many people to express their thoughts and put key aspects of their lives in a context that informs the communities where we live.

Some years ago I wrote a play called *Out From Here.* It dealt with out-migration from Ireland in the mid nineteenth century, and out-migration from Newfoundland in the mid twentieth century. While doing the research for that play I was taken by the similarities between the leavings from Ireland and the leavings from Newfoundland. It was sobering to realize that the forces that drove people from Ireland were similar, in kind, to the ones that drove men and women to go to "the Boston states" to make a living and to invent a dream. Like the emigrants from the famine lands many of the emigrants from this place never came back. Many of them, my relatives included, climbed steel and worked on building their individual dreams. That exodus from Ireland is further echoed now as men and women emigrate from Newfoundland and Labrador to do dirty work for great money in Alberta. The diaspora continues.

Nowhere was the reality of outmigration, diaspora if you will, brought home to me as when I did the dedication to that play. It was then that I more clearly saw the raw reality of outmigration: my three children were all gone from here. They left, for other green pastures, between the ages of 18 and 22. Today, they remain away, and like many others I am a long-distance grandparent. Like many others I live the loneliness of the long-distance family.

In the telling and poetic narratives found in this book we probe the meaning of home, place, and belonging. These narratives do not "make fools of writers". These narratives help us see and articulate what we take for granted around us. The eyes of others, notably visitors to this place, can make the sky clearer and the rocks more rigid in their solid wonder. As one writer here said, "imagine that". In scholarly tradition Singh and Devine have noted the themes that emerge from the various narratives. Given the variety and scope of the narratives such elaborated themes are most helpful. These narratives speak eloquently to the power and place of grandparents and to the significance of grand-parenting. Some of the narratives found here reflect a tingle of nostalgia. While the grandparents tell of raising large families, being very busy, working hard, there is a sliver of longing for far off days. While this sentiment is not universal in the narratives shared here, it probably speaks to a sense of belonging, of belonging to this place.

The place of respect given to grandparents as well as the expectations laid on people living in given communities is evident in the narratives. We might say, today, that these communal expectations were somewhat rigid and set the norm for acceptable behaviour. Linked in with expectations and generational norms was the reality of "going away". In time, and maybe always, there was a need for people to move because "you had no choice but to look for employment opportunities elsewhere." Elsewhere, what a word that is. No matter where it was, "elsewhere" was not here, not home, not this place. As John Munn said in the locally produced movie *John and The Missus,* "You're not telling me where to live; you're telling me where to die."

The phrase "emotional comfort" is a telling one when we think about the role of grandparents. I see the need for that emotional comfort with my own children, whose long-distance question often begins with, "How is Nan?" The connection is way beyond expectation or sense of responsibility; it is often a matter of the heart and soul. Another telling aspect found in many of these narratives is how grandparents are able to analyze, reflect on, and articulate their place in the world. Singh and Devine write about "local theorizing". This is it in action.

Another aspect of the narratives in this book is the significance of the physical house, and the notion of "home" [As the little girl in *Yesterday's Men* said, "Yes, we have a home but we don't have a place to put it"]. Likewise, the idea of being connected in a community where "everybody knew everybody" was often depicted by calling people aunt or uncle, who were not related at all. This adopted kinship speaks to the level of connectedness lived in many communities depicted in the narratives here. The sense of disconnectedness felt by many people after they had been "relocated" from isolated communities into larger towns and cities was akin to what people felt who left here to go to New York or who now leave for Fort McMurray. There is often, always, a missing of the vital connectedness of the lost or left community.

The loneliness of the long-distance family is evident in many of the grandparent narratives here. Many people speak of the effort to stay connected, but in many ways digital hugs just don't cut it. As my little grandson said, "Granddad, sometime you must come on the plane with us." When I asked him why, he said, "When I am in England I do not see you." This was for me a fond existential moment!

The studies in this book show that grandparents can be seen as receptacles of community values and as such are generational conduits for such values and cultural capital. This notion of the place of grandparents in passing on values, mores, as well as cultural and social expectations is significant. Many grandparents clearly see this process as part of their "job". Very often while grandparents might be telling about the trappings of culture, for example, "Jiggs Dinner every Sunday", they are in fact sharing more telling and deep-rooted aspects of life having to do with respect, dignity, and responsibility. Gems of foundational wisdom are found in these narratives. So very often the brightest sparks in a grandparent's life is a grandchild: cherished, coddled, loved, and adored.

The narratives in this book acknowledge the changing role of grandparents. Not even the role of grandparent can remain fixed when the community is spinning. There appears to be, according to narratives here, a more increased role for grandparents.

The reality of out-migration, that tangly relative of diaspora, is often referenced by claims like, "many of the young ones are gone away now." There is also an expressed sense, in many of these narratives that when people leave a community, "things are lost." Not least of such loss is the "lack of opportunity for [grandparents] to develop a close relationship and engage in grandparent-grandchild activities." Family is a key part of so many lives. Many of the grandparents given voice in these studies, "loved talking about their families and grandchildren." Grandchildren and the process of grandparenting, is a vital force in many people's lives.

One of the great contributions of the studies presented in this book is the way they help us see grandparents in a positive light. Elizabeth Davis, speaking about elder abuse, claims that helping society change the view of seniors will be a key aspect in curbing such abuse. This book makes a wonderful contribution to such a cause. One other thing this book does is put the whole concept of grandparenting in a historical and social context as well as it reinforces the ideal that "educators should acknowledge the diversity of family structures" that exist today. The whole notion of blended families becomes important when we realize that children from various family clusters are now extending the networks of grandparents. The reality is that children can have many grandparents. This can be both a rewarding and challenging generational reality. As is strongly advocated in this book, it is essential that educators, curriculum developers, and teachers appreciate the place of grandparents in their students' lives. Curriculum has often seen grandparents as sources of information, but they are so much more than that. It is also important to realize that the types of grandparents can have "different and distinct relationships" with their grandchildren. This book, in the sheer variety of relationships represented, is a most helpful view of the diversity mosaic of grandparents. This book continually puts the stated diversity found in grandparenting models into its larger economic and social context. This is crucial to a better understanding of the changing roles of and expectations placed on grandparents. As noted, "Grandparents are a diverse and vibrant group", and seldom represent a uniform "grandparenting style." There are also sobering moments in these narratives. Ones that cover the gamut from ideal grandparenting roles to ones that are tormented by the challenges of their children's lifes: they are all reflected here.

When I reflect on the contributions that grandparents make to families and communities, I am remind of an exercise I sometimes use with drama groups I work with. In that exercise I ask people to "take away" what they have contributed to the play. In short time it becomes evident that if individuals were to take away what they have done to produce the play there would be very little left. In similar fashion, if we were to take away what grandparents have contributed to us and our children we would, I believe, see massive gaps in values, mores, enjoyment, comfort, insights, information, knowledge, materials, kindness, and love. In short, we would be less than we are now.

The Loneliness of the Long-Distance Family

I know it is late but I will call anyway.

One distant night on that Green Island the people put their worry to bed.
They woke the next morning to see their potato plants smitten by the blue fog of blight.
The man-made Famine sneaked into the veins of the land and bled those who walked the soil.
The riddle remains of how the people of a green and fertile country came to starve to death.

I Wonder Why They Are Not Answering the Phone

Emigration went on bleeding Ireland as from a wound that would not heal
And they filled its boats with the people who called this place Talam an Eisc.
Dangling between desperation and hope the Atlantic offered a tumultuous line of promise.
In the crucible of the coffin ship, the children of the Green Island rode the Diaspora onto the wicked seas.
Salt of the Atlantic served as bitter balm for the memories of Famine.
Bold people, in tainted ships, came to this place and heard "welcome".

I Will Let It Ring a Little While More

New people lived the land and mastered the sea.
They fashioned a soul that would soften winters and inject promise.
In time, they became the people of the Rock.
Many of our people saw new horizons and moved from here.
There to build and to grow.
It is said that if my people were to reclaim their building half North America would fall down.

"Is that you Grandad?"

ACKNOWLEDGMENTS

First and foremost we want to thank grandparents in Newfoundland and Labrador who have never ceased to provide support not only to their family members and grandchildren living near ("non-diasporic" grandparents) and far away from them ("diasporic" grandparents), but also to their communities, generation after generation.

A number of people have contributed to this book. We want to thank the many contributors of chapters who have provided excellent work related to the topics of diaspora, grandparenting, community development, schooling, and listening to the voices of grandparents from the field. We feel it is our pleasant duty to record our debts of gratitude to them.

We want to thank John Hoben, Daniel Reid, Clar Doyle, Allyson Hajck, Kirk Anderson, Gord Ralph, Mary Cornelia Power and Joan Oldford for reading the earlier drafts of many of the chapters included in this book. Our special thanks to Clar Doyle for agreeing to write the Preface to this book. Further, we want to thank Rob Greenwood, Director of the Harris Centre, Memorial University, for having conversations with Amarjit at different times. This conversational engagement informed us of current initiatives that are being taken in the area of rural development in Newfoundland and Labrador in the context of regional, national and global policy making, governing, implementing, and evaluating discourses. The conversations helped us to sharpen our thinking and understanding of what needs to be done to sustain rural communities, families, and the life styles they offer to people in this province, in the context of the tensions that exists between lifestyles that are perceived as local and those that are urban and global.

The Faculty of Education and School of Social Work have been places of constant reflection and renewal for Amarjit and Mike, respectively. Colleagues and friends have contributed their time and their thoughts to this book, and the professionals working in the General Office, Financial and Administrative Services, as always, were most helpful and patient. We thank all of them.

We wish to thank our spouses Mary (Amarjit's wife) and Pauline (Mike's wife) for their tireless efforts and support in our completing this work.

I (Amarjit) want to thank my long standing friends Professors Gary and Gerry Gairola in Kentucky, and Ruth Larkin and Mike Hamnett in Hawaii, for encouraging me to continue and complete my various projects. I also want to thank those colleagues and friends who helped me in various ways in my professional and daily life. I know and they know who they are, so I do not need to name them here. I wish to thank Susan Bird and her family, Bowie Hannah, and especially the Power clan (my in-laws in Newfoundland and Labrador) for their help and kindness.

Both of us are grandfathers like many Newfoundlanders and Labradorians, whose grandchildren live far away from them. So like many, we are involved in distant grandparenting. Living in diaspora could be an inspiring experience in a sense that it encourages us all to engage in building and maintaining good, supportive relations with each other.

For me, Amarjit, living in diaspora and doing distant grandparenting has been a good learning process, because my siblings, my deceased parents, my daughter Neera, her husband Mori, and their two daughters - Tala and Uale'a, and my wife Mary C. Power and our son David, have all been a constant source of joy, love and support for me and each other.

For me, Mike, being a grandparent living in diaspora has taught me the value of time and building relationships from afar. My wife, Pauline and I, continually try to ensure connections and relationship development is an ongoing process as we grow with our children (six of them) and our grandchildren (five of them) both in this province and city as well as those in other provinces and other countries - to all of them, our gratitude and love.

Finally, we want to thank our series editor, Dr. Shirley R. Steinberg, http://www.educ.ucalgary.ca/werklund/ Chair and Director, The Werklund Foundation Centre for Youth Leadership Education, Professor of Youth Studies, The University of Calgary, and Project Leader and Director Paulo and Nita Freire International Project for Critical Pedagogy http://freireproject.org. In writing chapters in this book I (Amarjit) I have kept memory of Joe Kincheloe alive in my mind. And we want to thank Michel Lokhorst at SENSE Publishers, for giving us the opportunity to work on this project.

ABOUT THE CONTRIBUTING AUTHORS

People with a variety of backgrounds, professions and experiences have contributed to this book. They include university professors with doctorate degrees, specializing in different academic disciplines; registered Social Workers with BSW and MSW (Bachelor and Master of Social Work) degrees, and retired and practising teachers with M.Ed. (Masters of Education) degree with many years of teaching experience at different levels in the Public School systems in Newfoundland and Labrador, and Nova Scotia, Canada. Most of them work and live, or have worked and lived in small rural communities and have firsthand, nuanced knowledge and sensitivity to daily lived experiences of people living in those communities, including their own experiences.

AMARJIT SINGH & MIKE DEVINE

INTRODUCTION

Wanting to Voice One's Own Stories in Unsettling Conditions

ABSTRACT

In the introductory chapter to our book on the contemporary life of Newfoundland and Labrador grandparents, we set forth our agenda in compiling such a collection. Against a backdrop of globalization, we have chosen to examine the changing role of grandparents in Newfoundland and Labrador society. Despite historically being a rural community, the age of globalism has ushered in a wave of outmigration from this province that has resulted in many families living in diaspora. As a result, these global forces have changed family dynamics as well as the social identity of individuals, families and communities in Newfoundland and Labrador. As 'organic intellectuals' – that is, disseminators of local knowledge and emotional work – grandparents have had a vital role in shaping the culture of Newfoundland and Labrador communities for many generations. The nature of that role has been transformed in recent times, however, under disaporic family conditions necessitated by the modern global economy. By extension, the means in which they produce, reproduce, and transmit local knowledge to both their families and communities has changed. Thus, in this local/global dynamic situation, voices of grandparents have become a significant source of inspiration for those who want to sustain their communities in the era of globalism. As such, in listening to grandparents in this province, a traditionally overlooked social group, one can start to understand the changing nature and complex nuances of family life in communities in transition in Newfoundland and Labrador. Moreover, their voices can not only shed light on the past but also help address the problems and concerns of the present with an eye on shaping the future, within a global context, not only in this province but in similar places across Canada and the rest of the world.

Within the context of rural communities in a local-global society grandparents can play an important role in communities in transition. We suggest that to find answers to problems embedded in the voices of grandparents will require us to engage in a learning process that will require re-thinking in five areas: (a) education and schooling, (b) envisioning diverse life styles available that could be sustainable, (c) the existing programs that provide services to seniors as grandparents, (d) grandparents as leaders, organic workers and intellectuals, and (e) the value of

A. Singh and M. Devine (Eds.), Rural Transformation and Newfoundland and Labrador Diaspora: Grandparents, Grandparenting, Community and School Relations, 1–40.

small scale nuanced and community based research and implication of this type of research to the well-being of grandparents, families, communities and schools.

No space disappears in the course of growth and development: the *worldwide* does not abolish the local (Henri Lefebvre cited in, Wilson & Dissanayake, 1996, p.1).

...return migrants are often pushed or pulled back by economic factors, although ... the pull of personal or family ties is important. (Sinclair & Felt, 1993, p. 21).

...the outport [the small communities in Newfoundland] communities of today are very different...Outport people are...concerned about issues of representation and cultural appropriation...

...outport Newfoundlanders now want to tell their own story. (Kennedy, 1997a, p. 313)

...agency is a central psychological phenomenon that must be accounted for in any explanatory framework of human action. Broadly speaking, psychological agency refers to the human capacity for reflective action, and is based on the potential to imagine and create new ways of being and acting in the world. Further, "the question of agency also relates to how we choose to live our lives and responsibility we have for the decision we make." (Freie 2008, p. 1).

[all] men are intellectuals...but not all men have in society the function of intellectuals (Gramsci, 1971, cited in (Greaves, 2008)

...Intellectuals educate and discipline the entire culture... (p. 16, Ibid)

This book is about the contemporary life of grandparents in Newfoundland and Labrador- their families, schools, and communities. It highlights and celebrates their voices[1] as they live their daily lives in what has historically been a rural society which is rapidly going through economic, social, educational and cultural transformation. Newfoundland and Labrador became a province of Canada in 1949, and it continues to have a distinct culture. This introductory chapter elaborates in some ways on themes cited in the epigraphs.

Although our focus in this book is on grandparents' roles in Newfoundland and Labrador (sometimes referred in this chapter as Newfoundland but is intended to refer to the province of Newfoundland and Labrador), we contend that listening to their voices can shed light on the changing roles of grandparents in many other rural societies going through similar transformation under the influence of the current global economy. The fact is that there are more grandparents living now than before, and in the context of globalization,[2] there is an international trend of grandparents caring for grandchildren.[3] At the same time it is also noted that global forces have profound negative impacts on local rural communities in Newfoundland and Labrador[4] and in other parts of world. Globalism and other ecological factors have created job losses in rural communities in Newfoundland and Labrador, and appear to have accelerated the movement of people who leave this province to make a living. When people anywhere are caught in this sort of movement and psychological disposition – forced to leave their homes and places to go somewhere else to make a living and yet have strong feelings to one day return to their homes – they are said to be living in diaspora. Looking at what is happening around us in Newfoundland and Labrador suggests that many people from this province are now living in diaspora; their relationship with each other in many situations has become diasporic. "This pervasive pressure to leave is often experienced as a painful rupture from home and identity, and this loss is reflected in much Newfoundland literature" (Delisle, 2008a) p. 65.

Anyone who listens to stories of people leaving the province knows that this going away trend has not diminished the strong longing of many people to one day return to Newfoundland and Labrador; that is, their sense of home and place remain strong. In a real sense for many, the ever burning desire to return to Newfoundland and Labrador may never be realized, but their conversations reveal that this nostalgic desire never dies. Delisle (2008, *The Newfoundland Diaspora*) discusses the nostalgia Newfoundlanders feel about "going home". According to her, this "experiential nostalgia" helps displaced Newfoundlanders to define their social self and their personal identities.

A review of studies of various "local" sociologists by Delisle suggests that "… migrants often maintain connections to Newfoundland and Newfoundland culture by preserving ties with people back home, by maintaining a strong desire to return, by consuming Newfoundland products, and by establishing diasporic communities abroad (Delisle, 2008a, p. 65)." According to Delisle (2008a) this Newfoundland diaspora exists in part because Newfoundlanders often find it difficult to assimilate into their new homes in Ontario or Alberta, "…even though they are migrating to these parts of Canada as Canadian citizens (p. 66)." These trends presumably set by the forces of globalization appear to have changed family dynamics, social self and identities of individuals and communities in Newfoundland and Labrador.
In essence,

> Diaspora is both an appropriate and useful term to describe Newfoundland outmigration in that it captures the magnitude of the phenomenon, and connotes what I identify as five main aspects of the migration experience: (1) painful displacement and a condition of loss; (2) the continued connection to homeland; (3) the formation of diaspora communities abroad; (4) the construction of homeland in neo-national rather than regional terms; and (5) a sense of difference and marginalization in the new home. (Delisle, 2008b, *the Newfoundland Diaspora*, p. 8).

Delisle (2008b) indicates that,

> A 'Newfoundland diaspora,' then connotes… [a] continued attachment to homeland, often accompanied by a strong desire to return" (p. 15), and that diaspora,

... signals this [that Newfoundlanders are like any other immigrants working side by side in a factory in Toronto] (imagined or real) shared experience of displacement between Newfoundland migrants and other immigrants. It also suggests an ongoing sense of group identity, and link between these connections and Newfoundland as an imagined community (p. 17).

THE SCOPE OF THIS BOOK

Unsettling Impact of Globalization

Globalization produces unsettling conditions. However, these unsettling conditions have created opportunities to generate new and culturally sensitive local knowledge everywhere in the world to balance the impact of global knowledge which is often not sensitive to local needs. In the same vein, more than ever before, people in Newfoundland and Labrador now have learned to feel confident in their common sense ability to understand how their local society works and how the forces of globalization influence their everyday lives in many spheres (Baldacchino, Greenwood, & Felt, 2009; Felt, 2009; Galway & Dibbon, 2012; Greenwood, 2010; Kelly & Yeoman, 2010).

In the above local/global dynamic situation,[5] voices of grandparents have become a significant source of inspiration for those who want to sustain their communities in the era of globalism. Thus grandparents in Newfoundland communities are a critical and an active force in keeping hope alive in the possibility of the viability and revitalizing of rural communities and the life styles those communities can offer.[6] More specifically, grandparents everywhere make up a diverse and vibrant group of people, and as such grandparents in Newfoundland and Labrador are playing significant roles in keeping families, communities and schools together. Of more significance is the fact that they are playing this role at a very specific time when an increasingly number of individuals from Newfoundland and Labrador are living in diaspora. Therefore, it is important to listen to their voices and incorporate them into any discussion pertaining to imagining future sustainability of rural communities in Newfoundland and Labrador and rethinking of balancing of local/global rural interests. The collection of papers in this volume highlights several of these points.

There has to be a multiplicity of cultural, religious, political, economic and socially conducive conditions that would enable the publics (citizenry and non-experts) to have multiple voices, while at the same time enabling those who are the voices of the dominant forces to listen to the voices of the publics (Curry-Stevens, 2003; Flyvbjerg, 1998; Goodman, 2001; Hobgood, 2000; Mezirow and Associates, 2000). According to some observers this has not been the typical case of Newfoundland and Labrador culture and society. Historically, in Newfoundland and Labrador "outsiders" and a selected few nominated by the dominant forces of the day have been involved in producing knowledge in this province (Baldacchino et al., 2009; J. C. Kennedy, 1997a). Greenwood (2009, p. 281) states, "unfortunately, the province's history and political culture have resulted in a policy environment that limits real participation to very few players." As Greene (1999, p. 3) points out, "Until the founding of Memorial University in 1949, Newfoundlanders were denied the privilege of a post-secondary institution that could develop local studies."

Like the publics in many other countries, the publics in this province have generally been discouraged from producing knowledge based on their daily experiences in the public spheres and civil society,[7] and even reprimanded in certain situation for doing so (Hoban, 2011). On the whole, Newfoundlanders feel intimidated in recording and disseminating their experiential and observation – based knowledge. For example, we noted that one grandparent in one interview was not comfortable with having her story told in print even though no identifying information would be included. In some situations even highly respected local sociologists, with international reputation, felt intimidated while producing local knowledge (personal communication).

Greene (1999, p. 4) writes that, "On the personal level, the individual Newfoundlander, regardless of class, has historically shown an aversion to preserving written records; and the few who were courageous enough to perform the feat have always been denigrated as hoarders." On the other hand, according to Greene, "an oral tradition has held sway for centuries and remains still the richest source available for gaining an understanding of the everyday lives of the people of Newfoundland's past."

This situation has been changing as the number of educated people in this province grows (Galway & Dibbon, 2012; Sheppard, Brown, & Dibbon, 2009). Consequently, more and more people are learning about how "official/state" and "professional" forms of knowledge are socially constructed, preserved and strategically disseminated either to maintain the status quo or to change it (Finlayson, 1994; Neis & Felt, 2000a; A. Singh, 1991). Clar Doyle writes,

> "for many years from its foundations as a colony, Newfoundland remained a place in which creative culture was usually expressed verbally or musically, in the form of oral narratives, traditional drama and theatre, and vocal and instrumental music. Cultures in which oral tradition is strong become fertile ground for the development of written work as formal education improves" (2010, p. 117).

The improvement of formal, in-formal, and non-formal education in this province has contributed to the deepening of consciousness of people in Newfoundland and Labrador more than ever before. People in this province now feel confident in their common and good sense ability as intellectuals.[8] As such, we believe, they now, in more complex ways, understand how their society works and how local and global cultures influence their views and behaviors. For example, for us this trend became clear when, under the umbrella of educational reform in this province, the then existing denominational educational system was dismantled in 1997. Based on their understanding of social and cultural processes, parents, students, teachers, families and communities were able to use their agency in contesting the reorganization of the school system in highly sophisticated ways (Fagan, 2004; Galway & Dibbon, 2012;

McKim, 1988). However, they could not stop the reform that dismantled religious based denominational governance of schools in Newfoundland and Labrador. Never the less, they were able to point out the contradictions and mismatch of the "official" knowledge which guided educational reform (see news items that appeared at that time in the local paper, *Telegram*). Another more recent example includes the attempt by the provincial government to downgrade and reduce services to the Lewisporte area of the province that met with strong community reaction and had positive results. Also, the Hughes inquiry into the sexual and physical abuse of boys at Mount Cashel Orphanage in 1990 was as a result of the populace speaking out and "not putting up with" what was happening within that orphanage.

This changing cultural and social milieu of Newfoundland and Labrador society at the present time interests us the most. Specifically, for our pedagogical purposes in this book, we are interested in the ideas of common sense and good sense as these two concepts relate to the role of intellectual and intelligentsia as social categories in transforming Newfoundland and Labrador society, specifically, the rural sector of the society. Historically, but more recently much has been written and published *about* the possibility and sustainability of rural development in Newfoundland and Labrador (Wadel, 1969, 1973; House, 1999, 2001, 2003). However, in our reading of this literature we find that less emphasis has been generally given to the development for rural communities. Development for communities takes into account in robust ways what development means to members of communities in relationship to what it means to those who are perceived by community members as outsiders having more power and resources. Many societies in the world are rural societies and were colonized. It has been noted that after they emerged as politically independent nations, they adopted anti-rural development models. For example in Asia many people advocated self-reliant national development based on self-sufficient village economy. Their voices were ignored and labeled as backward and utopian by those who pushed for development models based on modernization theories in vogue at that that time. Thus, those who argued for anti-rural development perceived themselves as urban based local elites, intellectuals and intelligentsia, and forged dependent networks with the outside world. And in this way they alienated themselves from a great number of people who continued to live in the rural areas.

The anti-rural development models have many components. One of the principle components is the emphasis on central planning, control and coordination of the economy as a top down process. We will have more to say about the notion of modernity, globalization, role of intellectuals and intelligentsia in relation to the discussion of possibility of viable rural development in Newfoundland and Labrador in the last chapter of the book. Suffice to mention here is that many of the principles of Western modernity conceived as the universal project still echo in the thinking of rural policy and development practitioners and scholars in Newfoundland and Labrador and other rural locations in Canada. To be sure Newfoundland and Labrador has gone through the process of "nation-building" using modernization discourse as the main rationalization for doing so, especially after 1949 when it became the tenth province of Canada. This is not to say that those who have been engaged in this process have not gone beyond the thinking of modernity and modernization theories that were so prevalent in their dominating forms just after the time most countries became politically independent in Asia and Africa and started the process of nation-building. Historically, Newfoundland and Labrador has had pockets of 'resistance' to change and locals have successfully fought against change. Fogo Island is one such example. When the now infamous resettlement model was mostly forced upon rural and remote communities, Fogo Island people clearly and loudly said; "NO", and the people continue today to reside on this rural and remote island. Most recently (March, 2013), the provincial government increased its "incentives" for rural and remote community residents to relocate by more than doubling the financial packages available to them. The recent engagement of rural policy and development practitioners and scholars in Newfoundland and Labrador attests to this fact. These people are committed to Newfoundland and Labrador as place "… and the identity and social relationships that go with it that make rural communities and small, often islands, jurisdictions desirable and viable places for long term sustainable development" Baldacchino et al., (2009, ix-x). This increase in rural development literature has been, we believe and one can observe this trend, due to the emergence of certain types of intelligentsia and intellectuals in Newfoundland and Labrador in the last three decades.

This recent development mentioned above raises questions relating to functions of emerging intellectuals engaged in the development of society and culture in Newfoundland and Labrador at the present and of those who would function as intellectuals in future. According to many writers, there are many different and specific types of intellectual and intelligentsia in all societies in any given time (Aronowitz & Giroux, 1985; Ball, 1995; Doyle, 2010; Eyerman, 1987; Fuller, 2005; Giroux, 1999; Giroux, 2012; Gramsci, 1971; Llyod, 1983; Wright, 1978). Moreover, these writers claim that specific types of intellectuals and intelligentsia play different roles in transforming a society and culture in a specific direction in a given social-cultural-economic- political context. Thus both these types of people, according to these writers, are involved in the construction of knowledge and identity in their own self-images. Greaves (2008, p. 1) investigates Gramsci's theory of intellectuals and its relationship to the development of social self, and explains that, "…the concept of self is mediated in historical processes characterized by iniquitous social relations. It is not just a question of 'who we are' but also to what we attribute our loss of self?" Further, Greaves points out that" for Gramsci we are 'makers of ourselves,' but what have we made? Self-knowledge depends in, turn on gaining knowledge of the historical process in which our identity is constructed." And for Gramsci "intellectuals have had a vital role in history but this function reaches a zenith of sophistication in the capitalist era" (Greaves 2008, p. 2). Further, aspects of discourse on the social function of various types of intellectuals by these writers implies that citizens need to be alert or adopt an attitude which allows them to be critical or vigilant of the ways professional social science and state knowledge, produced by varieties of experts as intellectuals, is transformed into some kind of higher status knowledge that becomes untouchable by ordinary citizens. Specifically, in relation to the policy making process, the role of the experts as intellectuals, and their use of scientific rationality in the decision making process often becomes untouchable to the publics. So, it requires that citizens be familiar with at least some aspects of the on-going discourses. In this situation, citizens need to develop abilities and self-concepts that allow them to recognize how social science and professional knowledge can be given some sort of mythical status and how these forms of knowledge could become a source of symbolic violence. Therefore, social science and state knowledge, and social scientists can be and ought to be subjected to moral and ethical judgements without challenging the objectivity of social science research (Sen, 1983). As a category of intellectuals, social scientists, their products (intellectual capital) and the process of intellectual labor (i.e., how they choose questions, the priorities of their research, the selection of findings, and the publicity they give to their conclusions) are often open to normative scrutiny of their peers. But scientific actions — like all other actions, should be open to public scrutiny as well. This means that the work by social scientists is not above the collective social conscience of the larger society, i.e., it is not above the collective insights (amateur theories) ordinary citizens have about their environment and everyday living. These issues related to the production of knowledge by experts should be debated openly and citizens should have opportunities to participate in such debates. The media can play an important role in this effort. Also, public forums in the form of conferences, seminars, etc., could create opportunities for citizens and experts to discuss these matters openly through having dialogues with each other. This process of interaction and communication may make all involved feel empowered, i.e., individuals and groups may end up having some sense of power or control over their lives, by reducing real or perceived power gaps among them (ordinary citizens, professional practitioners and researchers working for the states and other private organizations), or may have potential to do so. It is hoped that under such conditions, any expected social and cultural change becomes meaningful to the publics. Further, participating in group discussions freely, responsibly, with a high degree of social consciousness enhances and strengthens democratic political systems as well as democratic life styles of citizens.

Aronowitz and Giroux (1985) discuss functions of many types of intellectuals in today's societies. According to them, unlike other intellectuals, transformative intellectuals engage themselves in creating conditions in schools, families and communities where new values and beliefs can be produced. This process in turn, they believe, will provide opportunities for younger generations as citizens in the larger society to become agents of civic courage who will not give up hope of changing institutions of society. By making despair unconvincing, the citizens will engage in activities which will make society more open, equal and just, and produce a democratic society which celebrates human dignity. We will have more to say about the functions of intellectuals in Newfoundland and Labrador in the last chapter in the book.

In our thinking, grandparents in general in all societies and cultures play multiple roles as organic intellectuals. Thus, from the very beginning in our approach to editing this book, we have seen grandparents in Newfoundland and Labrador as organic or transformative intellectuals. As such, this group of people is a reservoir of stories (see John Hoben's, Pauline Lake's, Pauline Finlay's and other articles in this book). If people only listen to grandparents, instead of just hearing them, the listeners will realize that grandparents stories tell us many things: under what conditions we as people in Newfoundland and Labrador grew up, what we have made of ourselves, and what we have lost and are losing in Newfoundland and Labrador – the place we love the most and do not want to leave, and the values and the culture of this land and its people. Their stories tell us what we need to sustain, and how to sustain what we desire having. As editors we are claiming here that, as organic intellectuals, grandparents have had a vital role in the history of development of communities and families in Newfoundland and Labrador, and in the reinforcing of the culture of the time. They continue to play this role even today through story telling. Grandparents as organic intellectuals in this province are vital actors in explaining to the younger generation of today and of the future about the potential of young generations in deciding what type of social self and identity they would want to develop – the social self and identity that would enable them in imagining and in making of Newfoundland and Labrador in that self-image. The readers will find that stories told by grandparents in many chapters in this book document this fact. Here we are also claiming that there is fundamental difference between the notion of listening and hearing. Listening requires paying attention to the voices of those who are speaking without any stereotypes and prejudices (e.g., a sense of empathy). It is trying to understand the deep meaning located in the voice of a person who is speaking, without imposing one's own interpretations of the speaking person's voice. Listening is only fully possible when a person feels safe to communicate with others what is in her/his mind. For these and other reasons, the authors in this book highlight the voices of grandparents in their respective chapters and leave interpretation of grandparents' voices, in large part, to the reader (Fook, 2012; Van Manen, 1997). Thus the voice of each grandparent is valued as it helps illuminate the meanings the grandparents attach to the shared experiences with their family members and communities in Newfoundland and Labrador.

Besides, in their later years of life grandparents play their roles in day to day living within a web of intersecting relations to their family members, who live near to them in varying but mostly rural communities, and also to those family members who live away from them in diaspora. In addition to playing grand parenting roles, one of the other significant intersecting relations grandparents have with their families and communities, entails focusing on their part, on needs and desires concerning their own overall wellbeing in later stages of life. These needs and desires are associated with living and ending one's life in terms of developing some personal and cultural perspectives on death and dying, and with one's sense of happiness and evaluation of life-long accomplishments and contribution in all spheres of life-social, political, psychological, spiritual, and economic. Thus the process of listening to stories of grandparents, and for that matter listening to life stories of anyone else, is a very complex undertaking. Here we are agreeing with ideas of those who research, write, teach and act believing that listening to others always has meaning and makes sense in specific situations and contexts. Through this process of contextual listening the authors in this book have collected more than one hundred and fifty-six direct quotes from grandparents of different backgrounds. Most of these quotes appear in many chapters in this book. These direct quotes represent the voices of grandparents, represent their concerns, and throw light on their grand parenting styles, hopes and suggestions.

Today in Newfoundland and Labrador many grandparents have higher education in a variety of professions and occupations. How these highly educated grandparents function today as intellectuals in relation to their grown up children will have profound impacts on their grandchildren and great-grandchildren in the future when their adult children set up their own households and become grandparents in the next twenty to thirty years. There are many grandparents in this group of intellectuals who have become diasporic grandparents because their children have moved away from this province to find work in other places with their families. These grandparents have become "distant grandparents" and are engaged in grand parenting roles from a distance. Singh and Oldford in the last chapter in this book write about future grandparents in Newfoundland and Labrador and what impacts they might have on their children. Many of the young adults of today, who would be grandparents in the next thirty years or so, are still deeply in love with Newfoundland and Labrador as home, place, and its beauty and safety. One can say that the parents and grandparents of these current young adults of today have done a good job in reinforcing Newfoundland and Labrador cultural values and identity among their children and grandchildren as Newfoundlanders. The questions Singh and Oldford raise in the last chapter are: Would these young adult as grandparents become diasporic grandparents, that is, would they end up living in diaspora like many grandparents of immigrant communities in North America do? Would they hold to unique Newfoundland individual identity or expand their "social self? Would this expanded social self enable them to be "local/global cosmopolitan Newfoundlanders and Labradorians" (LGCNL), as they have tried to imagine them to be in their last chapter? What implications, if any, might this new expanded self concept have on issues related to revitalization of rural communities in Newfoundland and Labrador? Would there be possibility of some sort of different forms of return migration and remittance process, different from what exists today? Would these new migration patterns fuel new type of local/global transformation of rural communities as it is happening in some other parts of the world?

Helen Buss (1999) in her book and the chapter in this book, and aspects of the research carried out by Jennifer Bowering Delisle, reviewed in the beginning of this chapter, shed light on the issues raised above. Singh and Oldford engage again with these questions in the last chapter of this book. They discuss the conditions in which it might be possible for future grandparents in Newfoundland and Labrador to develop Newfoundland and Labrador local global cosmopolitan social self (NLLGC), and thus become "local/global cosmopolitan Newfoundlanders." They work on this idea based on common sense knowledge and a perspective in social sciences, according to which the individual and society cannot be separated. They are interdependent on each other through a web of relationships. Both the individual and the society have many "social selves". The social self of a person changes with changes in her/his social experiences, aspirations, and expectations in a society which provides one with new opportunities and rewards. Thus, in turn, equipped with new experiences individuals bring about changes in the "collective social self" of a society, albeit, in many different shades (Aboulafia, 2001; R. Frie, 2008; Giddens, 1990; Giddens, 1991; Kaufman, 2003; Mills, 1971; Odin, 1996; Popkewitz, 2008; Vohs & Finkel, 2006; Zurcher, 1977).

Globalization, Loss, Creativity, Imagination, Hope and New Opportunities

The needs of globalization also trigger interest in creativity, imagination, and room for wonder for adequately responding to new challenges. Kelley and Yeoman (2010, p. 5) write that,

> ...as the twenty-first century unfolds, citizens worldwide grapple with unprecedented social and cultural changes and the challenging consequences these imply for the future. Locally and globally, many cultural workers – scholars, artists, writers, educators – agree on the importance of reconciling change, both through an estimation of the gains and losses accrued and by contemplating ways to move forward progressively and wisely in their wake. Given such a context, it is not surprising that a scholarship has emerged that investigates the nature of loss and addresses its charged and complex dynamic in productive, hopeful terms.

In this situation the voices of the grandparents and efforts of the contributors to this book in recording the voices of grandparents, and thus producing local knowledge, also celebrate the hope, creativity, imagination, and the possibility[9] of revitalizing of rural communities' cultural and life styles in the era of increasing "McDonaldization", "glocalization", "space war", and "grobaliztion" of nothing.[10] All the authors in this book discuss some reasons for grandparents' increased engagement at various sites[11] in enhancing the well-being of all members of their communities and families, as these grandparents also try to optimize their own well-being in the later years of life.[12] Doyle & Hoben (2011, p. 1) remind us that "as the voice of possibility, the imagination reminds us that control is never complete." As noted in the epigraph, Henri Lefebvre states that "no space disappears in the course of growth and development: the worldwide does not abolish the local" cited in Wilson & Dissanayake (1996), p. 1.

Also, the fact that no space completely disappears in the course of globalization and its overwhelming control over the development processes, is perhaps due to the ability of people and their imagination to produce local knowledge, which is unique to every culture or society: elders and the young possess various types of knowledge; women and men, farmers, fishers and merchants, schooled and not schooled people, all have different kinds of knowledge. In the context of interaction between global/local forces, people all over the world are engaged in simultaneously producing new local knowledge and preserving the local knowledge already possessed by them. They want to do this, among other things, to negotiate the direction of changes ushered by the forces of global modernity and the perceived undesirable impact these forces have on their social self and life styles (Giddens, 1990, 1991). As in other rural communities world-wide, people in rural communities in Newfoundland and Labrador want to produce their own version of local/global knowledge (Kennedy, 1997b, p. 313). In the tradition of social science research the work of many local researchers has emphasized the importance of the local (Felt, 2009; Fowler, 2007; Gmelch & Richling, 1988; Hiller & Franz, 2004; House, 1999; Kennedy, 1997a; Marlor, 2004; Mayda, 2004; Mills, 1971; Neis & Felt, 2000b; Neis, ; Newell & Ommer, 1999; Noel, 1971; R. Ommer & Sinclair, 1999a; R. Ommer & Sinclair, 1999b; R. Ommer, 2004; R. E. Ommer, 2002; Overton, 1985; Richling, 1985a, b; G. M. Sider, 2003; G. Sider, 1986; P. Sinclair & Ommer, 2006; Wade, 1973; Wadel, 1969; Welbourn & McGrath, 1996; Hanrahan, 1993; Byron, 2003).[13] Lawrence Felt points out that work of these local researchers cited here "...has revealed a complexity and resiliency in rural communities..." (Felt, 2009, p. 149). This book highlights, in local contexts, the voices and self-images of grandparents and their grand parenting styles in Newfoundland and Labrador. In this sense, we hope it reflects the character of Newfoundland and Labrador's resilient, innovative, diverse and optimistic people and their longing to stay at the place they call home.

Impetus to Conceive This Book

The impetus to produce this book, in part, comes from our desire as educators to produce "local knowledge" to meet the demands of local people, as well as of our students whom we teach in the contexts of multicultural societies and classrooms. As educators we have been engaged over the years in a larger pedagogical project.[14] We have been interested in the question: How could something that is "local", perceived "desirable" and "sustainable" be promoted and legitimized in the age of "globalism"? In our teaching and learning we have engaged ourselves and our students with discourses in the following areas: aging, globalization, social gerontology, micro and macro social work practice (with individuals, families, groups and community), Diaspora studies, transnationalization, and school-community-family relationships,[15] social change, and formation of the social self. Our current focus is on the changing patterns of Newfoundland and Labrador communities, especially the changing roles of grandparents and grand parenting practices in the context of globalization, and concomitant processes of "glocalization". Our students come from diverse backgrounds and bring with them rich social and cultural capital. In many cases they are directly involved in care giving to their own growing children, aging parents, aunts and uncles, and grandparents. We also teach courses to students who become professional teachers at all levels in the public school system, and who work in the areas of social work, community development, health care delivery systems, and who specialize in other academic disciplines. Many of our students pursue specialized higher education. These students bring with them field-based practical knowledge and experiences. Their field-based practical knowledge enables them to couch their voices in subtle nuances of everyday lived experiences. Students demand that this form of nuance based practical knowledge should be recognized in the development of curriculum[16] at all levels of training and educational institutions.

Thus, in producing this book, the contributors have tried to heed students' advice and voices in a variety of ways. They recognize the impact of the dynamics of local/ global forces on their own daily lives and on the roles grandparents are playing in this province. The authors are also conscious of the importance of local knowledge and local theorizing.[17] With such understanding the contributors to this book have produced local knowledge in the form of small nuanced studies,[18] based on their observations and experiences, while at the same time reflecting on life experiences of people living in small communities who are in constant communication with each other in the age of globalization dominated by the culture-ideology of consumption.[19]

Chapter Outline and Emerging Themes

We have thought of putting this book together within the perspective of reflective and critical pedagogy, and mainly for teaching, reading, and pedagogical purposes. In organizing the material in this book we make use of a number of pedagogical tools. The concept of voice as one of the critical pedagogical tools provides an anchor to various narratives that contributing authors have included in their respective chapters to this book. These authors have listened to grandparents' stories in the natural contexts of community and family settings. Through this process of contextual listening the authors in this book have collected more than one hundred and fifty-six direct quotes from grandparents of different backgrounds. Most of these quotes appear in many chapters in this book. These direct quotes represent the voices of grandparents, their concerns, and throw light on their grand parenting styles, hopes and suggestions for the well-being of their families and communities. Finally, in organizing the content of chapters we have identified forty one themes that have emerged from voices of grandparents found in various narratives. We list them in Appendix "A". We hope that this will give readers a taste of the voices of grandparents scattered throughout different chapters in the book. In this introductory chapter we have discussed some aspects of larger perspectives on globalization and development of rural Newfoundland and Labrador society and drawn comparison to other such rural societies elsewhere in transition. We also hope that readers will enjoy and relish grandparents' voices more fully when reading them in specific family and community contexts.

One of the underlying ideas in organizing material for this book has been that it is not only for people in small rural communities in Newfoundland, but for people in other rural communities globally who are experiencing rapid change, that the issues of self-representation and cultural appropriation have become very critical. They want to self-represent themselves in areas such as sustainability of their communities, families, lifestyle choices, cultural values, and for their very survival in term of being a distinct political, social and economic entity in the context of globalization; people all over the world desire, imagine, observe, plan, and act self-consciously, albeit in varying degrees, to sustain and expand some aspects of the local place and space in their own individual and collective self-images. The active, engaged, and entangled voices and practices of grandparents recorded and presented in this book can be seen as testimony to those concerns. Another underlying idea has been that, by listening to the voices of grandparents in Newfoundland, it can also shed light on the changing roles of grandparents in many other rural societies going through similar transformation in other provinces in Canada, and in other parts of the world as well. For this reason, we have included two chapters that include small-scale nuanced studies from Nova Scotia for sensitizing purposes. Further, readers will find that voices of grandparents are embedded in chapter content describing their experiences of school, family, community, and economic activities. The small scale nuanced studies discussed in each chapter serve to complement and deepen the meaning of other research-based content in each chapter with authentic and personally articulated experiences of grandparents.

In this book we have encouraged contributing authors to write from multiple perspectives in capturing the voices of grandparents in the context of everyday living. The authors have produced narratives that highlight the place of grandparents in families and communities that are transforming rapidly. In producing various narratives the authors have combined relevant multidisciplinary professional knowledge with their common and good sense experiences of everyday life in Newfoundland and Labrador. In this sense they have produced nuanced local knowledge with global implications.

In terms of specific steps taken in organizing this book, as editors we have done the following: first, as we expected, all contributors in their respective chapters provide a relatively extensive list of references, endnotes, relevant statistics taken from various sources and review of research carried out both at micro and macro levels in different areas of interest to them and to the larger publics at national, regional and global levels. Secondly, in today's society it has become common practice that in everyday discourses on various issues people frequently use such key words (Williams,1983) as modernity, modernization, progress, globalization, market, consumer culture, information age, post-modern society, diversity, identity, difference, racism, immigrants, multiculturalism, local and global culture, virtual reality, and other key words like these to make their points and arguments to persuade others to see and understand the "real world" from their own personal and collective perspectives (Mullaly, 2010). Thus different people with varied backgrounds have conversations which vary in levels of complexity and meanings, often ridden with conflicting interests and goals (Brah, 1996; Giddens, 1999). Often, people in their daily lives attribute their own common sense meanings to these key words. To be sure, everyone is not always looking only for differences. Some individuals are also looking for "unity in diversity", and want to "embrace the local and the global" (Giroux, 1993). For these and other reasons, we have added an extended list of endnotes to this introduction. These endnotes provide definition and meanings of some key concepts from the perspectives of well-known Western researchers and scholars in social sciences. These scholars, along with the general public, are interested in making good sense of common sense knowledge as public intellectuals (see Endnote 8). This they do by offering the publics a bigger framework to interpret every day experiences. We suggest that the material provided in the endnotes may be used as a pedagogical resource and guide by those who may want to expand their interests in issues discussed in this book further, and who might find themselves having a desire to know a particular topic in greater depth in a comparative and academic discourse framework. Here we are claiming that individuals will be in a good position to make sense of their surroundings if they feel comfortable communicating with each other by using everyday language and mixing it with the language of the professions, and the state (see Endnote 14). Thirdly, as editors we have encouraged all the contributors to write in a language accessible to all stakeholders and the general publics, such as family members and grandparents themselves who may not relish excessive specialized social science language and the language of the "experts" and "researchers" (Mills, 1971; Smith, 2002 ; Habermas, 1981, 1985). Those who are interested in the language used by social scientists, and who relish such language may find the material presented in the endnotes of some help. Fourthly, in the end of each chapter as another pedagogical tool, a number of reflection questions are listed. These questions, we hope, will lead readers to further inquiry, reflection and guided observations of grandparents' role as leaders engaged in mediating process of rural transformation with the goal of sustaining the local.

A Quick Overview of Changing and Multiple Roles of Grandparents

Like others, grandparents have to interact with different people in their everyday lives. Grandparent roles may include looking after the grandchildren, dealing with their own children and their spouses, in-laws, and school personnel, being aware of the provincial laws and services available and knowing grandchildren's friends. In addition, grandparents may also have relationships and struggles with their own parents and siblings as well as members of the community; these are not easy and straightforward tasks.

Caring for grandchildren also involves grandparents reflecting on their own later years of life, looking after their own health, spiritual and general well-being needs, wants and desires. Grandparents also struggle with understanding the social, political, cultural and technological changes that are taking place due to globalization and the impact of these forces on their communities and on the life styles of families, children and grandchildren. It is within the context of these multiple, complex changes that grandparents continue to develop their role throughout this stage in their life.

Grandparents also may have to deal with many conflicting situations involving all those other parties interested in the well-being of their grandchildren. This may be due to the fact that, like any group, grandparents as a group are not homogeneous. There is a great degree of difference and diversity in the opinions and life styles of grandparents. Many of today's grandparents are relatively young, well-educated, both cosmopolitan and local in outlook, and consumers of a variety of goods and services in their own right.

Some of these conflicts can be seen in the voices of grandparents which the contributing authors have documented in their respective papers. Differences of perceptions, for example, between grandparents and their children about what is nutritious food may cause conflict. How much should grandparents exert their opinions in opposition to grandchildren's mothers' opinion when it comes to disciplining the grandchildren? Should children be allowed to sleep when lights are on? Are grandparents spoiling the grandchildren with excessive care and loving them too much? Can grandparents discipline their grandchildren for excessive use of technology at home and at school, for example, use of IPods? Often grandparents express that they want to "be there" for their adult children and grandchildren, if they want or accept their involvement.

Grandparents, in their relationships with others, also need to understand the global context. A number of steps need to be taken to achieve this understanding. All parties need to understand and to contextualize emerging patterns of family structures in Newfoundland and Labrador. Also, they need to be aware of the dynamics of different types of families in Newfoundland and Labrador and the roles of grandparents in them. In addition, they need to imagine creating social and material conditions for further investigating the nature of the contemporary global trends by trying to understand the relevance of past meanings of Newfoundland and Labrador culture and society. Is it possible and relevant to uncritically continue to transmit local skills and knowledge from grandparents to children and grandchildren? Is it possible to persuade grandchildren and parents not to eat fast-food in the age of McDonaldization? To what extent is it desirable to expect grandchildren to accept rural life styles of Newfoundland and Labrador?

Investigating the nature of the contemporary global trends by trying to understand the relevance of past meanings of Newfoundland and Labrador culture and society, we believe, will enable grandparents to negotiate[20] with their families, their grandchildren, and the larger society and culture- both local and global – a meaningful orientation to spend the later years of their lives either in usual, optimal or pathological ways.

The stereotypical negative beliefs about the elderly and grandparents, based on an ideology of ageism, is that, as a group, they are lazy, disengaged, sick, a burden on families and a financial drain to society. However, research and common sense experience provides ample evidence that this is not always the case. The elderly and the grandparents, both as groups and individuals, are active participants, in their own special ways, in carving out the outcomes of their later years of life; quality of individual aging encompasses both an individual's orientation to the aging process and her/his definition of the family and community circumstances in which getting older is taking place. For example, Singh and associates (Singh, Kinsey, & Morton, 1991; Singh & Kinsey, 1993) studied lay health and self-care beliefs and practices of the elderly in four communities, including two communities in Newfoundland, and found that "lay persons [the elderly, most of them were also grandparents] are not only consumers of professional care, but are actively involved in the process of providing primary health care (p. 224)."

On the whole, as Singh, and Mehta (2008, pp. 126–127) point out, "…we should be sensitive to the idea that people [in different cultures] attach different meanings to old age; that they experience old age in varying ways depending upon their interactions with other people; and that the interactional context and process can significantly affect the kind of aging process a person will experience". Further, Singh and Mehta note that, "…old age is experienced in one's cultural contexts. Therefore, the importance of social context, cultural meanings, and values to the aging process should be kept in mind. All these factors are dynamic rather than universal or unchanging. Disengagement, low self-esteem, and dissatisfaction are an outcome of the interpretation and meanings generated in interaction between the aged and others". Another point to keep in mind, according to Singh and Mehta, is that, "…when dealing with the elderly [grandparents], given that participants vary in their commitments and the importance they attach to different issues and interactions, the diversity of outcomes should be kept in mind. Individuals of different social, economic, ethnic, racial and cultural backgrounds have different interests that may affect how they experience and react to aging [grand parenting]."

With regard to relationships with grandchildren, grandparents expressed high commitment to their grandchildren, which was also supported in earlier studies (Devine & Earle, 2011). For their own (adult) children, grandparents were also highly committed. The dynamics of the relationships in a change context were interesting in that adult children express the need for independence but will sometimes "pull in" the grandparents when a crisis arises, for example. It is this distancing and then being pulled in that creates tensions and the potential conflicts in grandparent to adult children relationships.

We hope that these papers will illuminate the importance of taking seriously the role of grandparents in helping Newfoundland and Labrador families, communities and schools in raising grandchildren in the present context in which increasing number of people from Newfoundland are living in diaspora-that is moving back and forth between their communities and places of work away and still maintaining their families intact, in a hope of returning to their communities permanently in near future.[21]

What Do We Need to Do in Newfoundland and Labrador?

Grandparents' voices as documented in this book give us, admittedly, partial glimpses of complex aspects of family lives as lived by people in Newfoundland and Labrador. Nevertheless they provide insights that can serve as the basis for us to raise several questions about the future of rural communities in transition in Newfoundland and Labrador. We suggest that to find answers to problems embedded in the voices of grandparents will require us to engage in a learning process that will require re-thinking in five areas: (a) the education system, (b) envisioning diverse life styles available that could be sustainable, (c) the existing programs that provide services to seniors as grandparents, (d) grandparents as leaders, and (e) the value of small scale nuanced and community based research and implication of this type of research to the wellbeing of grandparents, families, communities and schools.

(a)   *The education system*

The education system seems mostly geared to socializing the younger generation as individuals to participate in the economic system mostly as consumers, and not so much as citizens who are equipped with conceptual tools and with moral and ethical predispositions to ask: Are the contemporary consumption oriented life styles sustainable? (Lauder, Brown, Dillabough & Halsey, 2006). What is the future of family and community relations in a consumer oriented society and culture? Are we simply consumers of social services or do we have a voice in the levels of services as well as their accessibility, particularly within a rural context?

Newfoundland and Labrador society is seen as a rural society in transition. Therefore, it is important to re-think the dominant model of a consumption oriented educational system if we want to preserve the positive aspects of Newfoundland and Labrador society and culture, and at the same time reduce the possibility of the number of young adults who are forced to leave Newfoundland as home and live in diaspora, perceived as loss. Kelly (2009) writes that,

> …a reconceptualization of loss as a central and explicit component of an education that addresses the concerns of rurality enhances our understanding of what is possible. While it is important to understand the sociological conditions that frame the *physical* mobility of rural people, it is just as important to consider its affective, even psychic, dimensions as mobility relates to attachment, to belonging, to transience – and to loss. For whether one stays in or leaves a rural area (and the oscillations of mobility and transience are rarely so simply demarcated), indeed, regardless of geographical place attention to such affective dimensions, what William Pinar (1991) calls 'a social psychoanalysis of place' (p. 165), can reap rich insights into both the challenges and possibilities for education and /in rurality (p. 1).

Further, she states that

...an education that might begin to address the needs of places must first of all resist simplistic binaries of identity and locale, and ask broader questions about loss, vulnerability, and difference, and what these suggest for a *new* project of conviviality and sustainability within rurality. Such an education asks students to consider the responsibilities and challenges of staying and leaving and to understand the condition of citizenships and attachment (pp. 1–2).

We may add that such an education would also encourage educated people to reflect on the meaning of functioning both as public intellectuals and intelligentsia in different situations creatively and imaginatively (See endnotes 5, 6, 8 & 17).

(b)   *Envisioning diverse life styles available that could be sustainable*

There are many other learning models of encountering different and diverse life styles available that could be sustainable. Those learning models suggest, by implication, that new visions of local and cosmopolitan values and beliefs can be incorporated into reformulating social policy and programs for the young and aging population, and into implementing and evaluating those policies and programs. There seems to be spaces that are in-between the consumer society and sustainable life styles that could be realized through new ways of re-learning. For example, as a province Newfoundland and Labrador is becoming an "aging society", while at the same time it is experiencing labor shortages. Taking these two facts and other factors such as the prevalence of out-migration into account, businesses, educational institutions, professional and non-professional, non-governmental, and governmental agencies are taking new initiatives to attract locals and immigrants to participate in the labor market at the local level. In this context retired people, those who are preparing to retire, and their families are re-learning the meaning of retirement and the aging process in general. Specifically, they appear to be increasingly becoming aware of various perspectives on the aging process. We have already alluded to some aspects of this process in this chapter (see endnote 12) and elsewhere (Singh & Martin, 1982; Singh, 1982a; Singh, 1982b). Various initiatives are basically directed to an older workforce (50 to 70 plus). The goal is to explain to them that life does not end with retirement, and that there are businesses and organizations out there in Newfoundland and Labrador ready to re-hire them after retirement, many offering flexible work environments. In this sense, the basic idea behind these initiatives is to inform people that there are many alternatives to stereotypical ideas of aging. For example, to optimize one's aging process, one could learn to aspire and prepare oneself to find another occupation after retirement. These initiatives are new in this province (MacEachern, 2012). The trend to re-hire workers from an older workforce is well entrenched in many other countries and provinces. The flip side of this trend is that businesses are often looking for cheap labor in a global economy dominated by neo-liberal ideology to maximize their profits, usually disregarding issues pertaining to social justice (Noddings, 2005). From our perspective, the success of these initiatives would depend upon to the extent to which re-hiring policy of various stakeholders remain sensitive to the vexing issues surrounding the notion of social justice as it relates to the aged population in particular. In the absence of such sensitivity we imagine these initiatives could pit the young against the old Newfoundlanders and Labradoreans, and locals against the immigrants.

(c)   *The existing programs that provide services to the seniors*

As editors of this book we believe that to begin this learning process, the existing programs that are designed to provide services to the seniors (the elderly) in Newfoundland and Labrador may consider creating such in-between spaces (spaces between local and global contexts, see endnotes 5, 7, 8 & 11) within them, where the focus could be exclusively given to those seniors who are also grandparents, and whose families live in diaspora. Grandparents play a significant role by providing crucial and needed services to their families, especially to their diasporic ones. It is good to note global trends when considering the roles grandparents play in families that are going through rapid transformation. For example, grandparents in different countries are now advocating that they should be paid for the services they provide to grandchildren and their own adult children in the tough economic times, and that they should offer themselves for rent to families, schools, communities, and to the state and non-government organizations for valuable services they can provide based on their experience and knowledge. They believe these services have economic values which should be openly acknowledged publically and taken into economic planning and policy making processes. Their services should not be seen as a source of cheap labor similar to those that immigrants provide, and to "un-paid" labor provided by women all over the world to sustained the global economy – the economy that has still to figure out how to respond to issues related to social justice. Lest we forget, there is an increased prevalence of elder abuse- locally, nationally, and globally. Many grandparents are abused and exploited all over the world for various reasons.[22]

The issue of grandparents as a 'resource' is one that has a particular history in the Newfoundland and Labrador context. In situations where adult children have been unable to provide care to their own children, the state has historically provided programs and services for the children to reside with their grandparents. The historical context and underlying values have been those of providing 'free' care; the state providing minimal supports to the grandparents intended to cover only basic costs – the notion of providing care for altruistic reasons or being viewed as a family responsibility – global neoliberal ideology. Recently, the province has increased its support to such grandparents (and other relatives) which is more reflective of an acknowledgement of the value of the care provided, but also, possibly reflecting the realities of the challenges to provide out of home placements for children.

Meanwhile, consideration may be given to designing other new programs that aim just to create safe spaces where friends and family members could listen sympathetically to the voices of the seniors, both grandparents and those who are not grandparents. For we witnessed not only in Newfoundland and Labrador but also elsewhere, that listening to the voices of seniors, as opposed to merely hearing their voices, in their later years of life, enhances their physical health, along with their spiritual and general well-being. This viewpoint is also supported by research in social gerontology. (Attar-Schwartz, Tan, Buchanan, Flouri, & Griggs, 2009; Devine & Earle, 2011; Singh, Amarjit and Mehta, Kalyani., 2008; Thiele & Whelan, 2008; Turvett, 2006).

(d)   *Grandparents as Leaders*

Policy makers in this province may consider designing leadership programs for grandparents. Besides the lingering prevalence of ageism, grandparents all over the globe are engaged in lifelong learning. Grandparents are not a homogeneous group of people and as such exhibit a great degree of difference and diversity in their opinions and life styles. Many of today's grandparents in Newfoundland and Labrador are relatively young, well-educated, both cosmopolitan and local in outlook, and consumers of a variety of goods and services in their own right. They appear motivated to engage in conversations about how to envision various aspects of change that are taking place in Newfoundland and Labrador society and culture. Some of them are relatively more committed to envisioning actions and practices that contribute to the sustainability of rural communities and lifestyles in this province in the age of globalism. In valuing grandparents, we need to be careful that they are not regarded by government leaders as commodities or merely a resource to be used to engage them in ways that they are seen as "free resources" to exploit.

(e)   *The value of small scale nuanced and community based research and implication of this type of research to the wellbeing of grandparents, families, communities and schools*

Following Smith's (2002) observations (see Endnote 17) about the value of small scale nuanced and community based research, we have tried to highlight the idea that "everyone" – and not only the designated highly funded "experts" and "researchers" – can have the ability and desire to produce, and in fact can produce relevant and local knowledge in contemporary Newfoundland and Labrador society to make sense of their everyday lives. Expert knowledge with its technical rationality often leads to the increasing "colonization of the lifeworld" (Habermas, 1987, *The Theory of Communicative Action*, Vol. 2, p. 355.).[23]

Considering the tensions produced by the capitalist/corporate form of modernity between local and global interests (see endnote 4&.5) we suggest a systematic re-thinking may be an alternative option in Newfoundland and Labrador to ask questions such as: What sort of knowledge is being produced in Newfoundland and Labrador as a place? Does this knowledge support the desired commitment, love, and attachment to Newfoundland as a place to live and provide imaginative alternative life style options to citizens to invest in their communities for the future? What type of intellectuals is our education system producing? Do they function as local organic intellectuals or as intelligentsia? This last question is related to production of knowledge. Henry Giroux in his book *Border Crossing* (1993b) and Derlik (1996), provides some suggestions as to how the local organic intellectuals can function as a committed group of people dedicated to softening the strong and often harsh impact of capitalist globalization on their community members and surrounding environment in the future.

We hope, albeit in small ways, local nuanced knowledge produced by grandparents as amplified in their voices, and represented in many chapters in this book, becomes a pedagogical resource that can be used by teachers, students, social workers, health services providers, community development workers, policy makers, and by the common citizens to contribute to the decolonization of the life world in Newfoundland and Labrador, and also in other parts of the world.

NOTES

[1] We realize that voice is not something that someone gives to others. It is something to be engaged and critically understood. Voice is often problematic, yet it is central to any sense of personal action and power, that is agency. While a great deal has been written on voice as critical pedagogical category, no attempt is made here to review the literature on this category. However, it suffices to mention that the exercise of listening to the voices of both the diasporic and the non-diasporic grandparents in Newfoundland and Labrdor, and to all the stakeholders who are interested in their well-being, enables us to realize what forms of knowledge and cultures those groups bring in the form of cultural and social capital. It is important to know what sorts of cultural and social capital get produced and reproduced when different voices are engaged in real life situations. Once the grandparents come to realize that their voices are liberating, they can build on that freedom. They can feel confident in solving real and perceived problems pertaining to their daily lives in their own specific ways. We should remind ourselves that in this process of prioritizing the voices of the grandparents all parties involved are simultaneously teachers and learners. Part of the struggle for voice, in pedagogy, is to help the grandparents to develop a language that can serve as a means to empower them to socially transform their lives. Further, we should remember that lived experiences and language are linked together. We speak out of our lived experiences, for in fact there is no other way to speak. Therefore, if we do not have freedom to speak out our experiences, we might become voiceless. If the individual is voiceless, does it mean that the individual is negated? Silenced? Our orientation is that if grandparents in Newfoundland and Labrador, with the help of other stakeholders, can use their voices to produce "local knowledge" and "local theories" about their own aging process in relation to the larger debate in society about aging and grand parenting , they might be able to speak to their own specific reality with confidence. They could self-consciously reflect on their own construction of old age and on their own transformation. In writing this book we are claiming that integrating case studies presented in this book into pedagogical practices give us a site to engage the voices of grandparents in Newfoundland and Labrador and other stakeholders. For this way of looking at the struggle for voice, in pedagogy, see Doyle, Clar & Singh, Amarjit (2006). *Reading and teaching Henry Giroux*. New York: Peter Lang Publishing, Inc., Giroux, H.A. (1989). *Schooling for democracy*. London: Routledge, Giroux, H.A. (2003). *The abandoned generation: democracy beyond the culture of fear*. New York: Plagrave Macmillian, Giroux, H. A. (1993). *Living dangerously: multiculturalism and politics of difference*. New York: Peter Lang Publishing, Inc, Giroux, H.A. (1993). *Border crossing: cultural workers and the politics of education*. New York: Routledge.

[2] Globalization, and related terms such as globalism, globality and the like are defined in many different ways. Ritzer (2007) defines globalization as "the spread of worldwide practices, relations, consciousness and organization of social life." He defines globalism as "the monocasual and unilinear

view that the world is dominated by economics and that we are witnessing the emergence of the hegemony of the capitalist world market and the neoliberal ideology that underpins it." He defines Globality as "the view that closed spaces, especially those associated with nations, are growing increasingly illusory in the era of globalization." (p. 292)

3   Many grandparents are retiring at younger ages and they have more energy and enthusiasm to take on an active role in their grandchildren's lives. In the context of globalization there is an international trend of grandparents caring for grandchildren. There are more grandparents living now than in the past. According to Statistics Canada, Census of Population, 2001, for all children age 0–14 in Canada: 3.3% of the grandchildren shared a home with at least one grandparent, 2.9% of grandchildren lived in a multigenerational household, and 0.4% of grandchildren lived in a skip-generation household. For the population of children aged 0–14 years, Newfoundland and Labrador ranked number three in Canada with regard to the percentage of grandchildren sharing a home with at least one grandparent. In the case of Newfoundland and Labrador, these numbers were 5.3%, 4.6%, and 0.7%, respectively. Comparable numbers in the Northwest Territories were 5.4%, 4.1%, and 1.3%. In Nunavut these numbers were 9.7%, 7.4%, and 2.3 (Milan, Anne and Brian Hamm, 2003).

Further according to this trend, there was an increase in the number of grandchildren being raised by grandparents in Canada; between 1991 and 2001 there was a 20% increase in the number of Canadian children under 18 who were living with grandparents with no parent present in the home. Statistics Canada (2006) data indicate that there were 65,135 children living with their grandparents, and where the grandparents were their primary caregivers. The 2001 data for the same population was 56,790! These numbers show that the practice of grandparents raising their grandchildren is on the rise. This phenomenon is even more evident in the United States. According to the National Census Bureau, in 1996 over 1.4 million children were being raised by grandparents without the help of parents (Casper & Bryson, 1999). This was an increase of 37 percent from the 1993 census (American Association of Retired Persons [AARP], 1998)! In Australia in 2003, the Australian Bureau of Statistics reported that there were 23,000 grandparent families with children aged 0 to 17 years, and there are many Australian organizations that feel that this number is much higher! The same phenomenon was also witnessed in South Africa recently by two Newfoundland social workers. In the latest Social Work news letter entitled Connecting Voices, Green & Haley (2009) recount the following: "We marveled at the resilience and strength of the South African people... Approximately six and a half million people are living with HIV / AIDS in this country – that means one in four people. While it is difficult to imagine the impact on families, we witnessed it each day as we went into the townships. We saw grandmothers carrying children, cleaning clothes, gathering food and cooking. In 2005 there were over 2 million children orphaned because of AIDS – a number expected to grow to 5.7 million by 2015. The middle generation is dying, leaving a large and visible gap between the young and old. Grandmothers are filling this gap after burying their own children. As the Stephen Lewis Foundation says, 'grandmothers are the unsung heroes of South Africa' (p. 12)." While there is an increase in South Africa, it is sparked more by the health issues related to HIV/AIDS than in other countries.

4   Kelly (2009), in another context, writes about Newfoundland and Labrador: "In the past three decades the province [Newfoundland and Labrador], has been culturally reconfigured by the ecological crisis of the world's ocean, resulting in the collapse and closure of the province's historical *raisond'etre,* a five hundred years old cod fishery. The depopulation that followed – 12% of the total population in a 15 years period-resulted in a radical decline of community infrastructure. Schools, churches, fire halls, and medical facilities closed as a profound cultural disorientation grew. This orientation is still felt province-wide, but reverberates most profoundly in rural and 'outport' [small rural communities] places. Coincident with this demise the rise of an oil and gas industry, also fueled by global greed, overproduction, and disregarded for the finitude of planetary resource. Such circumstances of profound cultural (and ecological) crisis, loss, reorientations, and change drastically increase the stakes of leaving and staying [in rural areas]. They also heighten the need for more complex approaches to any efforts designed to ensure the viability and suitability of places." (p. 2) "Learning to Lose: Reality, Transience, and Belonging (A Companion to Michael Corbett), *Journal of Research in Rural Studies,* 2009, 24(11). In the same vein, the final report of the Newfoundland and Labrador Government's Royal Commission on Renewing and Strengthening Our Place in Canada, released in 2003, states that "with job losses in many parts of the province being so severe, and without sufficient growth in

employment opportunities elsewhere in the provincial economy, people have been forced to choose between unemployment and out-migration" (35).

5   Arif Dirlik points out that "the meaning of the local in contemporary discussion is uncertain" (p. 42) and any undertaking to define it "must of necessity be highly speculative." Benjamin Barber believes that the "local" is a politically contested concept. Dirlik claims that the local "is both a site of promise and predicament". He explains "what the local implies in different contexts is highly uncertain. Suffice it to say here that a concern for the local seems to appear in the foreground in connection with certain social movement (chief among them ecological, women's, ethnic, and indigenous people's movements) and the intellectual repudiation of past ideologies (primarily the intellectual development associated with postmodernism)" (p. 23). He further asks "why there should be a connection between the repudiation of past ideologies and the reemergence of the local as a concern is not very mysterious. Localism as an orientation in either a 'traditional' or a modern sense has never disappeared, but rather has been suppressed or, at best, marginalized in various ideologies of modernity. Localism does not speak of an incurable social disease that must sooner or later bring about its natural demise; and there is nothing about it that is inherently undesirable. What makes it [localism] seem so is a historical consciousness that identifies civilization and progress with political, social, and cultural homogenization and justifies the supersession of the local in the name of the general and the universal. Modernist teleology has gone the farthest of all in stamping upon the local its derogatory image: as enclave of backwardness left out of progress, as the realm of rural stagnation against the dynamism of the urban, industrial civilization of capitalism, as the realm of particularistic culture against universal scientific rationality, and, perhaps most importantly, as the obstacle to full realization of that political form of modernity, the nation-state" (p. 23). Henri Lefebvre writes that "no space disappears in the course of growth and development: the *worldwide* does not abolish the local" (p. 1, cited in Rob Wilson and Wimal Dissanake, 1996). The small scale studies that we have included in this book document how grandparents, families, and communities in Newfoundland and Labrador are attempting to come to terms with ongoing processes and forces of globalization as a contemporary manifestation of modernity. This manifestation is disrupting local communities and regions in this province into something else, whether nightmarish or the location for imagining alternative possibilities for the future. (see Endnote, 4).

6   The notions of voice, hope, creativity, imagination, and possibility are integral parts of critical theory and critical pedagogy. "The primary preoccupation of critical pedagogy is with social injustice and how to transform inequitable, undemocratic, or oppressive institutions and social relations." (Burbules, N. C. and Berk, R "Critical Thinking and Critical Pedagogy: Relations, Differences, and Limits," in *Critical Theory in Educational Discourse*, Popkewitz, T. S. and Higgs, P. (1997) (eds.). Butterworth's. According to Sullivan (1987:63) "a fundamental assumption of a critical pedagogy is that it is a broad educational venture which self-consciously challenges and seeks to transform the dominant values of our culture." Likewise, Leistyna & Woodrum (1996) assert that: "Critical pedagogy is primarily concerned with the kinds of educational theories and practices that encourage both students and teachers to develop an understanding of the interconnecting relationship among ideology, power, and culture... [that] challenge us to recognize, engage, and critique (so as to transform) any existing undemocratic social practices and institutional structures that produce and sustain inequalities and oppressive social identities and relations." According to Giroux (1997: xiii) pedagogy "involves the production and transmission of knowledge, the construction of subjectivity, and the learning of values and beliefs." Kellner (2000) explains, "Critical pedagogy considers how education can provide individuals with the tools to better themselves and strengthen democracy, to create a more egalitarian and just society, and thus to deploy education in a process of progressive social change." Kellner, Douglas. "Multiple Literacies and Critical Pedagogies." In *Revolutionary Pedagogies – Cultural Politics, Instituting Education, and the Discourse of Theory*, by Peter Pericles Trifonas, (2000) (Edi,). New York: Routledge, , Giroux, H.A. (1997). *Pedagogy and the politics of hope: theory, culture, and schooling: a critical reader.* Boulder, Colo.: Westview Press, and Steinberg, S.R. (2012). Critical *Qualitative Research Reader*. (Co-editor with Gaile Cannella. New York: Peter Lang Publishing; Weiner, E.J. (2007).

7   Mary Kaldor (2010). In Manfred B. Steger. (2010) (Ed.).*Globalization the greatest hits: a global studies reader*. Boulder: Paradigm Publishers, pp. 153–163. Taken from her book, *Global Civil*

Society: An Answer to War (Cambridge, UK: Polity Press, 2003: 1–12) describes five meanings of global civil society. She proposes "to set out five different versions of the concept of civil society in common usage and to say something about what they imply in a global context" (p. 158). These five versions are: Societas Civilis, Bourgeois Society (Burgerliche Gesellschaft), The Activist Version, The Neoliberal Version, and The Postmodern Version. Her book is subtitled an 'answer to war'. She says "This is because the concept of civil society has always been linked to the notion of minimizing violence in social relations, to the public use of reason as a way of managing human affairs in place of submission based on fear and insecurity, or ideology and superstition" (p.155). According to her, "The terms 'global' and 'civil society' became the new buzzwords of the 1990s. In this book, I want to suggest that the two terms are interconnected and reflect a new reality, however imperfectly understood." (p. 153). She says, "All versions of civil society are both normative and descriptive. They describe a political project i.e., a goal, and at the same time an actually existing reality, which may not measure up to the goal. Societas civilis expressed the goal of public security, of a civilized, i.e., non-violent, society. Bfirgerliche Gesellschaft was about the rise of market society as a condition for individual freedom, and the balance between the state and the market." (pp.161–162). According to Klador (2010), "The neoliberal version is about the benefits of Western, especially American, society; thus the goal is the spread of this type of society to the rest of the world. Globalization, the spread of global capitalism, is viewed as a positive development, the vehicle, supplemented by global civil society, for achieving global Westernization or 'the end of history'." (p. 162).

Further, "This version might be described as 'laissez-faire politics', a kind of market in politics. According to this definition, civil society consists of associational life—a non-profit, voluntary 'third sector'—that not only restrains state power but also actually provides a substitute for many of the functions performed by the state. Funding for democracy-building and human rights NGOs is somehow supposed to help establish a rule of law and respect for human rights." (p. 161)

According to Kaldor (2010), "The postmodern definition of civil society departs from the universalism of the activist and neoliberal versions, although even this version requires one universal principle—that of tolerance. Civil society is an arena of pluralism and contestation, a source of incivility as well as civility. Some postmodernists criticize the concept of civil society as Eurocentric, a product of a specific Western culture that is imposed on the rest of the world. Others suggest a reformulation so as to encompass other more communalist understandings of political culture. In particular, it is argued that classic Islamic society represented a form of civil society in the balance between religion, the bazaar and the ruler." (p. 160).

According to Kaldor (2010), "…for the activist version, the inhabitants of civil society can be roughly equated with civic-minded or public-spirited groups. Those active in civil society would be those concerned about public affairs and public debate. For the postmodernists, civic-minded groups are only one component of civil society. In particular, postmodernists emphasize the importance of national and religious identities as well as multiple identities as a precondition for civil society, whereas for the activists, a shared cosmopolitanism is more important." And, from the postmodernist perspective, "… it is possible to talk about global civil society in the sense of the global spread of fields of contestation. Indeed, one might talk about a plurality of global civil societies through different globally organized networks. These might include Islam, nationalist Diaspora networks, as well as human rights networks, etc. Further she writes that "The postmodern version has to be related to the break with modernity of which a key component was the nation-state." (160–161).

She explains, "The activist perspective…is a radicalization of democracy and an extension of participation and autonomy. On this definition, civil society refers to active citizenship, to growing self-organization outside formal political circles, and expanded. It is space in which individual citizens can influence the conditions in which they live both directly through self-organization and through political pressure". (pp. 159–160)

Further, "The activist version is about political emancipation. It is about the empowerment of individuals and the extension of democracy. For activists, globalization is not an unqualified benefit. It offers possibilities for emancipation on a global scale. But in practice, it involves growing inequality and insecurity and new forms of violence. Global civil society, for the activists, therefore, is about 'civilizing' or democratizing globalization, about the process through which groups, movements and individuals can demand a global rule of law, global justice and global empowerment. "The contemporary versions of civil society all have normative goals, which can only be fully explained in the context of globalization." (p. 162).

"Common sense, as described by Merriam-Webster, is defined as beliefs or propositions that most people consider prudent and of sound judgment, without reliance on esoteric knowledge or study or research, but based upon what they see as knowledge held by people "in common". Thus "common sense" (in this view) equates to the knowledge and experience which most people already have, or which the person using the term believes that they do or should have. According to the Cambridge Dictionary, the phrase is good sense and sound judgment in practical matters ("the basic level of practical knowledge and judgment that we all need to help us live in a reasonable and safe way"). Whichever definition is used "...common sense remains a perennial topic in epistemology and many philosophers make wide use of the concept or at least refer to it. Some related concepts include intuition, pre-theoretic belief, ordinary language, the frame problem, foundational beliefs, good sense, endoxa, axioms, wisdom, folk wisdom, folklore and public opinion."

"Gramsci gave much thought to the question of the role of intellectuals in society and stated that all men are intellectuals, in that all have intellectual and rational faculties, but not all men have the social function of intellectuals. ....Furthermore, he distinguished between a "traditional" intelligentsia which sees itself as a class apart from society, and the thinking groups which every class produces from its own ranks "organically". Such "organic" intellectuals do not simply describe social life in accordance with scientific rules, but rather articulate, through the language of culture, the feelings and experiences which the masses could not express for themselves. As educators Gramsci's ideas are important for us because his ideas about the education system correspond "with the notion of critical pedagogy and popular education as theorized and practiced in later decades by Paulo Freire in Brazil, and have much in common with the thought of Frantz Fanon and with ideas of Henry Giroux.

Greaves explains that for Gramsci (1971, p. 344; Gramsci 1995, p. 386), it is social activity that unites philosophy with the mass (Greaves, 2008, p. 11). Greaves writes "Gramsci contrasts 'common sense' with what he calls 'good sense.' He [Gramsci] conceives of good sense as a latent critical faculty in all humans, but it is one that suffers from underdevelopment and becomes choked in a bewildering superstructural babble created by the class opponent. The most important feature of good sense is the critical relationship it bears to practical activity." (Greaves, 2008; p. 12). In Gramsci's words good sense depends upon "overcoming bestial and elemental passions through a conception of necessity which gives a conscious direction to one's activity. This is the healthy nucleus that exists in 'common sense,' the part of it which can be called 'good sense' and which deserves to be made more unitary and coherent." (Gramsci 1971, p. 328, cited in Greaves, p. 12). Greaves explains that "Gramsci's overall point is that when one becomes conscious of the class function of ideas it is indeed possible to extricate good sense from common sense. Good sense exploits the faculties employed by formal philosophy, such as the ability to structure the mind logically and coherently, to think hygienically, interpret empirical data, and so forth. This does not mean everyone can become a great philosopher, but everyone can certainly come to a more systematic assessment of his or her social position in the world. Good sense is therefore loaded with historical potential" (pp. 12–13).

In Gramsci's words "[i]n acquiring one's conception of the world one always belongs to a particular grouping which is that of all the social elements which share the same mode of thinking and acting." (Gramsci 1971, p. 324, cited in Greaves, p. 13). In this sense Gramsci writes that "...although one can speak of intellectuals, one cannot speak of non-intellectuals, because non-intellectual do not exist" (Gramsci 1971, p. 9, cited in Greaves, p. 14). For Gramsci, then, "... intellectual must be 'studied concretely' in the context of living social reality." (Gramasci 1971, p. 6, cited in Greaves, p. 13.) Gramsci writes that "[all] men are intellectuals ... but not all men have in society the function of intellectuals" (Gramsci 1971, p. 9, cited in Greaves p. 14). Greaves explains that for Gramsci (1971, p. 8) "in terms of the generic human organism, the notion of non -intellectual labour is false. Everyone does it; any mental activity that involves the stringing together of thoughts in an organised way is an intellectual process, and the productive sphere involves such cognition at all levels." (Greaves, p. 14). Thus Greaves explains that the word intellectual in the modern world is tied "...to productive specialism and supporting cadres created by an extremely complex division of labour" (p. 15), and "the function of intellectuals can be set apart from other workers in two closely related senses: the disciplinary and the educational. Intellectuals educate and discipline the entire culture in which the conflictual labour process operates by projecting the specific realities of production as though these are trans-historical certainties common to all, and are therefore indisputable, moral, just and so on. In other words, intellectuals are defined according to hegemonic function." (p. 16).

Carl Boggs (1993, p. 3) states that intellectuals are both technocrats and social critics. The important thing is to note that in the production process each social group creates its own organic intellectuals. Gramsci writes "[e]very social group, coming into existence on the original terrain of an essential function in the world of economic production, creates together with itself, organically, one or more strata of intellectuals which give it homogeneity and an awareness of its own function not only in the economic but also in the social and political fields." (Gramsci 1971, p. 5, cited in Greaves, p. 16).

⁹   While writing in another context, Doyle and Hoben (2011) explore the relationship between imagination within the nexus of critical pedagogy and philosophy. They write that "we sometimes believe that creativity has to do with enduring characteristics or talent that is limited to certain people while others believe all people are creative" (p. 115). In a similar vein Maxine Greene is interested in transformations, openings, and possibilities. She claims that "one must have an awareness of leaving something behind while reaching towards something new, and this kind of awareness must be linked to imagination" (1995, p. 20, cited in Doyle and Hoben, p. 117). "The imagination is, then", according to Doyle and Hoben, "a staging ground for the conflicts and struggles of human existence in which identity and ideology contend.... The imagination allows us to break with hegemony by making accessible those realms and modes of existence which the monolithic voice of repressive power wishes to hide for our preview.... The imagination is the unseen hand which provides the impetus to go in reach of new horizons. Quite often wonder startles us with the unexpected beauty of our daily lives, a haunting place where we can hear the lonely songs of consciousness, moving outwards, seeking, searching through the endless possibilities to be claimed among love, and as-yet-unknown yearnings" (p. 124).

¹⁰ George Ritzer (2007) defines, "glocalization", "space war", and "grobaliztion" of nothing in these ways. McDonaldization is "The process by which the principle of the fast-food restaurant coming to dominate more and more sectors of American society, as well as the rest of the world; in the later sense, a form of cultural imperialism." (p. 263). Glocalization is "the interpenetration of the global and the local resulting in unique outcomes in different geographic areas." (p. 292) Ritzer (2007) writes that "to Bauman, what defines the global world is a 'space war' between those who have and those who do not have mobility. However, even those with mobility face grave problems." (p. 282) Grobalization of nothing is "the imperialistic ambitions of nations, corporations, organizations, and the like and their desire, indeed need, to impose themselves on various geographic areas." (p. 292) By nothing, Ritzer means ".... (largely) empty forms; forms largely devoid of distinctive content.. Conversely, something would be defined as (largely) full forms; forms rich in distinctive content.....A good example of nothing in these terms is the shopping mall (e.g. ,any of the malls owned by the Mills Corporation-Potomac Mills, Swagrass Mills, etc.), which is an empty (largely) structure that is easily replicated around the world. These malls could be filled with an endless array of specific content (e.g., local shops, local foods etc.-something!) that could vary enormously from one location to another. However, increasingly they are filled with chain stores of various types- nothing! Since more and more countries in the world have these malls, this is an example of the grobalization of nothing and of increasing global homogenization." (p. 267)

¹¹ For conversations about notions of sites, place, public spheres, pedagogy, cultural work and cultural workers, and their relation to the ideas of teaching, learning and education, curriculum development, and teacher education, see Singh, A. (1996)." World Englishes as a site for pedagogies of the public spheres," Revista de Langues para fines especificos, No. 3, Marzo-Abril, Universad de Las Palmas de Gran Canaria, Espana – Spain, 303–328, Singh, A. (2000). "World Englishes, curriculum change and global career opportunities," in Singh, A., Baksh, I.J. & Hache, G. (2000). Studies in Newfoundland education and society, Vol. 111, 773–750. St. John's: Memorial University, Newfoundland, Canada. Singh (1996: 311–312) noted that in the realm of certain forms of cultural studies and critical theory, the notion of cultural site and practice are talked about in a specific way. For example, Simon (1994) explains that a "cultural-political site is not an ordinary situation. It is a complex and conflictual location

where intricate representational forms are worked out and produced. It is a place where multiplicity of forces (determinations and effects) are at work to produce a particular practice. Different things can and do happen at a specific site at a particular time. A site is a place where different possibilities of uses and effects interact." A site is a contested terrain. According to Simon it is a place where, "the past is traversed to competing and contradictory construction." Further, he suggests that 'cultural workers intending to initiate pedagogies of historical reformation need an understanding of topography on which these struggles are taking place." (Simon, 1994:128) To struggle at a site means taking into account the specificity of the particular context in which one is located in relations to others. There could be many sites of production for a particular struggle. Simon (1994:128–129) provides a simple list of the sites of popular memory production…). See, Simon, I.R. (1993) *Teaching against the grain: Text for a pedagogy of possibility*. New York: Bergin & Garvey. Simon. I.R. (1994). "Forms of insurgency in the production of popular memories; The Columbus quincentenary, and the pedagogy of counter commemoration" in H.A. Giroux and P. McLaren (1994) (Eds*.). Between borders: pedagogy and politics of cultural studies*. New York: Routledge.

Following Simon, one can see how aging and getting old as sites could be taken up (e.g., integrated) by grandparents in Newfoundland and Labrador where they could engage themselves in various forms of struggles and negotiations with others. Occupying a specific location and doing grand parenting in the overall family structure in one's life course, old age and specific issues surrounding this location could be taken as sites at myriad places (e.g, in households and public venues, such as sports arenas, schools, business forums, embassies, airline counters, hotel lobbies, governmental offices, shopping centers, bus and train terminals, international trade centers, the information highway, movie theaters, temples, birthday parties, marriage ceremonies, religious festivals, national day celebrations, cultural parades, fashion shows, funerals, child birth celebrations and eating places). The contributors to this book, to some extent, show how grandparents in Newfoundland and Labrador use these places as sites. These sites can also be seen as expansions of the public spheres in which grandparents in province could have opportunities to voice their concerns. The concept of "the public sphere' was originally developed by Habermas (1962), *The Structural transformation of the Public Sphere*. According to Fraser (1994:75) "the idea of the 'public sphere' in Habermas' sense is a conceptual resource… it designates a theater in modern society in which political participation is enacted through the medium of talk. It is the space in which citizens deliberate about their common affairs, hence, an institutionalized arena of discursive interaction." She explains, "…this arena is conceptually distinct from the state; it is a site for the production and circulation of discourse that can in principle be critical of the state." Further, she asserts that "the public sphere in Habermas' sense is also conceptually distinct from the official economy; it is not an arena of market relation but rather one of discursive relations, a theater for debating and deliberating rather than for buying and selling. " She states, thus this concept of the public sphere permits us to keep in view the distinction between the state apparatuses, economic markets, and democratic associations, distinctions that are essential to democratic theory." Fraser has expanded this concept with respect to theorizing the limits of democracy in late capitalist societies. (See, Fraser, N. (1994), "Rethinking the public sphere: A contribution to the critique of actually existing democracy," in H.A. Giroux and P. MacLaren (1994) (Eds.), pp. 74–98, Op. Cit). For further discussions of concepts discussed above to the socialization of future grandparents in this province, who are at present students attending schools at different levels, see, Doyle, C (2006. , Singh, A.). *Reading and teaching Henry A. Giroux*, New York: Peter Lang Publishers, Inc., and Paulo Freire (2005). *Teachers as cultural workers, letters to those who dare teach*. Boulder: Westview Press.

[12] What does growing older mean if it is not simply the passage of time, having another birthday? In gerontology " increasingly, scholars argue that chronological age is a relatively meaningless variable … Age is only a way of marking human events and experiences; those events and experiences are what matters, not time itself … Time's passing is of concern only because it is connected, however loosely, with other changes: physical, psychological, and social." (p. 4 – see reference below) In gerontology" in the past, researchers searched for the "normal changes that accompanied aging; a most important part of this research was to distinguish normal age changes from pathological or disease processes that become more prevalent with age but were not caused by aging. With the growing knowledge about the modifiability and variability of physical aging processes, the distinctions among usual, optimal, and pathological aging emerged … 'optimal' aging is characterized by minimal loss of

physical function and a healthy, vigorous body; 'pathological' aging is aging accompanied by multiple chronic diseases and negative environment influences. 'Usual' ageing refers to the typical or average experience – somewhat in between pathological and optimal"... "Psychological aging processes include changes in personality, mental functioning, and sense of self during our adult years." (p. 5) Gerontologists make many generalizations in this area: "First, personality does not undergo profound changes in later life... For example ... the grumpy old man was very likely a grumpy young man. Although the developmental challenges and opportunities we encounter do vary through our lives, the strategy we use to adapt to change, to refine and reinforce our sense of self, to work towards realizing our full human potential are practiced throughout our adult lives." (p. 6) "Social aging is a multidimensional and dynamic force. It includes the transitions into and out of roles, expectations about behavior, societal allocation of resources and opportunities, negotiations about the meaning and implications of chronological age, and the experience of individuals traveling the life course and negotiating life stages." (p. 7) See, Morgan, L. & Kunkel, S. (2001) (2nd Edition). Aging: the social context. California: Pine Forge Press.

¹³ See Bibliography – Sociological/Anthropological Articles, Maritime History Archive, Memorial University, 2003–2005.

¹⁴ The 1970s saw the rise of critical pedagogy. It rose in resistance to so-called transmission approaches to education and curriculum. Therefore, in our reading we find that in critical pedagogy a distinction is often made between the pedagogical goals and curriculum goals of teaching and learning. Curriculum goals generally entail providing students the opportunities to learn the already existing forms of knowledge produced within the framework of dominant paradigms. Pedagogical goals require more than this. They are framed to bring about progressive social change. See endnote 7. Based on our research (see Doyle, C. and Singh, A., 2006, op. cit.) in the "field", we have developed the RCIT (Reflective and Critical Internship Teaching model), a model of teacher education designed to engage students with curriculum that aims at achieving both the curriculum and pedagogical goals. In this model we envision that generally there are three forms of knowledge production that dominate our daily conversations and lived experiences. We label these forms of knowledge as common sense knowledge, professional knowledge, official knowledge, and defined them as follow: common sense knowledge is taken for granted dominant cultural norms, values, attitudes, self -concepts, behavior patterns, and overall orientations which we have acquired through socialization in cultures and societies. It constitutes more of our personal opinions and idiosyncrasies. Professional knowledge is produced by various professionals, such as sociologists, psychologists, and so on, and their respective professional organizations. Official knowledge is produced by the state, i.e., various government apparatuses, such as the department or ministries of education, health, economic development, and so on. In building the RCIT model we find ourselves more inclined to accept the assertion that it is the ongoing conversations we have with others that makes it possible for us to live together and solve our problems. Therefore, the model encourages students to self-consciously combine the three forms of knowledge described herein when they engage in communication with others. We have found that when students do that, they feel more empowered. They are more likely to make sense of their environment (personal and social predicaments in which they find themselves due to their specific locations in general social structure) with more confidence. Empowerment also entails prefigurative politics and living. Kaufman (2003:277–8) writes that "prefigurative politics is based on the belief that we are creating the new world we are advocating as we go, and so we should try to build in the present, the institutions and social patterns of the society we are working toward." And "in prefigurative movements, we are reweaving the social fabric. We are creating an alternative social world, and the relations we create along the way lay the foundations for the relations we will have after we achieve our goals." See, Kaufman, C. (2003). Ideas for actions: relevant theory for radical change. Cambridge, Mass.: South End Press. Also see, Schon 1987, 1983.

¹⁵ See the "Special Issue: *The Morning Watch* Books Winter 2006 Vol. 33, Nos. 3–4 to Fall 2007 Vol. 35, Nos. 1–2 ". Amarjit Singh et. al. edited four books. These books contain efforts by many authors to produce local knowledge in Newfoundland and Labrador.

¹⁶ Giroux is one of the leading voices within the discourse of critical pedagogy. One of the important tenets of Giroux's thought about curriculum is that teachers and professors need to take seriously those cultural experiences and meanings "that students bring to the day-to-day process of schooling itself.

If we take the experiences of our students as a starting point for dialogue and analysis, we give them the opportunity to validate themselves, to use their own voices" (1981, p. 123). This suggestion does not fit well to "a predetermined and hierarchically arranged body of knowledge [that] is taken as the cultural currency to be dispensed to all children regardless of their diversity and interests" (p. 123). He further explains that the concept of hidden curriculum allows us to make "linkages between schools and the social, economic, and political landscape that make up the wider society, the hidden curriculum theorists provided a theoretical impetus for breaking out of the methodological quagmire in which schools were merely viewed as black boxes" (1983, p. 45). Giroux maintains that curriculum must not be limited to the domain of the few and the privileged, but it must center on the "particular forms of life, culture, and interaction that students bring to school" (2005, p. 104). He writes "critical pedagogy always strives to incorporate student experience as official curriculum content. While articulating such experience can both be empowering and a form of critique against relations that silence, such experience is not an unproblematic form of knowledge" (Giroux and Simon, 1989. p. 231). Giroux suggests, "instead of stressing the individualistic and competitive approaches to learning, students are encouraged to work together on projects, both in terms of their production and evaluation" (2005, p. 104). Like Giroux, we realize that that curriculum should go beyond the experience of students' lives. It should expand their boundaries and borders "while constantly pushing them to test what it means to resist oppression, work collectively, and exercise authority from the position of an ever-developing sense of knowledge, expertise, and commitment' (p. 104). According to Giroux and Aronowitz what we need is "really useful knowledge that draws from popular education, knowledge that challenges and critically appropriates dominant ideologies, and knowledge that points to more human and democratic social relations and cultural forms" (1994, p. 153). See, Giroux, H.A. (1981), Giroux, H. A. (1983). *Ideology, culture, and process of schooling*. Philadelphia: Temple University Press; London: Farmer Press; *Theory and resistance in education: a pedagogy for the opposition*. London: Hienemann Educational Book, Giroux, H.A. and Simon, R.I. (1989). *Popular culture, schooling, and everyday life*. Granby, Mass.: Bergin and Garvey, Giroux, H.A. (2005) (2nd.Ed.). *Schooling and the struggle for public life: democracy's promise and education's challenge*. Boulder, Colo.: Paradigm Publishers, Giroux, H. A. and Aronowitz (1994). *Education still under siege*. Westport, Conn.: Bergin & Garvey, Doyle, C. and Singh, A. (2006), op. cit.

[17] Many writers recognize the importance of local knowledge and local theorizing (Geertz, 1983; Schibeci & Grundy, 1987; Tripp, 1987; Smyth, 1989). This form of knowledge and theorizing helps people to enhance their well-being in the concrete context in which they work and live. We have found that in the Newfoundland and Labrador context of school-family-community relations, local knowledge and theories produced by teachers, parents, student and others help them to focus on the concrete relationship on which their daily lives depend (Singh, et. al., 1999).

Local knowledge and theories are discussed and defined in multiple ways and at different levels (FAO Corporate Document Repository, Title: What is Local Knowledge? United Nations): "Local knowledge is the knowledge that people in a given community have developed over time, and continue to develop. It is based on experience, often tested over centuries of use, adapted to the local culture and environment, embedded in community practices, institutions, relationships and rituals, held by individuals or communities, and is dynamic and changing. It is important to note that "local knowledge is not confined to tribal groups or to the original inhabitants of an area. It is not even confined to rural people. Rather, all communities possess local knowledge – rural and urban, settled and nomadic, original inhabitants and migrants. There are other terms, such as traditional knowledge or indigenous knowledge, which are closely related, partly overlapping, or even synonymous with local knowledge. The term local knowledge seems least biased in terms of its contents or origin. As it embraces a larger body of knowledge systems, it includes those classified as traditional and indigenous."

"Knowledge systems are dynamic, people adapt to changes in their environment and absorb and assimilate ideas from a variety of sources. However, knowledge and access to knowledge are not spread evenly throughout a community or between communities. People may have different objectives, interests, perceptions, beliefs and access to information and resources. Knowledge is generated and transmitted through interactions within specific social and agro-ecological contexts. It is linked to access and control over power. Differences in social status can affect perceptions, access to knowledge and, crucially, the importance and credibility attached to what someone knows. Common knowledge is held by most people in a community; e.g. almost everyone knows how to cook rice (or the local staple food). Shared knowledge is held by many, but not all, community members; e.g. villagers who raise livestock will know more about basic animal husbandry than those without livestock. Specialized knowledge is held by a few people who might have had special training or an apprenticeship; e.g. only few villagers will become healers, midwives, or blacksmiths."

And "The type of knowledge people have is related to their age, gender, occupation, labour division within the family, enterprise or community, socio-economic status, experience, environment, history and so on. This has significant implications for research and development work. To find out what people know, the right people must be identified. For example, if boys do the herding they may know, better than their fathers (e.g., where the best grazing sites are located). If we ask the fathers to show us good pastures, we might only get partial information. Development professionals sometimes think villagers know very little, when in fact the wrong people have been interviewed." Further, "It is important to realize that local knowledge – as with other types of knowledge – is dynamic and constantly changing, as it adapts to a changing environment. Because local knowledge changes over time, it is sometimes difficult to decide whether a technology or practice is local, adopted from outside, or a blend of local and introduced components. In most cases the latter situation is most likely. For a development project, however, it does not matter whether a practice is really local or already mixed with introduced knowledge. What is important before looking outside the community for technologies and solutions is to look first at what is available within the community."

"Local and indigenous knowledge refers to the cumulative and complex bodies of knowledge, know-how, practices and representations that are maintained and developed by peoples with extended histories of interactions with the natural environment. These cognitive systems are part of a complex that also includes language, attachment to place, spirituality and worldview. Many different terms are used to refer to this knowledge, these include: traditional ecological knowledge (TEK), indigenous knowledge (IK), local knowledge, rural people's/farmers' knowledge, ethnobiology/ethnobotany/ethnozoology, ethnoscience, folk science, and indigenous science." The reason "these many terms coexist [is] because the wide range of social, political and scientific contexts have made it all but impossible to for a single term to be suitable in all circumstances. The LINKS project promotes an all-encompassing approach to local & indigenous knowledge. For in many cultures, the 'rational' or 'objective' cannot be separated from the 'sacred' or 'intuitive'. Nature and culture are not opposed and circumscribed by sharp boundaries. Knowledge, practice and representations are intertwined and mutually dependent." (See: United Nations Educational, Scientific and Cultural Organization: Local and Indigenous Knowledge Systems LINKs)

[18] The usefulness of small scale, community and neighborhood based studies is well recognized by the social science community. Smith's (2002) comments on small scale research projects involving Maori communities are useful here, and so are presented in some detail. Smith writes about the concerns of Maori researchers in New Zealand and the challenges they face in articulating indigenous research agenda in the context of a highly institutionalized world of research. Her observations may throw some light on how to appreciate the place of small scale research done by local people who are deeply involved in the well-being of their communities. She points out that "...research is highly institutionalized through disciplines and fields of knowledge, through communities and interest groups of scholars, and through the academy." She reminds us that research is a political process since it "is also an integral part of political structures: governments funded research directly and indirectly through tertiary education, national science organizations, development programmes and policies." Further, like governments "corporations and industries fund their own research. Their research programmes can involve large amounts of money and resources, and their activities take place across several parts of the globe. Others like "non-government organizations and local community groups also carry out research and involve themselves in the analysis and critique of research. All of these research activities are carried out by people who in some form or another have been trained and socialized into ways of thinking, of defining and making sense of the known and unknown. It seems rather difficult to conceive an articulation of an indigenous research agenda on such a large scale." This is so, she explains, because "to imagine self-determination, however, is also to, imagine a world in which indigenous peoples become active participants, and to prepare for the possibilities and

challenges that lie ahead." (p. 124) She goes on to say that "... in addition to reasons outlined earlier … about the general regard for research by indigenous peoples, there is another reason for a reticence in naming an activity or project as research. Research is also regarded as being the domain of experts who have advanced educational qualifications and have access to highly specialized language and skills." The diasporic grandparents in Newfoundland and Labrador are interested in producing their own culturally relevant knowledge in the context of their own communities. But it is not easy to do so in real life situation, because they have to constantly engage the so called 'research experts'. Smith explains, "communities carrying out what they may regard as a very humble little project are reluctant to name it as research in case it provokes the scorn and outrage of 'real' researchers. Furthermore, indigenous communities as part of the self-determination agenda do engage quite deliberately in naming the world according to an indigenous world view." (p. 125) In this context one could appreciate the usefulness of the small scale studies. Theodoratus (1984–1989) also endorses the usefulness of small scale studies, and his 1984–1989 series compiles research on the presence of small ethnic communities in the United States and Canada that might otherwise not have been noticed by larger group projects.

[19] Ritzer (2007) defines Culture –ideology of consumption as "an ideology that affects people scattered widely throughout the globe with the greater reach and sophistication of advertising, the media, and consumer goods. Ultimately, a global mood to consume is created that benefits transnational corporations, as well as the advertising and media corporation."

[20] According to Thomas West (2002, p. 20) "the guiding problem of negotiation … is how to balance optimism with critique, how to remain hopeful about the possibility of doing more than simple expressing our differences while avoiding and resisting the colonizing strategies of negotiation that are disguised as civil discourse. Clearly, what is needed is to supplement these stances with a theory of 'critical negotiation,' an idea that comes to resemble more a borderland dialogical process or an ethics of social and political engagement and less a mere 'dealing'." Further, West points out that this theory of critical negotiation is supposed to do four things: 1. "recognize the role and effect of emotion during negotiation …, 2. understand that negotiation is a co-constitutive process …, 3. realize that how power relations are perceived before negotiation affects what is happening during negotiation …, and 4. insist on situating negotiation within its larger social and historical contexts …"

[21] Kelly (2009) reminds us that "the meaning of home, place and belonging have never been more highly contested than in these times of unprecedented migration, displacement, and exile, shifting national borders and identities, and multiple diasporas." (op.cit., p. 1) Further she points out that, like the fishing outports of Newfoundland and Labrador, "rural places now more than at any other point in history, are places of great loss-of people, natural resources, and, often as a result, of any vision of long term viability. In such places, loss as a persistent condition of life is vividly felt. Yet, what is often misrepresented in such circumstances as an acceptance of disadvantage is more often an intricate and, on many fronts, satisfying negotiation of abiding attachments, longing, and hopes set against a background of ecological and economic insecurity." (p. 2. Also see endnote 4)

[22] Information on elder abuse all levels is readily available on the Internet. Here we cite only few references that are relevant to the point we want to make. Missing Voices: views of older persons on elder abuse. World Health Organization, Geneva, 2002. International Network for Prevention of Elder Abuse, WHO/NMH/VIP/02.1, WHO/NMH/02.2. Also see, Strategic Plan to Address Elder Abuse in Newfoundland and Labrador: A Five Year Plan for 2005–2010. Developed by the Seniors Resource Centre Association of Newfoundland and Labrador; Abuse of Older Adults: Department of Justice Canada Overview Paper, June 2009, Department of Justice Canada.

[23] Retrieved from "http://en.wikipedia.org/wiki/Lifeworld"

"Habermas, whose social theory is grounded in communication, focuses linguistic meanings. It is the lived realm of informal, culturally-grounded understandings and mutual accommodations. Rationalization and colonization of the lifeworld by the instrumental rationality of bureaucracies and market-forces is a primary concern of Habermas's two-volume Theory of Communicative Action. For Habermas, communicative action is governed by practical rationality – ideas of social importance are mediated through the process of linguistic communication according to the rules of practical rationality. By contrast, technical rationality governs systems of instrumentality, like industries, or on a larger scale, the capitalist economy or the democratic political government. Ideas of instrumental importance to a system are mediated according to the rules of that system (the most obvious example is the capitalist economy's use of currency). Self-deception, and thus systematically distorted communication, is possible only when the lifeworld has been 'colonized' by instrumental rationality, so some social norm comes into existence and enjoys legitimate power even though it is not justifiable. This occurs when means of mediating instrumental ideas gains communicative power – like if someone pays a group of people to stay quiet during a public debate, or if financial or administrative resources are used to advertise some social viewpoint. When people take the resulting consensus as normatively relevant, the lifeworld has been colonized and communication has been systematically distorted. The 'colonization' metaphor is used because the use of steering media to arrive at social consensus is not native to the lifeworld—the decision-making processes of the systems world must encroach on the lifeworld in a way that is in a sense imperialistic". George Ritzer (2007, p. 287) explains colonization of the lifeworld in this way: "As the system and its structures grow increasingly differentiated, complex, and self-sufficient, their power grows and with it their ability to direct and control what transpires in the lifeworld (Habermas)."

REFERENCES

Aboulafia, M. (2001). *The cosmopolitan self George Herbert Mead and continental philosophy.* Champaign, Ill: the University of Illinois Press.

Aronowitz, Stanley & Giroux, Henry (1985). *Education under siege: the conservative, liberal and radical debates over schooling.* Masschustts: Bergin and Garvey Publishers, Inc.

Attar-Schwartz, S., Tan, J., Buchanan, A., Flouri, E., & Griggs, J. (2009). *Grandparenting and adolescent adjustment in two-parent biological, lone-parent, and step-families. Journal of Family Psychology,* 23(1), 67–75.

Baldacchino, Godfrey, Greenwood, Rob, & Felt, Lawrence (2009). *Remote control: governance lessons for and from small, insular, and remote regions.* St. John's, NL: ISER (Institute of Social and Economic Studies) Books, Memorial University of Newfoundland.

Baldacchino, Godfrey, Greenwood, Rob, & Felt, Lawrence (2009). "Geography, Governance, and Development: Challenges Facing the Small, Insular, and Remote". In Baldacchino, Godfrey, Greewood, Rob, and Felt, Lawrence. (2009), op. cit., pp. 1–15.

Ball, Stephen J. (1995). "Intellectuals or Technitians? The Urgent Role of Theory in Education Studies," *British Journal of Educational Studies, 43*(3), 255–271.

Boggs, Carl (1993). *Intellectual and the crisis of modernity.* Albany: State University of New York.

Brah, A. (1996). *Cartographies of diaspora: contesting identities.* London; New York: Routledge.

Burbules, N.C., & Rupert, B. (1997). "Critical Thinking and Critical Pedagogy: Relations, Differences, and Limits." In Popkewitz, Thomas S. and Philip Higgs. (1997) (Eds.). *Critical Theory in Educational Discourse,* Butterworth's.

Buss, Helen M., Clarke Margaret (1999). *Memoirs from away: a Newfoundland girlhood.* Waterloo, Ontario: Wilfrid Laurier University Press. *Cultural Logie,* pp. 1–21.

Delisle, J.B. (2008a). "A Newfoundland Diaspora?: Moving through Ethnicity and Whiteness", *Canadian Literature,* (196), 64–81.

Delisle, J.B. (May, 2008b). *The Newfoundland diaspora.* Vancouver: A thesis submitted in partial fulfillment of the requirements for the degree of doctor of philosophy.

Devine, M., & Earle, T. (2011). Grandparents: roles and responsibilities and its implications for kinship care policies. *Vulnerable children and youth studies, 6*(2), 124–133.

Dirlik, Arif (1996). The Global in Local. In Wilson, R. and Dissanayake, (1996) (Eds.), op.cit., pp. 21–45.

Douglas, J.A. (Ed.) (2010). *Rural planning and development in Canada.* Toronto: Nelson Education.

Doyle, C. (2012). "In the land of plenty: response to Henry A. Giroux," Aula de Encuentro, Revista De In vestatigacion Y communica Ciionn De Expeiencias educativas. Andalucia, Numero Especial, Ano xv, Junio de 2012, 15–27, Servcio De Publicacines E Intercambio, 29–38.

Doyle, C. (2010). Cultural Loss: What is taken from us and What we Give Away, in Ursula Kelly and Elizabeth Yeoman (2010). *Despite this loss: essays on culture, memory and identity in Newfoundland and Labrador.* St. John's: ISER Books.

Doyle, C., & Hoben, J. (2011). No Room for Wonder. In J.L. Kincheloe and R. Hewitt (Eds.). *Regenerating the philosophy of education: What happened to soul?*. New York: Peter Lang.

Doyle, C., & Singh, A. (2006). *Reading and teaching Henry Giroux.* New York: Peter Lang Publishing, Inc.

Eyerman, Ron et al. (1987). *Intellectuals, universities, and the state in Western societies. Berkely:* University of California Press.

Fagan, B. (2004). *Trial: the loss of constitutional rights in education in Newfoundland and Labrador: the Roman Catholic story.* St. John's: Adda Press.

FAO Corporate Document Repository, Title: What is Local Knowledge? United Nations.

Felt, Lawrence (2003). Small, Isolated and Successful: Lessons from Small, Isolated Societies of the North Atlantic, *Collective research papers of the Royal Commission on renewing and strengthening our place in Canada 4*, St. John's: Queen's Printer.

Felt, Lawrence (2009). A Tale of Two Towns: Municipal Agency and Socio-economic Development in Akueyri, Iceland, and Corner Brook, Newfoundland. In Baldacchino, Godfrey, Greewood, Rob, and Felt, Lawrence (2009).

Finlayson, A.C. (1994). *Fishing For Truth: A Sociological Analysis of Northern Cod Stock-Assessments from 1977–1990.* St. John's: ISER Publication. Memorial University.

Fook, J. (2012). *Social work: A critical approach to practice* (2nd Edition) Thousand Oaks: California. Sage Publications.

Fowler, Ken (2007). "School Life and Community Economic Challenge: A Newfoundland Case Study," *Canadian Journal of Education, 30,* 1.

Fraser, N. (1994). "Rethinking the public sphere: A contribution to the critique of actually existing democracy," in H.A. Giroux and P. MacLaren (1994) (Eds.).

Freire, P. (2005). (Expanded Edition with new commentary by Peter McLaren, Joe L. Kinchelo, *and Shirley* Steinberg). *Teachers as cultural workers. Letters to those who dare teach.* Boulder: Westview Press.

Frie, Roger (Eds.) (2008). *Psychological Agency: Theory, Practice, and Culture.* Cambridge, Massachusetts: A Bradford Book, The MIT Press.

Fuller, Steve (2005). *The intellectuals.* Icon Books.

Galway, Gerald & Dibbon, David (Eds.) (2012). *Educational reform: from rhetoric to reality.* London, Ontario: The Althouse Press.

Geertz, C. (1983). *Local Knowledge.* New York: Basic Books.

Giddens, A. (1990). *The consequences of modernity.* Cambridge: Polity Press.

Giddens, A. (1991). *Modernity and self-identity: self and society in the late modern age.* Palo Alto: California: Stanford University Press.

Giroux, H. (2012). "Higher Education, critical pedagogy, and the challenge of neoliberalism: rethinking the role of academics as public intellectuals," Aula de Encuentro, Revista De In vestatigacion Y communica Ciionn De Expeiencias educativas. Andalucia, Numero Especial, Ano xv, Junio de 2012, 15–27, Servcio De Publicacines E Intercambio.

Giroux, H.A. (2005) (rtEd.). *Schooling and the struggle for public life: democracy's promise and education's challenge.* Boulder, Colo.: Paradigm Publishers.

_____ (2003). *The abandoned generation: democracy beyond the culture of fear.* New York: Plagrave Macmillian.

_____ (1997). *Pedagogy and the politics of hope: theory, culture, and schooling: a critical reader.* Boulder, Colo.: Westview Press.

_____ (1993). *Living dangerously: multiculturalism and politics of difference.* New York: Peter Lang Publishing, Inc.

_____ (1993). *Border crossing: cultural workers and the politics of education.* New York: Routledge.

_____ (1989). *Schooling for democracy.* London: Routledge.

_____ (1983). *Theory and resistance in education:* a pedagogy for the *opposition.* London: Hienemann Educational Book.

_____ (1981). *Ideology, culture, and process of schooling.* Philadelphia: Temple University Press. London: Farmer Press.

Giroux, B.A., & Aronowitz (1994). *Education still under siege.* Westport, Conn.. Bergin & Garvey.

Giroux, H.A., & McLaren, P. (Eds.) (1994). *Between borders: Pedagogy and politics of cultural studies.* New York: Routledge.

Giroux, H.A., & Simon, R.I. (1989). *Popular culture, schooling, and everyday life.* Granby, Mass.: Bergin and Garvey.

Gmelch, G., & Richling, B. (1988). "'We're Better off Here': Return Migration to Newfoundland Outports." *Anthropology Today, 4,* 12–14. *Society and Culture.* St. John's: Breakwater Books, 1993.

Gramsci, Antonio (1971). *Selections from the prison notebooks,* (Ed. and Trans.). Q. Hoare and Smith. New York: International Press.

Geertz, C. (1983). *Local Knowledge.* New York: Basic Books.

Green, M. (1995). *Realizing the imagination.* San Francisco: Jossey-Bass.

Greene, John P. (1999*). Between damnation and starvation: priest and merchants in Newfoundland politics.* Montreal and Kinston: McGill-Queen's University Press.

Greenwood, Rob (2010). Policy, Power, and Politics in Rural Planning and Development in the Canadian State. In Douglas, J.A., op.cit., (2010), pp. 86–109.

Greenwood, Rob (2009). "Doing Governance for Development: The Way Forward for Newfoundland and Labrador," in Baldacchino, Godfrey, Greewood, Rob, and Felt, Lawrence (2009), op.cit., pp. 280–294.

Greaves, N.M. (2008). "Intellectuals and the Historical Construction of Knowledge and Identity: A Reappraisal of Gramsci's Ideas on Leadership". *Cultural Logic,* pp. 21–29. ISSN 1097-3087.

Haberma, J. (1962). *The Structural transformation of the Public Sphere.* Cambridge: Beacon Press.

Habermas, J. (1987). Theory of communicative action, Vol 2: Lifeworld and system: A critique of functional reason. Boston, MA: Beacon Press.

Hanrahan, Maura (1993). *Uncertain refuse: Lecture on Newfoundland society and culture.* St.John's: Breakwater Book.

Hiller, H.H., & Franz, T.M. (2004). "New Ties, Old Ties and Lost Ties: The Uses of the Internet in Disaspoa". *New Media Society, 6*(731), 731–752.

Hoben, J. (2011). Learning what you cannot say: Public school teachers and free speech, An exploratory qualitative study. Unpublished doctoral dissertation, Memorial University of Newfoundland, St. John's, Newfoundland.

House, J.D. (1999). *Against the Tide: Battling for Economic Renewal in Newfoundland and Labrador.* Toronto: The University of Toronto Press.

House, J.D. (Fall 1989). "A Sustainable Outport: A Model for Community Development." *Canadian Journal of Community Mental Health, 8,* Vol. 2, 25–40.

House, J.D. (1989). *Going* Away and Coming Back: Economic Life and Migration in Small Canadian Communities. St. John's, NL: ISER (Institute of Social and Economic Studies) Books, Memorial University of Newfoundland.

House, J.D. (2001). "The New Regional Development: is Rural Development a Viable Option in Newfoundland and Labrador?" *Newfoundland Studies* 17, Vol. 1, 11–31.

Kaldor, Mary (2010). Five Meaning of Global Civil Society. In Steger, Manferd, B. (2010) (Ed.). *Globalization the greatest hits: a global studies reader.* Boulder: Paradigm Publishers, pp. 153–163.

Kaldor, Mary (2003). "Five Meanings of Global Civil Society" *In Global Civil Society: An Answer to War.* Cambridge, UK: Polity Press 1–12.

Kaufman, C. (2003). *Ideas for actions: relevant theory for radical change.* Cambridge, Mass.: South End Press.

Kelly, Ursula A., & Yeoman, Elizabeth (Ed.) (2010). *Despite this laoss: essays on culture, memory, and identity in Newfoundland and Labrador.* St. John's, NL: ISER (Institute of Social and Economic Studies) Books, Memorial University of Newfoundland.

Kelly, Ursula A. (2009). "Learning to Lose: Rurality, Transciene, and Belonging (A Companion to Michael Corbett)". *Journal of Research in Rural Education, 24*(11), 1–4.

Kellner, D. (2000). "Multiple Literacies and Critical Pedagogies." In *Revolutionary Pedagogies – Cultural Politics, Instituting Education, and the Discourse of Theory.* Peter Pericles Trifonas, Editor.

New York: Routledge.

Kennedy, J.C. (August 1997). "At the Crossroads: Newfoundland and Labrador Communities in a Changing International Context." *The Canadian Review of Sociology, 34*(3), 297–317.

Kincheloe, Joe L., Hewitt, Randall (Eds.) (2011). *Regenerating the philosophy of education: what Happened to soul?* Introduction by Shirley R. Steinberg. New York: Peter Lang. Series: Counterpoints – Volume 352.

Leistyna, P., & Woodrum, A. (1996). "Context and culture: what is critical pedagogy," in P. Leistyna, A. Woodrum, & Sherblom (Eds.). *Breaking free: the transformative power of critical pedagogy.* Cambridge, MA: Harvard Educational Review, pp. 17.

Lauder, H., Brown, P., Dillabough, J., & Halsey, A.H. (Ed.) (2006). *Education, globalization and social change.* New York: Oxford University Press.

Lloyd, Christopher (Ed.) (1983). *Social theory and political practice.* Oxford: Clarendon Press.

Milan, A., & Hamm, B. (2003). *Across the generations: Grandparents and Grandchildren.* Statistics Canada.

MacEachern, Daniel (2012). "Employers increasingly looking to older workers to combat shortage," *The Telegram*, St. John's, Newfoundland, Sunday, September 29, 2012, pp. A17–18.

Maclaren, P., & Kincheloe (Eds.) (2007). *Critical pedagogy: Where are we now?* New York: Routledge.

Marlor, C.P. (2004). "Retrenchment and Regeneration in Rural Newfoundland." *Contemporary Sociology, 11*, Vol. 33, 696–697.

Mayda, Chris (Summer 2004). "Resettlement in Newfoundland: Again". *Focus on Geography, 48*(1), 27–32.

McKim, Wliiams A, (Ed.) (1988). *The vexed questions: denominational education in a secular age.* St. John's: Breakwater Books.

Mills, C.W. (1971). *The sociological imagination.* New York: Oxford University Press.

Morgan, L., & Kunkel, S. (r^d Edition) (2001). *Aging: the social context.* California: Pine Forge Press.

Mullaly, B. (2010). *Challenging oppression and confronting privilege* (2nd Edition) Don Mills: Ontario. Oxford University Press.

Neis, B., & Felt, L. (2000). *Finding our sea legs: linking fishery people and their knowledge with science and management.* St. John's, NL: ISER (Institute of Social and Economic Studies) Books, Memorial University of Newfoundland.

Neis, B. (1999). "Families and Social Patriarchy in the Newfoundland Fishing Industry," in Newell, D., and Ommer, R. (1999). (Eds.). *Fishing places, fishing peoples: tradition and issues in Canada's small-scale fisheries.* Toronto: University of Toronto Press, pp. 32–44.

Newell, D., & Ommer, R. (Eds.) (1999). *Fishing places, fishing peoples: tradition and issues in Canada's small-scale fisheries.* Toronto: University of Toronto Press.

Noel, S.J. (1971). *Politics in Newfoundland.* Toronto: University of Toronto Press.

Noddings, Nel (Ed.) (2005). *Educating citizens for global awareness.* Boston: Research Center for the 21 Century.

Noel, S.J. (1971*). Politics in Newfoundland.* Toronto: University of Toronto Press.

Odin, S. (1996). *The social self in Zen and American pragmatism.* Albany; State University of New York Press.

Ommer, Rosemary (2004). "The Resilient Outport: Ecology, Economy, and Society in Rural Newfoundland." *Canadian Historical Review, 85*, Vol. 2, 363–367.

Ommer, R.E. (Ed.) (2002). *The Resilient Outport: Ecology, Economy, and Society in Rural Newfoundland.* St. John's, NL: ISER (Institute of Social and Economic Studies) Books, Memorial University of Newfoundland.

Ommer, Rosemary & Sinclair, Peter (1999a). Outports Under Threat: Systemic Roots of Social Crisis in Rural Newfoundland. In: Byron, Reginald and Hutson, John. *Local Enterprise on the North Atlantic Margin: Selected Contributions to the Fourteenth International Seminar on Marginal Regions.* Scotland: Ashgate, 1999, 253–275.

Ommer, Rosemary & Sinclair, Peter (1999b). Systemic Crisis in Rural Newfoundland: Can the Outports Survive?. In Pierce, John T. and Dale, Ann. *Communities, Development, and Sustainability Across Canada: Sustainability and the Environment.* Vancouver: UBC Press, 1999, 49–68.

Overton, James (1985). "Living Patriotism: Songs, Politics and Resources in Newfoundland." *Canadian Review of Studies in Nationalism, 12*, Vol. 2, 239–259.

Pinar, W.F. (1991). Curriculum as social psychoanalysis: On the significance of place. In J.L. Kincheloe and W. Pinar (Eds.) (1991). *Curriculum as social psychoanalysis: The significance of place,* (pp. 165–186). Albany: State University of New York Press.

Popkewitz, Thomas, S. (Ed.) (2008). *Inventing the modern self and John Dewey: modernities and the traveling of pragmatism in education.* New York: Palgrave Macmillan, (1st edition).

Popkewitz, T.S., & Higgs, P. (Eds.) (1997). *Critical Theory in Educational Discourse,* Butterworth's.

Richling, B. (1985). "Isolation and Community Resettlement: A Labrador Example." *Culture, 5,* Vol. 2, 77–85.

Richling, B. (Winter, 1985). "Stuck Up on a Rock: Resettlement and Community Development in Hopedale, Labrador." *Human Organization, 44,* Vol. 4, 348–353.

Richling, B. (1985). "'You'd Never Starve Here': Return Migration to Rural Newfoundland." *Canadian Review of Sociology & Anthropology, 22,* Vol. 2, 236–249.

Ritzer, George (2007). *Contemporary sociological theory and its classical roots: The basics.* Boston: McGraw Hill, Higher Education.

Sheppard, B., Brown, J., & Dibbon, D. (2009). *School district leadership matters.* Dordrech, The Netherlands: Springer.

Schibeci, R., & Grundy, S. (1987). Local theories. *Journal of Education, 81*(2), 91–96.

Schon, D. (1987). *Educating the reflective practitioner.* New York: Basic Books.

_____ (1983). *The reflective practitioner.* New York: Basic Books.

Sen, Amartya (1983). "Accounts, Actions, and Values: Objectivity of Social Science," in Llyod, Christopher (1983) (Ed.). *Social theory and political practice.* Oxford: Clarendon Press. (Wolfson College Lectures 1981), pp. 87–108.

Simon, 1.R. (1993). *Teaching against the grain: Text for a pedagogy of possibility.* New York: Bergin & Garvey.

_____ (1994). *Teaching against the grain: Text for a pedagogy of possibility.* New York: Bergin & Garvey.

Sider, Gerald (1986). *Culture and class in Anthropology and History: A Newfoundland illustration.* London: Cambridge University Press.

Sider, Gerald M. (2003). *Between History and Tommorow: Making and Breaking Everyday Life in Rural Newfoundland.* Peterborough: Broadview Press.

Sinclair, Peter R., & Lawrence F. Felt (1993). "Coming Back: Return Migration to Newfoundland's Great Northern Peninsula." *Newfoundland Studies, 9,* Vol. 1, 1–25.

Sinclair, Peter & Ommer, Rosemary (2006). *Power and Restructuring: Shaping Coastal Society and Environment.* St. John's, NL: ISER (Institute of Social and Economic Studies) Books, Memorial University of Newfoundland.

Sinclair, P.R., & Felt, L.F. (1993). "Coming Back: Return Migration to Newfoundland's Great Northern Peninsula". *Newfoundland Studies, 9*(1), 1–25.

Singh, Amarjit & Mehta, Kalyani (2008). *Indian diaspora: voices of the diasporic elders in five countries.* Rotterdam/Taipei: SENSE Publishers.

Singh, A., & Doyle, C. (2006). *Reading and teaching henry Giroux.* New York: Peter Lang Publishing, Inc.

Singh, A. (2000). "World Englishes, curriculum change and global career opportunities," in Singh, A., Baksh, I.J. & Hashe, G. (2000). *Studies in Newfoundland education and society,* Vol. 111, 773–750. Also see *The Morning Watch* http://www.mun.ca/educ/faculty/mwatch/fall07.html, Winter 2006, Vol. 33, Nos. 3–4 to Fall 2007, Vol. 35, Nos. 1–2, ISSN 0384–5028.

Singh, A., Kinsey, B., & Marton, J. (1991). "Informal Support among the Elderly in Four Ethnic Cultural Settings in Canada and the U.S.A.," *International Journal of Contemporary Sociology, 28*(1–2), 57–83.

Singh, A., & Kinsey, B. (1993). "Lay Health and Self-Care Beliefs and Practices: Responses of the Elderly in Four Cultural Settings." In Masi, R, Menshah, L, and McLeod, K. (1993). (Eds.). *Health and cultures: policies, professional practices and education.* Oakville; Mosaic Press, pp. 197–228.

Singh, A. (1991). How to Manage or Make Sense of Recent Reports and Documents on the Quality of Schooling (Part I) and Social Theory, Political Practice and Experts – Making Sense of the Reports on the Quality of Schooling (Part II). In Singh, A. & Baksh, I.J. (1991). *Dimensions of Newfoundland Society and Education.* St. John's: Faculty of Education. Memorial University, pp. 7–34. Also see *The Morning Watch* http://www.mun.ca/educ/faculty/mwatch/fall07.html , Winter 2006, Vol. 33, Nos. 3–4 to Fall 2007, Vol. 35, Nos. 1–2, ISSN 0384-5028.

Singh, A., et al. (1999). Some observations on School-Community-Family Relations in Selected Schools in Newfoundland. *The Morning Watch,* pp. 1–9, (http://www.mun.ca/edu/faculty/mwatch/win99/singhetal.htm)

Singh, A., Martin, Wilfred, B.W., & Singh, R. (1991). The modes of self of South-Asian elderly in Canadian society: towards reconstructing interdependency. *Multiculturalism, XIII*(3), 3–9.

Singh, A. (1982a). "Theories of Social Gerontology". In Singh, A. and Baksh, I.J. (1882) (Ed.). Society and Education in Newfoundland, Vol. II. St. John's: Faculty of Education, Memorial University of Newfoundland, pp. 529–539. Also see *The Morning Watch* http://www.mun.ca/educ/faculty/mwatch/fall07.html , Winter 2006, Vol. 33, Nos. 3–4 to Fall 2007, Vol. 35, Nos. 1–2 , ISSN 0384-5028.

Singh, A. (1982b). "Some Dominant Views of the Elderly, Their Families and Caring for the Aged in our Society." In Singh, A. and Baksh, I.J. (1882) (Ed.). Society and Education in Newfoundland, Vol. II. St. John's: Faculty of Education, Memorial University of Newfoundland, pp. 540–549. Also see *The Morning Watch* http://www.mun.ca/educ/faculty/mwatch/fall07.html , Winter 2006, Vol. 33, Nos. 3–4 to Fall 2007, Vol. 35, Nos. 1–2, ISSN 0384-5028.

Singh, A., & Martin, Wilfred. B.W. (1982). *A symbolic interactionist orientation to the study of aging in Newfoundland.* St. John's: Institute for Research in Human Abilities, Research Bulletin No. 82–005, Memorial University of Newfoundland. Presented at the Seventeenth Annual Conference of the Atlantic Association of Sociologists and Anthropologists, St. Francis Xavier University, Antigonish, Nova Scotia, March 12, 1982.

Smith, L.T. (1999). *Decolonizing methodologies: research and indigenous peoples.* London: Zed Books Ltd.

Smyth, J. (1989). A critical pedagogy of classroom practice. *Journal of Curriculum Studies, 21*(6), 483–502.

Steger, Manfred B. (Ed.) (2010). *Globalization the greatest hits; A global studies reader.* Boulder: Paradigm Publisher.

Steinberg, S.R. (2012). Critical *Qualitative Research Reader.* (Co-editor with Gaile Cannella. New York: Peter Lang Publishing.

Sullivan, E. (1987). Critical pedagogy and television. In D.W. Livingstone (Ed.), *Critical pedagogy and cultural power.* MA: Bergin & Garvey Publishers, 57–75.

Theodoratus, R.J. (Eds.) (1984–1989). *The immigrant communities and ethnic minorities in the United States and Canada.* New York: AMS Press.

Thiele, D.M., & Whelan, T.A. (2008). The relationship between grandparent satisfaction, meaning, and generativity. *International Journal of Aging & Human Development, 66*(1), 21–48.

Trifonas, P.P. (Ed.) (2000). *Revolutionary Pedagogies – Cultural Politics, Instituting Education, and the Discourse of Theory.* New York: Routledge.

Tripp, D. (1987). *Theorizing Practice: The Teacher's Professional Journal.* Geelong: Deakin University Press.

Turvett, B. (2006). Grandparent power. *Working Mother, 30*(1), 77–77.

United Nations Educational, Scientific and Cultural Organization: Local and Indigenous Knowledge Systems LINKs (see these links for discussions on the notions of "local knowledge").

Van Manen, M. (1997). *Researching lived experience: Human science for an action sensitive pedagogy.* (2nd ed.) London, ON: The Althouse Press.

Vohs, K.D., & Finkel, E.J. (Eds.) (2006). *Self and relationship: connecting intrapersonal and interpersonal processes.* New York: The Guildford Press.

Wade, Cato (1973). *Now, whose fault is that? The struggle for self-esteem in the face of chronic unemployment.* St. John's: ISER (Institute of Social and Economic Studies) Books, Memorial University of Newfoundland.

Wadel, Cato (1969). *Marginal Adaptations and Modernization in Newfoundland; A Study of Strategies and Implications in the Resettlement and Redevelopment of Outport Fishing Communities.* St. John's,

Institute of Social and Economic Research. St. John's: Memorial University.

Welbourn, K., & McGrath, C. (1996). *Surviving in Rural Newfoundland*. St. John's: Writers' Alliance of Newfoundland and Labrador.

West, Thomas (2002). *Sign of struggle: The rhetorical politics of cultural differences*. Albany: SUNY Press.

Weiner, E.J. (2007). Critical Pedagogy and the Crisis of Imagination. In Maclaren, P. and Kincheloe (2007). (Eds.). *Critical pedagogy: Where are we now?* New York: Routledge.

Wilson, R., & Dissanayake (Eds.) (1996). *Global/Local: Cultural Production and the Transnational Imaginary*. Durham and London: Duke University Press.

Williams, R. (1983). *Key words*. London: Fontana.

Wright, Eric Olin (1978). "Intellectuals and the Working Class," *The Insurgent Sociologists, 8*(1) (Winter 1978), 5–18.

Zurcher, L.A. (1977). *The mutable self: A self-concept for social change*, Beverly Hills: Sage Publications.

PLACE, DIASPORA, NOSTALGIA, HOPE, AND POSSIBILITIES

ROB GREENWOOD

RURAL NEWFOUNDLAND AND LABRADOR

*The Personal and the Political in Sustaining Choices and
Sustaining Communities*

The Canadian Province of Newfoundland and Labrador has a history and geography
that has forged a people with a strong sense of shared identity, yet who demonstrate
many differences and contradictions, individually and collectively. They routinely
identify themselves as distinct from other Canadians, yet they have migrated across
the country in search of work for generations. They have a strong shared political
commitment to place when dealing with the federal government in Ottawa or
foreign multi-nationals, but they have many internal divisions: Labrador's sense
of grievance versus "the Island;" "baymen" versus "townies;" the second city of
Corner Brook versus St. John's. They pride themselves on their English and Irish
roots – the first colony of the British Empire – yet the Aboriginal people native to the
island are extinct, and the first Europeans to settle the province, the Vikings, did not
maintain a permanent presence. There is even intense dispute over terms like Newf
and Newfy; for many they are derogatory terms while for others – especially for
those who have moved to the mainland and who celebrate their Newfoundland and
Labrador heritage, – they are used with pride. (See Chapters one and thirty-eight)

Much of the mentality of the English and Irish who settled the province can be
linked to the industry that attracted them in the first place – the fishery. Cod, in
particular, was the basis of a rural economy, which resulted in hundreds of small
fishing outports strung around bays and peninsulas and on islands, close to the
fishing grounds. Merchants in St. John's and a few larger communities controlled
access to markets, provided supplies on credit in return for exclusive rights to
the dried salt cod. Local democracy was very slow to develop, and settlers who
operated in a cashless economy feared the property taxes that local government
would demand. The opening up of the interior of the island with logging and paper
mills, as well as the gradual development of mining on the island and in Labrador,
introduced additional employment and a cash economy. Employment on Canadian
and American military bases in World War II, followed by the extension of the
welfare state when Newfoundland voted (after two hard-fought ballots) to join
Canada, resulted in newfound wealth (Alexander, 1983; Royal Commission, 1986).

Compared to the rest of Canada, economic statistics in the newest Canadian
province lagged national averages for decades. Seasonal fishing and forestry
industries, and a large seasonal construction industry tied to major resource

A. Singh and M. Devine (Eds.), Rural Transformation and Newfoundland and Labrador Diaspora:
Grandparents, Grandparenting, Community and School Relations, 43–54.

developments and the push to establish roads throughout the province, meant that many workers depended on unemployment insurance for part of the year. While earned incomes remained low compared to elsewhere in the country, the province maintained the highest rate of home ownership in North America. Newfoundlanders and Labradorians had adapted their ability to survive through self-provisioning (building their own homes, heating with fire wood, hunting and fishing), with the cash economy. Many commuted seasonally to jobs on the mainland, or worked around the world in the marine industry, while maintaining their homes in rural communities. Large extended families and strong social capital in tight-knit communities accommodated modernization without sacrificing rural lifestyles and traditions (Royal Commission, 1986).

The collapse of the cod fishery and the declaration of a moratorium in 1992 brought this lifestyle largely to an end. Years of declining stocks, combined with increased mechanization in the forest industry and repeated efforts by the Federal Government to diminish dependence on unemployment insurance had placed increased pressure on rural communities. The moratorium, however, represented the largest layoff in Canadian history, and perhaps even more significant, a psychological blow to a culture and society founded on cod. From a total population of about 522,000 in 2001, the province's population dropped to approximately 506,000 in 2007. At the same time, the composition of population within the province was changing dramatically. Rural communities suffered out-migration, not only to the mainland, but also to urban centres within the province. The population was also aging significantly, partly due to out-migration of young families, but also due to a significant drop in fertility rates, as those families that remained had far fewer children than in the past. In 2007, for the first time in the province's history, more people were leaving the workforce than were entering it (Locke, 2011; Lynch, 2008/9; Clair, 2008).

Newfoundland and Labrador has changed a lot in recent decades and it's going to change a lot more. Remote commuting, where people keep their home in the province but commute for varying periods to earn wages on the mainland, is increasingly prevalent. In addition to the cod moratorium, the closure of two of the province's three paper mills removed entire workforces in the mills and in the regions that produced the pulp wood. Mining and mineral explorations continue to generate significant wealth and employment, but seldom is it located in established communities. Labrador West has become the province's very own Fort McMurray, and while some families re-locate, many workers commute within the province. New mines in Labrador and on the Island avoid the creation of communities dependent on non-renewable resources, and establish work camps for employees to live at home and commute for weeks or months at a time.

Meanwhile, the North-east Avalon region, including and surrounding the capital city of St. John's, is booming. The oil and gas industry has led to high paid jobs in the offices that manage the fields and in the broad supply chain that services the industry. Some workers in rural areas commute to jobs on the offshore vessels and platforms, but the bulk of activity is in the capital region. The provincial government is in the unique position of having significant growth in revenues thanks to the taxes and royalties paid by the oil companies. Expenditures have also grown rapidly, however, with significant infrastructure development in health, education and transportation around the province, but the bulk of permanent employment is concentrated in St. John's, further enhancing the North-east Avalon economic dominance. Rather than a two-track provincial economy, with the St. John's region versus the rest, there is more of a three-track economy of the dominant St. John's region, followed by regional centres enjoying relative population growth, with a third track of rural and remote communities suffering unprecedented decline.

The demographic trends reflecting and reinforcing these regional variations are multiple and complex. There is an overall aging of the population in all but a few communities. Even the booming St. John's region and the urban regional centres around the province have population pyramids that are not sustainable in the long term. Aboriginal communities in Labrador have the healthiest youth cohorts, but persistent educational and employment challenges will mitigate the opportunities for these young populations if the challenges are not met.

The aging populations in the urban centres of the province are enjoying the best of times. Provincial spending is fuelling stable or growing employment in public administration, health care and education. The provincial college system is targeted with substantial funds to meet the increasing skills shortages for oil, mining, mineral processing and potential hydroelectric development. Rural families are abandoning their home communities and moving into the urban centres, to be close to service sector employment and to services and amenities, especially health care. Little empirical evidence is available, but there are indications that workers commuting to mining employment and the Alberta oil sands are re-locating to the urban centres across the province for the same reasons – access to public and private services and service sector jobs for spouses. There are even reports of owners of fishing enterprises moving to urban centres, while operating their vessels out of rural communities during the fishing season.

The signs of prosperity are abundant throughout these urban centres. New shopping complexes, housing developments and rapidly rising housing prices, vehicle sales, recreational equipment sales, the list goes on. For people without the education, skills or employment to take advantage of these opportunities, rising housing costs are making affordable housing a new social challenge in a province long reputed to have the highest rate of home ownership in North America. For single parents, the prosperity around them can be out of reach without public supports for child care. And greater prosperity, combined with remote commuting and disrupted families, is leading to reports of greater alcohol and drug problems.

Finally, at the community level, outmigration of families from rural towns, and significant levels of remote commuting, diminish the pool of volunteers available for local government, volunteer fire departments and social organizations. Neighbouring communities, long protective of their independence, are finally exploring how to share services. For communities too distant from their neighbours for this to be viable, basic services and social supports are disappearing (Freshwater, Simms and Vodden, 2011).

There have been many innovative approaches to community and regional development in Newfoundland and Labrador. In the absence of strong local government, a vestige of the province's fishing history and concomitant lack of local democratic efficacy, a network of voluntary Rural Development Associations (RDAs) were established starting in the 1960s. Based on local community committees, with representation at the regional level, these community-based organizations were initially organized in opposition to government resettlement efforts. The Memorial University Extension Service played a key role in this process, and gradually the federal and provincial governments provided financial support for these organizations to employ a coordinator and implement community development projects. By the 1980s, the RDAs were no longer the only community-based organizations in their areas, as municipal government evolved, the Federal Government supported a nation-wide network of Community Futures committees, and a plethora of social and fraternal organizations made up a maturing civil society (Task Force, 1994; Baldacchino, Greenwood and Felt, eds., 2009).

By the 1990s, the federal and provincial governments demanded a more coordinated use of their community and rural development supports. The Task Force on Community Economic Development was established in 1994, in the midst of the fishery moratorium, to determine a new approach to community and regional development in the province. Significantly, the Task Force was not asked to consider how government's own departments and agencies were to better coordinate their efforts. The product was a network of 20 Regional Economic Development Boards (REDBs) in Economic Zones covering all areas of the province. The REDBs were to develop strategic economic plans for their zone and negotiate a performance contract with the federal and provincial governments to coordinate supports for development. Many RDAs have continued to operate without direct government operational support, and municipalities have played an increasing role in community development, while REDBs have had less than consistent support from the federal and provincial governments (Douglas and O'Keeffe, 2009; Vodden, 2009; Freshwater, Simms and Vodden, 2011). In 2012 the Federal Government announced that they would end funding to REDBs, and their counterparts in the Maritimes, and the Government of Newfoundland and Labrador responded by cutting their support to REDBs. There are numerous other non-governmental organizations throughout the province, with social, environmental and fraternal mandates, but other than those in the St. John's region benefitting from support under the Provincial Poverty Reduction Strategy, community-based organizations are crying out for more resources (Greenwood and Pike, 2011).

I have been fortunate to play a role in community and regional development policy in the 1990s, and in researching and writing about it since then. As founding Director of the Leslie Harris Centre of Regional Policy and Development (the Harris Centre) at Memorial University, I have also been able to collaborate closely with community, industry and government organizations throughout the province. I also have lived through many of the developments in Newfoundland and Labrador's evolution since the 1960s. Indeed, I have been one of the many who moved away to attend university and returned home (twice in my case) and my young family and I moved to Saskatchewan for five years, and like many, returned "home" (to take up the job at the Harris Centre) the first chance I got. I also have enjoyed the benefits of knowing both sets of my Grandparents, and my children have had the opportunity to know their Grandmothers as integral parts of their lives.

How do grandparents fit into this mix of prosperity, dislocation and restructuring? In part, they are a driver of some of these changes. Again, data is lacking, but there is evidence of many Newfoundlanders and Labradoreans returning to the province after working on the mainland throughout their careers. They are bringing pensions and savings and for the fortunate ones, windfalls from houses sold for many times what they were purchased for in Toronto, Calgary, Fort McMurray, Vancouver or elsewhere. They may wish to return to their home community, but if that is a rural town distant from health care, they will purchase or build a house in the nearest regional centre or in the St. John's region. In the title of his last book on regional development, Donald Savois captured a driving force in this trend: *Visiting Grandchildren* (2006). Savois' primary meaning was that grandparents in the Maritimes would have to travel outside the region to visit their grandchildren in Ontario or the west. Much of that is no doubt happening in Newfoundland and Labrador also, but many grandparents are also moving to regional centres and to the St. John's region to be close to their grandchildren – and to health care and other services.

For parents and children living hectic lives in these prosperous regions, these supportive grandparents are often the difference between assimilation into the North American consumerism-dominated sameness that is discussed in Chapter one in this book, and the continuation of some vestige of Newfoundland and Labrador's rural identity with its ties to the resource sector, outdoor recreation and community culture and connections. For families living on the margins of the prosperity in low-wage, insecure employment, or long-term unemployment, the presence of these grand parents may be all that separates them from extreme poverty.

My own family has benefitted enormously from my mother and my wife's mother, who have been available to babysit and support us as we went to university and built our careers. My mother-in-law has maintained her home in rural Newfoundland, providing a place for affordable summer holidays and a re-connection with family stories and connections, logging history and outdoor recreation. When I studied in England, and my wife was working, "Nan" stayed with us twice for extended periods to child mind. We could not have maintained a desirable standard of living and I may not have finished my Ph.D. without her. My mother lives in St. John's, and she has provided a window for our children into an extended family of fifty-four first cousins, seasonal visits to Old Perlican to pick berries, and a reliable source of cooked dinners.

A great unknown is how these economic and cultural benefits will continue into the future. Fertility rates in Newfoundland and Labrador are no longer at replacement level. The average child in the future will not have a brother or a sister, and their children will not have an uncle or an aunt. In the social history of Newfoundland and Labrador that lack of extended family is inconceivable. Literally. As the baby boom generation dies off, the children born in mainland Canada will not have the links back to this province. This province will hold some curious attraction in the diet and music of the diaspora, but the absence of those tradition bearers with a direct connection in their life experience with the province will be a difficult void to fill. Singh and Oldford in the last chapter discuss the conditions in which it might be possible for the future Newfoundland and Labrador grandparents to keep the links back to this province alive.

What of the life and life style of future Newfoundlanders and Labradorians and what place will grand parents have? Recent research on regional interaction in the province points to the emergence of "functional regions" where the majority of the population lives in communities that are within daily interactive proximity to one another. People live in one community, work in another and shop in another. The North-east Avalon and the province's regional centres all enjoy a greater critical mass than their individual populations would indicate. And the smaller communities which surround them are integrated into larger labour market and service areas than their historical conception of community would have conceived. With the continuing viability of the province's resource industries, at higher levels of productivity and with fewer people employed, these functional regions will continue to have propulsive economic activity. Emerging industries such as aquaculture in some areas, increased agriculture, pockets of small and large-scale manufacturing, and public and private sector services, will employ people for decades to come.

For many, these functional regions will present an ideal combination of access to urban services and amenities while maintaining easy access to outdoor recreation and rural lifestyles. For rural communities too distant to be part of such functional regions, the prospects are much bleaker. A restructured fish processing sector, with opportunities for longer employment periods during the year would enable some sustainable functional regions based on the fishery. Tourism will continue to offer seasonal opportunities to supplement other employment but tourism-dependent regions will resemble the original fishing communities in Newfoundland and Labrador. A small population of year-round "livyers" will maintain the community over the winter, until the population swells in the summer and fall with tourists and people with summer homes. This could be a very attractive lifestyle for retired and semi-retired people, but it is not consistent with the traditional rural community we picture in the province.

The potential for increased immigration is another uncertain prospect for the province. There is not a shortage of people in the world, and many would like to come to Canada. The experience to date, however, is that immigrants are attracted to locations that already have a lot of immigrants. The provincial government has advanced an immigration strategy and many municipal governments are implementing welcoming communities programs. As resource developments continue, particularly in mining and mineral processing, and possibly in hydro-electric development, significant demand for skilled labour is being generated. Temporary worker programs are being used increasingly to meet these demands, but this is not the sustainable population growth most communities hope development will generate.

What will the Newfoundland and Labrador family look like in fifty years? In one hundred years? The Celtic roots of the West Country English and the Irish who formed 98 percent of the settler population will no doubt persist to some degree. The stoic rural mentality that allowed poverty and deprivation to be endured with close family and community supports and good humor may continue to resonate. The attitude of "what odds" seems to be dissipating, though, as a more self-confident, better educated, wealthier population is not willing to "put up" with what they get. The unprecedented popularity of Premier Danny Williams was rooted in the confidence and pride of a millionaire Premier who was unwilling to settle for second best for anything. Whether you shared in this approach, its appeal to Newfoundlanders and Labradorians cannot be denied. What will today's parents pass on to their grandchildren? It certainly won't be the same as today's grandparents.

What grandparents pass on depends a lot on how they critically engage in the forces around them. Chapters one and thirty-eight in this book highlight how grandparents can be conceived of as organic intellectuals who combine formal and informal education and who can bring critical literacy to understanding the context of this province and society in flux. While many of the economic and demographic forces around us are beyond our control, how we engage them and make our own life decisions is influenced by our understanding and our values.

If we cede this critical engagement to outside intellectuals and ideas rooted in notions of modernity, consumerism and sameness, the result will be predictable. But places and people are not all the same, and it is how they assert their understanding and values within the forces they confront that determines the mediated outcomes that create the in-between accommodations Chapters and thirty-eight call for.

My own life, influenced by my grandparents and my parents, and my wife's mother – who was widowed when my wife was five years of age – have provided a grounding and countering to the values that dominated post-war Canada.

My mother was the youngest of ten, in a family that originated in the rural Newfoundland fishing industry. My grandfather, William Joseph Bursey – Will-Joe – was ambitious and entrepreneurial and like many Newfoundlanders of the day, he left his home town of Old Perlican in rural Newfoundland and travelled not to Canada, but to the "Boston States" where he learned the machinist trade. He fit in a trip to the "wild west" where he carried a six gun, helped with the wheat harvest, and returned to Chelsea, Massachusetts where he married my Grandmother, another Newfoundlander who had moved to the Boston States to seek a better life. Julia Colbourne had been sent to work as a domestic servant with a wealthy family after her mother and siblings were wiped out by TB in Carbonear – a disease that ravaged many Newfoundland and Labrador families prior to Newfoundland joining Confederation with Canada.

Will-Joe and Julia returned to Old Perlican with their first child, born in the US, and went on to have eight more children before they moved to the South Side of St. John's harbor, where my mother was born. Will-Joe had built up a fish processing and retail business and locating in St. John's made business sense. The family maintained close connections to Old Perlican and Will-Joe's parent's house stayed in the family as a summer home. The six brothers all started out working in the business and several continued in Will-Joe's company or branched out on their own. After my mother married a Canadian sailor, they settled in Toronto where my brother and I were born. My father was from downtown Toronto, but his parents longed for a rural lifestyle outside the city and by the time I was born my dad's father, Frank Greenwood, had taken early retirement from Bell Telephone and he and his wife Ethel purchased a small mixed farm near the Holland Marsh north of Toronto. My parents settled in a suburban neighbourhood, with my father commuting to downtown Toronto where he was in furniture sales.

It was a typical mix of rural and urban in post-war Canada. Most urban Canadians had rural roots. The growing suburbs were home to ambitious couples wanting all the "good things" for their families – new cars, washing machines, nice furniture, etc., etc. But people also complained about the "rat race," where working for wages, getting into debt, commuting to jobs in the city, all dominated daily life. Frank and Ethel were early contrarians, chasing their dream of a quieter life on a farm. When my father, Gary, grew tired of the rat race, with the daily commute in growing volumes of traffic into Toronto, my mother, Mona's, origins in Newfoundland presented the promise of an alternative lifestyle. When I was seven and my brother twelve, we made the move from the centre of the Canadian universe to the "slower pace" of Newfoundland. For the first seven years we lived with my mother's parents in their large house in the heart of the city – no commute, with the harbor in view, and a different world from Toronto. Uncles and Aunts and cousins came and went from the large house and a sense of extended family became normal. "Excursions around the bay" to Old Perlican were part of the seasonal cycle, to pick berries, catch trout, and learn family history through osmosis – mostly the uncles arguing over what really happened in various stages of community or family history.

My wife's family was more rural, but not without migrations. My mother-in-law, Madelaine Mercer, moved from the very remote, very small coastal community of Victoria Cove, to one of the new booming in-land communities that were part of the attempted industrialization of Newfoundland and Labrador. Millertown, on the shores of Red Indian Lake, was a magnate for workers seeking wage income as loggers. The paper mill in Grand Falls was downriver and the forests around Red Indian Lake fed log booms which emptied into the Exploits River. Millertown had grocery and hardware stores, a hotel and a rail line. Madeline, like my Grandmother and so many young woman of the time, was sent to do domestic work for a family, and in Millertown she met Horace Lane and they started their own family. Like his father and one of his brothers, Horace died young of a heart attack and my wife grew up surrounded by strong women who watched out for each other. Mechanization of the logging industry eroded jobs over time, and Millertown entered a long, slow period of decline. My wife, like one of her sisters, finished high school and left home at sixteen to study to be a lab and x-ray technician. She landed her first job at the children's hospital in St. John's, where we met and started our family.

Mona and Madelaine became good friends and our children have learned about Old Perlican and Millertown; they have had many visits, and they have enjoyed many family gatherings where the stories and values are shared. "Nan" and "Mama" have been ever-present in our children's lives, even when we lived in England and in Saskatchewan, coming for long visits and helping with babysitting. More importantly, they embody the histories and values and sense of place that they were raised with. For my wife and I, combining work and education while we raised our family, we are exposed to the academy with its peer reviewed research for international journals where theory is abstracted from context, while living in a particular context that is interpreted daily through the lens of the past and the present, rural and urban.

The notion of grandparents as organic intellectuals flies in the face of academic specialization and privileged access to "expert" opinion. Indeed, even within the academy the scholarship of engagement is frowned upon by most promotion and tenure committees. Collaborating with individuals and organizations outside the university takes time and presents risk in generating peer reviewed articles. Tier 1 or Tier 2 journals cater to academic disciplines on an international scale. Theory and evidence must be generalized to be transferrable and place-specific context may provide interesting case studies, but the focus must be on the universal – as if it exists anywhere outside of place and context.

My own career choices and academic pursuits have been influenced by these tensions. These tensions are discussed in Chapters one and thirty-eight in this book from the perspective of importance and necessity of doing small-scale local studies by "non-academics" and "non-experts", and from the perspective of colonization of knowledge, lifeworld, and decolonization of highly funded and institutionalized social science research. I did my Ph.D. at the Warwick Business School, one of the top-ranked business programs in the world, but I compared Newfoundland and Northern Norway in my thesis. I've always maintained links with university research during my career, most of which was in government policy roles, but I have been unwilling to focus on academic research that is not driven by local or regional issues or applications. I have worked in the university for almost a decade now, but it has been in the bridging role of outreach and engagement. There is an increasing interest in universities world-wide for this, largely due to government and community demands for more direct benefits from public expenditures on universities.

Individuals and institutions are constantly torn between these demands. We are inundated by the media, by specialized publications, and by peer pressure, to seek the "good life" of material possessions, international travel and urban cosmopolitanism.

But, if we are fortunate enough to have grandparents with alternate conceptions of what constitutes a good life, we are forced to consider what else is possible. Seldom is there a choice between all of one way and all of another. As noted in Chapters one and thirty-eight, we must mediate "in between" places. I have had to make several career choices where the balancing of values was integral to what I would do and where I would live. I have developed a simple schema to help with these situations, and I think it has evolved from my balancing of family history and values with professional and material aspirations.

The schema is quite straight forward. My wife and I moved to Saskatchewan when our children were young and my wife had just completed her education degree, after changing careers working in the hospital (with a gap of three years living in England and having two children). The job market for teachers in St. John's was very tight, and I was ready for a change in my job in the Provincial Government. I was offered a great position in the Saskatchewan Government, and while we would miss our families, a few years away while the children were young would advance our careers and be an adventure.

When it came time to consider returning to Newfoundland, five years later, our daughter was about to start high school and if we did not leave then it would have been difficult to uproot the kids. I was by then working as a consultant – I left the Government position to escape a dominating Minister, and a position with a Crown Corporation was eliminated in a restructuring that eliminated all the Vice Presidents. I had an offer with a Crown Corporation in New Brunswick, and there was a evolving possibility of a position at Memorial University.

Weighing the options led me to break them down by three primary criteria: fulfillment, family and money. Fulfillment related primarily to the nature of the job – how much it related to my professional interests, my training and the opportunity to grow professionally. Family is where the demands of the job in terms of hours and travel come in, and their impact on time with your spouse and children. Based on the importance of extended family, and location, resulting from the family influences I have outlined, family also took into account where the job required me to live and would it be close to our mothers, siblings and cousins. And money does matter. How much would you make? What was the growth potential? What were the benefits? Job security can also factor in under this.

Each job option presents a different mix on each of these criteria. Make enough money and you can probably take a little less fulfillment and a little more demand on your time away from family. If you don't have any options, you take what you can get: you have to live. At different stages of your life, different factors carry more weight. It is harder to be away from your children when they are young. It is harder to be away from your parents when they are very old.

This schema provides a simple tool for individuals and families to balance the conflicting demands of career, family and material wellbeing. The three are all linked, but when you assess different career or job options it allows you to do so with a conscious, deliberate consideration of what matters most, or what are the trade-offs.

There are in between spaces. Every individual has their personal values, and they are influenced by their relationships and the demands they place on them. Having the grandparents I have had, and the influence of mine and my wife's parents on our children, has had a tangible impact on the choices we have made. Grandparents as intellectuals highlights that their influence is about ideas and interpreting reality, and pointing out to the current generation, who at one point in their life course will become grandparents, that there are many in between spaces available to them and to their own children to choose.

Reflection Questions

1. The "long commute" of many Newfoundlanders and Labradorians has resulted in a new model of commuting or living away for lengthy periods of time. In the past, people in the province often went to the Labrador fishery in the summer and worked as loggers in the winter and would be gone for several months, returning in the fall. Later, men working on offshore draggers would be gone from home for 10 days and home for two days. The new model, the long commute, is slightly different than in the past. How might this different model affect families and communities differently?

2. The oil boom and increased centralization of people in the province to larger centres is juxtaposed to the decline of rural and remote communities. How does the loss (and closure) of rural and remote communities impact those who are 'forced' to move to larger 'more prosperous' centres? What are the continued links between rural and urban communities?

3. Grandparents are discussed in this chapter as a tremendous support to their families in providing many types of care, not the least of which is child care. What are the concerns that may arise from a social policy perspective as grandparents are being viewed more as a resource to families and to community, given the neoliberal ideology of government often attempting to offload programs, services and care to the community's informal network such as grandparents?

4. The author describes his sense of place in Newfoundland and Labrador and 'reconnecting' with his roots. Choose another chapter in the text that describes the experience of diaspora and compare and contrast this author's experience with another author in this text.

REFERENCES

Alexander, D. (1983). Atlantic Canada and Confederation: Essays in Canadian Political Economy, comp. E.W. Sager, L.R. Fischer, and S.O. Pierson. Toronto: University of Toronto Press.

Baldacchino, G., Greenwood, R., & Felt, L. (Eds.) (2009). Remote Control: Lessons in Governance for/ from Small and Remote Regions. St. John's: ISER Books.

Canadian Rural Revitalization Foundation (CRRF) and Rural Development Institute (RDI) (2005). Final Report, National Rural Think Tank, April 28, 2005, "Immigration and Rural Canada: Research and Practice," www.brandonu.ca/rdi

Clair, Michael (2008). "From Out-migration to Immigration: *The Changing Policy Landscape.*" *Newfoundland Quarterly, 101*, 2 (Fall), 34–37.

Douglas, D., & O'Keeffe, B. (2009). "Rural Development and the Regional Construct: A Comparative Analysis of the Newfoundland and Labrador and Ireland Contexts," in G. Baldacchino, R. Greenwood, and L. Felt (Eds.). Remote Control: Governance Lessons for and from Small, Insular, and Remote Regions. St. John's: ISER Books, pp. 77–113.

Freshwater, D., Simms, A., & Vodden, K. (2011). "Defining Regions for Building Economic Development Capacity in Newfoundland and Labrador," St. John's: Harris Centre, November.

Greenwood, R., Pike, C., with Kearley, W. (2011). *A Commitment to Place: the Social Foundations of Innovation in Newfoundland and Labrador.* St. John's: Harris Centre. www.mun.ca/harriscentre

Greenwood, Rob (2009). "Doing Governance for Development: The Way Forward for Newfoundland and Labrador," in G. Baldacchino, R. Greenwood, and L. Felt (Eds.) *Remote Control: Governance Lessons for and from Small, Insular, and Remote Regions.* St. John's: ISER Books, pp. 280–294.

Kearley, Wade (2008). "Where do you draw the line? Regionalization in Newfoundland and Labrador: A comparative synopsis of selected stakeholders' input." St. John's: Harris Centre, January 25.

Locke, Wade (2011). "A Prosperity Plan for Newfoundland and Labrador: Defining the Realities and Framing the Debate," Memorial Presents, Harris Centre, June 8, www.mun.ca/harriscantre.

Lynch, Scott (2008/9). "The Absence of Opportunity: Understanding the Dynamics of Intra-Provincial Migration within Newfoundland and Labrador." *Newfoundland Quarterly, 101*, 3 (Winter), 36–39.

Reimer, B. (2007). "Immigration in the New Rural Economy," *Our Diverse Cities: Rural Communities*, 3 (Summer), 3–8, http://canada.metropolis.net/publications/index_e.htm

Savoie, D. (2006). *Visiting Grandchildren: Economic Development of the Maritimes,* Toronto ON: University of Toronto Press.

Storey, K., & Shrimpton, M. (1989). *Impacts on Labour of Long-distance Commuting Employment in the Canadian Mining Industry.* ISER Report No. 3, Institute of Social and Economic Research, Memorial University of Newfoundland, St. John's, NL. *Royal Commission on Employment and Unemployment.* 1986. Report. St. John's: Queen's Printer.

Task Force of Community Economic Development (2005). Report, "Community Matters: The New Regional Economic Development," St. John's: Task Force.

Tomblin, S., & Braun-Jackson, J. (2006). "Managing Change Through Regionalization: Lessons from Newfoundland and Labrador." St. John's: Harris Centre.

Tomblin, S., & Braun-Jackson, J. (2008). "Managing Change through Regionalization: Lessons from Newfoundland and Labrador." St. John's: Harris Centre, Memorial University. www.mun.ca/harriscentre/Reports

Tremblay, Reeta & Amanda Bittner (2011). "Newfoundland and Labrador: Creating Change in the 21st Century." In John Biles, Meyer Burstein, Jim Frideres, Erin Tolley, and Rob Vineberg, (Eds.) *Integration and Inclusion of Newcomers and Minorities Across Canada.* Montreal and Kingston: McGill-Queen's University Press.

Vodden, Kelly (2009). "Experiments in Collaborative Governance on Canada's Coasts: Challenges and Opportunities in Governance Capacity," in G. Baldacchino, R. Greenwood, and L. Felt (Eds.) *Remote Control: Governance Lessons for and from Small, Insular, and Remote Regions.* St. John's: ISER Books, pp. 259–279.

HELEN M. BUSS, (AKA MARGARET CLARKE)

MEMOIRS FROM AWAY, A NEW FOUND LAND GIRLHOOD (AN EXCERPT)

I have come to Victoria, British Columbia, as I do for a week each February, to read the memoirs and personal papers of pioneer women whose manuscripts are kept here in the public archives. But from the moment I arrive my first thought is not about my research, but about writing an introduction to the memoir stories that have cropped up like wild flowers among my other writings. I wrote the first drafts of these memoirs in Florida, that paradise of remembrance where everyone comes from somewhere else, where Canadians can feel really Canadian because they miss listening to the CBC. I visit Florida often because my parents have an apartment by the sea and some time ago, when I had a year of study leave, they lent it to me for several months so I would have a quiet place to work away from the Canadian winter.

Spending an extended time in Florida, I found myself writing about the Canadian identity that I adopted, or that adopted me, as a seven year-old Newfoundlander; the American difference reminded me constantly of what it was to be Canadian. Being Canadian is real in Florida, because you know you are not American, whereas here in Victoria, in my own country so to speak, I often find myself uncomfortable, as if I were a Newfoundlander from the old-time outports in a merchant's town parlour.

The invention of my Canadian identity began when I was a very little girl, the day after the referendum votes of adult Newfoundlanders were finally all counted and we became part of the Canadian nation. My father and the history books tell me that our coming to Canada was a much more complex process than I remember, with run-off elections and weeks of getting in the outport vote that finally tipped the scales toward a decision that most of the city folk of St. John's did not want. The tentative announcements gradually became real only over days, weeks. But I remember it differently.

In my remembering it all happens one late night, in our living room at our home on Craigmillar Avenue, with my father's friends smoking cigars around my mother's folding card-table, its surface strewn with maps and statistics. My father made predictions, while others denied their validity; it was an intense male world which my mother stayed well away from, and which I watched through the glass-panelled doors that looked into that room full of men. These are the kind of moments memory's imagination shapes for its myth of the self; all time delays, all nonessentials of character and plot fall away and only the archetypal necessities of

A. Singh and M. Devine (Eds.), Rural Transformation and Newfoundland and Labrador Diaspora: Grandparents, Grandparenting, Community and School Relations, 55–70.

identity remain: the mother in the kitchen, the father's world behind the little squares of glass, and later, my territory, the garden under the maple trees.

The maples had been planted by my father many years before, when he could not have known of their aptness for my secret Confederation ritual. That morning, after his night of cigar smoke and statistics, he told me I was now indeed a Canadian. Or perhaps it was later, after the negotiations that he had shared in, helping to get the best deal possible for the future of communications in Newfoundland. Anyway, it was some morning after, whenever it was, that I stood under the maples and turned around and around, facing each of the four corners of my world, saying aloud, "I am a Canadian; I am a Canadian; I am a Canadian; I am a Canadian." I greeted each point of the compass, there in the dizzy pleasure of my turning, not knowing what travail I was taking on.

Some days now I feel like the only Canadian. Some days I feel like the last Canadian. Some days I feel that being a Canadian is impossible. I like to think that all of these feelings are essential to being a Canadian. Every Canadian must feel this alone. All Canadians must feel that their own personal history is the one that makes them Canadian and since no one else has had quite the same history, they live alone in their Canadian identity. When we talk of being Canadian we speak not of national myths, but of our own lives. To be a Canadian is to be an autobiographer.

Now, a lifetime later, I am here on the island at the other end of Canada looking at apartment condominiums, playing with the prairie dweller's dream of retiring "to the coast." My bread and butter is back in Calgary, where the messages pile up in my mailbox and on my e-mail at the university, and my job awaits, as secure as anything academic can be in the Province of Alberta. Alberta feeds me well, but does not make me feel at home; something about its efficiency, its wealth, the smoothness of a politics that aims always at an unproblematic optimism, makes me feel unreal. Each summer I pack my research notes, full of the anonymous stories of women gathered in Canadian archives from Victoria to Ottawa, and travel back to Manitoba, the place where I made my marriage, raised my children, became that thing we call, in an ancient and strange phrase, a doctor of philosophy. Better to call me a doctor of memoirs, a job description you won't find a lot of call for in the classifieds. Manitoba, where I spent most of my adult life, had no job for the kind of doctor I had become, so decades after we went away from Newfoundland because of my father's job prospects, I went away again. And like any Newfoundlander, I went once more westward for a job. But, like any Newfoundlander I want to come back to whatever sod is called "home." The Manitoba that will not hold me still holds a small piece of real Canadian territory dear to me, the always-unfinished cottage on the shore of Lake Winnipeg, the place that has been ours for the last quarter century. In these times, that is a long time. The pine walls of its interior are full of my changes. Each summer, as I work my research inside them, they declare my history and its lessons: "don't you get too high-falootin' girl, with your doctorate and your professorship; remember the woman's life that feeds it. Remember all the diapers and dishes and Tuesday-evening suppers prepared on the run before night classes in Middle English, all the bittersweet poems of wifehood and the comfort stories for children alarmed in the night. Remember all the lies and truths you had to tell yourself and others in order to learn about language in this place." Each summer, Manitoba grounds me, centres me, makes me feel real for a while.

When I began my study leave, I came to Manitoba for the summer to write and read, before heading for Florida in the late fall. I began to conceive of a trip to Newfoundland at the end of the year, a kind of reward for working hard. Maybe that's what caused the memoir stories to begin. I had been back to my birthplace only twice since I left in 1955. The first time, in 1969, I went with my husband, two kiddies and a truck and camper. We touristed through Prince Edward Island, along the Cabot Trail and spent only five days in Newfoundland. My mother's sister, Aunt Helen, was alive then and was good to me as she had always been. My father's brother, Uncle Leonard had become the owner of my childhood home and he invited us to the best dinner of fresh salmon I have ever eaten. I went alone to walk through the neighbourhood. Standing by the familiar graveyard just south of our home, for the first time in my life of busy wifing, mothering, teaching-a life in which I felt all too real-I felt like a ghost haunting a former life. I remember not liking that feeling. It was the beginning, I think, of being overly conscious of my disconnectedness from my own lived life, the uneasy way you have to feel in order to be driven to words, driven by desire for those small moments when, writing, you live inside your own experience, your own body. I avoided Newfoundland for over two decades after that time, finally going in the early nineties in the guise of researcher-a comfortable otherness-in search of women's stories. Every place I looked, I found the stories belonged to someone else; they were not mine. A lively research was already underway. Cousins were kind, hospitable, but I did not feel at home. They had lives in this place; I did not.

Generous with memory and talk, in the way Newfoundlanders are, my Aunt Jean took time out from dying of cancer to remember my childhood. We spent an hour together and when we said goodbye, I knew I would not see her again. She would be a memory, like my Aunt Helen and Aunt Thelma, the women whose stories had enlivened my childhood years. Discouraged by not finding a suitable topic for research, depressed by the passing of so many in my parents' generation, whose lives had been Newfoundland for me, I opted for being a tourist, searching each day a different arm of the Avalon Peninsula, as if I were a lady from Manitoba here to take photos to show my kids during the long prairie winter. For a few days I imagined that I was the mother of such a tightly knit prairie family, not the mom of grown children living thousands of kilometers from where home used to be. Several times we drove the circle of my childhood territory, the limits of my walking and bike-riding in old St. John's: west along Military Road where it becomes Harvey Road up by the Catholic Cathedral, past the place where I used to go to Holloway School, past where the street becomes LeMarchant Road, past the building which used to be Prince of Wales College, my school from grades six to nine, along to where LeMarchant becomes Cornwall Avenue and then down the hillside of Craigmillar

Avenue, past my house to Topsail Road, down Water Street, along the harbour and up King's Bridge Road to our bed and breakfast near the new version of the Newfoundland Hotel.

Each time we drove the circle I would remark on how the old St. John's seemed lost in the larger city built since my childhood. Each time I would marvel that the limits of my childhood took only twenty minutes to circle in our car. Each time my husband would slow down near my house on Craigmillar (now not owned by our family) and ask if I wanted a photograph, if I wanted to get out and walk around the neighbourhood. Each time I refused; it was too cold; it was too windy: it was ghosting time again. Months later, when I saw the photograph he took of me leaning against the *Peter Pan* statue in Bowring Park, I realized how hard it must have been to be with that woman in Newfoundland, her face full of her loss, her fear, her anger: a woman haunted by unmade stories.

But this time would be different. The memoir stories had started to happen and I would have a research purpose: the research of my own life. I would banish the ghosts through having a living reason for being in Newfoundland, especially since, as my plans grew, my parents decided to join us. I would be taking my Mom and Dad, Kathleen and Harold, home with me. Harold and Kathleen have been home dozens of times since they left with their five children in tow to move to the prairies in 1955; they have seen the changes in their home place, watched the growth of highways and suburbs and shopping centres, seen their Newfoundland and their generation gradually disappear. They admire the progress, mourn the deaths. Now they are getting a little too fragile to go on their own, so they will fly to St. John's where we will meet them after our long drive from Manitoba. Their plans are simple, a week at their favourite bed and breakfast with their son-in-law and daughter to take them to all the old places that are part of them, visits to the few living folk they love, then off to Nova Scotia, where there is a sister, a son, a daughter-in-law, and a granddaughter to visit.

My own plans are more grandiose. Since these memoirs have begun to grow, I have become ambitious for material. I plan with a singleness of focus that only a writer bent on inspiration can. My plans quickly become massive enough for a Russian novel. I will travel back over the territory of my life, all my Canadas, from my research into the past in Victoria, through the Calgarian present, to a month of reflection and preparation at the Manitoba cottage. Heading eastward by car we will stop first at the mill town in Northern Ontario where I began my teaching career, then take the Great Lakes route to Toronto to see my daughter and join the family, now mostly settled in southern Ontario, where we will celebrate my mother's eightieth birthday with a gathering of the clan. After swallowing half a continent, we will visit my brother Hal and his family in Cleveland and absorb a chunk of America on the way to the Maritimes. My appetite for Canada regrets that we cannot taste Montreal and our French connection, my Aunt Denise, who graciously married my Uncle Jack a few decades back so that we could have Quebecois cousins, but we are taking the American route to the Maritimes where our eldest son has settled, and to Halifax where my youngest brother will take us to Peggy's Cove and we will deep-breath some sea air, readying our palates for our Newfoundland destination. Yes, I was ambitious for this writing.

But ambition makes fools of writers. A couple of weeks before our departure I am explaining our itinerary to my husband-it seems I have not let him in on all the details of the Russian novel-when he suggests that we go by air instead of attempting such a long drive. I brush aside his concerns with distance; this is a symbolic journey, not to be contaminated with thoughts of the actual size of the continent. And haven't we already savoured half of America and Canada in our year of study and travel? Didn't we successfully drive to Florida in the fall, and in spring cross the south and west of the whole of the United States of America? Hadn't we picnicked by the Rio Grande, tasted the wine valleys in California, supped a full month on the archives in Victoria? Weren't we the intrepid pair who had gloriously flown to France for academic papers and more wine valleys? Weren't we the stubborn Canadians who singlehandedly mastered the Paris subway system to return again and again to the Spanish embassy to win visas, despite turbot wars and bureaucracy, in order to get lost in the slums of Barcelona on our way to drink deeply of Gaudi and Miro? Hadn't we gorged on auto-routes at 140 clicks per hour, and bitten off forbidden pictures of the Mona Lisa? Hadn't we gobbled up two continents already this year? What was another 10,000 kilometres? Besides, driving to Newfoundland would be fun. What I wanted to tell the man whom I expected to do most of the driving was that it would be part of my research and therefore sacred, but I knew by the doubt in his eye that such an argument was out. So I bargained instead. I said I would do all the driving (a promise I had no intention of keeping), if he would have cruise control installed in the car. While I flew to Quebec City to give yet another paper our car was cruise-controlled. Days later, when my airplane brought me back into the bright Winnipeg summer, I was still in a complete state of denial about the difficulty of travelling so far, after a year of trips. I had become addicted to motion, addicted to not really belonging anywhere. As I checked out the cruise control and arranged for final engine servicing, as I packed for whatever the next five weeks of journeying might bring, I kept telling myself that this was a culmination of the memoir writing, this was the trip into the past that would make all the writing real, make me real, ground me in the place of my birth.

* * *

Coming into Port aux Basques on a sunless day deciding between rain and fog, we watched the long, low stretch of rock narrowing the barren grey of the sea between our ferry and landfall. Startled by the sudden appearance of dwellings rising unexpectedly in the momentary breaks of light, I am amazed that *people* live here! Yet there will be times on my visit when, as my mainland carefulness falls from my manner and my speech speeds to its childhood rate, and as Newfoundland women with no reticence about expressing their opinions make me dare to be downright rude by prairie standards for middle-class females, that the phrase becomes joyous: "people *live* here." And in short seconds of forgetfulness I will almost feel at home; I will come into possession of a keen desire to be one of the people who lives *here.*

When I am away from this island place I tend to forget the most impressive ability that Newfoundlanders possess: their exceptional ability to express what they think and feel. It is not something I am used to anymore. In the daily places I live people so often do not trust language to say what they mean, do not seem to know what they feel and refuse to speak what is on their minds. Conversation becomes a game in which we all try to mask ourselves from the other. Here, again and again, I meet people confident enough in the value of their own language-making, and in the listener's ability to hear them without perversion, that communication constantly startles me. Like some long lost endorphin circling a runner's brain, some substance would suddenly begin to zip through my chemistry and talk would begin to have meaning. These are moments when I forget I am from away and I almost feel I am from here.

Like the day we sailed to Julie's Cove with a childhood friend. Anchoring in the perfect circle of the cove, we go ashore and are guided through the undergrowth beyond the cove's beaches to find the now-deserted settlement which is marked only by a grassy bank where the houses would have been. Farther up the densely treed hill we read its story in the language of the graveyard's headstones. They tell us succinctly of brothers drowned, of wives dead in birthing and children taken by disease. No words are wasted, but their brevity speaks volumes. These bleached-white testaments tell the history of so much of Newfoundland, the brave, tenuous communities of interconnected families, the generations of lives spent in these small worlds of the coves, their ultimate diaspora. It would not be surprising if we were to meet someone from Sudbury or Seattle or Singapore climbing up through the underbrush to see her ancestors' graves.

After exploring the Northern arm, the communities off the TCH, the great parks along the way, and as we approach the Avalon Peninsula, the idea of walking in my old neighbourhood starts to become difficult. The memory of feeling like a ghost when I went there in my twenties, my refusal to set down my foot there when I had come a few years ago, had built a kind of anti-nostalgia in me: the dread that some fragile adult identity would disintegrate by the very act of touching the ground. So this time, to give me courage, I had booked us into rooms a few blocks distant from my home on Craigmillar Avenue to force myself to set foot in the neighbourhood. I wanted to face the ghosts, even if I was one of them. The evening of our arrival in St. John's I went walking in the cemetery that had been both my childhood playground and my childhood terror. It is not well kept. I can remember when the caretaker who lived on the property had every path trimmed and all the fences in fine repair. Now his house is gone from its space on Topsail Road and the paths are unkempt and shabby. No kid would want to violate the rule of no bike-riding on these scruffy paths. I walked all over the cemetery until it felt as ordinary to me as a backyard in need of a trim. I tramped down Topsail Road and up Craigmillar Avenue until every inch of my old grounds felt as unmagical as the streets of Calgary. I walked past my house several times, surreptitiously glancing in the front windows as I did. Inside, people seemed to be having a dinner party. Talk and food and candlelight filled the dining room. How nice. How civilized. How good that the place is unhaunted by me, that life goes on in wonderful ordinariness without any notice of the middle-aged woman from the Prairies pausing on the street outside. I confess that I turned toward my lodgings with a slight feeling of let down that had not yet become relief.

And then I saw the snails. Do you know that feeling when a memory long lost suddenly leaps full-blown in your head? It feels like a flower is blooming in your forehead, as in time-lapse photography where the bud becomes a rose in a mere second of fecundity. The front of my head actually tingled as I bent down to examine the sidewalk in the late twilight. Yes, there they were, a dozen or so snails marching across the sidewalk, their delicate shellhouses, swirled brown and beige and white, carried delightfully on their backs as they went to and fro from whatever chore took them from the curb of the street to the cement and stone wall of the large garden of one of the more prosperous houses east of the cemetery.

When I was a child and became tired of all the playmates of my immediate neighbourhood, I would head east down Topsail Road towards the larger homes that marked a neighbourhood of more prosperity, older trees, more established families. You might not notice the difference today, as these more spacious homes become old, their large gardens not kept to the old standards of my childhood. Along here, amongst the handful of ''mansions,'' in a smaller, but still impressive home, lived a little girl whom I played with only rarely. I thought she was rich and so went to her house only when I was curious about the rich. This little girl (whose name escapes me) and I used to occasionally check on the snail settlement. There they would be, parading back and forth between street and garden wall. She and I would pick them up by their shells and carefully stroke their little tails, their creepy-crawly underbellies, and especially their little wiggling antennae. Oh, how that tickled our fancies, those soft, delicate wands, against our little girl fingers. Oh, how we shivered! Oh, how we laughed!

We would play as gods with our little colony, lining them up one by one, or in ranks. We would turn them north when they wanted to go south, and south when they wanted north, and watch in amazement as they found their way back to whatever direction they intended before they were disturbed by the unseen fates, small girls bent on haunches, knees at our faces, intent on ordering the world of snails. I remember one day the little girl told me that in France people ate snails. At first I was unbelieving, then, because she seemed so sure of her knowledge (she was, after all, rich), I was astounded, disgusted and worried in turn. "Would you eat snails?" I asked.

"Oh no," said she. "What would the garden do without them? They turn the soil you know." Sometimes, even if you are only six years old, you have enough sense to know when you are in the presence of poetry. And now the poetry of snails had survived the road changing from gravel to pavement, survived the pathway moving from foot-worn to concrete, and had gone on year after year in the same place for fifty years. They were here for me now, in the twilight, at the moment I had returned from away.

No longer comfortable on my haunches, I leaned against the garden wall and watched them for a while, feeling the flower of memory bloom in my head. I began to feel an amazing relief, then joy, that I had returned to such a scene of my childhood home. The snails have stayed with me, a scintillating visual image, from that moment to this, urging me on in these acts of memory.

Since the growing of images into similes and metaphors and the translation of them into symbols in my business, if this were a classroom instead of memoir I would probably ask my students to read the image of snails that carry their houses on their backs into a metaphor of the writer embodying language. Yet lately I find the working of language as symbol just a little embarrassing, the feeling I get when my students ask that inevitable question: "Did the writer really know that he was making all those different meanings? Did he really mean for us to see them?" More and more these days I want to stop my patient explanation about the complex relationship of writer, text and reader, stop my careful rhetoric of the importance of empowering ourselves to work with the complexity of language outside of authorial intention, and tell them that the use of metaphor and symbol is just a bad habit we have fallen into since we first came to believe that the word was somehow divine, that God was the word and the word was God. Symbolic language, I want to tell them, is all just the elaboration of an authoritarian belief system, outdated and oppressive. I do not tell them this because I know language has a tendency to become symbolic the moment we speak or write, like it or not, so we had better know how it keeps doing that, even when we are trying hard not to let it get away from us. I am trying hard right now.

But stumbling into the snail metaphor through this writing makes me realize once more the wavy line between memory and fact. Now that I reread what I have recounted to you as my memory of the snails and the little girl (whose name I still cannot remember), I realize much of it may be invented out of mere fragments of actuality. So, if you are one of the kids at the back of class who doubts the whole literary enterprise, here's my full confession. Yes, I can honestly testify that I used to play with snails at that spot on Topsail Road and I did know a little girl who-I suddenly remember at this moment of writing-came from a family who owned a jewellery store. I seem to remember her last name was Silver, but perhaps that would be too symbolically apt to be true. Whether or not I played in particular with her among the snails or some unremembered child is undecidable. I know someone told me about the French eating snails, and I think it happened while playing with the snails, and I do accurately remember (I think) being shocked. But you'll be relieved to know that my childhood was no more fanciful or poetic than any ordinary childhood and so the part about turning the soil and realizing poetry, well, that's just what decades of education in the literary tradition makes you do. Besides, isn't it worms who turn the soil? After an hour or so at my word processor, language just takes over, has its way with me. I'm sorry. I apologize. One thing I can guarantee you: when I went to Newfoundland and saw those snails on the sidewalk of Topsail Road just east of the cemetery I was one happy woman. It really did make me feel real in that place, driving out the fear of ghosts and old half-baked stirrings of who-knows-what traumas of childhood. Women writing today are encouraged to find dreadful things in their pasts. I was really happy to merely find the snails.

I slept well that night and seeing the snails made it easier to go about the Avalon Peninsula enjoying the old places, enjoying my parents memories, without feeling I was a ghost with no solid flesh to hold my identity together. The snails "actualized" me as we would say today, and I am grateful for it. I hope nobody puts out slug poison in that garden and kills them before I get back to Newfoundland again. And I'm sorry I made up that eco-romantic line about turning the soil. So there you have it: confessions of a sometime fiction writer trying to walk the constantly moving line between what happened and what is made from what happened. Forgive me, for I was only trying to make things real. In compensation, let me tell you a story about my parents, one I will call "Harold and Kathleen in Newfoundland." My parents are so real, they're super-real.

The Newfoundland and Labrador tourist book has adopted for its motto the phrase that is a typical reaction of their citizens to any new fact, fancy or phenomenon: "Imagine that!" I can remember hearing the phrase constantly as a child. It seems to me now that it was a way adults could show both approval and disbelief at the same moment. Maybe they were just being noncommittal, maybe they were suspending disbelief, but I think it is a healthy reply to make to a child, who having meandered through some probably awkward and highly improbable description of events, half concocted, half actual, hears an adult say "Imagine that!" Better than to have him tell you you're a liar, stupid or otherwise at fault. Better than having some patient parental unit of the present day try to be helpful about the difference between reality and fantasy. "Imagine that" had many tones and shades of meaning, from true amazement with a real exclamation mark to a slightly ironic twist with disbelief just below the surface. But whatever its tone, it always gives you the benefit of the doubt, allows your version of things to stand.

Taking Kathleen and Harold around the Avalon Peninsula left me in a continuous "imagine that" condition. Since I am the product of a late-twentieth-century, pseudo-socialist, historically conscious, ecologically sensitive ideology, the idea that one would want to tour anything except natural or historic sites dumbfounds me. On the other hand, my parents, unrepentant admirers of technological "progress," (they have dragged me through everything from NASA's Florida museum to the CN Tower) wanted us to go to see the building of the deep-sea oil rigs at Bull Arm. Dad had been there before, so he was doing this for our benefit. We were reluctant; he was insistent. And I ended up enjoying the tour. Imagine that.

I think he took me there to be impressed with the giant concrete circle being built in the middle of the Bay, and the enormous dockside complex that would eventually sit atop the circle when it is finally anchored out at sea. And I have to admit, at an intellectual level it is an impressive idea, that humans can make such an artificial island, and that if we are really lucky, and our science is right, it will survive the North Atlantic. But what impressed me most was the enormity of the human effort that made it possible. One of my Newfoundland cousins had gone all the way to Korea to help supervise the installation of the electrical systems in one of the pods that will be at the top of the artificial island. And his expertise was only one of thousands needed to make this project happen.

The young woman who guided us as we toured the site in a school bus recited the statistics of how many people are fed each day, how many eggs must be cracked, potatoes peeled, steaks grilled and fish fried, described the lock-step system of supplying, servicing and supervising that must go on when the crews are working three shifts a day during the "continuous pour" of concrete that makes the giant circle possible. She was quick with accurate statistics when I asked how many women and in what capacities were employed on the site. I'll have you know that this Newfoundland project has managed to employ more women directly in the technological and building side of this project than just about anywhere. I forget the statistic, but I was impressed at the time. "Imagine that," I thought.

As we walked up the stairs to the viewing site to see the giant grey structure circled by the bright blue water, I thought of the graveyard at Julie's Cove and all the ways Newfoundlanders have had to reinvent themselves to make a living on their island. Our guide described the new techniques that have made it possible to keep work on the project going nine months a year, through fog, storm and all but the coldest winter days. It sounded difficult; it sounded dangerous. I remembered a story from one of my school readers about a boy from a tiny outport who-on an everyday journey from one place to another-took terrible risks with sea and fog. I especially remembered the low-key reaction of everyone, including himself, when he managed to come safely to land. Despite our guide's sureness about the way the project has improved upon already-sophisticated Scandinavian technology, and her careful explanation of the stress tests the models of the rig have undergone that show it will resist all that nature can hand out-all perhaps except an earthquake under the sea-I had my doubts. Newfoundlanders would still be taking risks with sea and fog. "Imagine that," I said carefully in response to our guide's articulate enthusiasm.

Another day, attempting to wean my parents from their preference for sites of Newfoundland progress and industry, I convinced them to come to the archeological digs at Ferryland, where Memorial University has unearthed several layers of habitation that help them reconstruct settlement of that part of the island, one of the earliest (except for the brief Norse visit) white settlement in North America. We dropped my husband at Witless Bay from where he would go on a boat ride to photograph sea birds-puffins, murres and kittiwakes. My parents said they had seen enough birds in their day so they and I headed on to the digs. The university people have the site nicely laid out so that you can observe the various processes of an archeological dig safely at the same time as the workers and students continue their painstaking exploration. Once again, a well-informed young woman guided us. My parents have a tendency to distract such guides by trying to guess which part of Newfoundland they come from. This is not easy, since young people in Newfoundland today often have only trace remains of their local accents. My parents are persistent and quite good at this guessing game, and the guides are patient, perhaps understanding the dislike my parents' generation have for depersonalized guided tours. Kathleen and Harold, quite insistently, work to establish a more personal relationship, asking biographical questions, offering up their own backgrounds in return. This young guide seemed determined to tell us something about the site and even though my father interrupted to correct her history a couple of times, she did manage to do quite a good job of our education.

However, somewhere between showing us the well that was built by the first white inhabitants and explaining the way the workers had laid out the vegetable garden to imitate the first one on this spot, Dad and I noticed that Mother was missing. After a brief flurry of excitement we found Kathleen, being escorted carefully and very slowly, out of the forbidden-to-the-public depths of one of the digs, while she questioned her young male companion for details of his place of origin and his parents background. Father questioned her in turn: "How did you get down there, Kathleen?"

To this she replied, "How do you think? I walked, of course!"

I scolded her: "But you're not supposed ...."

She interrupted me with a haughty, "There's nothing wrong with asking a boy where his people are from." This desire to locate origins made me remember the typical question asked by adults who did not know me when I went on my childhood visits to my mother's birthplace in Carbonear. They did not ask "Who are you?" but "Whose child are you, my maid?"

I learned to say, "I'm Mom Osmond's granddaughter, Mrs. Arthur Osmond that is. I'm her girl Kathleen's child." And to those who further inquired, "and who would your father be, then?" I would reply, "Harold Clarke, from Victoria village, who was Aunt Ann's son who used to live up in the 'Burnt Woods.'" These were correct answers to questions of identity in those days.

On the way back to Witless Bay, mother regaled us with all that she had learned down in the digs. Some of it was even about archaeology. Imagine that. When his boat docked my husband was ecstatic over the sea birds and whales he had seen. He leaned in the car window, tried to persuade us to take the next trip by telling us how the whales had come right up to the boat, followed them, churning and surfacing and singing beside them. Aboard the boat the captain's son had sung sea shanties and then all the mammals, those aboard the boat and those in the water were inspired to sing together. Kathleen and Harold were polite during this recitation; they had seen many whales in their lifetimes, sung many a sea shanty, knew the difference between a whale and a whale of a story.

"Imagine that," they commented politely.

Our best day was full of sunshine on a blue-green ocean, perfect for a visit to the birthplaces of my parents on Conception Bay. But the trip did not start out easy. On each of our day trips I would haul out the map of the Avalon Peninsula, preparing to act as navigator from behind as my husband drove (it's strictly men in the front, women in the back with Kathleen and Harold on board). Each day my parents would insist that I put the map away. "We know exactly where we are going," they would exclaim. Miles later on there would be mild doubts: "We should have come to that turnoff by now." Or, "this corner is all changed." I took to memorizing the route on the map before they woke up in the morning, and then whispering it into my husband's left ear from my place behind him in the back seat. But my parents voices, both absolutely convinced of their own routes (which were often different) would assail him from his right and right rear. This particular morning our driver tried to call above our voices that he could hear no one. (My husband does not shout; he is from the Prairies and the strong, silent school of manhood). We all continued giving directions. Finally, observing that my husband was becoming quite disoriented, I had to shout them down. So that my mother would not take my edict personally, and, so as not to be seen to favour myself, I made the rule that no one in the back seat could give any directions.

This put the burden of navigation firmly on my father, and I insisted that he take the map. In fact, I threw it over the seat at him. He took it in hand, carefully displaying his ability to compromise, and never once opened it on the rest of our journey. We found our way to the town of Victoria, to Salmon Cove and Crocker's Cove and on to the regional centre at Carbonear despite the fact that father generally did not notify us as to where to turn until we were on the wrong road. Then he would ask with the wonder of a man who knew his way home blindfolded, "How come you didn't take the road to Victoria back there?" After turning the car around in several driveways, my husband finally learned to ask "which way?" at every intersection.

Carbonear, Victoria, Salmon Cove and Crocker's Cove. The circle of these four places loop the memories of my parents' childhood and youth as well as the history of my family and its four centuries in this place. As we approached the road to the "Burnt Woods," Harold's birthplace, my father warned me that we would probably not be able to get very far on it. He had been here a few years back with my brother Peter and they had not made it all the way up the Church Road to the old homestead. This was all the challenge I needed. I would go where no brother had gone before. Despite the fact that the road quickly became as rough as an old river bottom, I managed to get the car all the way to a small bridge that my parents assured me was only a short walk from our destination. We walked on and quickly found the only remains of my grandmother's house, a small grassy field and the foundation stones of a root cellar.

We picnicked on the stones as we took photographs and Kathleen told us of how, as a young woman, she would come from Carbonear to visit her cousins in Victoria and walk with them up this road in the evening in the hopes of meeting Harold. As she talked, my father left us, heading up the slight incline of the former road. I did not expect him to go far; we had already tired him with the walk from the car and our explorations toward the stream that bordered the property. After a little while, when he failed to return, I joked to my mother that maybe the fairies had taken him. Her face smiled, but her eyes held another, less confident, look. I had a sudden panic about an old man of eighty-five, who only a few years ago had had heart bypass surgery and even now only barely controlled his tricky heart with a pacemaker and medication. What was I thinking of, allowing him to go off by himself! What would my brothers and sister say if I lost him in his birthplace?

It must have been a good half kilometre before I caught him. He was striding with considerable energy toward the horizon. I remembered being told by my Uncle Rich of my grandmother heading off into the woods, her head captured by the fairies; I remembered my own daughter's tendency, as a small child, to keep walking briskly in a straight line toward the horizon whenever I let her out of my arms and I thought of the way I tend to lose my consciousness in walking and end up far from where I intended to be. I had to call to him to make him stop. When I told him I was afraid because of the story of grandmother and the fairies he laughed and explained to me the history of the forest around us; how it had been burned before settlement (thus its name), had grown back into a thick rich forest by his youth, and now could only manage the small scattered growth we saw around us because of all the woodcutting that had gone on since his time here. He told me about the other homes that had been along the road, about his brother Rich coming up here to look for the horse that had strayed, about the berry picking and the vegetable garden and the swimming in the creek long, long ago.

By the time we returned to our picnic spot he was eighty-five again and very tired. I hiked down to where we left the car, examining the ruts of the road as I went to see how I might avoid scraping the car bottom, and with considerable care and caution, managed to bring the vehicle to where he was. By then a man with a fishing pole had walked out of the woods and father and mother were busy acquiring his history. He was a Clarke of a different family, and although friendly he seemed unimpressed by the fact that my parents knew his grandfather, as later the young university student mowing the grass in the cemetery would not be surprised that our name was Clarke like hers; the graveyard was full of them.

In Salmon Cove we had a hard time finding the place where my Aunt Susie, father's sister, had lived with Uncle John all those years of her married life. Mother went into the post office where they remembered Susie and pointed to the spot. By then we had had a whole morning of finding traces of houses and graves, and my parents were tired, but agreed that we could go to see the Sands at Salmon Cove, since I remembered it as the most beautiful ocean spot of my childhood. Its grey-black sands were still stunning and the larger world has now realized this beauty for it has been made into a nature reserve.

I intended to head back to St. John's by the fastest route since my parents seemed so tired. I had underestimated the energizing power of remembering. When we returned to our car they were all enthusiasm again, explaining how we must go back to Carbonear by the Crocker's Cove route so we could see the land our ancestors settled in the first years of the 1600s. On the way, they both kept up a running commentary of their youthful exploits as each hill and dale brought new memories. At the sight of Carbonear Island we were told the story of mother's teaching days in Crocker's Cove, when she took the students to Carbonear Island to relive their ancestors' defence against the French invaders, and we heard father's recitation of the battles between the Newfoundlanders and the French. I had heard these stories often before and had regretted their anti-French subtext, but here, in this treeless, exposed ocean place, they began to make sense. Given the unprotected nature of this landscape our ancestors must certainly have been the underdogs.

Suddenly, my father commanded that the car be stopped. "Here it is; here it is, the ancestral home." Ahead of me, glimpsed between the shoulders of my husband and my father, jutting narrowly into the ocean, was a small rocky peninsula with grass enough for maybe a goat. None of the trees and brooks of Victoria village, none of the town life of Carbonear, no sandy strand to walk on. This was certainly the most disadvantaged place we had seen that day. The rocks descended steeply from their small grassy tops to the ocean below. How could they have lived here, in this treeless place unprotected against the wind coming off the ocean on three sides?

"Father, you could hardly cultivate a cabbage on that land."

My parents laughed. "Fish, my dear, fish. They cultivated fish flakes." I pictured the various houses that must have been raised on that barren ground over the years since 1600, from the sod huts of the dangerous times of early settlement to the salt-box style, two-storey wooden houses of my great-grandparents' era. I pictured a house surrounded by fish flakes. The small sheltered place where the grass grew greener must have been where the cabbages were planted. I pictured those hundreds of years of bloodlines, the fishermen, the sailors and the working (always working) women going on in this place generation after generation. All of their energy and toughness, all of their foolishness and failure, all of their hearts' blood, pounding away inside me. Imagine that.

The place gave Harold and Kathleen even more energy. For the rest of the day they traipsed their tired juniors around the whole of Conception Bay: a visit to mother's family graveyard, a chat with a very much alive Aunt Ann, my mother's sister-in-law; a drink with old friends of my parents. By the end of the day, driving back into St. John's, I felt as if I had lived all my life in my parents' memories, not my own. St. John's, my own childhood place, felt unreal again. I felt I was detached from myself again, floating in a dream of white grave markers against craggy rock shimmering on an ocean of bright turquoise memory. I needed to see things separate from my parents; I needed to do it alone.

But there seemed no moment, in the few days left of our visit, to be alone. We drove my parents to see old friends and relatives, and at sunset we went to Signal Hill to watch the sun set over the city and the lights gradually come on until St. John's became a necklace of light glittering in its reflective harbour. Another day, Dad insisted that we see the Newfoundland Maritime Museum. Fortunately, we discovered that we happened to be in St. John's on the day the "tall ships" were arriving and we joined the crowds on the South Side, facing the larger crowds across the harbour in downtown, and the folks up at the Battery and Signal Hill, to cheer the vessels as they navigated the narrows. This last event reminded me that I had never been to Fort Amherst, the rocky promontory that is at the end of the South

Side Road. My father assured me there was not much to see, since no restoration had taken place, but to humour me they went along to investigate on our last evening. There is no place to park at the end of the South Side Road, so my parents stayed with the car after we convinced a local resident to let us park our elders and our car in the man's parking space. Freed of Kathleen and Harold we went to explore the old lighthouse and the rocks that met the Atlantic over the low red granite of the cliffs.

My tendency to walk fast meant I lost my husband at one point. He told me later he had found a ledge of rock where some young women were sharing a case of beer, and he had asked if he could take their photograph. They had agreed, laughing, asking him if it would be used by the police to arrest them for their illegal activity. He stayed for a beer.

So I walked back to the car without him, and managed a few minutes of being alone. If you walk back from Fort Amherst at sunset, you see a different view from the panorama that takes your breath away on Signal Hill. This is no tourist photo opportunity to be captured with one perfect picture which you can blow up into a poster and say to your friends, "Now, here, see! Isn't my homeland beautiful?" To walk back from the low cliffs of Fort Amherst is to see the city as a moving picture. At first it is hidden from you, only the deep trench of the narrows and the cliffs of Signal Hill beyond can be seen. Then the city comes into view, not from the lofty height of the hill, but at eye-level across the harbour so that you see the daily workplace of the waterfront against the impossible steepness of the streets that tail up from it towards the upper town. To see the city from this place, from where I had never seen it, made me sit down on the rocks to take it in, street by street, building by building. It was as if my own childhood were over there, on the north side among those buildings. It was as if I, on the south side of the harbour, was separated, not by time but only by space, from a place where I still belonged. I tried to imagine what kind of woman I would have become if I had not left that place when I was a month short of fourteen. I pulled my knees up to rest my chin and meditated for some time, watching the city move from daylight to darkness. But I could not imagine that, could not imagine the Newfoundland woman I might have become; I was from away, and even if away had become only a harbour's width it could not be spanned by my imagination.

As I returned down the narrow road, the sounds from the homes built against the cliffs of the South Side Hill seemed magnified. People's voices, the sounds of dishes being washed, music playing, television, all the ordinary sounds of a summer evening were intensely alive, intensely real. I was away from them and I understood that being from away helped me hear them with the keenness of those who cannot come home.

Each time I have left Newfoundland in past years it has been in conditions of stress, with a profound sense of being glad to get away safely. My parents tell me that when I was a baby and we moved to Nova Scotia during the war, the ferry was darkened for fear of submarine attack. When I was a teenager and our family left for the West, we rushed to our airplane during a break in days of late winter fog. I was ecstatic that the long overdue flight was actually taking off. As I watched my mother shed tears for leaving her home behind I could hardly wait to discover the prairie city that was our destination. Returning from our camper trip in the sixties with our young children, we had met gale force winds heading back down the west coast to cross on the ferry at Port aux Basques. The chains that held our camper to the truck tugged and jerked, groaning with the effort of hanging on. A few years back, on our last visit, we took off during a May rain-squall and the plane bounced its way to sunshine at 30,000 feet. Looking down through the breaks in the clouds I could see icebergs, formidably close to the coastline.

This time we set out from Placentia, choosing the fourteen-hour ferry ride to North Sydney rather than the long drive to the west coast of the island to catch the Port aux Basques ferry. Being notorious for motion sickness as a child, I had worried about so many hours on the water. But the day was a gift of sunshine, warm winds and an ocean as smooth as the proverbial glass of that worn image. I sat on deck most of the day, watching the shore recede, caught by the play of light on water, hypnotized by the wind around me, the parting of the waters ahead of me. Newfoundland had given me a "sun rays crown her golden hills, and summer spreads her hand," kind of day, just like the old anthem I sang as a girl promised me in those days before I became a Canadian. It was a gentle leave-taking, one that made me want to come again; one that invited me to realize why I had come back to this place. It was for the memoir stories, the ones that were creating the new self, the self that would contain this place inside me. At this moment, in the wind of the ferry deck with the island of my girlhood slipping behind me, I wanted more than anything to return to those stories and make them ready for you. Imagine that.

REFLECTION QUESTIONS

1. This author's remembering of her life in St. John's, Newfoundland, was a very young child. Her return to St. John's as an adult brought back a 'flood of memories', and created a sense of deep unrest within her very being. Provide your own analysis of this sense of deep unrest.

2. Sometimes when we 'make a new life' in another province or another part of the world, the return "home" is "not the same": we may feel out of place in this place we call home – a true sense of diaspora. Analyze the underlying meanings that may be behind this 'out of place' feeling as you yourself may have experienced or how others may have explained it to you.

3. The term "imagine that" is one that is not uncommon in Newfoundland. What is your understanding of the term as used by the author in this chapter?

4. Describe your own "sense of place" within the context of your experiences as it relates to where you come from – as where you identify as home.

DAVID BALDWIN

REMITTANCE, THE NEW WAY TO WORK IN NEWFOUNDLAND AND LABRADOR

INTRODUCTION

Newfoundland and Labrador has seen its fair share of economic prosperity over the past 50 years. Large projects such as Churchill Falls, Hibernia, Terra Nova, and the Voisey's Bay Mine have brought millions of dollars to the local economies of Newfoundland and Labrador. These projects have also allowed many families to earn good livings and enjoy the finer things of life. With an increase in material things comes more responsibility to pay for these things, and look for the next big project to keep up this lifestyle. When the large jobs are over like those mentioned above, many workers have to look for work in other parts of Canada like Alberta, Ontario, Offshore Drill rigs, and the North West Territories. Sometimes workers leave the country and go to places like Africa, Mexico, and Holland. However, as the world becomes more dependent on oil and natural gas, large companies will do anything to get experienced workers. With the demand for a skilled workforce, many places throughout the world are now offering the opportunity for skilled workers to travel to these distant places and work and live for free, and provide travel to and from the province. This has created a new family dynamic of remittance where people in local communities are rising above the poverty line. This has created a Newfoundland Diaspora where Newfoundlander's send money home because they want to continue to remain part of their families (Singh, 2007).

Many national governments have focused on the growth of remittances, their impact on poverty alleviation and development (Singh, 2007). Remittance is allowing people to be away for short periods of time while families stay at home and receive money that was earned in other places. With an increase in money comes an increase in spending. This spending often benefits local towns and other tertiary businesses which in turn improves their standard of living. The flow of money from other parts of the world seems to have a trickledown effect where many people benefit. This paper will discuss the issue of remittance and Diaspora of several people from the fictitiously named town of Sandy Book Newfoundland, where the population is very scarce, and how remittance is allowing this little town to prosper.

Background Stories of People Interviewed

The first person that I interviewed was a man whom I have called Tom. Tom is a man in his 50's who is getting ready to retire. Tom is an electrician by trade, and has

A. Singh and M. Devine (Eds.), Rural Transformation and Newfoundland and Labrador Diaspora: Grandparents, Grandparenting, Community and School Relations, 71–78.

worked his way up the seniority ladder to become a project manager for a company in Northern Alberta. Tom has not always worked away from home, but over the past 5 years has worked in Alberta because of the lack of work in the province. Tom has worked on a lot of major jobs including Hibernia, Terra Nova, and the Voisey's Bay project. After working in these jobs Tom developed a lifestyle that required him to look for large well-paying jobs. As Tom mentions, "small little jobs do not pay well enough for me to stay here anymore". From contacts that he made while working in these jobs, Tom was contacted from Alberta after he finished work here. Tom indicated, "I never even had enough time to take holidays after Voisey's Bay before Alberta called me to become the project manager on the Horizon Oil Sands Project in Northern Alberta".

The second person that I interviewed was a man whom I have called Calvin. Calvin is a man in his 40's who has a sick wife at home, and two children that are in postsecondary schools. Calvin is an electrician by trade, and works on the Grand Banks of Newfoundland and Labrador on the Hibernia Platform. Calvin has not always worked away from home, but over the past 5 years has worked offshore because the scheduling allows him to be home more often with his sick wife. Calvin has worked on a lot of major jobs including Hibernia, Terra Nova, and the Voisey's Bay project. Calvin mentions, "I like working offshore because the pay is good, and I get an isolation allowance". Calvin indicates that being offshore allows him to provide for his wife who cannot work, and pay for his children's educations. Calvin was also called from Alberta, but turned them down in favour of the offshore because it is closer to home.

The third person that I interviewed was a man whom I have called Shane. Shane is a man in his late 30's who has a wife and two school aged children. Shane is an electrical instrumentation technologist, and works off the coast of Nigeria. He works on the Ekpe Phase II oil platform that is run by Exxon Mobile. Shane, contrary to Tom and Calvin, has worked away from home ever since he started working. Shane has worked on a number of projects in the offshore sector, and was contacted from Nigeria about 10 years ago to work in their natural gas fields. Shane mentions, "I have to work away to pay for the big things I have around me, and provide the things to my children that I never had as I grew up". Shane indicates that being on the other part of the world is a tough pill to swallow, but he would not be able to move home and settle for low wages.

Work Scheduling

Tom indicates that the job he is working now is quite enjoyable and the pay is substantial. Tom is one of several people in the community who work for the same company; he works on a rotation period of 20 days away and 8 days home. The company provides air travel to and from the site, and provides accommodations and food while he is away. Tom is pleased with this arrangement because he is making money as soon as he gets on the plane to leave.

Calvin also indicates that he enjoys his job on the offshore, but sometimes questions whether or not to continue with his job because his wife has good and bad days. Also, when accidents occur in the offshore, they are bad as can be seen on March 12, 2009, when a crew of workers going to the offshore platforms went down into the Atlantic Ocean and only one crew member survived. Calvin indicates, "You always have things like this occurring in the back of your mind, and family members think about it even more". However, Calvin likes his offshore routine because it allows him to work on a 2 and 2 rotation where he works for two weeks and is home for two weeks. He thinks working in places like Alberta and having 8 days home would not be enough to spend with his family. Like Tom, Calvin also enjoys the fact that when he is offshore he is making money and not spending any.

Shane also indicates that he likes his job living abroad. Shane indicates, "If I never liked it I would not be doing it". Shane's schedule is a little different than that of Tom and Calvin, Shane has to work overseas for two months before he gets three weeks off. Shane, like Tom and Calvin, gets all living and travel expenses paid for. Shane mentions that being away for a couple of months makes it more special when he is home for three weeks.

Life on the Road

Life on the road can be a difficult situation for some people, but the gentlemen I interviewed seemed to accept that life on the road is a necessity if you want to live comfortably. Globalization has made this a reality because remittances are making people want to enjoy the finer things (Singh, 2007). In Tom's case, he has lived out of a suitcase all of his life, and his wife has grown to accept this. When I interviewed him, she mentioned that she likes for him to be away. This might have been sarcastic, but she said that they enjoy the time he has off, and thinks back to when he worked in Newfoundland and was gone for twelve hours a day seven days a week. The shift he works now, allows him the time to unwind, and spend time with his family.

In the case of Calvin, he sometimes finds it difficult to be away from his wife with her good and bad days. He admits that it was much easier being away when his children were in their late teens living at home. Now that they have moved on, he is finding it more difficult to be apart. Calvin also has a family made up of "trust networks" (Singh, 2007). Calvin is providing money for the physical care of both his mother and father. His father lives with his wife, while his mother lives in a compassionate care home. Calvin's mother has Alzheimer's disease, and needs constant care and supervision. He believes that remittance is allowing him to feel at home even though he is not there. He indicates that the money is good, and is allowing him to pay for his children's educations, and provide the care for his wife and parents.

Shane also finds it difficult to be away from home on certain occasions. Shane is a person who was recently married and misses his wife, and sharing time with his children. Shane indicates that he has to put those things at the back of his mind because the money is too good, but admits that he misses seeing the birthdays, anniversaries, and holidays. Having small children makes it more difficult because sometimes children can be a handful with only one parent in the home. His kids are getting to the age now that they want to test the authority of the mom. He said, "The most difficult time to be away from home is during Christmas, because those are the times when family get together to celebrate traditions and a phone call is not the same." However, Shane said that technology is allowing him to communicate with his family better than any time before. Computer programs allow him to see and hear his family while on the road. He said, "It is like the wife and kids are in the next room".

Remittance Benefits for Families

Many people throughout the country look for places with high economic prospects for work. They often travel to these places seeking employment where they send money back home-a form of Diaspora. In turn, their households use this money to make investments for the future, increasing their child's education, and increasing their material possessions.

One interesting thing that I found when interviewing these three men is the fact that they all have decided to make investments. All three men contribute regularly to RRSP's, Bonds, and other high interest savings accounts. Also, Tom and Shane both have ventured into shares of companies that work abroad. All men indicate that these investments will allow them to retire early in age where they can move back home to enjoy their retirement. They like the idea of investing because they like the idea of ownership and all the prestige this brings.

Another thing that I noticed when I interviewed these men is the overall consensus on the importance of education. While Tom and Calvin did go to a trade's college, all men wanted their children to go to a University to get a higher education. Tom said, "I want my son to work at something a lot easier than what I did". I then asked him about the obvious high standard of living he was enjoying, and he replied, "I was lucky, think how many electricians that are not". He did have a good point because there are many skilled people who are still trying to make ends meet. Tom also explains that, "I did my time in the trenches where I was cold all the time and wet, it is only in the past 20 years that I have been able to work without my tools". This is a good realization because many people view only those successful people, and fail to realize that a trades job is the same as any other job, some get paid better than others.

Each man wanted to support their children when they went into postsecondary. Tom indicates that his son cost him over $50,000 to complete his degree. $50,000 is a lot of money that not every family can afford. Tom started saving for his child's education when his son was born. This helped offset some of the costs when his son went through school.

Calvin, whose children just started higher education, expresses that, "Last year, both my children went through about $25,000 in tuition and living expenses". Like

Tom, Calvin starting putting away bond money for his children when they were born. However, Calvin has used his investments to pay for his children's educations thus far. According to Calvin, "the bond money is there now when I need it".

Shane, like Tom and Calvin is saving for the time when his children attend postsecondary. However, Shane is not putting away money in bonds because today they have no value like they had years ago. Instead, Shane is putting money into a high interest savings account, and will take the money out when his children need it in the future.

The standard of living for all men that I interviewed was quite high. Every man, in the last 10 years purchased a bigger home, bigger truck, and bought things like snowmobiles, boats, and sports cars. All of these things are good indicators of high standards of living. Also, the children of all of these men enjoyed similar lifestyles as they grew up. Each child had the best of clothes, shoes, and recreational vehicles. All men indicated that they have taken on the added responsibility of paying for things in the family that other members cannot afford. Calvin, as mentioned, pays for his parent's accommodations. Tom was responsible for paying for the funeral arrangements for both his parents. These costs are large in nature, and a substantial salary is needed to pay for such things. Remittance has allowed these men to make good money away, and help pay for things in their families (Singh, 2007).

Remittance Benefits for Home Towns

As was mentioned above, remittance has allowed people to work in other places, and send money back to families for their enjoyment. Remittance has even been seen as a way of alleviating poverty and increasing development (Singh, 2007). According to Kuptsch and Martin (2004), $1 in remittance spending can generate $2 to $3 in local economic activity. I can see such a thing when I go home and take note of the different things happening in my town. I am always amused by the amount of infrastructure that is being created. A small town with no source of employment seems to be doing quite well.

The employment is there, but not in the town. The town of Salmon Cove has a great deal of people who live abroad working, and come home on different rotations. This has resulted in an increase in the amount of money flowing through the town and neighbouring communities. The town of Ships Harbours is a good example of how remittance is helping improve neighbouring communities. Ships Harbours, once a traditional fishing town was devastated when the local fish plant left the community. As a result, many people retrained, and starting working abroad. Ships Harbours is surrounded by several communities such as Sandy Brook, West River, and North Harbour that are all experiencing the benefit of remittance. As a result of remittance, Ships Harbour is starting to see an influx of business.

Business is coming in many forms such as car dealerships, malls, stores, fast food restaurants, and new schools. When people go away to work, they spend their money home. Like Tom, Calvin, and Shane, all men after working away purchased new homes. These homes take an abundance of building materials that were supplied by a new hardware store that was erected in the community. With so much housing accruing in the area, a hardware store was needed to meet the demand.

Another thing that people buy when they come home from abroad, are new cars. In the past 5 years I have seen 3 new car dealerships created in the area to meet the demand of remittance workers. Tom, Calvin, and Shane, like others, recently purchased new trucks which seem to be a status symbol in the area. Trucks are not cheap, but everyone has one. The need was there for such distribution, and as a result, car dealerships were created.

The town of Ships Harbour has always had a mall that supplied neighbouring areas. For years the mall was falling down, and stores were, leaving in favour of richer areas. Ever since workers have been going away to work and sending money home, the mall has improved. Stores are moving back into the area, and trendy shops are opening up that you would only see in an urban environment.

All of these new businesses create jobs and bring money into local towns. This is great because it can employ workers from the area who wish to work at home. Jobs are being created that at one time where simply not necessary. Some of these jobs are given to school aged kids who can learn to make a living, and this too creates a trickle-down effect that can help other business. Local businesses that were feeling the pinch after the closing of the fish plant are again feeling the prosperity of new money. It's sad that our community lost its fish plant, but it seems as if the community is richer then it has ever been.

CONCLUSION

With increased demand for petroleum, comes increased demand for skilled workers. Companies will need to look and compete for these skilled workers if they want to meet the demands. Newfoundland and Labrador is a prime example of a province that has a large population of remittance workers who work elsewhere and travel back home. As Newfoundland and Labrador waits for the next big job, its workforce is gaining experience in other parts of the world. This work is creating Diaspora in Newfoundland and Labrador because remittance is allowing many families to earn good livings and enjoy the finer things of life. Diaspora is creating a new family dynamic where families enjoy a loved one's presence for short periods of time, but feel the economic benefits continuously. Being away from loved ones for an extended period of time can create some problems, but as in the case of the three men interviewed in this paper, the advantages far outweigh the disadvantages (Singh, 2007). Local communities are starting to see growth after a continuous decline in out migration. Remittance is allowing local communities to take money and create infrastructure that in turn creates local employment. The flow of money from other regions may draw local skilled workers from the province, and many fear that this could cause problems for Newfoundland and Labrador when it comes to future development at a result of people going away to work. This outflow of people is serious business when it comes to national economies (Tilly, 2007). However, after discussing the issues with the men of this paper, I have learned that many Newfoundlanders will come home again when the work starts and the money is good. However, this is a problem because now the province will have to compete with other provinces for skilled workers. Globalization is causing workers to spread all around the world, and companies having to provide incentives to get them there. One thing is sure; globalization does not seem to be slowing down.

REFLECTION QUESTIONS

1. Each of the men interviewed in this chapter stressed the need for higher education for their children (University). However, each of these men are obviously very successful in their careers. Why is education so important to the men, despite their financial success?
2. What are the potential impacts of parenting children in the family models described above?
3. Rural communities are often described as 'dying' in Newfoundland and Labrador as well as in other provinces. What does the voice of this author tell you about rural communities and possibilities for the future?
4. The 'shift' models presented in this chapter present some unique dynamics in terms of family life, community life and life experiences overall. What are some of the most significant dynamics or issues in this type of lifestyle?

REFERENCES

Kuptsch, C., & Martin, P. (2004). Migration and development: Remittances and cooperation with the diaspora. http://www.gtz.de/migration-and development/download/dokumentation-plenum2.pdf
Singh, Supriya (2007). Sending money home-maintaining family and community. *IJAPS, 3*(2), 93–109.
Tilly, C. (2007). Trust networks in transnational migration. *Sociological Forum, 22*(2), 3–24.

ALISON GEORGE

ALBERTA'S OIL SAND WORKERS AND THE ROLE
OF GRANDPARENTS

Grandparents play a significant role in the lives of their grandchildren when their parents are forced to migrate to the workforce in Alberta. Grandparents can be role models, teachers, family historians, and can help their grandchildren discover their identity. Since Alberta's oil boom a large number of men and women from Newfoundland and Labrador migrate to Alberta to work in camps. It is estimated that "a minimum of 5,500 Newfoundlanders travel back and forth to work in Alberta" (Beaton, 2008, p. 177). As a result of this grandparents are being called upon to help with care giving responsibilities. The women of the family are faced with added pressures of family life as their spouses can no longer help to provide this care on a regular, full time basis. This article will explore the challenges migratory workers face and the important roles that grandparents have in the lives of their grandchildren. For this paper, data was collected through personal interviews of 3 male migratory workers from Newfoundland and Labrador who work in Alberta's oil field whom I will identify as Jim, John, and Cliff. As well, to compliment the paper, I interviewed grandparents who will be identified as Lori, Liz, and Andy.

Many men and women from Newfoundland and Labrador are forced to move away to be able to provide financial security for their family. The men that I interviewed had no other choice but to leave home to seek work in Fort McMurray, Alberta. All of these individuals have technical trades backgrounds and said that, at the time when they decided to go away to work, there were no jobs for them in Newfoundland. Jim said "I would stay home if I could find a job and make enough money to be able to provide a good life for my family" (Jim, personal communication, July 20, 2010). All of the men interviewed work in blocked time approximately 3–4 months at a time, with a break home approximately every 2–3 months. John said that "I try to schedule my work around certain times of the year so that I can be home with my family on special occasions such as Christmas, Easter and summer vacation" (John, personal communication, July 20, 2010). Most of the individuals interviewed indicated that they try to work in the fall, spring and part of summer when they feel that they are not needed as much at home. For example, John said "I want to be home in the winter because I can help shovel and make sure the kids get to school safely" (John, personal communication, July 20, 2010). While Cliff mentioned "I like to be able to be home in the summer with my family because my kids are off school so

A. Singh and M. Devine (Eds.), Rural Transformation and Newfoundland and Labrador Diaspora:
Grandparents, Grandparenting, Community and School Relations, 79–82.
© *2013 Sense Publishers. All rights reserved.*

they can spend some quality time together and engage in activities such as camping and fishing" (Cliff, personal communication, July 20, 2010).

Grandparents' Role from Their Son's Perspective

Grandparents provide ongoing support to their families so that life is a little bit easier with the absence of the spouse. They can be solid support networks that are there for their children and grandchildren. Grandparents can play a major role in the growth, development and education of their grandchildren. Cliff said "that this statement is especially true when I return to work because my children lean on my parents for guidance and support" (Cliff, personal communication, July 20, 2010). Cliff also mentioned that, "when I go away I have the support of parents to babysit, attend school concerts, and help out with lunches and homework" (Cliff, personal communication, July 20, 2010). John also agrees with the previous statement saying "If it wasn't for my parents I am not sure how my wife and I would be able to do it" (John, personal communication, July 20, 2010).

Grandparents' Role

Today grandparents can play an active role in the lives of their grandchildren; their duties can range from primary to occasional caregivers. I asked Lori (grandmother) what she thought her role was in her grandchildren's life and she said; "I worry about my grandkids as if they were my own children and that when my son goes away to work it's my responsibility that my grandchildren have a good meal on the table and make sure that they have a safe home environment" (Lori, personal communication, July 20, 2010). Grandparents provide unconditional love and stability for their grandchildren. Andy mentioned that his "5 year old grandson comes to breakfast every morning asking for a cup of tea and wanting to hear stories" (Andy, personal communication, July 20, 2010). Research has shown that;

> most children enjoy hearing grandparents tell about their lives when they were growing up. Grandparents who are able to share the rich heritage of the past with children give them a deeper, broader foundation upon to base their own lives and to build new knowledge. (Lee, 1985, p. 4)

When asked, "What role do you play within your family when your sons go away to work?" Liz said; "I cook, clean and take care of my grandchildren".

The common role and duties from the grandparents that I interviewed was to babysit, provide meals, and to provide a safe loving environment (Liz, personal communication, July 20, 2010).

When asked; "Does caring for your grandchildren when your sons are away have negative effects on your life? Do you feel tired from taking care of your grandchildren?", Lori stated; "my grandchildren give me energy that I didn't even know I had; they bring so much joy to my life that it wouldn't be the same without them" (Lori, personal communication, July 20, 2010).

Grandparents and Grandchildren Relationship

Intergenerational relationships are positive for the development of children. Research shows that the earlier children are made familiar with older adults, the better their perceptions of them are. Children's negative perceptions about the elderly increase as they grow older, so developing positive relationships at an early age helps reduce negative perceptions (Spence & Radunovich, 2007).

This is also supported by Theodore, (1984), as cited in Downs & Walz, (1981), who states, "Adults who have had a strong relationship with their grandparents tend to be much more positive to the value and importance of older citizens than those adults without such bonds to grandparents" (p. 48). Grandparents are significant in the transmission of values, morals, and beliefs to grandchildren. Children who have close relationships with their grandparents learn the value of family relations and history. They learn about life and history through listening to their grandparents' stories about their past and their growing up. Grandparents help their grandchildren discover themselves and find their own identity. They accomplish this by transmitting knowledge about their culture and history so the children can have a greater understanding of who they are and where they came from. Grandparents can be objective when listening to their grandchildren about life issues and provide advice without making judgments. Many times grandparents can act as mediators between the child and parent because sometimes parents are quick to make judgments and draw conclusions about their own children.

Grandparents are teachers to their grandchildren; they can teach them the importance of family, telling them the history of their roots, and their religious background. Grandparents are more likely to teach their grandchildren about faith and religion. Every Sunday Lori watches church on T.V and her grandson comes up to watch it with her. She says that "if you don't have faith then you don't have anything at all...faith is what gets you through the difficult times" (Lori, personal communication, July 20, 2010). All of the grandparents interviewed expressed the importance of passing down rituals and family traditions. Littler (2008) confirms this notion that "The importance of the role of grandparents in passing on faith and belief to their grandchildren is well established in Jewish and Christian tradition" (p. 52). Also, research reports that "if grandparents are regular churchgoers, then 61% of young teenagers are also likely to be regular attenders, with a further 18% attending occasionally" (Littler, 2008, as cited in Brierley 2002, 42; p. 52).

Intergenerational relationships not only have a positive effect on children but on grandparents as well. "Grandparents not only enjoy spending time with their grandchildren, they also find that involvement with their grandchildren is equally beneficial to their own health and wellbeing" (Singh, 2010, p.4). Andy mentions that his "grandchildren keeps me on my toes and makes me feel young again". This is supported by Spence & Radunovich (2007), "developing connections with a younger generation can help older adults to feel a greater sense of fulfilment (p. 1).

CONCLUSION

After several decades of the phenomena of migratory workers heading to Alberta oil fields one can draw tentative conclusions about the role of grandparents in the nurturing of their grandchildren. The family unit is obviously impacted by the migratory phenomena. The interactions between families will continue to be paramount in supporting young families where one of the parents is working out of the province. The extended family and role of the grandparents cannot be underestimated and this role will continue to be vital in support of the family unit as there seems to be no end to the migratory workers availing of the work in the Alberta's oil fields. From the interviews and research provided it demonstrates that grandparents are very instrumental in the lives of their grandchildren with the absence of the primary caregiver. They help their grandchildren to discovery themselves and help form their own identity. They tell stories about life lessons that transmit values and morals to them. Migratory workers depend on their parents to support, encourage, and to be involved in their daily lives of their grandchildren.

REFLECTION QUESTIONS

1. What are the implications of 'family life' when one parent, often the father, is absent to 3–4 months at a time, as in the cases described above?
2. How might the role of grandparents differ when one parent is absent for long periods of time?
3. How might the impact on the parent who is absent, differ when grandparents are involved versus when grandparents are not involved in the life of the other parent and the children?
4. How might the relationships between the grandparents and the grandchildren differ, when one parent is absent and assuming that the grandparents 'step in' to help?

REFERENCES

Beaton, E. (2008, August). No man's land. *Chatelaine*, Retrieved from http://www.eleanorbeaton.com/userfiles/file/Chatelaine%20-%20Oil%20Patch%20Widows.pdf

Lee, I.K. (Year n.d.). Joys of grandparenting. Department of Agriculture, Washington, D.C. Arkanas University.

Littler, K. (2008). 'Who says grandparents matter?' *Journal of Beliefs & Values*, 29(1), 51–60.

Singh, J. (2010). Mainstream Research on Grandparents.

Spence, L., Radunovich, H.L. (2007). Developing intergenerational relationships. This document is FCS 2282, one of a series of the Department of Family, Youth and Community Sciences, Florida Cooperative Extension Service, IFAS, University of Florida, Gainesville, FL 32611.Retrived from http://edis.ifas.ufl.edu/pdffiles/FY/FY100700.pdf

Theodore, H.B. (1984). An evaluative study of the role of the grandparent in the best interests of the child. *The American Journal of Family Therapy*, 12(4), 46–50.

SENSE OF COMMUNITY AND COMMUNITY PROFILES: GRANDPARENTS AND GRANDPARENTING STYLES

ANNE MARIE FREAKE

PROMINENCE OF GRANDPARENTS

Grandparents are a vital part of society and in the lives of their children and grandchildren. They are contributors to both community and community culture, through sharing their wisdom and strength. Grandparents can be involved in the community in many ways, including spending time with their children and grandchildren, volunteering with community organizations and fundraisers, and attending church. A grandparent whom I had the privilege of interviewing is Mary Statford. Mary grew up in a tiny Newfoundland community of forty-seven families and now lives in a small city. She raised her own family and enjoys the company of her adult children and grandchildren.

Mary Statford is a seventy-five year old wife, mother and grandmother. She has been married to George Statford, who is eighty-five, for the past fifty-three years and they appear to still be very much in love. They have five adult children – three daughters and two sons. They also have five grandchildren – four granddaughters and one grandson. Two daughters, one son and one granddaughter live within a twenty minute drive, while one daughter, one son and four grandchildren live on the mainland.

Mary described the small community that she grew up in as a "close-knit community." The only family that she had in the community was her immediate family, which consisted of her parents, siblings, herself, her paternal grandfather, and step-grandmother. She wishes she had met her paternal grandmother and maternal grandfather, who had died before she was born. Mary excitedly told about the two story house that she grew up in with her family, even showed a painting of the house, and also explained how her grandparents were an important part of her daily life.

Even though Mary did not have many extended family members living in her hometown, she felt the community was close and like family. Mary stated, "We knew everybody in the community; it was only a smaller community. I mean, people who weren't related to us, we used to call, out of, what is the word, ahh, we used to call them aunt and uncle. There was a man and a woman next door to us and they were older and I always called them aunt and uncle. A lot of people do that, I think it was out of...a sense of dignity or something, respect." Rural Newfoundland and Labrador is known for this distinct respect, addressing the elderly as aunt and uncle, even if there is no kinship involved.

Mary attended a two classroom school where the two classrooms were downstairs, with a church upstairs. Concerts and other events were held inside the church, with the help of the two teachers and many other members of the community, who were

A. Singh and M. Devine (Eds.), Rural Transformation and Newfoundland and Labrador Diaspora: Grandparents, Grandparenting, Community and School Relations, 85–90.

always eager to lend a hand. Nearly the entire community attended church services, which were conducted by a United Minister from a nearby community. Mary kept her religious faith close to her heart when she moved away from home and tried to instill those beliefs in her children. Many of the activities that both adults and children participated in occurred outside in the fresh air. Mary stated, "I played hopscotch. In the winter we would skate on the ponds; there were a couple of ponds we would skate on after school. Summertime, there wasn't much to do in the summertime. We went berry picking when the berries were ripe."

Mutual support helped Mary and her family members survive in a rural area. When food was scarce or when there was sickness or death, community members came together. Mutual support can be defined as "helping others and being helped in a climate of good will, mutual respect, mutual reward, common ground, and collaboration; recognition of needs and appreciation of strengths; and personal and interpersonal efforts toward a common purpose" (Steinberg, 2002, p. 5). When other members of the community needed assistance, Mary's family too provided this support.

When Mary completed Grade Eleven, she moved from her small town to a larger centre, to see what the world had to offer. Mary worked for several years in a photo shop, which she took great pleasure in and is proud of. At this time, she met a young man named George, they began courting and later married. Mary and George moved to a neighborhood in a nearby community, where they still reside today. Mary decided to stop working in order to start and raise a family, while George worked as a surveyor.

Today Mary and George are not as involved in the community as they once were. When their children were young, they were involved in girl guides and other structured activities. Mary felt strongly about having the children involved in these types of community activities, to help them grow in confidence and character. Both of their daughters were involved in brownies and girl guides, as were their granddaughters. Mary expressed dissatisfaction over one of her granddaughters leaving girl guides to pursue dancing, but she is still proud of her.

George worked as a surveyor and was responsible for surveying a large part of the TransCanada Highway in the province. George is proud of his work accomplishments and loves to tell stories of his time on the road. He wrote a song about his life entitled, "The Man in Brown," which speaks of his working experiences and a little of his private life. George spent a lot of time away from his family, on the road with other men, building roads, tearing down houses and fences etc. The work was labor intensive, but as George expresses through song, he enjoyed it.

The neighborhood where Mary and George have resided since the sixties provides mutual support, as was provided in Mary's hometown. Those living there for decades have been in each other's lives through marriages, births and deaths and have become close friends. They still visit each other today and enjoy playing card games. Although they do have a car, Mary and George prefer to stay at home most days, spending time talking with their children and grandchildren and reminiscing about their lives. One of Mary's main hobbies is reading books about Newfoundland and Labrador's history; she has dozens of books, which she has read and reread. Mary also enjoys collecting cookbooks and trying new recipes.

A neighborhood can have either a positive or negative effect on those who live there, depending on the support provided. There is a "powerful environmental impact that living in a particular area has on the health, well-being and life course of individuals who live in that area (Pierson, 2008, p. 10). A close-knit, supportive neighborhood such as Mary and George's, where many of the same families have lived for over forty years, has a positive impact on those individuals and contributes to their health and well-being.

Sadness spread across Mary's face when asked how her relationship is different with her children and grandchildren who live away. She said, "I still love them just as much as the ones that are here you know, but when you can't spend all that much time with them, you know." She said that she usually speaks on the telephone with the majority of her children and grandchildren weekly; they try to maintain as much contact as possible. Mary's son and his family came to visit this past summer in July and her daughter, husband and two children came to visit in October. They try to come back home to Newfoundland every year.

Mary's granddaughter, who lives nearby, often drops by for visits and sometimes stays for sleepovers on the weekends. Mary told the story of when her granddaughter was entering kindergarten, her daughter was considering putting her into a French immersion program. Mary explained to her granddaughter what that meant and helped convince her daughter and granddaughter that French immersion was the best option for her granddaughter's future, reminding them that two other grandchildren went to a French immersion school on the mainland and that they are doing well. This shows how Mary has an important impact on the decisions and lives of her family and is highly respected.

Having grandparents, particularly grandmothers, involved in the lives of their grandchildren can have a positive impact on young children who externalize negative behaviors or are short tempered. Grandmothers often have more experience in caring for children and thus, may understand more about children exhibiting negative behaviors. They can pass this wisdom on to their children, to assist with their child rearing practices. Grandmothers can also engage in positive interactions with their grandchildren and act as positive role models (Barnett, Neppl, Scaramella, Ontai, & Conger, 2010, p. 7). Mary has demonstrated that she has her grandchildren's best interests at heart, and wants to be as much a part of their lives as possible, which benefits both her and her grandchildren.

In a recent study on adolescents and the involvement of their grandparents, it was found that adolescents respected their grandparents and viewed them as an important part of their lives. Many grandchildren felt an emotional closeness to their grandparents, which had positively impacted them, providing them with more supervision and guidance (Attar-Schwartz, Tan, & Buchanan, 2009, p. 7). Mary and George speak with their two young adult grandchildren often, and have a close relationship with them, even though they live on the mainland. Mary and George feel that they are positively impacting their lives, through sharing their values and opinions.

Mary stated, "Grandchildren are really priceless." She has many funny stories about her grandchildren when they were younger, one in particular about her grandson, who wanted to remain her "favorite grandson" when another grandchild was being born. Mary enjoys passing on her belongings to her grandchildren. She gave one of her granddaughters a porcelain cat that she had asked for. Mary also made a photo album for each of her children and grandchildren, which holds pictures of them from birth to present day. Just like her grandchildren, those photo albums are priceless.

Upon leaving her dying community, Mary took many of the community's values and attitudes with her to her new community, and passed them on to her children and grandchildren. For example, respect for elders, addressing them as aunt and uncle even when not related, was passed on. Mary's daughter, who still lives at home, calls the lady across the street aunt, and slept at her house for two years, after the elderly lady's husband passed away. The values, attitudes and behaviors that Mary passed on to her children can be viewed through social learning theory. This theory emphasizes that "human behavior is learned during interactions with other persons and with the social environment" (Hardcastle & Powers, 2004, p. 35). As Mary was a stay-at-home mom who spent much time with her children, they learned her values, attitudes and behaviors and were influenced by what she said.

Many young adults in Mary and George's community, like two of their own children, are moving to the mainland to secure employment and raise their families. An implication that this outmigration has on the community is that it changes the family dynamics, especially for Mary and her family. Growing up, Mary lived with her parents, siblings and grandparents and learned from them. In contrast, Mary does not have any grandchildren living in their community, with only one living in the same province. She does have regular contact with her grandchildren, but cannot be as involved in their lives as much as she would like and would be able to if they lived nearby. Her grandchildren are not getting enough exposure to their grandparents, who have many positive values, attitudes and morals that they would like to pass on. Mary feels that because they live so far away, her grandchildren are not able to learn the same respect and receive the same guidance as they would if they were near.

An implication of the outmigration of young people on the community and on the Province as a whole is that it becomes difficult to pass on these morals and values through the generations. The same issues that are impacting Mary and her family are impacting families across the province. Years ago, extended family lived nearby or shared a household, often working together in the fishery. This daily contact helped with the positive development of the children and created close families ties.

Even though more families are being separated by distance, with increasing life expectancy, there are more individuals becoming grandparents and great-grandparents. And thus, more children are able to develop relationships with grandparents. In a study on Grandparenting in the 21st Century: Issues of diversity in grandparent-grandchild relationships, grandparents expressed "the best thing about being a grandparent was witnessing the development of their grandchildren" (Stelle, Fruhauf, Orel, & Landry-Meyer, 2010, p. 6). Mary is proud to be part of her grandchildren's lives, to watch them grow and learn. Although Mary and George have only one grandchild residing in the province, they are able to speak with their other grandchildren regularly and see them almost every year. This regular contact enables Mary and George to still witness their grandchildren growing and learning.

Grandmothers are generally more concerned with maintaining close emotional ties and relationships with family members whereas grandfathers are more often concerned with giving advice about getting an education and retaining a job (Bates, 2009, p. 4). This may be partly due to the fact that women are socialized to be more emotionally expressive and responsive than men. Generally, men often discuss the news, sports and work rather than feelings and emotions.

Grandparents, such as Mary and George, are an important part of society. They carry with them values, attitudes and morals that can be passed on to their children and grandchildren. Grandparents, adult children and grandchildren can benefit from being involved in each other's lives, learning from and contributing to the well-being of one other. Grandparents are contributing to community by being a part of their children and grandchildren's lives and passing on their values, attitudes and behaviors. They can also contribute more formally through volunteering within the community. Each grandparent contributes in his/her own way, depending on their personality and abilities.

REFLECTIVE QUESTIONS

1. What are the implications of relationship development of grandparents with grandchildren who are 'away'?
2. In what ways do adults help ensure the 'transmission of culture' to the (grand) children?
3. Community may be broadly defined. How are grandparents and grandchildren part of the same community, even when they live in different countries?
4. How is the relationship between adult children and grandchildren different with their (grand) parents? If they are similar, how are they similar?

REFERENCES

Attar-Schwartz, S., Tan, J., & Buchanan, A. (2009). Adolescents' perspectives on relationships with grandparents: The contribution of adolescent, grandparent, and parent grandparent relationship variables. Retrieved on December 1, 2010 from http://www.sciencedirect.com. qe2a-proxy.mun.ca/science?_ob=MImg&_imagekey=B6V98-4W99VTF-1-9&_cdi=5892&_ user=1069227&_pii=S0190740909001194&_originsearch&_coverDate=09%2F30%2F2009&_ sk=999689990&view=c&wchp=dGLbVzz-zSkWA&md5=26339b6efbb2f7e87c09c6b368a4cbf2& ie=/sdarticle.pdf

Barnett, M.A., Neppl, T.K., Scaramella, L.V., Ontai, L.L., & Conger, R.D. (2010). Grandmother involvement as a protective factor for early childhood social adjustment. Retrieved on November 23, 2010 from http://web.ebscohost.com.qe2a-proxy.mun.ca/ehost/pdfviewer/pdfviewer?vi d=3&hi d=7&sid=eb9d4a6f-5b77-446a-953ed4f1da67c570%40sessionmgr12

Bates, J.S. (2009). Generative grandparenting: A conceptual framework for nurturing grandchildren. Retrieved on November 25th, 2010 from http://web.ebscohost.com.qe2a-proxy.mun.ca/ehost/ pdfviewer/ pdfviewer?hid=11&sid=bb211a93-6e68-4ff5-b6f849f207297de6%40sessionmgr13&v id=4

Hardcastle, D., & Powers, P. (2004). Community Practice: Theories and skills for social workers (2nd ed.). Toronto: Oxford University Press.

Pierson, J. (2008). Going Local: Working in communities and neigbourhoods. New York: Routledge.

Stelle, C., Fruhauf, C.A., Orel, N., & Landry-Meyer, L. (2010). Grandparenting in the 21st century: Issues of diversity in grandparent-grandchild relationships. Journal of Gerontological Social Work, 53(8), 682–701.

Steinberg, D.M. (2002). The magic of mutual aid. Retrieved on November 24, 2010 from http://pdfserve. informaworld.com.qe2a-proxy.mun.ca/649002_751318387_902225339.pdf

ASHLEY CURNEW

THE ROLE OF GRANDPARENTS IN THE DEVELOPMENT OF COMMUNITY

Mark Twain once said that the universal brotherhood of man is the most precious possession (Moncur, 2010). One can only assume that this brotherhood that Twain spoke of is one that is comprised of a sense of belonging, the sense of belonging that parallels among members of a community, whether it be a geographic community or a community of people with similar characteristics or ideas as to how the community should be organized. Lee (1999) states that community organization has been a fundamental attribute of society throughout history, whereby people are purposefully brought together to organize their labour to achieve some development or adjustment in the life of the group.

Understanding Community and the Role of Grandparents

Community is nothing new to residents of Mercedes Creek. The tiny town of only 1500 has a history as interesting and diverse as the people who reside there. One resident, who will be referred to as Mrs. Lane, spoke fondly of her childhood and the relationships she witnessed among community members, familial and non-family relationships. She recalls that, in Mercedes Creek, respect was a fundamental concept valued among community members, respect was to be shown toward all people but in particular, toward grandparents/elderly residents. Individuals were always referred to as Mr. X and Mrs. X no one was addressed informally by their first name, unless they were a close relative. Grandparents, as the elders of the community, were a highly esteemed subsystem of the community and passed on the tradition of respect for others to young children, who continued the cycle by passing this tradition on to their children. Grandparents and elderly citizens were seen as the cornerstone of family and thus, were treated like proverbial gold. When an elderly person walked into the room, the common courtesy was to give that person your seat, especially if you were a younger person, as the general expectation of children was to be seen and not heard. When grandparents/elders spoke, you listened, and when they told you to do something, you did it, and without complaint.

Mrs. Lane recalls how her grandparents played a key role in her development – grandparents were as influential as parents during the upbringing of children in Mercedes Creek in the 1940's. Furthermore, Mrs. Lane attributes her strong understanding of the importance of community to her grandparents. Lee (1999)

A. Singh and M. Devine (Eds.), Rural Transformation and Newfoundland and Labrador Diaspora: Grandparents, Grandparenting, Community and School Relations, 91–100.

states that a community can be a group of people subject to laws, which may not be agreed upon by all, as there are a variety of meanings for understanding the notion of community. Mrs. Lane recalls that while her father was frequently gone away for work, her grandmother would often help ease her mother's burden of raising eight children, by stepping into the missing parental role. "Grandma would help around the house, cook meals, bathe the children and help the household to run smoother for mom". Mrs. Lane stated that she often spent a significant amount of time around her grandparents and that they had a tremendous effect on how she viewed her community and her role as a member of Mercedes Creek. Her grandparents helped demonstrate what it meant to be a neighbour and a community member in the way they always stepped forward to help with the building of a new home, the planting of a neighbour's garden, or helping out a Mercedes Creek resident who was sick or physically unable to manage particular tasks on their own. Mrs. Lane states that she learned from a young age to help your neighbor in any way you could and that the sense of community partnership was a responsibility of all residents. "You looked after one another, it was the unspoken rule. You did for others what you'd expect them to do for you, if you ever needed them". Mrs. Lane said that she rarely saw her grandparents in conflict with another community member and that they would nod to everyone they saw on the street and ask how he/she was doing. Seemingly, in the process of ensuring community involvement, this created an even closer, more tight-knit town where neighbours were an extension of the family tree.

As mentioned previously, there was a close bond between Mrs. Lane's grandparents and the next generation of children. Mrs. Lane explained that because her dad was often away in other parts of the province working to support the family, this placed a lot of additional stress on her mother to raise the kids and run the household. As a result, Mrs. Lane's maternal grandmother would spend a significant amount of time with Mrs. Lane, her siblings and the children's mother, the family system was viewed as the centre of the community. Mrs. Lane's grandmother continually told Mrs. Lane that blood was thicker than water and that when your family was in need, your responsibility was to do whatever you could to help them. Mrs. Lane witnessed this family tradition of helping one another through the close relationship between Mrs. Lane's grandmother and mother. This was a continuation of the concept of community demonstrated to Mrs. Lane by her grandparents, in the way they helped out neighbours and other community residents. The importance of assisting your community was passed on to residents of the next generation, not restricted to children, but it was assumed that family would help family. Children were often taught by grandparents and parents that the common practice was to help your friend and neighbour whenever you could. Mutual support was a strong community trait of Mercedes Creek and children were taught from a young age that community existed for those that lived there. Mrs. Lane stated that there was no social welfare system in the early days, so people relied on each other for help. As Hardcastle, Powers, and Wenocur (2004) state, mutual support is helping your community and its members in time of need and this was a value held dearly and practiced by Mercedes Creek residents.

Mrs. Lane personally witnessed her grandparents' demonstration of community, in their thorough involvement in her life, in the lives of her siblings, as well as in the lives of other children of the youngest generation. Mrs. Lane described the close relationship she had with her grandparents, who both played a monumental role in her child rearing. As previously mentioned, Mrs. Lane's grandmother was frequently around and helped in the raising of the children while Mrs. Lane's father was away. Mrs. Lane stated that her grandmother taught her many life skills how to knit and sew, how to bake and cook, as well as how to do laundry – all of which were typical responsibilities of women during the mid-twentieth century. Chores were not done for an allowance but rather out of expectation, you did out of love and respect for your family. Mrs. Lane noted that her grandfather was an instrumental person in demonstrating the sense of community partnership that existed between members of the tiny rural town of Mercedes Creek, as he would often come to the aid of a community member who was taking on a big task. He also tried to look out for all third generation children, not only just those who were family. If he saw children doing something that they shouldn't be doing, he would scold them and tell them why it was wrong. And because grandparents were highly respected, children would typically apologize for their actions and run back home. There was no backtalk to elders/grandparents because it was common knowledge that these people were to be respected; any knowledge that they passed on to children was usually for the well-being of the children. Furthermore, discipline was viewed as necessary. A smack on the behind often did the trick, although some parents went too far with their discipline. Mrs. Lane stated that she didn't think of it as overly strict but as a necessary means of teaching grandchildren wrong from right and she feels discipline was one of the main reasons why she stayed on the right path. Grandparents encouraged their grandchildren to attend school; however, if money was needed, children were expected to quit school and go to work. It was the expectation that you pulled your weight and helped your family with whatever skill set you possessed. The socialization of children focused on helping your family and community in any way you could and that showed through in the closeness of community members.

Religion was another attribute that was passed down from grandparents to subsequent generations. Grandparents instilled in their children a strong sense of religion and spirituality, which was passed on from these children to their own children. Mrs. Lane said, "You were expected to go to church and to say your prayers". Grace was said before every meal and it showed the appreciation you had for the blessings you were given. There was an understanding passed down to children from parents and primarily grandparents that not everyone was as lucky and we should be thankful for the many things we had and thank God for those blessings. "We attended church every Sunday and religious deities were scattered throughout our home. Subsequently, the Knights of Columbus was one of the religious groups that our grandfather participated in, and he convinced my father to join as well. My brothers looked up to my dad and grandfather and they talked about following the family tradition of joining the Knights of Columbus when they grew up. A taboo attribute of religion at that time was when young people from different religious branches began dating. This often put into question how the children of this budding couple would be raised. Thus, my grandfather would always say that the best men were from the Roman Catholic Church and I'd be a fool to look elsewhere".

Another organization that Mrs. Lane's family was heavily involved in was the church hall, where Mrs. Lane's grandmother and mother would often volunteer, along with other ladies in the community. They would prepare meals for weddings, funerals, baptisms and other social gatherings; providing cookies, salads, sandwiches and peeling vegetables for a big a boil up. This meant that all the ladies were expected to pitch in and lend a hand to help out their fellow community members. Knitted goods as well as homemade crafts were supplied to local craft fairs held at the church and to events sponsoring local organizations. Social inclusion was a strong element within the church, so no one was excluded from volunteering to help community causes. "A helping hand was a helping hand and it was appreciated," adds Mrs. Lane.

Paid work was often associated with hard labour in Mercedes Creek. It meant working long hours on the water or down underground. There was no way of getting around it. If you wanted to put food on the table for your family, you had to put in the effort. Sometimes this meant leaving town or leaving the province, says Mrs. Lane. Mrs. Lane's father was frequently away working, which made life difficult for her mom, who had to raise a house full of children on her own. Hence, her grandparents played a crucial role in her upbringing. The primary industry in Mercedes Creek was mining and often grandfathers would set the stage for future generations by using their clout in the mining organization to help second and third generation men get jobs in the mines as well. It was not work for the faint at heart and it would often take the good out of you but it meant you could remain in your community with your family and help make life easier on them. The town of Mercedes Creek attempted to make changes for the better by putting forth various initiatives to help the economy, similar to the concept of local development. When times were tough, community members would gather together to achieve a particular goal, which in many cases would be to help the economy and provide jobs for local residents (Lee, 1999). Informal and formal leadership from members of the community would help coordinate the idea and get volunteers interested in helping with the project, which was typically easy in Mercedes Creek where people didn't shy away from hard work. Social participation was a key attribute of town members and benefited community development projects immensely. A vegetable garden in the community was one such initiative that proved to be successful for a number of years and extremely beneficial to the residents in terms of employment, promoting self-sufficiency of the town, as well as educating residents on the gardening process. This idea also helped bring residents together as a community, as most residents would work closely and help the other out when necessary. The fact that the community of Mercedes Creek had consensus on many town initiatives, such as the vegetable garden, meant that the projects were more likely to prosper. As Lee (1999) suggests, action in a community without consensus is more prone to division and failure; it is important for town members to be on the same page regarding town initiatives, in order for these projects to survive.

Unpaid work in the community was widespread. Neighbours would help each other out on a regular basis, whether it was helping a sick neighbour fix up their shed, or helping a friend put a wooden fence around his garden. The task was never too big when multiple hands pitched in, and this is why community involvement was such a beneficial tool to all members involved.

Mrs. Lane states that she began to witness her community getting smaller as she grew older. It was not unusual for some residents to leave the town fresh out of school, to look for work. If you weren't interested in fishing or mining, then you had no choice but to look for employment opportunities elsewhere. Often some of the men would leave to look for jobs in St. John's and vicinity, the lucky ones who were successful at finding employment would work at loading and unloading ships or working around the docks. When females sought employment, they would usually work at housekeeping in hotels in urban centres and these women would work hard to earn payment in the form of room and board or a small compensation. Females like males, were typically forced to leave home when they reached a certain age, as it was too expensive for their families to support them, along with raising the other children. Families were frequently large in numbers which meant that when you were old enough to work and live on your own, you moved out and began taking care of yourself. The most significant decline in community began when the primary industry of Mercedes Creek shut down in the 1960's. This meant a substantial loss of employment for people living in Mercedes Creek and as a result, many families moved away. Most people moved to more urban areas where there were more opportunities for employment. However, regardless of the type of occupation you held, the concept of helping family was always at the forefront of people's minds as many of them would send money home to family.

Despite all the struggles and relative defeats suffered by the community of Mercedes Creek, Mrs. Lane still speaks fondly of her hometown. She states that there is a resiliency among community members; "you can't hold us down we're as tough as nails." However, the once tight-knit community has seemingly dispersed and separated. The population has dwindled from the high numbers in the 1960's when industry was at its peak to a current population of 2700 people (Mercedes Creek, Community Profile, 2010). The declining population has not necessarily equated to a closer community, suggests Mrs. Lane, where she attributes a change in the values and principles held by community members as another reason why the community has fallen apart. Although, she feels the community is still strong in the relationships between members of the older generations where grandparents, like herself, reach out to help one another when possible, and nod their head to each other, to indicate non-verbally "how are you today, friend?" The various community groups that existed when Mrs. Lane was growing up still exist; however, they have a much smaller following than in previous years. Mrs. Lane attributes this decline to the decline in religious participation. "People don't attend church today like they used to and those that do are my age still have that rooted sense of spirituality and thanking God for what we have." The Knights of Columbus and St. Michael's Parish Ladies still exist but the members of these community groups are older individuals who have a strong religious affiliation and an appreciation for helping their fellow community members. Work opportunities within the community are still rather limited, especially in the paid sector, the primary paid industries that employ some of the residents are healthcare, education and construction. Unpaid work does not occur as frequently as it did in the 1960's when Mrs. Lane was growing up, which Mrs. Lane attributes to a lack of opportunities and a lack of respect held among members of the younger generation. Mrs. Lane stated that when she was young, you were expected to help the elderly without being asked, you shoveled their driveway, picked up their mail, ran errands, and cut firewood for those with wood stoves.

With the decline in population and changing societal attitudes, there appears to be a disjointed sense of community and/or a lack of understanding as to what community used to mean to the tiny town of Mercedes Creek. Mrs. Lane noted that there has been a two-fold decline in the population, as not only are young people leaving the town to seek employment elsewhere, but many members of the older generation (Mrs. Lane's friends and fellow grandparents) are dying. The impact of such a decline in population has meant less discussion regarding community between grandparents and grandkids, as well as less opportunity for grandchildren to observe their grandparents interacting with other grandparents in a manner that reflects the mutual support function of community. This has led to a slow decline in the sense of community among residents and fewer community members helping one another. Mrs. Lane also reports that the friendly demeanour that was so prominent is now rare, which she blames on the lack of societal values that promote community interdependence. A change in societal values with regards to respecting elders/grandparents has also impacted the way in which young people value and treat grandparents. A higher number of grandchildren no longer see a need to go out of their way to help elderly people or to initiate conversations about how to foster a better sense of community between residents, there appears to be more of a desire among the younger generation to remain isolated from their fellow community members. As a result, the sense of community has diminished in Mercedes Creek. Some residents remember the days when neighbours were more like family, those are the grandparents, like Mrs. Lane, who struggle to keep the concept of a true community alive in the town. The long term care/continuing care social worker in the town also helps to encourage community by promoting events that bring people from all ages together, to socialize and mingle where discussions can occur about the good old days. One of the advantages of people leaving the town, which Mrs. Lane struggled to come up with, is the fact that many of the people who remain in Mercedes Creek do so because of their innate appreciation of the town. Many of the first people to leave when an opportunity arises are those with a poor perception of Mercedes Creek, that it is negative and degrading. These negative opinions can often be upsetting for long-time residents of the town, who are proud of their community, its history and potential for success. With the negative-focused people out of the town, there is a more positive community attitude towards Mercedes Creek. Mrs. Lane states that had these people stayed, the town would still be relatively separated, as it is not necessarily the quantity of people but rather the views held that have changed the way the town of Mercedes Creek functions.

Mrs. Lane is relatively new to the role of a grandmother. Her only grandchild is two years old and resides on the mainland, in Ottawa. Mrs. Lane notes that despite her positive affinity towards Mercedes Creek, her son was quick to move to seek employment elsewhere. He met his would-be wife at university and they later moved to Ottawa in search of job opportunities. Mrs. Lane says that she tries to visit as often as possible but it's not financially possible. Since the death of her husband ten years ago, finances have been a little tight. However, her son usually attempts to make a trip home with his wife and their new baby daughter every summer but this is not always possible. Mrs. Lane notes that telephone conversations and cards have helped her stay close with her son and his family, although she wishes to see her granddaughter grow up. She states that she cannot wait for the little girl to grow up and hopefully come visit Mrs. Lane in the summer. Mrs. Lane said that as long as she's alive, she'll keep the values of community close to her heart and pass those values on to her granddaughter. She notes that it would be nice to have her son and his family closer so that she could see them regularly, but the tiny town of Mercedes Creek is not the optimal place for young families to start out, as there are few employment opportunities.

Mercedes Creek is typical of most rural towns in the province of Newfoundland and Labrador; it has a strong historical heritage that is emergent in an elderly population that is declining. With an employment rate of only 37.9%, which is much lower than the provincial average of 63.3%, there appears to be an undeniable truth that the town has lost a significant percentage of its population due to lack of resources and employment opportunities. As mentioned previously, the population of the once thriving town was close to ten thousand when at its peak in the 1950's before the primary industry shut down; now, at a population of approximately 2700, the town has seemingly lost its community cohesion, which can be attributed to the deaths of many of the elders who desired to maintain the community ties and mutual support that one were an integral part of Mercedes Creek. The change in societal views, morals and values has changed the tiny town. In a world where the elderly/grandparents are no longer viewed as an important source for wisdom and knowledge, it is easy to see why the young people of Mercedes Creek have become disjointed from the sense of community. Further, Mercedes Creek is now a predominantly tourism-based community whereby there are few employment opportunities for residents, thus leaving to seek employment elsewhere is the only alternative to ensure a financially viable life for young people and their families.

Systems Theory views the community as a social system made up of parts that are interrelated and interdependent, each subsystem relies on the other to function (Hardcastle et al., 2004). It seems apparent that in recent years the community system and its subsystems have become more decentralized and less coordinated with one another due to a change in the overall values of the townspeople. Societal values are more in line with beliefs to "fend for yourself" versus the "do onto others as you would want done onto you" values that were strongly held in the 1960's when the idea of community was more prevalent. This shift in thinking could have a lot to do with the different way of socializing children today, children are being socialized to be independent and self-sufficient. Mrs. Lane feels that this quest for independence has gone too far, whereby these independent children become independent adults who refuse to help others or accept help themselves. There is hope though; Berkman and Ambruoso (2006) state that the number of grandparents raising grandchildren has dramatically increased. This means that grandparents, like Mrs. Lane, have more opportunity to pass their values and beliefs about community and helping thy neighbour onto their grandchildren. This provides hope as it may reignite the flame of community cohesion and togetherness. However, the shift in vision as to what the community of Mercedes Creek should look like is a good example of how societal values can impact the behaviour of community members. A community where residents once held strong ties to each other and to the community is now disjointed and separated. This is the reality in many rural towns across Newfoundland and Labrador today. Thus, as a social worker, discovering the beliefs held by community members is crucial to obtaining a complete picture of the community in context, and in helping to show current residents how their community used to be and how it can be again.

Mark Twain once said that the universal brotherhood of man is the most precious possession (Moncur, 2010). This opinion is shared by Mrs. Lane, who was taught from a young age that your community is what you make it and that belonging to a community is something to be treasured Mutual support and social participation are elements of community that Mrs. Lane feels are lacking today. There is less of a focus on reciprocity where people put into the community what they want to get from the community and more of a belief that people should be able to exist in relative isolation (Hardcastle et al., 2004). As long as there are vocal members like Mrs. Lane left to share their stories, there is hope that current residents can come to understand what community really means. The concept of community will survive in the stories and traditions that are passed down through the generations, stories that demonstrate what it means to not only live in a community but rather to be part of a community.

REFLECTION QUESTIONS

1. Provide your own analysis of the statement or thinking that it is the more negative people that have left the community and the ones who stay are more committed.

2. How does the notion of "everyone fending for themselves" fit with the previous sense of community, the contradiction?
3. The paper suggests that grandparents/elderly were much more respected in early/ mid twentieth century than today. What are some indicators that support this statement and what indicators refute this statement?
4. How is the transmission of culture and family continued in this paper and is it likely that it will be effective with the newest grandchild and other grandchildren in the future?

REFERENCES

Berkman, B., & Ambruoso, S. (2006). Handbook of Social Work in Health and Aging. Oxford: Oxford University Press.

Cox, C.B. (2000). Empowering Grandparents Raising Grandchildren: A training manual for group leaders. New York: Springer Publishing.

Hardcastle, D.A., Powers, P.R., & Wenocur, S. (2004). Community Practice: Theories and skills for social workers (2nd ed.). Oxford: Oxford University Press.

Lee, B. (1999). Pragmatics of Community Organization. Mississauga, Ontario: Common Act Press.

Loue, S., & Sajatovic, M. (2007). Encyclopedia of Aging and Public Health. New York: Springer.

'Mercedes Creek' Account Selection Page – Community Accounts. (n.d.). Community Accounts. Retrieved November 26, 2010 from http://www.communityaccounts.ca/communityaccounts/onlinedata/accountselectionpage.asp?_=vb7FnYmXulCv0q.Yjp-Fg5upv7iUko66rJp3zA__

Moncur, M. (2010). Community Quotes. Retrieved from November 26th 2010 from http://www.quotationspage.com/subjects/community/

Shulman, L. (2009). The Skills of Helping: Individuals, families, groups, and communities (6th ed.). Belmont, CA: Brooks/Cole Cengage Learning.

Toledo, S., & Brown, D.E. (1995). Grandparents as Parents: A survival guide for raising a second family. New York: Guilford Press.

CRYSTAL FITZPATRICK

GOAT ISLAND

Gone But Will Never Be Forgotten Grandparents as Contributors to Community & Community Culture

"Nan, can you make me some tea and toast?" Nan and toast are two of the most common words spoken at the home of these grandparents. Mrs. Jane Byrne, more commonly known as Nan, makes the best toast in the world as suggested by her seven children, 13 grandchildren, and husband of 53 years, Mr. Jack Byrne (pop). Jane and Jack married on November 5th, 1957, in the small town of Goat Island located on the Northern Peninsula of Newfoundland and Labrador (NL). Jane and Jack, who remain happily married today, raised their family on Goat Island and continued to live there until 1998, before moving to St. John's, NL.

Goat Island was a traditional fishing community, first settled by the French in the 1500s. The community of Goat Island was formed by a distinct group of people who shared a culture, traditions and community bond (Lee, 2002). Fishing was the backbone of the community and was classified as men's work. Pop said that you spent more time doing unpaid work than paid work. Unpaid work included preparing the fish for salting or drying on flakes, cutting and storing firewood, and hunting for moose and ducks. Gardens were common within the community and everyone grew potatoes and cabbage. Many families had mini farms where they raised sheep for wool and goats and hens for food, eggs and meat. During the fall, men would mend traps and nets to prepare for next summer. They would also cut down logs to build homes, sheds, bridges and boats, which was often a community project where everyone helped out. Women completed the housework and the bulk of childcare duties, helped prepare the fish for winter, and performed garden duties. They would also prepare the wool for use to make socks and gloves.

The Role of Grandparenting

Growing up on Goat Island in the 1940s presented many challenges for families living in the area. In recalling their experiences as grandchildren, Nan and Pop stated that they learned from a young age that the only means of survival at that time was to take advantage of God's creations – becoming a part of the wind and water and rock and soil, and recognize the importance of self-reliance for survival. Pop's grandfather played a big role in teaching him the ways of the land so that he could contribute and provide for the family. He remembers his grandfather telling him that survival

A. Singh and M. Devine (Eds.), Rural Transformation and Newfoundland and Labrador Diaspora:
Grandparents, Grandparenting, Community and School Relations, 101–108.

was your main purpose in life and teaching him how to hang in during tough times. A sense of identity was created within him through endless stories of the importance of a family name and a loyalty to the land that your family before you made a living from. Pop's grandfather showed him the importance of having faith in a community based on hospitality, kindness and assistance. His grandfather told him that love was key and never to mistake a strength for a weakness. "Basically," Pop said, with a smile on his face, "He taught me what it meant to be a true Newfoundlander." Pop's grandmother died before he was born.

As for Nan, the majority of her memories involve her grandparents. Her mother died giving birth and her grandparents played a big role in providing mutual support to her father in raising the children. When Nan was not outside playing with friends, she was helping to care for her sisters and performing the woman traditional duties of baking bread, washing clothes, cooking and cleaning. From an early age, Nan learned the importance of family and the give and take relationship that makes a community. Like other community members, Nan felt a deep sense of pride, and had faith, in her community.

Nan and Pop's grandparents instilled in their grandchildren a sense of emotional comfort with their way of life and the importance of everyday being a learning experience. Contact with grandparents "constitutes a medium that enables communication and social interaction, leading to the transfer of knowledge and skills" (Hurme, Westerback, & Quadrello, 2010). Nan and Pop's grandparents did just that, through demonstrating the importance of creating a bond and mutual support among community members. The community was close-knit with close friendships, and regardless of the circumstances, there was always someone to lend a helping hand. Friendship was valued in the community and residents treated one another as equals. People had very little with regards to material things so there was no jealously because of material things.

Religion was a top priority to Nan and Pop, in the raising of their children. The rosary was said every morning and night, along with night time prayers. The spiritual aspects of life helped create a sense of purpose in a higher power than simply accepting the circumstances of their lives (Lee, 2002). Pop said, "Because we were devoted to the sea, the only thing we had to protect us at times was the higher power. Beliefs brought our community together and provided us with courage to persevere in difficult struggles."

"Respect," Pop said, "is the last piece of the puzzle to ensure unity within a community. The older adults had the knowledge needed to survive during those days and without them, we would not have known the tricks to the trade." Pop holds a strong pride in his community due to the guidance of older adults and the knowledge of culture and traditions he gained. Both grandparents admit with smiles that they would not have known how to survive or raise a family without the support and guidance from their grandparents.

After they married, Nan and Pop had seven children in a 12 year span. Nan and Pop remarked that with so many children, they could not spend as much time with each child as they would have liked. Nan and Pop noted it was a struggle but they did the best they could with what they had. They are still close with their children today.

"In modern society, grandparents have a variety of established roles such as providing childcare, acting as playmates, and/or providing financial support for their immediate family" (Lee & Gardner, 2010). The grandparents have adopted a similar role within their own family providing safety, security, love, and a sense of family and history, and have piqued the children's interest in values and traditions of the past (Lee & Gardner, 2010). Nan and Pop feel they are getting a second chance and are experiencing children in a new light. They are using time with their grandchildren to share the values, traditions and family rituals of the past in the hope that their grandchildren will carry on the traditions into future generations. This form of grandparenting is known as symbolic grandparenthood (Hurme et al., 2010). Pop acts as mentor to the boys in the family, doing his best to transcend the traditional values of men as good providers, and teaching them life lessons as his grandfather once did (Stelle et al., 2010). In relation to childcare, Nan practices the traditional woman's role of caring for the children, preparing their meals, ensuring they are washed and dressed, and teaching the girls to knit and bake bread. This works well for the grandparents and grandchildren; the grandchildren are learning different perspectives and about all aspects of life (Stelle et al., 2010).

Nan and Pop have close relationships with the majority of their grandchildren, especially those who live in the same community as them. The grandchildren who live nearby usually go to Nan and Pop's for afterschool childcare and snacks, which helps create and maintain a close bond. All family members come together for special family gatherings as Christmastime and during anniversaries. Nan and Pop's oldest grandchild has relocated to St. John's, but there is still constant contact by phone every day and the grandchild comes home to visit because Nan and Pop do not travel much anymore. Two grandchildren are living in Ontario and Nan and Pop admit that they are not as close to them as they would like. However, they do their best to see them once a year and keep in contact via phone and send cards at Christmas and to acknowledge birthdays.

The Good Ol' Days are Gone

'The good ol' days are gone' is a common saying by the elderly throughout NL, especially by Pop whose heart breaks at the thought of Goat Island becoming a ghost town, and unfortunately this is the reality of today. The permanent population of Goat Island never surpassed 135 people, with the majority of men fishing to provide a living for their family. After the cod moratorium in 1992, the bottom fell out of the barrel and ended the 400-year tradition of inshore fishing in the region. As a result, many residents moved to larger urban centers such as Stephenville and St. John's and throughout Canada. The term 'brain drain' could be used to describe this move, which is defined as the "transfer of resources in the form of human capital and mainly applies to the migration of relatively highly educated individuals from developing to developed countries" (Docquier & Marfouk, 2006). The community of Goat Island was built on the fishery and once the fishery closed, there was no other means to earn a living. Thus, people were left with no other choice but to leave the area to seek "a new identity that entails self-transformation that often means a commitment to further education and training" (Stockdale, 2004). These displaced workers who left their community of Goat Island to build a new life outside of the fishing industry would never return again, "becoming foreigners in their own community" (Stockdale, 2004).

Today Goat Island has a population of approximately 25 people. The grandparents left in 1998 due to Nan's heart condition, and Pop admits that only because he loves Nan more, he would not have left at all. Nan and Pop still spend their summers in Goat Island and for them, it will always be home. Goat Island is dying and those who hold a strong emotional bond to the community are experiencing grief and hearts are breaking because their livelihood is slowly disappearing. Nan and Pop instilled in their children the will to survive and determination to make a life for themselves, but now with tears in his eyes, Pop fears that future generations will no longer be raised with the same values.

Goat Island Today

The current population in Goat Island consists of middle aged and elderly people; no longer are the streets filled with screaming children. Relationships among those still living in the community remain strong and mutual support is still evident; however, people are finding it hard to cope so they tend to stick to themselves. There are fewer people to help those remaining and fewer homes to visit, particularly during the Christmas season. Fewer lights in few homes make for a lonely atmosphere at night.

In relation to work for the middle aged folks, during the fall there are make-work projects enabling individuals to collect their Employment Insurance benefits. A few work in nearby communities performing home-care duties and working in the forestry. Middle aged relatives tend to live with and care for their parents. Unpaid work still consists of cutting and preparing firewood for use, participating in the limited food fishery, maintaining homes, and looking after the elderly. Religious practices are disappearing and few formally attend Church, but instead practice their faith on their own. With so few people in the community attending mass, it has been difficult to maintain the cost of heating the Church.

Analysis of Goat Island

Upon reflection, Pop stated, "It took us a long time but I think we finally accept that Goat Island will never be the same again." Even though Nan and Pop's hearts still break at the thought of it becoming a ghost town, their memories provide emotional comfort, and they know that regardless of where they are, Goat Island will always be a part of them. "Earning a living from the sea is who we are but it is not who our children are or grandchildren will be," says Pop. "If people had stayed, it would have been very challenging to earn a living. The community existed only because of the fishery and died when the fishery died." Nan and Pop would rather see the community die than see their grandchildren suffering for the sake of struggling to keep the community alive with no economic resources.

In assessing the loss of the community, the grandparents agreed that the biggest loss they see is in the local community spirit and the willingness to survive. Pop noted that since the population of the community started to decline, people never got over it and are now struggling to move on. "Back in the old days, everyone shared a bond with people around them but now people living in the community are not as close knit as they used to be. There are fewer visits and less communication on a daily basis." Pop believes that even though the population has decreased, it should not mean that people should give up living.

Nan and Pop both feel that they gained more from their experience of living in Goat Island than they lost. They admit that it is not as easy as it once was to teach others the culture and traditions of the community, but they think it should be an individual responsibility now as grandparents to pass on the culture and traditions as generations before them did. Nan and Pop call their house in Goat Island a cabin, and through their stories and visits there, they are doing their best to pass on its culture to their grandchildren. Pop loves bringing his grandsons down on the wharf and to the stage to share stories of the old days so they can learn about the way of life back then. Nan and Pop say that even though they are not living in Goat Island anymore, they still carry a sense of pride for the community and will rise to defend it. "We are doing our best to create a sense of belonging and connectedness to each other and are trying to instil the values of hard work and a sense of identity for future generations, but in a different way. No matter where we go or where our life paths will take us, we carry the feel of the place with and within us and no matter how small the community gets, no one can take that away from us."

Nan and Pop believe that it is their responsibility to form their own community within their family in order to educate the children in traditional values and beliefs. "Even though the fishery is gone and our community is slowly dying, we still have a story to tell and a commitment to our culture and our family to ensure the past will never be forgotten. You can take the man out of the bay, but you can't take the bay out of the man."

Social-Psychological Theory would best describe the feelings the grandparents are experiencing. The perspective emphasizes "how each community member feels about him-or herself and how they interact with others" (Kirst-Ashman, 2008). It views community members as bound together for psychological and social reasons, sharing similar concerns. Also, it creates a sense of well-being, and "we" among current and past residents in the community (Krist-Ashman, 2008). Culture and traditions will be lost as the community slowly dies, however, my grandparents did make a good point in saying that individuals need to take it upon themselves to pass on the traditional culture and beliefs of the old days. Creating a non-geographical community based on the educational foundation will help to serve a number of purposes to enhance members' sense of well-being (Krist-Ashman, 2008). Creating these strong relationships with grandchildren can help provide a feeling of belonging, connectedness and a sense of identity regardless of where you live or where life will take you.

The harsh reality for many rural communities in NL is out-migration due to lack of employment opportunities. Nan and Pop have realized this but have decided to work with the community to reclaim their livelihood and help promote the culture of the land and its people through enhancing tourism. The grandparents are doing their best to turn the signs of weaknesses into strengths by educating their grandchildren on the values and culture of the past through social learning. They are teaching them the human behaviour and practices of the past to take with them in their current social environments such as the skills of fishing and system knowledge such as the importance of having pride in and loyalty to a community (Hardcastle & Powers, 2004).

"Employment creation is viewed as a central component to rural regeneration" (Stockdale, 2004). In today's society, higher education levels are required for people to make a living. "Human systems cannot exist without a relationship to its environment. They must exchange information and resources with other systems and act on that information to maintain itself and flourish" (Hardcastle & Powers, 2004). The reality is, without the systems and networks available, Goat Island is unable to survive. Regardless of the want to keep the community alive, without the readily available systems for people to earn a living, it is not going to function or survive. In order for rural communities to survive, communities need to "become increasingly involved in their own futures" (Stockdale, 2004). New creative ways need to be established to keep traditional fishing communities alive.

Nan and Pop identify themselves as residents of Goat Island and will continue to pass on their knowledge and traditions to their grandchildren in hopes that the past will never be forgotten. Considering the current situation, they do not see anything else that they can do. They are saddened by this reality but are doing their best to find the strength within themselves to keep the community alive in their memories. In quoting Pop, "This is my homeland, the place I was born in, no matter where I go, it's in my soul, my feet may wander a thousand places but my heart will lead me back home."

REFLECTION QUESTIONS

1. "Where are you from?" is a common question that Newfoundlanders and Labradorians ask others. For Newfoundlanders and Labradorians this is a common, matter of fact question. However, it has a deep meaning. In thinking about this question, what does it mean for you?
2. The transmission of culture is taken on by the grandparents in this paper. Is cultural transmission an individual responsibility or a collective responsibility? What are the implications of each view?

3. A sense of identity is formed through our relationships with others. How have your grandparents influenced you in your sense of identity?
4. The grandparents in this paper have accepted the loss of their community. How does this process (accepting loss) happen, from your perspective?

REFERENCES

Docquier, F., & Marfouk, A. (2006). International migration by educational attainment (1990–2000) in C. Ozden and M. Schiff, (Eds.), International Migration, Remittances and the Brain Drain, Chapter 5, Palgrave-Macmillan.

Hardcastle, D., & Powers, P. (2004). Community Practice: Theories and Skills for Social Workers (2nd ed.). Toronto: Oxford University Press.

Hurme, H., Westerback, S., & Quadrello, T. (2010). Traditional and new forms of contact between grandparents and grandchildren. Journal of Intergenerational Relationships, 8(3), 264–280.

Kirst-Ashman, K. (2008). Human Behaviour, Communities, Organizations, and Groups in the Macro Social Environment: An empowerment approach (2nd ed.). Belmont, CA: Brooks/Cole.

Lee, B. (2002). Pragmatics of Community Organizing (3rd ed.). Mississauga: Common Act Press.

Lee, M., & Gardner, J. (2010). Grandparents' involvement and support in families with children with disabilities. Educational Gerontology, 36, 467–499.

Stelle, C., Fruhauf, C.A., Orel, N., & Landry-Meyer, L. (2010). Grandparenting in the 21st century: Issues of diversity in grandparent-grandchild relationships. Journal of Gerontological Social Work, 53(8), 682–701.

Stockdale, A. (2004). Rural out-migration: Community consequences and individual migrant experiences. Sociologia Ruralis, 44(2), 167–194.

HEATHER SMART

THE INFLUENCE OF GRANDPARENTS WITHIN FAMILIES AND COMMUNITIES

Some people view their community as a geographic location and the place where they live, work or go to school; they often do not gain a true sense of community, or recognize that it is much more than this. Homan (2011) describes communities as interlocking systems and relates the importance of tradition and culture to these systems. Our communities are a part of who we are and each person living within a community contributes to it in one way or another. Although there are formal leaders within communities, community and community culture are highly influenced by informal leaders, such as grandparents. This paper will explore the subject of grandparents as contributors to community and community culture, through an interview with a grandparenting couple, who will simply be referred to as Grandpa and Grandma.

Grandpa and Grandma grew up in Little Brook, a small, rural community in Newfoundland. They describe Little Brook, then and now, as a tight-knit community in which most residents know one another. Little Brook has become an aging community; however, recently several young families have moved back and are raising their children there.

As children growing up in Little Brook, Grandpa and Grandma experienced the true meaning of community. They both discussed growing up in large families and having their grandparents live nearby. They talked about the tradition of having a mid-day "Jiggs dinner" at their grandparent's house every Sunday, and Grandma described feeling as though grandparents were the backbone of not only individual families, but also of the community. She recalled this Sunday tradition as an opportunity for the whole family to get together and remembers that her grandparents would ensure there was space for all. She recalls her grandparents having to set places for family members to sit and eat all over their home, in order to make room for everyone. However, that didn't matter, as her grandparents would express that the sense of "togetherness" was important to them and the family as a whole.

During these dinners, Grandma's grandmother would teach the children to cook and have them help with bringing the vegetables in from the garden. The children were active participants in the lives of their grandparents, and the grandparents made sure that the children were learning family traditions and community culture when in their presence. Beland and Mills (2001) discuss the importance of grandparents being active participants in the lives of their grandchildren; this participation has always

A. Singh and M. Devine (Eds.), Rural Transformation and Newfoundland and Labrador Diaspora: Grandparents, Grandparenting, Community and School Relations, 109–116.

been believed to be an important part of society's social and family networking. The intergenerational learning of family tradition and culture through interactions, attitudes and perceptions displayed in such relationships allows children to develop a strengthened bond with their grandparents, their family and their community. Learning about their grandparents' past and how they lived encourages children to develop a sense of appreciation and a level of respect. It is apparent that Grandma's grandparents were successful in this, as many of her stories demonstrate the pride she has in her family and community.

Grandpa also described his grandparents as being active participants in his life. He explained that the main occupations in Little Brook were those of a woodsman or farmer and it was common for the men of the community to go into the woods to work from Monday to Friday. When the men of Grandpa's family returned home for the weekend, there was always a family dinner, usually held at his grandparent's house. Grandpa recalls that two of the most important lessons he learned from his grandparents through traditions such as these weekend dinners were the importance of family and of respecting family, community members and even the community itself. Grandpa spoke of times when his family had to live off the land. His father worked in the woods and the family grew vegetables on their land, not to sell, but to feed the family. He recalls that crops were often shared among community members to ensure that each family had enough to eat. Many adults would volunteer to help one another on the farms within the community and teenage boys were often hired in the summer to assist with the crops.

Ofahengaue, Toafa & Moala (2008) state, "Grandparents play an intrinsic and inherent cultural role reserved for the preservation and transference of family, community, and cultural values, beliefs and practices from one generation to another." Both Grandpa and Grandma demonstrated their belief in this, as they shared stories of learning from their parents and grandparents. Grandma spoke of helping her mother and her grandmother make bread, cook, do laundry, sew, knit and quilt. She expressed great pride in learning such important cultural traditions and hopes to someday pass them down to her granddaughter. Grandpa helped his father and his grandfather cut wood to heat their homes, carried the wood to the house or stored it in the woodshed, helped out in the garden, and went fishing and hunting. He expressed great pride in learning such skills and talked about how much he enjoys sharing them with his daughter, who loves to fish and take part in outdoor activities. He too spoke of his excitement in being able to pass along these traditions and skills to his grandchildren.

Growing up, Grandpa and Grandma recall the churches and schools as playing a major role within the community. In Little Brook, there were four dominant religions: Salvation Army; Anglican; United; and Seventh Day Adventist; however, each church welcomed members of all religions. The schools in Little Brook were also denominational when Grandpa and Grandma attended, but later became non-denominational.

Each church in Little Brook held Sunday school classes for the children, in which both Grandpa and Grandma took part. Grandpa reported that his family would go to their church on Sunday mornings and might then go to another church on Sunday evenings. The churches brought the community together, not just religiously, but also socially. It was common for a church to be used for community concerts, fundraisers and other community-based functions. Grandpa and Grandma describe the whole community attending any and all social functions and remember these social events as being named "a time." Grandma recalls hearing her parents and grandparents state, "There's a time at the church tonight." However, it was stated, "a time" would always bring the community together; children, parents and grandparents would all be involved in planning the events. Whether it was a Christmas concert being put off by the children, or an anniversary party for a couple in the community, everyone did their share.

With respect to leaders within the community, Grandpa and Grandma viewed their grandparents and other community elders as maintaining this role. Little Brook did not have a community council when Grandpa and Grandma were children, so whenever an issue arose, it was always discussed among the elders of the community. The elders were viewed as the most knowledgeable, as they were the most experienced members of the community. Aside from the elders, clergy and teachers were also seen as informal leaders.

Grandpa and Grandma recall that throughout the week, members of the community would generally care for their own families. However, on the weekends when men returned home from working in the woods, it was common to see community members helping one another or working together to repair community churches or schools. The children were free to roam the community, as parents knew other members of the community were always watching out for their safety. Grandpa reported that as a child, if you did anything out of line, your parents would often know about it by the time you got home. This was how close knit the community was. Everyone looked out for everyone else and there was always a level of respect among all community members for doing so.

When talking about when and why people began to leave Little Brook, Grandpa recalls that his grandparents had no need or intention to leave and if they did, it would have been a difficult task, as transportation options were very limited during this era. Grandpa then explained that his parents' generation stayed in Little Brook and raised their families there. He believes this was because many people did not complete their education; rather, they began working early to help their family, then married young and had children. Grandpa also thinks his parents stayed in Little Brook because his grandparents were there, because of the closeness of the family. As Grandpa and Grandma attended school, the importance of obtaining a post-secondary education in order to secure employment became prominent. In order to acquire such a level of education, many people, such as Grandpa, had to leave Little Brook and move to urban centres such as St. John's, Newfoundland and Toronto, Ontario. Grandpa chose to go to St. John's and Grandma soon followed. Once Grandpa finished his education, he obtained a job in St. John's and he and Grandma settled there, married and began their family. This was a difficult move for Grandpa and Grandma to make, as St. John's and the communities surrounding it were bigger and less personal and Grandpa and Grandma found it strange not knowing their neighbours or anyone else in the community.

Although they no longer live in Little Brook, Grandpa and Grandma still feel as though it is their home. Grandma describes St. John's as the place in which they live, but whenever someone asks, she still refers to Little Brook as home. In fact, Grandpa and Grandma plan to retire in Little Brook and have already begun the process of building a house there. Grandpa and Grandma state that they will find it difficult to leave their children and grandchild, who also reside in the St. John's area; however, they also feel it is important that their granddaughter have the opportunity to experience rural life.

As grandparents, Grandpa and Grandma see Little Brook as a safe, friendly community in which their granddaughter can experience many cultural and traditional aspects of life that are difficult to experience in an urban area. Grandma excitedly plans for her granddaughter to visit during the summer when she can take her berry picking, sightseeing and exploring surrounding communities. Grandpa also wants to take his granddaughter boating and ski-dooing, teach her to fish, swim and skate and bring her to the family cabin where her mom went every summer as a child. The Grandparents also express their wish that their granddaughter develop a sense of community and be near her extended family, as her great-grandparents and several aunts, uncles and cousins also live in Little Brook.

Grandpa and Grandma recognize that there have been many changes in the community of Little Brook since they left over 30 years ago, describing it as somewhat more "loosely-knit" than it was. Although the churches still provide residents with religious services and social events, not as many people attend; thus, less socialization among community members occurs. Many of the families that made up the community have left to find employment and new families have moved in. Thus, the aspect of all community members knowing one another has diminished. Although the socialization among adult community members in Little Brook has declined, that of the children in the community has not. Today, there are numerous groups and activities in which children partake, most with a high involvement rate. These include school groups, sports teams, religious groups, and girl guides/boy scouts.

There have also been physical changes within Little Brook since Grandpa and Grandma moved to St. John's. The community, once known for its rich farmland, no longer has that luxurious resource. Some of these farms are no longer maintained, as the owners have passed away and their children left the community years ago to obtain employment and chose not to return to the farms, having settled and had families in more urban areas. Other changes in the community include abandoned, older houses that are no longer maintained and the closure of two general stores and a teenage "hangout," which was owned by Grandma's parents.

Grandpa and Grandma recognize that the pattern of youth leaving Little Brook in order to further their education and obtain employment has affected the community.

Many of the original family names will soon be lost from the community, as the older generation passes away and much of the community culture and traditions will die with them. Also, much of the families' histories are being forgotten, as those who know the stories are growing older and their children and grandchildren are living away, making it difficult to pass these stories down through the generations. On the positive side, the population of Little Brook is recovering, as the area is becoming popular with retirees, many of whom have no previous ties to the community but are attracted by the quality of life and proximity to a larger town with many amenities (banks, supermarkets, hospital, shopping malls, restaurants, etc.). Grandpa and Grandma feel that, had the younger generation stayed within the community of Little Brook, there would have been little opportunity for employment, resulting in high unemployment rates and an increased dependence on social services. This belief is consistent with the research conducted by Giroux (2008), in which he discusses the effects of minimal job opportunities in rural areas creating high unemployment rates among vulnerable groups.

When asked to describe their relationship with their 19 month old granddaughter, Grandpa and Grandma's faces light up. They boast having a very close relationship with their granddaughter and her parents, whom they visit with and speak with on a daily basis. Grandma's early retirement was decided upon as a result of her wanting to provide childcare for her granddaughter. Grandma stated, "I couldn't imagine allowing my granddaughter to be cared for by a stranger. If this person had two or three young children to watch, who's to say my granddaughter would not receive poor care or not have her needs properly attended to. I just couldn't chance it." Grandpa agreed and expresses feeling lucky to be in a situation whereby he and his wife could afford to have Grandma take an early retirement. He is also happy they could ease the minds of their daughter and her husband, knowing their daughter is receiving the highest level of love and care without the worry of having to pay for childcare. The type of relationship Grandpa and Grandma have with their granddaughter is common within today's society and that of past generations. Robbins, Scherman, Holeman and Wilson (2005) state, "Grandparents often provide support for their children who have young children of their own. The support can be monetary, advice giving, baby sitting or emotional support. This role changes depending on the perceived needs of the family, and the grandparents' situation."

Grandpa and Grandma discuss how much they enjoy living only a 15 minute drive from their granddaughter and how convenient this is, both for allowing them to visit regularly and to help their daughter and her husband whenever they need assistance. They are able to take their granddaughter to their home for sleepovers every second weekend. This allows their daughter and her husband to have time to themselves, while also providing Grandpa and Grandma with quality time with their granddaughter. When discussing the amount of time they currently spend with their granddaughter, the grandparents feel saddened that this will not be possible once they move back to Little Brook, in a couple of years. However, they express excitement that their granddaughter will be able to visit them in Little Brook and stay for extended visits. Grandpa and Grandma describe their children doing this when they were young. Grandpa and Grandma would sometimes visit their parents for a weekend and then return to St. John's while their children stayed with their grandparents for a week. They believe such practices are good for the grandchildren, as it allows them to spend time learning the traditions and cultural beliefs of their family, while strengthening their bond with their grandparents. It is obvious, through discussing their relationship with their granddaughter, that Grandpa and Grandma have very positive feelings with respect to their grandparenting role (Sands, Goldberg-Glen & Thorton, 2005).

Grandpa and Grandma's daughter and her husband express deep gratitude for the excellent care Grandpa and Grandma are providing for their daughter. Their son-in-law discussed how advanced his daughter is for her age and credits this largely to Grandma engaging her granddaughter in educational play. Their young daughter can count to ten, knows the alphabet, can talk in sentences, remembers the words to numerous children's songs and stories and is partially potty-trained. Were it not for the high level of care provided by Grandma, this child would likely not be at this learning level. Grandma describes how much her granddaughter loves to look at books and have stories read to her and states that much of her time is spent reading to her granddaughter. If she was being cared for by anyone else, especially someone caring for several children, their granddaughter could not be given the time and attention needed to read her numerous stories throughout the day. However, Grandma recognizes the need for her granddaughter to interact with other children her age, which is why she brings her to a community playgroup one day a week.

Grandpa and Grandma's ancestors and other families first settled in Little Brook because of its rich farming and forestry resources. Early settlers on the coast in this area made a living by fishing, but realized they needed further resources in order to maintain their communities and provide for their families. It was for this reason that some of them moved to Little Brook to cut timber for building boats and houses and to provide vegetables to the fishing villages. From there, these activities grew to the point of Little Brook being one of the largest farming and logging areas within the province of Newfoundland and Labrador.

As most people worked in one of these industries, the community became very close-knit and there was a general interdependence among families. This strong sense of community continued throughout the generations and was still dominant in Grandpa and Grandma's generation. However, over that period of time, while the community grew, people became more mobile as the railway, and then highways, were developed. Children who did not want to follow in their parents' footsteps began to move away to find employment and later to further their education.

As the families dispersed throughout the province and beyond, family values and morals that were developed over the years began to fade, largely as a result of infrequent contact, especially between grandparents and their grandchildren. The community culture is also changing, as the younger generations have left Little Brook and retirees have recently begun moving in. However, this recent in-migration by retirees has benefitted the economy of the general area and the province and may also strengthen the sense of community in Little Brook, as people inter-mingle, not only at social events but also through their everyday activities.

Grandparents play an important role within communities today and have done so in the past. They are often the backbone of both families and communities, in that they keep the cultural values, attitudes and traditions of the community alive. Without our grandparents, our sense of community and our knowledge of our history would be severely weakened. It is for these reasons that so many communities hold their elderly population in such high esteem. Grandpa and Grandma are living proof of this and of the fact that the values provided by grandparents can be maintained, despite the mobility of the generations.

REFLECTION QUESTIONS

1. In this case study, the grandmother took early retirement to care for a granddaughter. How does this sense of responsibility by grandparents fit (or not) with your notions of grandparents' involvement in the lives of their adult children and grandchildren?
2. Grandparents providing care to grandchildren helps develop a strong relationship between the grandchildren and grandparents. How do you see this involvement affecting the adult children and their spouses?
3. What are the changing impacts of religious life on community?
4. What are some positive aspects of community where individuals and families are more 'independent'?

REFERENCES

Beland & Mills (2001). Positive portrayal of grandparents in current children's literature. *Journal of Family Issues, 22*(5), 639–651.

Giroux, S.C. (2008). Rural parentage and labour market disadvantage in a sub-saharan setting: Sources and trends. Rural Sociology, *73*(3), 339–369.

Homan, M.S. (2011). Promoting Community Change: Making it happen in the real world (5th ed.). Brooks/Cole, Cengage Learning.

Ofahengaue, V., Toafa, S.G., & Moala, K.O. (2008). Grandparenting in the tongan community: A cultural model. *Journal of Intergenerational Relationships, 6*(3), 305–319.

Robbins, R., Scherman, A., Holeman, H., & Wilson, J. (2005). Roles of American Indian grandparents in times of cultural crisis. *Journal of Cultural Diversity, 12*(2), 62–68.

Sands, R.G., Goldberg-Glen, R., & Thornton, P.L. (2005). Factors associated with the positive well-being of grandparents caring for their grandchildren. *Journal of Gerontological Social Work, 45*(4), 65–82.

Smith, B. & Smith, B. (2010, November 4th). Personal Interview.

JENINE BATEMAN

A GRANDMOTHER'S CONTRIBUTION TO COMMUNITY & COMMUNITY CULTURE

The term 'community' can encompass many aspects, including the place you live and the neighbourhoods, relationships, and organizations you are involved in (Hardcastle & Powers, 2004). Whether we try or not, we are all part of a community. For this paper, I will be looking at grandparents as a community and will analyze their contributions to the community and to community culture. I have interviewed a grandmother for the purpose of this paper and have focused on her life growing up, how her grandparents demonstrated the importance of community, and how she, as a grandparent today, demonstrates the importance of community. By looking at the past and present, I will examine the changes in values, attitudes, and morals and assess the implications of these changes on the community, and on Newfoundland and Labrador as a whole.

About the Grandmother

The grandmother, aged 77, was born and raised in Storm Island, a small, coastal community of Newfoundland. The grandmother estimates the population of the community was around 1400 when she was younger, whereas today the population is only 718 (Community Accounts). The grandmother, along with her five siblings, was raised by their single mother, since her father died when she was a young child. At the age of 17, she was married to her husband, a 21 year old who had moved to the community from Rouge Island to seek employment in the fishery. Together, they built a home in Storm Island and raised 14 children. The grandmother still resides in the small, coastal community of Storm Island and has been widowed for two years. She currently has 23 grandchildren and 21 great grandchildren.

The Grandmother's Grandparents

The grandmother has few memories of her grandparents as her grandfather died before she was born and her grandmother died when she was 15 years of age. At this time, the community relied mainly on fishing for survival, which she describes as 'hard work but pride work.' The grandmother describes her growing years as a comfortable way of life. "No one was trying to outdo someone else since most

A. Singh and M. Devine (Eds.), Rural Transformation and Newfoundland and Labrador Diaspora: Grandparents, Grandparenting, Community and School Relations, 117–124.

people worked in the fish plant... They had all the same jobs...No one had electricity or fancy things... Everyone was equals." There was community support and a strong bond between community members because of this. She notes that, "It did not matter who it was that needed help – a relative, friend, or stranger, you would do what you could to help them."

Her grandmother's close friends would regularly come to the house to visit and have general conversation. She recalls the elderly in the community being private people and there was no such thing as jealousy or gossip. She also recalls the community members being very family-centered, with private matters staying within the home and not being discussed outside the home. The younger adults, their own children, and their grandchildren were very respectful of the elderly in the community. The grandmother recalls having to refer to the elderly individuals as 'aunts' and 'uncles,' even though there was no relation and if they were strangers they were referred to as 'Sir' or 'Madam.' The children had chores appropriate for their ages. For example, the oldest daughter took care of the younger children, the boys carried water, and the girl did the dishes. She recalls that, as a young child, her grandmother did not expect her grandchildren to do any chores.

The children and grandchildren were involved in the bond of the community in the sense that they would have to learn how to fish, knit, and make bread, which was taught by the elderly of the community. "Certainly, your parents taught you things but since the older men were retired from fishing and the older women's children were grown, they were the people that had time to teach you things." This is how the traditions and beliefs were passed down through the generations.

The grandmother's grandparent's involvement in the community was very much religious-oriented. Storm Island was an Anglican community. "Everyone went to church and you went twice a day, in the morning and in the evening." She recalls being required to wear a dress and hat for church. The only organization she recalls her grandmother being involved in was the Anglican Church Women, where she would get the prizes ready for card games and collect the cards. The grandmother is unsure of her grandparents' paid work but does know that they had gardens and animals, such as chickens and sheep. The women were the ones who cared for the garden and animals since the men worked outside the home. She states that they did not have to worry about firewood because they had a coal stove.

The grandmother cannot recall people leaving the community when she was a child. The only time people left was when the men went to work in Nova Scotia. "My grandfather and father both worked over in Nova Scotia and the money was good there... a lot better than working at the fishplant. They would work on the fishing docks and be gone from July to December." She cannot remember anyone leaving until after her marriage to her husband in 1950. She says that some young people in the community that were around her age were beginning to leave for urban centres such as Halifax and Toronto. The grandmother does not know why they left but speculates that it was for jobs that were not fishing related.

As a Grandparent Today

The grandmother has lived all of her life in Storm Island. She has seen the community at its best and at its lowest. When asked how she views her community today, she replies that the community is a dying, outport. "Storm Island had it all at one point. There were restaurants, a movie theatre and grocery stores and now we got nothing... Everyone is moving away to bigger and better things." The community has lost many of its organizations and community spirit is wavering. She enjoys the summer months when everyone from away comes home to visit. "The community comes alive for a month or two, it's a nice thing."

The grandmother feels that she has good relations with her family, friends, and other members of the community. She describes her relationship with her friends as being open. "We have a little gossip and talk about what is going on in the community... We may talk about issues in our families...We have electricity and more money to have people come over... We are much more outgoing now." Her five siblings have either passed away or have moved from Storm Island. "They moved where their children lived... My brother is in Nova Scotia and my sister is in central Newfoundland...I guess that's why I never moved cause most of my children stayed in the community." As for non-relatives in the community, she says that no one is a stranger and having lived in Storm Island for 77 years, she knows many people in the community. "Doesn't matter if you don't know them, you treat them like your friends and family anyways."

Religion is still seen as important to the grandmother; she regularly reads the Bible and religious magazines but no longer attends church services. She attended church services until her children had grown. She spoke about a bad experience in church which resulted in her no longer regularly attending services:

> It was in the 70's when it all happened. We had a minister who was absolutely rude. This one time in church there was a band playing and the music was beautiful and a lot of people went to church to listen to the music. Everyone was enjoying the service until the minister started preaching on how people only came to church to listen to the music and he started asking for more money. Well, that was it for me. I never went back there again. I don't need to listen to him preach about money and there is nothing wrong with having a band play in the church. What odds!

Since that bad experience, she only attends church services on special occasions, such as weddings and funerals, but adamantly states that 'she always paid her church.'

As a grandparent, she is saddened by the lack of religion in the community. She was always required to attend church services as a young girl and Sunday was a day of rest, but it is different now as only the older populations regularly attend church services. "It is sad that people do not go to church anymore and when the old ones are all gone, they might as well board up the church... The only time people tend to go is Christmas Eve."

The grandmother did not participate in any community organizations, explaining that she had raised all her children and never had time for doing anything outside the home. When the children were all grown and moved out of the home and her husband retired from the workforce, the grandmother and her husband travelled a lot, visiting her children, grandchildren, and other relatives throughout Newfoundland and Nova Scotia. The grandmother did not have paid work but she did have a garden where she and her husband grew vegetables and flowers. She stopped gardening ten years ago as she was no longer physically capable of doing it.

Many of the community traditions and culture are gone or are slipping away, notes the grandmother, as she talks about her dying community. She is saddened by this as Storm Island is the only home she has ever known but she accepts the fact that it is dying. When the fish plant shut down, people left for other jobs because they had no choice. This brought much loss to the community, in terms of loss of businesses and community spirit. When asked if anything had been gained out of people leaving, the grandmother replied "Nothing, we never gained a thing out of it...The children grew up and moved on elsewhere...They went to school and got good jobs. They don't look back, why would they?"

The grandmother says things could have been different since the community was close and there was so much tradition and pride in the community. "The tradition is gone cause you can't teach knitting over the phone and anyway, the young ones don't want to know any of the traditions. The grandkids are growing up in Nova Scotia and Alberta and they don't have that Newfoundland pride and do not know much about the culture, cause they don't live in it."

The grandmother describes her relationships with her grandchildren as being excellent. She has 23 grandchildren and 21 great grandchildren scattered throughout Canada in provinces such as Nova Scotia, Alberta, and of course, Newfoundland. The majority of her grandchildren live in Newfoundland, with most residing in Storm Island and surrounding areas, and others residing in central and eastern Newfoundland. The grandmother describes being close to all her grandchildren but notes it is different for those living further away. She states that her grandchildren from away call frequently to check in on her and during special occasions. She reports that the grandchildren in Alberta cannot come home much but they do keep in contact through phone calls. She describes going to her daughter's house in Storm Island to see updated pictures of the grandchildren on the Internet [Facebook] and using a Webcam to talk to her children and grandchildren [Skype]. She said that it is a nice way to keep in contact with the children and grandchildren, and it allows her to see their faces. She gets frequent, sometimes daily visits from her grandchildren, who reside in the community and in surrounding areas. They usually come for meals or visit after supper. The grandmother mentions that she sometimes babysits her grandchildren.

Analysis of the Community over Time

From interviewing this grandmother, I have gained an understanding of grandparent contributions to the community in the 1930's and in present day. Sadly, there have been many changes in that timeframe that have negatively impacted the community. Storm Island was once a booming community with many resources, strong bonds, a sense of pride, and rich culture. Today, the community is dying and has little to offer. The community has changed in its traditions and culture, for instance, back then men worked in the fishing industry and women were housewives. They did not have much choice of an occupation, and had to work living off the land. The children learned at young ages their roles within the community, since they lived and observed it every day. The theory that applies to this situation is Social Learning Theory where we learn from observation and learned behaviours (Hardcastle & Powers, 2004). The grandmother grew up in the community when fishing was the dominant source of employment. At a young age, she observed and learned from her grandparents the traditional roles, values, traditions and beliefs. Now that she is a grandparent, she has the responsibility of passing along the same to her grandchildren. The fishing industry has died but she still passes along the pride of being a Newfoundlander from Storm Island and the history of the community. She teaches her grandchildren how to make bread and knit and when her husband was alive, he would take the children out in the boat to go fishing.

Storm Island can be understood by looking at Systems Theory. Kirst-Ashman (2008) defines Systems Theory as "interactions of individuals, groups, families, organizations, and communities in the macro social environment. The different systems are interrelated and function as a whole." For Storm Island, some of the systems included the fishery occupation, religion, relatives, friends, and community facilities. Systems Theory also relies on homeostasis, and for this community, there is little stability and balance. The out-migration of the younger populations and grandchildren living in other communities and/or provinces has changed the values and attitudes of the community and the traditions, pride, and outport culture. Sadly, due to the loss of the different systems, Storm Island is failing.

Some changes seen as positive include the new role for grandparents as caregivers of their grandchildren and the use of new media (Internet, Webcams) which allows grandparents and grandchildren to maintain regular contact. The new caregiving role is related to Social Learning Theory as grandparents are able to pass along the traditions and culture by spending quality time with their grandchildren (Bullock, 2004; Gregory, Ruby, & Kenner, 2010; Lee & Gardner, 2010; Ofahengaue Vakalahi, Toafa, & Moala, 2008; Kemp, 2007). New media is an excellent way for grandparents to keep in frequent contact with grandchildren who do not live nearby and enables them to transfer knowledge and skills to their grandchildren (Hurme, Westerback, & Quadrello, 2010).

Values, attitudes, and morals have changed over the years, along with the traditional ways of living. As stated earlier, the people of Storm Island are in despair because the community is losing resources and businesses. More and more people are leaving and moving to other parts of the island and to other provinces and thus, will not experience the pride, identity, and culture that they would have experienced living in the rural Newfoundland outport of Storm Island. It is now up to the grandparents to preserve this and pass it along. When speaking with the grandmother, she describes how relationships have changed over the years. Long ago, community members provided assistance and support such as giving clothes and food to needy families, and no one gossiped or talked about matters within the home. Nowadays, community members are more outgoing and the mutual support provided is more emotional to help them cope with the out-migration (Shulman, 2009). This mutual support can help preserve community bonds and culture as members are there for one another. The role of religion has also changed over the years. Years ago, religion and the church were respected, with the church being an important part of the community and a place where community members obtained many of their values and morals. Nowadays, the church does not appear to be as important and those values and morals seem to have diminished.

A dying community has resulted from out-migration. The fishery was the dominant source of employment for Storm Island and it was how people identified themselves as being Newfoundlanders. When the fishery closed and people had to move away to find another source of income, their identity and pride became shattered. Storm Island currently consists of an aging population due to the outflow of young adults and their families, which Stockdale (2004) refers to as 'child drought.' This has many implications for grandparents and for the preservation of the community's culture and traditions. It is difficult for grandchildren raised in urban centres to identify with the culture of a community such as Storm Island, or for those raised in other provinces to identify with the culture of a province such as Newfoundland and Labrador. Many young people leave smaller communities such as Storm Island to seek employment or obtain their post-secondary education. These individuals may never return to their home community to work. Docquier & Marfouk (2006) refer to this as 'brain drain.' This out-migration of young people impacts community development and growth, and results in the demise of community services, facilities, and the community itself (Stockdale, 2004). The likelihood of these individuals returning to their rural hometowns is slim as they undergo social transformations when exposed to the different lifestyles and cultures of urban centres and gain independence (Stockdale, 2004).

CONCLUSION

Newfoundland and Labrador's culture is distinct and unique, and Newfoundlanders possess strong provincial pride. Within the province, each community has its own distinct bond and traditions. This paper examined the community of Storm Island, the grandparent community within Storm Island, and grandparent's contribution to the community and to community culture. Through interviewing the grandmother and discussing her role in the community today and her grandmother's role in the community years ago, it is clear to see that the community and its values, attitudes, and morals have changed over time. These changes have implications for the community of Storm Island and for the province of Newfoundland and Labrador.

For example, grandchildren residing in other provinces cannot identify with being a Newfoundlander and may not learn from their grandparents the province's customs, culture, and traditions. Slowly, the small outports of Newfoundland and Labrador are dying and along with them, their sense of community, bond, and culture.

REFLECTION QUESTIONS

1. Rural communities are dying and, according to the literature, this trend is not likely to change. What are the implications of accepting this change? Why would it be important to work to stop this trend?
2. One industry towns are always vulnerable to major changes should the industry change. What, if anything, should be done to guard against this vulnerability?
3. What is the impact (positive and negative) of the diminished role of religion in community?
4. Analyze the phenomena of grandparents moving from their own communities to be with adult children and grandchildren.

REFERENCES

Bullock, K. (2004). The changing role of grandparents in rural families: The results of an exploratory study in Southeastern North Carolina. Families in Society: *The Journal of Contemporary Social Services, 85*(1), 45–54.

Community Accounts (2010). Isle aux Morts Profile. Retrieved November 23, 2010 from http://www.communityaccounts.ca/communityaccounts/onlinedata/accountselectionpage. asp?_=vb7FnYmXuICvOq.Yjp-Fg5upv7iUko66uJR4kWI_.

Docquier, F., & Marfouk, A. (2006). International migration by educational attainment (1990–2000) in C. Ozden & M. Schiff, (Eds.). International Migration, Remittances and the Brain Drain, Chapter 5, Palgrave-Macmillan.

Gregory, E., Ruby, M., & Kenner, C. (2010). Modelling and close observation: Ways of teaching and learning third-generation Bangladeshi British children and their grandparents in London. *Early Years, 30*(2), 161–173.

Hardcastle, D., & Powers, P. (2004). Community Practice: Theories and skills for social workers (2nd ed.). Toronto: Oxford University Press.

Hurme, H., Westerback, S., & Quadrello, T. (2010). Traditional and new forms of contact between grandparents and grandchildren. *Journal of Intergenerational Relationships, 8,* 264–280.

Kemp, C. (2007). Grandparent-grandchild ties: Reflections on continuity and change across three generations. *Journal of Family Issues, 28*(7), 855–881.

Kirst-Ashman, K. (2008). Human Behaviour, Communities, Organizations, and Groups in the Macro Social Environment: An empowerment approach (2nd ed.). Belmont, CA: Brooks/Cole.

Lee, M., & Gardner, J. (2010). Grandparents' involvement and support in families with children with disabilities. *Educational Gerontology, 36,* 467–499.

Ofahengaue Vakalahi, H., Toafa, S., & Moala, K. (2008). Grandparenting in the Tongan Community: A cultural model. *Journal of Intergenerational Relationships, 6*(3), 305–319.

Shulman, L. (2009). The Skills of Helping Individuals, Families, Groups, and Communities (6th ed.). Belmont, CA: Brooks/Cole.

Stockdale, A. (2004). Rural out-migration: Community consequences and individual migrant experiences. Sociologia Ruralis, *44*(2), 167–194.

NATASHA SPURRELL

GRANDPARENTS AS CONTRIBUTORS TO COMMUNITY AND COMMUNITY CULTURE

Over time, communities have changed significantly, along with the role of grandparents. Rural communities, especially those in Newfoundland, have experienced a substantial shift demographically, socially and economically. The prevalence of these paradigm shifts have created increased roles for grandparents who reside in rural communities (Bullock, 2005). This paper will share the perspective of a grandparent, and discuss her role as a grandparent and as a member of her community. It will examine how the community and relationships within it have changed over time, from both a family-oriented and community perspective. Outmigration of community members and the impact of this outmigration on the community will also be explored.

Grandma grew up in a small rural coastal community in central Newfoundland. During her childhood and adolescent years, the small town was heavily populated with a strong sense of community and families were much larger than they are today. According to Wilkinson (2008), the increased number of children in families positively influences social cohesion of the community. This is congruent with Grandma's experiences as she describes the involvement of extended family and non-relatives as greater in years past. The roles of parents were also different – one parent sought employment and the other cared for the children. Grandma's mother did not work outside the home and thus, there were rare occasions when she and her siblings would have caretakers aside from their parents. Furthermore, she stated that there were always larger groups of children so there was always someone watching them and ensuring their safety. She recalled that if they were to get in any trouble as children, it would not take long before her parents would find out, as the news in the community traveled quickly.

Grandparent roles were also significantly different in comparison to today. Grandma remembers her grandparents' warmth and kindness and the traditional family gatherings on Sundays where they would eat Jigg's Dinner. Furthermore, she stated there was never a time that she visited her grandparents when there were no sweets in the home or knitted socks and outerwear for the grandchildren. She could also not recall a time when she was in the presence of her grandmother without her parents also being there. Nonetheless, her grandparents did play a significant role in her upbringing as they taught her the importance of community and traditions, which she has passed on to her own children and grandchildren. This is congruent

A. Singh and M. Devine (Eds.), Rural Transformation and Newfoundland and Labrador Diaspora: Grandparents, Grandparenting, Community and School Relations, 125–132.

with the findings of Stelle, Fruhauf, Orel and Meyer (2010), of how the role of grandparents was to teach their grandchildren the respected roles, culture and rules that exist within family and society.

The role of grandparents in the lives of their grandchildren is often influenced by personal characteristics such as age (Lee & Bauer, 2010). The advanced age of Grandma's grandparents and their deteriorating health influenced the grandparent-grandchild relationship substantially. She stated that had her grandparents been younger and in better health, her experiences with them may have been very different.

During her childhood and teenage years, Grandma enjoyed time with her peers, playing outdoor games and hanging out at local restaurants. She stated, "There were many restaurants back then, one every few blocks, very different from today as there are only two or three left in the community." The majority of her peers were cousins, thus furthering the close connections to extended family. Many pastimes consisted of visiting neighbours, relatives and friends. Families were very close, not only the nuclear family, but also the extended family and distant and non-relatives.

Grandma has a very close relationship with her four children and eight grandchildren. Her relationships are exceedingly positive with much emotional, social and economical involvement. Today, grandparents are seemingly younger and assistance with childcare is more of a vertical process. Grandparents are providing caretaking roles rather than the horizontal involvement of aunts and uncles that used to exist in the family dynamic (Harper, Phil and Ruicheva, 2010). Grandma stated, "With the disparity that currently exists in family dynamics, and as a result of the transitions in the rural workforce, the family that once surrounded children is no longer available; grandparents are taking on a larger role."

When I asked about the role of religion, Grandma responded "it was of great significance for families. It was a time that the family and community would all come together." In addition, the church held many social functions, including concerts for all ages. She stated that "the church was the rock of the community and was very powerful in bringing everyone together." As a child, she was actively involved; she attended Sunday school and during important holidays she remembers her Sunday school group commuting to different households throughout the community where they would sing hymns and enjoy each other's presence. She stated she was never bored as she was very close to church, friends and relatives.

Communication in Grandma's time was primarily face to face, as phones were not easily accessible. She recalled having to go to the post office in order to use a telephone. Therefore, there was limited contact with people who resided in different geographical areas. This isolation brought the community closer together and added to its 'close-knit' feeling. Further, as most of her family, including aunts and uncles, were within the same geographical area, extended family involvement was significantly higher as many visitations took place.

Grandma could not remember a time growing up when she was employed. However, she did perform much unpaid work. The whole family, including the young children, would help out with chores and basic upkeep of the family home. This included splitting wood with her father and helping to store it for the winter, along with raking the grass and putting it in blankets. Grandma stated that "growing up in a family of eight meant lots of work, and all family members were expected to do their share." In addition, she remembers pulling potatoes from the vegetable garden and having to clean them afterwards. She stated, "There was a lot of gardening work to be done and children were not hesitant in helping as it was natural at that time for them to participate in such labour." Other community members, such as friends of her parents, would also contribute in helping families with preparing wood for the winter and the vegetable gardens. Grandma said, "Back then we would always give away vegetables or potatoes to our neighbours and extended families." It was common for the community members to pool their resources and share their labour and talent for the good of the community (Bracken, 2008).

At a time when the fishing industry was at its peak, there were not many reasons to leave the community; Fall was an exception when men went away to obtain lumber and this was only for a few weeks of the year. When this particular Grandma was asked why people might have left the community, she replied "to get married." She got married and left her hometown when she was seventeen years old to reside in a neighbouring community. Those who moved permanently, like herself, moved often as a result of marriage, to join a spouse living in another community or province. The community was still heavily populated at this time. There was much business and prosperity and, as a result, many people did not leave to seek work elsewhere; instead leaving was based on personal choices as opposed to economic difficulty that affects these rural communities today (Wilkinson, 2008).

Today, this rural community has changed drastically. The population has declined considerably, along with the industries that once prevailed. Furthermore, the community is considered an aging community as many youth have left to seek higher education or employment. This has severely impacted local businesses such as restaurants, convenience stores, and local gathering places and hang outs. Consequently, activities for youth have diminished significantly. The youth center, skating rink, and local activities that once existed within this community are no longer present. Furthermore, churches play a smaller role in her community; many of the previous churches have been amalgamated and still the congregations are substantially lower. Thus, community members do not come together like they used to.

Grandma still remains relatively close to her peers. However, she stated, "It's not the same friendship we once shared." As a result of being a 20 minute commute to her former hometown, oftentimes rather than personally visiting her peers, much contact takes place over the telephone. Similarly, relationships with her siblings have also been significantly impacted as they also relocated to surrounding communities. She stated, "When we were growing up, my aunts and uncles were much involved in my life; today there is little to no aunt/uncle to niece and nephew involvement."

When asking about her personal participation and the community's participation in paid and unpaid work, she stated, "It's very different than it once was in the past." With the technological advancements and machinery that exist in today's society, the unpaid work such as gardening and splitting wood is more easily done than it once was. Thus, her grandchildren no longer participate in unpaid work. She was employed for most of her life whereas her mother was a stay-at-home mom. Grandma asserted that, "It's impossible to obtain a decent livelihood today on a single income with four children."

Community involvement and organizations have also become more prevalent according to Grandma. Her own children were involved in many community activities including girl guides, scouts, cadets, and local sports and clubs within the community. Currently, the diversity of community involvement for her grandchildren has been amplified further. They are involved in numerous after school programs, skating clubs, and a vast amount of sport associated activities.

The structure of the community has also drastically changed. There are more hierarchies within the community today and there is stricter enforcement of laws. Grandma remembered little about the involvement of town council and their role within the community in years past but feels their role to be very significant today. With respect to the informal leaders of today, she believes them to be large business owners and the wealthier people of the community. In the past, these leaders were the senior population as they obtained knowledge on house up-keeping, as well as cultural aspects, thus they were well respected (Lee, 1999).

With the rapid decline in the main industry of her hometown and surrounding communities came a significant decrease in the population. According to Grandma, "This has presented many hardships for the community as families have been separated as a result of one parent seeking employment outside of the community, which sometimes resulted in the entire family relocating as well." Consequently, the relationships that once existed between children and relatives are now rare. Older relatives were active role models for children. They taught children many different roles such as fishing, hunting, baking, and knitting, which back then were necessary for a decent livelihood. Today, these activities and roles are almost obsolete. She stated, "It's hard to see the traditions and our way of living back then falling apart." It's also difficult for her to watch her own immediate family leave the community in order to obtain a decent living. As well, their inability to come together due to the geographical distance that separates them makes it hard for traditions within the family to be passed on to the younger children. Consequently, reinforcing their culture is very difficult (Hannan, 2009). Further, she recognizes that there is not much left for children, as with the decline in the population came the extinction of many businesses, which directly affected the resources available to community residents. However, her sense of safety and pride still remains within this small community.

The role of grandparents has substantially changed as life expectancies are significantly higher, along with a decrease in generational distance between families. In the past, morality rates were significantly higher, thus children and grandparents had little involvement due to the generational distance and lower life expectancy.

Today, with the changing generational distance, family members are living simultaneously together. Grandparents are younger and spend more time than ever before with their grandchildren, as the prevalence of multi-generational families is now a familiar phenomenon and has become more widespread (Lauterbach and Klein, 2004).

During my interview with this particular Grandma, it became evident that the role of grandparenting has increased substantially compared to her childhood experiences with her grandparents. In the process of the interview, her grandchildren were present as they have been living with her for the past five months due to an abrupt illness of one of their parents. She stated that she is challenged in many aspects of being the temporary, sole caretaker for her grandchildren, since they are only 6 and 8 years old. She stated, "It has been awhile since I have had to provide that type of care as my own children are in their mid-thirties." Also, with limited space in her home, acquiring private time is difficult, as well as ensuring adequate space to meet her grandchildren's needs (Bullock, 2004). Financially, it has also been difficult as the needs of her grandchildren are quite different than those of her children. As a result of becoming their primary caretaker, she has had to miss multiple days of work, which has further impacted her financially. In her rural community, there are not many resources that can be utilized in relation to childcare services, and she has little knowledge of any services that exist within the community that may aid her in caring for her grandchildren (King, Kropf, Perkins, Sessley, Burt & Lepore, 2009).

Four of her grandchildren reside in the same community as her, while the other four reside out of province. She stated, "The relationships with the four who are in the community are very different than with those away but I love them all the same." The amount of contact with her grandchildren who live nearby is abundant, as she visits twice a day. Grandma stated that she provides childcare frequently and attends many of their social activities. In relation to the other grandchildren who reside outside of Newfoundland, although she talks to them about three times a week, this contact is limited as it is telephone versus visual contact. Further, she has only seen these grandchildren approximately five times for short visits and they are now teenagers. Thus, it is evident that the role of grandparents is influenced by variables such as geographical location and grandparent age (Hurme, Westerback, & Quadrello, 2010).

It is evident that throughout Grandma's life experiences, much has changed within her community. Years ago, the fishing industry was at its peak and income was provided by one parent rather than two. Families were more cooperative, along with the community as a whole. Community members provided assistance with the building of houses and sheds and in times of crisis, such as a death in the family, the community became actively involved and brought baked goods and donations to the homes of those who were grieving. There was a strong sense of community with members actively involved as their livelihoods depended on each other.

During the cod fishery, all family members would contribute in order to sustain an adequate livelihood for the family. Children were more responsible than they are today and were more actively involved in the family life. After the cod moratorium, residents of Grandma's community were forced to leave if they wanted to obtain a decent standard of living. Those who did stay faced many challenges and hardships in locating work that could provide a decent living (Davis, 2006). With the decreasing population, many businesses and resources that once prevailed were depleted.

The role of education is of higher significance than it was 30 years ago. Natural resources have diminished along with the skills needed of yesteryear, which led to an increase in out-migration of residents seeking training and education. With this came a loss of community cohesion as the elder role models that existed, and the interactions that occurred between them and the children, slowly faded and became non-existent. Although there is still a sense of pride in the community, the notion of cohesion has diminished incredibly.

Although much has changed in relation to the roles of families, depopulation, and the economy, there are still many positive aspects that remain in this community. The sense of safety still remains in the community as people are able to leave their homes unlocked when away, and community members still lend a hand to each other when needed. Grandma stated, "The community is very welcoming, scenic, and beautiful and will always be referred to as home."

Although emphasis is placed on rural communities and the widespread issue of depopulation that is occurring in these small locations, the province is also being drastically influenced. In 2002, the province of Newfoundland and Labrador had the highest out net immigration in Canada. Further, a large number of the population within this province are becoming more urbanized, especially youth, as they are seeking higher education and outside employment opportunities (Blake, 2004). Thus, not only are rural communities struggling, but it can be said that the rural economy within Newfoundland and Labrador has created a hardship on the province as a whole.

Rural communities of Newfoundland and Labrador have changed significantly over the last few decades. With the changing roles in economics, socialization, and demographics, much of the cultural and traditional ways of living in rural communities are slowly disappearing. Men and women who once lived off the rich resources that their community provided are being forced to urban centers in order to provide a decent livelihood for their families. Furthermore, with the prosperity of globalization and the natural resources of the community becoming more obsolete, dual income households are becoming more prominent. Consequently, the role of grandparenting has changed substantially in order to adapt to the increasing needs of caretaker roles within these rural communities.

REFLECTION QUESTIONS

1. From this case study, it appears that, as a very prosperous community, the 'adjustment' to the decline in the community is more apparent and difficult. Provide your analysis of this statement.

2. This case study is an example of the high levels of involvement of the grandmother in the lives of the children in or near the community. This is contrasted with the grandchildren who are 'away'. Discuss this impact between both situations as it relates to grandchildren.

3. Some issues with outmigration may be defined within the context of the 'lure' of better economic times and the need for higher education. How might each of these factors impact community and what values are implicit in these 'lures'?

4. The move towards the nuclear family being the 'norm' versus the historical role of extended family may be viewed as a loss. In what ways might the change be viewed as a positive?

REFERENCES

Blake, R.B. (2004). The resilient outport: Ecology, economy and society in rural Newfoundland. *Canadian Historical Review, 85*(2), 363–367.

Bracken, J.S. (2008). Defining rural communities: Future considerations for informal and non-formal adult education in rural communities. *New Directions for Adult and Continuing Education, 117*, 83–92.

Bullock, K. (2004). The changing role of grandparents in rural families: The results of an exploratory study in southeast North Carolina. Families in Society: *Journal of Contemporary Social Services, 85*(1), 45–54.

Bullock, K. (2005). Grandfathers and the impact of raising grandchildren. *Journal of Sociology and Social Welfare, 32*, 43–59.

Davis, R. (2006). All or nothing: Video lottery terminal gambling and economic restructuring in rural Newfoundland. *Global Studies in Culture and Power, 13*, 503–531.

Hannan, A. (2009). Rotumans in Austraila. *Social Alternatives, 28*(4), 34–38.

Hurme, H., Westerback, S., & Quadrello, T. (2010). Traditional and new forms of contact between grandparents and grandchildren. *Journal of Intergenerational Relationships, 8*, 264–280.

King, S., Kropf, P.N., Perkins, M., Sessley, L., Burt, C., & Lepore, M. (2009). Kinship care in rural Georgia communities: Responding to the needs and challenges of grandparent caregivers. *Journal of Intergenerational Relationships, 7*, 225–242.

Lauterbach, W., & Klein, T. (2004). The change of generational relations based on demographic development: The case of Germany. *Journal of Comparative Family Studies, 35*(4), 651–663.

Lee, B. (1999). Pragmatics of Community Organization (3rd ed.). Canada; Common Act Press.

Lee, J., & Bauer, J. (2010). Profiles of grandmothers providing childcare to their grandchildren in South Korea. *Journal of Comparative Family Studies, 41*(3), 455–475.

Stelle, C., Fruhauf, A.C., Orel, N., & Landry-Meyer, L. (2010). Grandparenting in the 21st century: Issues of diversity in grandparent-grandchild relationships. *Journal of Gerontological Social Work, 53*, 682–701.

Wilkinson, D. (2008). Individual and community factors affecting psychological sense of community, attraction and neighbouring in rural communities. *Canadian Sociological Association, 45*(3), 305–329.

JODY MORRISON

NAN "M" ABOUT CHURCHVILLE: BACK TO THE BASICS

[Note: Churchville is a fictitious name. Also, any personal names, or geographic names with an asterisk (*) have been changed to protect the identity of individuals or the community].

"After the church at the bottom of the lane burned down in 1892, my Grandfather took the Blessed Sacrament to St. Patrick's Church. He was a young boy at the time; he walked out and back...that's how long he was on the property...I was born and reared here," shares Nan M of her 79-year affiliation with Churchville, over a cup of tea and several cigarettes. Born in 1931 during the Great Depression, Nan M was the second oldest of five children, all of whom are still alive today. Nan M's paternal grandfather lived with her family until his death, when Nan M was nine years old. His wife, Nan M's grandmother, died before Nan M was old enough to remember her. Nan M's other set of grandparents, the McManns*, lived just up the road. Pop McMann worked with Newfoundland Power driving the "long cart" – a horse-drawn cart that delivered electrical poles to their destinations, but most others in the community worked in agriculture.

Churchville was predominantly a farming community, made up of just three roads at the time: Little Harbour Road*; Blue Tree Road*; and Flannery Road*. Nan M's family lived on Little Harbour Road, along with about a dozen other families. Limited technology in the community required much energy intensive activity. Transportation was customarily by foot, unless good timing proffered a neighbourly horse and carriage (sleigh in the winter) to hasten a journey. St. Joseph's School, a single level building located directly across from Roncalli Church*, provided the educational forum for the Churchville children. In winter the snowdrifts were cumbersome. As there were no snowploughs, students were forced to navigate the deep gulches on their way down the hill, and again on the way back up. Electricity was introduced in the late 1930s, allowing families to use electric lamps, but woodstoves were still required for heat and cooking. Washing was done with the tub and scrubbing board.

Money and resources were tight, and the values of the community represented this reality. Citizens of the community prided themselves on being self-sufficient, resourceful people who grew their own food, cut their own wood, and made their own clothes. Nan M's mother made all of her clothes. Nothing was wasted. She boasted, "Once a coat got shabby, what you'd do then is, they'd take the coat apart, turn it inside out, and when it was finished, you'd have another new coat...

A. Singh and M. Devine (Eds.), Rural Transformation and Newfoundland and Labrador Diaspora: Grandparents, Grandparenting, Community and School Relations, 133–138.

and you know how the collar wears on a man's shirt? There was nothin' wrong with that! They took that collar off, and turned that around. That's the way we were reared."

During the winter those living in Churchville were isolated from the city of St. John's, and oftentimes each other. Nan M says that she did not see a doctor for the first time until she was 17 years old. "You prayed to God you didn't get sick, and if you did, you cured yourself." Poultices, Mercurochrome, and Iodine were staples of first aid. "If you had an itch, you scratched it 'til it didn't itch anymore. An ear infection was treated with hot olive oil. If you had something in your eye, they told you to blow your nose to get it out." If an ambulance had to be called in deep winter, the ailing individual had to make his/her way down to Blue Tree Road to meet the ambulance, as the emergency response vehicle could not circumnavigate the deep drifts of snow on the Little Harbour Road.

In the event of an individual passing from this realm into the next, the town of Churchville was also equipped. Individuals were waked in their own homes. A local resident, Mr. McMann, built the caskets. A room was cleared out in the home and set up for the wake. Nan M remembers that her grandfather was not dressed up in a suit when waked, but was instead "covered with a brown shroud, with some kind of gold cross on it." Neighbours would visit the home of the waking individual to pay their last respects.

Nan M remembers her parents' relationship with her grandparents as reinforcing the values of independence and self-sufficiency within nuclear families. "You could go there (to visit) but we didn't go for suppers or anything. We never had that... not that we weren't close, but that's the way it was back then. You always had your supper in your own house. Once you got out and married, then you were on your own, kind of thing. You could come to visit, but to say you got together to have a party or something...no." The attitude at Christmas was similar; there was not much socializing or gift exchanging.

Nan M's Grandmother McMann was the only one with a telephone in the community. There was a powder magazine at the top of the road that stored TNT. When it was needed in town, a call would be made to Nan M's uncle and it was his job to deliver it, thus Grandmother McMann got a telephone, and the rest of the community had access to one in case of emergencies. "We didn't know nothing... what was going on in St. John's; we had no radio. We just knew what was going on within the perimeter of Churchville."

Independence was valued and taught at an early age; it was ingrained through social learning (Hardcastle, 2004). Young children were required to do their share of the chores, and to do it right the first time or they would be asked to do it over. There was a lot of labour intensive activity including woodcutting, planting, weeding, cooking, childcare, and fetching water from the well. Contribution was expected, and necessary, by all family members. Nan M says her mother was pregnant every two years, so at eight, nine, and ten years old, she had to wash dishes daily after all three meals. To this day, Nan M says she hates doing dishes.

The prevailing attitude at the time dictated that people minded their own business, and did not interfere with what did not directly concern them. Thus, everybody got along. Nan M says, "there were not enough people around to fight anyway." Children were sent out of the room when adults were talking, outside in the summer, in a bedroom in the winter. Children had no idea what was going on; they knew if something was going on, just not what exactly. Nan M recalls there would be no heat, and they would be "up in the room froze to death." It was a time when children respected their elders, would never dare talk back to their parents, and assumed their fair share of responsibility around the home. They had little in the way of material possessions, knew better than to demand much, instead they made use of the scant resources they had. A cardboard box could be utilized in any number of ways, but the all time favorite was as a slide zipping down the hill from Little Harbour Road to Blue Tree Road in the wintertime. "It was a wonder we weren't killed, banging into fences and stuff." While they did not have a lot in terms of possessions, Nan M lit up when she spoke of how much fun they had, reminiscing nostalgically about coming home soaked with snow-filled boots.

Roman Catholic was the dominant religion of Churchville. Nan M says that back in the day, church was the place to mingle. Everyone in the community met at Mass on Sundays, and at First Friday Devotions. It was unheard of not to go to church. During Mass, women were required to have their heads covered and wore dresses; women and girls did not wear 'long pants' at the time, regardless of the day of the week, and dresses went past the knee, always. When asked if they dressed up for Mass, Nan M exclaimed: "Oh my God, yes! Dressed up with whatever they had. Don't know how dressed up they were...no rich people around. They were dressed well though." Fasting was required before Holy Communion and First Friday Devotions. Children attended First Friday Devotions from 8–8:30 a.m. and then promptly returned home to have their breakfast of toutons and molasses, and then beat it back down the hill for their morning lessons at St. Joseph's School. Catholic values were strongly incorporated into the school curriculum, reinforcing what was taught at home and the overall Catholic culture of the community (Engebretson, 2008). Sundays were revered as a time of rest. The cooking of Sunday dinner was the extent of permitted labour on the Sabbath.

In addition to Church activities and functions, other venues occasionally presented social opportunities for Churchville residents. If one was willing to make the trek to the old York Theatre on Water Street, he/she could catch a movie. A well-attended annual garden party took place every summer. Mummering was done at Christmas: someone might have an accordion, and a group would go from neighbour to neighbour, long enough for a song, drink and maybe a piece of fruitcake. A couple of times a month, dances were held at the parish halls in Churchville and neighbouring communities. Stack's Bus would transport dance-goers, allowing intergenerational mingling amongst people from differing communities. At the time, women from Churchville did not indulge in drinking alcohol and would have a Pepsi or Coke instead; they did however "go for a puff behind the barn."

Nan M was only 11 years old when her mom died. Five young children were beyond the physical caring capacity of her father, who was still a relatively young man. At the time of his wife's death, Nan M's father was working at a local hospital as a personal care attendant making about $50/month. Given the limited resources at the time, five children would have been an excessive burden to any family in the community. Thus, Nan M and her two sisters spent the next five plus years in Belvedere Orphanage for Girls operated by the Sisters of Mercy in St. John's. Nan M's brothers stayed with Mrs. Gibbons* "across the road," a friend of Nan M's mother. Regular contact was not kept with her father while in the orphanage as there were no phones and he was busy working. However, any child who had a place to go to was required to leave for the two-month break in the summertime. Nan M left Belvedere at 15 years of age and returned to her father's house; she did not return to school as she obtained employment at the hospital in which her father was employed. Her sisters returned home the following year, and Nan M then helped care for them.

Nan M moved to Toronto at the age of twenty "green as they could come." She met her husband while there, also a Newfoundlander. They married in 1954 and moved home two years later, eventually ending up back in Churchville and building a house on her family property. Life did not get any easier for Nan M as her husband was a drinker, and she assumed primary responsibility for the rearing up of the seven children that they shared. "I got through it; the youngsters got through it. As much upset I got, I kept it off the floor." Nan M practiced the learned values from her childhood of keeping adult 'talk' away from her children and minding her own business.

Nan M has ten grandchildren, with six living nearby, and four residing on the Mainland. Nan M adamantly insists that there are no differences in her relationships with any of her grandchildren; she enjoys them all equally and loves to see them coming. Barnett, Scaramella, Neppl, Ontai and Conger (2010) state that this is usually the case with maternal grandmothers, but of course there are always exceptions. Nan M notes that she has a closer relationship with her daughter's oldest child, a 27-year-old grandson who drops by frequently, helps out around the house, and offers his services as a chauffeur. Barnett et al. further state that the mother-daughter relationship influences more direct involvement with the daughter's children (and this supports Nan M's current level of closeness with her daughter's son). According to Nan M, her teenaged grandchildren are involved with friends, love interests, and other outside distractions, so there is somewhat of a generational 'stake' in that family ties are compromised by this developmental stage (Villar, 2010). However, Nan M's teenaged children do make regular appearances, usually in the context of larger family functions such as family dinners – common occurrences given that most of Nan M's children live close by, four who currently live in Churchville. These special family gatherings undoubtedly contribute to the positive feelings Nan M expresses towards her descendents (Hurme, Westerback, & Quadrello, 2010), and reflects the positive relations that Nan M has with her own children, that is evident by the shared behaviours and values that have been passed down (Hayslip, 2003).

Nan M noted that she is affectionate with her grandchildren, something she was not with her own kids, likely because she now has the privilege of less daily pressures (Barnett, et al.). Nan M does not remember experiencing much in the way of physical affection as a child. She reflects that she was so busy as a parent that she did not really get the chance to show her children much affection, similar circumstances perhaps as experienced by her own parents.

The dynamics of Nan M's family are quite interesting and show signs of carrying the seemingly detached "mind your own business" cultural attitude from Nan M's childhood. Nan M's adult children can go weeks or months without speaking or visiting each other, even two sons that live adjacent to each other in the same house. But when help is needed, as was the case when Nan M's son with multiple sclerosis needed money to receive treatment in Europe, the family pulled together to support their brother in his quest.

Most original residents of Churchville bought property there and passed it down through the generations; this provided an incentive for younger people to stay and build their own homes in the community. As development increased and interest in farming waned, land was sold with several new sub-divisions being constructed in Churchville. Some people left as they married, or decided to seek employment elsewhere, but many stayed or returned after an absence. Nan M believes the use of land for building houses is a positive thing, especially with the community benefits of paved roads and water and sewer.

On the downside, Nan M feels that basic values have been lost. The independence to which she proudly referred is gone. It is still evident in her though, as she is a strikingly independent senior, who only asks for assistance if hard pressed. It has also been ingrained in her children through social learning (Hardcastle, 2004), and is particularly noticeable in her single parent daughter of three children, and in her son who lives very independently with multiple sclerosis.

Religion is not given as much credence as it once was. Nan M feels that the older generation still holds their faith close to their heart, but she acknowledges that the younger crowd does not so much; most do not attend Mass regularly, and the rules have certainly slackened over the years. She commented on some of the fashions young women are sporting, stating her father would "roll over in his grave if he saw what they were wearing today." Morals have changed drastically too. She quips, "Girls are on the pill at 14 and 15 years of age; we never heard the word 'sex'!" One theme that was repeated throughout our discussion was simplicity. Nan M stated simply, "We had nothin', but we were happy. They got so much stuff today, they don't know how to have fun." Nan M believes 'less is more,' and that appreciation of the basics has been lost in our current state of excessive materialism.

Having an intimate connection to Churchville, the author notes the sense of community that still permeates the area. Regardless of how many 'strangers' move in and how much affiliation there is with metro St. John's, the original families of Churchville maintain their connection with each other. A visit to a local corner store or Tim Horton's bears witness to innumerable social interactions among community members. Community pride is resonant, with many residents still strongly tied to Churchville's history and its solid roots.

REFLECTION QUESTIONS

1. The notion of "minding your own business" and not talking about others is a dominant theme in this case study. How might these concepts strengthen community?
2. Having fun is a theme from the grandmother's younger days. What kinds of social benefits were possibly gained with having fun?
3. Relationships with grandchildren change as the grandchildren mature. There appears, in this case, to be a distancing. How would you characterize this change in relationships between grandma and some of the grandchildren?
4. Land ownership and transferring land to the next generation has played a significant part in this community. Analyze the significance of the land in this case.

REFERENCES

Antonucci, T., & Jackson, J. (2007). Intergenerational relations: Theory, research, and policy. *Journal of Social Issues, 63*(4), 679–693.

Barnett, M.A., Scaramella, L.V., Neppl, T.K., Ontai, L., & Conger, R.D. (2010). Intergenerational relationship quality, gender, and grandparent involvement. *Family Relations, 59*, 28–44.

Engebretson, K. (2008). The Catholic school called to dialogue: A reflection on some consequences of the ecclesial unity of the Catholic school. *Journal of Beliefs and Values, 29*(2), 151–160.

Hardcastle, D., & Powers, P. (2004). Community practice: Theories and skills for social workers (2nd ed.). Toronto: Oxford University Press.

Hayslip, B., Henderson, C., & Shore, R.J. (2003). The structure of grandparental role meaning. *Journal of Adult Development, 10*(1), 1–11.

Hurme, H., Westerback, M.A., & Quadrello, T. (2010). Traditional and new forms of contact between grandparents and grandchildren. *Journal of Intergenerational Relationships, 8*, 264–280.

Personal Communication. November *30*, 2010.

Villar, F., Triado, C., Pinazo-Hernandis, S., Celdran, M., & Sole, C. (2010). Grandparents and their adolescent grandchildren: Generational stake or generational complaint? A study with dyads in Spain. *Journal of Intergenerational Relationships, 8*, 281–297.

NADINE VATER

GRANDPARENTS AND COMMUNITY

Shelton (fictitious name) is a rural community located on the West Coast of Newfoundland. Approximately 1200 people reside in the community. Mr. Joe Bodrow (fictitious name) was not born in Shelton, but he was raised there and continues to reside there today. Mr. Bodrow (69) is married to Mary Smith (60), also from Shelton. Mr. Bodrow and his wife are parents of three children: May (36), George (33) and Rhonda (29), and grandparents within the community of Shelton. Mr. Bodrow describes what Shelton was like when he was a boy, what it is like today, and how the community has changed over time. He also discusses his role as a grandparent within the community.

Mr. Bodrow was born on Hartley's Island, which is located in the Bay of Islands. Many people populated the island as it was close to the water and fishing was the form of livelihood for many families' years ago. However, families residing on Hartley's Island were forced to resettle in 1961, mainly due to the lack of continuous community development. Vehicles or electricity did not exist on the island and there were a lack of teachers willing to go there to teach the children. The island eventually became isolated and people relocated to Shelton and Drodge's Cove, communities directly across the bay from Hartley's Island. Many people who once lived on Hartlye's Island own cabins there today, and visit in the summertime to share good times with friends, their children and grandchildren. This gives them a sense of belonging with other people from the island and offers their grandchildren a sense of what life was like for their grandparents when they lived there.

Mr. Bodrow explained that growing up for him was different than it is today. They never had so much as people do today. As young children, Mr. Bodrow and his brothers had chores to complete. They helped their father and grandfather cut wood, pack it away and lug water, as there was a lack of running water at that time. They were expected to help their parents with the necessities of survival, which are things that young children do not have to do today. "Now mind you, we did get to play with our friends but the chores had to be done first," explained Mr. Bodrow. He stated that children's roles are certainly different within the community today.

Mr. Bodrow had a close relationship with his grandparents while growing up. "My grandparents often looked after us and fed us because times were hard back then." Mr. Bodrow mentioned that several of his eldest siblings were raised by his grandparents. They all lived in the same geographical area, thus he had constant contact with his grandparents. Grandparents were important within the community

A. Singh and M. Devine (Eds.), Rural Transformation and Newfoundland and Labrador Diaspora:
Grandparents, Grandparenting, Community and School Relations, 139–146.
© 2013 Sense Publishers. All rights reserved.

many years ago as everyone helped look after the children in the community. Grandparents played a vital role in the lives of their children and grandchildren and within the community.

Mr. Bodrow maintains close relationships with other grandparents within the community of Shelton who are approximately his age. He stated that, "every now and then, me and my buddy will take our little grandsons for a walk." He verified the importance of close relationships with grandchildren if the opportunity is available, as some people do not have that option. Mr. Bodrow described the pleasures of having a close relationship with his grandparents and other grandparents within the community while growing up and stated that he would like for his grandchildren to have the same opportunity.

Mr. Bodrow explained that his interactions with the younger generation are limited as the majority of his friends are near his age. He stated that, "many of the young ones are gone away now." Most of his interactions with the younger generation are with those who are friends of his children. He maintains relationships with those individuals as they are sometimes present when he visits his children. He had closer connections with the younger generation when his children lived at home, as their friends spent time there. He also mentioned that he has interactions with fisherpersons of the younger generation, as they have contact during the fishing season. However, that is the extent of his relationships with younger persons within the community.

Mr. Bodrow described his relationships with his children as very good. He has two daughters, a son, and four grandchildren and described his relationships with his grandchildren as perfect. Mr. Bodrow sees two of his three children at least four to five times a week. His eldest daughter and two grandchildren reside out of province, thus their physical contact is minimal. However, they speak regularly. When he does see his grandchildren, Mr. Bodrow strives to engage them within the community. Ochiltree (2006) states that [m]ost grandparents enjoy time with their grandchildren, taking them out to playgrounds, on various other excursions, and having them in their homes for visits and sometimes for sleepovers (p. 25). Mr. Bodrow often takes his grandchildren for walks within the community or to the local park for them to engage in interaction with members of the community including other children, parents and grandparents.

Religion is important within communities. Bounds (1997) states that [r]eligion is a critical component, although often ignored, of these postliberal shifts in community/ civil society (p. 4). As a Roman Catholic child, Mr. Bodrow was required to attend church regularly and he continues to be a regular church attendee. Mr. Bodrow and his wife generally attend church once a week on Saturday evenings. Mr. Bodrow enjoys his grandchildren accompanying them to church and requests that his children bring his grandchildren to the community on Saturdays so that they can do so. Mr. Bodrow believes it important to expose his grandchildren to religion.

Mr. Bodrow is a supporter of the community church. He mentioned that, "we usually puts $20.00 in one of the church envelopes and gives it to the parish every Saturday evening." The local parish often arranges fundraisers and Mr. Bodrow donates items that are needed for these fundraisers. For example, the local parish collects firewood and sells tickets for a fundraiser. Mr. Bodrow often retrieves wood and donates it to the local parish to help with the fundraiser. The local church also has a food bank. Mr. Bodrow and his wife donate non-perishable food items to the food bank to help support the less fortunate families within the community.

Shulman (2008) suggests that, "mutual support occurs when group members provide emotional support to one another" (p. 290). Mr. Bodrow stated that if a person from the community passes away, he and his wife, along with many other community members, attend the funeral to pay their respects. The community comes together to provide empathy, sympathy and support for the family. This demonstrates a sense of community as a support system develops to support community members. Mr. Bodrow also acknowledged that when grandchildren experience a dilemma with their parents, they often turn to grandparents for emotional support and comfort. He has responded to calls from his grandchildren in Nova Scotia needing his support. He has also experienced his young grandchildren turning to him for support when they are being disciplined by their parents.

When Mr. Bodrow was 14 years old, he began helping his father and grandfathers in the fishery on Hartley's Island. When he was 17, several years before resettlement, he left for Nova Scotia where he began his own fishing career. He eventually purchased his own large seining boat and returned to Newfoundland when he was 23 years old to make Shelton his home. Mr. Bodrow identifies himself as a fisherman within the community of Shelton, even though there are many other fishing communities within the area. He explained that there are, "seven or eight other boats and if we see fish, we will radio them and let them know. And they do the same for us." A sense of community is demonstrated here as the fishermen of Shelton help one another out. Mr. Bodrow also mentioned that, "if people lose their lobster traps in a storm of wind, all of the fisherman usually give 20 or 30 traps each to help them out so they can get back fishing right away and make money." Peck (1987) states that, [c]ommunity is something more than the sum of its parts, its individual members (p. 60). Independent people work together to help one another. It is expected of you to help other fishermen and the same is expected of them. Mr. Bodrow explained that many fishermen employ their sons and grandsons on their boats. He stated that he would have enjoyed the presence of his grandsons on his boat; however, they are much too young to become part of the fishing community.

Although Mr. Bodrow is not a formal member of any organization within Shelton, he is an active participant when something is needed within the community. Currently, the town council of Shelton is preparing to construct a new graveyard for the Roman Catholic Church. Mr. Bodrow has been helping to sell tickets to fundraise for construction of the new graveyard and has also donated money to help support these costs. Mr. Bodrow expressed the importance of investing in the needs of the community in order to "keep it alive."

Mr. Bodrow remarked on his role within the community as a grandparent performing unpaid work. Since he is now retired, Mr. Bodrow and his wife provide unpaid child care to their youngest daughter. Ochiltree (2006) states that, [s]ome grandparents see providing child care as their role and responsibility and even their pleasure (p. 27). Mr. Bodrow enjoys caring for his youngest grandson during the week as it provides an opportunity for them to interact and engage in activities together. He noted that many grandparents today help care for their grandchildren while their children work, as his son's mother-in-law also provides childcare for her grandchildren.

Many people have left the community of Shelton. Mr. Bodrow even left the community as a young man to begin his fishing career. He assumes that people have left and are currently leaving the community due to lack of employment. Many years ago, the majority of people went to Nova Scotia to begin fishing or to Toronto to work in the factories, as there was lots of work up there then. Mr. Bodrow noted, "Nowadays, people are leaving to go to Alberta where work is plentiful and the money is good." People who leave Shelton usually go to other provinces with higher employment and higher wages. Few move to nearby communities.

Mr. Bodrow explained that by people leaving the community, things have been lost. Firstly, more people are leaving the community, therefore there is a decline in population. Subsequently, there is less being put into the community. Berkley and Economy (2008) state that [e]veryone in a community has something to contribute to the process, and everyone in a community should be invited and encouraged to do just that (p. 5). Although people are encouraged to give back to the community, it is difficult to do when people are leaving to make careers and find jobs elsewhere because few exist within the community to give back. Mr. Bodrow explained that with people leaving Shelton, there are less people to support the churches, local businesses, the needs of the community, as well as other individual community members.

With the younger generation and their children leaving Shelton, they are possibly leaving behind parents and grandparents. This can impact relationships between grandparents and their grandchildren. As Mr. Bodrow has a daughter and two grandchildren residing in a different province, he explained that his relationship with those grandchildren is restricted. A lack of opportunity exists for them to develop a close relationship and engage in grandparent-grandchild activities.

The only benefit that Mr. Bodrow can see of people moving out of the community is that, "they are making good money for themselves and supporting their families." He mentioned that another good thing about people leaving is to see them come back. People returning, after being gone for many years, demonstrates the importance of community and the ties that people maintain to their community after being away for significant durations.

There is little employment within the community of Shelton and if people were to stay, there would possibly be increased poverty. Economy-wise, little would have been contributed. Business would eventually die as people would not have the money to be spending to keep businesses, organizations and churches thriving. However, increased support for community members and relationships between grandparents and grandchildren would be created and maintained.

Mr. Bodrow stated that Shelton is different today than it was years ago, even just a decade ago. People within the community do not visit one another as often as they once did. "Christmas used to be a time for visiting friends and family and now you barely see anyone, let alone any other time of year." Mr. Bodrow noted that he has less friends today than he had years ago. Many have passed on or have moved away. He added, "you still might maintain a bit of contact but there are no visits like it used to be."

Mr. Bodrow maintains relationships with most of his family and there are several that he sees regularly. There are a few family members that they invite over regularly for meals and accompany on vacations. Mr. Bodrow is very supportive of his family and would offer assistance if needed. He reported that he is close with his children and grandchildren, but he would be more satisfied if he had further physical contact with his daughter and grandchildren who reside in Nova Scotia.

The role of religion has also changed, according to Mr. Bodrow. Nowadays, few people attend church in Shelton. It appears that religion is fading and the Church is not as important to the younger generation. A Roman Catholic priest from another community holds church services in Shelton, as no local priest exists anymore. There are few people who attend church services, and those who do are elderly community members. Very few children attend. Mr. Bodrow fears that in years to come, there will be no church services in the community as few people support the parish and fewer children are becoming involved.

Although Mr. Bodrow was not a formal member of any community organizations in the past, nor is he now, he did mention that he does support the community where it is needed. He supports the church and the construction of community sites, such as the new graveyard. He supports fundraisers and donates needed items to the community.

Mr. Bodrow mentioned that he is retired but he still tries to, "give the other fishermen a hand during the season." He often assists the local fisherpersons in preparing their traps for the setting day. He also assists them with taking the traps out of the water once the season is over. This helps him feel like he is a fisherman again as he misses not being an active participant within the fishing community. Fishing remains strong in Shelton; Mr. Bodrow explained that he will continue to help other fisherpersons strive to do their best at something so joyful.

Both of Mr. Bodrow's children, George and Rhonda, reside in the nearby city, which is approximately a 20 minute drive from Shelton. His eldest daughter, May, resides in Halifax, Nova Scotia. George has one son, Jake (3), and Rhonda has one son as well, John (2). Mr. Bodrow explained that he sees both George and Rhonda quite often, as well as his two grandsons, as they exchange visits regularly. May has a daughter, Susan (12), and a son, Don (9), who Mr. Bodrow does not see as often, as they live in another province. Mr. Bodrow sees them about four times per year. May and her family usually visit Shelton during the summer months. Mr. and Mrs. Bodrow visit them in the spring, summer and early winter, usually at Christmas time. He usually speaks with his daughter and his grandchildren in Halifax every two to three days.

Mr. Bodrow expressed his longing to have his daughter and grandchildren live closer so that he could participate in various activities with them. He mentioned, "even just to take them out in the garage like I do with my other grandchildren and let them pick around at my stuff." Mr. Bodrow feels like he is missing important parts of his grandchildren's lives. He feels like he is not fulfilling his role as a grandparent. He stated that, "it is hurtful when you visit your grandchildren and they barely know who you are and they act shy around you. That is hurtful for me." He does not experience this with his grandchildren who live close by. Geographical distance can impact relationships between people and Mr. Bodrow experiences this with his grandchildren who live in another province.

The community of Shelton has certainly changed over time, according to Mr. Bodrow. The importance of religion has diminished and is gradually disappearing. The crime rate seems to be on an incline. Mr. Bodrow reported that within the past several years, boats have been broken into and items have been stolen. The values and morals of the younger generations are distorted, according to Mr. Bodrow. "When we were young, we would have never thought about destroying someone else's stuff. Our parents and grandparents would have killed us." In his generation, the community together enforced discipline. Nowadays, the police are more likely involved as younger people have less respect for their parents and grandparents and are more likely to reject compliance.

Mr. Bodrow explained that since more people are moving away to other provinces, relationships between grandparents, parents and grandchildren are suffering. Communities are growing apart and people are becoming more differentiated. As a result, communities lose their connections and closeness. Given a smaller population, there are less people to interact with within the community. Nowadays, many people have other means of doing things which can impede community closeness. For example, many people now use oil as their main source of heating. Therefore, the community is less involved with one another as fewer people use wood as a heating method. Grandparents do not have the opportunity to take their grandchildren into the woods to teach them how to cut wood, which was huge when Mr. Bodrow was growing up. "People are doing their own thing now and no one cares about what anyone else is doing."

With fewer individuals within a community, the reputation of the community can be impacted. Most rural communities are considered friendly and close. According to Hardcastle (2004), [c]ommunity suggests people with social ties sharing an identity and a social system (p. 92). With more individualization among community members, the less caring, giving, and supportive they may seem. A community is more than just individual people; it is a group of people (Lee, 1999, p. 15) who work together to create a cohesive community that provides a supportive environment. This is demonstrated in Mr. Bodrow's explanation of a fishing community. People have social ties and work together to help one another. When individuals fail to work together, there will be a reduced sense of community among its members and the reputation of rural communities will weaken. The same applies to grandparents within communities. With younger people relocating, relationships between families are impacted. Caring, involved, friendly communities are created through relationships between members. With the interruption of relationships, communities are at risk.

Newfoundland is considered a friendly province. Without continuous community development, rural communities are at risk of dying. The reputation that Newfoundland has of being a friendly province will disappear with fewer rural communities. Connections are necessary for communities to thrive and be maintained. It is important that the younger generation maintain contact with relatives and non-relatives of all ages, especially grandparents. Hall (1999) notes that as grandparents have life experiences and often know how to do things, grandchildren benefit by learning from their grandparents. Therefore, it is important for grandchildren to maintain close relationships with their grandparents. Generosity, cohesiveness, connections and support among members are what keep a community animate. Without these tactics, communities may deteriorate, and possibly die, simultaneously losing their reputation.

While learning about the history of Shelton in relation to grandparents and community, it is clear that decades ago, grandparents, parents and children generally remained within the same community. Nowadays, parents are moving away with their children, impacting the grandparent-grandchild relationship. Younger generations have differing values and morals than grandparents within the community. Grandparents are concerned about their grandchildren and their relationships with them, the connections between community members that keep the community thriving, and the lack of importance of religion. According to Mr. Bodrow, religion is important within a community and for its members. Maintaining social relationships and community ties with members, including children, is vital to keep communities prospering.

REFLECTION QUESTIONS

1. Despite fairly regular contact with his grandchildren Mr. Bodrow stated he sometimes feel hurt when the grandchildren away hardly know him. How would you interpret this statement?
2. Self-identity and community identity are often defined as separate concepts. In this case study Mr. Bodrow identity as a fisherman is intertwined with his identity as a community member. Explain.
3. Connections with and involvement of community members in community development is defined in a formal sense. Although Mr. Bodrow is not involved in community organizations formally, he is very involved in an informal sense. How might the formal definition of involvement in community development be inadequate in this case?
4. Diaspora may be defined in a number of different ways and in a number of different contexts. Name and explain how this concept applies in this case study.

REFERENCES

Berkley, B., & Economy, P. (2008). Giving Back: Connecting you, business, and community. Hoboken, N.J.: Wiley.

Bounds, E.M. (1997). Coming Together/Coming Apart: Religion, community, and modernity. New York: Routledge.

Hall, C.M. (1999). The Special Mission of Grandparents: Hearing, seeing, telling. Westport, Conn.: Bergin & Garvey.

Hardcastle, D.A., Powers, P.R., & Wenocur, S. (2004). Community Practice: Theories and skills for social workers (2nd ed.). Oxford: Oxford University Press.

Lee, B. (1992). Pragmatics of Community Organization (2nd ed.). Mississauga, Ont.: Common Act Press.

Ochiltree, G. (2006). Grandparents, Grandchildren and the Generation in Between. Camberwell, Vic.: ACER Press.

Peck, M.S. (1987). The Different Drum: Community-making and peace. New York: Simon and Chuster.

Shulman, L. (2008). The Skills of Helping Individuals, Families, Groups, and Communities. Blemont, CA: Brooks/Cole Publishing Co.

SACHA ANDERSON

THE ROLE OF GRANDPARENTING

A Journey Through Time

When asked, grandparents will often identify their role in the community as a connection to the past and the future (Barusch, Smith, Steen, & Peter, 1996). Grandparents often act as role models and mentors within their families. This paper will explore the role of grandparents and how this role has changed over the years, through the eyes of "Rita" (fictitious name), a seventy-two year old widow and mother of four. Rita lived on Cabot Island (fictitious name) before resettling to Lants (fictitious name). This paper will also explore how community has changed over the years in terms of community leaders and organizations, religion, employment opportunities, and relationships between community members.

In the initial stages of our interview, Rita described what life was like for her growing up in Lants, NL. Rita resettled to Lants from Cabot Island when she was a young girl. Newfoundland's resettlement program was aimed at "rationalizing" population distribution and concentrating people into growth centers where new industries were expected to take hold (Kenney, 1997). Although Rita does not recall the specifics of her family's resettlement, she still remembers her parent's many discussions surrounding leaving their home on Cabot Island. Rita's father, Charlie, explained to her on many occasions that it was necessary to leave so Rita and her brother would have more educational opportunities.

Rita remembers growing up in her family's two story home, where they did not have electricity or running water; she laughed and stated that to use the bathroom, she and her brother would have to take a pail "down behind the house." Rita recollects that when her family resettled to Lants, her maternal grandmother lived with them until she passed away when Rita was fourteen. Consistent with the findings of Chan and Elder (2000), Rita described her relationship with her maternal grandmother as "very close," which was in contrast with her relationship with her paternal grandparents. Rita stated that her maternal grandmother played a significant role in her upbringing as she was involved in Rita's everyday life, whereas her paternal grandparents seldom visited from their home in Fields. Rita remembers her maternal grandmother teaching her valuable life skills such as how to sew, bake, knit and keep house. Moreover, Rita feels her own grandmother's involvement in her childhood has heavily influenced how she views her role as a grandparent.

When asked if her grandmother played a role in the community, Rita responded that her grandmother did not participate a great deal, however she was part of church

A. Singh and M. Devine (Eds.), Rural Transformation and Newfoundland and Labrador Diaspora: Grandparents, Grandparenting, Community and School Relations, 147–154.

groups. Her grandmother's lack of involvement in her new community illustrates the diaspora she felt in having to leave the place she called home and attempt to integrate into a new town, where roles within the community had already been established. Individuals and families who resettled in the 1900s had to adapt to the status quo, governance, culture and economy of their new community. However, it is evident that Rita's grandmother chose not to accept, but rather endure, the norms of her new place of residence; thus increasing the probability of her feeling like an outsider in the community (Nesbitt-Larking, 2008).

Rita and I discussed her sense of community with regards to her peer relationships. Rita stated that she does not feel as connected to her community as she did in previous years; "everyone is just so busy now days, with all the technology and things to do." However, when Rita described years past in Lants, she laughed and recalled garden parties, dances, and picnics where everyone would come together and mingle; there'd be dancing and food, but not a lot of alcohol like there is today. When asked if she had strong peer relationships with those in her community, Rita, replied "Oh yes, lots of friends, adding her group of friends is what made her community home for all these years. We've all been friends for as long as I can remember, even though we don't visit as much, we are still friends."

During our interview, I inquired about Rita's relationship with the younger adults in the community. Interestingly, as Rita has adopted two of her grandchildren, her relationship with the younger adults of Lants is much the same as it is with the older adults. Rita stated that most of the younger generation is, "very accepting, even on hockey trips, they never treated me any different." Although Rita said she wouldn't call them friends, she feels that she has a good relationship with the younger ones. Currently, three out of four of Rita's biological children, while neither of her adopted grandchildren, are living in the community. Rita describes her relationships with her children as close and feels as though there has never been a time where she was unable to be there for her children and vice versa.

Growing up, Rita recalls religion playing a huge role in her community. "We went to Church every Sunday and attended Sunday school." The Church was involved in just about everything. Rita noted that the Church was one of the main leaders in Lants, and, "pretty well everyone gave money to the Church; It was expected." Rita remembers her mother and grandmother being involved with the Anglican Church Women (ACW) group, as she is today. Rita feels that her involvement in the ACW group positively impacts her relationship with the community and its members. "We do cold plate dinners, Christmas food baskets..." says Rita.

Lants was once known as a dual industry town; the main sources of employment were the Canadian Newfoundland Railway (CNR) and the cod fishery. Rita remembers when her father and first husband worked at the CNR for eighty cents an hour. "Pretty well everyone worked at the CNR, with the exception of the fishermen of course." Although most people worked for a wage, Rita recalls many forms of unpaid work. "The men would always help one another out, building their skiffs, doing the wood, and baiting the lines." When the town was readying to receive electric power, her father helped put in the power lines. "I don't recall if it was paid work, but I don't believe it was." Women also performed unpaid work in the community through helping the ill with their housework, caring for children, salting fish, and baking for community events. With regards to paid work, Rita remembers most women being homemakers, while some did work at the drug store and bank.

When asked about any formal community groups that Rita and her first husband were involved in, Rita responded that men and women participated in separately. For example, the men had their dart league and the women had bingo, cards, and the ACW. Rita recalls the men going moose hunting, fishing, and rabbit snaring together. Although these groups were informal in a sense, they performed a significant function in the community, while contributing to the cohesiveness of its members (Lee, 1999).

Years ago, Lants was a lively, well to do community; jobs weren't scarce in the past. However, with the advent of technology, finding employment with the main employer, Downsview Fisheries, is not an easy task. "They have machines that will do most anything; I'd say that if that wasn't the case many of the young people would still be home", said Rita the advent of technology and modern transportation have made it possible for people to move back and forth between provinces for employment (Barnett, Scaramella, Neppl, Ontai, & Conger, 2010).

It is not uncommon for young people to leave rural areas for employment, or to pursue post-secondary education (Jamieson, 2000). Rita described the summer and Christmastime as very lively as students return from school and those who work away come home on their holidays. Rita discussed a new phenomenon in Lants where the men, in a significant number of families, go away to work two weeks on and two weeks off. When asked why families chose this way of life, Rita replied, "Well this is home, and I suppose they might be hoping to get a job in town eventually." Rita noted that this change in family dynamics has influenced involvement by grandparents. "A lot of my friends help out with their grandkids while the men are away. Even some grandparents have chosen to move too, so that they can provide childcare for their grandchildren."

Rita and her daughter left Lants in the early 1980s, after the death of her first husband. Rita lived away for approximately twenty-three years, returning frequently to visit her children and grandchildren. When asked why she returned, Rita stated that she missed her family, friends, and home. Since returning in 2004, Rita feels that much has changed with regards to the various aspects of community. "it's difficult to put into words, but things are just different, things have changed." Rita believes that one of the biggest changes in the community is that of "helping one another or lack of today." In the past, there was no such thing as having to hire contractors to build homes, and sheds; Everyone did their part. When asked if this was the case with all generations, Rita replied that it was not and that those adults who are currently in their forties and fifties still help one another up around the cabin and around the house. Rita added that people have more extravagant homes than in the past; she attributes this to the employment opportunities community members have found in other provinces.

Rita feels the role of children in the community has changed considerably. In the past, children learned life skills from their parents and grandparents; today, there is an increased focus on attaining a higher education as a means of supporting oneself. Years past, children were viewed as helpers and were expected to contribute to their family's livelihood, childrearing, and housework. Children were allowed to roam and explore Lants without parental concern. "I always knew someone was watching them," states Rita. Rita feels much has changed since she parented her biological children to now; "There was never such a thing as babysitters, but today that seems to be the only way."

Interestingly, Rita feels the role of grandparents has not changed much over the years. Grandparents still play a substantial role in the upbringing of grandchildren and remain a key support in families (Stelle, Fruhauf, Orel, & Landry-Meyer, 2010). Even though grandparents today do not have the same opportunity to teach their grandchildren life skills like years ago, they have evolved to meet the needs of their grandchildren growing up in the twenty first century. I know grandparents who learned to play the wii through spending time their grandkids.

Although community members are still involved with community groups and organizations, it is not to the same extent as they were involved years ago. Rita noted that the younger generation does not seem to be involved with the card clubs and dart leagues; rather the groups are aging along with those involved. It's always been the same crowd for as long as I can remember. She further states that although people are still active participants, the peer relationships just aren't the same.

When comparing past and present religious involvement in the community, Rita notes this to be one the biggest changes in the community. The congregations and monetary contributions of community members are steadily declining; like the community groups, only the older adult population seems to be interested. The church is no longer a predominate agent of social control, rather the town council, RCMP, and minor hockey association have assumed the role of major leaders in the community. There was a time when families went to Church in a time of need; today, they look to alternative organizations and agencies.

In recent decades, with the increased cost of living and lack of employment, more women have joined the labour force. Women are considered to be flexible, educated, and skilful workers (Lie, 2010). Rita believes that women's advancement in the labour market is an example of a predominant change in the community. In the past, a woman's main responsibilities were the upkeep of the home and caring for her children. Rita stated that just as many women work as men do now, and although she feels this is a grand advancement, children are left in the care of babysitters, daycares and family members, including grandparents.

Out-migration of community members has the potential to reduce informal support networks (Shucksmith, 2000). As Rita discussed, a considerable number of community members have left Lants, which has contributed hugely to the decline of Newfoundland culture. "There just isn't enough young people to carry on traditions." Rita stated that this decrease in population and loss of familial relationships have left older adults in the community feeling disconnected and isolated from their community (Shucksmith, 2000). When community members leave for extended periods of time, the probability of them returning is decreased. Out-migrants are exposed to new cultures, trends, and traditions that make it harder for them to return (Fine, 1999).

Rita feels the traditions and closeness of the community has diminished with the out-migration of community members. However, she feels, that "some good has come of it, as the town is attempting to keep young adults in the community through offering new programs and services. We've got the new stadium, the pool, and the mall, lots of things for people to do now." Rita doesn't believe things would be different if people didn't leave; "I'd say everyone would be unemployed, but there would be a lot more people around, that's for sure."

As a result of increased life expectancies, multigenerational families have become the norm of the twenty first century. At present, grandparents will experience the role of grandparenting for thirty years or more, allowing for a substantial increase in grandparent-grandchild contact. However, the actual value of these relationships is dependent on a number of variables: geographic location, quantity and quality of contact, etc. (Barnett, Scaramella, Neppl, Ontai, & Conger, 2010).

Rita is a grandmother and great-grandmother to twelve children spread out across the country. Rita describes her relationships with her grandchildren as very good, regardless of their geographic location. Rita explains that she has always valued her relationships with her grandchildren, and makes an effort to treat everyone equally, although there are times she will talk with one grandchild more than the others. However, Rita feels she is not as close with her great grandchildren; They have their other grandparents, and they are all so far away.

As all of Rita's grandchildren live away, she does not see them as often as she would like. Rita has grandchildren in St. Johns, Halifax, British Colombia, Toronto, Ottawa, New Brunswick and Calgary, all of whom she speaks with quite often. Rita tells of how her grandchildren have different names for her, depending on where they've grown up. "Some call me nana, nanny or nan, while the ones in Toronto call me grandma. Most of Rita's grandchildren are adults now and some have children of their own. We speak about once a month, I suppose it's because everyone is so busy." When asked how often Rita visits or is visited by her grandchildren, she explains that she tries her best to see everyone equally. However, Rita admits she sees those who still live in Newfoundland more frequently, as the distance and cost of travel is not as great. Notably, Rita has just returned from a visit to Ottawa, where she visited with her granddaughter, who recently had a baby boy.

Interviewing Rita has provided a community profile of the town of Lants over time. It is evident that much has changed in the community over the years, since the cod moratorium. Rita recalls that when growing up, there was always lots of paid and unpaid work to be done. Family dynamics have also changed. Years ago, couples had numerous children; today, the average is one or two per household. Notably, technological advances in medical care have increased the life spans of older adults, allowing them to remain in the role of grandparents for longer periods of time.

Although the life skills taught by grandparents today differ from those taught in previous years, grandparents still play a large role in the upbringing of children in Lants. Furthermore, grandparents are viewed as a vital resource of information and a familial support to their children, grandchildren and communities. Interestingly, although the role of grandparents appears to be much the same, because of their increased life expectancy, they have more time to spend with their grandchildren, thus allowing for more intimate relationships to be developed. Furthermore, how this bonding occurs has changed significantly. In years past, the only means of bonding took place during visits, whereas today, travel and technological advances such as SKYPE and inter-gaming systems like the Wii, allow for daily contact even if miles apart.

Although the cod fishery is no longer one of the dominant employers in Lants, Downsview Fisheries remains key to the towns' survival. In my interview with Rita, it was evident that the people of this community hold great pride in Downsview Fisheries.

Interestingly, Rita could not recall any real leaders in her community from years past; she noted that they, were "all in it together." In contrast, today she sees many leaders in the community; however, older adults do not see them as such. For instance, hockey coaches and the town manager and mayor all play a significant role in leading the community, but Rita does not believe they hold much power. This may be attributed to the fact that these leaders continue to hold the value of respecting one's elders and very seldom will they make decisions that impact older adults without consulting them first.

It is apparent that much has changed in the town of Lants since the 1900's when the resettlement initiative was launched. Although community values, morals and attitudes are basically the same, they have indeed been modernized in an attempt to be socially acceptable. The people of Lants still help one another when needed, but as a direct result of increased technology and everyday demands, they have adapted to the stressfulness of the twenty first century. Family dynamics have been altered in an effort to stay close to home while providing for one's family, but still, grandparents are an invaluable resource. The once outport people of Lants interact with the outside world more so than ever, while many have no choice but to leave and join it (Kenney, 1997). But like Rita, many Lantsers eventually come back to their invaluable roots and traditions of hard work, kitchen parties and Christmas mummering.

REFLECTION QUESTIONS

1. Rita resettled back in Lants upon retirement. One of the biggest differences she sees is how people don't help one another out like they used to do. How might one account for this change? What is the impact from a community development perspective?

2. Some grandparents moved out of province to provide child care to their grandchildren and, presumably, to ensure ongoing and regular contact with them and their adult children. What does this say about the supposed changing roles of grandparents in relation to grandchildren?
3. Lants is a community with two industries historically. The former railway; now the ferry service, and the fishery. How does this impact on community development and community cohesion?
4. Child care, both historically and, to some extent, today is more care free. There is a sense that, possibly to the smaller community, all adults care for the children when they are out and about. How is this a positive and how is it a concern?

REFERENCES

Barnett, M., Scaramella, L., Neppl, T., Ontai, L., & Conger, R. (2010). Intergenerationalrelationship quality, gender, and grandparent involvement. *Family Relations, 59*(1), 28–44.

Barusch, A., & Steen, P. (1996). Keepers of community in a changing world. *Generations, 20*(1), 49.

Chan, C.G., & Elder, G.H. (2000). Matrilineal advantage in grandchild B grandparent relations. Gerontologist, *40*, 179–190.

Even-Zohar, A., & Sharlin, S. (2009). Grandchildhood: Adult grandchildren's perception of their role towards their grandparents from an intergenerational perspective. *Journal of Comparative Family Studies, 40*(2), 167–185.

Fine, B. (1999). A question of economics: Is it colonising the social sciences? *Economy and Society, 28*(3), 403–25.

Hardcastle, D., Powers, P., & Wenocur, S. (2004). Community Practice: Theories and Skills for Social Workers (2nd ed.). United States: Oxford Press.

Jamieson, L. (2000). Migration, Place and Class: Youth in a rural area. *The Sociological Review, 48*(2), 203–223.

Kenney, J.C. (1997). At the crossroads: Newfoundland and Labrador communities in a changing international context. *The Canadian Review of Sociology and Anthropology, 32*, 297–317.

Lee, B. (1999). Pragmatics of Community Organization (3rd ed.). Canada: Common Act Press.

Pratt, M., Norris, J., Cressman, K., Lawford, H., & Hebblethwaite, S. (2008). Parents' stories of grandparenting concerns in the three-generational family: Generativity, optimism, and forgiveness. *Journal of Personality, 76*(3), 581–604.

Rutherford, M., DeQuine, J., Harrington, M., Moffett, A., Narayan, C., & Navon, A. (1999). Simply Grand. *Time, 154*(15).

Shucksmith, M. (2000). Exclusive Countryside? Social inclusion and regeneration in rural areas. York: Joseph Rowntree Foundation.

Stelle, C., Fruhauf, C., Orel, N., & Landry-Meyer, L. (2010). Grandparenting in the 21st century: Issues of diversity in grandparent-grandchild relationships. *Journal of Gerontological Social Work, 53*(8), 682–701.

VOICES OF GRANDPARENTS:
COMMUNITY-FAMILY-SCHOOL RELATIONSHIPS

LINDA COLES

NEWFOUNDLAND AND LABRADOR DIASPORA

Grandparents' Perceptions of Their Roles

The role of grandparents in the fifties, sixties, and seventies, in Newfoundland and Labrador, was different than it is today. Back then, from patriarchs to matriarchs, the grandfathers and grandmothers were highly respected and revered as experienced seniors within the family unit and within the community. Both children and grandchildren, alike, venerated and held in high esteem the grandparents of the family. Grandchildren were often positioned as listeners who deferred to grandparents in all aspects of the daily lived experiences. Within this context, grandparents were seen as the wiser, older members of the family, viewed with some element of the sacrosanct and sometimes even feared. Grandchildren moved into their spaces and learned their ways and have become the grandparents of today.

INTRODUCTION

The exigencies of our economy have caused thousands of people to move away from Newfoundland and Labrador and, at times, from rural to urban areas within the province. Newfoundlanders and Labradorians have been out-migrating from the province since the 1890s. The out-migration of Newfoundlanders and Labradorians was fuelled once again, in 1992, when a downturn in the fishery led to the cod moratorium. According to Statistics Canada (2001), between the 1996 and 2001 census, 47,100 people moved away from Newfoundland and Labrador.

Over the past couple of decades a mass out-migration, from rural areas in particular, left in its wake the closure of schools, homes, and businesses, as it became necessary for young and old to leave their homes to find work in other parts of Canada and the world. Only those who have personally experienced the out-migration truly know what the real impact has been for their families and communities. Raising the voices of those who have been directly affected by the out-migration leads me to grandparents.

This chapter explores grandparents' perceptions of their lived experiences with their roles within a 21st century context and a Newfoundland and Labrador diaspora. The Newfoundland and Labrador diaspora, within Canada, occupies a unique potential for promoting extended family relationships, from a distance, between grandparents and their families. But how are Newfoundland and Labrador grandparents living

A. Singh and M. Devine (Eds.), Rural Transformation and Newfoundland and Labrador Diaspora: Grandparents, Grandparenting, Community and School Relations, 157–176.

and experiencing their roles within this Newfoundland and Labrador diaspora? This chapter illuminates the roles of Newfoundland and Labrador grandparents through the perspectives of the lived experiences of a small group of grandparents.

Research Question

Because there is little research that goes directly to grandparents to explore their experiences, a qualitative phenomenological study dedicated to understanding their lived experiences as grandparents best lends itself to examining the research question, What are grandparents' perceptions of how they experience their roles from within their lifeworld? The central phenomenon to be explored is grandparents' perceptions of their roles in today's postmodern world from within a Newfoundland and Labrador diaspora.

The purpose of this study is to uncover and describe the essence of grandparents' roles as articulated by them. Van Manen (1997) notes that; "The essence or nature of an experience has been adequately described in language if the description reawakens or shows us the lived quality and significance of the experience in a fuller or deeper manner" (p. 10).

Some of the underlying questions guiding this work are: What does grandparenting mean in today's world? What are the underlying themes and contexts that account for their view(s) of their roles as grandparents? What types of roles do grandparents fulfil? What types of roles do they prefer? How are grandparents' lifeworlds positioned within the context of a Newfoundland and Labrador diaspora? What are some of the challenges faced by grandparents in a diaspora? How do grandparents reconcile their roles within the changes brought about by new technologies and new literacies (Kress, 2003; Barrell & Hammett, 2000; Luke, 2000)?

Background and Rationale

As mentioned previously, and as confirmed through my conversations with the three adults, the role of grandparents in the fifties, sixties, and seventies, in Newfoundland and Labrador, was very different than it is today. Over the last half of the twentieth century and on the cusp of the 21st century, advancements in technology (e.g., distance education and the fishery, in particular), changes in the male/female ratio in the workforce, the loss of resources (e.g., people and cod), the financial status and overall health of grandparents, and exposure to different literacies and the global community, have brought about changes in the demographics of Newfoundland and Labrador. The impact of these changes has been felt in the rural and urban areas of the province.

Some of the hardest hit changes have been the school system (with a reduction in the number of students in the K-12 system and the closing of schools), evolving demographics (with an imbalance of young people and seniors) and changes within the extended family structure. More than two decades ago, Leahy-Johnson & Barer (1987) claimed that contemporary society was witnessing the evolution of the family from an extended family unit to the nuclear family structure, which isolates extended family members such as grandparents (Leahy-Johnson and Barer, 1987).

The roles of individuals, within the once closely-knit family unit, have changed as modern thought emphasizing direction, order, coherence, stability, simplicity, control, autonomy, and universality has given way to postmodern thought emphasizing diversity, fragmentation, contingency, discontinuity, pragmatism, multiplicity, and connections. This shift has had significant implications for the immediate and extended families in communities throughout Newfoundland and Labrador.

While Newfoundland and Labrador grandparents play a role in the lives of their grandchildren, the out-migration of people from the province to other parts within the province, has had an impact on the roles of grandparents. In the diaspora, some grandparents have followed their children and grandchildren to places within or outside of Newfoundland and Labrador, while some have left their children and grandchildren here in Newfoundland and Labrador to move away to work. Other grandparents have chosen to remain behind in the province of their birth. Whatever the individual choices and circumstances, grandparenthood, one of the oldest social roles in human experience (Knox, 1995), is feeling the impact of the changes that have been brought about by a Newfoundland and Labrador diaspora. While still a key part of the extended family unit, some grandparents' roles and relationships are changing as a natural progression of social, cultural, and technological evolution.

During the mid-to late-20th century, in Newfoundland and Labrador, one's grandparents would also be the next door neighbours. They generally lived in very close proximity to their grandchildren and this constituted a somewhat seamless extended family. Children could drop in next door with their grandparents as easily and effortlessly as if it were their own home. It was generally expected that grandchildren would respect and be obedient to their grandparents who would, in turn, give a watchful eye and show concern for the well-being of grandchildren. Sometimes grandchildren would be asked to help with some of the household chores for grandparents and at times grandparents might give guidance to grandchildren. However, that was a few decades ago. Today, within a Newfoundland and Labrador diaspora, the grandparents of the 21st century are navigating transitions in a wave of constantly changing roles. Within the navigations and transitions lies the space for illuminating the lived experiences of Newfoundland and Labrador grandparents.

As an initial foray into this study I had conversations with three adults about the grandparents in their past. A general theme from these adults was of grandparents who were kind, gentle, skilful, hard workers. In general, they experienced not 'doing a lot' with their grandparents but did try to 'lend a hand' in helping their grandparents. One adult in relating how much he enjoyed being around his grandparents, described them as being the 'quintessential grandparents,' despite not having done much 'with them.'

The discussions with these adults compelled me to explore the lived experiences of a small group of grandparents of today. I used phenomenological methodology to interview the four grandparents in order to glean, from their perceptions and insights, the essence of their lived experiences as a group of Newfoundland and Labrador grandparents.

Related Research

Over the years, the possible significance of grandparents' roles in the lives of children has been alluded to in research. During the late 1900s some researchers suggested that the potential is there for grandparents to play a significant role in the lives of children (Kivnick, 1982; Wilson & DeShane, 1982). These studies also indicate that the grandparent's role is an integral part of their own self-identity.

Emotional attachments between grandparents and grandchildren have been described as unique and the love, nurturance, and acceptance which grandchildren have found in the grandparent/grandchild relationship is different than anything they get from any other person or institution (Kornhaber & Woodward, 1981).

The position of grandparents within the family network has often been regarded as a dependent role and contrary to the norms of self-reliance and independence which were attributed to the nuclear family (Kivnick, 1982). However, according to Neugarten and Weinstein (1964) the traditional role of grandparents was one in which patriarchal or matriarchal control was the essence of the relationship with their grandchildren.

My review of the research indicates that while the voices and perspectives of researchers have been front and centre in discussions and debates about family relationships and the extended family, the voices and perspectives of grandparents have been consistently absent. On a local level, grandparents' perceptions of how they experience their roles in society, generally, have not been foregrounded in policies. For example, in Newfoundland and Labrador, Words to Live By: A Strategic Literacy Plan for Newfoundland and Labrador (2001) was developed without any direct input from grandparents about their grandparenting roles. Research on grandparents and grandparenting has tended to look outward at grandparents' lives from inside the world of official research practices. The spotlight rests on experiences and resources that reflect back comfortable, tidy images of grandparents in traditional roles.

While grandparents' perspectives have been absent, some researchers recognize that their perspectives are uniquely theirs and the need for them to be heard is a significant gap in the research. While his focus was on children, philosopher, Jean Jacques Rousseau's perspective could also be applied to grandparents when he noted that childhood, "has its own ways of seeing, thinking, and feeling and nothing is more foolish than to try and substitute ours for theirs" (Rousseau, 1956, trans. W. Boyd, p. 39).

The findings of Kornhaber's (1981) research suggest that, from the perspective of 5 to18 year-old grandchildren, grandparents have clearly identified roles as: Historians: Grandparents provide historical, cultural, and family sense of history; Mentors: Grandparents offer wisdom, teach children to work with the basics of life, and deepen sex role identity; Role models: Grandparents provide role modelling for future roles of grandparent, aging, and family relationships; Wizards: Grandparents are magical for children, telling stories, stoking the child's imagination; Nurturers: Grandparents widen the support system for children. These roles substantiate the need for the involvement of grandparents as participants in the research process in order for their voices to be heard and their views taken into consideration, with the development of policy and the evolution of health, political, and cultural practices which are designed to serve them. The relative neglect of grandparents' views in research calls for reconstructions of grandparenting as participants and citizens with perspectives and insights that need to be heard.

According to Kornhaber & Woodward (1981), "the complete emotional well-being of children requires that they have a direct, and not merely derived, link with their grandparents" (p. 163). The findings of their study of grandparent/grandchild relationships suggest that emotional attachment is a significant component for children. Using qualitative data gathered from 300 children 5–18 years of age, the authors identified a range of attachments prevalent between grandchildren and grandparents, including: the grandparent as the nexus of family connections; the grandparent as a constant in the life of the child; grandparents as teachers of basic skills; grandparents as negotiators between child and parent; grandparents as role models for adulthood; grandparents as links between past and future giving a sense of historical and cultural rootedness; grandparents as determinants of how the young feel about the old in society; and grandparents as part of secure and loving adult/child relationships next to parents.

These authors also suggest that the roles of grandparents are also linked to the growth and needs of grandchildren and grandparents. Shared time, shared place, shared activities, a commitment to family, and a sense of altruism on the part of the grandparents were found to be crucial in the nurturance of the grandparent/grandchild bond (Kornhaber & Woodward, 1981).

There are educational, social, cultural, historical, and moral reasons why grandparents' voices and their perceptions need to be included in matters that affect them and these matters include their place in the evolving society of a Newfoundland and Labrador diaspora. From a social and moral perspective, shifting from constructions of grandparents that view them as dependents and 'possessions' to constructions that view them as 'participants' and 'citizens', (Lloyd-Smith & Tarr, 2000) requires their voices, their insights, and perspectives.

Is there something very important and relevant missing when the perspectives of grandparents are absent from the research on grandparenting? While there has been a lot of fine research that has focused on grandparents within the context of extended families, researchers have not tended to go directly to Newfoundland and Labrador grandparents for their perspectives. To glean the essence of the "lived experiences" (van Manen, 1997) of Newfoundland and Labrador grandparents necessitates going directly to them about their roles, within a Newfoundland and Labrador diaspora. Consequently, the necessity of utilizing a phenomenological approach to access the voices and perspectives of grandparents, becomes apparent. Grandparents have views and opinions about things that involve them. Engaging their voices and perspectives can help to delineate particular themes of interest and concern and essences while empowering them to greater levels of participation and involvement as citizens.

Methodology

As suggested by Barritt (1986), the strongest rationale for a study is,

> the heightening of awareness for experience which has been forgotten or overlooked. By heightening awareness and creating dialogue, it is hoped research can lead to a better understanding of the way things appear to someone else and through that insight lead to improvements in practice (p. 20).

Phenomenology is the study of the essence of lived experience. A qualitative phenomenological approach is best suited to explore the research question. What are grandparents' lived experiences with grandparenting? Within postmodern thought the more naturalistic and interpretive approach of qualitative research lends "... special credence and value to proposals that...include participants whose meaning-making was overlooked in previous policy and research" (Marshall and Rossman, 2006, p. 209). I use interviews and conversation, to find out from grandparents about how they are experiencing grandparenting in their daily lives.

Phenomenological inquiry embraces the notion of keeping presence with participants, in this case grandparents, by entering into their field of perception, to see their lifeworld and their lived experiences (Creswell, 1998) as they see them. Van Manen (1990) presents the nature of hermeneutic phenomenological research as the study of lived experience, of essences, and of the experiential meanings as we live them. He claims that, "phenomenology describes how one orients to lived experience, hermeneutics describes how one interprets the texts of life" (p. 4). Relating this to research methodology, Van Manen suggests a series of research activities that are inherent in the researcher's methodical structure in phenomenological research as:

- turning to a phenomenon which interests us and commits us to the world
- investigating experience as it is lived rather than as it is conceptualized
- reflecting on the essential themes which characterize the phenomenon
- describing the phenomenon through writing and rewriting
- maintaining a strong and oriented pedagogical relation to the phenomenon
- balancing the research context by considering parts and whole.

This study explores the lived experiences of a small group of grandparents. These grandparents' expressions of their lived experiences are described and interpreted to illuminate the invisible, through core themes of phenomenology including: arriving at essences through intuition and reflection; committing to descriptions of experiences; and regarding, as primary evidence, the data of experience (Moustakas, 1994).

Participants

The research participants are four grandparents from Newfoundland and Labrador.

Margot (grandmother) – Margot was born and raised in a rural community in Newfoundland. She has been involved in the field of education for many years. Three of her grandchildren live in Newfoundland and the remaining six live in other parts of Canada. She and her husband, the grandfather, regularly visit the grandchildren who live away from the province. The three children who live in the province are in close proximity to the grandparents.

Jake (grandfather) – Jake was born and raised in a rural community in Newfoundland. He has been involved in the field of education for many years. His two grandchildren live in Newfoundland and in close proximity to the grandparents. He and his wife, the grandmother, have a lot of contact with their grandchildren.

Owen (grandfather) – Owen was born in a rural community in Newfoundland and since retiring from the fishing industry, spends part of his year in another province in Canada and the remainder of the year in a rural community in Newfoundland. His three grandchildren live with their parents in an urban area in the province. Owen and his wife (the grandmother) see them during periodic visits to the urban area and when they come to the rural area for visits.

Marion (grandmother) – Marion was born in a small community in Newfoundland. She now lives in the capital city. She is divorced from the grandfather. She has two grandchildren who live outside the province. She is very diligent about maintaining contact with her grandchildren and being there for them. Her current spouse plays a grandfather role for her children.

Data Collection

Van Manen (1997) advocates for searching; "everywhere in the lifeworld for lived-experience material that, upon reflective examination, might yield something of its fundamental nature" (p. 53). Creswell (1998) conceptualizes the data collection process as a circle of interrelated activities. These activities are: locating a site or individual; gaining access and making rapport; sampling purposefully; collecting data; recording information; exploring field issues; and storing data.

The data collection for this study happened in two phases during which the participants' perceptions of their experiences were obtained through rapport building (Appendix A), conversation and interviewing (Appendix B).

Interviews

During the initial phase, the focus was on getting to know the grandparents and opening up spaces for them to represent their lived experiences. The first conversation with participants focused on their own experiences with their grandparents (Appendix B).

The second conversation (Appendix B) was structured as an interview and was focused on their perceptions of their own role and lived experiences as grandparents.

Data Analysis

Van Manen (1997) suggests that in the conversations and interviews, "...one looks for the emerging themes; [and] in collecting anecdotes one has to recognize what parts of the text of daily living are significant for one's study...". (p. 69).

One of the first steps in data analysis in phenomenological methodology is the setting aside of the researcher's beliefs and experiences "...in order to acquire a clear lens in which to view experiences" (Finney, 2000, p. 7). Moustakas (1994) suggests that during this process the researcher is, "challenged to create new ideas, new feelings, new awareness and understandings...so that we may see with new eyes in a... completely open manner" (p. 86).

A second step in data analysis within phenomenology is the hermeneutic circle. Pollio, et al (1997), define this as, "an interpretative procedure in which there is a continuous process of relating a part of the text to the whole" (p. 49–50). During this process, themes are identified.

The Voices of the Grandparents

To facilitate my initial foray into the experiences of the grandparents, I engaged them in conversation, guided by questions about their experiences with their own grandparents, the number of grandchildren they have and about their homes, communities and interests. Conversation mediated my metaphorical entry into a shared space with the grandparents.

The participants talked about their experiences with their own grandparents and about how their role and their experiences with their own grandchildren were different from what they had experienced as children. It became clear that the grandparents' perceptions of their grandparenting experiences held truths that needed to be heard. Some of these truths became representations of themes. The participants' insights into their grandparenting experiences helped to elucidate aspects of grand-parenting which only they, as grandparents, are positioned to reveal.

Through the shared phenomenon of the grandparents' lived experiences, three themes emerged: (1) grandparents as backup and support. (2) grandparents as teachers and learners. (3) grandparents as friends. These themes serve as bellwethers of insight leading us into the essence of grandparents' perceptions of their roles.

Grandparents as Backup and Support

The theme of grandparents as backup and support represents a compelling, time-honoured commitment of grandparents to their own children and their grandchildren. According to Knox (1995), grandparenthood is one of the oldest social roles in human experience and a key aspect of their role is that of a surrogate parent. Jake, who sees his grandchildren fairly regularly, explained how he considers one of his roles to be one of support,

> I certainly do not try to be, nor do I have any desire to be, the parent, but I see myself always as a grandparent who is there when the need arises to spend time with my grandchildren or to care for them. However, in this role I follow the rules and expectations of the grandchildren's parents. I want them to experience this consistency.

> I don't want to change the rules on their parents. I believe it's important to be consistent.

> My wife [their grandmother] and I do things for the grandchildren to help our daughter and her husband, whenever we can. However, we don't try to do the child-rearing and when they are in our care, we don't treat them [my two grandchildren] any differently [with respect to parameters, values, and expectations] than we did our own daughter [when she was a child].

Jake spoke very fondly of his own grandparents and his relationship with them. He maintained that they were always very busy with trying to make a living so they didn't have as much time to have fun with the grandchildren as he does [being a retired educator and having the steady income of a pension].

While Margot spends a lot of time with her grandchildren who live in close proximity to her and her husband, she was adamant when she said, "we step in and do the caretaking only when the parents need us to help." As in the case of Jake's daughter and her husband, Margot's daughter and her husband are also working professionals. Margot pointed out that the "busy lifestyle of two working parents means that they need babysitting and daycare support from time to time." Margot believes that it is better for her grandchildren to be cared for by her and her husband, the grandfather. She claims that this will bring more consistency for the children because she said, "we know the parents' values and beliefs about child-rearing and we're in a good position to be able to carry out their wishes."

When she talked about her experiences with her own grandparents, Margot, like Jake, claimed that she had wonderful grandparents. However, her grandparents did not do any babysitting because they were too busy trying to make a living. They also did not engage in activities with them, as grandchildren. Margot told about her experiences with helping the grandparents. The supportive role fell to the children and grandchildren as they were considered to be responsible for helping the grandparents in any way they could.

For the grandchildren who live out of the province, Margot said that she goes to spend time with them on visits. However, in addition to the visits, whenever her daughters and their husbands have something in their working or social lives that need attention, Margot offers to travel to where they live to take care of the grandchildren.

Marion was very definitive about her commitment to her grandchildren, saying,

I have retired after working many years as a health professional so I have a lot of time to focus on helping my son and daughter with their children. I think at the core I have the same values as my own grandparents. I want to pass those on to my grandchildren. I don't want to be the babysitter, I want to be the grandmother. However, when the need arises, I will be there for my grandchildren and in turn my children.

Owen is a very conservative, quiet man and doesn't consider himself to be very good at household kinds of things such as cooking for children. He seemed to enjoy telling about his unsuccessful experiences with making spaghetti for his own daughter when she was a little girl. However, he was quick to learn how to help and give support with the care of his infant grandson when his daughter was in hospital for a few days. He told about how he paced the floor hour after hour trying to sooth his crying grandson. He sees himself as simply a backup support for when emergencies arise. He leaves much of the care to his wife, the grandmother. When I was in the presence of Owen with his grandson, I noticed that he took his crawling grandson and carried him in his arms when he observed him crying. However, as soon as the child's mother came into the room and the child continued squirming, Owen reinforced, in a very caring way, the parameters of his role as a grandfather, when he said,

Alright, Mother, here he is. He's yours. You can take him now.

He seemed to be suggesting that he would be there as a backup but as soon as the parents are around and available then he was more comfortable leaving the responsibility of the childcare to his daughter, the parent.

Owen remembers that, as a child, one of his grandmothers was very serious and somewhat strict with grandchildren. She would chide them for whispering or for giggling. She didn't babysit him at all. If his parents were busy in the gardens, or with haymaking and other jobs the children would, more often than not, be working (in their own way) with the parents. It was expected that the grandchildren would be obedient to the grandparents and provide support for them, when it was deemed necessary. For example, he remembers doing simple chores like picking berries and running to the general store next door, for his grandmother.

Marion only knew one set of grandparents because her mother was raised in an orphanage. Her statement seemed to capture the essence of what other grandparents had to say about their own grandparents and also about how they viewed their roles with their own grandchildren.

One's past experiences can influence the way you mother and grandmother. I have good feelings about my paternal grandmother. She was religious. She lived in Toronto and would return in the summertime to Clarenville. We would travel from Corner Brook by train, across the province, to visit with her. The visit was always a wonderful experience. I remember her being so busy and hardworking with cooking, cleaning, tending to the henhouse and berrypicking. While we were not in her presence very often, when we were, she certainly acted like a prudent parent towards us. Everything seemed to be right with the world when we were at her house. She was like a second parent to us. However, she didn't babysit us. I'm sure if there had been an emergency she would have cared for us. When we were around her she was like a backup for our parents. That's the way I am today with my grandchildren, except that I'm not working outside the home anymore. Being a retired professional I have more money than she had and this gives me more opportunity to buy things for my grandchildren.

I don't see myself as my grandchildren's caregiver or babysitter but I care deeply for them and feel as though I am a backup...just in case I am needed.

Grandparents as Teachers and Learners

The four grandparents in this study showed a lot of concern for their grandchildren's learning and overall success, both academically and in extracurricular activities. They also realized the necessity of themselves becoming lifelong learners in order to communicate with and keep pace with their grandchildren. While they had memories of their own grandparents praising them for some of their successes they could not recall their grandparents actually teaching them anything specific. They viewed themselves as being different from their grandparents, in this regard. Whenever there was an opportunity they were interested in teaching their grandchildren some of the skills that they felt they needed to acquire. They also considered themselves to be people who were willing to learn new things (especially when it comes to technological skills) so that they could communicate with their grandchildren.

Marion explained,

I think many grandparents of today are lifelong learners and they want to keep pace with changes in society and with their grandchildren. There's more of a tendency for us today to try to keep up with the child's interests, books, music, and activities...maybe this gives them that sense of entitlement that we so often complain about these days. Years ago we were expected, as children, to yield to grandparents' interests and wishes. Our grandparents tended to resist our ideas and our activities. As children, we would hear them say, "What is the world coming to? We were never like that." They wanted us to learn their ways.

For special occasions and when buying presents for their grandchildren, Margot explained,

Well, we're very aware of the importance of education and it's habitual that when we are looking for a gift for our grandchildren we tend to try to find things that have some educational component to them.

Marion had a similar outlook and pointed out that she has gotten to know which children's authors and titles are of a high quality. She explained,

Well, I buy good books for my grandchildren because I want them to be readers and I think this will help them to learn. I see myself as being one of their teachers. Education is very important to me and I want this for my grandchildren, so every opportunity I get I'm teaching them through reading or singing. I sing to them all the time. Just the other day I was on Skype with my 3 ½ year old grand-daughter who lives in Ottawa. She was happy to tell me, "Grandma, as I'm reading my book I'm practicing singing The Twelve Days of Christmas." I also email her. She has her own website.

For special circumstances I send her a book in the mail. Recently I sent her a book and put a note in it telling her to get well. I have learned to use the social media so that I can be in touch with my grandchildren. This helps to break down the distance for us and we don't seem so far apart. One day when we were on Skype my granddaughter called out, "Look at me, Grandma, I'm having cinnamon on my toast." Then later in the conversation, she said, "Good-bye Grandma and Poppy, I'm turning off the computer myself."

Owen, however, leaves the educating to the parents. He says that he usually gives them a toy for special occasions but doesn't focus too much on the educational aspects of the toys. He pointed out,

I try to get them interested in things I enjoy. I really like hockey so I gave each one of my little grandsons (ages one and three) a hockey stick and a soft puck for Christmas. I like watching sports on television and already my three-year-old grandson is enjoying it as well. I'm away from them for much of the year so I don't see myself as playing much of a teaching role. I tell them right from wrong and that's about it. My daughters are educated so they know a lot about what kinds of things they should have for their children to help them learn. We usually ask our daughters what they would like us to buy for their children.

Owen and his wife (the grandmother) are concerned with supporting their daughters and their daughters' husbands, in their plans for their children. While he sees a role for him in teaching them right from wrong, he basically leaves the teaching and learning responsibilities to the parents.

Margot, who spent most of her career as an educator, claims that she sees a role for herself with the teaching and learning. She has read to her grandchildren on Skype. She looks for any opportunities to support their learning and literacy development. She buys books for them, reads to them and takes them to drama productions, art exhibits, and musicals.

Like Margot, Jake sees a role for himself in terms of the teaching and learning. Even though his grandchildren live close by and he sees them on a regular basis, he uses every opportunity to write and read to them. He has already written a book about his past, to his grandchildren, in the hopes that when they are old enough to understand they will be able to read this book and learn about their heritage. Jake seems compelled to ensure that his grandchildren know about their roots. Jake also engages his grandson in conversation. Talk and experiential learning has been very much a part of their relationship with each other. For example, he talked about an activity, with his grandson, where they collaborated on decorating an outdoor tree. While the tree was being decorated, Jake kept his grandson engaged through conversation and hands on experiences with the decorating.

Each of the grandparents seemed to think that their grandchildren had very good, capable parents so they didn't feel the need to worry about teaching them. Owen described what seemed to be the perspectives of all of the grandparents in terms of their teaching role. He pointed out that, he believed he should,

> support their children's expectations for their children and when necessary to help but not to interfere with the child-rearing.

All of the grandparents seemed to recognize the importance of being able to communicate with their grandchildren using the technologies that are available to them. Owen, Marion, and Margot, who have grandchildren 'living away,' considered the use of e-mail, Skype and Facebook very important when it comes to keeping in touch with their grandchildren.

Margot said,

> It's as if you are there in the room with them. You can watch them grow. It's so real. In the past, if one lived some distance away from the grandparents they might not get to know them because they didn't have tools like Skype to keep the grandchildren close. Engaging with them through the social networking systems helps them to learn how to use these systems and it also helps to keep in touch.

Owen, shared some of the same sentiments, except that he didn't focus on the educational aspect of social networking,

> I did not know my other grandparents very well because we would go months and sometime maybe a year without seeing them. I knew that my other grandmother did a lot of knitting and quilting because she used to send those things to us when we were children. I hardly knew what these grandparents looked like. Today I see my grandchildren regularly through Skype but I still don't see myself as having a teaching role when it comes to my grandchildren. I leave that to the parents.

All of the grandparents saw some differences in terms of the roles their grandparents played with their learning. Owen and Jake claimed that their grandparents might have taught them practical kinds of life skills but in terms of literacy-type skills that was pretty much left to the schools. Any teaching that grandparents did was usually associated with religion, values, and life skills. Today both Owen and Jake tend to want to have fun with their own grandchildren so they teach them skills associated with play.

While Marion's and Margot's grandparents did not play much of a role in terms of teaching them and they did not try to learn new knowledge which would enable them to be able to relate to them as grandchildren, Marion and Margot themselves consider their own roles as grandparents to be very much involved with teaching and learning. They were very aware of what they could do to support their grandparents' learning and their own learning.

Grandparents as Friends

Each of the grandparents talked about how special it was to have grandchildren and they maintained that they enjoyed playing with them as friends and playmates would do. They saw themselves as very different from their own grandparents, in this regard. Jake suggested that,

> Even though I enjoyed being with my grandparents and they were kind and loving people, I don't think they saw me as someone to play with as I do my own grandson. My mother worked in town so my grandparents were caregivers while she was at work. My grandparents led very busy lives, just to make a living. So there wasn't a lot of time for play, especially during the daytime.

> However, I do engage in play with my own grandson. My wife takes on more of a caregiving role. Between the two of us we give a lot of attention to our grandchildren. We are very conscious of not spoiling them. Certainly there's an element of friendship.

Owen took a similar stance, and suggested that his relationship with his grandparents was positive. They lived next door so in a way they were almost like parents to Owen. He knew he could trust them and they wanted what was best for him. He enjoyed being around his grandmother, for example, but he didn't view her as a friend.

> She didn't play games with us. She gave us instructions and orders, and she would discipline us when necessary. I held her in high esteem and felt the need to be obedient to her. So if she asked me to run errands or bring in wood for her stove, then I responded immediately. It was the thing to do.

He pointed out how,

> In our time, it was expected of us. We knew that we had to support our grandparents in this way. If we picked berries we would give some of them to our grandmother. If we caught a fish we would share it with our grandmother. I think in today's world the grandparents are the ones who feel responsible for the sharing and the giving. Our grandparents always seemed to be above us and our friends, not our grandparents, were the children we played with.

Some grandparents saw their own grandparents as authority figures, as opposed to friends. Owen remembers how one of his grandmothers would try to discipline him and his siblings by using threats.

> She used to threaten us with the 'Booman.' She would say, "The booman will get you if you're not good." I wouldn't consider my grandparents as friends. They were grandparents and as grandparents they had a different role. I don't really see myself as a friend for my grandchildren, either. On second thought, I suppose there's an element of friendship in our relationship because I do have a bit of fun with them.

Marion, too, did not experience her grandparents as 'friends' or playmates. She said that there was the "odd time" when one grandmother would play cards with her but that was a rare occasion.

> They didn't play with us. So I didn't view them as friends. I think I saw my grandmother as a very special person but not a friend. I held her in high esteem. Today my grandchildren see me as someone to play with as well as a grandmother. My little grandson in Vancouver will question 'his poppy' about the way he says words. So it's almost as if he sees him as an equal and maybe a friend. Years ago, we would never question the way our grandparents talked or any of their behaviours.

Margot sees an element of friendship in her relationship with her older grandchildren. She told of activities which she engages in with her teenage and older grandchildren.

> We go to movies and the theatre together. We go for walks. I didn't do those things with my own grandparents. We lived somewhat separate lives, in this regard. My grandparents spent time with their age group and my friends were usually children.

CONCLUSIONS AND IMPLICATIONS

Van Manen (1997) explains the absence of a final conclusion by describing phenomenological research as a "poetizing activity" where interpretation and significance are left, in large part, to the reader. In this study the voice of each individual grandparent is valued as it helps to illuminate the essence of the shared experiences of Newfoundland and Labrador grandparents.

Along with changes in society has come changes in the status of grandparents and they are generally not viewed as having the same kind of authority and patriarchal or matriarchal control. Grandparents are enjoying their grandchildren and taking pride in their accomplishments and are more inclined to move into the pop culture and literacies (email, Skype, Facebook) of the grandchildren as they endorse a "pleasure without responsibility" orientation toward the role of grandparent. Grandparents are learning as the grandchildren are learning. Grandparents of today tend to have a natural role of a lifelong learner (e.g., in the use of technology) because they want to have meaningful experiences and conversation with their grandchildren. Because grandparents are deferring to grandchildren, in their willingness to learn what they need to in order to keep pace with them, this may contribute to a sense of entitlement in the grandchildren of today.

As the roles of women change and many return to work or wait until they are older to start their families, many grandparents have retired and are in a position to provide some childcare support. Another important contribution of grandparents, as referenced from the childhood experiences of the grandparents in the study, was that they gave them a sense of security regardless of the roles they played in their day-to-day living. All of the grandparents in the study felt that unconditional love for their grandchildren and even though they didn't view themselves as babysitters they did admit that they would embrace that role if it was necessary, in order to help their own children. The grandparents felt very positive about their grandchildren and claimed that they reaped a lot of joy from having them around. However, they all agreed that the rearing of the grandchildren was left to the parents.

Grandparenthood and the special relationship that occurs between grandparent and grandchild function as a resource by bridging the past, present, and future for grandchildren, giving a sense of security, aiding in ego development, and offering a vision of the future (Baranowski, 1982; Kornhaber & Woodward, 1981). All of the grandparents in the study were concerned about passing on stories and information about their roots and their culture.

Significance of this Study

The experiences of a particular group of grandparents provides a lens through which the roles of grandparents can be viewed from their perspectives. While the results of a phenomenological study such as this, are not meant to be generalizable, this type of inquiry can provide an informed starting point for future research on grandparents' perceptions of how they experience their grandparenting roles. The results will add depth and breadth to the limited knowledge that exists around Newfoundland and Labrador grandparents' perceptions of their lived experiences and may provide a general insight into grandparents' lifeworlds (Van Manen, 1997). As Barritt (1986) writes, "As with the child, at play, who creates meaning and self at the same time, so we, who try to understand human [the grandparent] experience, also contribute to its transformation" (p. 21).

REFLECTION QUESTIONS

1. The author refers to the notion of research in the area of grandparenting, historically, as the following: "...reflect back comfortable, tidy images of grandparents in traditional roles", the notion of 'packaging' and conceptualizing 'the truth'. What are some of the concerns with this "packaging of the truth"?

2. The author refers to the fact that, in the past, grandparents did not have time for grandchildren. How would you account for this statement, from the chapter, this text, and your own experiences?

3. The chapter suggests that the grandparent-grandchild roles have changed. In the past, grandchildren were expected to be there to help out the grandparents; today, grandparents are expected to help out the grandchildren. Discuss these changing roles.

4. The author talks about one theme being the grandparents as teachers. Some grandparents appear to not view life-long learning as education. How would you ensure that "education" is clearly defined and explored if you were doing this research study?

APPENDIX B

Interview Questions

The following questions were used to develop a rapport with the research participants and to guide the interview and conversation.

- Age (50s-60s; 70s-80s); Gender; Where do you live? How long have you lived here? Where did you live before?
- Why did you move? Are you retired if so, what was your occupation? If not, what is your occupation?
- What do you remember about your grandparents? Were your grandparents involved in helping you to learn?
- Do you feel that you have valuable things to say to your grandchildren? To share with your grandchildren?
- Do your grandchildren live in Newfoundland?
- Do you feel that other people listen to what you have to say?
- Do you make yourself heard when you disagree with people?
- Do you have influence within your family?
- Which of your skills do you share with your grandchildren?
- Do you share your family history with your grandchildren? Explain.
- Do you share your cultural experiences with your grandchildren? Explain.
- Do you try to teach your grandchildren?
- Do grandchildren learn from you? If so, what?
- How often do you see your grandchildren?
- Does your relationship with your children affect your relationship with your grandchildren?
- Do you take your grandchildren on outings?
- How do you communicate with your grandchildren? Which mode of communication do you use?
- Have you read to your grandchildren? Explain.
- Do you celebrate special occasions with your grandchildren?

- Do you feel that your grandchildren are an important part of your life?
- Do your grandchildren need you? Do you need your grandchildren?
- Are you involved in the daily life of your grandchildren?
- What is your favourite way of communication, generally?
- What is your favourite social thing to do with your grandchildren?
- How do you feel about your role as a grandparent compared to the roles of grandparents from your childhood?
- Do you use your expertise when it comes to dealing with belief systems?
- Is your relationship with your grandchildren different from your relationship with your own children? Explain.
- Do you feel that you are an effective Grandparent? Explain.
- What legacy will you leave your grandchildren (material or otherwise)?
- Thank you for your time, effort and interest.

REFERENCES

Barrell, B., & Hammett, R. (Eds.) (2000). *Advocating change: Contemporary issues in subject English.* Toronto: Irwin Publishing Ltd.

Barritt, L. (1986). "Human sciences and the human image". *Phenomenology and Pedagogy, 4*(3), 14–22.

Bowering Delisle, J. (2008). The Newfoundland Diaspora: A Thesis submitted in partial fulfilment of the requirements for the degree of Doctor of Philosophy in the Faculty of Graduate Studies (English): UBC.

Coles, L. (2008). *Children's lived experiences with readin: A phenomenological study.* Memorial University: Doctoral Dissertation.

Coles, L. (2011). "The books we like are not in that box." Children unveil their lived experiences with literacy in n elementary school. (Paper Presentation at the 17th European Conference on Reading: Lietracy and Diversity) in Mons, Belgium.

Creswell, J.W. (1998*). Qualitative inquiry and research design: Choosing among five traditions.* Thousand Oaks, CA: SAGE Publications.

Government of Newfoundland and Labrador, Department of Education (2000). *Words to live by: A strategic literacy plan for Newfoundland and Labrador 2000.* St. John=s, NL: Office of the Queen=s Printer.

Hiller, H.H., & Franz, T.M. (2004). "New ties, old ties and lost ties: The use of the Internet in diaspora." *New Media & Society, 6*(6), 731–52.

Kivnick, H.Q. (1982). "Grandparenthood: An overview of meaning and mental health". *The Gerontologist, 22,* 59–66.

Kornhaber, A., & Woodward, K.L. (1981). *Grandparents/Grandchildren: The vital connection.* Garden City, NY: Anchor Press/Doubleday.

Kress, G. (2003). *Literacy in the new media age.* New York: Routledge.

Kruk, E. (1995). "Grandparent-grandchild contact loss: Findings from a study of "Grandparent Rights" members". *Canadian Journal on Aging, 14,* 737–754.

Kvale, S. (1996). *Interviews: An introduction to qualitative research interviewing.* CA: SAGE Publications.

Leahy Johnson, C., & Barer, B. (1987). "Marital instability and the changing kinship networks of grandparents". *The Gerontologist, 27*(3), 330–335.

Lloyd-Smith, M., & Tarr, J. (2000). "Researching children=s perspectives: A sociological dimension". In A. Lewis, & G.   es (pp. 59–70). PA: Open University Press.

Luke, C. (2000). "Cyber-schooling and technological change". In Cope & Kalantzis, (Eds.), *Multiliteracies: Literacy learning and the design of social futures* (pp.69–91). London. UK: Routledge.

Moustakas, C. (1994). *Phenomenological research methods*. Thousand Oaks, CA: SAGE Publications.

Polio, H.R., Henley, T.B., & Thompson, C.J. (1997). *The phenomenology of everyday life*. Cambridge, UK: Cambridge University Press.

Sheffer, G. (2003). *Diaspora politics*. New York: Cambridge University Press.

Statistics Canada 2001. Census. <http://www12.statcan.ca/english/census01/home/index.cfm>.

Statistics Canada 2006. Census. <http://www12.statcan.ca/english/census06/release/index.cfm>.

Sussman, M.B. (1960). "Intergenerational family relationships and social role changes in middle age". *Journal of Gerontology, 15*, 71–75.

Van Manen, M. (Ed.) (2002). *Writing in the dark: Phenomenological studies in interpretive inquiry*. London, ON: The Althouse Press.

Van Manen, M. (1997). *Researching lived experience: Human science for an action sensitive pedagogy*. (2nd ed.) London, ON: The Althouse Press.

Wilson, K.B., & DeShane, M.R. (1982). "The legal rights of grandparents: Preliminary discussion". *The Gerontologist, 22*(1), 67–71.

PAULINE LAKE & MARLENE GEORGE

PARENTING TWO GENERATIONS

Reflections and Discovery

> The presence of a grandparent confirms that parents were, indeed, little ones, too, and that people who are little can grow to be big, can become parents, and one day even have grandchildren of their own. So often we think of grandparents as belonging to the past; but in this important way, grandparents, for young children, belong to the future. ~Fred Rogers

In this chapter we will share our reflections on the part our parents and grandparents played in shaping our present role in parenting two generations. We wish to honour our generations past for the legacy gifts we have received and are now passing on to our grandchildren. It is through this reflection that we have discovered the immeasurable value of the legacy of generations past that births the hope of generations to come.

Pauline Becoming a Grandmother

When I heard the news that my daughter and son were becoming parents and that both grandchildren were expected in the same month, nostalgia washed over me. I remembered my own journey as a new mother, my children as little ones, and the instrumental role my mother played in caring for me and my children. I was struck with the passing of time and with the wonder and awe of life as I awaited the births of my two grandchildren. I wondered what my role as grandmother would be. Dim memories of my grandparents became clearer.

My daughter, Karen and her husband lived in the same city as I did; my son, John and his wife lived in Alberta. I saw my daughter frequently and observed the new life growing within her. I was present for her baby's ultrasound and for her admission to the hospital. I remember feeling a cluster of emotions as I experienced the overwhelming worry and concern for my daughter, pride and respect in how she managed her labour and delivery and the incredible joy of seeing my daughter with her child. When I was given this little miracle to hold, I was overwhelmed with his little heartbeat, the warmth of his breath and the intensity of love I was feeling for my adorable little grandson, Benjamin. I had become a grandmother!

My son, John had left home and Newfoundland and Labrador (NL) at the tender age of 19 and was gone three years when his father died. Now, just six years after his father's death, he was becoming a father himself. He and his wife lived in

A. Singh and M. Devine (Eds.), Rural Transformation and Newfoundland and Labrador Diaspora: Grandparents, Grandparenting, Community and School Relations, 177–186.
© 2013 Sense Publishers. All rights reserved.

Alberta and, due to the geographical distance between us, our only contact during her pregnancy was by phone. When I received my son's anxious phone call that his wife was in hospital and required an emergency caesarean section, I was filled with concern and excitement. I thought about how my mother had experienced her daughter's stillbirth, death of a grandchild and the birth of two other grandchildren with disabilities. I was struck with the realization of how difficult these experiences must have been for her as a mother and as a grandmother. My tears of memory and concern transformed to tears of joy with the next phone call from my son, the proud father of a baby girl, my first granddaughter, Emma. It was two long weeks before I held Emma and looked at her amazing little face, a face I would always love, a face with a smile like her father's.

The anticipation of my grandchildren involved a period of waiting for something big to happen that I knew would forever change my children's lives and mine. It was a time of reflection and a time of discovery. In reflecting on the roles of my grandparents and my children's grandparents, I discovered a greater awareness of myself and the values, beliefs, and culture that shaped me. I embraced the spirit of generations past as I welcomed precious new breath into my life, my family and the world.

Marlene Becoming a Grandmother

That amazing moment when I became a grandmother was a moment more precious than years. It seemed time stood still briefly as I was conscience of the realization that this moment now marked my life over five generations. I was fortunate to have had three of my grandparents living for my growing up years. I had observed my own parents in their active grandparenting roles to our four daughters (as well as my husband's parents). Now in this moment, as I held my grandson for the first time, realizing he was bone of my bone, and flesh of my flesh, I was overwhelmed with the meaning of this moment in time.

I was present for my first grandchild, Camden's birth, which meant traveling in the wee hours of the morning once we got the phone call that Rachelle was in labour. It just seemed right that as her mom I would be present in the case room as she became a mom. I'm sure I broke every blood vessel in my face pushing with every contraction Rachelle had. After quite some time, and much hard work, the doctor announced her baby was too big to deliver and he prepared her for an emergency caesarean section. I felt relief for both Rachelle and baby yet I was saddened that I couldn't be with my little girl the moment my grandson was to be born (even though her hubby was). I cried, we prayed for the next little while and then came my son-in-law pushing this 11 pound 8 ounce baby boy back from the O.R. I had never seen a new born baby that big before (his mother was 9 pounds, 13 ounces). While I was overwhelmed with joy at the safe arrival of our grandson, this picture was not right. I remember questioning, 'where is my daughter? ...is she alright? ...why isn't her baby with her? It didn't seem right that we were passing around her baby boy and she wasn't present with us for this memorable moment, (she was not allowed to leave the recovery room until she began to have some feeling in her lower limbs). It was in those very first moments of becoming 'Nana' that I sensed my parental concern for now two generations. While I rejoiced in the safe arrival of my grandson, a new generation in our family, my concern for the generation before (my daughter, his mother) was none the less intense. As soon as Rachelle was back in her room and her bouncing baby boy was placed on her breast, he too settled, reunited with his mom who had carried him for all those months before. Seeing my daughter with her baby and witnessing her natural ability to bond and care for him was like watching myself in a mirror and feeling all those maternal feelings for what was now two generations.

When my grandson was born, I knew that I had already invested 24 years of parenting into this baby boy in parenting his mom, my daughter. I was very cognizant of the fact as well that my parents and my grandparents also had an investment in the life of this baby boy because of their parenting and grandparenting influence on my life. Lois Wyse said, "Grandchildren are the dots that connect the lines from generation to generation." In that moment more precious than years, when my grandson was born I rejoiced, another generational dot had been connected.

> *"Through their presence or their absence, our grandparents leave their lasting mark on generations to come." Author Unknown*

Pauline Remembering Grandparents

My mother's parents died before I was born, however I grew up listening to my mother's stories about them. Her father, "Poppa" worked as a whale fisherman on the Labrador and would be away from home for months. My mother told stories of the excitement when Poppa returned home and of what his presence meant to her mother and the family. He played games like "ducking for apples" and spoke "Eskimo" Inuit, teaching them to say the "Hail Mary" in the "Eskimo's" language. My mother told of her father's wisdom, of how well read he was, of his devotion to family and church and his generosity towards his neighbours. Her proud voice would drift off at the end of her stories when she would say, as if more to herself than to her children, how difficult it must have been for him to leave "mother". "Mother", my maternal grandmother, was a strong woman emotionally, however physically she was frail and often sickly. The only two pictures I remember of both my grandparents reflected Poppa's physical strength and "Mother's" frailty. I will always remember the sadness in my mother's face and voice as she spoke of her mother's gentleness, caring and strength in parenting seven children, mostly on her own. My mother told many stories of my grandmother's hospitality towards the poor and of her deep faith in God and church. As a child, I often wished that my mother's parents were alive for my mother and for me. I had a longing for grandparents who were strong and gentle, who would play games and tell stories and grandparents who would most certainly love me, grandparents who would be so different than the Nanny I had in my father's mother.

Nanny was left a widow at an early age and raised a family of five on her own by operating a general store, keeping boarders, ("rich" people from St. John's who came to our area to fish and hunt), and by taking in clothes to sew. I never heard stories about my grandfather and the only picture I saw was a large oval framed one that hung in our parlour. Nanny was 85 when I was born and I remember her as a small woman with white hair tied back in a bun who always wore a black dress with a white apron tied about her waist, black stockings and black shoes. For the fourteen years I knew her, she perched herself on the couch in our kitchen by the window that looked out at the entrance of the general store that was now operated by my father. As a child, I felt that Nanny thought the shop was still hers because she always had a say in what my father did there. Nanny had the biggest bedroom in our house and I was not allowed to go into her room without permission from her, permission that I seldom received. She had no time or interest in music or "carrying on" and her cane would tap loudly on her bedroom floor if such "carrying on" took place after her early bedtime.

As a child, I thought that nanny didn't have much interest in me, that she didn't want to "be bothered" with me and therefore I didn't relate much with her. She did shock me once when she gave give me 10 cents for a Bible and she often played the card game, crib with me; however, I was sure she cheated because it seemed she always won. In spite of the lack of affection I felt for her, Nanny's presence was a comfort of sorts, she was like a fixture that would always be there. There was a definite routine to her day that my family's life went around. I knew she was significant in my life because she was my father's mother. She was a focal point of our family life and when she died at 99 years, I knew someone really important had died. As a child, I did not realize the value of this hard working and loving grandmother, however I do remember the silence and emptiness in our home when she died and the loneliness I felt not having her perched on our couch.

Marlene Remembering Grandparents

My treasured childhood memories of my Nanny Brace and Nan and Pop Canning are certainly measured for their quality and not quantity. Those memories were limited to three precious weeks during the summer when my family made our annual pilgrimage back from the 'mainland' to the homeland, Newfoundland, to reconnect to our roots. My parents were Salvation Army clergy and were transferred from Newfoundland in the mid 60's to communities in Nova Scotia and Ontario. From the time I was four until I was eighteen, the highlight of my year was our return trip to two rural Newfoundland communities (Birchy Bay and Green's Harbour), my parents' hometowns. These communities and the homes of our grandparents became the epic centre of all that breathed Newfoundland and HOME to me. It was no easy or inexpensive task back in the 60's and 70's for my parents to pack up four children every summer and head back to Newfoundland for three short weeks but it was a non-negotiable. Mom and Dad valued their relationship with their parents and extended family so much that trips to Disney World or southern climates paled in comparison to the pull that brought us back to Nan and Pop's every summer of my growing up years.

There was always a warm welcome awaiting us at Nan and Pops (and Nanny Brace's too) as we walked across the garden with suitcases in hand (no driveways back then) to get to their house down by the water. In the early days there was no running water or indoor bathrooms in either of my grandparents houses but we always seemed to adapt quickly to brushing our teeth from a cup, recycling Eaton's and Sears' catalogues in the out-house, and having our Saturday bath in the big wash tub. I remember the light of the kerosene lamp and Poppy with his straight leg crossed sitting by the radio listening to the evening news. My grandfather loved to tell stories and the kitchen table was the gathering place for family tales, songs and laughter. My grandmothers, although they didn't know each other well, were in many ways similar. They were diligent homemakers, hard workers, and loving mothers to their children and grandchildren. It's not that they said it a lot but their presence spoke of love and home and you got the feeling they were glad to have you there. Both my paternal and maternal grandparents were devout Christians who were very involved in their local Salvation Army church community. They were people of prayer. I often heard my grandparents pray at church and around the family table. They demonstrated in their lifestyle a slogan of The Salvation Army, "Heart to God and Hand to Man." I'd heard the stories of the early years when many times my grandparents' home became home for travellers along the coasts of Newfoundland (before the roads were through) and often clergy and denominational teachers found 'home' at my grandparents' house as well. This spirit of hospitality continued through the years and generations because as teenagers there were a number of times when our friends found 'home' at our house as our parents welcomed them into our family. My siblings and I would also bring our 'mainland' friends to Newfoundland to visit with us at Nan and Pop's as well and they were always welcomed.

My grandparents have given me a legacy not of material riches or grandeur but a legacy of hospitality with their "open heart – open home," unwritten policy. They have given me spiritual roots that are not pious or self-righteous but of people who walk humbly before their God. They have instilled in me the absolute high priority of staying connected with family through the years and across the miles. I recall with tear glazed eyes even now the hard farewells as our family and extended family would gather at the end of the garden on the morning of our departure for another year. My Nan and Mom would embrace and the tears would flow. What followed was similar to a funeral procession as this deep rooted family would ache with the anticipated separation for yet another year. We traveled away in those days. Since then my grandparents have traveled away to their heavenly home and though they are physically absent, their presence of legacy is leaving their lasting mark on generations to come. For this I am thankful.

> The very fact that you don't look or act or feel like the grandparents of even a generation ago does not mean that you are less, but that you are more — in effect, an evolved form of grandparents, primed to do a bigger and more challenging job than any group before you. ~Arthur Kornhaber

Nana Pauline

I always loved the Matryoshka nesting dolls. I like how each doll fits into the other. When I became Nana, my role as daughter, granddaughter, and mother became nested in my role as Nana and I became more as a person. It was like a big wind had taken my children and I into another place as my son and daughter welcomed their own children. When my next two grandchildren, Sean and Olivia were born, I was overjoyed with sheer delight and gratitude at their births. I now had confidence that I would establish my own unique relationship with them as I had with their older siblings. The great wind had brought me to a place of truth in that, long after my grandparents and my children's grandparents are gone, their gifts of self will continue to resonate over time. I am more confident that in being who I am, I am able to build my own precious link with my grandchildren. I am living the amusement and joy of my children's paternal grandmother's words, "Every crow thinks her own is the blackest". I am confident that when my grandchildren snuggle up with their paternal great grandparents, that they feel the meaning of those words too.

I wanted to be the best Nana I could be and in the beginning I had a mix of joy and anxiety of how I was going to accomplish this role. I wanted to be an "expert" whenever my children called for support and advice. However, with new kinds of diapers, came new information on feeding, blankets and sleeping positions and I was often the one who needed to learn and to be open to new approaches. There was a period of a year that my four grandchildren and their parents lived in another province. It was a very unsettling time for me. I wondered what the effects of the geographical distance would be on my relationship with my grandchildren and wanted to provide my children with support in their parenting roles. Isn't that what grandparents do? Nanny had provided order and consistency in my life by her very presence. My children had their paternal and maternal grandparents living in close proximity, playing an active role in their daily lives providing them with attention, care and guidance. How was I to grandparent children who lived in another province of Canada? My daughter and her family have since moved back to Newfoundland, however, I continue to have my two granddaughters living away.

Then, there is the dilemma of being one of the "young crowd" of "Nanas". I work full time outside my home and am involved in volunteer activities related to my work. I take educational courses and attend conferences nationally and internationally. When my first two grandchildren were born, I was completing my Masters of Social Work degree. I and my second husband also enjoy ballroom dancing, hiking and travelling. HOW CAN I BE THE NANA I WANT TO BE? Simply said, I trust that my grandchildren will know me by the love that they feel from me and the priority I give them in my life. I find creative ways to balance the demands of my work life with ways to see my grandchildren and to provide assistance to my children in their parenting roles.

I prioritize the relationships with my children and grandchildren. My daughter and family are living just five minutes from me and I have frequent contact with them. We share meals together, I arrange monthly sleepovers with my grandsons, Ben and Sean, pick them up once a week from school and schedule times to see them participate in sports and other activities. Everything from sharing a treat at Chapters to taking them for several days once a year while their parents are holidaying provides me with the opportunity to build relationship with them and to be a part of their lives.

I am no longer concerned about how the distance will prevent me from establishing a relationship with my son's two daughters. I am thankful that my son and his wife prioritize a yearly visit home and I visit them once or sometimes twice a year. We have regular phone contact and we use skype. My son and daughter-in-law email pictures on a regular basis that keeps me included in what my granddaughters are doing. My granddaughters, at three and seven years, phone me themselves which is just wonderful. I have also stayed with my granddaughters for several days to allow their parents to holiday and to give me an opportunity to '…have them all to myself'.

With my four grandchildren, I share stories of childhood (mine and their parents), take them to church to share how I express my spirituality and participate in their interests and activities. Knowing that I would treasure my grandchildren is not a surprise to me. The example of grandparenting that I witnessed in my children's grandparents and in the presence and stories of my own grandparents are rich with stories of love, attachment, commitment, growth, forgiveness and choices based on spiritual values. These stories have not stopped for they have become part of my story that I continue to share with my children and grandchildren.

Our stories also have unexpected turns. I did not expect to experience the heavy grief of becoming a widow at 45 years of age. I now understand on a deeper level Nanny's black clothing. I did not expect to remarry at 57 and widen my family circle to include my husband's three children and his son's daughter, Mikinlee. I know that my husband's children's acceptance of me will play a significant part in how my relationship with Mikinlee will evolve. Regardless of how I am accepted, I know that I have accepted my widened circle. The good news is that when right lessons are learned and absorbed into our attitude of living, there is an openness to cherish everyone. I am thankful for Mikinlee who regardless of bloodline, will add beauty to my life and I look forward to my Nana role in her life.

I regard my grandchildren as the great gifts of my life and I am awestruck everyday with what I receive from them. They have blessed me with the opportunity to see my children, Karen and John, as loving and caring parents and my son, Neil and his wife, as a devoted and loving uncle and aunt who arrange holidays and time with their nephews and nieces. My grandchildren's sense of wonder and their eagerness for adventure has helped me to rediscover my sense of wonder in things I had come to take for granted. My grandchildren's joy is spontaneous and springs up when I least expect it. It is as if life is magical and everything is a miracle. Their playfulness, laughter and joy increases my fascination with life, enriches my sense of self and influences how I participate in my relationships, my work, and my activities. They have stirred echoes of generations past and have given me a greater potential for love and life. My grandchildren have helped me to step aside and let my children become adults as I continue to love them as adults. And someday, when I am gone, they will, I know, remember me.

Nana Marlene

Prior to my grandson's birth, my daughter established that I would not be called 'Nanny', or 'Grandma' but my distinct title would be, 'Nana'. In all of the generations of grandparenting in our family, I would be the first, Nana! I approved of this distinct title that belonged only to me (his paternal grandmother is 'Nanny'). I became a grandmother at the age of 47 (going on 35) so in my mind too, 'grandma' and 'nanny' belonged to ladies much older than I.

I am extremely close to both of my grandsons and have been from the moment of their births. In many ways I feel like their second mother because I am my daughter's first choice caregiver for them if she is not with them and even at times when she is with them and needing a rest.

I was supposed to travel to Thailand the summer Camden was born but it was impossible for me to leave Rachelle and her first born baby at such a critical time. I recalled the first three weeks after Rachelle was born, my mom was out of the province and I missed not having her with me as I adjusted to this new role. I was determined that if at all possible I would spend the first few weeks with Rachelle helping her to adjust to the wonderful world of 'mommy-hood.' I did the same when her second son was born. In fact I was scheduled to be in London, England on work related business for eight weeks around the time Cullen was due to be born. Much to the dismay of my professional organization, I had to turn down the opportunity when Rachelle announced her second baby was due during that time. In the heart of this Nana, there is no professional development opportunity that is worth missing the birth of my second grandchild and being there for my daughter at this special time in their lives – parenting two generations. I purposefully schedule 'Nana' days to spend special times with my grandsons. My husband and I are both very active in the lives of our children and grandchildren and I am so thankful to be living in the same community as them. This is a blessing that I did not have a generation before.

In my professional work role I am required to help people navigate through many stressors in life and often I am asked what is my stress management plan. I am happy to report the healing power of spending quality time with my grandsons whether we are having a 'snuggle' or exploring the world when I am Nana, I am stress free.

Our grandsons are learning the importance of family ties that are binding over four generations. My parents, who are now retired and living in the same community, are actually more active in the lives of their great grandsons than they were able to be in the lives of their grandchildren (because of geographical distance). Although my parents are in their mid-seventies, my grandsons look forward to those afternoons spent with 'Nanny' and 'Poppy' Brace.

Being a Nana has become so much more fun and intimate for me than being a 'grandchild' was and it may have something to do with the old saying 'absence makes the heart grow fonder.' As a child, 'absence' kept me from having a truly intimate relationship with my grandparents and this is something I longed for. Today our family is experiencing a paradigm shift in having four generations living in the same community – something that, as a child, I could only have dreamed of. This reality perhaps gives roots to my strong desire to be very present (often) in the lives of our grandsons.

I can't honestly say that being a "Nana" is more fun than being a "Mom" because I dearly loved raising our four daughters, but I can say 'parenting two generations' is more fun than parenting one!

Reflection/Conclusion

In sharing our stories, we have a heightened awareness of the influence of the journey of generations past as we map out our own journey as grandparents in another time.

We are discovering that our path as grandparents is being marked by what was absent in our relationship with our grandparents as well as what was present. The absence of physical presence with Marlene's grandparents has heightened her desire to be physically present with her grandchildren. On the other hand Pauline is discovering that the desire to bridge the distance with her grandchildren who live away is rooted in the active grandparenting modelled by her children's grandparents who were physically present in their lives.

Our reflections of grandparenting have provided us the opportunity to revisit how we felt as grandchildren in our relationship with our grandparents and to discover new meaning in those experiences through the eyes of an adult who is now a grandparent. For example, in reflecting on "Nanny", Pauline realized a new appreciation for the strength of a woman who, in the early 20th century, independently raised her family of five without assistance, which explained her lack of permission for leisure in her life and in the life of others.

In reflecting on the deep attachment to family and place prioritized by Marlene's parents, it is no surprise that Marlene and her entire family are now residing permanently in Newfoundland near extended family. For Pauline the deep attachment to family and place motivates her to ensure that she brings a flavour of Newfoundland and Labrador and its rich culture to her son and grandchildren who are living away.

In comparing the experience of grandparenting in the previous generations to grandparenting in the 21st century, the technology of today has enabled more ability for contact regardless of distance and place. For example, in the 60's and 70's, Marlene's grandparents were limited in how they could have contact (yearly visits and letter writing) with grandchildren living away compared to the various social media options available today (i.e., email, skype, facebook). Therefore grandparents today have many more options to have contact with their grandchildren.

Although time and society have changed significantly, the relationship between grandparent and child was valuable then and continues to hold value today. A common theme in our reflections is the value of having the desire to maintain family ties and to build relationship across generations. Our shared experience supports Lois Wyse words, "Grandchildren are the dots that connect the lines from generation to generation."

REFLECTION QUESTIONS

1. Pauline describes quite vividly, her recollections of her maternal grandparents through stories that she heard from her mother. How would you describe the 'relationship' development of grandparents who were/are deceased? What is the significance of this form of connection?
2. What are the positive and the negative aspects of the possibilities for relationship development between grandparents and their grandchildren today?
3. What might have been some of the 'realities' of living 'away' from ones home province in the 1960s and 1970s, as was Marlene's reality?
4. How would you characterize the commitment of both grandmothers to grandparenting in this chapter?

REFERENCES

The_presence_of_a_grandparent_confirms_that_parents. (n.d.). *Columbia World of Quotations.* Retrieved October 03, 2012, from Dictionary.com website: http://quotes.dictionary.com/The_presence_of_a_grandparentconfirms_that_parents Wyse, L. http://www.brainyquote.com/quotes/quotes/l/loiswyse399215.html
Author unknown http://write-on.hubpages.com/hub/quotes-grandparents-day-grandparenting Korhaber, A. http://www.grandparents.com/grandkids/grandparents-day/grandparents-day-quotes

JOHN HOBEN

THE FORGOTTEN CATALOGUE

Grandparenting, Learning and the Threat of Diaspora
in Rural Newfoundland

BEING BORN INTO STORIES

As Richard Kearney (2002) says, "we are made by stories before we ever get around to making our own" (p. 154). Grandparenting entails much memory work, as the forms of caring they embody are part of the forgotten catalogue of local knowledge which help us to collectively navigate an uncertain present. Grandparents are endowed with the experience which comes from living, and that lends a sensitivity to the importance of the happiness which comes from loving, caring human relationships. In grandparenting we see how we can grow and learn from our own experiences, and thereby gain new insight into the pitfalls of needless fears and insecurities which come from living too worldly, introverted or "busy" lives (Hebblethwaite & Norris, 2011). Despite prevailing stereotypes about the diminished human capacities brought about by aging, "grandparents are often seen as both the symbolic and instrumental safeguards of the succeeding generation during times of strain or reorganization" (Hayslip, Shore, Henderson & Lambert, 1998, p. 164).

This is a learning relationship which shows both humility and the value of deep emotional engagement—the idea of the importance of perspective taking and everyday experience as opposed to the conventional educational emphasis on accumulated knowledge (Strom & Strom, 2011). In this way children and grandparents mediate a new social horizon in ways which work across and between local spaces; this relationship between grandparents and grandchildren is midwifery, a form of surrogacy vital to giving birth to new ideas. This form of education is not didactic, rather it is narrative, experiential and imaginative in nature, it takes love as its aim and point of departure. Rather than being representative of declining life, or the end of one's productive capacities, in this way grandparenting is a site of powerful productive and imaginative capacities which can alter society for the better by connecting real life experiences to hopeful narratives of past and place.

Focusing on Musgrave Harbour, a small community of approximately 1200 people located on the North East Coast of Newfoundland, this chapter considers how grandparenting enables us to make sense out of diaspora by allowing us to develop a critical literacy of self-in-place. Using critical autobiography, I examine the relationships between my parents, my in-laws and their children, all of whom are

A. Singh and M. Devine (Eds.), Rural Transformation and Newfoundland and Labrador Diaspora:
Grandparents, Grandparenting, Community and School Relations, 187–206.

touched in some way by the ever present threat of diaspora given their participation in seasonal and migratory working patterns. Grandparents, I maintain, play a crucial role in orientating community members to place by using past memories to create a deep and sustained sense of belonging. Rather than living in the past, grandparents teach their loved ones how to live in the moment, to imagine, to love, to risk opening oneself to others, helping those they love to develop a critical and informed notion of time, one infused with a vital sense of hopeful agency. Seeing the past-as-praxis, grandparenting teaches us to create a more caring and loving society by taking up themes which are rarely talked about in the rhetoric of modern educational outcomes and objectives; namely love as an interpersonal and deeply transformative social force.

Stepping Over Shadows

Many of these stories were told with humor. In fact this was a method grandparents often used in storytelling and in teaching. While this might seem like a simple matter of mood, of being carefree or lighthearted, it was also a life perspective, and a tool for coping and encountering life in ways which fostered both resiliency and enjoyment. The grandparents also often spoke of the importance of seeking continuity with the past, in a way which said that the past was always re-created in ways which echoed the voices and experiences of those who had gone before them. The family history was a way of teaching and commemorating in ways which reassured grandchildren that they were part of a story that mattered, both as a future project and a present inheritance. Grandparenting seen in this sense, is a metaphor for the local and the personal forms of connections which offer us meaning and direction in an increasingly fragmented and disorientating world. Globalization, ecological challenges, crises in global capital and modern anomie all suggest the need for all of us to learn to be at once more self-sufficient and inter-connected, albeit on terms which are not solely of someone else's making. As Madigan (2011) points out in describing the work of Hans-Georg Gadamer, this is because the past is never simply the past—it is part of what makes us who we are.

> [W]e cannot step over our shadows....people are connected in a continuous thread with their past, with traditions, and with their ancestors. This is not an epistemological quest because we are historical beings, living out traditions that have been bequeathed to us by others. And although we may be taking up traditions in different ways, they are still the source of who we are and how we shape and live our lives. The echoes of this history are inadvertently and deliberately inviting us into both past and new ways of being in the present. We live in a world that recedes into the past and extends into the future, so rather than pitting ourselves against history, we need to remember, recollect, and recall it. The address of tradition is not just something arching from before, for we are in tradition (p. 64).

This ongoing process of reflecting on the past is more than simple nostalgia and seeks to avoid the type of melancholic attachments which arise from an inability or unwillingness to acknowledge loss (Kelly, 2010). Instead it is mindful of the fact that history is narrative and interpretative and that the social conditions structure the life world we inhabit. This means that the stories we tell each other are of crucial importance since they frame and structure our agency along with the intensive cultural work that grandparents perform as they frame the conditions for the articulation of collective memory in the present moment.

The grandparents who form the focal point of this chapter are from Musgrave Harbour, a small community of approximately 1200 people located on the North East Coast of Newfoundland, a Province often affectionately known as "The Rock". This community was traditionally a fishing community and up until the early 1990's a fish processing plant provided seasonal employment for many of the residents. Many other young people find seasonal work in Ontario in the construction industries or in Alberta working either in construction or in the oil and gas industry, others work as truck drivers in the far north. There have also always been a number of small boat owners who take part in the inshore ground and lobster fisheries, as well as a growing number of owners of large modern steel long liners, as well as share men who fish shrimp and crab hundreds of miles offshore.

The community has a K-12 school with a student population of approximately 150 students. While there have been plans to bus high school students to a nearby school in Carmanville, partly due to community opposition, these students now remain in Musgrave Harbour. There are also a growing, albeit small number of summer home owners, many with family connections to the community who vacation in the community during the summer months. The population is overwhelmingly white, Protestant and English speaking. There are three Churches in the small community, representing the Pentecostal, Salvation Army and United Church of Canada. Although there were many other small businesses and grocery stores in the community in the past, at present there remains only a sole gas station, a single grocery store, a takeout restaurant, and a motel. In recent years there have also been a number of small cottages which are rented, primarily during the summer months as well as a bed and breakfast establishment.

The Moulands, my wife's family, live in the southern part of Musgrave Harbour near the beach. Bernice and Wince, married for 39 years, have 5 children, 9 grandchildren and one great grandchild. Bernice Mouland (nee Simms), age 65, originally came to Musgrave Harbour in 1970's from Little Bay, Green Bay. From a large family of 15 children, her father worked as a deckhand in the coastal shipping trade and in the forestry sector. According to Bernice, Little Bay was a small, tight knit and close community nestled in the hills and uneven coastline of southern Green Bay. While there she lived a busy life, helping her mother and sisters with chores around the house, and playing outside with her friends and cousins. Later she would move to Stephenville with her infant son, Clyde, to live with her sister Ivy to take more schooling. It was here that she met Wince who was also enrolled in an "upgrading course" at the local college.

Also from a large family, Wince's father worked as a fisherman, logger and trapper, while his mother stayed at home to raise 9 children. Wince worked in Musgrave Harbour as a fish plant worker from the mid 1970's until the early 1990's when the local plant closed due to the ground fish moratorium. After that time he began working in a larger plant some 30 miles up the shore in Wesleyville where he presently works. Together they have five sons and one daughter. All of their children, with the exception of their daughter (my wife) who works in the St. John's area as a general practitioner, live in the same community as their parents. Their sons are experienced trades workers—a carpenter, a plumber, a heavy equipment operator—and the oldest son, Clyde works as an experienced crab and shrimp fisher.

Clarence and Ruby Hoben, my parents, have been married for the past 48 years. Clarence, aged 71 is a retired vice principal and Ruby, his wife, aged 77, once worked as a teacher while a young woman and now is a housewife. Ruby is a lifelong resident of Musgrave Harbour while Clarence moved to Musgrave Harbour from the Burin Peninsula while a young teacher where he met his future wife. Ruby's father was a fisherman and lighthouse keeper, assisted closely in his work by his wife, Myrtle. During the first 9 years of their marriage they lived with Ruby's parents in the same house where she grew up along with Clarence's two youngest brothers who were initially aged 6 and 10 when they came to live with their sister-in-law and their family after their mother died of cancer at the age of 49. While there they developed close bonds with Ruby's mother who took on an important care giving and emotional role. Clarence's father worked on deep sea trawlers year around his entire life, while his mother was a stay at home mother for seven children. Originally, from the Burin Peninsula Clarence is part of a close extended family made up of four brothers and three sisters. A retired vice principal he has lived in Musgrave Harbour for the past 50 years. Clarence and Ruby have two children: my sister Gail, aged 37 who works seasonally in Ontario and who owns a home in Musgrave Harbour along with her husband, Sean, a construction worker and their 12 year old daughter Courtney; and, their son, John [me], aged 38, lives 5 hours away near St. John's the capital city with his wife and their two daughters aged 1 and 4.

The comments you will read here came out of a series of conversations with family members in which I simply told the participants that I wanted to hear stories about place and grandparenting. These include a long group session with four grandparents that forms the heart of the chapter and an interview with two of the grandparents' children who have the most experience with leaving home to find work, and who also rely on grandparents for child care and emotional support. The reflections are written about my home community, a place in which I have not lived for more than twenty years.

Car Bonnets and the Eaton's Catalogue

As Ricoeur points out, "time becomes human to the extent that it is organized after the manner of a narrative" (cited in Porter Abbott, 2008, p. 4). Time here is an extension of human community and identity, it is the narrative space from which human activity and meaning flows. If we can say time has meaning only in so far as it affects human relationships, the relationships these grandparents talked about were characterized by love, by simple fun, and by teaching the importance of place through everyday skills such as baking, snaring rabbits, cutting firewood and sharing stories. As Clarence said when he plays with his grandchildren he gets a sense of, "relaxation and the enjoyment of seeing them growing and developing". Grandparents were teachers who lent their grandchildren a sense of the importance of time-in-place and of the need to find happiness and self-fulfillment in a growing sense of community and personal identity. The significance of this bonding and teaching about place has perhaps an even greater significance in rural areas since "close relations and friendships, combined with the existence of desired property, contribute to a rural orientation and eventual return by migrants from the cities" (Traphagan, 2000, p. 367).

Stories matter because, "distance emphasizes differences, be they real or imagined, and it is imagination that both inspires and sustains the construction of place myths: the connoted, embellished identities attributed to places" (Hopkins, 1998, p. 65). Seemingly aware of this danger, the grandparents combined narratives of place with the importance of learning practical skills which helped with everyday life. While this was seen as being part of a type of practical care, quite often it was also simply fun, reflecting the close connection between family leisure and generativity, the desire to make a contribution to the future through human social relationships (Hebblewaite & Norris, 2011). Grandparenting was centered on an ethic of care and play that grew out of accumulated wisdom and the unique perspective afforded by the grand-parenting-life-space. As Bernice, a grandmother of 8 said, "it's like it says on a picture I have at home on my wall, 'if you knew how much fun your grandchildren were, you would have had them first' [laughs]. "Being a grandparent makes you feel good, it makes you feel young". Part of these leisure activities involved practical skills such as baking, cutting and gathering wood, or building fires, or, hunting. As Bernice went on to say, "I make cookies with Sophia. When she was out the house she put her apron on and she helped me make buns." Likewise, according to Wince, "We had ours down to the woods and boiled the kettle and we put out snares and they put out theirs too. We go down every year. They enjoy it." As Bernice added, "They enjoy it plus they learn things—outdoor skills. They help you get your wood."

Place, however, had a definitive content that was communicated through describing real tangible experiences. In this sense it was more than simple "alterity [whereby] the rural is represented as some place other than urban, as some time other than the present, as some experience other than the norm" (Hopkins, 1998, p. 78). Although there was hardship and often loss, in their lives, the grandparents also spoke of the close relationships to the sea, land and to each other enjoyed by past generations. Grandparents also described the lack of physical activity of their grandchildren's generation which they contrasted with their own lives as children when they performed chores for their parents, played hide-and-seek, rounders, tiddley, swam, walked, jumped ice pans, played house or simply relaxed outside in the fresh air. As Wince said, "You don't see any youngsters outdoors now, not a one." As Wince put it, "the first time I rode a pedal bike I was a young man". "We didn't even have a slide but we used to ride down over the hill on a car bonnet. But it was fun. We would all get on the car bonnet and go down over the hill flying, had the time of our lives". These memories of play were also set against a realization of just how little monetary wealth they and their families possessed at the time. As Wince said, "when we were growing up we had to use the Eaton's catalogue for toilet paper". The forgotten catalogue which Wince mentions in his story about growing up in rural Newfoundland is more than a funny story, it is another example of how the humor and the harshness of everyday reality can be bridged by improvisation and by sharing the stories about the most seemingly mundane aspects of everyday life. The grandparents' efforts to involve their grandchildren in play, then, was both a form of memory work as well as an attempt to "facilitate the establishment of common interests and experiences, that, in turn, enabled the development of strong intergenerational bonds" (Hebblewaite & Norris, 2011, p. 125).

In many ways this local form of knowledge creation and meaning making was much different than that advocated by formal schooling. In fact, some of the grandparents told stories which contrasted survival based forms of community knowledge with academic knowledge that was seen as disconnected from local time-and-place. Local knowledge also represented a "concern with memory..... [that] emerged in response to crisis: with cultures, as with individuals, memory becomes problematic when continuity with the past is threatened" (Sheridan, 2008, p. 23). One of the informants [Wince] told with pride, the story of his father's choice to go to work instead of attending school since it became a means of supporting his family in the community where was born and bred. As he goes on to say, "My own father never went to school in his life. When he was old enough to go to school his father asked him 'Everett you can go furring with me and have a pair of boots or you can go to school. So he went furring with my grandfather and he was at that all of his life". Schooling in comparison offered only deferral and diversion from the types of work which allowed a young person to become part of the community by learning skills which enabled them to become self-sufficient. Clarence, for example, told of his own father's work with similar pride, a man who was forced to leave school and go to work on the deep-sea fishing fleet at the an early age because of his own father's sudden, unexpected death. As he said, "Dad himself he was on a banker when he was thirteen years old. He had his thirteenth birthday aboard a schooner, a banker, on the Grand Banks."

Culture provides us with, "the opportunity to pick and poke at our identities, personal and communal, as well as to represent ourselves to the world and to ourselves" (Doyle, 2010, p. 119). These narratives were stories of learning to survive in rural communities where life was often unpredictable and harsh, though it likewise offered independence, autonomy and close family connections. Interestingly, these stories often were ways of connecting the personal to something much larger and more profound than the individual self. As Wince emphasized, "I tell my grandkids all the time what it used to be like when I was growing up". Without romanticizing the past or glossing over its hardships, the grandparents felt a strong sense of connection to the small community in which they lived, in part because of the sense of personal connection they had to the physical environment, but also because they felt a sense of agency that was rooted in the local histories, family narratives and the local dialects which created a rich fabric of human knowledge and natural beauty.

Narrative had a crucial role to play in communicating the value of work and place. What did become clear in my conversations was that "these men and women do have firm ideas about their labor: what it is worth, when it is alienated from them, and when they can control it" (Roseman, 2002, p. 32). Although many of the stories conformed to traditional gender roles in which woman performed domestic work while the men were wage earners and performed outside work such as cutting firewood, performing carpentry work, and hunting and fishing either recreationally or as a means of making a living. Despite this, however, these relationships were also quite counterintuitive and complex. Both Ruby and Bernice worked outside the home as wage earners, one later in life as a shopkeeper and the other as a young school teacher in the community in which she was born. Likewise, Bernice often spoke of her love of catching rabbits or working in the woods. Even when traditional gender roles were taken up, it was often clear that this work was valued by both grandparents and grandchildren alike as important, necessary work which enriched the family environment as a whole.

Resiliency-in-place was a response to hardship which could be opposed to leaving and the threat that "changes that would so far transform them that they would no longer be fit to perceive the world as it truly is, and no longer therefore be able to claim the persons whom they were" (Lamb, 2002, p. 18). Survival was about creating responses which kept alive one's ability to lay a claim on the past and to say that one belonged to a particular place. Many of the stories focus on hardships without being either unduly fatalistic or glib in their treatment of this theme. Indeed, hardship often took the form of a problem which can be explored, and often, solved—or at least mitigated—by hard work, thinking, communicating with others and drawing on shared family and community resources. While both families often spoke of the moratorium in this regard, the grandparents also acknowledged that in many respects life in rural communities was now better than it had been before: standards of living had improved, the fishery had diversified, people had become more adaptable, and many had, in the interim, gained other forms of education or skills.

Yet, the grandparents also recognized that technology and progress was a double edged sword. In some ways, the past was seen as an idyllic place which kept traditional family ties alive, but it was also one in which the demand for labour was great, yet, since it was largely unskilled labour, wages were low. As Ruby said, "In those days they didn't have any trades." Grandparents also emphasized that in the past mobility was limited. For Clarence growing up seeing his grandparents who lived in another community was rare since "Wasn't so easy to get around back then. They didn't have vehicles." As Wince added quite pointedly, "They had to walk". Adding an example, he told how, his maternal grandparents would walk from Deadman's Bay to Musgrave Harbour, a distance of about 14 miles on Sunday evening to go to church before leaving that night to walk back home again. Although it offered more options for children and grandchildren, technology also sometimes represented the threat of diaspora, of losing one's attachment to family and place, and of making existing ways of life rapidly redundant. In this sense, technology, which replaced human labour and disconnected people, facilitated control of local populations and was regarded with suspicion. Quite often technology seemed to be implemented in institutions or businesses with little or no output from locals and hence was seen in such circumstances as potentially damaging. Computers were one such example, one that altered the focus of young people's lives. As Wince said, "When I was small with my grandparents we had nothing. Now they spend their time on computers." Another was automated machinery which had been installed in the local fish plant and which threatened locals' job security. For them, technology increased the distance between community members and the environment in which they lived.

In many ways Musgrave Harbour is like, "many rural communities [that] have suffered depopulation and job loss as their economies have struggled in the changing national and global marketplace" (Bullock, 2005, p. 44). Given this broader socio-economic context it is not surprising that showing grandchildren how to live was also an important part of grandparents' "jobs", a task that was often seen as being centered around an ethic of community and care. As Bernice said, "You try to teach them right from wrong. If you know they are doing something wrong you tell them not to do it." Mostly, however, they saw their role as one of caretaking and providing moral guidance. Indeed, even these accounts were also told with good humor, as Clarence said "You pick them up when then fall and then you say dammit, why do they always fall on my watch". When I asked Clarence whether they taught their grandchildren anything he replied simply with a laugh, "No, thats' the parents' job". Although they joked about being permissive, grandparents also note the importance of having some form of discipline. Sometimes one grandparent was seen as more permissive or accommodating than the other. As Wince pointed out [laughing], "Bernice is a grandparent and youngsters do what they like. I had to look after Emma so when she came down with me I wouldn't let her touch anything and right sudden she said, 'when Nan is here I can do what I like' and I said, 'Nan is not here now'. [laughs]"

As Fromm (1974) notes, "While we teach knowledge, we are losing that teaching which is the most important one for human development: the teaching which can only be given by the simple presence of a mature, loving person" (p. 98). In part this maturity and love were the result of the unique life positioning grandparents occupied. For Ruby grandparenting was an interesting time because you possess a great deal of life experience but are still young enough to provide the same mentorship and guidance as a parent. As she went on to say, "You have more time for them than you did for your own children. You can pass them back when you get tired" [laughs]. Indeed, Ruby spoke fondly of her own memories of playing in a shop owned by her own grandfather, one which went bankrupt in one of the island's bank panics. For these grandparents, then, this idea of substitute parenting hinted at a role which for many outport parents was becoming increasingly important given the growing number of parents who work in places like Alberta and Ontario. As Wince emphasized, "Now the grandparents carry their grandchildren everywhere…If you go to the school now most of what you see is grandparents carrying youngsters to school in the morning and picking them up in the evening."

In many ways, then, grandparents talked subtly about the need to pass on traditional forms of knowledge, primarily by sharing time with their grandchildren and doing things together. This is important since, "adolescents report that they view advice from adults to be more credible and worth consideration when it is offered after carefully listening to the way teenagers feel and think about events and situations" (Strom & Strom, 2011, p. 921). Wince spoke about this role as he talks about his teenage grandson, Clyde, as he links the activity of gardening to both present and past. In Wince's words, "When we were growing up they planted what they could survive off. Little Clyde helps me with the garden sometimes. He helps me with the potatoes. Picking them up when I dig them up at the end of the year." This was a truly intergenerational skill set since as he pointed out: "I learned a lot from my grandparents when it comes to sowing gardens".

"Creating memory on the ground" (Holc, 2001, p. 68) always begins with a set of collective and individual choices about place and context. Often practical knowledge had strong connections with local cultures and ways of life. Wince's youngest son, Sheldon, began working as a carpenter in the last two years of high school by doing work for people in the community, including installing siding on neighborhood houses on his own, skills which he developed both on his own and by working with his father, or as he put it "it was something that I picked up here and there". This is a trade which he loves and he said that he always knew that he wanted to be a carpenter. Carpentry for him provided a sense of identity as well as a link to local knowledge and ways of thinking and living. They are part of his "loyalty to home, or the ground of a previous identity, to anchor alterations of the self within the boundaries of will and intention" (Lamb, 2002, p. 33). Carpentry was a skill that many of his brothers, friends and relatives shared. Both of his brothers were capable carpenters, one had built his own house, not uncommon in the community, and his father had built his own house as well as a number of sheds and outbuildings which stood on the premises. In Musgrave Harbour worthwhile knowledge was practical, ready-to-hand and helped a person become both self-reliant and capable of helping others.

The activities which young people and grandparents shared, then, were one way in which both young parents and youths developed strong identities centered on a sense of agency strongly connected to place and past. The past was important because it was also a source of local knowledge that had been tested and proven. By relating this knowledge to their grandchildren grandparents were also signifying that they were beginning the process of maturing and becoming productive adult members of the community. It appeared grandparents took youths seriously as individuals and future adults, a role which is of increasing importance given the challenges faced by this "forgotten population" in contemporary rural areas of Canada and North America (Jackson, Marshall, Tirone, Donovan and Shepard, 2006):

> The restructuring processes that shape power dynamics and inequities not only affect adult members of the community but also youth (MacDonald, 1998; McDowell, 2000). Youth, in turn, influence the ways in which power relationships within the community evolve. Some argue that youth are often the 'forgotten' sector of the population or what has been termed the 'neglected others' (McGrath, 2001) because they do not wield political power in the same fashion as adults. Indeed, when speaking about issues of power and power inequities, youth are rarely viewed as key stakeholders because within our society and culture, youth (up to a certain age at least) are outside of the formal political structures given that they cannot vote and are considered the legal dependants of their parents and guardians. As a result, adults shape almost all aspects of the daily lives of youth at home and at school. (p. 233)

Children, then, "serve as social, emotional, and economic 'linchpins' for households that span...borders" (Orellana et al., p. 586). Grandparents and parents alike recognized that each child authored his or her own story and it is neither possible nor desirable to try and protect young adults from the outside world. In this sense small town life was not simply an escape from the world, it was a way of finding personal meaning and family connection in a space which simultaneously exists beside, and challenges, contemporary modernism. As Ruby's daughter Gail, for example, reflects on her time working in Ontario she emphasizes the importance of allowing children to exercise their own judgment in deciding whether they want to leave. In her words, "Now that my daughter is older now I try to talk to her and see what she would prefer. I think on the kid's part it makes them grow up faster too-more responsibility on them that way. They are not living such a sheltered life as we did growing up in such a small community....like years ago people would go hunting and things and leave their kids home, sort of the same way with different circumstances." As Gail's comments suggests, then, the challenge for many rural residents in the modern age is learning to make sense out of one's experiences of hybridity by developing a crucial literacy of identity-in-place.

Of course, the degree of influence grandparents have on youths will depend upon many factors including the time grandparents and grandchildren spend together, the emotional bond which they share, the ease with which they connect to youth, culture, and the degree of mutual trust and respect which exists. At times however, grandparents noted the great contrast between their own upbringing and that of the present generation of youths. As Clarence points out speaking about his own childhood, "we had chores to do", this included cleaving wood, bringing in wood, fetching water, caring for animals, and helping with house cleaning. These were also chores which they performed for their own grandparents who often had to work until they were well advanced in age or rely on family caregivers. In contrast to the material abundance of kids today Wince pointed out how they would often perform many difficult chores for their own grandparents in the hopes of earning the twenty five cents needed to see a movie at the community theatre. As Lenz (2011) points out, "Individuals always belong simultaneously to different "remembrance environments" in which that being worth remembering, i.e., the contents and the ways of remembering, as well as its importance for the regulation of present-oriented interpretative authority and formative power can vary considerably" (p. 321).

I'm all Right Where I'm to?, Migration and Hybrid Identities

As Kelly (2010) notes, "there are many diasporas, each born of varying degrees and kinds of difficulty" (p. 19). It was clear that different types of mobility practices evoked different types of feelings and thoughts in the grandparents, their children and grandchildren. This depended on the reasons for going, the distance, cultural differences, whether community could remain intact, whether the new place somehow evoked memories of home, and the duration of the move. For some, however, migration and the threat of leaving only underscored the importance of deep roots to home. In many respects, it was interesting to consider these stories in the context of stories about traditional mobility practices. As Barbara, the wife of Everett, Bernice's second oldest son, emphatically stated, "I'm all right where I'm to." For her, life in a rural community offered greater freedom and more intense personal and familial attachments. For this young nurse who, like her husband, drove two hours each day to work in Gander, a small town which served as a regional service center, moving away meant making many personal compromises, it was a life of exile and disavowed loses. In her words, "People who are gone up to Alberta they have to make it sound good. But when they come home they still don't have any more in the garden." As she went on to emphasize, "They could be gone for half the year. Money is not everything; I think time home with your family is just as important, that stuff you can't get back".

Migrancy was closely related to the idea of resiliency that was also a theme present in the grandparents' stories of the past. As Ruby said, "They had hard times." Ruby also spoke of a great uncle who was shipwrecked for several weeks and was eventually picked up off the coast of Spain and another uncle who drowned while hunting sea birds. The grandmothers also told stories of how their own mothers and grandmothers worked in the fisheries by helping to dry fish, raise children, cook clean and make do with the household's often scant supplies. The women in their stories were strong, resilient and optimistic, finding meaning in lives which were often tough but lived in close proximity to the sea, the land, and to strong loving bonds which connected families and close friends. The past represented a time of hardship and simple virtue: a time when the boundaries of self and place seemed much more meaningful and secure. As Ruby said of her own mother, "She worked for years in St. Johns in the service (what you would call housekeeping) and she worked in Twillingate for a doctor over there. In St. John's she worked for two older women. The three of them (her mother and her two sisters) used to work in the same house, one would cook, one would clean and another would do the dusting. Then she got tired of it, she came home and met dad and got married. She went fishing with dad, she went in the woods, she went lobster catching, she lived on the island with dad where he was a lighthouse keeper."

These patterns are longstanding and "comfort, connection, and insight in the face of loss are essential to prevent counterproductive and even destructive responses, and to promote healing, growth and change" (Kelly, 2010, p. 31). Ruby also spoke of her own parents' work in the seasonal fishery when much of the community travelled with their families to the Whadam's island over 10 miles offshore to be closer to the summer fishing grounds. There was a church, a store, many stages, wharves and houses, a community store, a lighthouse, and even, a plant for rendering cod liver oil. These stories were told with fondness, were seen as emblematic of a type of mobility which made both economic sense without causing deep disruptions in family or community ties. Unlike resettlement which was a top down move, the cod moratorium, or even, the economically motivated seasonal migrations of the present day, moves by their ancestors to take part in summer fisheries (including the Labrador fishery), or to work seasonally in logging camps were seen as a "normal" albeit necessary part of one's cultural existence.

Unfortunately, within this small community migration was a common experience often related to "a necessary accommodation to global capitalism's 'need' for 'flexible' labor, as justified over the last several decades through a rhetoric of economic and social 'restructuring'" (Roseman, 2002, p. 32). Wince and Bernice, for example, had nephews who, like many community members, worked in the pool cleaning business. This was a form of seasonal work which gave them a decent, albeit somewhat modest income that allowed them to live at home for a good part of the year. Wince's sister and her husband, like many others, had left the community to work in Fort McMurray. But their own children also left: this included Gail, Clarence and Ruby's 37 year old daughter, and Sheldon, Wince and Bernice's 35 year old son. Indeed, all of the grandparents spoke of the difficulty of seeing their children work away while leaving their children and families at home. Wince spoke of the difficulty of seeing his son, Sheldon work away for much of the year as a carpenter who worked in Canada's high Arctic. For him, this was a hardship for grandparents and grandchildren alike and one which reminded them of the importance of family and place. As Ruby said, "sometimes the parents simply have no choice", recognizing the tension between economic and emotional factors caused by family migration (Orellana et al, 2001).

But experiences of migration and stories of home also helped to forge alternative conceptions of community and place. As Lamb (2002) emphasizes, "there is not diasporic community without a dream of homecoming, nor any diasporic idea without a relation to home" (p. 32). Ruby's own daughter worked in Ontario with a company which produced office equipment while her son-in-law worked in the seasonal construction industry. Like many Newfoundlanders Gail and her husband, Sean, lived in trailer parks during these times, often with many other members from the same or neighboring communities. While many had formerly lived in apartment buildings, often in low rent areas, they found such an arrangement was more flexible, allowed them to live in more rural areas which gave them more space in a more open, natural setting. In addition, it was also a more economical arrangement and circumvented many practical problems associated with intermittent renting.

In light of these complex migrational patterns, grandparents are increasingly taking on conventional parenting duties in relation to their own grandchildren, often out of simple necessity (Bullock, 2005). Ruby's own 12 year old granddaughter, Courtney, who once attended school in Ontario, now prefers to live with her grandparents in Musgrave Harbour until the school year ends. The alternative is not very attractive since, as Clarence puts it, "You don't get to know them the same. You only see them once or twice a year, so you don't seem them growing and changing." For many local families, grandparents were important for logistical and financial reasons, since they offered child care services and lodging for children who chose to remain at home while migrant parents pursue seasonal employment. Indeed, within the community, some grandparents actually move into their children's' home while their adult children pursued seasonal work abroad, combing house sitting and child care duties. Yet, despite these supports, moving away was still difficult for the parents. For Gail going away was something which she did with reluctance. In her words, "I look at it now as something that must be done. I prefer not to, but on the other hand I feel a little bit better knowing that my daughter is with her grandparents rather than her being up there and being in school and crying all day long. I think she is more content. I would rather stay home and not go away but you do what you have to do for survival. So grandparents are really important in that way."

Remaining with one's grandparents for these few months of the year also offered young adolescents the chance to explore their family roots and develop a deep sense of place. Yet, while it did offer the chance of prosperity for some, the migrant lifestyle often led to circumstances where migrant rural workers "accept wages and working conditions that others, that is, urban laborers are loath to accept" (Quataert cited in Roseman, 2002, p. 26). Distance also meant disconnection and loss of the types of relationships which, to rural people, helped to define who they are. As Gail put it, "I think [Courtney] has become very close to her grandparent by having to live here part of the year. So I like that. I think that family and family roots are very important. But it is very, very difficult to have to leave Courtney. How I deal with it…[by] thinking of it as only short periods of time." This lifestyle of migrancy can be contrasted with the close ties of their parents' generation since as Wince points out "I lived right across the road from my [paternal] grandparents all my life". But close family linkages are beneficial for grandparents and grandchildren alike since, as Gray, Mission and Hayes (2005) argue, "The quality of the relationship between children and their grandparents can have an impact upon the wellbeing of the grandparent as well as on the developmental outcomes for the child" (p. 16).

Although these were not "miminal families", community members who leave often faced challenges as a result of their migratory lifestyle (Traphagan, 2000). While diaspora often forces us to grow, to deepen our sense of our own gradual efforts at claiming agency and transformation, it also brings risks, often the risk of being marginalized or treated as an outsider. Gail, for example, told of an incident where a co-worker told them that, "the new girls got the best of both worlds because you can work summertime and sit on your asses all winter and not do anything". After they reported his comments, their manager did, in fact, take the employee to task. Fortunately, these experiences of prejudice and stereotyping were rare and did not, "suggest a certain lack of agency in the lives of these women: a problematic passivity that means they sacrifice certain aspects of their identities rather than attempt to negotiate and reconcile every role they wish to fill" (Sheridan, 2008, p. 23). However, diaspora could not fragment the strong sense of community many of the informants felt. Indeed, diaspora was something which was experienced through communities, showing the relational and cultural dimension of individual identity. This sense of community was an important means of orientating oneself to new places and ways of life. In Gail's words, "I find that Newfies stick together. No matter where you go... What one Newfie does, the others will eventually do. As for the communities in the trailer parks, I like it....you feel more safe and secure. You tend to trust Newfies more because you know them or somebody you know does." Once again then, we see how exile "blends the pleasure and the pain – the advantage and the disadvantage – of not being where you ought to be" (Lamb, 2002, p. 32).

In many ways, "home and the loss of home constitute a recurring motif of modernity" (Mufti and Shohat in Sheridan, 2008, p. 24). While loss creates new identities and attachments the process is often not without stress, especially since many migrants have to compete for scarce resources and cultural capital in unfamiliar surroundings. Indeed, moving often brought conflicted feelings since, as Gail pointed out, "It's really stressful and you have feelings of guilt because you are leaving your child-it's almost like between money and responsibility but in the other way you have to live and provide necessities". As she went on to add, "Me and Shawn often discuss maybe we should settle for a low paying job but then would she suffer in other ways because she would not have dental care or eye glasses. You can become very depressed and I lose sleep over it. You kind of dread it. When we got off the boat I started crying and said, 'Oh God Sean, we are finally home'"

While it is tempting to see such life arrangements as overwhelmingly negative, they in fact represent an expanded sense of family, place and home in which children can become simultaneously attached to place and literate in navigating complex modern environments. In many cases, these experiences are rich and unique—a part perhaps of the rich ongoing history of "these enigmas of migration and settlement" (Lamb, 2002, p. 25). The Moulands' youngest son, Sheldon, for example, worked throughout the far north as a carpenter and spoke excitedly about seeing the rugged beauty of the Canadian Arctic, including large parts of the North West Territories, Hudson Bay and the Baffin Island, and even had the opportunity to observe a narwhal hunt. Although he had worked in the Province, including Gander, St. John's and Labrador, as well as spending a year in Calgary, at, present he has settled into working for a company based out of Halifax which hires skilled workers to work 2-month-on-1 month-off shifts in Canada's far north. In his view, wages here were much lower than elsewhere in Canada and were substantially less than what he could make working in the North. As he said," the money is the biggest thing, you will triple your wages". Yet despite the financial incentives Sheldon still found leaving hard, despite this he still saw the benefits of working away while living at home—in his words, "you got to do what you got to do". As he noted when the time to leave begins to draw near "you spend more time with your kids and you treat them differently". But this lifestyle also brought challenges, as his father noted, Wince: "Sheldon works 12 months a year and he is only home once or twice every two or three, or four months and she [his wife] is working too so you knows it has to be hard on them".

"The choice of which lives and whose histories to invoke through the practices of cultural memory entails a preceding process, implicit and explicit, of identifying a[n]....experience "worth" remembering" (Holc, 2011, p. 68). Sheldon shared Gail's dread of leaving his family, and yet he was also more ambivalent about the effects of hybridity on his community and his own family. In many ways he recognizes this new reality is complex, as opportunities and new experiences often exist side by side with experiences of dislocation and temporary hardship. He is acutely aware in many respects of the limitations of the local economy, recognizing that the benefits of the Province's burgeoning oil industry are largely limited to the capital city of St. John's, meaning that rural economies are largely dependent on the seasonal fishery and the incomes of those who work in Toronto, and more often, Alberta's booming oil economy. In this sense, he does not cast himself as a victim but as someone who makes difficult choices for the good of his family and for his own personal growth. And yet, despite this he retains strong, deep personal and familial attachments to his home community, he owns his own home, and together with his wife who works in a medical clinic is able to provide his young family with a good standard of living.

This sense of choice, of choosing to leave and of enjoying one's work was part of a set of "memories other than those that culture compels us to tell and also to live by" (Widerberg, 2011, p. 330). Despite his longing for home, Sheldon also pointed out that while he spent much time away he also felt that in many ways he spent more quality time with his children and family than many working people since when he was at home he could afford to spend much quality time with his family. Despite this, as his wife worked a full time job as a medical assistant, Sheldon noted the importance of his parents in helping with children care, particularly when he was away. Learning to combine practical strategies of resiliency with a developing migrational literacy, then, is an important part of learning to respond to "the images of backwardness and also limited economic and educational opportunities" which in many ways comprise the dominant images of rural areas around the world (Traphagan, 2000, p. 367). Yet, despite the advantages they bring, such choices are not without costs. Although he did not speak much about it, about ten years ago I also remember how Sheldon was working with a construction crew in Labrador as a young carpenter. A light company plane that regularly carried crew and materials north crashed just after takeoff killing the owner-pilot and a number of his coworkers. This was a terrible tragedy which touched in some way nearly everyone who lived on our shore. It was a flight he was initially scheduled to be on, but a last minute change of plans meant he was home when the plane went down. As this big genial man sits in my living room I am reminded that he often flies on small planes throughout the North. For me, these little facts reflect the quiet strength of the people of my hometown, a strength born out of a determination to make the best of sometimes trying circumstances, with a big smile and a welcoming outstretched hand.

Where Else Can We Live But Days?

In the Colony of Unrequited Dreams (1999) Wayne Johnson gives us a portrait of a Smallwood who is quirky, enigmatic, ambitious and always on the move: he works in New York as a poor reporter, walks across the island on the railroad tracks to garner support for a railway workers union, born in an outport he spends his teenage years living in town where his grandfather was a well-known boot maker, as a union organizer he becomes champion of the island's scattered inlets and coves only to later zealously promote industrialization and large moneyed interests, a father of confederation and a pig farmer, protean, laughable and, yet, in many ways, a strange figure of national myth. Yet, as large as Smallwood's imaginative shoes loom, the real hero(ine) of the novel is Sheilagh Fielding, a newspaper columnist and Smallwood's witty, townie love interest. Despite her aristocratic, hard drinking, wry demeanor, she is a woman who knows where she is at; and, paralleling Smallwood's ability to navigate the two worlds of town and bay, Fielding is able to navigate the class divisions which divide Newfoundland culture, in a way which makes us love ourselves—her acerbic wit becomes a metonym for Newfoundlander's own burgeoning post-colonial consciousness. Self-congratulatory tendencies aside, Johnson's book haunted by the ghost of Judge Prowse and an anemic intellectual elite caught in the thrall of cronyism and colonialism, shows us how writing and the imagination can help us to transform the possibilities offered by exile and diaspora. The unrequited dream, Johnson suggests, teaches us how to love with dignity and to bear loss with grace.

Strangely, in many respects, diaspora takes its meaning from time. Time marks degrees of separation. Family history, in contrast, is a story that cannot avoid the personal or the intimate, indeed it seeks them out, as being central to one's existing sense of self and place. These are the historical actors then in this unfolding story. For some "telling stories is as basic to human beings as eating" (Kearney, 2002, p. 3). While some might object to a narrative analysis in an historical account, or even one in which one's own family is involved, as Kearney (2002) notes, the stance which the author takes in relating narratives of history is different than the definitive authoritative one ascribed to him or her by empiricism. It is, "a form of understanding that is neither absolute nor relative, but something in between. It is what Aristotle calls phronesis, in contrast to the mere chronicling of facts or the pure abstraction of scientific theoria" (p. 150). Rather, it "is closer to art than science; or, if you prefer, to a human science than to an exact one. Like the architect's ruler, it is approximate but committed to lived experience" (Kearney, p. 150).

Dream work and memory work often overlap: they feed upon each other and the waxing and waning sense of our place in the world. My father recently told me how he was reminded of my grandfather, at my recent PhD convocation. He told me how seeing me walk across the stage reminded him of three Lionels: one who was there [Lionel is my middle name], one [my uncle] who became a medical doctor [and who lives on the mainland], and one who couldn't read [my grandfather]. As my father said for a man who had to go to work when he was 12 after his own father's death, "he didn't have a chance". The irony is however, that he did impress the value of education upon others, and as clichéd as this may sound, for me it does emphasize the importance of memory and family history to our sense of who we are. The past in this way can be a form of agency, much as aging itself can be a form of strength rather than a continual reminder of loss.

Our sense of place is rapidly changing. While we do need new forms of ethical and social solidarity to replace the old frameworks of nationalism in order to meet the challenges posed by a broken environment and exploitative globalism, it is unclear just how this may be accomplished. In some small way perhaps storytelling and providing spaces for encountering others, can provide some semblance of hope. We can choose to remake local spaces from the inside out, as it were, by taking advantage of the hybrid identities which have evolved from rural communities and their encounters with global capitalism. For Gail, for example, her experience working in factories with co-workers from all over the world opened her eyes to the reality of the different types of oppression and marginalization that displaced people face. As she put it, "It really opens up your eyes to what is going on in other countries. When you buy something you don't think about where it comes from whether it was made by a little kid who only makes $3 an hour but they have no other choice but to do it and feed their family so it really makes you think". Migrant lifestyles provide a unique mix of vulnerability and learning opportunities, as displaced workers gain firsthand knowledge of other cultures and communities which provide new insights on their own communities and lives. This lends us hope since, "Through memory, a new relation between the past and the present is created, one that can give structure to past and present experiences" (Widerberg, 2011, p. 330).

Place means little though, without the love that animates memory and the dreams which give our lives meaning. However, in modern society love is reserved for the family unit, often conceived of as an institution born out of romantic love and functioning as an important source of social solidarity. All learning in the end comes down to the fundamental question of what is there that is worth caring about—who am I, is another way of articulating the age old question of what should I love? This is because love is what animates us, it is what defines the boundaries and unending possibilities inherent within the human condition. Indeed, Phillip Larkin once wrote a short arresting poem that reminds me of the difficulty of finding solace in a world where so many traditional social institutions have been fragmented and broken.

Days

What are days for?

Days are where we live.

They come, they wake us

Time and time over.

They are to be happy in:

Where can we live but days?

Ah, solving that question

Brings the priest and the doctor

In their long coats

Running over the fields.

Larkin reminds us that science can never replace or erase the human need to make sense out of the world though the use of narrative and imaginative language. In a sense, this is where we live: in those narrative spaces created by our encounters with the world, continually informed by present experience and our ongoing sense of the past. Grandparenting, I have suggested, is a vocation which only makes sense within this precise commemorative frame. Grandparents are not simply occupying a receding, nearly forgotten past; rather, they play a vital and ongoing creative role in creating a space where we can find our common humanity. Indeed, the "answer" to Larkin's question is perhaps more metaphorical than metaphysical. His poem suggests the needs of finding solace, of making do in a world which often fails to offer us any readymade solutions. Dealing with diaspora as a type of existential condition, as a starting point for meaning making, requires a sense of the history which led us to such a place, and the need for stories which provide us with a sense of hope, which provide an assertion of the importance of caring and love. Although education remains preoccupied with "content" grandparenting reminds us of the importance of care as a vital, social and personal process. Quite simply, they offer us a way of comporting ourselves: to the past, in the present and for the future—a future in which many of us will become grandparents ourselves. Perhaps we can find a meaningful place to live in this small thought—a tiny seed sending out delicate white tendrils, blind roots searching out the deep—reaching breathlessly into a vast sleeping unknown.

REFLECTION QUESTIONS

1. In this chapter, there is a variety of experiences that current and former adults (in their various roles) have shared. Name one particular experience that stands out for you and explain why it has a deeper meaning.
2. One example includes Sheldon, who works in the far north of Canada. How is this story of a near tradgedy connected to the history of Newfoundland and Labrador (and Newfoundlanders and Labradorians) as it relates to diaspora?
3. The use of the narrative (voice) of others is one research method that provides a unique way to "understand" the lived experiences of people – what are some of its limitations?
4. From the stories in this chapter, how would you describe the emerging/changing face of rural Newfoundland and Labrador?

REFERENCES

Bullock, K. (2005). Grandfathers and the Impact of Raising Grandchildren. *Journal of Sociology and Social Welfare, 32,* 43–60.
Doyle, C. (2010). "Cultural loss: What is taken from us and what we give away" In Kelly, U.A. & E. Yeoman (Eds.). *Despite this loss: Essays on culture, memory, and identity in Newfoundland and Labrador,* (pp. 117–127) St. John's, NL: ISER Books.
Fromm, E. (1974). The Art of Loving. New York: Harper & Row.
Gray, M., Misson, S., & Hayes, A. (2005). Young Children and Their Grandparents. *Family Matters, 72,* 10–17.
Hayslip, B.J., Shore, R.J., Henderson, C.E., & Lambert, P.L. (1998). Custodial grandparenting and the impact of grandchildren with problems on role satisfaction and role meaning. *The Journals of Gerontology.* Series B, *Psychological Sciences and Social Sciences, 53*(3), 164–73.
Hebblethwaite, S., & Norris, J. (2011). Expressions of generativity through family leisure: Experiences of grandparents and adult grandchildren. *Family Relations, 60*(1), 121–133.
Holc, J.P. (2011). The Remembered one: Memory Activism and the Construction of Edith Stein's Jewishness in Post Communist Wroclaw. *Shofar, 29*(4), 67–97.
Hopkins, J. (1998). Signs of the Post-Rural: Marketing Myths of a Symbolic Countryside. *Geografiska Annaler.* Series B. *Human Geography, 80*(2), 65–81.
Jackson, L.A., Marshall, E.A., Tirone, S., Donovan, C., & Shepard, B.C. (2006). "The forgotten population?: power, powerlessness, and agency among youth in coastal communities". In R. Ommer & P.R. Sinclair, (Eds.). Power and restructuring: Canada's coastal society and environment. (pp. 209– 232) St. John's: ISER Books.
Johnston, W. (1999). The colony of unrequited dreams. New York: Doubleday.
Kearney, R. (2002). On Stories. New York: Routledge.
Kelly, U.A.M. (2009). Migration and education in a multicultural world: *Culture, loss, and identity.* New York: Palgrave Macmillan.
Kelly, U.A. (2010). "Learning from loss: Migration, Mourning and Identity" In Kelly, U.A. & E. Yeoman (Eds.). Despite this loss: Essays on culture, memory, and identity in Newfoundland and Labrador. (pp. 17–34) St. John's, NL: Iser Books.
Lamb, J. (2002). Metamorphosis and Settlement. *Journal of New Zealand Literature, 20,* 18–38.
Lenz, C. (2011). Genealogy and archaeology: Analyzing generational positioning in historical narratives. *Journal of Comparative Family Studies, 42*(3), 319–327.
Madigan, S. (2011). Narrative Therapy. Washington: American Psychological Association.
Musil, C.M., Gordon, N.L., Warner, C.B., Zauszniewski, J.A., Standing, T., & Wykle, M. (2011). Grandmothers and caregiving to grandchildren: Continuity, change, and outcomes over 24 months. *Gerontologist, 51*(1), 86–100.

Orellana, M.F., Thorne, B., Chee, A., & Lam, W.S.E. (2001). Transnational Childhoods: The Participation of Children in Processes of Family Migration. *Social Problems, 48*(4), 572–591.

Porter Abbott, H. (2008). The Cambridge Introduction to Narrative. Cambridge: Cambridge University Press.

Roseman, S.R. (2002). "Strong Women" and "Pretty Girls": Self-Provisioning, Gender, and Class Identity in Rural Galicia (Spain). *American Anthropologist, 104*(1), 22.

Sheridan, L. (2008). Memory, Nostalgia, Identity: Bernice Morgan's "Waiting for Time" and Deirdre Madden's "Nothing Is Black". *The Canadian Journal of Irish Studies, 34*(2), 23–29.

Simon, R.I. (2005). The touch of the past: Remembrance, learning, and ethics. New York: Palgrave Macmillan.

Strom, P.S., & Strom, R.D. (October 01, 2011). Grandparent education: Raising grandchildren. *Educational Gerontology, 37*(10), 910–923.

Traphagan, J.W. (2000). The Liminal Family: Return Migration and Intergenerational Conflict in Japan. *Journal of Anthropological Research, 56*(3), 365–385.

Widerberg, K. (2011). Memory work: Exploring family life and expanding the scope of family research. *Journal of Comparative Family Studies, 42*(3), 329–337.

PAULINE FINLAY-MOLLOY

GRANDPARENTS PASSING LEGACIES THROUGH STORY TELLING AND ACTIVE LIVING

All human beings, whether they realize it or not, pass on the most important parts of their heritage to their children and grandchildren, which includes an understanding of what they value, from their earliest recollections to old age. The totality of these beliefs, memories, gems, whatever society wishes to call them, encompasses the culture of communities. In this paper, Newfoundland communities, to varying degrees, pass on their culture to others, often using the oral tradition of storytelling and active participation, as in past generations.

For the purpose of this study, five interviews carried out in the summer of 2011 with five grandparents from Newfoundland communities are discussed, along with my experience as the grandmother of three little girls. The range of ages of these grandparents is 56 to 81 years. All grandparents, with the exception of one, have been married over 35 years. In the discussions, often the pronoun "we" was used, rather than "I" as most activities and caregiving with the grandchildren was done with both grandparents present.

The first interview was with a grandmother from the west coast of Newfoundland. She has one grandchild, who she believes will be her only grandchild. This grandchild lives in British Columbia. Another grandmother lives on the Avalon Peninsula and has three grandchildren, with only one grandchild who is living thousands of miles away. The grandparents, in this case, feel that they offer much to the education of the two grandchildren who live nearer to them. The only grandfather in the study, who also lives on the Avalon Peninsula, shares numerous stories of his involvement in passing on his culture to all of his seven grandchildren who live on the island of Newfoundland, but not all in his hometown. The grandchildren all live within a 90 minute drive from him. He tells stories about all the adventures and bonding that takes place during his weekends and holidays with the grandchildren. The oldest grandparent in the study, an eighty-one year old grandmother from the Southern Shore, tells about her 34 grandchildren and 15 great grandchildren. She recounts stories of a close-knit loving relationship with all of her 13 children's offspring. She discusses how storytelling is a big part of all or most aspects of their social times together, from when the grandchildren were very young to now, as they are growing older and having families of their own.

The grandmother from the west coast of the Island feels that her only grandchild has a close connection with all of her grandparents who live on the island. This past

A. Singh and M. Devine (Eds.), Rural Transformation and Newfoundland and Labrador Diaspora: Grandparents, Grandparenting, Community and School Relations, 207–216.

summer the little girl, aged 11 years, came home to spend a month with both sets of grandparents, alternating a week with the maternal grandparents and then a week with the paternal grandparents. This grandmother in her fifties says that she wants to have a close bond with her only grandchild, and desires being remembered kindly by her. "I want her to remember me as a safe haven. I'm here to listen to her and direct her path to some extent. I want to help her to be a person who can make her own decisions, not to follow the crowd." Over the years her grandchild lived with her and her husband. The grandparents helped to look after the child while the daughter went to school and worked. She explained how she felt lost when her daughter and her son-in-law moved away to attend university. "Since they've been away you lose all of the closeness. We miss not being able to see her when she's in a concert and not being able to share in her accomplishments day to day. We do a lot when she's here or when we go to visit them." She also considers what her grandchild is missing out on in their lives. "She is not able to share parts of our lives, such as trips to our cabin, quadding and skidooing." Communication with her granddaughter is a big part of her life. Often the child will contact her on Skype and say "Let's chat!" She loves to tell about all the small projects they do together. "We have little conversations. We write letters as she enjoys getting letters and then she writes back. We read books on Skype, books about polar bears, lessons about being conscious about the world." This grandparent, who used to babysit children, worked in a bank and then helped out in her husband's electronic business, believes that, through her hard work, she is a good role model for her grandchild. When asked how she treats her grandchild different from her two daughters, says she doesn't think so. "I do a lot of the things that are the same, that I did with my own children." When asked how she passes on her Newfoundland culture to her grandchild, she was modest in her answer. "Her other grandparents have taught her the accordion and square dancing. Her great grandfather is 102 and he plays the accordion. They also teach her tap dancing and Newfoundland songs. In school she's done research on Indians of Canada and other groups in our country. And we always tell her stories about what it was like when we were young."

The second grandmother who lives on the Avalon Peninsula in a small outport most of the year, feels that she and her husband are very close to all three of their small grandchildren. In discussing her own grandparents, she says she remembers being 'half scared' of her mother's mother, who lived a short distance from her small community (population <200). She described the difference between her grandparents and her and her husband as being very unlike their relationships with grandchildren nowadays. She said "They were not all over you like we are with our grandchildren." Although one grandson lives in the United States, this grandparent talks to all of her grandchildren often. Of the grandchild who lives thousands of miles away, she says "He loves to talk. We use Skype every day. We talk to them all here in Newfoundland. Every second day I'll talk to him. His mom puts him on the phone or on Skype." She takes her role as a grandparent very seriously. When asked how she saw this role she said "My role is to set a good example and help them enjoy themselves. One day I rolled down over the lawn with my grandchildren. They loved it. It made me feel young again". Parents need to keep their children involved and she sees it as a challenge today.

These two first grandparents appear emotionally close to their grandchildren, very similar to the author's relationship with her three small granddaughters. When my grandchildren visit our small community, my husband and I take them trouting, go on picnics with them, read to them and play games as well. The second lady interviewed states "We take them to the beach, wash their clothes, make cookies and bread with them, read them stories, play games and get them ready for bed." When I visit my grandchildren I have an activity planned each day and certain rituals that the grandchildren love. One ritual that helps them develop a sense of story is our story writing activity. I buy them three cheap journals from the dollar store and each day we sit together at the table and discuss what kind of story we will write today. In each book I will scribe their little stories, asking questions to direct their attention. Then we read each story two or three times. I think this helps them with the whole process of storywriting. Later that day I'll ask each of them to tell me the story or retell it to Mom or Dad or Poppy.

This second grandmother, who is the same age, worked on the fish plant for many years and now works at H & R Block seasonally. She and her partner like to make sure they do quality activities with their grandchildren. "We take them to the Salmonier Nature Park, swimming at Northern Bay Sands, whale watching at O'Brien's Tours and we've taken them to Signal Hill and Fort Pepperal. My husband knows a lot about Newfoundland history. He is always telling them stories about our province. He watches the Discovery Channel a lot. He knows quite a lot about so many topics." She remarked that their relationship to their grandchildren changed as they grew and have different needs. She said "They follow our examples and we've adapted sometimes to their maturity." When asked how her grandchildren learn about their Newfoundland culture, she replied "My niece teaches them Newfoundland songs. My brother-in-law plays accordion and my uncle, too. Two of my grandchildren play the flute and one would like to play the guitar." The grandmother compares what activities she did with her children to what her grandchildren do with her and her husband "They love listening to their grandfather telling stories, comparing what it was like when we were kids and the way things are done now. They have big campers to go out of town on the weekends. We used to take our kids on a trike and go to a cabin. Or we'd go to a small park and have a picnic." This grandmother and her partner did not need to take responsibility for daycare, but at times they babysat for the parents to have a night out or they attended a concert or sports event with the children. She spoke proudly of the help they give. "Sometimes we help them out with babysitting, doing homework with two of the grandchildren, and doing projects. One time my husband got wood off the beach for a school project. Another time he loaned one child a compass which he brought to school and explained it to his class." When asked how she'd like to be remembered by her grandchildren, she replied "I'd like them to remember us for all the things – fun times together – our cultural adventures." In this case study, the stories and outings together with children and grandchildren helped reinforce the grandparents' values and cultural connection. The children experienced a kind and loving relationship with their grandparents and enjoyed spending time with them.

The third grandparent hails from the northeast coast of Newfoundland and was an educator all of her life, along with her husband who was a school principal. Today she is an energy worker who studies all over the world. Like me, she believes that learning is a lifelong pursuit and that travel is a big part of a person's learning. She has one daughter and two grandchildren who live on the west coast of Canada. She has memories of one grandparent. She was a very cautious person. "I remember her cutting up a candy cane at Christmas time so I wouldn't choke. Another time she reprimanded me because I was digging a hole and she was afraid someone would fall into it." She described this grandmother as a strong, capable person, a take charge type. She said whenever she used her sense of humor as a child, her relatives told her that she was like her grandfather, who had died when she was two years old. She thinks she is different than her grandparents in that "there is a lot more physical touching-ramsing, we call it!" Her grandchildren love being around her and she gives several examples. "They still fight over who is going to sleep with me. If my husband is there, they come down to the bedroom and get in the bed in the morning. I like to lie down with them and read them stories." Over the years she helped out her daughter. "I flew up to Toronto to look after them when my daughter was working all summer." Being active clearly shows grandchildren what a grandparent values in life. "Our two grandchildren travelled to the Yukon to visit us when we lived there. They travelled to Alaska with us four times. In the Yukon the granddaughter would go to my workplace with me and put on a lab coat and count the bottles for the ointments I was making. My husband and I have taken the two of them to the zoo and theme parks in Florida. We are always being active with them." Visits back and forth are a part of this family's history. This grandmother elaborates further on her visits to their home. "When I'm up with them I cook with them. I teach them Newfoundland recipes-toutons, cod au gratin, old fashioned fudge using my mom's recipe, and anything with blueberries in it." She says it's a bit different when they come to Newfoundland. Her husband takes a more active part when they are in their home.

He sits with them and makes porridge for them.

He tells them stories of when he was a boy in England. He tells a story about a dog protecting him all the time. They ask for this story all the time so he retells it. He was lucky because he had grandparents for a long time. He talks to them about a photo of our granddaughter and her great grandmother (paternal). He shows them symbols such as Bobbie hats, and tells them legends of Robin Hood. I tell them about Daisy, a big sheep. We named all the sheep in our rural community where I grew up. We have an hour of storytelling before they go to sleep. I might keep them up longer than usual.

There seems to be a deep bond among grandparents, great grandparents and grandchildren.

Relationships with the grandchildren have changed as the children matured. They can do more things now, as they get older. I am able to communicate with them on a more mature level. It makes a huge difference in their lives, in their self-esteem and sense of worth. We touch them at a level of who they are, their heritage and where they are. It gives them a true sense of identity. It helps them see beyond their family and keeps them grounded. It makes them feel better about their place in the world.

The oral tradition of storytelling is a big part of the bonding in this family. Also, they listen to Newfoundland music together. They own lots of traditional music. They attend the Downeast festivals with their mother. The grandmother teachers them Newfoundland sayings. "One of their favourite sayings is How's ya gettin on? (wink click, click). My granddaughter can do it with the winking and clicking!" The grandparents also buy Newfoundland books and read to them. Challenges for grandparents years ago, this grandmother notes, is that "Life was hard. Often boozing aged them and there was lots of violence. Parents may have had addiction problems, and grandparents had to take over. They had to provide longer term assistance when single parents couldn't handle it on their own." This grandmother described her role as a grandparent to be "Pure Joy". She proudly displays herc omputer where she alternates photos of her granddaugther and grandson as the screen saver. She hopes her grandchildren will remember her in a loving way. "Physical contact is so important. We have time for the big walking hug and many marathon hugs." She looks forward to her weekly contact on the phone and on Skype.

The fourth grandparent is the grandfather of seven children who spent most of his life in the heavy equipment industry. He worked in management and often teaching skills to others. Both he and his grandchildren live on the Avalon Peninsula. He remembers the lack of contact with his own grandparents. "There was one grandfather I saw on one occasion. The other grandfather didn't live long. Everybody seemed to be too busy back then, trying to survive. They weren't fun to be around. There was no interaction with grandchildren. The women were doing chores-knitting socks or cooking dinner." I found this to be the case with my own grandparents. If my grandmother was in the garden with her flowers, I could look over the fence but I was not allowed to enter. I had to sit quietly and was not allowed to touch anything in my maternal grandparents' house. It was a very cold way to grow up, with grandparents who didn't seem to want you to be around. This grandfather believes that grandparents in his day didn't think about spending time with you. Back then they saw grandmothers mainly in the house where they'd try to enlist your help. They wanted you to help them with physical activity. They might get you to feed the hens or go for a bucket of water. They might offer you a cookie or a bun. They'd give you 15 cents for the garden party. Sometimes, he said, they gave you a dime or fifteen cents but it was not a weekly thing. I didn't experience this with my grandparents, either maternal or paternal. No money was given to me, but in her old age, my maternal grandmother gave loonies or toonies to my children, and occasionally she gave my sons a five dollar bill. Often, as this grandfather emphasized, they would just tell you to go outdoors and play. When asked if grandparents had changed over the years, the grandfather remarked "Oh, yes! They are like chaulk and cheese!" One point that was emphasized by this person was that he loves spending time with each of his seven grandchildren and he doesn't treat either one differently. "I take them hiking to the community pastures. I never do anything differently. I give them the same amount of money. I'm always teaching them things and telling them about their ancestors and the way they lived. I take them exploring for fossils and they've even found 500 million year old fossils!" It is clear to see that this man sees his role in grandparenting as a teacher. He said

> I don't feel like I'm stuck with them. I pass along everything I know, not just by telling them but with physical activity. I encourage them to participate in physical activity-softball, golf and soccer. I encourage them to get a good rounded education.

There appears to be a close connection between this grandfather and all of his grandchildren.

> We always had interaction with them. They used to stay at our residence on holidays and weekends. One time one of my grandsons made a comment when he was leaving "I certainly loves to be out here." I'd make up an agenda before their visits. The list would include: bonfire, visits to beach at Spoon Cove, hikes on Feather Point.

I didn't ask any questions about his wife but he seemed to glow when talking about his grandchildren. He described the interaction as "excellent" and "a barrel of fun". He listed off all the exciting things he does with them. "I taught them to feed the horses (keep your fingers outstretched), eat outdoors, fill bird feeders, identify bird species, cook up different meals for them, stuff they're not used to." Every time he sees them he feels "on top of the world". He described his feelings as "nothing but plus/plus". One sentence summed it up suscintly. "Every time I see them they give me a big hug and a big kiss-nothing is better than that!" As a writer, artist and fossil enthusiast he believes he passes on his love of nature and the past to his grandchildren. "One key to continuing family lore and culture is story telling. I gave each family a copy of the stories I've known and told." He writes down many stories and types them, then gets a copy of the book for each family. He believes there should be more interactions between grandparents and children and parents. He sites various challenges nowadays for parents. "They need more involvement with children. There should be scheduling for parents to spend more time in the home. Often the use of technology is unsupervised." When asked what he sees as his role with his grandchildren he says "Talk to children. Don't talk down to them. Get involved. Teach them everything you know. Always ask for their input as well." This grandfather shares his stories he's written about Newfoundland culture. He shares with his grandchildren's classmates. He has been invited into schools many times by his grandchildren.

> They have read some of the stories I've written. I've made small sailing boats with them, boats to go across the Atlantic. I get the materials, and let them put the boats together. I give them a pill bottle to glue on and to put a message in. They screw the bottle onto the boat.

From the conversation I knew this grandparenting style had much in common with my own. I cut out foldable books and the children put them together, and all three granddaughters are involved. I tell them stories about Newfoundland of long ago, how my grandparents and great grandparents lived. My husband and I try to keep them active while we are around them, when they visit us. We go to the beach and build ice forts, make a camp fire and roast weiners and marshmallows and occasionally some caplin. We tell them about the lighthouses at Cape Pine and Cape Race and how my ancestors were lighthouse keepers and fishermen and why we have lighthouses. We take them to the edge of the ocean and tell them about the bountiful ocean and how our ancestors worked hard to feed their families.

The grandmother interviewed last is an expert at being a grandmother. At a ripe old age of 81 she has 34 grandchildren and 15 great grandchildren from her 13 offspring. She lives in a small outport on the Avalon Peninsula and travels to see her children and grandchildren with her husband. She never misses a wedding or dance. She is still active and lively in her community. She has a great sense of humour and made me laugh many times talking about her grandchildren. When asked what her role as a grandmother is she stated:

> Talk to them. Put them on the right road. We tell them about going to church. I don't try to tell them anymore. I tell them right from wrong. Some of them are mature enough to listen. I baby sits them. Sews for them. Teach them how to knit and sew and cook. Tells them stories.

After her father died this grandmother had been placed in an orphanage for three years. When her mother remarried she had to take her home. She didn't remember her grandfathers because they died when she was young. Her mother's mother died when she was young also. She remembers her paternal grandmother who used to haul her over to her own place on a slide called a Mancat, like a horseslide only smaller. This grandmother was sweet to them, especially after her father died so young. She used to help her in her garden and pick berries and give them to her. She had a very nice relationship with her grandmother, the only grandparent she remembers. Her job was chiefly of homemaker with the family growing to 13 children she was kept busy. She worked at the peat for a couple of years but stayed home after that. When asked how she helps her children and grandchildren these days, she said

> When my son goes back and forth to Iqaluit, his wife looks after the nest. We, my husband and I, go out and we bring in the clothes and pack it up. I

cook for them and look after their son. Over the years we have done plenty of babysitting and homework with the grandchildren. I helped them with essays and speeches. I drew witches and pumpkins with them. Now we keep in touch mainly by phone and Facebook. They bought us a computer so I can check up on them and see their pictures. We are always on the phone, telling the latest news. I'll tell one person and they pass it on.

When asked how it affects her own mental and physical health she responds "I feel really good. It gives me great self-esteem to be able to do what I can for them. I am really proud when they come for a visit, to see us. They're all over me when they come. Some of them listen 100% of the times and some say 'Mother, that's bull,' some of them like to listen to the stories we tell them. It makes me feel good to know that they are interested." She had lots of ideas about the challenges faced by parents and children today.

There are lots of challenges. You wonder who the children are resorting with. No discipline any more. They can get in with the wrong people and be in prison for life. Parents need to tell their children to be in at a certain time and know where they are going. Years ago when we were raising our children we had no money to give them. Now they have too much and too much money is given to children.

Several of her grandchildren lived with her when her daughters had children at a young age.

I had one grandson who was very sick and towards the end had seizures. We prayed a lot and we treated him like one of our own children. We took it one day at a time. It was very difficult when he died. But we knew we did our best for him. A granddaughter stayed with us until after kindergarten. She was sweet and she was no trouble. It was hard when our grandson died but we had good neighbours and family. You did what you had to do back in them times. Nobody had much back then.

When asked what suggestions she has for grandparents she said "Keep close with them right when they're able to know them. So they are able to have good memories when you're gone. You want them to remember you in a good way, not in a contrary way. Sing songs and tell stories so that they know about their past and won't forget it." She spoke about teaching one of her daughter's children the old songs, trying to get them to remember all the words. The interest is there and some of them will take the time to learn the songs.

All of the grandparents enjoyed being interviewed. They loved talking about their families and grandchildren. One grandparent said her grandchildren are her pride and joy and she could talk about them for hours and never get tired. Another said it was pure joy to be grandparents and she liked to share her happiness and memories with others. The grandfather said it was an honour to share his fondest memories of time spent with his grandchildren.

It has always been a positive to me to express an opinion that might in the end result in helping someone else. I think the main benefit in gaining education is to then continue to pass it on to others. Talking to grandchildren is a huge reward for a grandparent. Sharing knowledge and stories and listening to their ideas is a priceless benefit. Unfortunately, parents don't always have time to participate in the maturing of children. Sometimes they do but they have a negative feeling and show an attitude such as, why should I bother to take my child to a function when some other person will take him/her.

The experience cemented the author's view that Newfoundland grandparents love their grandchildren and want to help them along life's pathway. It further strengthened her conviction that grandparents who are devoted to their own children continue to be devoted grandparents. The values and legacy passed on in words and deeds shape the communities and show what spirited people Newfoundlanders really are. The consistent support of grandparents helps build a strong base on which new families bond together and thrive. The words of the grandparents speak for many grandparents on the island of Newfoundland.

REFLECTION QUESTIONS

1. Towards the beginning of this chapter, one grandparent referred to being an influence on the grandchildren, "…to a certain extent." From your own experience, how would you interpret this comment?
2. Sometimes when we ask people about "passing on culture", it may not be clear to them. How would you describe the notion of "…passing on culture?"
3. Some of the grandparents describe having lots of "fun" with their grandchildren. How does this concept of "fun" fit into the role of grandparents?
4. Some interviewees described their grandparents being 'cold' and not paying much attention to them. What might account for this approach by grandparents of "yesteryear" within the context of their culture at that time?

CATHERINE LEE-IVANY

"IT'S WONDERFUL TO BE A NEWFOUNDLAND GRANDMOTHER"

Keeping in Touch with Grandchildren in Person and Through Technology

ABSTRACT

As grandparents generally live longer they play an even more important role in the lives of their grandchildren. This means grandparents are passing along family history, traditional skills and offering important advice and guidance to their grandchildren. Grandparents are also able to spend time in delightful recreational activities with their grandchildren. Some are lucky enough to have their grandchildren living nearby so they can see them on a regular basis, while others make connections through technology. I spoke with two grandmothers and asked that they share the experience of their own lives with their grandparents, and then tell me how their own relationship with their grandchildren compares today. I then spoke with several of their grandchildren to find out just how important their relationships with their grandmothers are to them. One group of grandparents-grandchildren sees each other quite often, while the other keeps in touch by phone and computer with occasional visits. All of the individuals I spoke with value their grandparent-grandchild relationship.

Introduction

The grandparent-grandchild relationship is one that is valued in today's society. This relationship may also have a very positive effect on well-being on both sides.

> Grandparents are living long enough to enjoy a lengthy life as grandparents, they can keep in touch more easily with grandchildren, they have more time to devote to them, and they have more money to spend on them. They are also, less likely to still be raising their own children (Mitchell, 2009, p. 231).

Many grandparents today enjoy playing a very active role in the lives of their grandchildren. Some may play a large role to help when both parents are working, some show their unwavering support by attending their grandchildren's activities, and some delight in the closeness that technology provides when their grandchildren don't live nearby.

A. Singh and M. Devine (Eds.), Rural Transformation and Newfoundland and Labrador Diaspora:
Grandparents, Grandparenting, Community and School Relations, 217–230.

In today's society where often two parents are working, grandparents may play a role in bringing children back and forth to school, or providing care when school is over.

> Grandparents often have more time than working parents to support young people in activities and are well placed to talk to their grandchildren about any problems the young people may be experiencing. They were also found to be involved in helping to solve the young people's problems, as well as talking with them about plans for their future (Tan, Griggs, & Attar, 2008, p. 1).

Most children and adolescents really welcome this time spent together as I found out in my interviews. Not living close to grandparents wasn't of the utmost importance in keeping the relationship together either, as many "did not view physical proximity as bring necessarily important as they used modern technology to communicate" (Tan, Griggs, & Attar, 2008, p. 1). All did agree that they would prefer to live close to their grandparents. The grandchildren and grandparents I spoke with did not live together, but all stated this intergenerational relationship had a positive impact on their lives. "The continued existence of intergenerational bonds is actually positive for family life in the United States" (Tutwiler, 2005, p. 45). I suspect this is the same for Canada and especially, for Newfoundland and Labrador.

As no two people are alike, no two grandparents view their role in exactly the same way.

> Grandparents as a group are not homogenous. As a group they are quite diverse with their own unique cultural backgrounds. The reason to highlight this diversity is to suggest that this particular group may have something to offer that a younger generation of parents lack (Singh, Review of Research: Why Focus on Grandparents? (working draft), 2010, p. 1).

Certainly, grandparents have a lot to offer grandchildren. Grandparents wish to leave a legacy of themselves to their grandchildren and share their stories and lessons they have learned in their own lives. In my paper I will talk about my own experience with my grandparents and I will explore what life was like for a grandchild in an isolated rural community in the 1930s and 1940s and for a city grandchild in the 1940s and 1950s. Through interviews with "Audrey" and "Lorna" and their grandchildren, I will look to see how these two grandmothers view their role today and how their grandchildren are a source of happiness, self-fulfilment and satisfaction.

> The quality of the grandmother's relationship with her grandchild is one of the main factors affecting the degree of psychological well-being she experiences and that greater involvement leads to greater satisfaction in the role of grandmother (Shlomo, Taubman, Ari, Findler, Sivan, & Dolizki, 2010, p. 47).

VOICES

My Own History with My Grandparents

Grandparents play an important role in our families and in our society. They are where we come from. Family research is invaluable to human knowledge and understanding starting with reflection into how our own families have shaped who we are. I wasn't lucky enough to spend a large part of my life with grandparents, and, therefore, it is interesting for me to conduct some research with people who have been grandparents for a long time, and ask some questions to the grandchildren who have been fortunate enough to have them.

My father grew up in a rural community, The Goulds, on a farm just outside of St. John's. His father, who was a farmer, died of cancer in 1964, three years before I was born. My father's mother died in 1968 at 56 of a sudden heart attack while she was getting ready to go out. My mother grew up in Harbour Grace, a rural fishing and fish plant community about an hour drive outside of St. John's and her mother died of cancer at age 61. I still have some very vivid memories of my grandmother. Nanny was a very quiet and ladylike woman. She would never raise her voice and she always had candy, nickels and dimes for us in her purse. We saw her at least a couple of times a month but I don't recall ever spending any time with her just myself or of her teaching me any skills. I remember she loved to sew. Her illness meant she had been sick from the time I was four or five.

My mother's father, Pop, was a widower for six years before he suddenly passed away of a heart attack. I would take the yellow, Fleetline bus out the "old road" to Harbour Grace from Mount Pearl, to spend many weekends with him. Years before he worked at a Printing Press business and the top of his finger had gotten caught in some machinery and it was cut off. I remember that as a very vivid detail about him. He made his own bread and whenever I stayed with him we always had fresh bread in the morning with tea. Pop would always pour his tea into his saucer and drink it from there. Years ago, drinking tea from a saucer to cool it was common and passed down from the British tradition. Today it would be considered a breach of etiquette. At night he would heat up big beach rocks and wrap them in a towel or blanket and put it at the end of my bed to keep my feet warm. I remember he always wore a suit and tie whenever he left the house.

I have another vivid memory of my grandfather from a weekend I went to stay with him in Harbour Grace. I went to a Saturday night dance at the local school when I was thirteen years old. I was waltzing with a boy I really liked when I saw my grandfather come in through the door, dressed in his suit and tie with his overcoat and hat. He had come to bring me home to make sure I got there safely. I remember feeling mortified that Pop was there and I was waltzing with a boy. I remember him patiently waiting for me until it was over so he could take me home.

For most of my life I didn't really think about my grandparents much as they had been part of my life for such a short time. Now I find myself looking back at not just my own grandparents, but the notion of what it means to be a grandparent and how that has changed so much in our society...and perhaps how it has stayed so much the same. I believe my grandparents did help to shape who I am today.

I had an unexpected encounter with my biological grandmother when I was twenty-eight. After being adopted as an infant by wonderful parents and given a great life, I discovered my biological roots were not far from the town I was adopted into. I hadn't really thought much about searching or even put any effort into it. I was simply driving on the TransCanada Highway passing Soldier's Pond, when the idea came into my head. Ten years before, my Mom had told me the name of my birth mother, she had seen it by accident in court when the adoption became official. When I returned home I looked up the name in the phone book and in two calls I had found my birth family. Newfoundland is indeed a very small place.

My birth mother had moved to Toronto shortly after my birth and had a son four years later. She was one of only two girls in a family of ten children. Her father died when she was a teenager from a sickness he contracted from working in the mines on Bell Island, leaving her mother to raise a family of ten by herself in a small outport community. I was the first grandchild. As it was 1967, society deemed that I would not be raised by a single mother. My grandmother insisted in no uncertain terms, that I would be put up for adoption and that was that. My biological father was a boy in the same community who was already engaged to another girl in the community, who was also pregnant. My biological mother, I never refer to her as anything else as I grew up with a mother, was so distraught that she left for Toronto and she has been there ever since. She never married and was afraid to tell her mother she was pregnant again in fear that she would be forced to relinquish her son as well. She didn't tell her mother until the day she had her son and her mother was back in Newfoundland, too far away to force her to do anything.

When I met my grandmother she was a very small woman of 81. She had tremendous strength and respect from her family, that was very clear to see. She gripped me by the hand and told me she had prayed every day that God would let her see me before she died so she would know what became of me. I told her I believed her prayers had been answered because I never had any intention in looking for any one until the divine thought on my solitary drive home on the highway.

She got to sit with her daughter and myself at her own kitchen table and have tea and buns. She showed me family albums and pointed out who everyone was. She died within a year after I met her.

I wish I had more time to spend with my grandparents. I would have liked to get to know them better and have them all see what I have made of my own life. I would have liked to interview them and collect their stories rather than hear them from other relatives.

THE GRANDMOTHERS' VOICES

"Audrey"

Audrey was born by a midwife on an island off the coast of Newfoundland in 1932. The place she was born is now a ghost town. It was only ever accessible by boat and the population only reached around one hundred people. It had its own post office from 1941 to 1965 until it was resettled, or depopulated by Joey Smallwood's government.

Everyone was a fisherman or worked with the fishery and the community was very close knit. The community had its beginnings in the 1500s after the English claimed fishing rights to Newfoundland waters; the community survived and thrived until 1965. Its history includes a run in with the notorious pirate Peter Easton. But with no cars, electricity or plumbing, it could not survive the social shift of Newfoundland moving into Confederation with the Fisheries Household Resettlement Program. Premier Joey Smallwood wanted all Newfoundlanders to have access to a reasonable level of government services, telephones, electricity, healthcare facilities, schools, roads and post offices and he wanted to modernize the fishery ("No Great Future" Government Sponsored Resettlement in Newfoundland and Labrador).

Audrey was born the second oldest of eight children. Her parents and both sets of grandparents came from the same community. Audrey says, "My parents and my older brother and I lived with my father's parents for a while when we were building our home. My mother's parents were older. It was my grandfather's second marriage because his first wife died young. My grandparents had fourteen children and my mother was the youngest."

Audrey remembers helping with dishes when she was a little girl and running errands. She remembers, "One time I told my grandmother I didn't like her because she liked my older brother best and then I went and hid under the bed. My brother was Nan's boy and he got away with everything. He was her first grandson."

Audrey grew up on an island where they grew and produced a lot of their own food and supplies. "My grandparents grew their own potatoes, turnip, cabbage and beet. I remember turning over grass to make hay. We were the only people who owned a cow at this time. My grandmother made her own butter, cream and cheese."

For most of the men on the island, working meant going away for long periods of time to fish. "My grandfather and father owned a schooner called the Olive and Jesse that went to Labrador for fish. They would be gone all summer."

There was a lot of work for the women to do while the men were gone. Women tended gardens and animals and made hay. Women also worked with the fish carrying heavy barrels. "We would put fish in the barrel and me and my mother would bring it up to the flake to dry."

"My grandfather also had a store on the island. He was the merchant. There were also 3–4 other schooners on the island as well."

Audrey had some wonderful memories of her grandparents.

All of my grandparents were religious. There were two Anglican churches on the island, one in our community and one in a nearby community. One set of grandparents sat in the front seat of the church and the other set sat just behind. This showed their status in the community. We shared a minister with a larger area and he came once a month. Men in the church filled in on the other Sundays and my grandfather was a lay reader. The Bible was an important text book at this time. Audrey says, we had to learn a lot of the Bible. Everyone learned because that's what was expected.

Boys spent a lot of time with their fathers and grandfathers. I learned to knit with my grandmother; caps, mittens and scarves. We ordered wool from the Eaton's catalogue. Grandfather would bring back treats from St. John's when he went with his fish. He always brought tomatoes for his wife and barrels of apples in the fall. I remember my first coat that wasn't handmade. My Uncle bought it for me in St. John's. It was dark green and I thought the world of it. I thought I had my fortune.

Audrey said time spent with her grandparents was often working time as something always needed to be done. "Yes, I'm a different grandparent with my grandchildren. I'm more outgoing. I guess my grandparents were too busy. I remember some evenings with my grandmother. If she took up her knitting I could sit with her and knit."

Audrey lives in Mount Pearl and has five children. Four children live in Newfoundland, her oldest boy lives in Alberta and has done so for almost thirty years. They keep in contact by phone on a regular basis with visits every two years or so. I am married to her youngest son. Audrey has been married to her sweetheart, from a neighbouring community on the island where she was born, for fifty-five years. They have four grandchildren ages thirty-one, thirty, twenty-two and ten. She also has two great grandchildren ages six and two. Audrey has been involved in all of their lives.

Audrey says, "Being a grandmother is very satisfying. I attend all of their functions, dancing, drama, music, brownies, and confirmation – whatever they have going on. I have babysat for them after school, have them down often to stay overnight and sometimes bring them out around the bay." Audrey and her husband have another home near where their old community was resettled where they spend a lot of time.

Audrey left her community when she was young to pursue a teaching career. She attended Prince of Wales Summer School on LeMarchant Road in St. John's and then taught Primary and Elementary grades for six years moving from Trinity Bay, Bonne Bay, Channel Port aux Basques, Stephenville, and New Harbour. Eventually she and her husband settled into St. John's and then Mount Pearl to raise their family. Her husband worked and she stayed home and raised her children.

"All of my grandchildren and great grandchildren live nearby and visit us often. We also speak on the phone but we don't communicate using technology as we don't use a computer."

"Lorna"

Lorna, the second of five children, was born in 1941 at the Grace Hospital in St. John's. Lorna's grandfather on her mother's side was a surveyor in the mines of Bell Island. He eventually went into politics with Joey Smallwood and became Minister of Highways and then Finance.

I remember having my picture taken near a big piece of machinery when the Kenmount Road overpass was being built. My grandfather on my father's side was a verger, or caretaker for the Anglican Cathedral and the model school. Both of my grandmothers were housewives.

There was quite a class difference between both sets of grandparents. My grandparents on my mother's side were a lot of fun and there were a lot of social activities. We would get paid for polishing silverware and washing floors. We were volunteered, we didn't volunteer. They always favoured my older sister. She might get paid $10 and I would get paid $2. We lived only a twenty minute walk from them and we would see them at least once a week. In the 1950s, quite often my grandfather would pick us up after Sunday school and go for a drive. In the winter we would go to Kent's Pond skating with the old fashioned two blade skates.

I asked Lorna what were some important lessons she learned from her grandparents. She said, "We were taught respect and manners by our grandparents. Mom would let things go but grandmother would give us a rap on the fingers."

Christmas time was an important time for Lorna's family. "Christmas dinner was at our house and Boxing Day dinner was at my mother's parents' house. We were only allowed to see my father's parents on Christmas Eve when we delivered gifts. Class was important back then."

Lorna says, "I don't remember time spent with only one grandchild. I remember attending a Mason's garden party as a little girl but I was with my sister. I don't remember spending time with them by myself."

The class divide between the two sets of grandparents was a wide one.

My father's parents were only five minutes away but we only saw them once a month. My mother was more interested in the social activities of her own parents. But on Christmas Eve, we would pack up the sleigh with parcels and go delivering gifts. We'd have to have Purity Strawberry syrup and Nanny's homemade fruitcake. This is my biggest memory of them. I felt more loved there even though there were dark, dinghy, wooden walls compared to my other grandparents with the large house and modern architecture, teak and glass...but it was all for show. My father's parents were warm, friendly and family oriented. My mother's parents were social climbers and politicians. My father's mother taught me how to crochet. My mother's mother taught my mother and older sister how to sew...but not me.

Lorna married her sweetheart (this writer's own father's younger brother) almost fifty years ago.

My mother was against it as he was only a lowly farmer's son. He joined the military and our three children were born in Germany and France and we have lived all over the world. Our three children now live in Alberta, Ontario and Nova Scotia. We have four grandchildren, two are sixteen, and one eleven and one twelve. Two live in Ontario and two live in Nova Scotia.

I asked Lorna how she is different as a grandparent than her grandparents. She says, "I don't show favouritism. In my own heart I have opinions sometimes but, I don't let the kids see that. I try and support them in ways with no pressure. When we're together we play Scrabble and other board games and talk."

Lorna has lived near her grandchildren at some times in their lives. "When I lived nearby I did babysit and I still fly up to babysit when their parents want to go on trips. Being this far away from them makes grandparenting only somewhat satisfying. I wish I was closer."

Lorna's children or grandchildren have never lived in Newfoundland and have only been here for some holidays. Lorna says "I am a grandmother, a playmate and an electronic penpal or techno-grandma. My grandchildren and I share email and chatting online. My grandchildren create movies of themselves and send them to us sometimes and we also talk on the phone at least every two weeks."

But Lorna admits,

the computer used to be used more to communicate but now they're more interested in their friends. It frustrates me sometimes that they don't have the same respect for their parents as my children had for me. I do share childhood stories with them about what it was like when I was a little girl and what their parents were like when they were little children.

THE GRANDCHILDREN'S VOICES

I interviewed some of the grandchildren to see what their thoughts were on their relationship with their grandmothers. Some I met in person and others I interviewed over the computer. I posed a series of questions to find out how they viewed their grandparents so I could find out how much they knew of their grandmothers' stories, and what important lessons and legacy they see being passed down to them.

Ciara (10): Audrey's Granddaughter

Ciara's other grandmother (her mother's mother) lives in Dublin, Ireland and she is now 91. Ciara says, "We try to visit her every year but I spend a lot of time with my grandmother here," pointing to Audrey.'

My grandmother and I used to go for walks and play school almost every time I came here. I come to see her at least every two or three days. We try to come at a good time because I have so many things going on. I'm in dance and acting and music. She always comes to see me in my shows.

Ciara thinks she and her Nan are alike in personality and get along very well.

When Nan and Pop take me around the bay she would read me a story every night before I'd go to bed and we like to play card games and board games together. I also help her make bread and cookies. I always feel very happy when I am with my grandparents and I love to be with them. I think if I'm here and we making cookies together then that's good for her physical health.

Alyssa (21): Audrey's Granddaughter

What have you learned from your grandparents (especially your grandmother) (skills, ideas, life lessons etc.)

My grandparents have always taught me an important thing-education is always your number one priority. Growing up they took care of me each and every day after school, and never once let anything get in the way of me finishing my homework. Whenever I faced a problem, they helped in the best possible way they could. My grandmother kept me busy when I visited. She showed me how to bake her famous homemade bread, hem a pair of pants, make chocolate chip cookies from scratch, and how to knit myself a winter scarf. She believed exercise is what kept you young so we walked every single day, which is most likely why I find myself to be so dedicated to my workout routine today.

How much time do you spend with your grandparents now? How much time did you spend with them growing up?

Growing up I spent nearly every day with my grandparents. From as early as I can remember they've always looked after me whenever my parents needed them to. From elementary school all through high school I spent every day after school with them, for hours on end. As I've gotten older, my time spent with them is becoming less and less. Between my part-time job and my university courses, I have very little free time as opposed to when I was younger. I've always cherished the time spent with my grandparents, so I try to make as much effort as possible to see them whenever I can.

How often do you speak to your grandparents during a regular week?
"On average, I speak to them about 4–5 times during a week. It could be more or less depending."

Do you ask what it was like when they were your age, or younger, with their grandparents?

Often times in the past I've asked them how different things were when they were growing up. It shocked me hearing the amount of change they've seen as they got older. I can't imagine how both exciting and overwhelming they found it adapting to their constantly changing surroundings. They even tell me today they will never get used to the concept of "texting." Just like them, I will never get used to the concept of actually using an outhouse.

What do you most like to do with your grandmother when you are with her? With your grandfather?

My grandfather is a quiet man, and tends to keep to himself more than my grandmother does, or so I've noticed. Whenever I'm around we'll just sit and listen to the radio, enjoying each other's company. My grandmother on the other hand, has a competitive side when it comes to cards. When I was younger she would be generous enough to let me win from time to time, but now I can tell she puts her game face on. I can't visit now without having at least a game or two, but it is always enjoyable to do so. My grandmother also enjoys shopping once in a while, so my mother and I will spend a day taking her out to wherever she would like to go.

How much do you know about the place where your grandparents grew up?

We have often spoken about the place in which they grew up on our trips out to the cabin. From what I've been told, it is now nothing but a ghost town. The island was only accessible by boat, and I believe there was only one main road (which was not paved of course). They had only a one room schoolhouse, which accommodated the increasingly small population. The majority of supplies had to be brought in from off the island, as there was only a small convenience store for the necessities.

Do you ask questions of your grandparents about when your own mother was young?

I've never really asked about my mother to be honest. We have talked at many points over the years about what her life was like growing up compared to what mine has been like. I've always had my mother around to answer any questions I had about her life as a child, so I never really felt the need to ask my grandparents. Although I think it would be very interesting to hear it from their point of view, considering what a crowded household they had!

Do you keep in contact with your grandparents using technology? (Facebook, MSN, email) Why or why not?

My grandparents actually only just got a computer in the past year or so, and they didn't even bother to install the internet on it which will go to show how much they actually use it. I don't think they have ever really had the interest in having a computer actually, my Nan just enjoys playing card games on it. So we normally keep in contact by phone, and we are always back and forth between my mother's house and theirs, so we are always in touch somehow.

Tommy (16), Jenna (11), Rebecca (16), and Jaclyn (12): Lorna's grandchildren.

What have you learned from your grandparents?

Tommy: I've learned about the value of being patient. My grandparents gave me a sense of family.

Jenna: How to put icing on cookies.

Jaclyn: From my grandmother I have learned how to knit, play a variety of different card games, and if you prank her she doesn't get mad, she gets even. From my grandfather I have learned lots of facts about the World Wars and our history.

Rebecca: I have learned from my grandfather that there are never too many cat pictures that one can email. I've also learned about the Air Force and other historical facts. I've learned how to knit from my grandma, although I forget. She has also taught me how to bake, and do my own laundry. My nanny and poppy have taught me that you're never too old to have fun.

How much time do you spend with your grandparents?

Tommy: About a week or two a year, but, more often when I was younger and living in the Valley here in Nova Scotia.

Jenna:One week or a few days a year.

Jaclyn: Because I am from Ontario and my grandparents are from Newfoundland, I see them approximately one week a year.

Rebecca: I spend about one or two weeks with my nanny and poppy a year. This is because I live in Ottawa and they live in Newfoundland.

Do you ask about what it was like when they were your age with their grandparents?

Tommy: No, I never thought to ask.

Jenna:Not usually.

Jaclyn: No I have never asked my grandparents that question before.

Rebecca: Not that I can remember. Probably not, because I know it was way different from nowadays.

What do you most like to do with your grandparents when you are with them?

Tommy: Visit, talk and just hang out together.

Jenna:Ask questions about them.

Jaclyn: With my poppy I like to visit the war museums and listen to his stories about our world histories. With my nanny I like to play games and watch game shows. I like to listen to the stories from when my Nan was a girl. I like to make "frogs" with Nanny and Rebecca. Frogs are a cookie made on the stove with sugar, cocoa, butter, milk and rolled oats heated up on the stove then dropped on a cookie sheet. Nanny makes the best frogs!

Rebecca: When I'm with my grandparents, I enjoy just spending time together, baking, watching a movie, or visiting the local attractions, either around Ottawa or in Newfoundland.

How much do you know about Newfoundland? Now? At the time your grandparents were your age?

Tommy: I learned most of what I know about Newfoundland through Social Studies in school, such as when they joined confederation, over-fishing of cod and its economic repercussions.

Jenna:I know quite a bit about Newfoundland now but very little about Newfoundland when my grandparents were my age.

Jaclyn: I know facts from taking many tours of historical sites such as the Titanic museum, Signal Hill and whale watching.

Rebecca: Newfoundland was not part of Canada when my grandparents were born. But now I know interesting facts about it, and the role it played in the World Wars.

Do you ask questions of your grandparents about when your parents were children?

Tommy: No, that's something I never really thought to ask.

Jenna:Yes, a lot.

Jaclyn: Yes, I do ask about the prices of different things and about different technology and I compare their old lifestyle as a kid to mine now.

Rebecca: I do ask my grandparents about my parents, sometimes. Just to see if they did bad things, so that they can't get me in trouble...hehe.

Do you keep in contact with your grandparents using technology? (Email, Facebook, MSN, etc.)

Tommy: No, I use all of the above, but I'm not good at keeping in touch with my grandparents or most other family members from away, with the exception of my cousin Rebecca.

Jenna:Yes, all the time.

Jaclyn: Yes, we used to do video calls with nanny and poppy a couple of years ago.

Rebecca: I used to talk to nanny on MSN and Webcam. Not so much anymore. Now it's by telephone, talking or the occasional text.

CONCLUSION

Being a grandparent is a very important role in today's society and passing down one's story and legacy is very valuable. It may be a challenge to do this when family members don't live nearby and other forms of communication must be used to keep the family members connected and the relationship intact. Both Audrey and Lorna agree that it is an important, enjoyable and worthwhile role. Lorna says she wishes her legacy to be, "The only thing I wish for all members of my family is love, happiness and a long happy life. Hopefully, my husband and I have taught them the basics for achieving these goals. And to also have fun living life to its fullest. From my parents and grandparents I have learned to love and to hold dear all the good things that have happened to me." Audrey says she wishes her legacy to be,

> that my grandchildren know the joy of life and the importance of spending quality time with your family. I hope I have passed this down by sharing traditions like playing cards and baking. From my parents and grandparents, I have learned to work hard, to go to church regularly and to be kind to people who are not so well-off. When I was growing up, my grandmother would put a piece of salt beef in a basket and fill it with vegetables and give it to a family who needed it. We had cows, sheep, pigs and hens and we always shared with others who didn't, especially during harvest time.

Grandparenting is a joyful role to play. "Positive grandparent identity meanings, may encourage a heightened sense of well-being by providing a sense of authenticity, meaning and purpose" (Shlomo, Taubman, Ari, Findler, Sivan, & Dolizki, 2010, p. 45). All the grandchildren agree as well that their grandparents play a very important role in their lives and they all treasure their time spent together. Grandparents are a wealth of love, attention, wisdom and family stories to be cherished.

REFLECTION QUESTIONS

1. We may be inclined to think of grandparents as a homogenous group. However, this author's description of her maternal and paternal grandparents is quite different. What are the implications of a bias towards homogeneity?
2. How might families deal with situations where an adult child is not the biological child. What are the challenges, concerns and opportunities?
3. In this chapter, what lessons do we learn in terms of the role of grandparents (grandmothers AND grandfathers) in terms of cultural transmission? What gets (possibly) saved and what is in danger of getting lost, and why?
4. What are some of the differences in the reality of grandparenting today?

REFERENCES

"No Great Future" Government Sponsored Resettlement in Newfoundland and Labrador. (n.d.). Retrieved July 18, 2011, from Memorial University of Newfoundland Maritime Archive History: http://www. mun.ca/mha/resettlement/rs_intro.php

Mitchell, B.A. (2009). Family Matters: An Introduction to Family Sociology in Canada. Toronto: Canadian Scholar's Press Inc.

Shlomo, S.B., Taubman, O., Ari, B., Findler, L., Sivan, E., & Dolizki, M. (2010). Becoming a Grandmother: Maternal Grandmothers' Mental Health, Perceived Costs, and Personal Growth. *Social Work Research,* 45–57.

Singh, D.A. (2011). Cultural and Social Capital, Parents' Involvement and Academic and Social Achievement of Children in Schools: Reflecting on Some Suggestions From a South Asian American Mother. St. John's: Memorial University.

Singh, D.A. (2008). Grandparents Research Notes. St. John's.

Singh, D.A. (2010). Review of Research: Why Focus on Grandparents? (working draft). St. John's: Memorial University.

Tan, D.J.P., Griggs, D.J., & Attar, D.S. (2008, June 4). 'Involved' grandparents significantly associated with better-adjusted grandchildren. Retrieved July 26, 2011, from University of Oxford Press: http://www.ox.ac.uk/media/news_releases_for_journalists/080604.html

Tutwiler, S.J. (2005). Teachers as Collaborative Partners: Working With Diverse Families and Communities. New York: Routledge.

Interviews in person and by email with various individuals.

JEFFERY CHARD

RETURNING TO OUR ROOTS...VEGETABLES

Growing Your Own Food

The world today is a fast-changing place. The advance of technology has fuelled a drive towards globalization in all aspects of our lives. As a result, the economic structure of our society in North America, and specifically here in Canada, is undergoing a transformation. In the past few decades there has been a noticeable change in the basis of our economy. Through such movements as the industrial revolution, our society has changed from an economy based on natural resources, such as farming and fishing to an economy based on consumption. "Given the proliferation of goods on the marketplace, our constant exposure to commercial messages, and the energy we invest in acquiring consumer goods, one could argue that the consumption activities dominate much of our everyday lives" (Mitchell, 2009; p. 144). Many families today are caught up in the notion of modernity; they feel the need to be modern at any cost. Families must have a certain type of home, a specific type of car, brand name clothes, the latest cell phone, a large screen television... the list could go on and on. The desire to 'keep up with the Jones' is driven by the commercial nature of our society. "Almost everyone everywhere wants all of the things they have heard about, seen, or experienced via the new technology" (Steger, 2010; p. 16). But is this a good way to live our lives?

This writer proposes that there may be a different, simpler way of life that may be more fulfilling than the somewhat artificial and unsustainable lifestyle many of us are living. This idea of choosing a simpler lifestyle is not a new one. One need only look to the Japanese concept of Wabi-Sabi to understand this lifestyle a little better. Wabi-Sabi is "the Japanese view of life (that) embraced a simple aesthetic that grew stronger as inessentials were eliminated and trimmed away" (Ando, n.d.; p. 1). Followers of Wabi-Sabi know the pleasure and fulfillment associated with "finding beauty in imperfection and profundity in nature, of accepting the natural cycle of growth, decay, and death" (Ando, n.d.; p. 1). While this philosophy of adopting a more natural way of life is present in other cultures such as the Japanese, it is also present in our own Newfoundland and Labrador culture. We need only to look to our past to see this simpler, more naturalist way of life. The roots of Newfoundland culture is based on traditions brought to us by our largely Irish and English ancestors which revolved around the practices of farming and fishing. The practice of growing or gathering your own food, a more natural practice than shopping for it in a supermarket, is still alive in many rural parts of our province.

A. Singh and M. Devine (Eds.), Rural Transformation and Newfoundland and Labrador Diaspora: Grandparents, Grandparenting, Community and School Relations, 231–242.

Many people, even in urban areas, are starting to recognize the value and pleasure that accompanies growing your own food. If an internet search were conducted one would be bombarded with sites devoted to the notion of urban families growing food in their own yards. Various reasons for adopting this change in lifestyle have been identified including economic reasons, political reasons, food security, and personal reasons. While this activity is usually recreational inside city limits, "it provides residents, in particular the most vulnerable, with a way of meeting their needs independent of fluctuations in international food prices." (http://openalex.blogspot. com/2008/06/urban-agriculture-vs-food-riots.html) With the increasing population in many cities throughout the world, there is also a need for greater amount of food. Urban agriculture has been suggested as a means to help provide for this need, though it hasn't really been explored to its full potential. Indeed, it could be a viable option if taken seriously. As stated in this article http://renewcanada.net/2009/urban-food-production-no-joke/ "a backyard garden four times the size of an ordinary door, can supply a household of six people with fresh vegetables for a year."

While the idea of raising crops in urban areas has been gaining momentum in recent years, the concept has been alive and flourishing in rural parts of our province since people have been living here. Older generations have been growing food and raising animals as a means of survival for years and this tradition has continued, despite the fact that it is no longer necessary for survival. This writer`s own grandparents, even while participating in seasonal work in such areas as construction, grew root vegetables, raised livestock, hunted and fished to provide for their families, and many grandparents today still engage in these activities. While the writer`s grandparents are no longer living, his father-in-law and a grandparent to four, still actively engages in self production of food in his small garden located in his small rural town of Blaketown, Newfoundland. This writer conducted an interview with 59 year old Reginald Stanford (Reg) regarding his views on this traditional way of life and its place in modern society' (Appendix A).

Reg has always been both a practitioner and advocate for embracing the more traditional ways of life of our ancestors. This now retired school teacher has lived this self-sustaining lifestyle for as long as he can remember, growing his own vegetables as a child in his family garden became anew when he became older and began his own family.

> I guess I really started it for myself after I finished University. I was a teacher, so I had my summers off and it was a good time to grow potatoes, carrots, cabbage, onions…stuff we ate all the time. In more recent years I grew other things like strawberries, raspberries, peas, tomatoes, parsnip, turnip, beets, even grapes…all kinds of things really.

Aside from growing crops, Reg also embraced many other activities fitting with a more rural lifestyle, such as

> fished many different species like cod and lobster, herring and other water species. I also hunted quite a bit, and still do. Moose, rabbit, turrs, ducks, all of

these animals added to my food supply as well. My wife and I also pick a lot of berries from the surrounding areas; it's something that we enjoy doing a lot.

When asked why he maintained this lifestyle, Reg gave some of the same reason previously mentioned in this paper, including saving money and the fact it was something that he enjoyed. One reason that was not mentioned and perhaps the most important one to Reg was that the quality of home grown food is much higher in his opinion. "I find that the quality of the food you grow yourself is much better than anything you can buy in a store, no matter how fresh they say it is. Most of the produce you buy in supermarkets is full of pesticides and who knows what else. Much of the meat you buy there is treated with preservatives, dyes and hormones... all those additives can't be good for you." Another important aspect of food growing that Reg mentioned was the desire to pass this way of life on to future generations, particularly his children and grandchildren. "I can't help but think of my grandkids, and what kind of future they are going to have. I hope that I can teach them some of what I know about fending for themselves." Traditional ways of life have been dying out in many parts of our province, and many grandparents are trying to combat this trend by showing their grandchildren that this simpler way of life has advantages of their own. When asked about this, Reg commented "It seems to me that most young people today are too busy or too caught up in their own lives to take time for something like this. Because it does take time, but it is time that can be enjoyed and valued."

Throughout the process of the interview many concepts were raised by Reg, but perhaps the most interesting would be how values have changed in Newfoundland from generation to generation.

I find that most people today can't do very much for themselves, that they expect other people to everything for them, you know? When I was growing up we had to do everything for ourselves, there *was* no one to do things for you... we did it out of necessity. We cut our own logs, built our own houses, grew our own food, hunted and fished for ourselves. I don't think many people do that anymore.

This supports the idea that many families today are greatly affected by modernity, and have a much different perspective than those in the past. As Richard Hooker states "we see ourselves as having lost tradition, that is, that our behaviour patterns, our rituals, etc., are all new and innovative, that we are not repeating the past." (http://www.wsu.edu/~dee/GLOSSARY/MODERN.HTM).

This is perhaps not the perspective for people to adopt as we can learn a great deal from our past, and the people around us. Perhaps one of the most effective ways to help future generations to see the value and importance in these more traditional ways of life, such as food growing, is to include it in our school programming. Many professionals agree that "Environmental education in schools is seen as an important strategy in achieving environmental improvement" (Loughland, p. 2). While children may be taught about environmental concepts in school, a food growing project or program could be much more influential as it incorporates the power of experiential learning. Experiential learning is the process of making meaning from direct experience, and many schools in other parts of the country have implemented food growing projects into their schools to give students the hands-on experience needed. "The most important thing that students get is accountability and responsibility. They're taking care of life…They learn the bigger picture, and how what they are doing in the garden affects them and the earth." (http://vancouver.ca/commsvcs/ socialplanning/initiatives/foodpolicy/tools/pdf/Evergreen_SchoolGdns.pdf)

These projects can take many forms, but most agree that they are very worthwhile as they can accomplish so much. Although this writer is aware of adult related community gardens, such as that offered at Memorial University`s Botanical Gardens, he is not aware of other such student based projects of this type in other parts of Newfoundland. Some educators seem to have thought about it before. Reg is one such person.

> As a teacher I always wanted to take something like this on. There is so much potential with a food growing project set up in a school. It can span across so many parts of the curriculum. From healthy living, Phys Ed., Economics, Science, social consciousness, writing skills, health… there are so many areas that it can cross. It could be a real cross curricular project that the whole school could get involved in! Guest speakers could be brought in from places like local farms; the Department of Agriculture, etc. Scientists could be brought in help students check the pH levels in the soil. The students could take field trips to places like the Experimental Farm in St. John`s to learn how to approach this project. Nutritionists could come in to show the differences between home grown food and the kind you get from supermarkets. It could really show a different, alternate lifestyle that might appeal to more environmentally sensitive students! There are so many projects that could be done!!

Indeed, one food growing project called the Cornell University Mosaic Garden Program does incorporate many of the ideas Reg mentioned. The following activities are undertaker by the students in this program:

Garden history – Youth ask gardeners to create a visual time-line documenting garden History.

Interview – Youth prepare and conduct interviews of gardeners focusing on gardening practices.

Mapping – Youth ask gardeners to draw individual plots and entire garden, eliciting comments from gardeners about planting practices. Youth locate gardens on larger map of their community.

Seasonal calendar – Youth ask gardeners to draw a calendar showing plant penology and garden practices through the season.

Soils measurements – Youth and gardeners conduct pH and other soil tests and collect soil samples for nutrient analysis. Youth interview gardeners about soil problems.

Venn diagram – Youth ask gardeners to diagram important factors in the garden and resource flows (e.g. material, human) to and from the garden and broader community.

Action – Youth work with gardeners to identify needs/problems in the garden and take some action to address them. (Doyle, p. 4)

Many of these activities could easily be incorporated into the curriculum here in Newfoundland and Labrador to create a productive and dynamic learning experience for the students that would help them connect to their communities and breathe new life into dying traditions. This writer, along with Reg, believes that implementing this type of program into the community of Blaketown could be done.

> Crescent Collegiate would have the space to start something like this up. I think that they own a large piece of land behind the school that would be perfect for a project like this. I think the key would be to get everyone on board though... all the staff, the students, the community... everyone. There would probably have to be a lead teacher who is into this lifestyle and knows about farming and growing crops, but the whole school would have to get involved in it too. You would need to create an atmosphere of excitement around it to get it going, I think.

As Reg stated, there would need to be a lot of support put in place to make something like this viable. The support of the local school, school board, and department of education would be an absolute necessity. Funding would be required to get the project up and running, as well as personnel to implement and maintain it. There are already many existing templates or program outlines to adopt, such as one suggested by Evergreen and their initiative of Growing Healthy Food on Canada's School Grounds. One of these programs could be adapted to fit into the needs and requirements of specific schools and communities.

Aside from support for the school community, there also needs to be support from the local community as well. As Reg mentioned previously, this type of project needs to be embraced by the whole community, given the school would most likely have to draw upon resources in the community to run the food growing program. Just getting the land itself prepared for farming would be a big effort, one that the local community volunteers could assist with.

> It would be a big undertaking to clear off the land behind the school and get it ready for farming. But there are a lot of people in this community with back hoes and heavy equipment that could help out. There are local businesses that make soil and fertilizer and compost.... There are plenty of local resources that could be tapped to make it work.

Getting the community involved would not only cut down on the costs for such an endeavour, but it would also help establish important ties between the school and community, as well as give the community a sense of investment in the school and the students.

But perhaps the biggest local resource that could be harnessed could be the knowledge that resides in many of the older generation in the community, the grandparents. As Reg states, "there is a lot of local knowledge as well, in human resources. The older people around here know how to grow things in this area, they could offer their assistance to help get it started." Getting the grandparents involved in the school, to share what they know with the students, some of whom may be their grandchildren, could go a long way in creating the intergenerational bond that many think is lacking in today's society. Reg echoes this sentiment,

> I think by bringing in the community you are also helping to create a bond between the younger generation and the older generation, a bond between grandparents and grandchildren. Traditions and culture would be passed down that might otherwise be lost. A real sense of community could be fostered.

Obviously there are many positive aspects to establishing a food growing program in a school community so why are there not more of these programs here in Newfoundland? There could be any number of reasons, and Reg suggests a few.

> There might be some problems with space and commitment from students. Most schools don't have the space to put aside for this, as they would need a greenhouse and space outside as well. The plants would need to be tended over the summer, and protected from being destroyed… stuff like that needs to be looked at as well.

This writer believes that these difficulties could easily be overcome if there was really a desire to establish such a program. Some believe that there might be other, bigger obstacles to contend with as well, most revolving around politics. There are many regulations and policies in places, as well as public opinion that must be considered in organizing and planning programs such as these. Zoning regulations, agricultural laws, community by-laws… many things could impede implementation of a food growing program, especially if it is located in an urban area. Reg suggests that governmental policies not only work against projects such as these, but also against many of the traditional ways of life in Newfoundland and Labrador.

> Government often makes it very hard to do it. There are so many policies and regulations in place that limit the things you can do to be self-sufficient. The restrictions on fishing, hunting, where you can farm… all of these things are obstacles to this way of life. There is so much red tape! Now I know some of these rules are done for conservation measures, but many of them just seem to be put in to promote the urban lifestyle, with no regard for how life is different in rural areas. The values are different in both places and the urban values seem to be more important to those in the government.

Overall, this writer believes implementation of a program such as this in my local area would have many more benefits than drawbacks. Many of the obstacles could be overcome with careful planning and organization. The notion of restoring at least one of the traditional ways of life, uniting generations, and creating a strong close-knit community make this project one that should be carefully considered in many schools and communities. After all, to quote a grandfather, "We really do need to consider stuff like this for the future. I want my grandchildren, and great-grandchildren, to grow up knowing about their heritage and to know about their roots."

REFLECTION QUESTIONS

1. Do you think that youth would be interested in learning farming skills? Why/ Why not?
2. What is the significance of developing, within the school curriculum, a course or part of a course on farming?
3. How does the role of grandchildren enter into this chapter, from your perspective?
4. Do you think that the skills of farming as highlighted in this chapter, are considered to be of value in your province/state, country: why/why not?

APPENDIX A:

Interview with Reg Stanford

Me: Are you aware of the concept of modernity? If so, what are your views on this subject?

Reg: Well, I am not really sure what the term means specifically, but I think I can figure out what it means. I assume you are talking about the tendency for people to want all things that are modern or new. Am I correct?

Me: Yes, that is the gist of the concept. Though there is a little more to it than that.

Reg: Yeah, well, I don't really subscribe to that philosophy myself. I tend to relate to an older set of values. I mean there are some good things about being modern, such as improvement in equal rights and advances in healthcare, but I don't put a lot of weight in modern things.

    I find that most people today can't do very much for themselves, that they expect other people to everything for them, you know? When I was growing up we had to do everything for ourselves, there *was* no one to do things for you... we did it out of necessity. We cut our own logs, built our own houses, grew our own food, hunted and fished for ourselves. I don't think many people do that anymore.

Me: Are you aware of the growing trend for many people in urban areas to start growing their own food?

Reg: I think I have heard about it before, but I didn't realize that it was becoming in vogue again in urban areas. I think it's a great idea though because you never know what is going to happen in life. There might be a disaster, or something might cause food supply to be cut off, then what are you going to do? If you can't grow it, then you are pretty much screwed.

Most people in cities think that beef comes from the supermarket, and that veggies come from bins in stores, they wouldn't know the first thing about growing their own. But I think the idea of growing your food is good, it fits into the idea of the recycling effort that many cities are promoting. Growing the food, composting organic waste, using the soil to grow food again... it's the perfect way to recycle!

The biggest obstacle to growing your own food in a city is that everyone is too crowded! There is no space in most cities to plant food, the building lots are tiny, and there isn't enough room to get a decent crop.

I think I remember something from a few years back that might be a good idea for growing food in cities though. I think people used to rent land from nearby farmers and plant and grow their own veggies in the land they rented. Kind of like a community plot. Like if Lester's Farm in St. John's rented small plots of land they weren't using to various people in the city so they could grow what they wanted there. That could solve the space problem.

Me: I know that you are in the practice of growing your own food. How long have you been growing your own food?

Reg: Well, I guess I have been at it for most of my life. I remember that my father used to grow potatoes and it was my job to make sure that they were fertilized, trenched, dug up... I pretty much took care of it all. I guess I really started it for myself after I finished University. I was a teacher, so I had my summers off and it was a good time to grow potatoes, carrots, cabbage, onions... stuff we ate all the time. In more recent years I grew other things like strawberries, raspberries, peas, tomatoes, parsnip, turnip, beets... all kinds of things really.

Talking about food... I never just grew food either. I used to get it from all kinds of sources. I always had my own boat so I fished many different species like cod and lobster, herring, stuff like that. I also hunted quite a bit, and still do. Moose, rabbit, turrs, duck, all of these animals added to my food supply as well. My wife and I also pick a lot of berries from the surrounding areas, it's something that we enjoy doing a lot.

Me: Why do you do this? Why not just buy the food?

Reg: Well, the main reason that I get my own food... hunt and grow food I mean, is for quality. I find that the quality of the food you grow yourself is much better than anything you can buy in a store, no matter how fresh they say it is. Most of the produce you buy in supermarkets are full of pesticides and who knows what else. The meat you get there is treated with preservatives, dyes and hormones... all those additives can't be good for you.

Another reason I do this is because I really enjoy it. I feel like it is part of my culture, part of my heritage, part of me! I mean, if I can do something I enjoy and that is good for me, why not?

I guess another reason I do this is because it does save me money in the long run. I mean it's not a big factor, but it does help financially. If I think about it, I estimate that I am saving 5 to 10 grand a year by growing and hunting my own food and cutting my own wood for heat. It all adds up over time. I save money by not having to buy the products, I don't use fertilizer because I compost and use that in my soil, it's totally natural and I waste very little.

In more recent years my reasons have changed a little though. I can't help but think of my grandkids, and what kind of future they are going to have. I hope that I can teach them some of what I know about fending for themselves. I have two granddaughters that are always up in the garden with me, or out fishing in my boat; they seem really interested in this stuff and I hope my two grandsons will be the same way. They are too young yet to really know what it is all about, but they certainly seem to want to get into all of it too!

Me: Do you think other people in your community share your views?

Reg: There are some people in this community that do grow their own food as well. Ron Butt, Woodrow Reid, Byron Brooks... actually, there are not a whole lot left that still do. Those that do still do it are mostly from my generation...

Me: Do you think younger people in today's society see value in the practice of growing your own food?

Reg: No, not a lot. Like I said, it is mostly the older generation that is doing this now. It seems to me that most young people today are too busy or too caught up in their own lives to take time for something like this. Because it does take time, but it is time that can be enjoyed and valued. If there are some younger people doing this in urban areas now I would think that it is because the younger generation is much more health conscious than mine and this is a very healthy way to live, in my opinion. I think that younger people today are more socially and politically aware as well. This can come from that as well. Like I said before, I think young people might see the value in it, but they just don't have the time and space to do it in an urban area. As I mentioned before though, I do hope that I can pass some of what I know on to my grandchildren, to help preserve this way of life and to give them a better quality of life as well.

Me: Do you think there would be value in trying to implement a food growing component into the school system?

Reg: Yes! As a teacher I always wanted to take something on like this. There is so much potential with a food growing project set up in a school. It can span across so many parts of the curriculum. From healthy living, phys ed., economics, science, social consciousness, writing skills, health... there are so many areas that it can cross. It could be a real cross curricular project that the whole school could get involved in!

I envision this as being most appropriate in an elementary or junior high school. Probably upper elementary actually, and Jr. High. I know I have heard about projects like this in places on the mainland, but not here in Newfoundland. I think they have a green house in St. Francis School, but I am not sure how it is used.

I think this could be done, but there might be some problems with space and commitment from students. Most schools don't have the space to put aside for this, as they would need a greenhouse and space outside as well. The plants would need to be tended over the summer, and protected from being destroyed…stuff like that needs to be looked at as well.

Me: How would you envision this in your local school? Who would run it? What kinds of support would be needed?

Reg: I think it would be a difficult, but very worthwhile thing to start around here. Crescent Collegiate would have the space to start something like this up. I think that they own a large piece of land behind the school that would be perfect for a project like this. I think the key would be to get everyone on board though… all the staff, the students, the community… everyone. There would probably have to be a lead teacher who is into this lifestyle and knows about farming and growing crops, but the whole school would have to get involved in it too. You would need to create an atmosphere of excitement around it to get it going, I think.

I think the most important part would be getting the community involved. It would be a big undertaking to clear off the land behind the school and get it ready for farming. But there are a lot of people in this community with back hoes and heavy equipment that could help out. There are local businesses that make soil and fertilizer and compost…. There are plenty of local resources that could be tapped to make it work. Also there is a lot of local knowledge as well, in human resources. People around here know how to grow things in this area, they could offer their assistance to help get it started.

Guest speakers could be brought in from places like local farms; the department of agriculture… places like that. Scientists could be brought in to help students check the pH levels in the soil. The students could take field trips to places like the experimental farm to learn how to approach this project. Nutritionists could come in to show the differences between home grown food and the kind you get from supermarkets. It could really show a different, alternate lifestyle that might appeal to some students! There are so many things that could be done!!

I think by bringing in the community you are also helping to create a bond between the younger generation and the older generation, a bond between grandparents and grandchildren. Traditions and culture would be passed down that might otherwise be lost. A real sense of community could be fostered. Any crops that are grown could be sold at a community fair or market as a fund raiser for the school too. Or kids could take what was grown home and start a garden in their own yards… it could be really big!

Me: Do you have any other suggestions or comments on this topic to offer?

Reg: Well, I just wanted to say how rewarding I find it to grow my own food, to be self-reliant. It is something that should be promoted, but government often makes it very hard to do it. There are so many policies and regulations in place that limit the things you can do to be self-sufficient. The restrictions on fishing, hunting, where you can farm... all of these things are obstacles to this way of life. There is so much red tape! Now I know some of these rules are done for conservation measures, but many of them just seem to be put in to promote the urban lifestyle, with no regard for how life is different in rural areas. The values are different in both places and the urban values seem to be more important to those in the government.

Some other obstacles that I see doing this in urban areas is the fact that people complain. I know that if I made my compost in a city that my neighbours would be complaining about the smell and such... that is more common in a city, I think. Take my neighbour for instance; he raises chickens and turkeys in his backyard, right next door to me. It can be noisy at times, and the feed sometimes attracts pests, but it is something he likes to do, and we are able to get fresh eggs anytime we want. I think the trade off is well worth it. I don't know if people in cities would agree. Maybe they could rezone parts of the city to farming-residential, so people who want to do this type of farming could live here and do so with other like minded people! It's just a thought.

Me: Well, thank you so much for your time. I really appreciate you helping me out.

Reg: No problem, anytime. I hope it helps out. We really do need to consider stuff like this for the future. I want my grandchildren, and great-grandchildren, to grow up knowing about their heritage and know about their roots.

REFERENCES

http://openalex.blogspot.com/2008/06/urban-agriculture-vs-food-riots.html
http://renewcanada.net/2009/urban-food-production-no-joke/
http://www.wsu.edu/~dee/GLOSSARY/MODERN.HTM
(4)http://vancouver.ca/commsvcs/socialplanning/initiatives/foodpolicy/tools/pdf/Evergreen_ SchoolGdns.pdf Growing Healthy Food on Canada's School Grounds – Evergreen, March 2006
Ando, T. (2010). *What is Wabi-Sabi*. Course Notes, Ed 6440.
Steger, Manfred B. (Ed.) (2010). Globalization, *The Greatest Hits:* A Global Studies Reader. Boulder: Paradigm Publishers.
Loughland, Tony , Reid, Anna , Walker, Kim & Petocz, Peter (2003). 'Factors Influencing Young People's Conceptions of Environment', *Environmental Education Research, 9*(1), 3–19.
Doyle, Rebekah & Krasny, Marianne (2003). 'Participatory Rural Appraisal as an Approach to Environmental Education in Urban Community Gardens', *Environmental Education Research, 9*(1), 91–115.

AMY BLUNDON

THE ROLE OF GRANDPARENTS

The role of grandparents in family life is ever-changing. They play many roles, from mentor, to historian, to loving companion and to child-care provider. Strong intergenerational connections can result, giving grandchildren a sense of security of belonging to the extended family. The degree of the involvement of grandparents varies from one household to the next, often depending on a variety of circumstances such as proximity to grandchildren, relationship to parents, type of family structure, health of grandparents and interest. In this paper I will address the different roles of grandparents in the family, highlighting some of the joys and stresses of grandparenting. Different family structures will be identified and how grandparents may sometimes feel pressure to become involved in family life to strengthen the family. I will discuss supports for grandparents in a changing society. Finally, I will provide three examples, including my own personal experience, of the important role grandparents play in families today.

There are many factors which affect the type of interactions that occur between grandparents and grandchildren. These factors include culture, race, ethnicity, gender, family structure and traditions. "It is common knowledge that various cultures seem to have different types of family systems. In the United States and Canada and the countries of northern Europe, the nuclear family, father, mother and the children, appears to predominate. In almost all of the rest of the world, extended families, the grandparents, father, mother, children, but also aunts, uncles, cousins, and other kin are considered to be "family" (Georgas, 2003, p. 1). In Japanese culture for example, the first son takes care of the elderly parents. The parents co-reside with his family. As a result, this close proximity allows for grandparents to develop strong relationships with their grandchildren, passing on cultural traditions (Mitchell, 2009, p. 222). Tan et al. discuss the traditional role of grandparents in white Anglo-American families, stating that grandparents often did not interfere with the upbringing of their grandchildren. However, this is changing with increasing lone-parent families, where the grandparents are becoming the "replacement partners (i.e., confidant, guide, and facilitator) and replacement parents (i.e., listener, teacher, and disciplinarian)" in families (2010, p. 995).

Modernization hypothesizes that increasing economic level and industrialization in a society results in the rejection of traditional values and culture, and inevitable convergence toward a system of "modern" values and increasing individualization. One of the consequences of modernization is the transition

A. Singh and M. Devine (Eds.), Rural Transformation and Newfoundland and Labrador Diaspora: Grandparents, Grandparenting, Community and School Relations, 243–250.

of the extended family system in economically underdeveloped societies to the nuclear family characteristic of industrial societies (Georgas, 2003, p. n.a).

However, Georgas argues the theory that families throughout the world will converge to a universal nuclear family type is unlikely. Instead he believes that family relations are too complex and subtle to respond uniformly to economic changes, most likely because of different cultural "sensitivities." In addition, he states that, despite changes in the forms of family, certain patterns of family life remain constant across cultures over time, and certain basic human needs remain resistant to any type of change in social organization. Grandparents for example, have a desire to be a part of an extended family and this alone will contribute to keeping the closeness of extended families intact.

Grandparents today do not fit the stereotype of a grey-haired individual who stays home with nothing to do. Rather, today's grandparents have active social lives, are often physically fit, tend to have better health and continue to work late in life. Many studies reveal "an automatic expectation that they [grandparents] take up the role of being a child care provider" (Goodfellow, 2003, p. 15), helping with the raising of grandchildren as parents work longer hours outside the home. There is an increasing demand on grandparent contribution in families where one parent is the predominant child care provider, as a result of being a single parent or the other parent having to leave for work for extended periods of time. In Newfoundland, in recent years one parent, typically the father, leaves the province to find work. As a result, grandparents are often called on to become the "extra" support these families need, offering emotional, financial and structural support. According to Goodfellow, "with continuing changes in family composition, the increase in blended, step and sole-parent families, and the rise in maternal employment, it is possible that grandparents may be the only significant and stable family member in the lives of many young children" (2003, p. 18).

Traditionally, grandparents had the role of mentor, historian and loving companion. They provided families with love, encouragement, patience, acting as role models, teaching skills and talents to other members of the family. They shared stories about the past, traditions, rituals, their own childhood and family, contributing to the family identity. I remember my own grandmother sharing stories about where her ancestors were from, County Cork in Ireland. She always told stories with such enthusiasm and pride, describing details her father had once told her. It was her great grandparents who migrated to Newfoundland, yet her stories were so vivid, it felt like she had lived them. As a result, I have always felt a connection to Ireland. Grandparents also pass on values and morals, and provide a positive image of aging for grandchildren. Faith was a very important part of my grandmother's life. Witnessing her experiences of joy and contentment with her faith helped me to develop my own values and faith. Although she had a difficult life, losing her husband and two children, she was always positive and happy, praying daily and embracing God in everything she did. Her optimistic attitude provides a model by which I try to live my own life. Grandparents offer a listening ear, while maintaining objectivity, which is difficult for parents to do. They have flexibility and are fun.

Today's grandparents have additional roles; they step up as caregivers when families are in need. With an increase in the breakdown of families, such as separation, divorce or remarriage, grandparents' services are in higher demand. However, as Tan et al. suggest, many times grandparents are just filling the gap between time and money poor parents, and the parenting needs of their grandchildren (2010, p. 1009). In many Newfoundland families, both parents work outside the home. This is often a financial necessity; however, with both parents working, there is additional stress on the family structure. Finding child care is an issue, especially with children under the age of two. There are very few daycare centers equipped to take babies and, if they do, it is at a much higher cost. This financial strain puts pressure on grandparents to become involved with the responsibility of childcare. Also, long work hours means less time devoted to quality family time. As a result, grandparents often fill in to entertain the children. I will provide three examples of how grandparents contribute to family life with regard to providing child care for young children. In all three families, the father leaves for extended periods of time, four to six weeks, to work, leaving the mothers home to juggle full-time work and family responsibilities. All three families are made up of a mother, father and one child under the age of three. Each of these families lives in a city with no extended family nearby. In each of the three families, grandparents play a key role in the functioning of the family unit.

In the first example, both parents are successful in their careers. The father's work routine is one month away, and then he returns for one month. The mother works full time and is currently attending school to upgrade her education. Both parents dedicate a lot of their time to their professions, requiring assistance from their extended family. Since they do not live close to any extended family, the maternal grandparents spend a lot of time commuting. There is a close relationship between the mother and her parents; as a result, the bond between the maternal grandparents and the grandchild is close. They assist with many practical problems that arise when the father is away working. The mother in the first family provided the following example; "When work or school demands more of my time, my parents never hesitate to help. They will jump in the car and stay with me, helping with my daughter or they'll come in to get my daughter and bring her around the bay. They have done this at least five times this past year." The flexibility of the grandparents provides the family with the support it needs for both parents to succeed professionally, while the child is happy and content to spent time with her nanny and poppy. The grandparents do not provide full time child care, but have the flexibility to step in and assist with providing support when needed. It is important to note that both grandparents work, the grandfather has a fulltime job and the grandmother a seasonal job. However, both grandparents can rearrange their schedules to accommodate their adult child's and grandchild's lives and appear happy to do this. In fact, the mother reports that often the grandparents will request opportunities to spent time with the grandchild, regularly taking her for weekly visits. The grandparents discussed the joy of spending time with their granddaughter, taking her to different activities, such as the museum and fire hall, where the grandfather is the acting fire chief. "There is so much pride when we get to take our granddaughter out and show her off. It's very exciting. I've wanted to be a grandmother for so long, now I get to really enjoy it." Both grandparents were in their early fifties and were physically active and healthy.

In the second example, the family has a similar work arrangement; the father works away bi-monthly and the mother is a fulltime manger. When they had a daughter, the maternal grandparents moved in full time to assist the mother with childcare whenever her husband was away with work. In this case both grandparents are retired, they are in their mid to late sixties, and this is their first grandchild in 12 years. The mother discussed the relief of having her parents help to take care of herself and her child. "Mom is great! Not only does she take care of my daughter but she cooks, cleans and does all the housework. All I have to do when I get home is put my little girl to bed. I love having her stay with me." The grandparents described the joy of getting to spend so much time with their granddaughter. They felt needed and since they were not working felt obliged to assist their adult child juggle a full time job and motherhood. In our conversations, the grandmother expressed concern about their home around the bay; "I wish we lived a little closer. It's hard being so far away from our other family and friends. I spend a lot of time on the phone trying to stay in the loop when I'm in town. We worry about the upkeep of our house too. I always worry about the water freezing." The grandfather also expressed dissatisfaction, "I find the time long, I get bored when I'm in here. There's no place like your own home." The grandmother also said many times how exhausted she felt trying to keep up with a one year old, "I don't know where she gets her energy. By the time 8:00 comes, I'm ready for the bed." Although they assisted with child care, the adult child had a lot of flexibility with her job and was able to accommodate the grandparents with breaks so they could return home and fulfill their own responsibilities when necessary. This flexibility was appreciated by both grandparents.

In the final example, the family also has a father who goes away for work, usually four to six weeks at a time, and a mother who works full time, in a lower paying job. They have a daughter who is two years old and is in fulltime daycare. Although childcare is not an issue, the grandparents have left their home to live with their adult child and grandchild while the father is away working. They take care of the finances, they drive both the mother to work and the child to daycare, and they take on household responsibilities. In this example, both grandparents are in their late sixties and retired. They say it is necessary to take care of their only child and their granddaughter, stating it was unacceptable for them to try and manage on their own. "This is our only child; of course we're going to help. What kind of parents would we be if we didn't give her a hand?" Since this was their only child, they did not feel a sense of loneliness for home; rather they felt more connected to family and home when they lived as an extended family. They did mention how exhausting taking care of a young child was, but that they preferred it over other activities. They felt immense pleasure with being needed to help take care of their family.

In each family I interviewed, the grandparents willingly participated in their grandchildren's lives. In each example, there was a close relationship between the parent and the grandparents, which encouraged increased involvement with family responsibilities of their adult child. Each family had times when only the mother was present, putting additional pressure on daily life. All the grandparents felt their assistance was needed, gladly offering help to their adult children. The level of involvement depended on the comfort of the parents and grandparents, as well as the grandparents' availability. In the first family, although the mother gladly accepted help through regular visits, her parents had their own commitments. They were both still working, had active social lives and were unable to provide full time care. Also, since finances were not an issue and the grandchild was in full time daycare, the grandparents' role was to relieve the mothers periodically, to give her time to catch-up on work or school, time to herself, or an opportunity to have a social life. During stressful times, such as the end of a term at university, the grandparents gladly adjusted their schedule to accommodate their adult child. In one instance, the grandparents discussed taking the child for a week to help the mother with a very stressful, busy time with work and school.

> Once this year when we were both working, we had to rearrange our schedule to help our daughter. She had to write a paper for school and had parent-teacher interviews. I was really worried about her, she was really stressed. Her father and I worked different shifts, I worked night shift and he worked days, so we could take our granddaughter so her mother could get everything done. It was exhausting, but we managed. It was worth it too, to help our daughter get through the week.

They described the close relationship they had with their granddaughter, how comfortable she felt being with nanny and poppy. They explained how she would cry because she did not want to leave them, always hugging them and saying how much she loved them. They discussed how wonderful being a grandparent was; how they got to play with their grandchildren, spoil them and give them back to the parents for the difficult stuff like discipline or tantrums. All children can benefit from a large circle of caring adults present in their lives. Grandparent contact exposes them to different environments and to points of view based on a long life experience.

If one parent is absent, a grandparent can also provide a missing gender role model. In each of the families I interviewed, there was a close relationship between the grandfather and grandchild. They fulfilled the male role model in the child's life while the father was away working. There appeared to be no issues of being anxious, worried or sad from any of the children while the father was absent. In fact all the children appeared very happy and content, and since the grandparents continually supported the family and were present, there were more opportunities to develop close relationships with adults in their lives. According to Tan et al, "closeness and informal involvement of grandparents are associated with reduced adjustment difficulties among grandchildren" (2010, p. 998). In the first family I interviewed, both the mother and father explained the relief they felt that they had other adults to count on to take care of their child.

> It's such a relief to have someone who can take our daughter and there is nothing to worry about. The first time I left her, I wrote pages of "how-to" notes to my mom; she just took them and laughed. They really listened to my rules and were great with my daughter, it was such a relief. I trust them completely with her and she adores them. Now every year my husband and I go down south for a week. It's great, I know my daughter is okay and we can focus on our marriage. I figure I give 51 weeks to my daughter, my husband should get at least one.

All parties were excited by the vacation, the parents because they got to concentrate on their marriage, the grandchildren and grandparents because they got to spend time together. This comfort level with grandparents sharing child care provided stronger bonds with all members of the family.

In each of the families I interviewed, grandparents had a positive view of participating in child care duties. However, many grandparents experience times of dissatisfaction with their role in raising grandchildren. In the second family I interviewed, the grandparents were feeling exhaustion. They were happy to be involved with their grandchild and help their adult child balance the stress of family life, but felt restricted in their activities. The grandfather discussed feelings of boredom which is common for grandparents who step in to become full time child care providers. Often grandparents have experienced active work lives up to when they start caring for grandchildren; to go from busy work challenges to staying at home with small children is a difficult adjustment. Some grandparents may feel a sense of disempowerment. The grandmother stated, "babysitting is occupying my time, but not my mind." Being able to communicate openly with adult children about personal needs is important for grandparents to be content with child care duties. In this family, the mother gladly rearranged her schedule, holidays and other activities around her parents' lives. She recognized their contributions to her family and understood they needed breaks from the routine of childcare. When they expressed a desire to go home, around the bay for a few days, she would arrange alternate childcare or take time off of work. Having a strong relationship with her parents provided this family with high levels of satisfaction for all its members.

In the third family I interviewed they experienced different types of stress associated with their role in the family. They were not needed for child care, but they took over the role of financial and emotional support for the mother and grandchild. The mother in this family was unable to drive, get groceries, and complete other routine activities without assistance from her parents. She relied on them to be her taxi, help her pay bills and daily household chores. Although the grandparents were thrilled to have such an active role in their daughter's and grandchild's life, financially it was a strain. They contributed to their daughter's family, while trying to pay their own bills and take care of their own home's upkeep. They were both retired and had access to fewer funds, which meant they often did without fulfilling their own wants and desires. Both grandparents admitted to wishing they were able to relax and take trips now that they were finally retired. "I always imagined retirement as a time to reward all my years of hard work. Instead, I'm penny pinching, trying to run two households."

The increasing role of grandparents in formal and informal child care requires that family members are respectful of their experiences and satisfaction with their role in the family. Intergenerational support requires trust and collaboration between parents and grandparents. The grandparent's role as child care provider should be discussed in an open, honest way, revealing any dissatisfaction or stress. Grandparents must be recognized for their role as family supporters. Many families today include grandparents in the lives of their families. In two of the families I interviewed, the grandparents were encouraged to participate in activities with the grandchild. For instance, the grandchild's weekly gymnastics class was alternated between the parent or the grandparents participating. Also, during special days at daycare the grandparents were recognized along with the parents. Encouraging and demonstrating the important role grandparents play in families will help to strengthen the level of contentment with participating as child care providers. They will feel like they are a part of the family unit, not just an employee. Another way to make grandparents feel appreciated is to incorporate their traditions into the family's daily life. I remember my own grandmother's tradition of making homemade bread; although my mother enjoyed making bread, they shared this responsibility. They took turns and celebrated how different the technique and taste was. Also, my mother was never very religious, yet she encouraged my grandmother to share her beliefs about her religion and faith with me and my siblings. That became a very powerful bond between us and our grandmother. My memory of my grandmother's role in my family is extremely positive. I lived with my grandmother until I became an adult, she guided and taught me as much as my parents. She was my child care provider and a respected member of our family. The distinction between her role as a grandmother, parent and friend was blurred; I considered her all of them. My parents included and respected her in our family life. She was an equal member of our family. My own views of the role of grandparents in a family are shaped by this model of my parents and grandmother's relationship. I believe that surrounding a child with loving adults who participate in child care activities is invaluable. If grandparents have the time and are willing to contribute to family life, they should be respected and celebrated.

REFLECTION QUESTIONS

1. Do you think that the role of grandparents in the province of Newfoundland and Labrador is different than in other provinces? Why or why not?
2. Sometimes grandparents' involvement, particularly if the grandparents do not live close, has an impact on their own lives. How does this reality fit (or not fit) with the nostalgic notions of grandparents in their 'golden years'?

3. In one example above, the parents were very involved in their careers. What possible strains may develop between grandparents and adult children in this type of situation?

4. Grandparents provide respite to parents who often feel the stress of work and family life. What are the positive impacts of the role of grandparents as respite providers and what are other potential positive impacts?

REFERENCES

Georgas, J. (2003). Family: Variations and changes across cultures. Online Readings in Psychology and Culture (Unit 13, Chapter 3). Retrieved on July 25, 2010 from http://orpc.iaccp.org/index.php?option=com_content&view=article&id=47%3Ageorgas&catid=33%3Achapter&Itemid=15

Goodfellow, J., & Laverty, J. (2003). Grandparents supporting families: Satisfaction and choice in the provision of child care. Australian Institute of Family Studies. *Family Matters, 66,* 14–20.

Milan, A., & Hamm, B. (2003). Across the generations: Grandparents and grandchildren. Current Social Trends, Statistics Canada. Retrieved on July 25 from http://www.statcan.gc.ca/kits-trousses/pdf/social/edu04_0004a-eng.pdf

Mitchell, B. (2009). Family matters: An introduction to family sociology in Canada. Toronto, Canada: Canadian Scholars' Press Inc.

Tan, J., Buchanan, A., Flouri, E., Attar-Schwartz, S., & Griggs, J. (2010). Filling the parenting gap? Grandparent involvement with U.K. adolescents. *Journal of Family Issues, 31*(7), 922–1015.

STEPHANIE SAMSON

THE AFFECTS OF DIVORCE ON GRANDPARENTS

The Roles They Assume

It is said that the love for your own child is one that cannot compare to any other feeling experienced. Most parents love their children unconditionally throughout their entire lifetime. Having a child and working diligently to raise them into a well-rounded human being is a task that all parents should be proud of. Often when a child grows they look for a life partner, someone whom they can have children with and the cycle goes on. Sometimes this union between two people can take a bad turn and may result in separation. No parent wants to see their child go through the pain of experiencing a marital separation. This pain can affect the parents significantly and can change their role in the relationship between their child and grandchildren.

The separation of two adults, whether mutual or not, can be quite traumatic for all parties involved. When the idea of reuniting is out of the question then the word divorce can be heard. Divorce is "the formal dissolution of a valid marriage by judicial decree" (Mitchell, 2009, p. 179). Once a family has come to the decision of divorce their effects ripple through their children, their parents, extended families, and friends. When a parent sees their child going through such a huge ordeal, they often times try to support them as best they can. In the case of divorce with children involved, grandparents can also play a major role.

Grandparents can find themselves in situations after divorce that they may enjoy or dislike. There are various roles that grandparents can assume after a divorce takes place. Some common roles are as follows; grandparents as parents, parenting their adult child, hater or peacekeeper, and an explainer.

For the purpose of this paper I conducted some research that I will be including. I have attached three case studies of personal stories that are relevant to this topic. The first case study is that of Jenny and then her Grandmother's story. Also, Sara, a child of a divorced family who was raised by her grandparents was kind enough to share her experience with grandparents and their relation to divorce. Throughout this paper I will use quotes from interviews that I conducted with these individuals.

Grandparents as Parents

The trend of 'grandparents as parents', is one of the most popular in the research on roles of grandparents after divorce. According to (Milan and Hamm, 2003, p. 4), "The 2001 Census counted more than 474,400 grandparents who shared households

A. Singh and M. Devine (Eds.), Rural Transformation and Newfoundland and Labrador Diaspora: Grandparents, Grandparenting, Community and School Relations, 251–260.

with their grandchildren." If parents are battling custody or have gone their separate ways then grandparents may assume the role of parents because of their ties to these children. Oftentimes grandparents can be a support block for a single-parent trying to raise children and so they end up spending more time with the children than the biological parents. Most often the home of grandparents can be a place of stability. Children need stability when their home may be crumbling. "While nearly half the grandparent households with a grandchild include the child's mother, about a million families in the United States are made up of grandparents raising their grandchildren without one of the children's parents" (Rothenburg, 1996, p. 2). Whether a parent lives there or not, in some divorce cases grandparents can be seen assuming the role of the parent and having sole responsibility of raising the children. Tremblay, et al. (2010, para. 3) point out that "Whether it be in terms of offering temporary child care, gaining visitation rights after the divorce, or seeking custody over grandchildren who have been abandoned or abused, today's grandparent is more involved in "kinship care" than ever before. After raising their own children most grandparents have the ability to raise children. They see their grandchildren as their responsibility because their child has failed as a parent or are not able to assume the role of raising the child."

Raising children as a grandparent can be quite difficult. As most grandparents are older in age, having the physical and emotional energy to care for a child can be demanding. If the children are of a young age then playing with them can be a task in itself. Usually if the children are older the task is a little less physically exhausting but may be more emotionally straining. Finances can also cause a problem. Many elderly grandparents live on fixed incomes and are therefore burdened with the cost of providing for children again. Also, once people reach a certain age they change their lifestyle to suit their needs. Most elderly have taken on the lifestyle of retirement so "instead of a quiet retirement, sweetened by delights of occasional visits with grandchildren, many grandparents have taken on the role of surrogate parents to their grandchildren" (Rothenburg, 1996, p. 2). If they are left to assume the role as a parent then these dreams of retirement may be placed on the back burner.

In case study number three Sara's story of how she grew up in this situation is explained. Sara states "being raised by my grandparents was no different than if I were raised by my biological parents. If anything it was better!" Her situation was a pleasant one and she felt that her life was not changed significantly because she grew up with her grandparents. She was very lucky in having this type of life. Some children grow up with grandparents as their parents and for various reasons such as old age, or stern rules, children grow up having a much different lifestyle than they would have if they were to be raised by their parents. Sara stated; "My grandparents were very involved in our school life and we were involved in all sorts of community activities."

Parenting Their Adult Child

Caring for their adult child during or after the process of divorce can be an important role. As a parent it is crucial to be able to provide your child with the emotional and financial support that they need. As a grandparent during divorce they may once again become very close to their own child. They need to be the "back bone" for their child and support them in their decision to divorce. Sometimes adults feel that they have let their parents down by failing their own marriage. Parents need to reassure their child that they support them in their decisions.

The supportive role by grandparents can affect both the grandparents and the grandchildren. Grandparents may feel burdened by their child's troubles and this can be emotionally, and sometimes financially, draining. As an older person, dealing with these burdens may not be easy. Also the grandchildren can be affected. Children may feel that their grandparents are always spending time with their parents and not spending quality time with them. They may feel negatively about their grandparents' visits and involvement in their parents' divorce. They could feel left out when their grandparents seem to spend more time and attention on their parents rather than on them.

Often times during divorce the children in the family end up living permanently with one parent and visiting the other. Research suggests that the children often live with their Mother. If possible, a maternal set of grandparents may spend a lot of time with their daughter after separation to help her deal with the emotional loss of a partner. In this type of situation the grandparents will be there to support their daughter and not as the fun loving, giving grandparent. Children will look to their grandparents for attention and when they do not receive the amount that they need they can dislike their grandparents. If they see their grandparents giving support to their single-parent, children may be upset that their grandparents are supporting the decision of their parents to divorce.

Hater or Peacekeeper

Watching your child go through a divorce can be a very emotional period in a parent's life, especially when children are involved. Being supportive can sometimes, come as a challenge, depending on the reasoning behind the divorce. One type of role that grandparents can take on is a parental role as either a hater or peacekeeper.

If the divorce is an ugly one then strong emotions can be "generated by grandparents' sense of outrage at the way their son and daughter had been treated by their ex-spouse" (Ferguson, 2004, p. 38). This type of anger can have an effect on the adult child and the grandchildren. Often times the grandparent is very open about their feelings. Ferguson stated, "Mothers had occasionally to remind grandparents that they must not express their angry feelings about the child's father in front of the child" (p. 39). This is similar for situations in the father's family. Grandparents who take on this role need to be cautious of what they say in front of the children as this may cause the children to make a judgement on their feelings about their grandparents.

On the other hand grandparents can take on the role as peacekeeper. This position is a hard one to take but is more beneficial for everyone. "It is often better for the grandparents to step back, as difficult as that may be, until the divorce kinks are worked out" (Metzler, n.d., para. 9). Being neutral will be difficult but will create the best results in the end. Having nothing to say will increase their chances of having relationships later with their child and grandchildren.

Jenny grew up in this type of situation. Her Grandparents took on a peacekeeper role when her parents divorced. Her Grandmother explains it as "something I had to do in order to keep a good relationship with Jenny and her sister. I was afraid that if I intervened I would make her Mother mad and she would not let us have a relationship with them." They felt that they wanted to be supportive but in a positive light. In case study number one I further explain Jenny's situation. She stated, "I am very grateful that my Grandparents kept this role and I am very lucky to have had them in my life during such a difficult time." Also, in case study two a summary of her Grandmother's interpretation of the role is included.

Explainers

During divorce children can have a hard time between picking sides, dealing with emotions, worrying, etc. Grandparents can help alleviate these types of problems and feelings. Having someone who is not directly involved, such as a mother or father, explain the reason for divorce can make understanding clearer for children. Grandparents are considered to be wiser than parents and so their view is usually more profound for children.

Adult children also need a shoulder to lean on during the process of divorce. Having a parent who can help by listening and conversing can be a great help when going through a traumatic time.

As mentioned earlier these are just some of the main roles that grandparents can play when their children decide to divorce. There are many other roles such as; stable generation, family historian, blind eye, etc.

Grandparents can play a major role in a child's life during the process of divorce. They can provide stability and support during the trauma of this transition. Whatever role they decide to hold they most often want to be involved in the children's lives. Having grandchildren should be considered a blessing and losing a relationship with them because of divorce will break the hearts of both grandparents and grandchildren.

If grandparents are going to take on the above roles during divorce they must first take into consideration the situation. Thinking about the parents and children before taking on a role will help make sure that the grandparents do not step into a situation where they are causing a problem. Relieving stress and helping make the situation easier is the goal grandparents need to achieve. Showing support, love, and time "can be an important aspect of a grandparent's role" while great help in aiding their family get through the rough time that they are experiencing (Ferguson, 2004, p. 38).

CASE STUDY 1

Jenny

Relating to the role of grandparents during divorce is an issue that Jenny can personally associate with. During her high school career her parents had a falling out and the result was a divorce. During this transition she confided in her grandparents who open-heartedly supported her through this rough time. They supported her emotionally and financially. They would constantly speak in a positive light toward her situation and her grandmother would reassure her that "everything was going to work out and she would eventually look back on it and consider it a bump in the road of life." She would also tell her that "everything happened for a reason." This was reassuring that something good can come out of something bad. Happiness is something that she felt years after their divorce. Her parents were not happy when they were married and so after the divorce she could actually see them happy.

Jenny would consider herself to be what people refer to as a "worrier". At the age of sixteen she was told by her father that he and her mother were getting a divorce. That moment was very heartbreaking for Jenny. She remembered it quite clearly. She was visiting him at his work and while there he gave her an envelope and said "give this to your Mother. These are the divorce papers she needs to sign." Jenny was mortified and angry. The reasoning behind this decision was pathetic and divorce did not seem to be the answer to her. But Jenny did not have an opinion and so during the winter of her eleventh grade year her father moved out of their house and the process of divorce began. The day he left is still very vivid in her mind. As he left he told her that "this decision has nothing to do with you. I want you to visit me a lot and to look after your Mother for me."

Living in a small community was also a major factor in her situation. Her community had a population of about four thousand people. Gossip travels very quickly in a town that size and so that story of her parents' relationship quickly spread. She was constantly asked questions by people about her situation which made her very uncomfortable. This made Jenny's decision to leave town every weekend to go to her grandparents even more purposeful.

Jenny's Christmas that year is much like an episode that someone would experience during another state of mind other than their everyday self. She remembers being very upset all of the time and worrying about problems that were outside of her control. For instance, she worried about her father living on his own, her sister living without her Father in the house, her mother supporting them with her low wage job, etc. These worries were alleviated by the relationship she had with her grandparents.

Once Jenny's grandparents got wind of the news that her parents were divorcing they decided to take on the peacekeeper role. They stressed that their reasoning for this decision was to "not make bad blood between her Mother" and them. They were always mild people and if they felt angry, which she is sure they did, they did not make it evident. On weekends she would drive the hour trip to their house where she would stay until Sunday night. Jenny would sit with them and share her thoughts and feelings. They always listened, especially her grandmother. She would just nod her head and smile while Jenny had little nervous breakdowns about how this could be happening to her. Once a week they would come to Jenny's house to visit. During these visits they would never mention her Dad and would always be very kind to her Mother about her decision. They wanted to make sure that she knew they would support her during any decision she made during her life. They would always say "if that is what you guys have chosen to do then that's all we can do." They would always reassure them that everything would be ok. They would often ask them questions about school or friends and make note of all the positives that were going on in their lives like school plays, great report card marks, skating competitions, etc.

If it were not for Jenny's grandparents she felt that her parents' divorce would have had a greater effect on both her and her sister's lives. They did not take on the role as parents but they were much like parents to Jenny in giving her the feeling of stability, love, and support. They reminded her that she was always welcome at their home and if she needed anything to let them know. They once told Jenny that she could not move in with them because she could not leave her Mom and sister who needed her around. Jenny remembered her grandmother saying "you are the rock of the family and it will never crumble if you keep up your strength."

CASE STUDY 2

Jill (Jenny's Grandmother)

Jill is the one who was Jenny's rock during her parents' divorce. She welcomed her into her home every weekend while Jenny tried to escape her heartbroken life. She lived about an hours' drive from Jenny's community and this drive was well worth it. While at her home she would sometimes forget how shaken her life was and feel like she was normal again. In conversation Jill would remind Jenny of her role in that traumatic time of her life.

Jill stated that it was difficult to take on the role of a peacekeeper during Jenny's parents' divorce. She mentions "biting her tongue" during the whole ordeal. Jill and Jenny's grandfather did have strong, angry feelings toward her parents for deciding to divorce and giving up on their marriage. Jenny's grandmother said "I could have crowned them when I heard the news. I was hoping that if I did this it would knock some sense in them." She wanted to make sure not to create any hard feelings so she would not have to miss out on a relationship with Jenny and her sister.

Having to keep quiet was hard but in asking about changing her role she said "I would not have changed it." She felt that "it was a good move to take on this role and I am glad I did." Jenny was very fortunate that she felt supported by her Grandmother during that time. Jill knew that this role would be the most beneficial for everyone. She said "I told her mother to let me raise ya but she wouldn't hear any part in it." So she did not persist and Jenny's mother did not want to separate Jenny from her sister.

CASE STUDY 3

Sara

At the age of twelve Sara's mother and father went through the divorce process. She and her siblings, one sister and one brother, lived with their grandparents while their parents worked through the divorce. Then they both ended up moving away. Sara's experience was quite different from Jenny's experience.

Sara loved her parents and grandparents so much. She said that "I did not love my parents any less because they gave us to Nan and Pop. I knew that it was probably the best thing to do at the time. I am not mad at them." After her parents' awful divorce they both decided that they were not able to raise three children on their own, so Sara's maternal grandparents decided that they would take over the role of parents for these three children.

Sara's grandparents lived in the same community as Jenny's. Although her parents' divorce was very public in the town where they both lived, Sara did not feel the same hostility toward community members as Jenny did. She was much younger when her parents divorced so people did not ask her about her situation. Also being raised by her grandparents was not abnormal because they were young and very supportive such as a set of parents would be. She describes it as being a normal childhood and would not have changed anything if she was older and her opinion may have mattered.

Sara describes her living with her grandparents as good. "They were the best guardians you could ask for and I never felt any different than you because I lived with my grandparents and you with your parents. I guess the young age of my Grandparents was a bonus too." They were closely in contact with the children before the divorce so moving in with them did not seem like a large transition. Her grandparents raised them until they were old enough to leave home and head off to university.

Sara says that she had a good relationship with her grandparents and doesn't believe that she lived a different life than anyone who was raised by their own biological parents. She said "they gave me all the ingredients that a set of parents would, like love, support, commitment, and they showed me how to be a good parent myself." Her grandparents did all the things that parents would do: support school events, place the children in groups, and hold birthday parties. She feels that they did a great job raising her and her siblings and wishes she could have some way to thank them.

During conversation with Sara she mentioned that

they would always want to be called grandma and granddad. They did not want to take the place of our parents but knew that they were in a different situation than most grandparents. They would often buy us gifts to give to our parents during holidays. We liked doing this. I remember going to visit my mom one summer for a week, but she would come home for a week or so most summers.

She would also try to make it home at Christmas and other times during the year. Dad was a little harder to see. He would call and send presents and money but we probably only saw him once a year.

My grandparents raised us as they did their own children so some values were a little different than my friends who were being raised by their parents. They would make us sit together and eat supper every night and go to church on Sundays. This did not hurt us but up until we lived with them we never went to a church other than at Christmas. I think they did a great job raising us and we really appreciated them to the fullest. We still do today.

Both Sara and Jenny were in families where divorce affected their entire families. Grandparents' roles can be important and whether they are taking on a lead role in their child's divorce or explaining the situation to their grandchildren, they are obviously important members of the family and their help and guidance can be appreciated.

REFLECTION QUESTIONS

1. The author refers to one role of grandparents in divorce of their adult son/daughter as being that of peacekeeper. This role, in essence, silences the grandparents. What are the possible outcomes or implications for the grandparents who assume this role?
2. The author refers to being a 'single parent'. What is your definition of 'single parent'? How does your definition fit (or not fit) when the second parent may not have physical custody of the child but is quite actively involved in the daily life of the child(ren)? Would you see 'singleness' being more on a continuum than a black and white definition?
3. How might the supportive role of grandparents differ when the grandparents live close by versus when the grandparents live in another province?
4. How do you see your community (geographical and/or school) playing a part in the life of children whose parents are divorced?

REFERENCES

Bridges, L., Roe, A., Dunn, J., & O'Conner, T. (August 2007). Children's perspectives on their relationships with grandparents following parental separation: A longitudinal study. *Social Development, 16*(3), 1–16.

Ferguson, N. (Autumn 2004). Children's contact with grandparents after divorce. *Family Matters, 67*, 36–41.

Hilton, J., & Macari, D. (1997). A comparison of the role of Grandparents in single-mother and single-father families.

Metzler, L. (n.d.). When parents divorce: Keeping communication alive with your grandchildren. I-parenting. Retrieved on July 31, 2010 from http://www.grandparentstoday.com/articles/parents-and-grandparents/when-parents-divorce-1905/2/

Milan, A., & Hamm, B. (Winter 2003). Across the Generations: Grandparents and Grandchildren: Statistics Canada.

Mitchell, B. (2009). *Family matters*. Toronto: Canadian Scholars Press, Inc.

Pruchno, R. (1995). *Grandparents in American society: Review of recent literature*.

Rothenburg, D. (1996). *Grandparents as parents: A primer for schools*. Urbana, IL: ERIC Clearinghouse on Elementary and Early Childhood Education.

Soliz, J. (2008). Intergenerational support and the role of grandparents in post-divorce families: retroactive accounts of young adult grandchildren. *Qualitative research reports in communication, 9*(1), 72–80.

Tremblay, K., Barbar, C., & Kudin, L. (May, 2010). Grandparents: As parents. Retrieved on July 28, 2010 from http://www.ext.colostate.edu/pubs/consumer/10241.html

MARGARET ANN CLEAL

CONTRIBUTIONS OF GRANDPARENTS IN TODAY'S SOCIETY

ABSTRACT

The focus on grandparents in today's society is extremely important because, as educators, we are seeing more and more emphasis on the role the grandparent is playing in the lives of the students we teach. "Grandparents are raising increased numbers of children in their home... [It may be a] skipped generation or intergenerational form in which the family consists of grandparents and grandchildren, or the family may be multigenerational and include grandparents, adult children and grandchildren. Even in the latter grandparents....take on the major responsibility for raising the child" (Tutwiler, 2005, p. 43). For the purpose of this paper, to show the changing role in the grandparent over the last three decades, I interviewed three grandmothers, born in the 1930s, 1940s, and 1950s. Through their personal experiences with their own grandparents as well as the experiences they have with their own grandchildren, I will attempt to show change not only in the view of their own grandparents, but the role that grandparents play in society today. Next I will discuss how this affects the school and community and finally I will conclude with my own personal beliefs of the roles of grandparents.

INFORMAL INTERVIEWS

Grandparent 1: Born in a Small Community in Newfoundland, at Home, in 1930

With tears in her eyes, this very "young" 81 year old spoke about her childhood. She lost her mother at a very young age and couldn't even remember much about her. She described her beautiful smile, but wondered if that was only because of what people told her. When her mom died, the three children, three girls, were left in the care of the father who was a fisherman and would be gone for long periods of time. "My own grandparents didn't play much of a role in our upbringing although they lived close by, they couldn't take on the responsibility of rearing the children because of ill health and at that time money was very tight." (Personal, Grandmother 1) Finally, her siblings and her were separated and placed in Foster Care. Her two sisters were placed in very loving homes, yet, she wasn't as lucky. "I was placed in a home that although it had lots of material things, it didn't have

A. Singh and M. Devine (Eds.), Rural Transformation and Newfoundland and Labrador Diaspora: Grandparents, Grandparenting, Community and School Relations, 261–270.

love." The home she stayed in didn't treat her well, and she often told that she was a real live Cinderella. She was responsible at a very young age for much of the cooking and cleaning.

> It taught me that to get ahead in this world I had to work hard and get out of the place I was in. I dreamed of a loving family, a loving home and I didn't care if I had a rug underneath my feet....I would live in a shack if it was filled with love. I often wondered what my life would have been like if my mom had survived. (Personal, Grandmother 1)

This lady moved to Statin Island, New York in the United States when she was 17 years old, where she remained until she retired. She raised her own children there and finally, had a "real" family. When her grandchildren arrived, she made sure she was an active part of their lives.

This lady told me about how important being a nanny was to her.

> I loved to spoil my grandbabies and they visited my house often. I was involved somewhat in their upbringing, with advice and support, yet sleepovers weren't a common occurrence. I made knitted goods, home-made bread and my children and grandchildren visited for meals, especially on Sundays. At that time, the mothers were house makers, rarely worked outside the home, and the fathers were the breadwinners. My grandchildren didn't need me for child care services and really it wasn't my role to do so.!

If someone was sick, she would stay with the family in their own homes to help, and very rarely did the grandchildren stay with her. When it came to education, she encouraged her grandchildren to become what they wanted to be, and when they attended college, "I would often send them a package of goodies and sometimes a little money....this was a big treat for them." Story telling was an important aspect of their relationship because she wanted her grandchildren to know about her own young life that wasn't so great at times. In their urban community, very few grandparents had responsibility for their grandkids.... "It just wasn't the norm. Mothers raised their children, fathers worked, and grandparents were just that, grandparents...loving them and then returning them." (Personal, Grandmother 1)

We spoke briefly of how she compared grandparents today to when she had her grandchildren very young.

> Grandparents today take on much more responsibility than they did in our generation. I have friends who practically raise their grandchildren. They provide babysitting, meals, almost move in with them. Some of these children too I believe expect too much from their parents (who are the grandparents) and place responsibility on them that should ultimately be their own. They cannot enjoy their grandchildren like we did. They are pressured and stressed with the decisions of their upbringing. This is so different than it was. (Personal, Grandmother 1)

Also she explained that grandfathers now play a bigger role than they did in her day. "My husband certainly loved our grandchildren and he would light up when they visited, yet he didn't seem to have time to spend with them as grandfathers do today. He worked, worked and then worked some more and he just didn't make the time to spend with them that grandfathers do today." She pondered on the changes and when I asked if she thought the relationship was better, she paused for a moment, and then quietly spoke,

> I cannot say that it is better or not. It is different and I know that the children probably do benefit more, yet I don't think the same respect is there. Grandparents were held with high respect, and I just don't see that the same. Grandchildren expect more from their parents and their grandparents, and I cannot say that it's a good thing. Spending time with them more? Great! Yet I think grandparents should not have the pressures that are placed on them today, yet being involved in their lives I think is great!

Now she and her husband enjoy dual citizenship in Canada and the United States and she is residing where she was born. She is still in contact with her grandchildren, and as young adults, they do not visit frequently and she believes this is because they have families of their own. She sees the relationship of grandparents and grandchildren today different, as they seem to be more involved in each other's lives. "I would love my grandchildren and great-grandchildren to visit our beautiful home in rural Newfoundland that overlooks the water." (Personal, Grandmother 1). She said that someday she hopes they will be able to experience going to bed and listening to the water lull them to sleep, just as she held and rocked them to sleep as young children.

Grandparent 2: Born in Rural Newfoundland, at Home, in 1944

This lady explained that she was one of ten children and although her grandparents were living when she was very young, she couldn't remember much about them. Both of her grandfathers were fisherman and at the time, it was the only occupation in their community. They lived near the water and watched for their own father to come home from fishing, because he too was a fisherman and because there weren't many forms of communication, the only way they knew their dad was coming home, was when his boat appeared in the harbour. The children spent most of their time doing chores because with a large family and the dad not present because of work, everyone had to do their share to keep the house functioning – cutting wood, caring for the cattle, cooking, making bread, and caring for the younger children. Their family was Catholic and they practiced their faith together, especially each evening before bedtime…they all gathered in the parlour to say the rosary. This was a very important tradition that is still part of their family. Her brother, sister and herself still carry on this tradition of saying the rosary together before bedtime.

One of her grandparents lived next door to the family, and according to older siblings, they didn't have a great impact on their upbringing.

We visited and helped them out, but we didn't stay with them. We had to do chores for them but each week we gathered on a large hill for a family picnic which involved our grandparents but really I cannot remember too much of them... Sunday was a family day and there was absolutely no work that was to be done. We had to attend church, enjoy a traditional Sunday dinner together as a family and then everyone packed a picnic for the hill." (Personal, Grandmother 2)

This was something they shared with their grandparents and especially when their grandfather was home, it was a special time. When her grandmother (her mom's mom) became ill, her mother took the lady into their family home to care for her.

Mom told me there was an infant in the house, as well as a twin that was fourteen months old, plus five other children at the time, and my father spent most of his time at sea. This took a toll on my mother because my ailing grandmother suffered from undiagnosed dementia, and really she was like another child. She remained with the family until her death, about eight months in total. Although I cannot remember it a whole lot, I can remember my grandmother being in an upstairs bedroom and me being scared. I didn't like her and I think it was because the memories that I have about her are not pleasant ones. We were sheltered from her mostly but there were times when I had to go to her room to sit with her or see what the fuss was about. I didn't like it at all!! (Personal, Grandmother 2)

My father was a very loving man and he fished when he was very young in an effort to help out his own family, who struggled like most other families did at the time. There was plenty to eat, yet there were no extras to share. When he was in Portugal there was a stowaway found on the boat. He was ten years old and his parents placed him on the boat because they couldn't afford to keep him and they hoped that by going to Canada he would be given a better life. The captain, my father said, was a cruel man who meant business, and when they found this young boy, the cap' (Dad called him) wanted to throw him overboard. There was no way that he was going to let this happen, so he fought for his life and well, Dad won. He took the young boy, who he called Tony into his bunk, shared the rationed food, and brought him home when the boat returned to Wild Beach Newfoundland. When he returned home to his own parents, this trip he not just had himself for his parents to keep, but also this young boy Tony. They took him in and raised him like he was one of their own. He was unofficially named Tony Hannam, our family name, and he remained there until he was old enough to move away. He didn't keep in contact with the family, but his grandson did look us up a few years ago and visited the small community where his dad was raised. My dad was kind and when he spoke of Tony, he always had tears in his eyes. My grandparents took Tony in even though they struggled themselves. (Personal, Grandmother 2)

She was very proud of her parents and one of the most important lessons she learned from them was respect.

My parents were strict, very strict, yet they were very hard working. They were loving individuals who placed their family at the center of their lives. This is what I wanted to foster in my own children. We learned at a very young age that with love came respect. We had traditions that I wanted to keep alive in my own family. (Personal, Grandmother 2)

Today with three of her children grown and married, the love and respect that they have for each other reflects the love and respect that was instilled in her in her upbringing. She remained home to care for her children while her husband was a Financial Supervisor, but finally they retired and can enjoy the new role they have acquired in the last few years – that of a grandparent!

This is one of the most important roles that I see as I look back on my life. Yes, my children were very important to me but to have grandchildren is very different. I cannot explain the feeling that I had when I found out that we had a granddaughter…I have three boys and well to have a little girl in our family was certainly something to be proud of. I really didn't care if it was a boy or a girl, but Nanny started buying frilly dresses and of course bows, something I didn't buy when my own were young. (Personal, Grandmother 2)

She has two grandchildren and unfortunately, because of employment, they live in Central Canada.

Unlike my own father, my son and his family live where he is employed because he plays an active role in the lives of his children. Because of technology…. phones, and the computer, I have daily contact to my grandchildren. The computer keeps us very close through the use of the web cam and sending pictures and videos back and forth. The bonds we have formed have been made possible because of the advances in technology.

Also she sees the advances in transportation as an added benefit that enables her to strengthen her ties with the grandkids….

If my son's family needs me, I am on a plane and by their side in less than three hours. I was there when both of them were born and have spent extended periods of time with them to help with day care expenses. I wish they were closer so I could really help the way I wants to. Someday…someday…we may get them home to stay. (Personal, Grandparent 2)

Then she states "Nanny and Poppy will not have to read their bed-time story to them on the phone." She looks forward to a visit soon from her granddaughter who will be staying for a month. She will return with her in the fall to visit with her four month old grandson.

She spoke about what she thought about the role of grandparents in our society and she told me that grandparents certainly play a much more important role than what they did when she grew up.

> It seems that grandparents are more involved in their grandkids lives now and in every aspect. The grandparents help out in every way they can, and sometimes too much is expected because some of these grandparents are still working in an effort to keep not only their children going, but their grandchildren too! I also think too that sometimes grandparents overstep their boundaries. I don't give my opinion on things unless I am asked about it....yet some of my friends seem to make decisions for their grandchildren without even being asked.... then they wonder why there is tension. We are lucky and we are comfortably retired for a few years, so now we can enjoy this new role in our lives....like I said before I wish they were closer so right now I could squat the chops off my little ones. (Personal, Grandmother 2)

Grandparent 3: Born in Small Community on the Burin Peninsula, 1955

This individual was one of five children who lost her own father at a young age. This was detrimental to the family because he was the main breadwinner and their family struggled to make ends meet. Their family was very close and when they were able to work, they did to contribute to the family.

> Everyone had to pitch in because, well, mom didn't work and because she didn't have much education, she really couldn't work, so she thought. Sometimes we had boarders in our home and mom provided meals and cleaning for them. At that time, our rooms were very crowded because if we had boarders, we lost our bedrooms and all children sometimes bunked together. (Personal, Grandmother 3)

All five children received university degrees and education was an important part of their lives. "When we lost dad, mom always told us that we needed to get our education because she didn't want us to have the hardships that she had. Hard work was a part of our family as far back as I can remember and everyone in the family had a specific role to play." Her grandparents she remembers vaguely but she remembers having to help them as they seemed "aged" to her, yet looking back on it, they died young – early 60s. She laughed "because I will soon be there, so that is really young!" (Personal, Grandparent 3)

Both she and her husband are retired teachers who raised their three children very close to the community she grew up in. Now two of the three children are married and they are very proud grandparents of little "Lilly". The pride that both of them show for their children and their only grandchild is evident by the way they speak about them. "What kills us the most is the fact that our children are scattered throughout the country, and "Lilly" is in British Columbia. When my husband retired, I was still teaching, so we knew the direction that our children's lives were taking, and we knew we would want to be with them as much as we could, so he spent three years in an isolated community up North teaching so we could not only enjoy our retirement, but be able to travel when we needed to, to be with our children, and now little Lilly." (Personal, Grandmother 3)

They spend every opportunity they can to be part of the grandchild's life. "I was there when she was born and I spent the first two months helping to care for my granddaughter. My husband, not being so brave around childbirth, opted to stay home until our little bundle of joy arrived. I just don't think he wanted to his own little girl in pain...he is a bit of a wimp!!" They set up an Education Fund for Lilly when she was born and contribute to it on a monthly basis. The phone, texting and computer, keep the closeness possible and "I even babysit each day while Erin gets her lunch." Through the use of Skype, Lilly talks to Nana as her mom prepares lunch. She recognizes her voice and when she met recently, she immediately went to Nana. "This is the only thing that keeps me sane, because we want to be an important part of Lilly's life." Poppy reads a book to Lilly and Nana and Lilly sometimes sing together. "Recently, I had surgery and little Lilly's daily kisses always made me smile." Again the advances in technology and transportation enable them to be closer to their grandchild; yet, the availability of work in the area doesn't allow them to move closer. Also financially they can visit, but they said that not everyone is able to do this.

Certainly the role of grandparents has changed over the years. My own mother was involved in my children's lives and spent a great deal of time at our house, yet she respected our roles as parents and even though she spoke her mind when she wanted to, she knew that ultimately it was our decisions that had to be made with regards to our children. I knew I could depend on my mother at any time to provide love, care and support to our children, yet there was a respect factor there that didn't allow us or our children to step over the line. We knew our boundaries and I don't know if the young children today see the same boundaries. Sometimes grandparents spoil the grandkids with material things that they didn't have as children, but I really do not know if that is a positive thing. The more the children get sometimes, the more they expect. Then you have a respect issue again, and if the children are pretty well permitted to do anything when they are in the care of their grandparents, it makes it very difficult for the lives of the parent when they have to enforce rules in the house. It is great when grandparents take an active role in the children's upbringing, but there is a line that shouldn't be crossed...we are grandparents, not parents and we should be able to enjoy this role, not take it on as a stressful role. If I had to, I would in a heartbeat step in and bring Lilly home if her mom or dad was sick, and I would ensure that she was reared as best as I could, but not just because....like I see some young parents do, expecting their own parents to raise their children.... (Personal, Grandparent 3)

Changes in Grandparents' Roles

Throughout the interviews and using my own grandparent experiences, it was evident the role of the grandparent is changing. As a young child I was involved in my grandparents' lives, yet it wasn't to the extent that my own parents were involved in my children's lives. I loved, respected, visited my grandparents and looked forward to my grandmother's cookies and stories, but they weren't physically involved in the upbringing of their grandchildren. One important point was that because of the large families, it was nearly impossible for them to be actively involved in all of the grandchildren's lives. My grandparents loved their grandchildren, provided support yet it was the responsibility of the parent to raise the children – not the grandparent. As the Grandparent stated in the first interview, "it wasn't her role to do so..." (Personal, Grandparent 1). As I interviewed the last two grandparents, aged in their 60s and 50s, they were and wanted desperately to be involved in their grandchildren's lives, by reading to their grandchildren, communicating daily, providing financial support through Educational Funds, and whenever possible, physically being there for support. If their grandchildren lived closer, both would provide child care for them, so again, they would be helping financially. Both stated that as their grandchildren grew up, they wanted to be there for their first day of school, their ballet recitals and their hockey tournaments because they wanted to be active participants in their grandchildren's lives.

In asking the three interviewees their opinions on the changing roles of grandparents in today's society, many of the ideas surfaced that we have read about – the age of mortality has increased, therefore grandparents are living longer which is enabling them to spend more time with their grandchildren. Families are having fewer children, which in turn mean fewer grandchildren so the opportunity to have close relationships with the grandchildren is more possible. The change in technology and communication in our global world allows grandparent and grandchildren to grow together even though many miles may separate them.

Changing Role of Grandparents within School and Community

"Traditionally, grandparents served as a safety net for children in instances of the death of a parent, divorce or when children were abandoned." (Tutwiler, 2005, p. 44) This is forever changing because more and more we see grandparents during parent-teacher interviews, because they are assuming the roles of the parents. It may be for varying reasons, but Tutwiler continues on p. 44 stating that grandparents may be assuming the role of parents because "children [may be] born to young or teenage parents, [or] parents who are substance abusers, [or those] who engage in child neglect or abuse, or [those] who are incarcerated." In our area, the other important aspect of grandparents being involved in the child's upbringing is when one or both parents have travel outside the area and province for work, thus sometimes leaving school-age children in the care of their grandparents.

With this new role of the grandparents comes new challenges. Grandparents need to be able to care for and support their grandchildren in all aspects of their growth. If the grandparents are working, they may need to deal with finding competent child care, and financially this new role may be a strain. They will need to be involved in the education of the child from getting them prepared for school to learning to deal with academics. Depending on the age of the child, grandparents will need to be aware of the challenges of the child's peers as well as the risk that certain children and age groups may face.

How does the modernization of grandparenthood impact the school and the community? We have grandparents who are actively involved in children's lives within and outside school. They may be coaching a basketball team or going on a field trip with the class, they may be a special presenter in the class or they may be fund raising for the needs of the school playground. They may even be a court appointed guardian, and we, as teachers, have to be aware of the changing face of families. We have to embrace the role of the grandparents as one that is very important. Taking on the direct role of the parent may not always be the case, yet a grandparent may be involved in the life of the child by giving support in an extended nuclear family. These grandparents not only enjoy spending time with their grandchildren, but they want to be a part of their educational future. These grandparents provide love and support in an effort to foster growth and development of these children. They can have a very positive impact on the child's development.

CONCLUSION

"Grandparents today generally play an active role in the lives of their grandchildren, though there is diversity with respect to grandparenting styles." (Mitchell, 2009, p. 232) We have seen through the three grandmothers interviewed that even in the last three decades the role of the grandparent has changed and one grandma even stated "If I had known how great it was to be a grandparent, and have grandchildren, I think I would have had them first!!" Now grandchildren are able to have strong relationships with their grandparents for various reasons more so than they were able to 50 years ago. "Grandparents often look out for the well-being of younger relatives, help them when they can and try to mediate or create linkages between family members and across generations.....Some grandparents take a more "hands-off" approach, which might be because of age, health status, distance or because their children obstruct visit." (Mitchell, 2009, p. 232) Whatever the reason, grandparents are more often than not involved in the life of their grandchildren and we need to encourage their involvement with the development of the child in mind. Sometimes when the grandparents are the sole providers, it may be viewed negatively, but the "continued existence of intergenerational bonds is actually positive for family life."

(Tutwiler, 2005, p. 45) I look forward to the day that I will become a grandparent and I am sure that we too will be actively involved in the lives of our grandchildren!

REFLECTION QUESTIONS

1. This chapter highlights the 'changing role of grandparents'. What are the positives of this changing role and what are some of the challenges?
2. As you reflect on the many different voices of grandparents throughout this text, there are common themes. However, there are also 'alternate stories'. How have some of these alternate stories impacted grandparents and/or grandchildren?
3. "Grandparents are too invoved in the lives of their grandchildren today". Provide your own critique of this statement.
4. What are some of the changing roles of grandparents you see in each of these interviews?

REFERENCES

Mitchell, Barbara A. (2009). Family Matters: An Introduction to FamilySociology in Canada. Toronto: Canadian Scholars' Press Inc.

Singh, Amarjit. Grandparent Review 2, August 2010, Online notes.

Singh, Amarjit. Grandparents Research 3, October, 2008, Online notes.

Tutwiler, Sandra J. Winn (2005). Teachers as Collaborative Partners: Working With Diverse Families and Communities. New York: Lawrence Erlbaum Associates.

Strong Families, Strong School. A publication of the U.S. Department of Education and Partnership for Family Involvement in Education. (http://www.ed.gov/PFIE/edpub.html) and (http://ericweb.te.Columbia.edu/families/strong/involve.html)

SPECIAL THANK YOU

Special thanks to the three grandmothers I interviewed. They wanted their names to be left anonymous. Their thoughts and opinions were very valuable to the research I conducted.

NICOLE CULL

THE DYNAMIC AND DIVERSE ROLES
OF GRANDPARENTS

INTRODUCTION

The concept of grandparenthood is a relatively new one. Mitchell (2009) describes it as primarily a "post-World War Two phenomenon" and considers the research conducted by Cherlin and Frustenberg (p. 231). This modernization has occurred because of "declines in mortality, falling birth rates, technological advances in travel and long-distance communication, retirement and increased affluence, and more leisure time" (Mitchell, 2009, p. 231). People are living longer so they are reaching the stage of grandparent. Because of retirement and pensions they are able to have the money and time to devote to grandchildren.

The role of the grandparent has undergone change throughout the years. Tutwiler (2005) notes "grandparents served as a safety net for children in instances of the death of a parent, divorce, or when children were abandoned" (p. 44). Today, death, divorce, and abandonment are still factors involving the grandparent in raising grandchildren. But other factors have to be considered. Sometimes, people find themselves becoming grandparents due to teenage pregnancy, children born to substance abusers, or to children left behind due to parent incarceration (Tutwiler, 2005, p. 44).

Grandparents who find themselves thrust into the role of grandparenting are met with unique challenges. Some who have retired are living on a fixed income and find the financial obligations quite stressful. Others struggle with supporting school work and keeping up with the social and physical demands of a young child.

Demographic changes in Newfoundland have expanded the role of grandparents in their children and grandchildren's lives. Due to a weak economy out migration for work has steadily increased. Consequently, the father leaves the province for labour in places like Alberta. The oil companies set up a schedule of work that allows many to work for 2–3 weeks successively and then the workers fly back to Newfoundland for a week to ten days break. This cycle is repeated throughout the year. Many mothers find themselves in essentially single parenting roles for a good portion of their time. This puts extra pressure on them to maintain the home, property, parenting, school work, and family, as well as in some cases, maintaining their own employment outside the home.

In these cases, grandparents are called upon to help with the children. Grandparents can be seen dropping off and picking up children from school. They are the first

A. Singh and M. Devine (Eds.), Rural Transformation and Newfoundland and Labrador Diaspora: Grandparents, Grandparenting, Community and School Relations, 271–280.

call after the parent if the child is sick at school. Grandparents have the free time due to retirement to attend school functions such as presentations, concerts, science fairs, and other functions. Essentially, they become their grandchildren's biggest cheerleaders. In some cases, grandparents also contribute financially to the family by sharing accommodations and paying their share of the household bills.

The following scenarios chronicle the role of grandparents in Newfoundland culture across four generations.

Four Generations of Grandparents

"*Henry the Great" Landry as he is fondly referred to by some 50 or so great grandchildren first dropped anchor in the sheltered harbour of Augus Shore, Newfoundland, some 150 years ago. He is the stuff made of legends. He waded ashore and scoped out the land. With a keen eye for detail he scanned the shoreline and the landscape he quickly spotted the large meadow where his sheep and cows could graze. Further up the hill he stooped and gripped a handful of soil. Its rich composition and texture indicated to him that he would have good success growing root vegetables like carrots, turnip, potatoes, and beets. If he was attentive, he would also cultivate some prize cabbage in this soil. The natural stream running through the meadow would give his livestock instant access to fresh water. The sheltered harbour was a haven from the harsh seas of the North Atlantic and the abundant fish in the waters would ensure his family had good access to good protein. Yes, this little town, the Place of the English, would become home for his new family.

Ever ingenious, Henry the Great staked out his land, all ten acres of it. He quickly had the land surveyed and it was granted to him by the government. The paperwork was in order and Henry got to work. A home was constructed, a chicken coop erected and the cows and sheep were set in the field to pasture. His fishing boat was ready and Henry didn't waste time. He was a hard worker and he became known as a good provider. Even when times were tough, Henry's family had enough.

Henry and his wife Lucy had a son whom they named William. William was educated by his father in the ways of work. Formalized schooling was a rarity but William was taught to read and write at home in between learning to be the jack of all trades like his dad. When Henry died, William was a young boy and he inherited the family estate. William continued to work hard and keep the enterprise going. When he married his young bride, Susan Penny, she came to a homestead complete with a house, chicken coop, fishing boat, cows, and sheep. Susan too knew the value of hard work and her gardens produced the finest of vegetables. From her fall harvest, the largest cabbage grown in the town was a part of the local church Thanksgiving display. She churned butter from the cow's milk and the eggs from her 200 hens fetched the family some much needed extra cash. Todd recalls, "My cousins and I would visit Nan L. in the morning hoping for an egg for breakfast. Sometimes she hesitated because she had to fill her customer orders. But if we waited long enough she would eventually give us an egg!"

Todd and Susan are siblings, the children of William and Susan Landry's daughter Velma. When Velma married Charlie Watters, William and Susan gave them a piece of property on the ten acre homestead so they could build their own home. This tradition continued for as many of their children as desired it. A generation later, grandchildren such as Todd, two other siblings and several cousins were also given a plot of land by Pop L., so they too could build their own homes. Even today, several family members still live within that ten acre area.

When asked about the influence of their grandparents on their lives, Susan and Todd were quick to recall specifics. In his words,

Nan L. was the scholarly type. She was interested in academia and could recite countless poems by heart. She would entertain us with her recitations and challenged us to learn some too. She always had a short proverb ready to teach us a little lesson as we worked or played alongside her.

In fact, she was dubbed the most intelligent woman in the British Empire. One did not need an invitation to visit or come to dinner at her place. The door was always open.

Todd said that Pop L. and his dad were workers. For them,

Formal education was not a priority for them. The demands of family and survival dictated that they work all the time and reading or studying could be interpreted as a way of getting out of work. However, Nan L. and Mom advocated for learning and helped with homework and maintaining school attendance. Nan L. gave me (Todd) my first thesaurus when I was a young boy and it fuelled in me a thirst for language that is still with me today.

In fact, he is the author of four published books that have become Canadian best sellers and used in university reading lists as a commentary on society in Newfoundland.

Susan told me about the day her mother came to visit and brought with her a small coin purse from Nan L. "I looked inside and found Nan's wedding band. Pop L. had passed away a few years before and Nan had passed on her ring to me. I put it on my finger then and still wear it to this day."

Pop and Nan L. did not necessarily contribute financially to the extended family in the sense that they provided cash. However, they did share their gardens and livestock with them. Susan recounted, "It was not unusual for either of my grandparents to slip a penny or nickel into my hand. They always did so with the admonishment to not tell the others. Years later, we discovered they told all of us this." Todd tells the story of when Pop L. passed away. "His will was read and his money was left to his 25 grandsons. By the time his estate was settled, we all stood to inherit $13.00." No, this is not a typing error! "We all gave it back to the estate to purchase a headstone for his grave."

Greater than any of the material things children could expect from grandparents, Nan and Pop L. gave love, compassion, a listening ear, a love for life and learning. Who could ask for anything more?

(*T. Watters, personal communication, July 18, 2011)
(*S. Lesher, personal communication, July 25, 2011)
*Names have been changed to protect the privacy of the interviewed parties.

Shari's Perspective of Nan W. (Velma)

Shari says,

> I don't ever remember a time when Nan W. was not available. She was a business woman and ran the second largest store in town where you could purchase items ranging from building supplies, to clothing, to flour and vegetables. She was shrewd with her resources and could make a dollar go a long way.

Perhaps this was because of her life experience during the depression where everything had a use and purpose and nothing was wasted.

Nan and Pop W. raised 8 children together. They also co-parented with their daughter Susan to raise her son Michael. Susan became a single mom in 1971 while attending college. She studied for three years so Nan and Pop W. cared for Michael, her son, and even after her graduation they continued to care for him while Susan established herself in her career and got married. By this time, Michael was 5 years old and his grandparents were so attached to him that they said he would stay with them for the school year but spend some summer holidays with his parents in the city.

At the age of 50, Nan W. was widowed. She was lonely and grieving and wanted Michael to continue living with her until he graduated from high school. Then, he moved to the city to attend college and live with his parents.

Shari said that

> Nan W. has always played a strong role as a grandparent. She has concerned herself with the spiritual wellbeing of her grandchildren by taking us to church and Sunday school. She was instrumental in seeing that some of us attend summer camps. She was present at all our school functions from concerts to graduations. Even today, she makes an effort to attend school and community functions for her great grandchildren.

She has travelled across the province of Newfoundland to attend the graduations and weddings of her grandchildren.

Shari remembers that

> Nan W. was always around. Our family always took summer holidays out of town. It was not unusual for Nan to be part of our travels. When my parents took a holiday together during the school year, Nan always moved in and took care of us and the house. She cooked our favourites and was careful to remind us to do our homework. Having Nan in our home made for seamless transitions.

For all intents and purposes, I am pretty confident our teachers were unaware that my parents were out of town. Nan was and is amazing!

Today Nan W. lives with her daughter and family and as an 81 year old, she jokes that she "can still jump over the head of some of her children." Sometimes, "I am not so sure that she isn't correct. She has an abundance of energy and keeps herself very busy with knitting, housecleaning, visiting, church, learning how to Facebook, and even doggy sitting."
(*S. Landry, personal communication, July 28, 2011)
(*V. Watters, personal communication, July 18th, 2001 and August 9, 2011)

Todd's Role as a Grandparent

Todd married Myra Wilson in 1969. They have four children, one son and three daughters ranging in ages from 41 down to 30 years old. There are currently six grandchildren ranging in ages 6 months to 7 years. Todd attended college when he finished high school and had a short one and a half year stint as a teacher. When he married, he moved back to Angus Shore and secured the role of Postmaster with Canada Post. Over his 35 years of tenure he was promoted to Field Service Postmaster and was responsible for the auditing of some 30 rural post offices. Myra was primarily a stay at home mom although she did work seasonally in the fish processing industry. Her financial contributions were greatly appreciated in the family coffers.

All four of their children have completed post-secondary education ranging from college diplomas to university masters degrees.

Todd recounts

we have had to help with caring for a grandchild for an extended time when our second daughter was hospitalized. We cared for her two year old daughter exclusively for 7 weeks because our son-in-law had to work. With our daughter's inability to work they could not afford daycare so we stepped in to help. In fact, we would have kept her longer!

Annually, they try to visit each of their children who live away from Newfoundland, always finding a project or two to do around their properties.

For the most part Todd and Myra have enjoyed the luxury of being strictly grandparents. In their words,

We *borrow* our grandchildren for the night for the occasional sleepover. Myra reads them bed time stories; she plays games with them, and tries to learn how to play Super Mario on the DS. I (Todd) take them outside to dig holes to plant seeds in my garden. We pick berries and I am looking forward to when the grandchildren are old enough to build little projects in my workshop.

They explore birds' nests and anthills together. At the end of the visit, Todd and Myra return the grandchildren to their parents and "we wonder how we ever had the energy to raise four of our own children." At times, they are called upon to pick a grandchild up from school or to babysit for an hour here and there. Financially, "we do not have to contribute to the livelihood of our children and grandchildren but we occasionally give monetary gifts towards holidays just to help out because we can." When asked if he enjoyed being a grandparent, Todd glibly replied, "If we knew that grandkids were going to be this much fun we would have had them first!"Yes, being a grandparent is a privilege and Todd and Myra said they,

> made a conscious decision to not interfere with the parenting styles used by their children in child rearing unless it is solicited. We are 'old school' in our parenting style having raised our children in a different generation and our methodology is not always relevant to current child raising practices. So, when our grandchildren ask for our permission to do something, we always ask what did mom or dad say so that we can be consistent with the parents.

As grandparents,

> we worry about the societal conditions in which our grandchildren are being raised. The prevalence of drugs and alcohol; the need for greater safety from strangers, and the financial stressors of raising a family today are just a few of our concerns.

In all of this, "we have a strong a sense of pride in watching our grandchildren grow, perform at piano recitals, or sing at school concerts and church functions." There is a great satisfaction that they can still relate to the things their grandchildren are doing. The generation gap is not too wide.

Todd is quoted saying, "as parents to four adult children, I am proud of my children and experience a great sense of accomplishment because they share my strong work ethic, high morals and beliefs." He counts it a success to see these values being perpetuated to the third generation. Environmentally conscious, Todd has pursued organic gardening all through his life and it is not uncommon to see his grandchildren helping out in the vegetable patch.

(*T. Watters, personal communication, July 18, 2011)

Susan's Role as a Grandparent

Susan is the daughter of Velma and Charlie Watters, sister to Todd. She is the namesake of Nan Landry. Susan spent 37 years in her career as a lab technician and manager. She thrived on the challenges of the science nature of her job. Susan and her husband David, co-parented Michael-now aged 39- with Velma and Charlie, and raised two other children, a daughter and son.

Susan and David have two grandchildren; a 12 year old granddaughter, Brianne and a 5 year old grandson, Tanner. She said,

> I have only seen Tanner a few times in his life because he lives in Ontario. Other than annual visits, I have watched him grow up through Skype, Facebook, and

pictures. But, we try to talk on the phone regularly-as much as a little boy likes to talk on the phone!

Brianne, their granddaughter, is Michael's daughter. Due to ongoing divorce proceedings, it has been necessary for Brianne to be out of the home and while her father has been granted sole custody, it has been better for Brianne to live with her grandparents for the interim. This living arrangement has been in place for two years.

Her grandfather (David) and I are the primary caregivers for Brianne but her father makes monetary contributions toward anything beyond basic care such as music lessons and Tae Kwon Do, or a new bicycle. I (Susan) help with homework and attend all school functions including parent-teacher interviews.

While they attempt to teach Brianne responsibility by giving her chores such as feeding her dog and the bird, she has to be reminded to follow through from time to time. After all, she is still just a kid.

Susan acknowledges

being a grand*parent* at my age brings with it many challenges. After I retired from my career it would have been nice to have had the freedom to travel at will. Having to be available for Brianne's schedule makes it difficult to do the simple things like make an appointment for a haircut just because I want to.

However, she is quick to highlight the positives.

I (Susan) stress excellence with Brianne in her school work and work closely with her to excel in school. Brianne is an honours student and this past school year was the only student in the entire school body who received a perfect attendance award.

As grandparents, Susan and David are very involved in school activities, making sure that Brianne has as many opportunities as possible to be involved in as many activities as reasonable. Susan notes that there is hardly anything more heart-warming than hearing Brianne comment, "I'm smart just like you grandma. My dad told me how smart you were when you were in school." And it is true! Susan excelled in school and graduated a year early at the age of sixteen.

Being a grandparent keeps me active and in good mental health. It keeps me current with what is going on in school today. Parenting keeps me young because I am constantly interacting with younger mothers. It motivates me to get out of the house and attend social events relevant to Brianne.

In Susan's words

In a perfect world, I (Susan) believe grandparents should fill the gaps as parents need them to in the lives of their grandchildren. It is the simple interactions such as reading a book, taking them swimming, or having the occasional sleepover that build the relationship between grandparent and grandchild. The role of grandparents is very important in creating a different bond than with parents by extending relationships beyond mom and dad.

(*S. Lesher, personal communication, July 25, 2011)

GrandParenting: Pedagogy and Practice in Schools Today

To facilitate good home and school relationships, educators should acknowledge the diversity of family structures existing in Canada today. According to Mandell and Duffy (2005) forty years ago one could wrap up the term *family* with the concise definition of a "social group characterized by common residence, economic cooperation, and reproduction. It includes adults of both sexes, at least two of whom maintain a socially approved sexual relationship, and one or more children, own or adopted, of the sexually cohabiting adults" (p. 3). Today this definition is woefully inadequate as it fails to address the complex variety of family forms in Canada. The Varnier Institute of the Family defines family as "any combination of two or more persons who are bound together over time by ties of mutual consent, birth and/or adoption or placement and who, together, assume responsibilities". Schools must be supportive of all family structures and "reject the notion that other family types are substandard" (Mandell & Duffy, 2005, p. 76).

When grandparents are raising their grandchildren then it is likely they are involved in their education. This task can be challenging for grandparents and to bridge the gap it is important for schools to use strategies to build collaborative partnerships with the family. Recent studies suggest that commitment, communication, equality, skills, trust, and respect are some of the characteristics of positive home and school relationships (Blue-Banning, Summers, Frankland, Nelson, & Beegle, 2004). Of these, "family members stressed that communication should be honest and open, with no hidden information and no *candy-coating* of bad news" (Blue-Banning et al., 2004, p. 173).

Bridging the gap between the home and a multi-generational family can be achieved through some family friendly teacher strategies. Teachers can refer to permanent student records to ensure they are using correct surnames of parents and or guardians and address all communication accordingly. For communication purposes, teachers can use the term *family* rather than *parents* and also be sensitive when using statements such as "have mom and dad sign this" (Ray, 2005, p. 75).

Raising a child can cause great demands on a grandparent's time and financial resources. "Teachers should be careful about making requests that involve time or money, such as '*send in cupcakes tomorrow*' (Ray, 2005, p. 75). Another way to support the home is to offer a flexible meeting schedule for parent-teacher conferences. Grandparents often find supporting homework to be a challenge so schools who offer after school care and tutoring are providing great family support (Ray, 2005).

CONCLUSION

The concept of family has changed with time. The kinship family is defined as one in which the grandparents provide primary care to their grandchildren. The responsibility can put constraints on seniors' time, finances, and physical and emotional well-being. When grandparents are providing care to school age children the education of these children adds another stressor. It is important for schools to bridge the gap between the family and the school. Ray (2005) suggests "it is time for teachers to stop looking at families as *traditional* or *non-traditional*. Today's families are richly *diverse*, and teachers must work hard to meet the needs of *all* children from *all* family types" (p. 76).

The key to success between the school, family and community is partnership. Such partnerships "can improve school programs and school climate, provide family services and support, increase parents' skills and leadership, connect families with others in the school and in the community, and help teachers with their work" (Epstein, 1995, p. 701).

REFLECTION QUESTIONS

1. At the beginning of this chapter the author quotes Mitchell (2009) as stating that grandparenting is a new phenomenon – mostly since the Second World War. How would you challenge this statement?
2. Grandparents today are often quite concerned about their grandchildren 'getting into trouble" (i.e., drugs, etc.). What are some ways that the school and/or the community can educate grandparents?
3. Many stories of the grandparents in this text talk of very positive aspects of grandparenting: what are some of the major challenges?
4. In this chapter one grandparent talks of how her retirement years are very different than she had imagined, due to child care responsibilities of a grandchild. How can the state support grandparents in these types of situations?

REFERENCES

Blue-Banning, M., Summers, J., Frankland, H., Nelson, L., & Beegle, G. (2004). Dimensions of family and professional partnerships: Constructive guidelines for collaboration. *Exceptional Children, 70*(2), 167–184. Retrieved from http://web.ebscohost.com.qe2a-proxy.mun.ca/ehost/pdfviewer/pdfviewer?sid=465e4ade-3ddb-46e5-885d-8bd8e0e46d3b%40sessionmgr14&vid=5&hid=112

Epstein, J.L. (1995). School/family/community partnerships. *Phi Delta Kappan, 76*(9), 701–729. Retrieved from http://web.ebscohost.com.qe2aproxy.mun.ca/ehost/detail?sid=2c784c62-e1b8-48d5-a6a2-3d77bece308a%40sessionmgr113&vid=4&hid=112&bdata=JnNpdGU9ZWhvc3QtbGl2ZSZzY29wZT1zaXRl#db=aph&AN=9505161662

Mandell, N., & Duffy, A. (2005). *Canadian families: Diversity, conflict and change* (3rd ed.). Toronto: Harcourt Canada.

Mitchell, B.A. (2009). *Family matters: An introduction to family sociology in Canada*. Toronto: Canadian Scholars' Press Inc.

Ray, J.A. (2005). Family-friendly teachers: Tips for working with diverse families. *Kappa Delta Pi Record, 41*(2), 72–76. Retrieved from http://vnweb.hwwilsonweb.com.qe2a-proxy.mun.ca/hww/results/results_common.jhtml;hwwilsonid=F4IPXPJJH4J5PQA3DIOSFGOADUNGIIV0

The Vanier Institute of the Family (2006). Retrieved August 8, 2011 from http://www.vifamily.ca/node/2

Tutwiler, S.J. Winn (2005). *Teachers as collaborative partners: Working with diverse families and communities*. New York: Lawrence Erlbaum Associates.

KIM MCCARRON

GRANDPARENTS' ROLES IN CHANGING SCHOOLS, COMMUNITIES AND FAMILIES

INTRODUCTION

As our family structures continue to evolve and change so too do the roles of grandparents in our communities and family units. Due to declining job opportunities on Cape Breton Island with the loss of major industries such as the fishery, steel and coal production, there has been an increase in out migration to the west for employment. This trend has separated families, spouses and children from one another creating new sets of circumstances where grandparents play a major role in the "kinship care" and raising of their grandchildren. Coupled with the financial strain of gaining an education and finding a job, most families require two household incomes to have a comfortable living; this adds to complications in areas of family life such as child rearing and care. Therefore, many questions can be raised about the new emerging roles of grandparents, their contributions regarding support that keeps their families intact, and how this corresponds to their community, schools and family in various parts of Cape Breton.

This is an account of six grandparents from various local communities within the County of Cape Breton in Nova Scotia. The study was a qualitative one involving interviews with a convenience sample of grandparents that constituted one male, and five females ranging from 54 to 80 years of age. The participants also had a mixture of cultural backgrounds such as Scottish, Irish, Italian and Lebanese heritages. All families were born and raised in local communities on Cape Breton Island, having significant involvement with their grandchildren on a daily basis. However, none of the participants in this study had sole custodial care but they provided voluntary supportive care in the raising of their grandchildren. The degree of grandparents' involvement varies from one household to the next, often being influenced by a multitude of circumstances such as family structure, proximity to grandchildren, relationship with parents, parental employment and demographics, health and age of grandparents, and interest or importance of grandchildren in their life course. In this paper, I will use, recent literature, my own personal views and the views of my participants to discuss the emerging roles grandparents have within the "family", now and in the past, while emphasizing the "pleasures and pressures" of grand-parenting.

A. Singh and M. Devine (Eds.), Rural Transformation and Newfoundland and Labrador Diaspora: Grandparents, Grandparenting, Community and School Relations, 281–292.
© 2013 Sense Publishers. All rights reserved.

Method of Data Collection

There were five participants that were interviewed for this qualitative research paper. All participants were interviewed by the researcher on one occasion, interviews which lasted between 30 and 45 minutes. All interviews were recorded, with permission of the participants being interviewed. After the interviews, the recordings were transcribed into computer files and care was taken to assure participants that no identifiable information would be in any subsequent report.

Review of the Literature

The definition of family is multi-faceted and continuously changing and evolving. How we define "family" is largely rooted in our personal experiences and cultural perceptions which can be attributed to a variety of factors that are forever changing. Our families' histories have a remarkable impact on the direction in which our life evolves (Mitchel, 2009). The relationships that people form with their families not only make significant differences to themselves but to society as a whole. Wendy Mitchel (2008) states that, "the twenty-first century family faces many demographic changes but despite this, the importance of intergenerational relationships remains" (Mitchell, 2008 p.126). Grandparents therefore, still remain an integral part of family life. With the evolution of family life there are new emerging roles of grandparents as child care provider, spiritual guide, teacher, historian, role model, emotional supporter, and a loving companion. Tutwiler (2005) describes grandparents as ranging in age from 40 to 80 years old, with the median age being 57. This is quite a span in age range and offers individuals who have a diverse "bank" of life experiences and unique cultural backgrounds that can benefit families and communities. Therefore, grandparents are a heterogeneous group, providing different types and levels of care with different personal support needs (Mitchell, 2008). Thus, many individuals remain grandparents for one third of their life span or over 25 years.

The literature surrounding grandparents demonstrates that the experience of grandparenthood is complex and diverse. Grandparenthood is an important part of the life cycle for most people, both as personal experience and for its impact on parents and grandchildren (Drew, Richard, & Smith, 1998). Grandparents often play pivotal roles in the lives of grandchildren, often assuming the role of voluntary caretaker due to a variety of reasons such as death, divorce, parental employment on evening or night shifts, multiple jobs, parental child abuse, substance abuse or parental incarceration (Strictton & Leddick, n.d.). The relationships between grandparents and their grandchildren also have largely been affected by the emergence of new family types and the woman's permanence in the workplace (Viguer, P. & Carols, J., 2010). In addition, demographic changes such as decreased birth rate, death rates, increased life expectancy, aging population, increased affluence for grandparents, retirement, better health, and more leisure time have established new parameters for grandparent's respective roles and relationships in the family unit (Viguer, P. &

Carols, J., 2010; Mitchel, 2008; Drew et al., 1998). Jendrek (1994), discusses that these circumstances that lead to grandparents providing care for their grandchild can be either formal (via court orders or decisions) or informally (the grandchild either lives with the grandparent or spends a good portion of time with the grandparent). According to Tutwiler (2005), "approximately 4 million children lived in homes where grandparents were the primary caretakers, which represented a 44% increase over the previous decade."(p. 44). In fact, one in 10 grandparents have been the primary support of a grandchild at some time in their lives (Miles, n.d.).

There are many factors which can affect the connections that occur between grandparents and grandchildren. Depending on a family's culture, race, ethnicity, gender, family structure, geography and traditions these interactions can vary. For example, in the Japanese culture, the first son takes care of the elderly parents by co-residing with his family. This allows grandparents to develop strong relationships with their grandchildren, passing on cultural traditions (Mitchell, 2009, p. 222). In many Asian cultures, multigenerational families have been a traditional way in serving the needs and caring for young people and elderly adults (Settle, 2009). In Canada and the United States the "nuclear family" is predominant, consisting of a husband, wife and their children (Tutwiler, 2005). There is a growing body of research that suggests that family structures are evolving and different structures are becoming more evident such as single parent families, same sex-families, adoptive/ foster families, and intergenerational/ multigenerational families (Mitchell, 2009; Tutwiler, 2005). Therefore, with greater health and financial security in the older generation we are seeing a larger role being taken by grandparents in regards to supportive care of their grandchildren.

There are many positive aspects related to grandparents raising grandchildren. In the Ruiz and Silverstein (2007) study, they stated that the response of grandparents as a second-line of defense against emergent fissures and fractures in the family may be especially valuable for the well-being of the grandchildren and their developmental process (p. 794). Sue Miles, program leader of family development at Western University states, "Providing grandchildren with a sense of security by helping them to grow in their self-confidence, self-identity, self-respect and self-esteem brings joys as well as challenges in parenting. Grandparents often experience a self-renewal through their grandchildren." (p. 1) This renewal can be both biological and emotional; experiencing emotional self-fulfilment, gaining social networks, and being able to support the positive development of a generation that carries a family forward (Miles, n.d.). Also, it can be argued, from the perspective of evolutionary biology, grandparents have a genetic predisposition to ensure the quality and success of their grandchildren, therefore, this network can provide resources to cope successfully with the stresses of life providing a cushion of support (Ruiz & Silverstein, 2007).

According to the literature, there can be many negative aspects related to grandparents raising grandchildren as well. Some researchers report grandparents raising their grandchildren are more likely to be living in poverty, in overcrowded conditions, to suffer from social isolation and have a disability, depressive symptoms or psychological issues (Tutwiler, 2005; Mitchell, 2009; Minkler & Fuller-Thomson, 1999). Tutwiler (2005) states, "Many grandparents do not have the financial resources to take care of a child because many are on fixed incomes and others may have to reduce work hours to care for the child" (p. 44). Obviously, becoming the primary care giver to your grandchildren is a life-changing event for grandparents. Sometimes, when grandparents assume parental roles for their school age grandchildren they can run into legal issues if they do not have legal custody. For example, according to Strutton and Leddick (n.d.), "when a child is enrolled in school, certain documents must be presented or the child will not be permitted to register such as social security card, immunization records, proof of residency, birth certificate, records from previous schools and any special services if they may have been receiving" (p. 111). A grandparent raising their grandchildren is a mounting trend, therefore it is important that grandparents recognize and are aware of their rights so that they can meet the needs of their grandchildren socially, economically, and academically.

As the literature shows, there are many benefits and drawbacks to grandparents' involvement in their grandchildren's upbringing. However, the level of involvement varies depending on a variety of factors and different family structures. The following is the local narratives of five grandparents and my own personal views on the level of involvement they play in their own grandchildren's lives and how that plays a role in the emotional, physical, economical and psychological health of their family units.

Local Narratives

Grandparents provide their children and grandchildren with physical and emotional support for a variety of different reasons. Traditionally, grandparents were seen as the patriarchs of the family providing mentoring, lineage, love, encouragement, passing down skills, traditions, and customs that were meant to strengthen family units. In my own experiences, grandparents share stories about traditions, rituals, the past and their own childhood and family, contributing to our identity as individuals and a family as a whole. I had the opportunity to know both sets of my grandparents, all of whom had a very big impact on my life and on who I am as an individual today. Although, two of my grandparents died of cancer when I was only 7 years old, "both were young themselves at the age of 56 and 57", I still have strong memories of who they were as individuals and the role they played in my life. Both sets of my grandparents were very actively involved from a very young age, whether it was telling me stories about their heritages (Lebanese, Irish and Scottish), teaching me how to cook, taking me to sporting events, picking me up from school, playing a role in child care when my parents were working shift work or just feeling love and affection from them, those memories are still very vivid. Both my grandmothers were housewives, one of my grandfathers worked at the Sydney Steel Company and the other had a family run printing business. I remember my grandmothers always cooking homemade food, and scrubbing floors, walls, doing laundry and making sure that the house was spotless. There was always a home cooked meal on the table and fresh baked goods. My grandparents provided me with values, morals and a positive image of what grandparents should be for their grandchildren. Financially, both my grandparents contributed to my education paying for half of my first year of college. Religion was also a very important aspect of my grandparents' lives. Being devoted Catholics they were involved in many aspects of the Church and community events. Although my grandparents played a huge supportive role to my parents when they were a young age, I now see a shift in responsibilities where later in the life of my grandparents, my parents played a significant role in the care giving of elderly and ailing parents.

The first grandparent participant that I interviewed was a 64 years old female who lived at home with her husband of 37 years. Both grandparents in this household worked for a living. The grandmother interviewee was a Licensed Practical Nurse but is now retired and her husband still works but travels out west for employment. Therefore, the grandmother plays more of a supportive and involved grandparent role than her husband. Together they have one child, a daughter who lives in Truro, Nova Scotia with her husband and four children ages, 11, 9 and 7 year old twins. This is at least a three and half hour drive from their home but she sees them on a regular basis. "I talk on the phone to them every day and travel up there every 6 weeks or so, I go up there more than they come down but it's easier for me 'cause I'm retired". As a grandparent she provides voluntary supportive care for her grandchildren when she is visiting or when her daughter needs assistance when her husband is traveling for work and she is working herself as a teacher. Her role in the family ranges from providing occasional care, to playing with them, cooking for them, taking them to school, to parks, to sports or extracurricular activities, helping them with homework, washing their clothes, getting them ready for bed etc. Basically, the grandmother plays a very involved role in "grand-parenting" her grandchildren and providing care and support when needed or when she is visiting. She finds her role satisfying but stressful at times stating, "Sometimes I find it satisfying, its different than raising your own kids, there is less responsibility, however, sometimes I feel obligated to watch them and I find it very tiresome". Also in regards to discipline she sometimes has a difficult time, "Sometimes they don't listen, like most kids and they fight with each other…I get frustrated and upset 'cause I only had one child and I don't know what to do when they are fighting or who to blame or who to holler at." Overall, her relationship with her grandchildren is something she cherishes and it keeps her young, "I love when they pay attention to me and give me hugs and kisses, makes me feel good". There are times that she feels that she is taken for granted and that her daughter expects too much but most of the time she is happy and willing to help out.

The second grandparent interviewed was a 57 year old female who lived at home with her husband of 35 years. Both grandparents in this household work for a living and the grandmother being interviewed is currently working fulltime as a hairdresser. Their family consists of two daughters and three grandchildren ages 9, 3 and 1. Both grandparents play active roles in their grandchildren's lives doing activities with them such as providing child care, taking them to sports, helping with house work, washing clothes, getting them ready for school, for bed, playing with them, or cooking for them. "We only can do what we can do, but when they need something we get it". One of her grandchildren, the 3 year old, has some health issues and they provide financial assistance to their daughter when they have to travel back and forth to Halifax for appointments but they are glad to do it because they are in a situation in which they can provide some extra funds. When asked how providing care for her grandchildren made her feel she stated, "Sometimes it drives you crazy, sometimes it's great, it all depends on the situation". Being involved in the daily life of her grandchildren was both satisfying and tiring at times. She valued the time she got to spend with them and enjoyed providing voluntary supportive care and doing activities with them. However, sometimes "I feel like my husband and me are taken for granted and my children expect things" which can be frustrating at times for the couple. Although, she was very clear that her children are great to invite them over for meals or take her to doctors' appointments; basically, if she needed something they would be there for her. Overall, she enjoys the time she spends with her grandchildren and finds immense pleasure and fulfilment from it.

My third set of grandparents were a married couple of 54 and 55 years of age, with two daughters and two grandchildren ages three and one. The couple has been married for 32 years and currently sold their house to their youngest daughter and her family. The grandparents are living temporarily with their youngest daughter, husband and two grandchildren while they build their new house. During their younger years both individuals worked full-time raising their own children. The male participant worked in the Steel plant and the female was a medical secretary. Presently, the grandfather is still working full-time and the female is working part-time hours which enables her to play a role in child care for her daughter who works shift work as a nurse in the hospital and whose husband is a carpenter. Both grandparents are very involved in the daily activities of their grandchildren, cooking for them, bathing them, getting them dressed, changing diapers, child care, taking them on overnight excursions, taking them to or picking them up from day care, helping with house work etc. The grandmother stated, "My grandchildren are an important part of my daily life; they make me feel young and needed." The grandfather had similar feelings stating, "When my first grandchild was born it felt unbelievable like my life had come full circle, I would give my life for my grandchildren; they mean the world to me, even though I love my children my grandchildren come first now". Both grandparents expressed immense joy in getting to spend so much time with their grandchildren and valued the flexibility they had in their own lives to step in and assist with support when needed, never feeling obligated to help. The grandmother stated, "I look after them twice a week since my job went part-time and my daughter went back to working full-time shift work as a nurse… I offered to look after kids to save her money and we also offer money for bills, rent while we are living here to help my daughter and her husband out." The grandfather seemed to play a role of "head of the family", everyone went to him for financial advice, or practical problems, and was a bit of a softy when it came to disciplining the grandchildren. "I have a hard time with discipline, it's not like bringing up my own children, I interact more socially with my grandkids; they run all over me". Both grandparents took pride in the upbringing of their own children and felt their grandchildren were a reflection of their own parenting and given that they are in a different stage in life it allows them to have a deeper connection to their grandchildren which made them feel contented. The grandmother stated, "it makes me feel good when they want you when they are going to bed at night and they ask for you instead of their mother or dad...makes you feel like what you are doing with them on a daily basis is meaningful". They also mentioned how exhausting it can be taking care of two small children but they would rather spend time with them than do other activities because of the relationship they have built with their grandchildren. The grandchildren are very comfortable being with the grandparents and often got upset if they were to leave, always hugging them and expressing their love for them. The grandparents loved that they were able to do things for their grandchildren, "The relationship with grandchildren is different than that of my adult children because we can spoil them and do with them what we want with them but send them back cranky and not worry about it like you would your children."

The fourth participant was an 80 year old grandmother whose husband died of cancer when she was just 57. The couple had five children (two boys and three girls), 14 grandchildren and 3 great grandchildren. The grandmother lived a very fortunate life in the sense she never had to work, she was a "housewife" and her husband ran a successful printing business which they sold before his death, and she has lived off the money since his death. She still lives in her family home with one of her adult grandchildren who recently moved back home to start a career in nursing and needed a place to stay so she welcomingly opened her home. Growing up for this grandparent was much different than children now a day, "we didn't have all the material stuff these children (have; it is) different to live, now you need two salaries." This grandparent played a very active role in all of her grandchildren's lives being involved with child care when needed, taking grandchildren to sporting events, school, picking them up, buying them presents (holidays and birthdays), and just being present in their daily lives. "I was very involved with my grandchildren's daily activities, if the parents couldn't do it and if I was free I would do it. I loved taking care of my grandchildren; they keep me active, moving and young." When her first grandchild was born she recalls, "We were on top of the world, there were lots of pictures taken of the first one but as more and more came along we had less and less time to devote to them all." Not all of her grandchildren are in close proximity. Her daughter's family moved to Prince Edward Island about 15 years ago for work. Since then she has been able to keep in contact with her daughter and her four grandchildren through weekly phone calls and traveling but it's gotten harder as she got older, "I used to go over and visit a lot when I was young and could drive

287

over but now because of my age, I need to depend on people to take me, we still talk weekly." This grandmother also was very involved within her community through the Catholics Woman's League (CWL) (of a Catholic Church) in Sydney. The CWL acted as not only a religious group but a social club, putting on dances, baking for funerals, or other events to raise money for the church and keep the community close. The grandmother stated that,

now a days our community membership in the CWL has decreased because more young woman have to work and do not have the time to commit to the church, it's usually only those woman who are older or retired that can help out but back in our day, even with large families, church was a very important aspect of our life and community.

All of the participants in this study had different experiences with their own grandparents but none of them had any real significant involvement with their grandparents growing up. One participant is quoted in saying, "Grandparenting was different back then...as much as we were there we had limited exposure to them... they were no influence: my life at all...I had very little contact with them even though they lived across the street." Other participants remember doing chores such as helping with the baking or going to fetch water in the well. Most of the individuals interviewed had very little memory of their grandparents but there was strong correlations that they had specific gender roles such as the grandmother was strong, rock of the family, very thrifty with money, kept the family functioning, and were home makers while the grandfather usually went out to financially support the family by working. One participant has an interesting relationship with her mother's grandparents because she had the opportunity to live with them for a year. She recalls,

My grandmother was very thrifty; made a dollar last and really watched her groceries. My grandfather was a barber and made 50 cents a haircut which wasn't a lot of money. My grandmother didn't work and I was always amazed on how she ran a household, bought groceries with the little bit of income they had coming in; I was surprised what they could do compared to what we have now a day; she was very wise with her money.

What was evident in the interviews was that the roles of grandparents have changed dramatically than in years past. One participant commented,

The interaction between grandparents and their grandchildren is only going to get greater and greater because of the economy. Adult children are moving back in with family, grandparents are taking a bigger role than they have ever done in any generation other than in China, but in our culture grandparents are taking on a huge role babysitting, taking grandchildren on vacations with them, back in our day our grandparents didn't do any of that.

All of the grandparents felt as though they were very different from their own grandparent in that they were much more involved in their grandchildren's lives, providing physical, emotional and financial support. "We are much different from our own grandparents, we spend more money than they did on life, spoil them more ...what money we made we gave to our kids and our grandkids." She also expressed the importance of her grandchildren in her life, "My grandchildren are a very important part of my life, I don't know if they need me, but I need to see them." In regards to her great grandchildren she was amazed and overjoyed to have them, "It's unbelievable to think you would be still alive to see your great grandchildren. If someone told me that I would be here to see this, years ago I wouldn't believe it."

When asked about what potential challenges parents are faced when providing good care to their children, all of the participants expressed their concern with the fact that both parents must work in order to meet the families' financial needs. This factor is what most of them felt was the reason that grandparents role in the family unit has shifted so dramatically. On grandparent stated,

Now a days, I find both parents must work unlike years ago, so I think more grandparents look after the kids because when I was young my mother didn't work and took care of us kids." Another grandparent stated, "In today's economy, parents have to work, have to be educated, uneducated kids are far behind and the potential to look after their families is just not there, therefore they require more support from the older generation.

One grandparent stressed how times have changed and there is more risky behaviour occurring within schools and communities, "Parents have to worry about school-bullying, drugs, alcohol use, sexual activity at an earlier age, harder times financially, not enough home cooked food and faster paced society ". Also, most of the grandparents felt that their own children spoiled their children too much giving them too many material things and not enough interpersonal contact time. "Parents spend more money now than they did and spoil their kids even though what money we made we gave to our kids and our grandkids, I think more time needs to be spent doing activities with your children and grandchildren rather than buying them electronic toys."

Analysis

In each of the families I interviewed they all eagerly participated in the lives of their adult children and grandchildren. Although none of the grandparents had full custodial or primary care of their grandchildren all actively participated and had high levels of involvement in their daily activities. Most of the grandparents' had close emotional relationships with their grandchildren which increased the responsibilities and involvement they had in their own adult children's families. The level of involvement always depended on the flexibility of the grandparents' work schedule, their affluence, their health, their interest and their willingness to volunteer their services. Since finances or health seemed to be never an issue for any of the grandparents it allowed them to be actively involved in the grandchildren's lives relieving the parent periodically when needed.

All of the grandparents that I interviewed viewed the active involvement with their grandchildren as a positive experience that brought many emotional and physical benefits to their lives. However, there were times where the grandparents has some sense of displeasure in the role of raising their grandchildren such as feeling exhausted, mentally drained, or feeling obligated to care for their grandchildren but these emotions did not outweigh the perceived benefits. Some of the grandparents also expressed that their adult children sometimes had unreasonable expectations of them in providing support for their grandchildren. However, most family members were respectful of the roles the grandparents voluntarily choose and it strengthened family units.

Today's grandparents are much different than those of the past; they are younger, healthier, more socially active, more affluent, are still employed and express interest in being involved in the lives of their adult children and their families. Overall, all of the grandparents interviewed wanted to make sure that their interaction with their grandchildren was meaningful and that at the end of the day they were making a difference in their "life course". The roles they presently play with their own adult children and grandchildren is largely different than the roles previously played by their own grandparents such as in the level of involvement, emotional support, financial support, and interpersonal relationships between grandchild and grandparent. These new emerging roles seem to have strengthened family structures, and enabled those families who are experiencing change, hardship or conflicts to find a balance where the grandparents involved reduce the stress not only in the daily lives of their adult children but in the lives of their grandchildren as well.

CONCLUSION

Our family's histories have a remarkable impact on the direction in which our life evolves. The relationships that people form with their families not only make a significant difference to themselves but to society as a whole. The definition of family therefore, is complex and can take multiple forms because it is consistently under construction and mediated by the local culture. Grandparents have played a huge role in our family histories whether it is sharing stories of family roots, giving "life" advice, being patriarch of the family, etc. Advances in health care and increased life expectancy of older individuals, coupled with the changing economy and structure of the family unit has influenced a new emerging role of grandparents in families who are more involved in the daily activities and responsibilities of their adult children and grandchildren both formally and informally. With the direction that current research is taking in defining the roles of grandparents in changing schools, communities and families it will be interesting to see how the family structures and grandparent's roles will change and evolve with time.

REFLECTION QUESTIONS

1. In the literature review in this chapter, the author quotes research which indicated an increase in grandparents providing care, by 44%. To what to you attribute this major increase?
2. It is recognized in this chapter that there are 'many different family types". What are the potential impacts on grandchildren and on grandparenting with these many different 'types' of families in school and/or community?
3. The author in this chapter reflected on and quoted some grandparents and their struggles with their roles as grandparents. To what do you attribute these challenges in grandparenting?
4. One grandparent reflected that parents provide lots of material things for their children but do not spend enough time with them. What is your analysis of this statement?

REFERENCES

Drew, L., Richard, M., & Smith, P. (1998). Grandparenting and its relationship to parenting. *Clinical Child Psychology & Psychiatry, 3*(3), 465–480

Gruters, B. (2008). Exploring Local Economic Development: The Challenges of Cape Breton Island. Retrieved on August 4th, 2011 from http://www.communitywealth.org/_pdfs/articles-publications/outside-us/book-gruter.pdf

Jendrek, M. (1994). Grandparents who parent their grandchildren: Circumstances and decisions. *The Gerontologists, 34*(1), 206–216.

Minkler, M., & Fuller-Thomson, E. (1999).The health of grandparents raising grandchildren: Results of a national study. *American Journal of Public Health, 89*(9), 1384–9.

Miles, S. (n.d.). Grandparents Raising Grandchildren. Retrieved August 3rd from http://www.wvu.edu/~exten/infores/pubs/fypubs/240.wl.pdf

Mitchell, B. (2009). *Family Matters: An introduction to Family Sociology in Canada.* Canadian Scholar's Press Inc. Toronto.

Mitchell, W. (2008). The role played by grandparents in family support and learning: Considerations for mainstream and special schools. *Support for Learning, 23*(3), 126–135.

Pearson, J., Hunter, A., & Cook, J. (1997). Grandmother involvement in child caregiving in an urban community. *The Gerontologist, 37*, 650–700.

Ruiz, S., & Silverstein, M. (2007). Relationships with Grandparents and the Emotional Well-being of Late Adolescent and Young Adult Children. *Journal of Social Issues, 63*(4), 793–808.

Settles, B. (2009). Grandparents Caring for their Grandchildren: Emerging Roles and Exchanges in Global Perspectives. *Journal of Comparative Family Studies, 40*(5).

Somary, K., & Stricker, G. (1998). Becoming a grandparent: a longitudinal study of expectations and early experiences as a function of sex and lineage. *The Gerontologist, 38*, 53–61.

Strawbridge, W., Wallhagen, M., & Shema, S. (1997). New burdens or more of the same? Comparing grandparent, spouse and adult-child caregivers. *The Gerontologist, 37*, 505–515.

Stutton, J., & Leddick, G. (n.d). Grandparents as Parents: A Growing Phenomenon. Retrieved August 3rd, 2011 from http://www.counseling.org/Resources/Library/VISTAS/vistas05/Vistas05.art23.pdf

Szinovacz, M. (1998). Grandparents today: a demographic profile. *The Gerontologist, 38*, 37–52.

The importance of family life: information for family and seniors. Retrieved on August 1st, 2011 from http://www.grandmascraftguides.com/Family_Corner

Tutwiler, S. (2005). *Teachers as Collaborative Partners: Working with Diverse Families and Communities.* New York: Lawrence Erlbaum Associates.

Uhlenberg, P., & Hammil, B. (1998). Frequency of grandparent contact with grandchild sets: Six factors that make a difference. *The Gerontologist, 38*(3), 276–85.

TANYA FIFIELD

THE TIES THAT BIND

The Multi-faceted Role of Grandparents in the 21st Century

INTRODUCTION

Families in Cape Breton, Nova Scotia are dynamic and energetic, despite the impact of the struggling local economy on family well-being. Cape Breton's economy has taken more than its share of hard hits over the past few decades- closure of coal mines, diminished fishing industry, and end of the steel-making era. These realities caused already hard-working parents much anguish and uncertainty about their families' welfare and future. Single-income families had shifted to dual-income families with husbands and wives adjusting their roles just to provide for the basic needs of all members. Stemming from these realities, out-migration increased and has had a negative impact on many small and large businesses and institutions such as schools in the area. A steadily declining student population has resulted in school closures and the exodus of young professionals from the region. Few, if any, replacements to these lost industries have been established for unemployed steel, coal, and fishery workers. For those who have remained, they have had to adjust drastically to alternative types of employment-call centers being one "industry" that has provided some jobs for the unemployed. Over the past five years, many families have had one or both parents leaving the island to work in western Canada in various aspects of the oil industry. These parents return regularly to Cape Breton to assume their parenting role only to return to the West to resume their paid work lives in order to provide for their families back here on the island.

With the drastic changes in Cape Breton's economy over the past few decades, many families have had to make adjustments and create new avenues for meeting the needs of all family members, especially children. While many families have uprooted their lives and moved to mainland NS, neighboring provinces, or western provinces (such as Saskatchewan, Alberta, and British Columbia), other families have remained and have involved extended family members in their day-to-day childcare operations to help ease the burden of formal childcare costs. Grandparents have stepped in and fulfilled numerous child-rearing duties to help keep their extended families intact while adjusting their own lives in enormous ways to embrace new responsibilities.

Recent interviews with five grandparents revealed a wealth of information that paints a very different picture compared to their grandparents' lives sixty years

A. Singh and M. Devine (Eds.), Rural Transformation and Newfoundland and Labrador Diaspora:
Grandparents, Grandparenting, Community and School Relations, 293–308.
© *2013 Sense Publishers. All rights reserved.*

ago. The grandparents interviewed for this paper and their responses provides a glimpse into the lives of 21st Century grandparents, their changing roles, and their contributions to various institutions in society today.

What Does Family Literature Say?

Family demographics today are quite different from two or three generations ago. While the "nuclear family" was viewed as the dominant-culture, family norm in the 1950's, various structures of families emerged in Canada's multicultural society throughout the 20th century, thereby making it inaccurate to talk about "family" as if only one single form of it existed. Baker (1993) noted that

> in actual fact, various cultural groups tend to organize their family life differently, depending on such factors as their socio-economic backgrounds, their historical experiences in this country, their relations with other cultural groups, their religious beliefs, whether they were indigenous to the country or immigrants, and if they were immigrants, when they arrived (p. 8).

Families vary greatly in society and Canadian sociologist Emily Nett recognized this and pointed to extending the definitions of "family" to include those who make up the wider network of related persons to a family unit. Nett asserted that "the family is an abstraction involving ideal, expected, and observed behaviour" (Baker, 1993, p. 4).

Mitchell (2009) reports that, "the vast majority of Canadian women (80 percent) and men (74 percent) over 65 years of age are grandparents" (p. 231). Mitchell (2009) recognizes that although some claim that today's "family" is in decline, the fact is that "grandparents now have the opportunity to live long enough to watch their children (and grandchildren) grow up" as compared to grandparents and their low life expectancy in past generations (p. 23). Mitchell furthers this stance, stating "from this vantage point, this increased generational overlap of lives could easily be interpreted as creating both new opportunities and challenges for aging families" (p. 23).

Mitchell (2009) views grandparenthood, "as a distinct and nearly universal stage of family life" as a "largely post-World War II phenomenon" (p. 231). The "modernization of grandparenthood" has come about as a result of numerous factors, those mainly being "declines in mortality, falling birth rates, technological advances in travel and long-distance communication (e.g., e-mail, webcams), retirement and increased affluence (e.g., pensions), and more leisure time" (Ibid, p. 231). The changing demographics of grandparents and the implications of this- living longer and healthier- may be the reason grandparents are being called upon to support the raising of their grandchildren more often now than in the past.

Tutwiler (2005) acknowledges that an increasing number of children are being raised by grandparents today. Called the "skip generation" or "intergenerational form", these families can include grandchildren and their grandparents or the family may be "multigenerational" where grandparents live in the same household as their adult children and grandchildren (Ibid, p. 43). These family forms are increasing in Canada due to increases in divorce, child abuse, and parental drug use (Mitchell, 2009).

In this era of modernized grandparenthood, more grandparents are leading households where their grandchildren are residing with them. With numerous reasons why a parent becomes unable to care for their children, grandparents may find themselves as the primary caregivers for their grandchildren, returning to the child-rearing skills they employed when raising their own children a generation ago. Grandparents may assume the role of the custodial parent of grandchildren in situations where the parent may have died, divorced, or abandonment has occurred. "Grandparents are assuming the role of parents for children born to young or teenage parents, as well as for children born to parents who are substance abusers, who engage in child neglect or abuse, or who are incarcerated" (Tutwiler, 2005, p. 44). While none of the grandparents in this study were the legal custodial parents of their grandchildren, their provisions of care do involve financial considerations as well as time and attention to the various needs of their grandchildren. Additionally, there are grandparents in the Cape Breton region who have had to take on this new care-giving role and are doing their best, given the economic hardships of raising children today on low or fixed incomes and diminished health status. These grandparents have a keen interest in keeping their families intact.

Research indicates that a greater proportion of grandparent caregivers are rearing grandchildren who have emotional or behavioral problems or developmental delays (Smithgall et al., 2009). These authors note that

> By virtue of this demographic profile, kinship caregivers in general— and grandparent caregivers in particular—often suffer a 'compounded disadvantage'(Schwartz, 2004); that is by virtue of their gender, race, and age, many grandparent caregivers belong to three undervalued social categories and thus represent a marginalized population according to several indicators (Ibid, p. 167).

Cox (2007) notes from her research that grandparents who have assumed the primary care of their grandchildren require consideration for the unique problems they face in this role. Some grandparents are overwhelmed by the "special jargon" teachers and schools employ in communications and are not at all familiar with new math or technology. She recognizes the key role social agencies play in strengthening the relationship between schools and grandparent-led families, working toward "addressing policy and procedural changes that can facilitate grandparents' involvement and support" as well as "offering direct interventions" (ibid, p. 564). Tutwiler (2005) states that "teachers will want to be attuned to the vulnerability exhibited by these children, both at home and at school" and "will want to be aware of the types of support available for custodial grandparents" (p. 45).

Smithgall et al (2009) report from their findings that upwards of 70% of grandparent caregivers had indicated a need for mental health or counseling services for the grandchildren in their care. Additionally, "interviews with grandparent-caregiver families revealed the existence of current, unmet mental health needs among both grandparents and their grandchildren, and interconnectedness between the well-being of these grandchildren and their caregivers" (Ibid, p. 167). The implications point in the direction of making mental health services known and available to these families for their continued development and welfare.

Smith et al (2010) found that there are discrepancies between the perceived need to provide support groups for custodial grandparents and the actual use of these supports by grandparents. They report that there is a lack of research targeting the variables at play in grandparent usage of support groups. These researchers believe it is essential that "pediatricians, schools, day care centers, senior centers, and religious organizations be used to advertise the availability of support groups to custodial grandfamilies" in light of previous findings that indicate many grandparents are unaware of the existence of these supports (Ibid, p. 391). Grandparent unawareness of supports or services was reported in Hayslip and Patrick (2005). They note that "King, Hayslip, and Kaminiski discuss self-reported barriers to both formal and informal social support services. Interestingly, in this sample, about half of the grandparents reported having difficulties receiving the formal services they needed" (Ibid, p. 324). Schools must be attentive to the possible challenges faced by grandparent-led families and provide pathways to ongoing support and guidance to help grandparents reach self-sufficiency in the interest of the children involved.

NARRATIVES OF GRANDPARENT PARTICIPANTS

Interview Parameters

Through purposeful, convenience sampling, two sets of grandparents and a grandmother were chosen for the interview process of this small-scale qualitative study. Nagy Hesse-Biber and Leavy (2006) note that "the logic of qualitative research is concerned with in-depth understanding, usually working with small samples" (p. 70). Thus, a small sample size of five grandparents was selected from the Sydney and surrounding areas of Cape Breton and these participants willingly engaged in small-group and individual interviews (differences in interview structures occurred due to personal, conflicting schedules as well as health issues). The duration of each interview lasted between sixty and eighty-five minutes with responses transcribed and later re-written in narrative format by the interviewer. All participants were informed that their names and other possible identifying information would be excluded from the narratives and subsequent research paper and were assured that the information they provided would be respected and protected. All direct quotes of participants will appear within the context of the paper's subsections.

Demographics of Grandparent Participants

The grandparents interviewed for this study range between the ages of 65 and 74, and are White, middle class, of Scottish, French, and/or English descent. All interviewees are currently married: one couple has been married for forty-five years, the other couple for forty-seven years, and the remaining grandmother for fifty-one years. None of the grandparents have a university or college degree. All study participants are retired from fulltime employment with one grandfather working part-time in the winter months at a community rink in the local area. Two of the five grandparents have health issues or experienced serious health complications over the past decade.

One set of grandparents has three adult children (two daughters and one son- all married) and four grandchildren ranging in ages from two months to ten years old with two of these children living in the local area. The other set of grandparents has three adult children (two sons and one daughter – two married) and four grandchildren ranging in ages from four to ten years old with two living in the local area. The remaining married grandmother has two adopted adult children (both married) and four grandchildren ranging in ages from six to nine years old, all of whom reside with their respective parents in western Canada. None of the grandparents interviewed were custodial – the two sets of grandparents interviewed provided irregular, voluntary care for their grandchildren and one of these grandmothers had provided regular, voluntary care for two of her grandchildren during their toddler and preschool years when their mother returned to the workforce.

Grandparents' Childhood Memories

Four of the five grandparents interviewed grew up in various areas of rural and industrial Cape Breton, with the remaining grandparent living the first seventeen years of her life in rural Newfoundland before moving to the industrial region of Cape Breton to work in 1956. The grandparents had stability in terms of not being required to relocate and parents who were married and provided for their upbringing.

All interviewed grandparents came from large families. One grandfather was the youngest of four children and the other grandfather was also the "baby boy" of his family of seven siblings- four brothers and three sisters. He recalled that "my mother cried when I was born because I was a boy and not a girl. She had two boys and then a girl and another boy before me". One grandmother was the second youngest of three brothers and two sisters (with two sisters dying in infancy). In recalling her youngest brother's birth, she said "he had been born with two broken arms and the doctor set the breaks with cardboard. We were all born at home". Another grandmother was the oldest of her four sisters and two brothers. The remaining grandmother was the second oldest of four siblings – three girls and one boy – with nine years separating her from her youngest sister. She recalls her sister's birth as "very exciting because of our age at the time she was born, nine years was a big span of time between us".

Except for one grandmother, all grandparents interviewed had attended schools in Sydney and surrounding areas. One grandmother recalled that "I never got away with anything and the only time I skipped a class to go to the movies with a friend... my parents knew about it before I got home. My teacher, I'm sure, called them, keeping them up on our attendance". This grandmother valued her public education and took a commercial course in high school that paved the way for her direct employment with the steel plant for a few months in grade twelve then immediately following graduation.

The grandmother who grew up in rural Newfoundland recalled her home and schooling experience as difficult with many hardships, "but that was all we knew back then, we were very poor-hand me downs, patched clothes". She revealed "Our home didn't have running water, electricity, indoor plumbing, or an outhouse... a lot of days we only had tea and bread to eat". She was educated up to grade six in a one-room schoolhouse that was a forty-five minute walk from home. Her schooling from grades seven and up took place in a three-room school. In terms of her favorite subjects, she shared "I liked grammar and math best" recalling the engaging activities in her school books.

All participants recalled childhoods filled with outdoor sports and activities. One grandfather shared his early years growing up in Whitney Pier, Cape Breton and then later in a neighborhood in Sydney.

> As a child, I enjoyed swimming, hiking along back trails, seeing movies at the old military armories, and stealing apples – crab apples from around our place. I liked to play baseball in the summers and hockey in the winters. We were called rink rats see because we spent so much time hanging around the old forum.

The other grandfather grew up in Glace Bay and was an avid baseball and hockey player as well. He had a poignant memory of his youth that devastated his athletic future.

> When I was 13 years old, I was shot in the abdomen at close range by a friend and a doctor worked on me for twelve hours, he just happened to be at the hospital that day – he was a military surgeon who did surgeries out in the field during the war. There was no local anesthetic – I was in shock and he opened me up and removed seven and a half feet of my small intestines and did what he could...I almost died. He told my parents that if I was strong, I'd make it.

This grandfather said that this experience was "life-altering". He was left with no feeling in his left side due to irreparable nerve damage and as a result, his left leg lost much of its muscle mass and strength, thus the accident left him as a "*cripple*" and that is how he perceived himself from then on. "It changed the path of my life, it changed me. I kept it hidden."

The grandmothers recalled doing household chores as part of their childhood activities. One grandmother recalled, "We always had to do chores – wash the dishes right after meals and keep our rooms clean... but we were never asked to scrub the floors". Another grandmother remembered an incident involving a new purchase her mother had made, with money always being very tight.

> She bought me a new pair of shoes and I got them wet one day so we had a wood-burning oven in our kitchen and I put them in there to dry them out and well they burnt and were ruined. She got so mad at me and I cried, saying 'I didn't know'. That was a hard lesson I learned...the value of money.

This value was reiterated by the remaining grandmother who, as a young girl of thirteen, had her first job working at her uncle's grocery store, unlike any of her friends or peers at the time.

> I learned to look after money at an early age. I paid the bills for my parents and grandparents, taking the bus and navigating my way downtown to go and pay their income taxes and power bills. When I graduated from high school and moved into my job at the steel plant, I already knew how to manage my finances. I was really proud of that.

One grandfather recalled chores he carried out at home, "cutting the lawn, shoveling snow, general house repairs – like painting and maintenance of the roof. I also helped out in the garden". The other grandfather as a young boy "hauled wood and coal daily and at a neighbor's house too, I got $1.25 a week". Neither of these grandfathers carried out what was traditional women's work inside the home – their sisters and mothers fulfilled these duties.

Recollections of Parents

All but one of the grandparents interviewed indicated that their fathers and/or grandfathers were employed as steel workers in Sydney in the 1930's and onward. One grandfather noted "my father worked in the steel plant and my mother did household chores". These traditional roles were evidenced in all respondent commentaries. One grandmother recalled that her father "was a steelworker all his life and his father worked on boats and then moved on to work in the steel plant." The grandmother, originally from Newfoundland, noted that her father "worked at an asphalt plant and my mother looked after us and our home. She would do housework for some neighbors and picked blueberries for fifty cents a bucket to make some extra money".

Parental rules were a recalled memory, especially for grandmothers. One recalled clearly that, as a teen, she "was not allowed to go out with Catholic boys and to be home before dark... didn't venture far from home. We had church on Sundays and Sunday school after lunch". This memory points to the clear division between religions and societal expectations in Cape Breton's history. Protestants were not to marry Catholics and vice versa.

Experiences as Parents

All grandparent participants indicated many positive responses in their experiences raising their own children. One grandmother stated that her babies "were very healthy and really happy, especially my son who always seemed to be singing and dancing and my daughter – who was always attached to my hip – she was more shy". Another grandmother reiterated her babies' good health and described them in one summative word, "precious". All grandparents communicated that they loved and enjoyed their experience as parents. During hard times, the grandmothers indicated that they turned to "God and prayer", with one adding that it was most important "to believe in a higher power and be positive" and the other noting a prayer that helped her, called "Make Me an Instrument of Your Peace". All of these grandmothers stayed home to raise their families, with two returning to the workforce when their children were in upper elementary grades and junior high school. One grandfather stated that he was "car poor and college poor" in terms of the financial aspect of his instrumental role in raising his children. Three of the grandparents interviewed shared a common hope for their children – "to be happy in their lives".

Perceptions of Their Grandparents

All grandparents interviewed had some knowledge, as children, of at least one of their grandparents but many had no recollection of at least one set of their grandparents – either due to death or the geographical distance from where they lived. One grandmother had interacted extensively with one of her grandmothers, the only grandparent she knew personally while growing up. She stated, "My grandmother was crippled so I would visit her and help her around the house, help bring in her water in a bucket. She was old and wise". This participant reported that she sometimes stayed overnight at her grandmother's house, providing care by tending to her needs. She recalled that "both of my grandfathers were blind- probably cataracts…my memories of them are vague".

One grandfather participant stated that he found his grandmother, again the only grandparent he knew growing up, quite old-fashioned. He stated, "She lived with my uncle and his family, she was a quiet old woman, never saw her go out much. She held on to old Newfoundland traditions, had old-fashioned ideas… had a little different thoughts on old Newfoundland ways of doing things." A grandmother participant shared her recollections of her paternal grandparents who lived next door to them while she grew up, particularly memories of her grandmother. She recalled,

> I still remember things she taught me – the poor and those who didn't have enough to eat. She was the type of person who would find out who didn't have food and feed them… I still don't know how she found out this. She used to say 'don't throw food away'. I still remember that and if I go to throw out a piece of food, I would feel guilty. She had a lot to do with my upbringing and my

mother didn't mind her involvement. She taught my mother to cook and bake, even though she was my father's mother.

This participant also articulated how she shared some similarities with her paternal grandmother – "saving money and not wasting or destroying things, giving away things to others, there are always people who need". Two grandmothers recalled their grandmothers trying to teach them Gaelic, with one remembering "We would be out on the veranda, you know, the ones that wrap around the house, and she used to try to teach me some Gaelic while I brushed her hair".

Like other grandparents interviewed, the remaining grandfather and grandmother did not know some of their grandparents due to them having passed away before they had a chance to get to know them. This grandfather recalled his maternal grandmother being "short, French, and tough" who could not speak English when she married his grandfather and "she never asked me to do anything around the house", living just across the street from his family's home in New Aberdeen. When asked how these grandparents today are different from their own grandparents, all participants stated that they are much more involved in the lives of their children and grandchildren, with one grandfather stating, "We talk more, we're part of their lives, we share their lives." His wife interjected and stated "We love them." This grandmother's weight on the concept of "love" in terms of loving her grandchildren today was noted, as it was not apparent nor instilled in her own experience with her grandparents. One grandmother stated that she differed from her grandmother in that "I help to look after my grandchildren and I'm healthy" whereas her own grandmother did not carry out any childcare duties and suffered debilitating health issues.

Common thoughts were articulated by both grandfathers and two grandmothers in the sense that they believed that their grandchildren listened to them whereas they believed their adult children did not. This was evidenced in their responses, especially when it came to the question "Do you think your children listen sympathetically to your life stories?" Most participants stated that they felt their children "didn't care" and "were amused" or that "they're probably getting tired of hearing about them". One grandmother went further than these comments, stating, "they may listen but often laugh about them because of the difference between generations... lifestyles are different for each generation." The two grandfathers indicated that they liked to share their "growing up" stories with their grandchildren and thought that their grandchildren's reception of these was positive. This reinforces what Mitchell (2009) reports in that "some grandparents play an important role in passing down important family memories through the retelling of family stories as well as by reproducing long-standing family traditions" (p. 232).

Contributions to Grandchildren

Grandparents in this study share common lifestyles. They have the freedom to be regularly involved in the lives of their grandchildren but also have moderate fixed incomes that place certain limits on their financial spending as well as some physical limitations that at times, reduce the nature and extent of activity involvement. All grandparents interviewed indicated that they derive immense satisfaction from their involvement with their children and grandchildren's activities. One grandmother stated "there's certain things the girls like me to do with them – paint their nails – 'nanny has to do them' and their mothers are not asked to do this, just nanny". This grandmother recognized the meaningful role she plays in her grandchildren's lives, saying

> as young children and as our grandchildren, they have expectations of us, right, and because we don't live close by it's so important when they're here that we do these things with them". She added on to this line of thought by saying "we offer them support and we show a great deal of interest in their activities and how they're doing in their school work, how they're doing socially with their friends.

Overall, the three grandmothers indicated that they spend time teaching skills to their grandchildren-from knitting and baking to reading and tennis. One grandmother added to these by noting she "teach[es] them how to be better to each other", thus contributing to their social development and family's well-being.

These contributions have a spin-off effect. Grandparents in this study indicated improved mental and physical health when it came to involvement in their grandchildren's lives. One grandmother exclaimed "there's great satisfaction, mentally it gives us new ideas and our own physical health has improved – they [grandchildren] gave us reason to improve". Another grandmother noted that "providing care makes you feel good that you can contribute to their well-being and I feel that they appreciate it". The remaining grandmother added that her provision of care helps her to "stay young and positive". One grandfather, on this topic of care, stated that attending to these tasks "helps keep me active, on the job, doing different things". Both grandfathers indicated that they chauffeur their grandchildren to a host of school-related activities and sports events while the grandchildren's parents were working. Grandfathers picked their grandkids up from school, took them to dance classes, piano lessons, soccer games, and hockey practices on a fairly regular basis, becoming part of the grandfathers' daily and weekly routines.

Contributions to School and Community

Grandparents make significant contributions to the lives of their grandchildren as well as to their schools and the community at large. Both sets of grandparents indicated their involvement in their grandchildren's schooling and school-related activities. The two sets of grandparents attended numerous school concerts and presentations that their grandchildren were participating in. "We go to their Christmas concerts, dance competitions, musical presentations, and fundraisers". When schools host their "open houses", both sets of grandparents attend to support the events and show the school community that they are interested in the achievements of the upcoming generation. This serves to empower grandparents as key socializing agents in their grandchildren's lives.

They extended praise and other verbal and nonverbal positive reinforcements to their grandchildren's classes, friends, peers, and teachers. Both sets of grandparents try their best to regularly attend the soccer games of two of their grandchildren and join in the celebrations that follow. They recognize that their grandchildren take pride in seeing them at these functions. Community spirit is uplifted through these shared experiences and they communicates solidarity to community at large.

Challenges of Grandparent Caregivers

Grandparent caregivers in Cape Breton have expressed a number of stressors that sometimes impact negatively on their lives and roles. Personal health status at times affected the level of involvement grandparents could provide to their grandchildren. However, even during illness or complications, the grandparents were consistently interested in the affairs of their grandchildren, their daily activities, and new developments.

Child behaviors can be a significant source of stress for grandparent caregivers. With many grandparents looking after young grandchildren, discipline and nurturance are key areas that require consistency. At times, grandparents were required to enforce disciplinary actions in terms of loss of privileges or verbal reprimands. For the one grandmother who assumed full-time care of her young grandchildren when their mother's one-year maternity leave expired and she returned to work, this grandmother noted that in terms of childrearing strategies, "what worked for my own children should work for my grandchildren and using common sense". A grandfather noted that he didn't require learning strategies or skills in helping raise his grandchildren "but a general 'to do' list helped". Technological changes have produced a wide variety of children's toys and leisure activities to which grandparents have never been exposed. One grandfather noted that "kids have too much electronics, too much exposure to computers and technology". He seemed to recognize the limits these devices placed on his involvement with his grandchildren – their interactions with their iPods and digital games excluded him. This situation poses some challenges as grandparents try to navigate appropriate guidelines for time spent by their grandchildren playing video games, interacting with iPods, computers, and cell phones. Grandparents have no formal training in these technologies and attempt to instill positive work ethics with respect to school work in their grandchildren.

Interview Analysis

From the interviews with these grandparents, a number of similarities emerged. First, all of these grandparents highly value their grandchildren and their role they play in their lives. Despite the apparent differences in how their own grandparents interacted with them as children, these grandparents are able and willing to assist their children with the socialization and development of grandchildren. All grandparents look forward to the time they spend with their grandchildren and have not needed to rely on external supports to assist them in their childcare tasks. This is greatly due to their middle-class status, confidence in their abilities, and position in life. It helps that they are all retired and have an abundance of leisure time to devote to their extended families. This was especially evident in the grandmother who looked after her two grandchildren for a number of years when they were young with both parents working full-time.

All grandparents have personal interests that they share with their grandchildren and hope that new skills are carried down through the next generation. While they each have experienced and fulfilled traditional gender roles in their own lives, these grandparents hope that their grandchildren will further their education and gain independence in their adulthood, regardless of gender. The grandparents enjoyed their experiences raising their own families and were quite willing to lend their knowledge and wisdom to their children and grandchildren.

REFLECTIONS

From a personal note, I did not expect to be as emotionally affected by the stories that unfolded by these grandparents. Their recollections of their childhood memories and the hardships they experienced as children and young adults contrast sharply with my own upbringing and childhood. I had only one grandparent – my paternal grandmother – with whom I developed somewhat of a relationship with while young. My maternal grandmother died when I was an infant and my maternal grandfather, whom I met only twice, died when I was a pre-teen. Back in the eighties and early nineties, I can recall my family going to visit my grandmother and spending Sunday afternoons and evenings with her. She was in her eighties at the time and had limited mobility. Eventually, her health failed and we took her in and tried to look after her nutritional, emotional, and physical needs but we lacked knowledge and expertise. We sought outside agency support and she was moved to a private nursing home where she passed on within a few months.

Unlike the grandchildren in these families, I feel like I missed out on a whole generation of my family by not having them around to share my experiences – both successes and failures – in life. Grandchildren today, if given the opportunity to develop a relationship with their grandparents, can benefit significantly from these ties and connections. As one grandmother noted at the closing of her interview,

> Parents have to teach children that grandparents are people who care about them and the only way that can happen is if parents care themselves about this… they can't teach what they don't care about". She added "I think that families really need to make a great effort to visit each other to show they

care about each other especially in this age of technology... face to face communication may be lost if we don't recognize this.

Another grandmother mentioned that "families need to slow down and make time for 'family' given how fast-paced their lives are". For the grandmother who was separated by distance from her grandchildren, she shared "being separated makes your own children think about you a little more I think and makes them realize how important grandparents are to them and their children".

CONCLUSION

Grandparents are a diverse and vibrant group. They add a dimension to our society that improves the lives of their families, schools, communities and other affiliations. They are enjoying increased longevity and improved health as compared to their own grandparents due in part to marked improvements and advancements in medical research and health care. Grandparents wear many hats – parents, childcare providers, public employees, chauffeurs, retirees, board members, athletes, educators, and community service representatives. Some are retired and enjoy a leisurely lifestyle, some are fully employed and fit leisure into their schedules while others are employed part-time and have plenty of time to enjoy both their extended families and personal interests. Some grandparents are single, living with their children and their families in multigenerational households while others are raising their grandchildren as their sole custodians or co-parenting alongside their adult children. The role of grandparents in Cape Breton today is a multi-faceted one indeed.

Grandparents interviewed in this study are making significant contributions to their families, communities, and schools. From interview narratives, observations, and experiences with grandparents, it is safe to state that these grandparents are a valuable and integral component of our society. Consistently evident from the interviews and observations is the pride and care grandparents articulated towards their children and grandchildren in all facets of family life. From school presentations to family celebrations, grandparents add a special dimension of wisdom and acknowledgement to their families' accomplishments. Grandchildren in these families look toward their grandparents for guidance, love, nurturance, and attention, even if only visiting with them for a month out of the year.

As responses from the grandparent interviews demonstrate, today's caregivers are often sought and found within the extended membership of a family. Grandparents in this study were willing and able to take on both minor and major grandchild-rearing practices while their adult children fulfil employment responsibilities. These grandparents indicated high satisfaction with the responsibilities of taking care of their grandchildren and hope that their level of involvement continues into the future, regardless of their family's constantly evolving status or the hardships facing the island of Cape Breton. Schools recognize the important role grandparents serve and rely on their involvement to see the continuing progress of students in all grade levels of the public and private school systems.

Knowing what the challenges and issues are for grandparents raising their grandchildren will serve to make practitioners, educators, and policymakers aware of what needs to be done to best serve these families well into Canada's future. The demands placed on grandparents in the 21ˢᵗ Century require responsive and supportive public policies and therapeutic programs. Changing attitudes maintained by individuals in various positions within society will help reduce stereotypical attitudes and beliefs about grandparents as caregivers to their grandchildren. Intergenerational relationships, as indicated in this study, have only served to strengthen these family bonds and make families more resilient.

REFLECTION QUESTIONS

1. Reflect on and discuss how grandparenting roles change with changes in the economy as exemplified in this chapter.
2. The author suggests that supportive services are needed in school/community/ state for grandparents providing care. Discuss the implications of these changing needs on policies in schools and in human services organizations.
3. Reflecting on your own experiences, how would you characterize the roles of grandparents today compared to your own experiences of your grandparents?
4. As researchers, we immerse ourselves in the research. One of the potential impacts is our own emotional 'involvement' as mentioned by this author. What are the implications/concerns when the researcher becomes impacted by the research/ stories of other people?

REFERENCES

Baker, M., & Dryden, J. (1993). *Families in Canadian Society.* Toronto, ON: McGraw-Hill Ryerson.

Barnett, M., Scaramella, L., Neppl, T., Qntai, L., & Conger, R. (2010). Intergenerational relationship quality, gender, and grandparent involvement. *Family Relations, 59*(1), 28–44.

Cox, C. (2007). Grandparent-headed families: Needs and implications for social work interventions and advocacy. *Families in Society, 88*(4), 561–566.

Dolbin-MacNab, M., & Kelley, M. (2009). Navigating interdependence: How adolescents raised solely by grandparents experience their family relationships. *Family Relations, 58*(2), 162–175.

Fuller-Thomson, E., & Minkler, M. (2007). Mexican American grandparents raising grandchildren: Findings from the Census 2000 American community survey. *Families in Society, 88*(4), 567–574.

Hayslip, B., & Patrick, J. (2005). *Custodial Grandparenting: Individual, Cultural, and Ethnic Diversity.* New York, NY: Springer. Retrieved August 2ⁿᵈ, 2011 from: http://site.ebrary.com/lib/memorial/ Doc?id=10171382&ppg=342

Letiecq, B., Bailey, S., & Porterfield, F. (2008). We have no rights, we get no help: The legal and policy dilemmas facing grandparent caregivers. *Journal of Family Issues, 29*(8), 995–1012.

Lumpkin, J. (2008). Grandparents in a parental or near-parental role: Sources of stress and coping mechanisms. *Journal of Family Issues, 29*(3), 357–372.

Minkler, M., & Fuller-Thomson, E. (1999). The health of grandparents raising grandchildren: Results of a national study. *American Journal of Public Health, 89*(9), 1384–1389.

Mitchell, B.A. (2009). *Family matters: An introduction to family sociology in Canada.* Toronto, ON: Canadian Scholars' Press.

Smith, G., & Hancock, G. (2010). Custodial grandmother-grandfather dyads: Pathways among marital dissatisfaction, grandparent dysphoria, parenting practice, and grandchild adjustment. *Family Relations, 59*(1), 45–59.

Smith, G., Montoro Rodriguez, J., & Palmieri, P. (2010). Patterns and predictors of support group use by custodial grandmothers and grandchildren. *Families in Society, 91*(4), 385–393.

Smithgall, C., Mason, S., Michels, L., LiCalsi, C., & Goerge, R. (2009). Intergenerational and interconnected: Mental health and well-being in grandparent caregiver families. *Families in Society, 90*(2), 167–175.

Tutwiler, S.J. (2005). *Teachers as collaborative partners: Working with diverse families and communities.* New York: Lawrence Erlbaum Associates.

ANGEL MCCARTHY

SUPPORTING ROLES OF GRANDPARENTS IN HOLDING THE FAMILY TOGETHER

INTRODUCTION

The role of grandparents is ever changing in our society. As family life changes and faces its own unique challenges, grandparents play a unique role in providing support to their family of origin. This paper offers a perspective of what it means to be a grandparent today in Newfoundland's changing society. It chronicles the experiences of three grandparents and the role they play in their children's and grandchildren's lives. Grandparents play a different role today than they have in any other time. Due to increases in life expectancy, falling birth rates, lower mortality rates, retirement and prosperity, and technological advances in communication and travel, grandparents are often able to experience being a grandparent longer. As Mitchell notes, "grandparents are living long enough to enjoy a lengthy life as grandparents, they can keep in touch more easily with grandchildren, they have more time to devote to them, and they have more money to spend on them" (Mitchell, 2009).

THE GRANDPARENTS

Megan

Megan and her husband, Jeff, live just down the street from their grown son, his wife and their two children. Their other son, his wife, and their three children live in Nova Scotia. Megan is a 64 year old retired school teacher. Even though she has been retired from teaching for the past 15 years, she has not truly given up working. Over the years she has tutored students and worked as a substitute teacher in her grandchildren's school. Megan remains connected to her former colleagues. Her closest friend and colleague will often organize lunches for their group to get together. Megan is also connected to her grandchildren's school professionally as she shares teaching experience, advice and strategies to the staff and takes part in educational programs.

Megan's memories of her own grandparents are with great fondness. As the oldest of 11 grandchildren she spent her summers on the farm with her grandmother and grandfather.

My memories are wonderful. I had a wonderful relationship with my grandparents, they were like my second parents actually and every summer

A. Singh and M. Devine (Eds.), Rural Transformation and Newfoundland and Labrador Diaspora:
Grandparents, Grandparenting, Community and School Relations, 309–318.

when I finished school from the time I was 5 until I was 16 I was out with them. I left home on the last day of school and I never came home until the day before school started.

Megan would do everything with her grandparents and would do many things for them. Megan remembers travelling to bingo on the "bingo bus" from Cupids to Holyrood, shopping every Friday with her grandmother and helping around the farm by feeding the chickens, collecting the eggs and helping in the garden.

I used to help around the house a lot as I got older and I was able to do that. We used to go out in the garden. They always grew their own vegetables and they always had their own chickens and cows and stuff like that. So I would go out in the mornings and feed the chickens and collect the eggs and stuff like that that needed to be done. I always liked trailing along behind.

She recalls going out shopping for groceries and buying big barrels of flour which were stored under the stairs, and the weekly supply of meats which were kept in the well the years before her grandparents owned a refrigerator.

They used to buy their flour in great big barrels and we would put it under the stairs. I remember that she made the most delicious homemade bread ever. I used to say, "Nan I think you should start a bakery" because it was so good.

Megan believes that she has learned the importance of family from her own parents and grandparents. Everything centred on the family and the children, "the family had to be first. Family was always so important". She also notices the everyday things she learned from watching her grandmother such as keeping the house clean, baking and folding and putting things away in their right place. She comments, "Sometimes I do things and I say, 'O my gosh that's what Nan used to do'. Like if you are picking up something or you have a certain way to do something." She sees her relationship with her own grandchildren as a reflection of the experiences she shared with her own grandparents.

I think that [my relationship with my grandparents] is why I like having a relationship with my grandchildren because I know what it was like as a child and the things I did with my grandparents . . . so I always kind of think that this is important to have this relationship and that is why I developed a relationship with my grandkids.

Megan and her husband make an effort to maintain a close relationship both with her grandchildren who live down the road and the others [grown son, daughter-in-law, grandchildren] living in another province. When her oldest grandchild was born Megan spent a week once a month during the first year to help her daughter-in-law and to develop a relationship with her grandchild. Every year during the summer they drive to Nova Scotia and bring the grandchildren home to spend two weeks with them. "They are fun to be with. I just love it. When they go it is like I am lost."

Gary & Daphne

Gary is a 62 year old retired Medical Laboratory Technician/X-Ray Technologist and his wife, Daphne, is a 55 year old retired Administrative Assistant. The couple lives in Norris Point, approximately two and half hours away from their daughter and her three school age children. Their daughter returns to her home in Norris Point during the summer months when she is not attending the college. Their son lives in British Columbia with his wife and two children. Gary and Daphne are very active in all aspects of their grandchildren's lives. They wish they could be closer to their grandchildren in B.C., however, they visit and talk as often as they can. Gary continues to work part time when the need arises. They are enjoying their retirement and remain active in their community.

Gary has no early memories of his own grandparents. Daphne recalls her mother's parents as being "very pleasant, well liked people who were cherished by all who knew them". Her father's parents were opposites. She recalls her grandfather as being a warm and caring man while her grandmother was different from him in every way. As a child she recalls doing chores such as washing the dishes, cleaning the floors and emptying the overnight pail. Daphne feels that as times have changed she is different from her own grandparents as things are not as strict as they used to be. She reflects on what she has learned from her grandparents:

I think that my grandparents showed me the true value of family and things like 'hard work never killed anyone' but made them better in many ways. Take care of yourself and everything else will be taken care off.

As grandparents, Gary and Daphne feel their role encompasses much more than teaching the value of family and hard work.

Gary and Daphne are engaged in all aspects of their grandchildren's lives. They see themselves as the second "mom and dad".

We are the second Mom and Dad, who, if retired, have the most time available to spend raising our grandchildren. We help financially, with transportation, volunteering, attending camps and revues and outdoor activities of all kinds.

Gary and Daphne take their role as the second "mom and dad" very seriously. Last year they accompanied their 10 year old granddaughter on a school trip to St. Pierre et Miquelon. They were the only grandparents represented in the group which consisted of 24 children, as well as 6 parents and two teachers. Their granddaughter would not have been able to attend the trip without them because her diabetes requires close monitoring. Their involvement in the trip deepened their relationship to the school and the other families. They feel the role of grandparents has changed over the years, but has become a more in-depth experience as the families today rely more on support from grandparents.

Alma

Alma is a 79 year old grandmother living alone in Corner Brook in an independent living senior's cottage. Alma has 25 grandchildren and 18 great-grandchildren. She was married at the age of 19 and had 12 children with her husband before his sudden death in 1985. Her oldest child is in her early sixties and her youngest twins recently turned forty. Many of her children live in Corner Brook or the surrounding area including Rocky Harbour, Port Aux Basques and St. John's. Two of her daughters also live in Nova Scotia. Many of Alma's grandchildren are grown up and living in other parts of Canada with families of their own. Her small living room is crowded with photos of her grandchildren and great-grandchildren at various stages in their lives.

After her marriage Alma stayed home to raise her children while her husband worked outside the home. After the death of her husband she had to go back to work to support her two youngest daughters and herself. Alma has no early memories of her grandparents as they died when she was very young. As a grandmother and great grandmother Alma spends as much time with her family as she can. She says one of the difficulties today of being a grandparent is that many of her grandchildren and great-grandchildren live far away. She says, "When they are away you can't see them and when they come home you can spend time with them". Many of her grandchildren grew up alongside her youngest children, often playing together and sharing many of the same memories. She often provided childcare for her grandchildren as well as playing with them, cooking for them, bringing them to school and making sure they were dressed warmly.

> I took them to the park and we made cookies. We sang, took walks, and went for picnics. [I] cooked all their meals and made sure they were dressed warm when they went out in the winter time and kept them warm.

Today she continues to spend time with her family and great-grandchildren. She contributes to family life by preparing special meals, sharing recipes, knitting wool socks and mitts and sharing a story over a cup of tea. She sees her most important job as a grandparent is to love her grandchildren and support them. "I suppose that's it. I love them all. I spent time with all of them and I don't forget their birthdays".

The Role of Grandparents

Past generations of grandparents did not have the opportunity to watch their grandchildren grow up. These "intimate ties were of a relatively short duration compared to today" (Mitchell, 2009). Grandparents today are more actively engaged in the lives of their grandchildren. The grandparents I interviewed see their role as that of one to support family life. Megan comments on her role in her grandchildren's lives:

> As a grandparent I just feel I am the one that supports them, I don't want to be the parent. I just want them to know that nanny and poppy are there to help them and support them. I don't want them to bring a lot of things that mom and dad can deal with. Sure I will help you the best way that I can, but I just want to be a grandparent and enjoy it. Not so much a parenting role. I want to be a grandparent.

Megan sees her role as a grandparents as separate from her previous job as a parent. She enjoys spending time with her grandchildren and loves her role as the grandparent that supports and maintains the family connection.

The jobs grandparents perform for their grandchildren encompass everything from spending time together, teaching new skills, picking them up from school and providing child care for tired or overworked parents. They see themselves providing a secondary level of support to their grandchildren when they need it. Gary explains the unique role of the grandparent:

> As grandparents we are involved in almost every aspect of their lives. We are the home teacher for unsolvable problems, the carpenter to help build character and wellbeing, the doctor when they are sick, we are the cooks when they are hungry, the laundry person when clothes need cleaning, we are the big stuffed toy that they need to cuddle when things go wrong, or they need extra loving, the minister who help them learn their prayers and we are their hearts when all that love comes pouring out.

The unique role of the grandparent is influenced by the family situation and the needs of the family. As more and more families consist of two working parents or one parent working outside of the community the extended family is relied on more and more for support for everyday activities. Alma recalls how she often babysat her oldest daughter's children when her daughter was working and the children's father was travelling for work. This support was essential to the family as the father travelled at least one week out of every month and the mother maintained full time employment outside the home.

Gary comments on the importance of this support, "A well-developed family provides support to each other as well as those around them". Megan comments on the things she does with and for her grandchildren:

> I pick them up every day afterschool. Sometimes we will have it – Julia calls it "girls' night" – and she'll come down here and stay with me and Chris will stay home or pop will probably take the boys out fishing. They know that if they need us we are there to support them if they can't pick them up or if they need to go to something like Brownies or Cubs or whatever they are in. We are there to help them. We just help them whatever way we can.

Challenges to Family Life

As family life changes, so too does the role of grandparents. In many families both parents must work to support the family. In some cases one parent works away for periods of time or the family is forced to move away from their extended family to a new place. This complicates family life. The role of grandparents in supporting the family has become an increased necessity. Gary comments on the increased demands within the family:

> Some parents today haven't the luxury of grandparents around to seek help from. It is almost imperative today for the parents to hold down at least two jobs or both parents must work. There is a loud outcry from children today to be equal in all facets of their lives with other children. This heavy burden is placed on the shoulders of the parents who have to find a way to deal with the issues. Add to this food, luxuries, medical, education, mortgagees and the list goes on.

The pressure on parents is enormous. In order to meet the demands of their family they need the help that grandparents can offer. Alma felt that maintaining relationships with grandchildren and great-grandchildren living far away is challenging, but when they come home you can make the most of it by spending time with them.

Megan also commented that as family life changes, the relationship between children and grandparents can be challenged. "That's the changing world today because children are living in a different society. Some children have three and four or five sets of grandparents. They don't know who to go to." She sees her role as a grandparent to provide advice and an open ear to whatever her grandchildren feel they need to talk about.

Megan also noted that family life faces challenges as the children are under pressure and are exposed to more things at an earlier age than ever before.

> I know kids have a lot of challenges today, like peer pressure. They have to have somebody to talk to and somebody to go to and I think that's important that communication between parents and children. My grandkids talk to me about things you know and the girls are getting a little bit older so they talk to me about stuff. I feel comfortable with that and I know that they can talk to their parents about that. I think that open relationship is important and sometimes a challenge too.

As parents face challenges dealing with peer pressure grandparents can help their grandchildren by giving advice and simply listening.

CONCLUSION

Meeting with grandparents, reading about grandparenting and reflecting on the role of grandparents has brought back my own fond memories of my "fictive kin' grandparents (Mitchell, 2009). The role my own grandparents played in my life was very small as my grandfather died young and my grandmother was bed ridden from a variety of illnesses up until her death when I was 11. The importance of my grandparent role models in my life are some of my happiest childhood memories. When I was young they were in their early fifties and had raised a total of 16 children, five of their own and 9 foster children. They had many of their own grandchildren who they always had time to spend with and lessons to teach. Many of the experiences I remember are similar to those experienced by Megan with her grandparents. I recall spending the entire summer with them as well as almost every weekend during the school year. I would dress up to go to church, ride the tractor down to the creek to go swimming, help in the garden, pick blueberries and strawberries, go weekly grocery shopping and play with their grandchildren as if they were my own cousins. The role of these grandparents enriched my early years with pleasant memories of happiness and love.

As the family changes the role of grandparents as the "second mom and dad" as Gary said, is becoming more important. Grandparents are increasingly completing the everyday tasks of feeding, providing transportation, and emotional support to their grandchildren. You need only to talk to these grandparents or meet their grandchildren to see the love and respect between them. I recall Megan's granddaughter writing an essay on creating a new holiday called "Poppy's Day" because she loved spending time with her grandfather and she was "poppy's girl". During our school's Remembrance Day assembly Gary and Daphne's granddaughter proudly brought to school a poem her grandfather wrote that she had practiced reading and wanted to share with the school. Alma's grandchildren recall the special meals she prepared for them and the numerous Christmas mornings they spent together.

The relationship between grandparent and grandchild, while not the same as that of a parent, is a special and supportive relationship which benefits the entire family. Gary describes how he feels when he cares for his grandchildren, "There is no way to explain how one feels as every moment is a joy and blessing. This is a rare opportunity in life and we are lucky enough to be there and be involved". Megan would like her grandchildren to remember "what we did together. The fun things and how nan and pop were so important in their lives. I think that is important".

APPENDIX

Grandparents Interview Protocol

Personal Information

1. What is your age?
2. What is your current living arrangement?
3. Are you retired? If so, what was your occupation?

Do you keep in contact with former colleagues?
Are you still working if yes, what is your occupation?
How many children do you have? How many grandchildren? Ages?

Personal History

4. What are your memories of your own grandparents?
5. What were your grandparents like?
6. What kind of things did you do with and for your grandparents?
7. Are you different from your own grandparents?
8. In what ways are you different?
9. What have you learned from your own Grandparents?

Family

10. What is the living situation of each of your own adult children? For example, do they live next door, in the same community, in the same province, or in other countries?
11. Do any of your sons or daughters have to be away from a spouse because they have jobs somewhere else?
12. If they are away from their spouses/partners, do you know how they help each other to keep the family intact? What sort of help do you provide to your adult children, their spouses and your grandchildren in this situation?
13. How does keeping the family intact contribute to community wellbeing as a whole?
14. As a grandparent what do you think are some potential challenges to parents today providing good care to their children?

Grandparenting

15. In what ways do you help or support your grandchildren?
16. How would you describe your role as a grandparent?
17. What activities are you involved in with your grandchildren when you provide care for them (for example, play with them, cook for them, take them to school or park, take them to sport places, help them in their homework, wash their clothes, get them ready for bed, and so on)?
18. How would you describe how you feel when you are involved with providing care to your grandchildren?
19. What do you suggest should be done to improve interaction with grandparents and their grandchildren, in future and right now, given the way society and our communities are changing?

How would you like your Grandchildren to remember you?

REFLECTION QUESTIONS

1. How is the role of parent and grandparent differentiated in this chapter?
2. How does Gary's definition of 'grandparent' fit with your own experiences of your grandparents?
3. How do you see Megan's comment on the fact that some children have several sets of grandparents impacting on children?
4. The chapter refers to the 'changing role of grandparents' today. Given that some literature refers to families being more 'nuclear families' compared to the past, what is your analysis of how grandparenting roles have changed (or not)?

REFERENCE

Mitchell, B.A. (2009). *Family matters: An introduction to family sociology in Canada*. Toronto: Canadian Scholar's Press Inc.

ASHLEY PITTMAN

THE INCREASED ROLE OF GRANDPARENTS IN NEWFOUNDLAND FAMILIES

As today's families undergo amazing and radical changes in the way in which people live their lives, the role of grandparents is also shifting and changing (Power, 1993). Social scientists believe families are adapting to the technological, social, moral and economic changes in the wider society (Baker, 1984). As our world becomes even faster paced, families are forced to look to others to help care for the needs of the family. The role of grandparents can vary greatly from one family to the next. Some families may require minimal assistance from grandparents, and others may need grandparents to assume full legal responsibility for the care of children. I will examine this phenomenon in greater detail as well as discuss my own personal experience with my grandparents and the experiences of three grandparents and their role in the lives of their grandchildren's education.

In today's society, "there is no such thing as a typical family". In 2006, the following statistics were recorded regarding Canadian family structures: 38.7% of families were married with children, 29.9% were married without children, 15.6% lived in common-law relationships, 15.9% were single-parent families and 0.6% were same-sex couples (Vanier Institute of the Family, 2010, p.26). Families today can take multiple forms and have very different needs. The change in family structures can be attributed to many factors. One of these factors is that rates of separation, divorce and remarriage have increased drastically (Power, 1993). Other changes in families result due to multiple trends in society such as: "the evolution of a global economy, increasing respect for human rights, the emancipation of women, the migration of populations between and within countries and cities and many technological innovations" (Vanier Institute of the Family, 2010, p. 12). With all of these occurring changes, there has also been an increased life expectancy among seniors and a greater recognition of the role of grandparents (Singh, 2010).

Grandparents today are now living longer and have the potential to enjoy being a grandparent for a longer period of time.. They often have increased time to spend with their grandchildren and may have more money to spend on them than in the past. In Canada, 80% of women and 74% of men over the age of 65 are grandparents (Mitchell, 2009, p. 231). With such large numbers of grandparents under the young age of seventy, it is not surprising that at birth, 66% of children have at least four living grandparents (Mitchell, 2009, p. 231). According to Connidis (2001), three quarters of adults over the age of thirty still have at least one living grandparent.

A. Singh and M. Devine (Eds.), Rural Transformation and Newfoundland and Labrador Diaspora: Grandparents, Grandparenting, Community and School Relations, 319–326.

I myself, at the age of 26 still have four living grandparents and, in my lifetime, spent time with and can remember three of my four great-grandparents. Declines in mortality rates and falling birth rates have led to the increase in the number of grandparents and to a modernization of grandparenthood. Other factors that have affected this modernization are: technological advances such as email and webcams, travel advances, retirement and increased affluence such as pensions and more leisure time for elders (Mitchell, 2009, p. 231). In the past, grandkids would often receive letters or phone calls from their grandparents and see them a few times a year, however today, some grandparents correspond with their grandkids by email, see them on webcams and travel great distances multiple times a year to spend time with them when they don't live nearby.

In my family, I am closer with one set of grandparents. I see both sets of grandparents regularly however, as they both live within a ten minute drive from my home. My grandparents travel regularly when family away have young children. They have not missed a birth in another province and ensure that grandchildren in Newfoundland and grandchildren away have a close relationship with them. Being retired allows my grandparents to travel for significant amounts of time. When visiting family away, they often stay two weeks to a month. In this time, they assume the major care-giver roles in the household and enjoy it immensely. My grandmother does all of the cooking, baking and cleaning in the home while the family works, and my grandfather does odd jobs around the house. Some of my family members leave full construction jobs for my grandfather to perform during his visits and there is seldom a trip in which he has not picked up a paintbrush.

One of my sets of grandparents is quite religious and have instilled faith and values into all of their grandchildren. We attend church services together and never begin a meal without the grandchildren first saying a blessing. I visit my grandparents at least once a week and have a "Sunday dinner" meal with all of my grandparents' immediate family. My family and I look forward to this time together and it gives us the opportunity to discuss the week's events. Life is hectic; however, we all try to attend dinner on Sunday to spend time together as a family. I know that I can always depend on my grandparents for anything I need. They have so much wisdom and love to offer and never hesitate to help family members in need. I have learned an incredible amount from my grandparents such as past traditions and memories of the communities where my family is from. My grandmothers have taught me how to bake and cook and are still my favourite resource to call upon for recipes. Like many other Newfoundland children, my grandparents have always played a significant role in my life and still continue to do so today.

In today's society, there has been an increase in multigenerational households in which grandparents live with their adult children and their grandchildren. Casper and Bryson (1998) have identified five family structures in which grandparents live: 1) both grandparents (one or both parents present), 2) both grandparents (no parents present), 3) grandmother only (one or both parents present), 4) grandmother only (no parents present) and 5) grandfather only. In 2001, almost one in five seniors or

17.6% shared a home with their adult children and grandchildren (Vanier Institute of the Family, 2010, p. 26). The proportion of three-generational households has been rising, particularly in larger urban centres such as Toronto, Montreal and Vancouver. In some parts of the world, multigenerational households are common, specifically in Asia and high rates of immigration into Canada are increasing these practices in Canada (Vanier Institute of the Family, 2010, p. 74).

Many families in Newfoundland and Labrador become multigenerational households as grandparents begin to age and are in need of aid from their adult children. Instead of placing their parents into an old-age home, many Newfoundland families choose to have their parents move into their homes. Some of these families have created in-law apartments in which the grandparents can live separately from the family, but still be in their care, while others live within the main home with the family. It is also common for grandparents who live in small rural communities to move into larger communities to live with their families. As rural communities age and lose important services that seniors need, many grandparents move willingly or unwillingly to larger centres with closer access to hospitals and other services. One of the sets of grandparents that I interviewed spends the winters living with their family in the city and move back to their rural community in the spring. It is too difficult for them to live at home during the winter as the rural community in which they live can only be accessed by a small ferry and conditions are quite harsh during the long winter months. The grandparents spend the winter months living between the homes of their adult children and grandchildren and then in the summer months the younger grandchildren travel to the rural community in which their grandparents live to stay with them. This is a common practice for many families in Newfoundland as grandparents play a significant role in the lives of Newfoundland families.

For some grandchildren, grandparents play more than a significant role in their lives. For these children, their grandparents have become their full time caregivers and assume responsibility of the physical and emotional well-being of their lives. In 1997, approximately 4 million children in Canada lived in homes where grandparents were the primary caregivers (Tutwiler, 2010, p. 43). Fuller-Thomson et al (1997) offer many terms used to describe this type of grandparents: "grandparent caregivers", "off-time grandparents", "custodial grandparents" and "skipped generation parents". There are multiple reasons for grandparents assuming full responsibility for their grandchildren, however, "the majority of grandparents never anticipated that they would be raising their grandchildren" and "the role has been thrust on them at a time of life when their plans did not involve parenting" (Cox, 2008, p. 14–15). Reasons for which grandparents become primary caretakers of their grandchildren include: death, divorce, substance abuse, teen pregnancy, domestic violence, mental and physical illnesses, AIDS, crime, child abuse and neglect and incarceration (American Association of Retired Persons, 1998). According to DeToldeo and Brown (1995), "grandparents feel compelled for the care-giving and rearing of grandchildren because of love, duty and the bonds of the family" (p. 15). The median age of grandparents raising children is 57 but the ages range from 40 to 80 years of age and grandparents often care for their grandchildren from six months to over ten years (Tutwiler, 2010, p. 43). The most common age that children move in with their grandparents is as infants or of preschool age (Tutwiler, 2010, p. 44). Custodial grandparents provide their grandchildren with a sense of continuity, stability and security when it was unavailable to them at home with their parents (Heywood, 1999, p. 368).

Whether it is time spent through a multigenerational household, custodial grandparent relationship or simply active grand-parenting, it is estimated that children today will spend 50% of their lives with their grandparents (Singh, 2010, p. 6). Grandparents generally play an active role in their grandchildren's lives by providing leadership, support and assistance in raising children (Kornhaber, 1996). Grandmothers are generally associated with family relationships and care-giving while grandfathers are involved in practical matters such as giving advice (Mitchell, 2009, p. 232). Grandparents allow for the transmission of culture as they pass down family memories through the re-telling of stories and reproduction of family traditions (Mitchell, 2009, p. 232).

In Newfoundland, families also depend on the active role of grandparents in raising their children. In rural Newfoundland the breakdown of family structures is as follows: nuclear (58%), blended/divorced (15%), single (8%), grand-parents (4%) and Alberta widow (15%) (Upshall, 2009). An Alberta widow family structure occurs when fathers leave the family to go to work in the Alberta oil fields. The occurrence of this type of family increased after Newfoundland saw a decline in employment and Alberta saw an increase of employment for Newfoundland workers. When one parent leaves to go to Alberta, the other parent often depends on family members, specifically grandparents to help care for the children. Statistics Canada collected the following data regarding grandparent care in Newfoundland in the 2001 Census: 5.3% of children shared a home with at least one grandparent, 4.6% of children lived in a multigenerational household and 0.7% lived in a skip-generation household (Statistics Canada, 2001). As reflected in the Census, Newfoundland has much lower numbers of custodial grandparents compared to the country of Canada.

Although custodial grandparents are not as common in Newfoundland, the role of grandparents is still significant in this province. As work hours rise, family time decreases and the typical workday consisted of only 3.4 hours spent with family in 2005 (Vanier Institute of the Family, 2010). Some families, "have flexible though unstable work arrangements, others rely on elaborate social and family networks to fill in the gaps left by inadequate income or insufficient time" (Vanier Institute of the Family, 2010, p. 74). Women in Newfoundland have been entering the labour force in record numbers and men are no longer the sole breadwinners for their families (Lacey, 1989).

For the majority of families, the economic requirements as well as the personal aspirations of parents do not make it possible for one parent to devote himself or herself to the care of their children on a full-time basis. Therefore, they must turn to some form of supplemental child care outside of their own (Vanier Institute of the Family, 1986).

Grandparents are often left to fill the child care gaps left by working parents.

When it comes to school, grandparents often have significant roles in their grandchildren's education. No matter what type of grand-parenting role exists, the grandchild's education is usually intertwined into the relationship. For custodial grandparents schools can be intimidating places as they have been out of school for many years and are unfamiliar with many aspects of school (Cox, 2008). Grandparents often have difficulty understanding the new Math curriculum and technological advances that have taken place in the classroom. Helping with homework can be a difficult task for grandparents as their grandchildren enter into higher grades. Grandparents who are not primary care-givers of their grandchildren often enjoy being a part of their grandchildren's education. In the schools where I have taught, some grandparents are very active members of the school community. They volunteer regularly with school activities and attend all special events in the school. Those who are not active in the school community often drop off or pick up their grandkids from school or take them out for lunch. I have also been in contact with grandparents who assume care of their grandchildren while their parents are away on trips. In my experience, grandparents are welcomed and positive members of the school community.

I will provide examples of the role of grandparents in their grandchildren's education through the personal experiences of three grandmothers and one grandfather in Newfoundland. The first example involves the rural grandparents I discussed previously in my paper. The role of this set of grandparents has changed significantly since all of their children and grandchildren have moved out of the small rural community in which they live. When the oldest group of grandchildren lived and went to school in the community, the grandparents were more active in their lives. The grandmother reminisced, "When the grandkids were in school out here, I used to cook lunch for them every day". The school was just a short walking distance from her house, and she described how she used to cook something hot every day for her grandkids' lunch and even for some of their friends. When the kids were in school in the community, she said she attended as many events as she could; "I never missed a Christmas concert". One of their grandchildren spent more time with them than any of the others as his dad worked away on the boats a lot: "When my grandson's dad was away working, I would help his mom with school work and activities. He would come over after school and stay for sleepovers when they both went to work". It was clear that she enjoyed having her grandson stay with her and did not mind the responsibility associated with taking care of him. She told me that the parents of her grandson were quite young when they had him and often needed assistance in taking care of the child. This grandmother always encouraged her grandchildren in school and supported them as best she could: "My grandchildren's education is very important to me because I didn't get much education when I was young and I want all of my grandchildren to finish theirs". Even today, this set of grandparents support their grandchildren in their education as best they can. When they move to the city for the winter, they try to attend as many school functions as possible for each of their young grandchildren. The grandfather is most active in their school life while in the city as he finds the time spent in the city long and boring and being involved with his grandchildren helps to make the winter season go a little quicker: "When we go to town, I walk down to my grandkid's school every day if the weather is good to pick them and walk them home for lunch and again after school. It helps to break up the long days in St. John's and it makes me happy to see them". The grandmother would move into the city to live at a moment's notice; however the grandfather is not willing to leave his home and community. She would rather be in town close to her grandchildren and the rest of her family and feels needed and appreciated in the presence of her grandchildren.

The second example involves a grandmother and two of her grandchildren who vary significantly in age. The oldest grandchild is in high school and goes to her grandmother's house on the bus after school: "My granddaughter comes over every day after school. She wanted to go to a different high school to be with her friends and has to come to my house on the bus to do that". I asked if it was a burden to have a teenager in the house, and she responded by saying, "Although she comes to my house every day I don't see her too much. She has me make her a snack when she first gets home and then she goes in one of the bedrooms and I don't see her again until her parents come to get her". The youngest grandchild is in grade two and the grandmother tries to play an active role in his school life. "My grandson comes over to my house every morning to get the bus to school because his school bus will not pick him up at his house". She described how she made sure she was up and ready each morning to greet him and see him off to the bus. When he would get dropped off to her house in the afternoon, she said she always had a snack ready for him to eat before he sat down to do his homework. "I help my grandson with Math and sometimes reading when he visits after school". The grandmother also talked about her favourite school activity to attend, the school skating sessions. At the sessions, parents and grandparents could volunteer to meet the class at the skating rink and help their child get ready to go out on the ice. She said that she had been out on the ice a few times and enjoyed seeing all the young kids having fun together. Her grandson also loved having his grandmother with him: "He loves having me there to watch and support him".

The third example is of a grandmother who has eight grandchildren of various ages. Some are now finished university and one has not yet entered school. This grandmother described present and past school experiences with her grandchildren and the joy associated with being there for them. "My grandchildren have been a very important part of my life since they were born and I always enjoyed them telling me about their work and play at school". Her active role in her grandchildren's education was evident as she described all of the events that she tries to attend. She attends concerts, assemblies and field trips whenever possible. If the parents could not attend these events, this grandmother made sure someone was there to support the children: "When their parents could not attend school events, I would always go". She was quite proud to be a part of her grandchildren's education and spoke very highly of their education. "I enjoyed talking with their teachers and their friends. It is so nice to see their classrooms and all the information in the corridors". The grandmother also talked about how she cared for the children from time to time before and after school if their parents needed them to be picked up or taken to school. Her discussion of her involvement in her grandchildren's education was detailed:

> I was always involved in my grandchildren's lives. School, music, hockey and figure skating, if they needed me to do something for them they knew I was there to ask. I made costumes, ice cream cakes and cookies for class parties, and volunteered. I was involved in whatever activities they needed me to be in school. Outside of school, we have lots of fun playing board games, reading stories, baking together and having sleepovers.

This grandmother also had the unique opportunity to act as a custodial grandparent to two of her granddaughters after their mother and father divorced. "My two granddaughters came to live me for four months. Their mom was transferred out of province and I was responsible for all of their care and school activities". She described the experience as a pleasure and said she would not hesitate to do it again. The grandmother was positive about all aspects of their care, including their schooling. "I enjoyed every night sitting to the kitchen table with them helping with their homework. It was a challenge sometimes though because neatness was not a priority for them. They would say, "Oh nanny, you are too particular"". Before I ended my interview with this grandmother, she wanted to be sure I understood her perspective on being a grandparent. She ended our interview by saying, "The biggest gift a grandparent can receive are grandchildren".

From school activities, to baby-sitting and full time care, grandparents take on a multitude of roles in their grandchildren's lives in all parts of the world. As stated by Hagestad (1985), "In a society where grandparents range in age from 30 to 110, and grandchildren range from newborns to retirees, we should not be surprised to find a variety of grandparenting roles and styles with few behavioural expectations regarding grandparenting" (p.36). As the role of grandparents changes in today's society, we must recognize and celebrate the contribution grandparents are making in the lives of our children.

REFLECTION QUESTIONS

1. In this chapter (and other chapters also) the parents are usually professional people (middle class). How might the experience of grandparents and the experiences of adult children and grandchildren be different where the parents are of a different (lower) socio-economic class?
2. At one point in this chapter, the author states that the grandparents often talk about the place 'they are from'. How and why is this sense of place so important to families?

3. The concept of 'multi-generational households' may be one that people generally in community may identify with, as we often see ourselves are having moved more to the nuclear family model. How do you reconcile the differences in 'perception' and reality – what accounts for the difference?
4. From this chapter, the role of grandparents in the education of their grandchildren is highlighted. How important and relevant are grandparents in this regard?

REFERENCES

American Association of Retired Persons. The grandparent study 2002 report. Author, Washington, D.C. (2002). Available: http://assets.aarp.org/rgcenter/general/gp_2002.pdf

Baker, Maureen (Ed.) (1984). The Family: Changing Trends in Canada. New York: McGraw-Hill Ryerson.

Casper, L.M., & Bryson, K.R. (1998). Co-resident grandparents and their grandchildren: Grandparent-maintained families. Population Division Working Paper Series, 26: U.S. Bureau of the Census.

Charlie Stelle, Christine A. Fruhauf, Nancy Orel & Laura Landry-Meyer (2010): Grandparenting in the 21st Century: Issues of Diversity in Grandparent–Grandchild Relationships, *Journal of Gerontological Social Work, 53*(8), 682–701.

Connidis, I.A. (2001). Family Ties and Aging. Thousand Oaks: Sage.

Cox, Carole (2008). Supporting Grandparent-Headed Families. *The Prevention Researcher*, 14, 14–16.

De Toledo, S., & Brown, D.E. (1995). Grandparents as parents: A survival guide for raising a second family. New York: The Guilford Press.

Fuller-Thomson, E., Minkler, M., & Driver, D. (1997). A profile of grandparents raising grandchildren in the U.S. *The Gerontologist. 37*(3), 406–411.

Hagestad, G. 1985. "Continuity and connectedness". In Grandparenthood, Edited by: Bengtson, V.L. and Robertson, J.F. 31–48. Beverly Hills, CA: Sage.

Heywood, Elizabeth McConnell (1999). Custodial grandparents and their grandchildren. *The Family Journal, 7*(4), 367–72.

Kornhaber, A. (1996). Contemporary Grandparenting. Thousand Oaks: Sage.

Lacey, Beth (1989). Child Care Arrangements in Newfoundland. St. John's, NL: Women's Policy Office, Government of Newfoundland and Labrador.

Mitchell, Barbara A. (2009). Family Matters: An Introduction to Family Sociology in Canada. Toronto, ON: Canadian Scholars' Press Inc.

Myles, J., & Morgan, S. (1995). Commentary: Rural families as a model for intergenerational relationships. In V.L. Bengtson. K.W. Schaie. & L.M. Bunon (Eds.). Adult Intergenerational Relationships: Effects of social change. NY; Springer Publishing. 61–66.

Power, Mary B. (1993). A school and its families: A feminist ethnography of divergent realities. ProQuest Dissertations and Theses.

Settles, Barbara H., Zhao, Jia, Mancini, Karen D., Rich, Amanda, Pierre, Shawneila & Oduor, Atieno (2009). Grandparents caring for their grandchildren: Emerging roles and exchanges in global perspectives. *Journal of Comparative Family Studies, 40*(5), 827–845.

Singh, Amarjit et al. (2010). Review of research: Why the focus on grandparents? Faculty of Education, Memorial University of Newfoundland and Labrador.

Statistics Canada (2001). 2001 Census: Age and Sex Profile: Canada. Retrieved August 02, 2011, from http://www12.statcan.gc.ca/english/census01/home/Index.cfm.

Tutwiler, Sandra J. Winn (2010). Teachers as Collaborative Partners. New York, NY: Routledge.

Vanier Institute of the Family (2010). Families Count: Profiling Canada's Families IV. Ottawa, ON.

NADINE O' RIELLY

GRANDPARENTS' ROLES IN SCHOOL, COMMUNITY AND FAMILIES

I believe society has changed drastically within the last three decades. "The number of children raised by grandparents has more than doubled in the past thirty years" (MacNab & Keiley, 2009, p. n.a.). Some of the values that society once held are disappearing and new ones are being formed. What was once valued in society has been replaced by some other ideology(ies). I'm not saying that all values in Newfoundland society have gone extinct, but even as a thirty year old woman, I can see differences from when I grew up. I can only imagine the changes that my parents or even my grandparents see in society. This paper will focus on grandparents and the impact they have in our lives. I will discuss how they empowered communities and school and I will also talk about how important they are in the lives of children. I will be focusing specifically on Newfoundland grandparents and will discuss how their role has changed, yet still show some similarities from the past. I interviewed three grandparents and they provided me with some great insight that I will share to through this paper. I will also provide some stories of my own grandparents and how they have affected my life in such a positive way. I will use the term "grandparenting" throughout my paper referring to the ways grandparents care for their grandchildren.

After reading some of the literature on grandparenting in different cultures, I want to highlight some very interesting facts that I have learned. Different cultures bring with them different beliefs on what grandparents are expected to do and how they do it. Asian grandmothers are more likely than Asian grandfathers to provide care for their grandchildren. Fifty-percent of children in urban China are cared for by their grandparents and Swedish working grandparents can take family leave to take care of a sick child. In Canada, grandparents may have different living arrangements within a family. Some may live in the home of the grandchildren and some may live away from the grandchildren. Grandparenting has gone from the traditional role to a more modern role which entails providing child care, financial support, house cleaning and sometimes as the sole provider. Grandparenting techniques within different nationalities still occur, but I have concluded that they all have one thing in common, which is providing love and support to their grandchildren. One of the grandparents that I interviewed had this to say about grandparenting. "I feel proud and lucky that I have them. Although it can be tiring at times, it is a good tired. I look for every opportunity to show them off as a grandparent".

A. Singh and M. Devine (Eds.), Rural Transformation and Newfoundland and Labrador Diaspora:
Grandparents, Grandparenting, Community and School Relations, 327–334.
© *2013 Sense Publishers. All rights reserved.*

The big question that remains is why grandparents sometimes take on the role of raising a child, or in some cases, children. I often wonder where grandparents find the energy and strength to raise another family. They've raised their own families and now it's like they have to start all over again. After reading some very enlightening literature on grandparenting, I realized it has to do with one thing, which is the love for your family. Families may experience issues and difficulties that cause grandparents to step in and take over. DeToldeo and Brown (1995) state four reasons that they call the 'four Ds', for the increase in grandparents raising grandchildren. They include drugs, divorce, desertion and death. They also state that "drug abuse is the biggest reason for the increase in grandparent lead families" (DeToldeo & Brown, p. n.a.). I found this statistic so interesting because I look at the area in which I teach and there are numerous children who are being raised by their grandparents. I also realize there is a lot of drug abuse in the community and surrounding communities in which I teach. So it makes sense that there is a connection between the two. It seems in today's society some parents are not taking the responsibility of being a parent as seriously as they should. They give up when things don't go their way.

> There are always challenges to parenting. That has not changed. Teaching your children to be kind and caring is hard work and demands a lot of time and effort. With two parent families being the norm, finding day care that is in keeping with your beliefs is a major challenge. With both parents working, balancing work and home is particularly challenging when planning quality time together as a family, and even more difficult to ensure quality time as a couple.

Grandparents realize that children should not be exposed to such negative things (E.G., drugs) and, as grandparents, they are often wiser and realize something has to be done. There are also different living situations when it comes to grandparetning. Some grandparents may live with the child, they may live in a separate dwelling close by or they may live far away. There may be just the grandmother present, the grandfather or they may both be living. In a case whereby the Grandfather is raising a child, the child may look up to their grandfather because of the absence of a male role model in their lives.

Tutwiler states that

> grandparents are raising increased number of children in their home. This family structure may take the skipped generation or intergenerational form in which the family consists of grandparents and grandchildren or the family may be multigenerational and include grandparents, adult children, and grandchildren (Tutwiler, 2005, p. n.a.).

And Bengtson states that,

> Multi-generational relationships are increasingly diverse in function and structure within American society. I propose that the increase in martial

instability and divorce has weakened so many nuclear families, these multi-generational bonds will not only enhance but in some cases replace some of the nuclear family functions (Bengtson, 2001, n.a.).

There are about six million grandparents in Canada and each grandparent has on average 4.7 grandchildren (Statistics Canada). Grandparents play a special part in all our lives, but especially in the lives of children. I believe the role of grandparenting has changed in some ways over the years and one grandmother that I interviewed had a great outlook into this statement.

There are some differences, but most are related to geography. If you live in close proximity I think grandparents provide all the support they ever did. Children are more likely to move further from home in recent years, but with technology the gap seems to be smaller that the miles would suggest. Internet advances like Skype and long distance packages keep people in touch now in ways not possible years ago. As well air travel that once was for the rich is the norm now and allows longer and more frequent visits to children living away. Having said this, the age of grandparents is probably rising as children are waiting longer to have families. In these cases elderly grandparents may not have the energy to provide the same experience that the younger ones could in earlier days.

Grandparents are not just responsible for summer visits or bringing a treat when they visit, they take on responsibilities for child care, schooling, finances, medications, socializing and many more. I remember as a child living in a small rural island in Newfoundland, our community was very close knit. Everyone knew each other and socialized with each other. Many homes included two parents, children and usually a grandmother or grandfather or sometimes both. My friends talked about their Nans and Pops as if they were their friends. They were so close to them and they had formed relationships and bonds that could never be broken. "All I want is my grandchildren to know that they are always safe and welcome in grandma's house and that they are loved unconditionally. I like to think I don't need any new strategy to achieve that". I did not have the opportunity to ever live with my grandparents, as they moved to St. John's even before I was born. The only time I saw them was during the summer. However, when I did see them it was like I never missed out on anything. As I reminisce about my grandparent it makes me a little teary eyed. As a child you don't really appreciate the stories they tell you and the things they do for you. My pop would sing us old time songs and tell us stories about when he was a child and my Nan would always be in the kitchen baking and cooking, which was the traditional role at that time. I think as a child I had a closer relationship with my grandfather because he was the one that seemed to have the energy for playing with us and taking us different places. All my friends and most kids in my school growing up had at least one grandparent living on the island. I sometimes felt a little jealous and envious of the special things they all did with their grandparents.

The full gamut...from feeding, playing games, making crafts and cookies to bathing, dressing and bedtime storytelling. They could be visiting or having sleepovers or I could be in their home providing total care. I like to talk to them about when their Mom or Dad were young and to do special things with them that they will remember specifically to us...like camping or fishing or making "my" chocolate chip cookies.

For me, there has always been a stigmatization of what grandparents look like and what they do. However, there is an ever changing role between the traditional roles of grandparenting and today's role. Grandparents of the older generation were seen as frail, grey haired, wearing aprons and sitting in a rocking chair napping. However, in today's society grandparents are far from that. Many grandparents are active, young at heart, young in age, more physically fit and have lots of energy. The average age of grandparents is fifty-seven years old and some are much younger and older than that. Grandparents are important in the formation of their grandchildren's character and perspective on life. Grandparents have lived through childhood, adolescence and adulthood and know the rights from the wrong and what constitutes a good decision over a bad one. They have experienced good times and bad and wins and losses, which has in turn made them more experienced in understanding the importance of family bonds. "When my grandson is in my house, I feel like I have more energy".

Grandparents in Newfoundland's society play a very important role in the empowerment of schools. Many families in Newfoundland consist of the father going away to Alberta or somewhere in western Canada working periods of time and then having some time off and returning home. You will find this kind of working arrangement in almost every community in Newfoundland. It is becoming more prevalent with the outcry for skilled trade workers, of which Newfoundland has an abundance. Due to economic hardships and labor shortages, many families have to do this to support themselves. This is the type of situation whereby grandparents step in and help out. Grandparents may move in to their children's house or vice versa. I think it's wonderful seeing children at school being dropped off by grandparents and picked up and seeing them being involved in school events. Most of our volunteers are grandparents of kids who attend the school. Grandparents always seem to have a greater appreciation for teachers and discipline than the parents do. This may be due to the fact they have the "old school societal values", which seems to be drifting into the distant past.

According to Tuminello,

Tapping into the pool of grandparents is an opportunity that a school should not miss. It is a win-win situation. The children will realize that they are important enough for grandmother and/or grandfather to visit. School is emphasized as a very important place. And grandparents will experience a most precious moment with their grandchildren, the priceless time when they all share an educational endeavor together! Such an experience can certainly widen the vision of everyone involved, paving the way for better understanding of the importance of the educational setting of the children (Tuminello, 2002, n.a.).

Grandparents also play a very significant role in the empowerment of a community. They can be seen as the people who have to keep traditions alive and thriving. Grandparents tell stories to the young and old, they are the ones that people depend upon for information about the past, information about members of the community, etc. On a personal note, my great Uncle was the person whom everyone went to for information. He didn't have his own kids, but thought of us as his grandchildren. He knew everything about the history of the community. He kept those memories alive by always relating back to the past when having a conversation with someone. Even though he was deaf since the age of 18, he was a very knowledgeable person who had no trouble communicating with others. It was a passion of his to talk about the past and maybe it was his way of keeping connected to his own roots. He passed away two years ago at the age of eighty-eight. My father definitely inherited the gift of a great memory from his uncle. My father is also full of information and facts that he shares with his family and other members of the community. It is so enjoyable to listen to and it makes the feelings of community and where you come from even more liberating. He always says "that you should know these stories so you can pass it on to your children". Now that he is a grandfather, he is looking forward to telling old stories and singing old songs and showing his grandson some old Newfoundland traditions that seem to be disappearing. We need more people like this in the community to embrace the richness of traditions and beliefs. This is what makes a community special.

I had an opportunity to hear from different grandparents during my research in completing this paper. I will take this opportunity to discuss the types of families and give examples of how they feel towards grandparenting in Newfoundland and some aspects of grandparenting that really hit close to my heart. In the first set of grandparents I interviewed, the grandfather is retired and the grandmother works part time. They are both in good health, with no major medical conditions. The grandmother is in her late fifties and the grandfather turned sixty this year. They say that being grandparents is the best feeling in the world. "We would do anything for our grandson. Providing love and support is what family is all about and we are fortunate enough to give that love and support". I also had an opportunity to interview the father who works away from the home four weeks on and then four weeks home. "During the time that I'm away working, my parents call my wife every day to check and see how things are. They also visit quite often now and feel very lucky that they can do this". This relationship between the parents-grandparents and grandchild is very strong and healthy. The grandparents are there to provide guidance and help and the parents have no trouble accepting this help. "The more love that surrounds my grandson, the better". This makes me think about all the grandchildren and children in the world that don't receive love from anyone and feel sad and lonely each day. When interviewing this set of grandparents I got the feeling that being from a small outport community, their sense of old traditions and heritage was a big factor in how they viewed themselves as grandparents. "We want our grandson to grow up knowing his heritage and culture. We want him to play on the beach catching hermit crabs, climb trees and experience the feeling of the salt water against his face while riding in the boat". They did all these things with their own children and they have seen how much they enjoyed it. "It's a part of who they are".

The next interviewee was a grandmother of four grandchildren. She is fifty-six years old and still works full time. This grandmother is a very active woman and doesn't know the meaning of slowing down. "I enjoy looking after my grandchildren so much because I'm more knowledgeable now than I was when I first started having my own kids." I know the grandmother personally and I'm quite aware of how much her grandchildren love her. Her style of grandparenting is much like the first set of grandparents that I interviewed. She viewed them as precious beings that deserve all the love in the world. "I don't know what I did before I had grandkids. My life must have been missing something and now I feel complete as a mother and grandmother". She does make an effort to make sure that not all long weekends and holidays are booked up with travelling and visiting. She states it is important to remember that you do have your own lives to live as well. This grandmother of four also had quite an insight into many questions that I asked relating to grandparenting, family and society.

I have provided many different kinds of support at various times. Financial support to assist in a mortgage down payment, emotional support when my daughter's marriage broke down. Child care for vacation or due to the birth of a child and help relocating to a new home or university. There are also some small things I try to do that provide some help like painting walls, washing floors, hemming pants, taking things to the dump...even cooking a meal can be a help at times. I try to buy them all a scattered thing and buy clothes for my grandchildren to help ease the financial burden of their parents. I pretty much would do anything if they were in need and sometimes I do like to do things just because they are my children and I love them.

I did not have the opportunity to interview any grandparents that had zero contact with their grandchildren. However, I do know of grandparents who have no contact whatsoever with their grandchildren and barely any with the own children. No phone calls on birthdays, Christmas or even just a phone call to say "hi". I know of a recent incident whereby a grandparent missed their only granddaughter's birthday. How does that happen? I know that each and every one of our lives are busy and keep getting busier every day, but these are special times in a child's life when special memories are made that they will have forever. Children deserve good memories. I feel that sometimes there are issues between grandparents and parents because of the different grandparenting types that occur. One type may work for one family but may cause problems in another. That's why it is so important to keep the lines of communication open. Parents and grandparents are not the only ones who suffer. The grandchildren also face the risk of losing something so valuable. Knox (1995) describes seven types of grandparent styles including formal, fun-seeker, distant figure, surrogate-parent, passive, family historian, and indulgent. Establishing a relationship that works for all members involved is truly the key to civilization. I see many families where they are always fighting, whether it's about what the parents are doing wrong or what the grandparents think is right. This is not a healthy environment for grandchildren and the adults have the responsibility to work these things out.

According to Tutwiber (2005),

In many ways the family is a small community. A family must provide love, support and a safe and secure environment while allowing freedom of expression without judgment. These psycho-social elements contribute to the total wellbeing of a family...all things important for a healthy community.

The role of grandparenting is continually changing and it needs to be highly valued. As an educator, I believe that celebrating grandparents is very important. Every year in my Kindergarten classroom, I have grandparents day. Students make cards, write poems or draw pictures to give to them when they come into the classroom. Grandparents are always invited to assemblies and awards day at the school, but I feel it is necessary for them to have their own day. It shows how much they are appreciated and respected in the school. Students also need to take time and think about all the things their grandparents do for them. Some may even come to realize that their grandparents are more like parents to them. Grandparents are gifts that need to be celebrated. It is important that grandparents seek out help if they see fit.

Many grandparents do not have the financial resources to take care of a child because many are on fixed incomes and others may have to reduce work hours to care for the child. Some grandparents are able to receive federal foster care benefits even though they are related to the child. Still others attempt to raise a child feeling that they have little support not only from welfare agencies, but from the legal, educational and health systems as well (Tutwiler, 2005).

There is one pertinent piece of information that sometimes seems to be put on the backburner. Life is like the revolution of the earth, it goes around the sun every year no matter what. Our lives will eventually come full circle as well, so inevitably most of us will become grandparents and have grandchildren of our own. It makes me think about what I consider to be important to me regarding my family. I want to instill in my grandchildren qualities that make them good and respectful individuals. Grandparents and parents have to work together to provide the best quality of life that children deserve.

REFLECTION QUESTIONS

1. The author briefly referred to situations where grandparents have little to no relationships with their children and, especially, their grandchildren. How does this model fit with the great majority of cases throughout this text? How do you account for this difference in relationships?

2. From your experience, how involved are grandparents in the lives of their grandchildren in the schools and in the community in general?
3. There is an underlying sense in this chapter and other chapters that grandparents may be struggling with their need (or sense of obligation) to provide care to their grandchildren (and their adult children) but juxtaposed to this need is the need for independence and living ones dream of a 'retired' lifestyle. Discuss these apparent conflicting needs.
4. In this and other chapters no grandparents have related that they do not enjoy grandparenting. Is it possible that it would be taboo to state otherwise – why/why not?

REFERENCES

Bengtson, V.L. (2001). Beyond the nuclear family: the increasing importance of multigenerational bonds. *Journal of Marriage and Family, 63*(1), 1–16.

DeToldeo & Brown as quoted in the "Working Draft", Dr. Amarjit Singh, August 2010.

Dolbin-MacNab, M.L., et al., (2009). Navigating Interdependence: How Adolescents Raised Solely by Grandparents Experience Their Family Relationships. *Family Relations, 58*(2), 162–75.

Tuminello, M.D. (2002). Grandparents' Day: a great school adventure. *The Delta Kappa Gamma Bulletin, 68*(4), 54–5.

Tutwiler, Sandra J. Winn (2005). Teachers as Collaborative Partners: Working With Diverse Families and Communities. New York: Lawrence Erlbaum Associates.

SHARON BROPHY

GRANDPARENTS RAISING GRANDCHILDREN

What the Smith Grandparents Have to Say

INTRODUCTION

People today are living longer and healthier lives and, as a result, have a better quality of life as well as more choices and benefits. One of those benefits is getting to watch their grandchildren grow up, something that many from past generations didn't get to experience due to high mortality rates and lower life expectancy. The senior years are often viewed as a time when many older adults look forward to retirement, a reward for the many years of hard work in the labour force and raising their families.

Today, as well as years ago, grandparents often played an important role in assisting with short-term care of their grandchildren. However, in recent years in many western societies, there has been is an increase in the number of grandparents that are now fulfilling the role of full time parents/caregiver for their grandchildren in the absence of the child's parents. This phenomenon is also evident in Newfoundland and Labrador and this will be the focus of my paper.

There are many ramifications when grandparents accept the role as care givers for their grandchildren, both positive and negative.

Aim of Chapter

The aim of this chapter is to explore the experiences of a set of grandparents who are raising their granddaughter in Urban Newfoundland. It is also my intent to highlight the experiences of this family, not only to determine if their Newfoundland experience is consistent with those reported in various literature studies, but also to identify any new experiences and challenges that they may face in raising their granddaughter. Their thoughts and concerns will be delivered on aspects that are relevant to raising a grandchild, such as: reasons for their care-giving, importance of the grandchild, strategies for coping, challenges, benefits, financial aspects, support mechanism, and future concerns.

Literature Review

There is an increase in the number of Canadian children being raised by their grandparents. Between 1991 and 2001 there was a 20% increase in the number

A. Singh and M. Devine (Eds.), *Rural Transformation and Newfoundland and Labrador Diaspora: Grandparents, Grandparenting, Community and School Relations*, 335–346.

of Canadian children under 18 who were living with grandparents with no parent present in the home. Statistics Canada (2006) data indicates that there are 65,135 children living with their grandparents, and where the grandparents are their primary caregivers. The 2001 data for the same population was 56,790! The numbers speak for themselves; the practice of grandparents raising their grandchildren is on the rise. This phenomenon is even more evident in the United States. According to the National Census Bureau, in 1996 over 1.4 million children were being raised by grandparents without the help of parents (Casper & Bryson, 1999). This was an increase of 37 percent from the 1993 census (American Association of Retired Persons (AARP), 1998)! In Australia in 2003, the Australian Bureau of Statistics reported that there were 23,000 grandparent families with children aged 0 to 17 years, and there are many Australian organizations that feel that this number is much higher! The same phenomenon was also witnessed in South Africa recently by two Newfoundland social workers. In the latest Social Work newsletter entitled Connecting Voices, Green & Haley (2009) recount the following:

> We marvelled at the resilience and strength of the South African people... Approximately six and a half million people are living with HIV/AIDS in this country – that means one in four people. While it is difficult to imagine the impact on families, we witnessed it each day as we went into the townships. We saw grandmothers carrying children, cleaning clothes, gathering food and cooking. In 2005 there were over 2 million children orphaned because of AIDS – a number expected to grow to 5.7 million by 2015. The middle generation is dying, leaving a large and visible gap between the young and old. Grandmothers are filling this gap after burying their own children. As the Stephen Lewis Foundation says, "grandmothers are the unsung heroes of South Africa" (p. 12).

The term being used today for this type of grandparent led family arrangement, is the "skipped generation", which is comprised of the grandparent(s) and the grandchildren; but an absence of either of the child's parents (Tutwiler, 2005). This type of household has yet another term to describe the distinctive family structure. Since the practice of grandparents raising grandchildren has become so common these days, the term "grandfamilies" was coined to describe it (Racicot, 2003).

Casper and Bryson (1998) have identified five family structures involving grandparents raising grandchildren: (1) both grandparents, some parents present; (2) both grandparents, no parents present; (3) grandmother only, some parents present; (4) grandmother only, no parents present; (5) and grandfather only.

There are a variety of reasons why so many children are now in the position of being raised in households maintained by grandparents. The most common reason is due to substance abuse by the child's parent (in the USA). Other reasons include: teen pregnancy, divorce, domestic violence, mental and physical illnesses, AIDS, crime, death, child abuse and neglect, and incarceration (American Association of

Retired Persons [AARP] 1998). Drug abuse is the biggest reason for the increase in grandparent led families. DeToldeo and Brown (1995) cite four reasons, that they call the 'four Ds', for the increase in grandparents raising grandchildren, they are: drugs, divorce, desertion, and death.

So why do grandparents take over the responsibility of caring for their grandchildren? DeToldeo and Brown (1995), say that there are many complicated reasons, but in the end, the reasons you take them in are straight forward and simple: "...love, duty and the bonds of family" (p. 15). But who takes care of the grandchildren when they are in the care of the grandparents? Bryson & Casper (1999) & Fuller-Thomson, Minkler, & Driver (1997) assert that the grandmothers were much more likely than grandfathers to be the person responsible for the care-giving and rearing of the grandchildren. Maybe this has something to do with society and its socially constructed gender roles.

There are many positive aspects related to grandparents raising grandchildren. According to Fuller-Thomson & Minkler (2001), grandparent caregivers reported greater closeness to their grandchildren than did non-caregivers. Fuller-Thomson (2005) indicated a number of studies that have been conducted that reveal other positive aspects of the grandparent as caregiver. He reported that a study conducted by Solomon and Marx (1995) revealed that the health and behaviour of children who were raised by their grandparents were similar to that of children who lived with both of their biological parents; this was evident despite the fact that they had less financial resources. The author also made note of a study by Minkler and Roe (1993). This study "found that grandparent caregivers were delighted with the love grandchildren provide and were relieved in knowing the children were safe and the family was kept together" (p. 5). Also, Fuller-Thomson (2005) reported that a study by Weibel-Orlando (1997) indicated that grandchildren who were raised by grandparents provided them with "extensive assistance" once they were grownup. According to Kornhaber (1996), some grandparents note that even though raising a grandchild is sometimes tiring and stressful, it increases their vitality and zest for life. Ninety percent of the grandparents in a study conducted by Hayslip & Shore (2000) reported that they would still take responsibility for their grandchildren if they had to make the choice again.

It was interesting to note that there were many positive benefits for grandchildren being raised by a grandparent. In the absence of their children, grandparents can serve as role models for their grandchildren. Wilson (1986); and Wilson, Tolson, Hinton, & Kiernan, (1990) note that when grandchildren are raised by their grandmother, they exhibit a number of positive behaviours, such as improved school performance, more independence in making decisions, less dependent on welfare, and fewer deviant behaviours.

It would be great to say that there were no negative aspects related to grandparents raising their grandchildren, but there are a number that are documented. Some of these aspects include personal, interpersonal, and economic consequences, including poorer physical and mental health. Minkler, Fuller-Thomson, Miller, & Driver,

(2000) note that grandparent caregivers have a higher incidence of illnesses such as hypertension, depression, diabetes, as well as insomnia.

Grandparents can find it stressful and exhausting if faced with raising a second family. DeToldeo and Brown (1995) note that it "can wear on your time, your energy, your finances and your spirit" (p. 21). They can feel a sense of loss, just as their grandchildren do. Strawbridge, Wallhagen, Shema, and Kaplan (1997) found that, over a 20-year period, grandparent caregivers were more likely to experience poorer physical and mental health than non-caregivers.

Financial hardship is another area that may be a concern for grandparents. Although many grandparents have some financial assets from their working years, most live on a fixed income and are experiencing financial difficulties. According to Fuller-Thomson (2005):

> many Canadian grandparent caregivers in skipped generation families were raising grandchildren despite substantial economic problems. Particularly troubling was the high percentage of grandparent caregivers and the grandchildren they were raising who were living in extreme poverty. More than 30% of skipped generation families had household incomes under $15,000 per annum (p. 18).

The additional cost of raising a child, or children, places an extra burden on their limited funds as grandparents are now faced with the additional costs of supplying money for such things as food, clothes, day care, recreation and school supplies.

Glass (2002) notes that there are a number of losses that a grandparent can experience when faced with parenting a grandchild, but "the most important of these losses include the grandparents' future goals, their traditional social life, their expected leisure activities, their anticipated independence that accompanies an empty nest, their perceived physical health, and their financial status" (p. 146).

When grandparents are faced with the task of parenting their grandchildren, they may also be faced with many tasks that they fell ill equipped to handle, such as the child's education and possible social problems. When grandparents are required to parent their grandchildren, their lives change overnight without any chance for preparation. Glass (2002) made a number of recommendations that were directed at the grandparents to help ease situations or problems that may occur. Two of the recommendations that were made included, become educated by participating in a parenting class designed especially for grandparents, to refresh their parenting skills as some of the basics have changed. The second recommendation was to acquire a tutor to help the child with their academics since grandparents may not feel confident in helping in that area. Stritof & Stritof (n.d.) also made several recommendations that would benefit grandparents' role as caregivers for their grandchildren: short term respite care, availability of affordable support groups and/or counselling services, telephone hot lines, free or affordable legal and financial advice, more money, and health insurance for the grandchildren.

What the Smith Grandparents Have to Say

In this section I will describe the results of an interview that I had with a married couple who are grandparents and raising their granddaughter. I came to know the grandfather over the past year at the school where I was teaching, the same school where his granddaughter went and where he was an active volunteer. I knew that he was raising his granddaughter, but didn't know any of the specifics. According to the teacher who acts as the librarian, he is a lifeline in the library. She commented that the work he does makes her job that much easier. Besides volunteering in the library, Mr. Smith also helps out in any way possible in the school, from putting things together to dismantling things, to helping with concerts, he is always there to lend a hand.

During a recent lengthy interview with these grandparents, it became much more evident how both the grandparents loved, cared for and adored this grandchild. In the following sections, I will address the experiences of the grandparents as revealed through the interview, how it relates to or conflicts with current literature on the topic of grandparents raising children as well as any new experiences or information not discussed in the literature review.

For the purpose of this paper, the grandparents and granddaughter will be referred to by fictitious names in order to conceal their identity. I will be referring to the grandparents as Mr. and Mrs. Smith and the granddaughter as Susan. Both grandparents were very open and willing to share information on their experiences raising Susan. Although the interview lasted over three hours and much valuable information was gained on the topic, a deeper understanding of their experiences would have been gained had there been more time for discussion.

The Smiths, now both in their seventies, have two grown sons, and a daughter whom they adopted when she was an infant. The daughter is the mother of Susan, the grandchild that they are raising. The sons are married and have children of their own, and all live in Newfoundland.

The reason why the Smiths assumed the parenting role for their grandchild was consistent with the reasons in the literature review. Domestic violence and mental illness were two of the reasons that the Smith grandparents took on the parenting role for their granddaughter, but most importantly, they acknowledged that they loved their daughter and granddaughter and felt it was their duty as a grandparent to care for them.

The grandmother revealed that she had to bring both her daughter and grandchild home from Alberta for several reasons; the daughter was suffering from an abusive relationship, an inability as a mother to care for her child, as well, the mother suffered from a bout of depression. The child's mother left their home shortly after returning from Alberta and has since re-married and separated. She has supervised visits with the child at the grandparents' house. Shortly after the granddaughter arrived home, the grandparents filed for the interim-adoption of Susan. When asked why they didn't just foster the child, they replied that they were concerned that the father would try to gain custody, and they couldn't allow that to happen as they feared for the child's safety. The Smiths adopted their granddaughter when she was five months old and they continue to be the sole caregivers for her today, nine and a half years later. The child's father doesn't have any contact with her and her other grandparents have limited contact, usually a phone call and gift on special occasions.

The literature on the importance of grandparents raising their grandchildren was also very detailed. Some of the literature related to the grandparents concern for the safety of their grandchildren. These finding were also consistent with those of the Smith grandparents.

When asked about the importance of raising the grandchild, Mrs. Smith responded that she felt it was important to be there for her grandchild, just as it was when she raised her children. She noted that when she and her husband were planning to marry and have a family, they wanted to have a house paid for so that she could stay home and raise the children and not worry about that expense. She felt that being home raising the children was the most important aspect of parenting. She expressed a belief that the working mother is what is wrong with children today, because mothers are absent in the raising of their children in favour of work; children miss out on important nurturing and social values. Mrs. Smith said that they love and care for Susan as if she were their own child; it is their moral obligation to do so. Mrs. Smith said that there is not a day goes by that they don't kiss Susan and tell her that they love her. Mrs. Smith said that "it is a job, if you want to do it right, you have to do things right". She hopes that other grandparents in the same position feel and look after their grandchildren the same way.

Much of the literature reviewed, stated that grandparents require coping mechanisms in order to better equip themselves for the task of raising grandchildren. Without being told how to cope, the Smiths realized the need for early intervention in order to make the change a success. A number of articles on the topic of caregiving by grandparents noted that it was the grandmother the majority of time that was responsible for the care of the grandchild. This was not the case with the Smith grandparents. Both grandparents shared the household tasks fairly equally, but Mr. Smith was responsible for the outside 'running around' aspect involved with Susan.

Mrs. Smith decided that in order to raise a grandchild, they would need to have a system; a sharing of responsibilities to make the process a smooth success. She noted that "you need to have a system at our age, this is not easy, and we have a good thing going and it alleviates responsibility for him and me".

The sharing of responsibilities at the Smith household is as follows: Mrs. Smith cooks the meals and cleans the house. She noted that her energy level is not what it used to be and that she tires easily, therefore she leaves "all the running around" to Mr. Smith. Mr. Smith's role is to bring Susan to school and to her various activities, help with her homework (while Mrs. Smith cooks supper), and make her lunch for the following day.

She noted that for the first three years that they had Susan, she had to care for her by herself as Mr. Smith was still working. But in those days, since Susan was still an infant, she could still easily do her housework as Susan slept through much of the day in her crib.

Numerous studies have concluded that there are positive advantages to raising a grandchild. The literature review was consistent with the benefits reported by the Smith grandparents, as the following were discussed as benefits: closeness to grandchildren, increased vitality and zest for life, and ensure safety of the grandchildren.

When asked about the benefits of raising a grandchild, Mrs. Smith laughed when saying "we're not going to get Alzheimer's, we don't have time to"! They feel very fortunate to have Susan. Both said that they are more active because of her and she makes them feel so much younger. Mrs. Smith noted that if she is having a bad day, all she needs to do is think about not having Susan in her life, and her mood brightens.

Besides keeping them mentally and physically active, they Smiths also note other benefits of raising Susan: they are able to watch her grow up, they can be a positive role model for her, they are comforted by the fact that they know that she is safe as opposed to wondering who has her or where she is.

There are usually challenges with all aspects of life and a grandparent raising a grandchild certainly has many challenges. These challenges vary depending on age, health, socioeconomic status, family support, knowledge and amount of resources, knowledge of raising children.

The Smiths noted several challenges that they faced when raising Susan. Mrs. Smith said that she missed the social aspect of spending time with her friends. For example, each year Mrs. Smith and her friends would normally go on a vacation, but because she doesn't want to leave Mr. Smith with all the responsibility of caring for Susan, therefore she doesn't go anymore.

They also find that discipline is a challenge. They expressed a concern that Susan, who is now ten years old, challenges them every day by wanting her own way, but they also stated that she is starting to listen and abide by their rules more these days.

Letting go is another of the challenges that they face. They mentioned that Susan is never out of their sight for more than ten minutes at a time! They want to protect her. Mrs. Smith said that it was easy when Susan was a young child, she was always in their sights, but now she wants more freedom and they are having difficulty with that. They said that they don't want to cut her off from other people, but in the same breath, they want to ensure her safety.

Another challenge that the Smiths mentioned was the lack of respite support. Even though they are eligible for 21 hours of respite for Susan, they are the ones responsible for finding the respite worker. For a young couple this might not be a problem, but for Mr. and Mrs. Smith it does pose a problem. They don't know any babysitters or respite workers, and neither do their friends, as it is not something that they have had to deal with for many years and they don't know of any supports in their area.

One of the major difficulties or issues that grandparents in many of the literature reviews reported was the lack of financial resources. Many grandparents reported that they had to dip into retirement saving and some even had to remortgage their house to pay for court cost and expenses incurred while they looked after their grandchildren. Many of the grandparents that were reported in the literature review studies were reported as living in poverty. This was not the case with the Smith family. The grandfather worked all his life, up until seven years ago and the grandmother worked prior to starting her family and again when her children were in high school. Both the grandparents had saved money for several years in order to pay for their house. Therefore a major financial burden was taken care of, and as a result Mrs. Smith was able to be a stay-at-home-mom with her children.

With regard to the financial aspect of raising Susan, the Smiths don't have any complaints. They have some government assistance, which they had to fight for initially. They mentioned that it is not much and it doesn't go a long way, and if they could get more it wouldn't go astray. Mr. Smith mentioned that they could have gotten much more had they taken Susan as a foster child, but they wanted the security of knowing that she was under their protection as opposed to receiving more money. Both grandparents make sure that Susan eats nutritious food and don't allow her junk food, and they make sure that she participates in a wide variety of physical activities. Many of these activities they used to pay out of their own funds until Susan's new social worker made them aware of funding for these programs.

Many of the grandparents in the literature reported that they didn't receive proper support for raising their grandchildren and didn't know where to seek help. This was consistent with the Smiths.

The support mechanisms for the Smith family were non-existent. As I already alluded to the fact that the Smith family didn't know of any babysitters for Susan, therefore they never went out together without her. When asked if they had any family or friends that helped out with her care, they both said no. They have really good friends, but they would never ask for their help with Susan, but know that if they ever need them, they will help. This was evidenced several years ago when Mrs. Smith had heart surgery and her friends were there to help in any way they could, from cooking the meals to looking after Susan. Therefore they know that help is there if there need it, but won't abuse it.

When I asked the Smiths what support mechanism they would like to see put in place for grandparents who are raising their grandchildren, they mentioned several things. They felt that a list of respite workers in their area would be a great help. They also noted educational session on teen issues, such as drugs awareness.

Mr. Smith felt that at the present time, he is quite capable with helping Susan with her homework and assignments, but that would probably change when she got into the higher grades, therefore tutoring services would be helpful.

Mr. Smith also mentioned that legal support would be a benefit. When they adopted Susan they had to pay out of their own pocket for all the expenses. Mr. Smith also alluded to the fact that the past social worker wasn't much help in educating them on what services or financial assistance was available to them. He noted that the current social worker was much more helpful in offering suggestions and giving assistance.

Since the Smiths didn't have any supports available for respite, they created their own breaks by making sure that Susan was involved in some type of organized activity or sport. This type of planning or coping strategy wasn't evident in the articles read for the literature review, but it showed that they were creative thinkers; the results serving both parties.

Mr. Smith felt that it is important for Susan to participate in physical activity, especially given the fact that she is very energetic. There are a number of ways that he encourages Susan to be physically active. After school, Mr. Smith walks with Susan for exercise and they both go for bike rides. He has her enrolled in organized activities such as swimming lessons, cross-country running, skating lessons, gymnastics, and summer camps. The time that Susan is involved in these activities also serves as a break for Mr. and Mrs. Smith; a much needed break that they look forward to.

When asked if they had any concerns for the future, both grandparents said that they worry about the future for Susan. For now they have control over much of what Susan does, who she plays with, where she goes etc. But they fear what can happen when Susan is older and they don't have full control. Mrs. Smith fears that when Susan gets older, she may get involved with inappropriate kids and drugs and they won't be able to stop it.

CONCLUSION

It appears from the interview with the Smiths that many of things they experienced were the same as in the literature review. They were also able to reveal coping strategies not evident in my literature review that would be very helpful to other grandparents.

As mentioned above, it is evident from the literature that there is a growing number of children being raised by grandparents all over the world. Based on this, my recommendation would be that a program needs to be put in place to offer more support to grandparents in the areas as suggested by Mr. and Mrs. Smith. This is something that we as a society can and should do to cope with the growing number of grandchildren being parented by grandparents. This would also help to ensure that the grandparents feel supported for the job they have taken on. This is especially important as the literature shows that there are many benefits for grandchildren to be raised by their grandparents, thus keeping this part of the family unit intact.

REFLECTION QUESTIONS

1. Given the increase in grandparents providing care to (grand)children, what are some areas where government may want to consider policy development as a means to prevent (to some extent) children from coming into the care of the state?

2. Grandparents appear to be quite willing oftentimes to provide long term care to their grandchildren. Given the impacts of poverty on families, what are the implications for grandchildren growing up in poverty with their grandparents?
3. Should grandparents who adopt a grandchild be provided with supportive services? Why/Why not?
4. Some would argue that drugs were a problem in the days of grandparents (the 60s and 70s). Why do you think this issue and concern about grandchildren becoming involved in drugs appears to be a much bigger issue today?

APPENDIX A

Interview Questions

1. Background info:
   a. Age:
   b. Number of children _____ and grandchildren_____?
   c. Number of grandchildren in your care____?
   d. Are you the primary caregiver or do you share the responsibilities with another adult?
2. Home info:
   a. Can you tell me how your grandchild came into your care?
   b. Can you tell me your experiences of raising your grandchild?
   c. What are the benefits of raising a grandchild?
   d. What are the greatest challenges?
   e. What impact has becoming a grandparent as parent on your financial situation?
   f. Do you have any support mechanisms that you can access to help in your grandparent as parent role?
   g. What support mechanism would you like to see offered in the future, if they could be offered?
3. School/social info:
   a. How do you assist your grandchild with their school work?
   b. Do you volunteer at your grandchild's school? If so, what capacity do you volunteer?
   c. Are you physically active? Do you consider physical activity important for your grandchild? If so, how do you promote physical activity for your grandchild?
4. Future:
   a. Do you have any concerns for the future as a grandparent in a parent role?

REFERENCES

American Association of Retired Persons (AARP) (1998). Grandparents raising their grandchildren: What to consider and where to find help. Retrieved on July 18, 2009, from http://www.aarp.org/families/grandparents/raising_grandchild/

Australian Bureau of Statistics (2003). Family Characteristics, Australia. Retrieved on July 20, 2009, from http://www.abs.gov.au/AUSSTATS/abs@.nsf/allprimarymainfeatures/234CFF39BDFDFF80C A25745F00168760?opendocument

Bryson, K., & Casper, L.M. (1999). Coresident grandparents and grandchildren: Current population reports: Bureau of the U.S. Census.

Casper, L.M., & Bryson, K. (1998). Co-resident grandparents and their grandchildren: Grandparent Maintained Families. Paper presented at the Annual Meeting of the Population Association of America, Chicago, IL. Retrieved on July 20, 2009 from http://www.census.gov/population/www/ documentation/twps0026/twps0026.html

DeToledo, S., & Brown, D. (1995). Grandparents as Parents: A Survival Guide for Raising a Second Family New York: The Guilford Press. Retrieved on July 21, 2009, from http://books.google.ca/books ?id=UtvXN6AV1Y8C&dq=Grandparents+as+Parents:+A+S urvival+Guide+for+Raising+a+Second +Family&printsec=frontcover&source=bl&ots=npP7Ro_rQi&sig=i3ZRvL-4TrV3Mi0Zoh_QhgJP1 BQ&hl=en&ei=RxlpSumcMYbIMc_z9c8M&sa=X&oi=book_result&ct=result&resnum=2

Fuller-Thomson, E. (2005). Grandparents Raising Grandchildren in Canada: A Profile of Skipped Generation Families. SEDAP. Retrieved on July 18, 2009, from http://socserv.mcmaster.ca/sedap/p/ sedap132.pdf

Fuller-Thomson, E., & Minkler, M. (2001). American grandparents providing extensive childcare to their grandchildren: Prevalence and profile. *The Gerontologist, 41*(2), 201–209.

Fuller-Thomson, E., Minkler, M., & Driver, D. (1997). A profile of grandparents raising grandchildren in the United States. *The Gerontologist, 37*(3), 406–411.

Glass, J.C. (2002). Grandparents parenting grandchildren: Extent of situation, issues involved, and educational implications. Educational Gerontology, 28, 139–161. Retrieved on July 18, 2009, from http://web.ebscohost.com.qe2a-proxy.mun.ca/ehost/pdf?vid=4&hid=6&sid=dbd0ef21-259a-4ea6-87ce-7e214612c7fb%40sessionmgr4

Green, S., & Haley, B. (2009). Volunteering in South Africa: An experience of Ubuntu. *Connecting Voices. NLASW, 13*(2).

Hayslip, B., & Kaminski, P.L. (2005). Grandparents Raising Their Grandchildren: A Review of the Literature and Suggestions for Practice. *The Gerontologist, 45*(2), 262–269. Retrieved on July 23, 2009, from K:\6440 Grad course\Grandparents\Grandparents Raising Their Grandchildren A Review of the Literature and Suggestions for Practice – Hayslip and Kaminski 45(2) 262 – The Gerontologist.mht

Hayslip, B., & Shore, R.J. (2000). Custodial grandparenting and mental health services. *Journal of Mental Health and Aging, 6*, 367–384.

Kornhaber, A. (1996). Contemporary Grandparenting, Sage Publications, Thousand Oaks, California.

Minkler, M., Fuller-Thomson, E., Miller, D., & Driver, D. (2000). Grandparent caregiving and depression. In Hayslip, B. & Goldberg-Glen, R. (Eds.), Grandparents raising grandchildren: Theoretical, empirical, and clinical perspectives (pp. 207–220). New York: Springer.

Minkler, M., & Roe, M. (1993). Grandmothers as caregivers: Raising children of the crack cocaine epidemic (as cited in Fuller-Thomson, 2005). Retrieved on July 18, 2009, from http://socserv. mcmaster.ca/sedap/p/sedap132.pdf

Mitchell, B.A. (2009). Family Matters: An Introduction to Family Sociology in Canada. Toronto: Canadian Scholars' Press.

Racicot, L. (2003). Understanding the Needs and Issues of Grandfamilies: A Survey of Grandparents Raising Grandchildren. A Pilot Study. Retrieved on July 18, 2009, from http://www.eric.ed.gov/ ERICDocs/data/ericdocs2sql/content_storage_01/0000019b/80/1b/6f/72.pdf

Solomon, J.C., & Marx, J. (1995). "To grandmother's house we go": Health and school adjustment of children raised solely by grandparents (as cited in Fuller-Thomson, 2005). Retrieved on July 18, 2009, from http://socserv.mcmaster.ca/sedap/p/sedap132.pdf

Statistics Canada (2003). Age groups, number of grandparents and sex for grandchildren living with grandparents with no parent present, for Canada, Provinces and Territories, 1991 to 2001 censuses – 20% sample data. Retrieved January 16, 2003, from http://www12.statcan.ca/english/census01/ products/standard/themes/RetrieveProductTable.cfm?Temporal=2001&PID=62722&APATH=3&GI D=355313&METH=1&PTYPE=55496&THEME=39&FOCUS=0&AID=0&PLACENAME=0&PR OVINCE=0&SEARCH=0&GC=0&GK=0&VID=0&FL=0&RL=0&FREE=0

Statistics Canada (2006). Age group of child, number of Grandparents and sex for the grandchildren living with grandparents with no parent present, in private households of Canada, provinces and territories, 2006 Census – 20% Sample Data. Retrieved on July 20, 2009 from http://www12.statcan.gc.ca/english /census06/data/topics/RetrieveProductTable.cfm?ALEVEL=3&APATH=3&CATNO=97–553-XC B2006025&DETAIL=0&DIM=&DS=99&FL=0&FREE=0&GAL=&GC=99&GK=NA&GRP= 0&IPS=97-553-XCB2006025&METH=0&ORDER=&PID=89035&PTYPE=88971&RL=0&S= 1&ShowAll= &StartRow=&SUB=&Temporal=2006&Theme=68&VID=&VNAMEE=&VNAMEF =&GID=614135

Strawbridge, W.J., Wallhagen, M.I., Shema, S.J., & Kaplan, G.A. (1997). New burdens or more of the same? Comparing grandparent, spouse, and adult-child caregivers. *The Gerontologist, 37*, 505–510.

Stritof, B., & Stritof, S. (n.d.). Raising Grandkids: A Growing Trend. About.com. Retrieved on July 23, 2009, from http://marriage.about.com/cs/grandparenting/a/raisinggrandkid.htm

Tutwiler, S.W. (2005). Teachers as Collaborative Partners. Working with diverse families and Communities. Mahwah, NJ: Erlbaum Associates.

Weibel-Orlando, J. (1997). Grandparenting styles: The contemporary American Indian experience (as cited in Fuller-Thomson, 2005). Retrieved on July 18, 2009, from http://socserv.mcmaster.ca/ sedap/p/sedap132.pdf

Wilson, M.N. (1986). The Black extended family: An analytical consideration. *Developmental Psychology, 22*, 246–256.

Wilson, M.N., Tolson, T.F.J., Hinton, K.D., & Kiernan, M. (1990). Flexibility and sharing of childcare duties in Black families. *Sex Roles*, 22, 409–425.

SHEENA MILLS

THE ROLE OF GRANDPARENTS

Grandparents are a vital part of today's family and grandparenthood is a distinct stage of family life. Grandparents take on many direct and indirect roles in the lives of both their adult children and grandchildren. It can be difficult to define exactly what a grandparent is since they mean so many different things to different individuals. There are three recognized categories of grandparent caregivers;

1. The custodial grandparents – this group has legal custody of their grandchildren. Some major problems have occurred in the parents' lives and the grandparents then takes over the role of the parents.
2. The "living with" grandparents – this group does not have legal custody of the grandchildren, but they live with them and receive daily care from them.
3. "Day care" grandparents – this group offers assistance to the parent(s) of the child. They perform the regular role of a grandparent: enough care since the grandchildren return home at the end of the day.

The purpose of this paper is to analyze the role of "day care" grandparents in today's society. It will focus on the role, benefits and challenges of individuals in this category. I have had the opportunity to interview three grandparents, two grandmothers (hereafter referred to as Ann and Mary) and a grandfather (John), to determine their role as grandparents and also to briefly look at how their role is similar to or different from that of their own grandparents. It is important to note that there can be some overlap between categories. One grandmother, Mary, though she does not have legal custody of her grandchildren considers herself, "to be on par with (her grandson's) mom in the role of primary caregiver. I take care of virtually all of his personal needs and make sure he lacks for nothing."

Generally, in Canada, the title of grandparent refers to the majority of Canadian men and women who are more than sixty-five years old. New born babies usually have all four of their grandparents living. As children age, the number of living grandparents decreases. Grandparenthood has become modernized. Factors such as retirement, more leisure time, advances in technology with regards to communication and travel and a decrease in mortality have contributed to this modernization. Today, grandparents have more time to devote to their grandchildren, more money to spend on them and can keep in touch with them more easily than in the past. Grandparents are living longer and can enjoy this period of their lives as involved grandparents.

A. Singh and M. Devine (Eds.), Rural Transformation and Newfoundland and Labrador Diaspora: Grandparents, Grandparenting, Community and School Relations, 347–354.

Mary believes that grandchildren bring so much happiness to her life. Regarding her grandson, she states, "he is the absolute joy of my life!"

Today, grandparents play a very active role in the lives of their grandchildren. There is diversity with respect to grandparenting styles. For example, grandmothers tend to be more involved in matters related to family relationships and caregiving while grandfathers tend to be more involved in practical matters such as giving advice. However, John, a grandfather of four grandchildren proves that this is not always the case. He states,

> For the three boys who live in the city (St.John's) I was their primary babysitter from birth until they started school. I would be at their home at 8AM on most mornings and I would usually be with them until one PM. We spent a lot of hours strollering or walking the Rennie's River Trail, Kent's Pond, changing diapers, feeding, bathing, walking through the malls on wet days, etc.

Many grandparents are active when it comes to taking care of the grandchildren. Some are involved in passing down family traditions, telling family stories and instilling values and morals in the young children. Others take over for the parents when their professions and various commitments do not allow the parents to do so. John states that he and his wife are "usually on call when their parents need help – transportation to or from school, to sporting events." On the other hand, some grandparents have somewhat of a detached role in the lives of their grandchildren and do not see them very often. This may be due to distance, health, age or unhealthy family relationships. According to John,

> The granddaughter who lives in (Nova Scotia) we would only see once or twice a year when we visited. So obviously we would not get to know her as well as the boys who live here in town. We spoke/speak to her a lot on the phone but it's usually her grandmother who has a better 'phone relationship'.

Grandparents play such an active role in the lives of their grandchildren because of need and/or want. With both parents working today to provide for their families, they often resort to grandparents to be the caregivers for their children. In some cases the parents cannot afford to place their children in some type of daycare or childcare facility, or to hire a babysitter. In other cases such facilities may not exist in the area in which they live. The most practical and sometimes less expensive route to take is to have the grandparents care for the children while the parents are at work or have other obligations to which they have to attend. Ann, a very involved grandmother of twelve said, "My youngest daughter, who lives in St. John's, is doing a 3 year course at College of the North Atlantic, and because her partner works out of the country, I go in regularly to look after her 12 month old son while she studies, does presentations, or writes exams." This grandmother is not alone in her connection to her grandchildren's social activities and education. Mary stated, "I attend all of his school functions, even attending any teacher meetings with his mom. Teachers at his school know to call me if they cannot reach his mom if need be." Sometimes both the parents and grandparents feel that it is in the best interest of the children to be with the grandparents.

Grandparenting helps both the children and the grandparents (Mader, n.d.). The role of grandparents is changing quickly and drastically. Grandchildren and grandparents can interact in quick and easy activities. There are challenges faced when caring for grandchildren but yet there are many joys and positive consequences. It gives grandparents a purpose and helps them fill the role of parent once more. Recalling the joy of a recent visit of her young grandson, Ann lovingly said, "The one year old was here for five weeks with his mom this summer and he heard the same lullabies and baby talk that his mom heard."

When it comes to caring for a child's basic needs, the caregivers (in this case the grandparents) need to be aware of certain factors. Since times have changed and a significant amount of time has passed since grandparents have raised their own children, there is much to consider. With younger children there is a lot of work involved when it comes to feeding, changing and soothing the child. As the child gets older he/she may demand a significant amount of attention and play. Grandparents need to recognize the importance of play, appropriate toys and activities to entertain children both indoors and outdoors. As healthy as many grandparents are today, entertaining and caring for a grandchild can be quite demanding. Mary enjoys,

> taking (her grandson) to movies, plays, swimming, skating and all and any sports he wants to be involved in…His aunties and I took him to Canada's Wonderland last summer and he and I are going to Disney World this winter…I have also tried teaching him gardening, I taught him how to ride his bike, his rollerblades and his scooter. We also colour, read and watch movies together.

In our modern society, families are smaller and there are fewer grandchildren. Many grandparents dote on the one or couple that they have. They help the parents by offering their services to care for the child or children when parents are busy due to work or other obligations. Today, grandparents are more closely connected with their families and grandchildren spend more time with their grandparents because of necessity and choice. They have a tendency to "spoil" them a little. Due to better retirement packages, grandparents are able to assist grandchildren financially. The grandparents also try to develop an interest in the grandchildren's interests. For example, some grandparents regularly attend the grandchildren's hockey games or even play video games with them. As Mary joked regarding her grandson, "He is trying, in vain, to teach me how to play Super Mario."

The ideal grandparents of today can be characterized by many different factors. They have a medium level of education and can help with homework and schooling. They usually live nearby, but not in the same dwelling as the family. They spend time with their grandchildren and regard it as both a duty and a pleasure. For instance, Ann said,

> I'm more involved with the two (grandchildren) that live close-by. I babysat one of them while her mother was commuting to St. John's to do courses

349

towards her master's degree. I took care of the other one from April to October every year until he started school. They spent a lot of time at our house – they're right at home here when their mother, who is a teacher, has to stay late after school, attend workshops, etc. Their father is a fisherman and during the fishing season is often gone for several days at a time. Nanny and poppy are always there to help out!! I attend all their school functions, and help out with school projects – heritage fair, bake sales, etc.

Many grandparents enjoy playing with their grandchildren and sharing stories with them about their own families and lives. Ann went on to say, "My spouse is not as involved as I am in the actual care of the grandchildren but he does keep them entertained sometimes with old stories, passes on old traditions connected with the fishery and with hunting." Through this sharing, the relationship between grandchild and grandparents becomes stronger. When the inevitable occurs and a grandparent does pass away, this sharing may have forged a bond that will keep the grandparent-child relationship alive.

My husband passed away last summer and up to that point he was very involved (in our grandson's) life....He was the father figure in his life, teaching him right from wrong, taking him fishing and in the woods, doing all the boy things that a boy needs his dad for. He would tell him stories of "when I was a boy" and teach him all about fishing and hunting,

said Mary who believes this will help her husband's memory live on.

There can be conflict between parents and grandparents especially when it comes to different opinions on child-rearing. This was also the case in the past when parents and grandparents shared a family home. "I would say that there was probably a power struggle for control of the household between the two women, my father's wife and his mother. But it worked surprisingly well, and I can only imagine what the situation would be like if it were the same for us," said John when recalling his own youth. However, grandparents are often available to step in when there is a breakdown of family relationships among parents. For instance, Ann has had to, "fill the void several times because of marital difficulties." Mary states that her husband "was a father figure for (my grandson) and he misses him very much so I try my best to make-up for that lack in his life. (His) dad is not directly involved in his life."

Unfortunately, grandparents do encounter challenges and difficulties which hinder them from being the grandparents that they wish to be. Health problems sometimes are a major encumbrance as well. They are limited in what they can do and in the care that they can provide. Sometimes grandparents have to change their relationship with others and lifestyles because taking care of the grandchildren often and for long periods removes them from their social network. It is difficult to discipline children today compared to in the past.

Studies have shown how important it is to have intergenerational relationships and this benefits children in their development. Statistically, grandchildren who receive care from grandparents achieve higher scores in school. This is due to the grandparents reading to and with their grandchildren as well as helping them with their homework. They have more free time to offer than the working parents. Working and single parent families are provided with the necessary assistance they need and require when their parent(s) step in to help. Also, the well-being and health of grandparents is positively affected by being involved with their grandchildren. They continue to be active as they engage in activities such as walking, playing and even helping out with sports.

Grandparenting offers many benefits. It makes the grandparents feel younger and more active. They enjoy their role in nurturing family relationships. Satisfaction is felt from being a caregiver. They like to pass on family history and traditions. One of the greatest benefits is to experience a greater purpose for living. Sometimes distance from grandchildren can be overcome through the sharing of experiences. Ann, who has grandchildren living in another area of the province said, "The grandchildren from St. John's spend lots of weekends with us. They like to hear stories from the past, go on walks, pick berries, go fishing with poppy and learn to knit from nanny."

When I was a child, unfortunately I had only one living grandparent. My father's parents had passed on before my birth. My mother's father had drowned when she was an infant and she was raised by her mother and step-father. I have been told that my paternal grandparents were two wonderful, loving individuals. On the other hand, I did not have much of a relationship with my maternal grandmother and none with my step-grandfather. It seemed they were more involved in the lives of their shared children and grandchildren and not in the step-children's families. I rarely visited their house and they rarely visited ours even though we lived in the same small community.

However, myself and my seven other siblings were very fortunate to have an uncle (my father's brother) and an aunt live next door. She was a young widow with four children when they married and they had no children together. He considered us his children. He was the most kind and gentle man. I visited their home almost every day and they would give me a treat, sometimes money, and tell me all sorts of stories about their lives from years ago. They were also very interested in hearing about what was happening in my life. Since their children were raised, we would get a call every Christmas morning to let us know that Santa had visited their house and left some goodies for us. We would rush next door and burst open the parcel that "Santa" had left. When we got older, they were always there to offer advice and sometimes financial help when times were tough. These two individuals, especially my uncle, were my grandparents. So, as difficult as it is to define family and there is a blurring of roles, it is equally difficult to define the term grandparent.

Grandparents of the past were very different than those of today. They had many grandchildren and this sometimes resulted in them spending a smaller amount of time with them. For example, sometimes a family would regularly visit the grandparents on a Sunday afternoon. Grandparents of the past lived shorter lives due to disease, poor health care and a shorter life span. Children were considered lucky if they had one or more surviving grandparents. The elderly were treated with a lot of respect back then.

The interaction of the grandparents interviewed with their grandchildren is very different from what they experienced in the past when they themselves were the grandchildren. When transportation and technology were much less developed, living in another town could be as much of a problem as living in another country. John recalled his experiences with his maternal grandfather.

> My maternal grandfather lived in Placentia, about forty miles of bad road from my home at a time when transportation was limited so I didn't see a lot of him – something the same as our granddaughter in Nova Scotia!! But I did spend several weeks during the summer months with him in the "big town" of Placentia and I have vague but special memories of these times.

Though distances are more easily bridged now than in the past, they still cause issues.

Similarly to today, some grandchildren of the past lived with their grandparents. John also said, "Our family lived with (my paternal grandmother) in her family home after my parents were married. Obviously we got to know her pretty well. She was primarily occupied with running the family general store which was probably our main source of income." However, this relationship was not as harmonious as most seen today. He continues, "But she certainly would not have been involved as a "babysitter". She played no role that I can remember."

Sometimes grandparents of the past helped raise their grandchildren and cultivated very close relationships. "I was partially raised by my grandmother … and she was a very important person in my life. My mom and I lived with her and my grandfather until I was 4 because my dad was away in Labrador working. Mom and I moved there with him when I was 4 and I did my first year of school there. I was so distraught with being away from my grandmother that I was allowed to come back … to live with her for the next two years," said Mary. At other times, living with a grandparent was not a happy experience. Ann wrote,

> My paternal grandmother…lived with our family (11 children) until her death at age 98.…She was a strong, independent woman, the matriarch of the family and as a child I was a bit in dread of her. When I got older I really grew to respect her determination and the effort she had to put in to raising her 5 children on her own.

These quotes illustrate how different the roles of grandparents today are from those of the past, even though some similarities do exist.

Through my interviews, I gained a different perspective on the role of grandparent and what I believe it should entail. Grandparents should play an active role in the lives of their grandchildren. It is beneficial to all people involved – grandparents, parents and grandchildren. It provides a purpose to grandparents and joy to both them and the grandchildren. Even though this paper focused on "day care" grandparents, there is some overlap between this group and the other two. The "day care" grandparent is, to me, the ideal representation of what a grandparent should be.

REFLECTION QUESTIONS

1. What is your understanding of the different roles played by grandmothers versus grandfathers? How do you account for this difference?
2. The author in this chapter (and authors in other chapters) refer to the notion that 'grandparents spoil their grandchildren'. Assuming this statement is true, what are some of the potential negative impacts on the grandchildren?
3. In this chapter the author refers to her relationship with her uncle and aunt as being similar to grandparents. Describe any situations you are aware of where such situations (blurring of boundaries) exists or existed.

REFERENCES

Mitchell, Barbara A. (2009). Family Matters: An Introduction to Family Sociology in Canada. Toronto: Canadian Scholars' Press Inc. Interviews with Ann, Mary and John* July 25th, 2010.
Singh, Dr. Amarjit. Mainstream Research and Grandparents.
Singh, Dr. Amarjit. The Voices and Well-Being of Some Diasporic Punjabi Seniors in North America. Guru Nanak Journal of Sociology.

* Names have been changed to protect identities.

PAUL JOY

THE ROLE OF GRANDPARENTS
IN TODAY'S SOCIETY

The experience of being a grandparent is unique for everyone. Grandparents often speak of the joy of being with their grandchildren. At the same time, grandchildren appreciate the fact their grandparents love them unconditionally. For some grandparents, seeing grandchildren may be difficult due to divorce, remarriage, or geographic distance. Whether you are a grandparent, step-grandparent, or a grandparent raising a grandchild, you are an important person in your grandchild's life. Grandparenting styles vary and each individual brings their unique 'self' to the experience including culture, ethnicity, gender, race, family traditions, family structure and personal history. Researchers who study grandparents have identified various roles including family historian, nurturer, mentor, role model, playmate, wizard, and hero (Uhlenberg et. al., 1999). Grandparents share their stories of the past about relatives, important events, family traditions or the grandparent's own childhood. Whether serving as the babysitter, the chauffeur, the confidante, or the caregiver, the challenge is to find a delicate balance between encouragement and control. Different grandparental structures will be identified in this chapter with examples from two very different grandparents that will clearly illustrate the critical role that grandparents often play in families today. For various reasons and circumstances, a new trend has arisen in which grandparents have come to play a new set of roles. I will examine this new set of roles that grandparents play in today's society.

Important to note is the fact that there are 6 million grandparents in Canada and that each grandparent has, on average, just under five grandchildren and that the role a grandparent plays is very dependent on geographical location (Statistics Canada, 2011). With such a large number of individuals owning the title of grandparent, the role they play can significantly affect their grandchildren in various ways. Grandparents play a significant role in school, communities and families. The frequency of visits between grandparent and grandchild is a very important indicator of the degree of influence the grandparent has over the child and is dependent on a number of factors such as geographic distance, quality of the relationship between grandparent and parent of the grandchild, the gender of the grandparent and marital status of the grandparents (Uhlenberg et. al., 1999).

There are numerous roles that grandparents play in a family. These roles are dynamic in that they will constantly change between the grandparent and their

*A. Singh and M. Devine (Eds.), Rural Transformation and Newfoundland and Labrador Diaspora:
Grandparents, Grandparenting, Community and School Relations, 355–360.*

grandchildren as they grow up. Grandparents offer children a broader range of knowledge, emotions and experiences than they encountered as parents. They also secure a special place in the family as a trusted adult, yet separate and different from the child's parents, and may provide a safe place for children to turn in times of stress when they feel they cannot approach their parents. Considering they are not responsible for the day-to-day care and discipline of their grandchild, grandparents can also assume the role of a pal, secret confidante, and a "light-hearted conspirator". Many grandparents treat their grandchildren in a more relaxed and permissive manner than they ever treated their own children. As a result, children often feel more comfortable discussing sensitive issues with a grandparent than with their own parents.

An advantage of being a grandparent is having a lot of wisdom that they may have acquired over many years of experience. Therefore, a number of the more seemingly major problems that new parents will face tend to be a simpler solution to a grandparent who has seen the problems previously. The fact of being able to turn to grandparents when faced with a problem can be both extremely helpful and comforting for their grandchildren. Boomers have long been said to be "reinventing" retirement, but the recent economic downturn has also started to reinvent the traditional nuclear family unit. There has been more of an emphasis placed on the importance of the grandparent's role today than in past which may have a lasting and significant effect on the workforce. For my paper, I will interview two sets of grandparents and focus on how they contribute to their families lives.

In the first example both parents are career orientated and both worked full time outside of the home until recently the grandfather retired. Both parents are physically active and dedicate a significant portion of their time outside of their home. The family resides in close proximity to one set of grandparents and other extended family and the other set resides on the other side of the province, visiting mainly during the holidays. The maternal grandparents live a few miles away from the grandchildren and a large amount of time is spent together. There is a very close bond between the mother and her parents and the bond between the maternal grandparents and the grandchildren is very close as well. The grandparents have two grandchildren in which one is a male under the age of three and the other is a six-month old female. Both grandparents are under the age of 60; the grandfather is 57 years old and the grandmother is 54 years old. This is a very average age for grandparents in today's society and by today's standards. Both grandparents are physically active and healthy, are very excited to be grandparents, and they enjoy their time with the children.

> I love playing with my grandchildren as if they were my own. I value every moment that I get to spend with them.

The grandparents in this example have a somewhat formal grandparenting style as well as fun-seeking style (Singh et. al., 2010). The grandparents adhere to what they consider to be the proper role for grandparents including spoiling the child with treats, babysitting, having lots of fun and playing with the grandchildren. These grandparents are like a playmate and although they worry about how their grandchildren will turn out, they leave most of the discipline to the parents. "I try to provide advice to my daughter about their discipline but she sees it more as interference in her parenting" said the grandmother. The grandchildren love spending time at the grandparents' home, often asking to visit them and not wanting to leave. The grandmother is still working while the grandfather is retired, allowing for flexibility with helping with the grandchildren. "Now that I am retired, I provide a lot of help both financially and emotionally in the raising of my grandchildren. I baby-sit my grandchildren while their parents go to work", explains the grandfather. It is not uncommon for the grandfather to baby-sit when the children are sick or to bring them to doctor/dentist appointments while the parents are at work. The grandfather has the flexibility to rearrange his schedule to accommodate his grandchildren's needs while, at the same time, he is more than happy to have the opportunity to spend more quality time with them. The flexibility of the grandparents provides the family with the support it needs for both parents to succeed professionally while the children are happy and content to spend time with Nanny and Poppy. The grandparents do not provide full time childcare but offer an alternative to step in and assist with providing support whenever they are needed. The grandparents actually request time with the grandchildren and it is not uncommon for the grandchildren to have sleepovers or daylong outings with the grandparents, including visits to the parks to feed the ducks or going for a drive around the bay.

In my second example, the grandmother is more involved in the lives of her grandchildren than the grandfather. In fact, the grandfather does not really have a relationship with any of his grandchildren. This grandmother, who was never employed outside of the home, has five children and is a grandmother of six grandchildren ranging in ages from fourteen to thirty two. As a result, this grandmother experiences a large age range with her grandchildren and therefore her experiences with each of them may vary. Three of her grandchildren live in British Columbia and, as a result, she spends very little time with them. "I find it so hard to be away from them. I feel that I am missing out on their childhood". In addition, two of her grandchildren have families of their own and require very little from her while her youngest grandchild lives just a few miles from her and is 14 years of age. This grandchild's parents are separated and the father still lives at home with her while the mother has her own place and is a single career woman. Therefore, the grandmother plays the role of the babysitter and chauffeur. The grandchild is picked up by the grandmother every day after school and is driven to any extracurricular activities that he may be involved in. Since his mother works in the Health Care Industry and works shift work, her grandchild spends a lot of time at her house. The grandmother loves the time spent with her grandson and is regularly heard praising him up and bragging about his latest accomplishments. "I was so proud of him when he made the school's basketball team", said the grandmother. The grandmother describes the joy of getting to spend so much time with her grandson as she is unable to see three of her grandchildren due geographical constraints and the other two grandchildren are mature adults. She is also a great-grandmother and makes special trips to see her young great-grandchildren although she considers herself too old to watch them and does not have the physical strength to lift the toddlers. "I don't have the energy to baby-sit my great-children by myself but I love spending time with them". This grandmother is 73 years old and is in fairly good health but does suffer from asthma and diabetes and had a heart attack 2 years ago that required open heart surgery. This grandmother takes on the role of a surrogate parent when the parents are involved in the actual caretaking responsibilities for the child. This usually occurs when the mother of the child is unemployed and unable to take care of her child. Thus, the role of taking care of the children falls squarely on the grandparents' shoulders.

After interviewing these grandparents, it appears that there is often a joint venture between parents and grandparents in teaching and caring for children. Although there may be some differences in parenting styles, parents and grandparents can develop guidelines and boundaries that each can live with. You may not realize the influence you have on your grandchildren until you hear them repeat something you said or imitate something you have done. Grandchildren bring love, energy, optimism, laughter, activity, youthfulness, and purpose to the lives of grandparents. At the same time, grandparents provide maturity, knowledge, stability, and unconditional love to the lives of their grandchildren. In today's society, it is much more common for both parents to have their own careers and lead extremely busy lives. Being able to call upon your grandparents to help with many of the practical everyday problems can be very valuable. The parents from example one stated that, "There have been many times that my father came over and babysat the grandchildren while my husband and I had to work. I appreciate everything that he does for us and we don't know what we would do without him". The underlying sense of responsibility that goes with this role is tremendous.

The role of grandparents in their grandchildren's lives can vary. Some grandparents can have very little influence on the grandchildren's lives while other grandparents can be the primary caregiver of their grandchildren. Grandparents often bridge the gap between parents and their children. One important thing, which seems to be missing in the lives of children today, is the sense of family, values, religious beliefs and principles. Thus, the grandparents can play a significant role instilling these values and beliefs back into their grandchildrens' lives. With changing times, children have started to question the authenticity of everything and have a hard time believing in things unless they are convinced otherwise. Globalization has eroded their sense of belonging and staying in touch with their culture and traditions. Consequently, grandparents play a vital role in passing down important family memories through storytelling and showing their grandchildren long-standing family traditions. They hope that this will help their grandchildren get in touch with their family roots and culture. Also, it is important for grandparents to look out for the well-being of their grandchildren and to try and create a linkage between members of the family. In addition, children can be very demanding but grandparents have the ability, without appearing to be pushy, and the time and experience to deal with their temper tantrums. Therefore, the task of parenting may continue into grandparenthood. Grandparents may actually be considered the pillars of the family and, as a result, can help parents and grandchildren in a magnitude of fashions by utilizing their experience and knowledge.

Recent changes in family and society have meant that the roles grandparents take on have changed. Many grandparents are playing a bigger role in the care giving of their grandchildren, resulting in additional pressures on their time, their health and their finances. "I try to provide as much help as possible in the raising of my grandchildren", said one grandmother. The increasing importance of grandparents, particularly as caregivers for children, has had positive effects on society as a whole and needs more support to continue to be effective. Changes in society over the last two decades have led to changed roles and greater responsibilities for many grandparents. Such changes include an increase in the proportion of families with young children where both parents are in the paid workforce, smaller family sizes (a subsequent reduction in the number of extended family members), an increase in the rates of abuse of drugs and alcohol and an increase in rates of separation and divorce. Therefore, contact between grandparents and grandchildren can be mutually satisfying and important for their well-being and development.

The majority of grandparents want to spend time with their grandchildren – although the roles they play in their grandchildren's lives may vary. Grandparents have a different and distinct relationship with each family of their grandchildren as well as with individual grandchildren (Roberto et. al., 1992). Some grandparents have quite formal relationships, some are informal and playful and some see themselves as the keepers of family wisdom, while others are content to be more distant figures. Families that have no grandparent contact in their lives may not be as stable and loving as those families with grandparents. There are grandparents who do not have a close relationship with their grandchildren. The contact that they have with their grandchildren depends not only on them but also on their relationship they have with their grandchildren's parents as well as the demands on the grandparents' time from more than one set of grandchildren. Therefore, grandparents are less likely to have a close relationship with grandchildren when they don't have a positive relationship with their grandchild's parents (Roberto et. al., 1992). Overall, the relationship between grandparents and grandchildren is constantly changing with the changing times in our society.

REFLECTION QUESTIONS

1. From your own experiences and reflecting on the role of grandparents, how has the role of grandparents changed?
2. "Early" retirement (i.e., retiring at 55 years or so) has influenced how grandparents are 'available' to their grandchildren? What are some of the issues (positive and negative) from the grandparents' perspectives as early retirees?

3. Several authors have discussed the increasing concerns for grandchildren (as stated by the grandparents) as it relates to drug abuse, for example. Considering that many of these grandparents were youth/teens in the late 60s and early 70s, how is this concern different today? What are its possible impacts on school and community?

4. We live in a global/local context. How has this notion of globalization impacted grandparent/grandchild relationships in today's society?

REFERENCES

Singh, Amarjit et al., (2010). Working Draft. Faculty of Education. Memorial University of Newfoundland. "Review of Research: Why the focus on Grandparents?"

Roberto, Karen A. & Stroes, Johanna (1992). Grandchildren and Grandparents: Roles, Influences, and Relationships. *The International Journal of Aging and Human Development, 34*(3), 227–239.

Uhlenberg, Peter & Hammill, Bradley G. (1998). Frequency of grandparent contact with grandchild sets: six factors that make a difference. *The Gerontologist, 38*(3), 276–85.

Jendrek, M.P. (1994). Grandparents who parent their grandchildren: Circumstances and decisions. *The Gerontologist, 34*(2), 206–216.

Statistics Cnada, General Social Survey, Family History. www.statcan.gc.ca.

DARREN REARDON

GRANDPARENTS' ROLE IN THEIR GRANDCHILDREN'S EDUCATION

The role of grandparents in their grandchildren's education has changed dramatically over the last generation. There are many factors which contribute to these changes such as a greater emphasis and importance placed on education, both parents working which results in required assistance from the grandparents, there are not as many grandchildren these days therefore more time to devote to the grandchildren, many grandparents are retiring at younger ages and they have more energy and enthusiasm to take on an active role in their grandchildren's educational lives.

I conducted an interview with a grandparent whom I know very well. I choose this grandparent because I am aware of the great amount of involvement he has with his grandchildren, although he feels, at times, he does not do enough. For the purpose of this paper I will refer to the grandparent as William. I asked William six questions (See Appendix) relating to the role he has in relation to his grandchildren's education. He was very interested in conducting the interview with me. I made certain that this interview would be confidential and the only person's privy to the information would be the interviewer (Darren Reardon) and my University Professor. William was very thorough in the answers he gave to the questions, at times other ideas came up that we discussed which I hadn't thought to ask. He spoke freely about being raised in his grandparent's home without too much, if any, contact with his biological parents. What William considered to be his major or primary role as a grandparent in his grandchildren's education was "to provide second level support." He felt that he didn't have any direct or specific role he just was "willing and available to help out whenever and wherever possible." This would include helping his "grandchildren complete their homework properly." If there were overnight stays by his grandchildren he would "ensure that completed homework was brought back to school, lunches were packed, grandchildren were washed, dressed, ate breakfast, and that they got to school safely and on time." William went on to discuss day to day or week to week duties or contributions to include "picking grandchildren up from school at least once a week", sometimes he would "stay at school with the grandchildren until parents arrived, drove grandchildren to extracurricular activities outside of school, attended school functions, assemblies, plays that grandchildren were involved in to provide encouragement and support", and he would "socialize with the grandchildren and provide incentives for the grandchildren to work hard in school." Although tangible incentives were not offered, intangible incentives

A. Singh and M. Devine (Eds.), Rural Transformation and Newfoundland and Labrador Diaspora: Grandparents, Grandparenting, Community and School Relations, 361–366.

of encouraging the grandchildren to become successful in life, being happy and healthy, making contributions to society, and doing these kinds of things for their grandchildren were incentives that were talked about.

In the opinion of William, he notes that "grandparenting has changed considerably during the last generation, especially when it involves contributing to grandchildren's education." William had some difficulty relating to this topic due to being raised by his own grandparents. Generally speaking, he mentioned that "grandparents a generation ago showed very little involvement in the education of their grandchildren. There wasn't as much emphasis put on education, grandparents themselves were less educated and felt they had nothing to offer or contribute. There were far less activities available for grandparents to become involved in. Lack of money also played its part, therefore grandparents didn't set up education funds for their grandchildren. Financially, there was more often than not, no support at all. Basically, when given the opportunity, grandparents would ensure their grandchildren's homework was completed."

Contributions given to grandchildren in reference to education was more indirect rather than direct (informal education). Indirectly, William would "help with the completion of homework." On occasion if William and his wife "were out shopping they would purchase some storybooks for the grandchildren to read." They would also "buy some school supplies such as crayons, pencils, and exercise books. "Monetarily there wasn't a great contribution given" by William and his wife because all of William's "children and spouses were working and earning a decent income. Both grandparents would "read to their grandchildren at any given opportunity."

William notes that his role as a grandparent may be "somewhat more active than other grandparents," however he has no means of measuring how active he really is, "especially when it deals with his grandchildren's education". He feels the "amount of time devoted to any grandchildren's education by any grandparents varies greatly and there are numerous reasons why some grandparents are heavily involved whereas others show little involvement." The number one reason, he notes,

is the geographical location of grandparents and grandchildren. For instance, the grandparents could be living in St. John's, NL while the grandchildren are living in Edmonton, Alberta which makes it much more difficult for grandparents to contribute to their grandchildren's education other than monetary contributions. Other reasons could be financial restraints on the grandparents, health and well-being, some grandparents may feel it is not their role to contribute and may feel out of place and uncomfortable even when they do want to contribute. They may feel as if they are overstepping their boundaries.

Many grandparents contribute to their grandchildren's education in their own special ways. Many times grandparents will sacrifice or put on hold their own plans in order to help out the grandchildren. William didn't necessarily like to call them sacrifices but he mentioned that there were many occasions where he would "change his plans for the benefit of his grandchildren." He has made "changes to vacation times", visiting his "cabin on the weekends, and not being able to sleep in on some mornings." There were a number of incidences where he cancelled his own "plans and did not postpone to another day just so that he could assist in helping the grandchildren." Many times he doesn't mind doing what he does for his grandchildren, because it gives him a sense of pride and responsibility. He knows that his own children and his grandchildren appreciate the giving of his time to make life a little easier for "the little ones".

Grandparenting Styles

The grandparent's age is related to how he or she interacts with grandchildren. Some grandparents are energetic and youthful adults, while others are frail and distant. Grandparents are often too focused on their own failing health to be involved with their grandchildren. Better health and physical mobility is one explanation for young grandparents to be more of the fun-seeking style grandparent. The surrogate-parent style is more typical of young grandparents.

Grandparenthood is one of the oldest social roles in human experience (Knox, 1995, p. 1). It wasn't until recently that the role of grandparents has become the interest of some scholars. This can be attributed to advances in health care. During the last 50 years, a ten year old had a greater opportunity of having two living grandparents; the increase being between 40% and 50%. It is estimated that children of today will spend, on average, 50% of their lives in the grandparent role. It is generally accepted that the grandparent role is a satisfying and meaningful one. There is an increase of humans living longer and a greater recognition of the grandparent's role.

In later life, the role of grandparents consists of social positions without normal expectations and, for the most part, unclear expectations. Much of the written literature gives a description of the tenuous role. Although there is a conception of vagueness when trying to figure out the role of the grandparents, there have been some attempts to classify grandparent behaviours.

The role of grandparents has increased due to improvements in health care which have increased the human life span and, in turn, the prevalence of three- and four-generational families. Knox (1995) has, through her research, found seven types of grandparent styles including formal, fun-seeker, distant figure, surrogate-parent, passive, family historian, and indulgent. The following will be a short description of each grandparent style.

Formal – are those grandparents who adhere to what may be considered the proper role for grandparents. This would include clear lines between being a parent and a grandparent, along with occasionally providing grandchildren with treats and babysitting which is something they also enjoy doing. These grandparents play their role from a distance. They see themselves as parents first, grandparents second. They only act as grandparents because their children have children. Most of the information that the grandchildren have about their grandparents comes from their parents through stories and descriptions.

Fun-Seeking – the fun-seeker is the grandparent whose interactions with the grandchild are informal and about having fun together. They are a sort of playmate for their grandchildren. They don't worry too much about spoiling their grandchildren with extravagant gifts. This style of grandparent does not feel responsible about how the grandchildren turn out. Grandchildren see their grandparents as more fun to be around than their parents. This may be the result of the grandparents putting them up to no good, getting them to do things that the parents will have to correct at a later time.

Distant-Figure – these grandparents can be described as loving grandparents but at the same time are known to be remote. He or she would generally visit the grandchildren only on holidays and special occasions like Christmas and birthdays. There is infrequent contact with the grandchildren. This style of grandparents seldomly shows up to spend time with the grandchildren. It can be due to the physical distance that they live away from the grandchildren or it could be a personal choice. On rare occasions the parent chooses not to involve the grandparents at all in their children's lives.

Surrogate-Parent – these grandparents are involved in the actual caretaking responsibilities for the child. This typically occurs when the mother of the child is employed or, for whatever reason, unable to take care of her child. This style of grandparenting is usually initiated by the child's parents rather than a choice of the grandparents. Assistance from the grandparent is needed based on a variety of reasons such as parental inexperience in taking care of the child, lack of parental preparation, continuation of education, or the absence of a father figure to assist in child care. This style of grandparenting is not common for most grandparents.

Passive – this style of grandparent tends to stay in the background but is available to help or assist with grandchildren when the need arises. These grandparents may serve as family watchdogs, who are ready to give a helping hand in times of need such as divorce, financial troubles, or illness. Most of the time this style of grandparents is reluctant to interfere. They will interact with grandchildren when invited to do so but rarely takes it upon themselves to make contact with the grandchildren.

Family-Historian – This style of grandparent is more involved in the social continuity of the family between the past and the future. These grandparents bring life to deceased or distant relatives who would otherwise not exist in the eyes of the grandchild. As the family historian, grandparents share stories about the past with their grandchildren. These stories may be about relatives, important events, family traditions, and the grandparent's own childhood as they were growing up. These stories of the family are passed on to the grandchildren through their grandparents. Grandparents act as the glue which helps bond the family together and contributes to family identity.

Indulgent – These grandparents are lenient towards their grandchildren and are not too concerned with spoiling them. Similar in nature to the fun-seeker grandparent. The indulgent grandparent is characterized by or giving to yielding to the wishes of their grandchildren. These grandparents can be gluttonous and be giving to the point of being excessive.

CONCLUSION

As I look at the characteristics of the different grandparenting styles, I see William as a combination of the fun-seeker and the surrogate-parent grandparent. He is always ready and willing to play and have fun with his grandchildren. He does not chide them when things start to get out of hand, nor does he pay too much attention to their parents when the noise level is too overwhelming. William is a very caring grandparent and has no hesitation whatsoever when he is needed to play the role of a parent. He is very grateful to have grandchildren and he will go to great lengths to make life a little bit better for his grandchildren. He takes great pride and responsibility in caring and helping out his grandchildren in whatever way he can.

REFLECTION QUESTIONS

1. The author referred to the grandparent making 'sacrifices' for the grandchildren. What are the connotations of the concept of 'sacrifice' and how might this concept be viewed by both parents and grandparents (either negatively or positively)?
2. The role of grandparents is contingent, in part, on their health. What other factors influence the role of grandparents?
3. Most, if not all, chapters talk about grandparenting in a positive light. What are some of the stresses or tensions with regard to grandparents in their roles as it relates to their grandchildren?
4. Of the seven types of grandparents identified, which type do you believe is most common and why?

APPENDIX

Interview Questions

1. What do you consider to be your role as a grandparent in your grandchildren's education?
2. What day to day or weekly duties do you perform?
3. In your opinion, how has grandparenting changed over the years?
4. What contributions do you give to your grandchildren's education?
5. Do you have a more active role as a grandparent than other grandparent's you know?
6. Are there any sacrifices that you give to assist in your grandchildren's education?

REFERENCE

Knox, M. The Grandparent Experience: An Investigation of Factors Related to GrandparentStyles and Emotional Satisfaction with Being a Grandparent. St. John's, NL. 1995. QE II Library (CNS). www. drurywriting.com/keith/grandparenting.htm

GORDON RALPH

GRANDPARENTING IN NEWFOUNDLAND AND LABRADOR

ABSTRACT

This paper attempts to capture aspects of grandparents and grandparenting in Newfoundland and Labrador under four headings: idealism and reality, child rearing practices, physical proximity and relationships, and testing continuity. It presents voices of grandparents in communities in which they live. The author had conversations with ten grandparents living in various communities across the province of Newfoundland and Labrador. No attempt is made to generalize beyond the statements by particular individuals. This type of study is meant to provide an informed starting point for futures research using other methodologies.

Grandparenting in Newfoundland and Labrador

Note: All interviews were conducted on the island section of Newfoundland and Labrador (NL).

No attempt is made in this report to generalise beyond the statements made by particular individuals.

Section One: Idealism and Reality

After interviewing grandparents both formally and informally a number of distinct patterns emerge. Asking people about their relationships with their children and grandchildren, initial responses are different than later ones. The first responses are extremely positive. By letting the discussion continue toward a more casual tone, it becomes obvious that the original positive responses may have been mildly exaggerated.

Greg, who lives in a medium sized community in eastern Newfoundland and Labrador, at first stated that there were no disagreements about child rearing practices between him and his son. However, later in the conversation when the interview was somewhat finished he said:

Sometimes I have to say to Charlie (his son) they're only kids, b'y, leave them alone.

A. Singh and M. Devine (Eds.), Rural Transformation and Newfoundland and Labrador Diaspora: Grandparents, Grandparenting, Community and School Relations, 367–372.

Greg felt his son was being too strict.

Brenda, who lives in a small community in central Newfoundland, at first stated there were no disagreements on child rearing practices. However, a week later in casual conversation, she stated that she wasn't going to feel responsible for the day-to-day things one has to do in raising a child.

> I'll give them love and affection but I've got a life of my own. I'm not going to feel guilty. I love my grandchildren but I'm only going to go so far. My mother wouldn't have any of my children alone with her in her house until they were toilet trained. She didn't expect anyone to help her raise seven children and I'm the same.

This comment suggests that she feels that her children would want her to become more involved with the day-to-day child rearing than she is prepared to do, though originally she stated that there were no disagreements on child rearing.

In studying family relationships it is not unusual for individuals to exaggerate the positive. This may be because one has had a quasi-religious level of significance which tends to be idealized. Max Weber presented what he calls Ideal Type Constructs. These terms accentuate, even exaggerate, reality rather than describe it specifically and accurately (Eshleman and Wilson, 1995). We might also consider the values placed on the family: "Values are social principles accepted by a society as a whole or by groups within that society. One example is the principle of one marriage for life. Many people do not have such a marriage, but may hold it as their ideal; that is, they value it" (Ward, 2002). The other influence is many cultures believe it is important for psychological stability to have been raised in a stable family. Though these two influences are not mutually exclusive they do suggest that the individual feels more adjusted as a result of these perceived wonderful influences.

Child Rearing Practices

One of the most contentious and varied responses relates to child rearing practices. Some grandparents feel that the parents discipline their children too harshly. An example would be what Greg quoted earlier.

Other grandparents feel parents do not discipline their children sufficiently and this tends to be a major source of tension between grandparents and their children. In some cases, it leads to grandparents avoiding contact with their grandchildren.

Mark, who lives in a large community in eastern Newfoundland, feels his grandchildren are not sufficiently disciplined.

> Whether it is finishing meals or going to bed, the children do whatever they want to. It is frustrating visiting them.

Mike, who lives in a large community in eastern Newfoundland, feels:

> ....too many sleepovers, too many video games and too much television...too structured but no real fun...no building things...no outdoor activities.

This suggests that the children's lives are controlled but inappropriately.

Clyde, who lives in a small community in central Newfoundland, feels that Dick, his son-in-law, tries to discipline his granddaughter but his daughter interferes:

> Dick tries to do the right thing and discipline my granddaughter and their mother comes behind and shags it up.

These comments suggest that there is a concern about the lack of discipline provided by parents toward the grandchildren. Freda, in casual conversation, said:

> I see my granddaughter once a year. And that is enough the way she's raising her. (The child lives in central Canada.)

Annette, who lives in a small community in eastern Newfoundland, states:

> The parents give in too much, spend too much on them. I don't know if the kids ask more or the parents are guilty.

Renee, who lives in a large community in western Newfoundland, has two grandchildren and says:

> One is completely spoiled.

Brenda (quoted earlier) said:

> One granddaughter, the youngest of three, is spoiled. The other four are fine.

Here we can see that some grandparents feel that their grandchildren are unnecessarily spoiled or indulged in.

Physical Proximity and Relationships

The relationship between grandparents and their grandchildren seems to be influenced by the physical proximity the children are to them.

Clyde (quoted earlier) says:

> One of my grandchildren lives in the same town as I do. I can't complain about him as I see him almost every day so if he's spoiled, it is my fault.

Renee says:

> I have two grandsons. The one who lives here is completely spoiled. The one that lives in western Canada feels that I love the grandson in Newfoundland more and I buy him more things. I know where this is coming from...the parents out west.

Elliot, who lives in a medium-sized community in western Newfoundland, says he has seven grandchildren – all living on the Canadian mainland and his relationship with them is exactly the same.

Brenda (quoted earlier) has five grandchildren, three living in eastern Newfoundland and two on the mainland and feels the relationship is exactly the same.

Mark (quoted earlier) said that he is more distant with three of the grandchildren. They live farther away and he sees them less frequently whereas his other three grandchildren live closer to him and he relates better to them because he sees them more frequently.

This discussion seems to suggest that if grandchildren are all living away, the relationship seems to be less differentiated than if one child or group of children live in closer proximity than the others.

Testing Continuity

One of the most interesting aspects of this analysis involves the present grandparents and their relationships with their own grandparents. This allows us to assess how family relationships have altered over six generations. Greg (quoted earlier) says:

My grandmother always had a dime for me. Now it's ten dollars. She lived in the same house. Grandfather died early. My wife Irene didn't know her grandparents and now her grandchildren are her life. She babysits them.

Clyde (quoted earlier) says:

Can't talk about my relationship with my grandparents as I didn't have any relationship with my grandparents. (Researcher: Would you say there was social distance?) Oh yes! Lots of social distance.

Annette (quoted earlier) says:

Everything is different. They were an old man and an old woman. We are closer in age and circumstance. More distant years ago. (They were) more to be looked up to. Now we joke and carry on with the grandchildren. Means (money) were different and we never spent time with them, never left, just never related.

Elliot spoke extensively about this difference and stated:

Grandparents didn't have any television. All news was by radio. No modern telephone. Life was simple. Both (grandparents) worked hard to provide the necessities. They fished and farmed and income was bartered. One grandparent trapped foxes and other animals and sold them in Halifax. The grandmother provided the necessities. I had to work the fields and sow potatoes. It was only in later life did they work hourly for money.

You did what you had to do to survive. You were part of a large family and you were required to pitch in. You did your share.

Totally, utterly different with my grandchildren.

Males did everything away. Now duties are shared equally. When I was young we could run free. Now there's preschool and everything is controlled.

Now kids are picked up and don't run free.

Betty, who comes from a large community in eastern Newfoundland felt:

Not much time spent with the grandparents. Mother's mother and father lived on the south coast and we spent little time with them.

I was frightened of my father's father, hard man. Respected all of them. Father's mother died young. Didn't know her.

The relationship with children is different because children are different.

Mike (quoted earlier) stated:

More things to talk about with grandchildren. Grandparents were more distant. They (grandparents) were there but more distant...they were there but not there. Little in common. Little to talk about. Today grandparents have more responsibility. Much more is expected of them. They help with child rearing which my parents never did.

Brenda (quoted earlier) stated:

I was close to my grandparents except my father's mother who thought she was Queen Elizabeth, though she lived next door. All the others were close. It could have been because her husband saw her son drown at two years old and couldn't do anything. I was closer to the grandparents who lived a couple of hours away. They were really friendly and close. I was close to my father's father. It was only my father's mother I couldn't relate to, she was distant.

Mark, who was quoted earlier, stated:

My grandparents were nice enough but distant. My mother's mother and father played a game where she hid us as small children because she told us her husband (grandfather) liked to eat young children. We went along with the game. We were never really frightened.

My father's mother and father were more distant...especially my father's mother...very serious. The house was always spotless. She had a child die at five. The doctor told her not to give the girl water and she died of dehydration. Maybe that affected her. I don't know. But she was distant.

This extensive commentary clearly articulates a tremendous difference in relationships between present day grandparents and their previous grandparents as contrasted with their present relationships with their grandchildren.

CONCLUSION

Of the varied aspects of child rearing, it becomes obvious that the most interesting and somewhat consistent aspect of these varied relationships is the big difference which exists between being a grandchild and being a grandparent. For many, Newfoundland was an agrarian society though pockets of the province were experiencing the Industrial Revolution, many of the values and attitudes of men and women born in the early part of the 20th century were shaped by a subsistence economy.

The other interesting aspect of this investigation is that some respondents would idealize their family relationships until later conversations provided otherwise. Other conversations appear to be mildly inconsistent with the prevalent Zeitgeist on family relationships.

REFLECTION QUESTION

1. This author refers to Weber's "Ideal Type Constructs" and suggests that, in essence, we present ourselves and our relationships to others in the public sphere as being quite positive. However, the reality is that relationships and relationships within families are very complex and ever changing. Analyze one of the chapters in this text within the construct of the Ideal Type.

2. Child rearing practices present as an issue between grandparents and their children. At least one statement refers to the notion that children are given things (games, TV to watch) in essence to keep the children quiet – this is related to the notion that children are to be 'seen, not heard' and, ironically, relates to many grandparents' attitudes when they were raising their own children. What might account for this incongruity?

3. Relationships with grandchildren in diaspora may or may not be the same. In this chapter some of the interviewees stated that their relationship with their grandchildren both 'away' and at home is the same. What might account for this seemingly inaccurate statement?

4. The author quotes several grandparents who refer to (mostly) not having a close relationship with their own grandparents. Within the context of society in the time of these grandparents, discuss how these relationships were different and some of the factors that may account for these differences.

REFERENCES

Eshleman, J., Ross & Wilson, S.J. (Canadian Edition) (1994). *The Family*. Allyn and Bacon, Massachusetts, p. 4.

Ward, Margaret (2002). *The Family Dynamic: A Canadian Perspective*. Nelson Canada, p. 11.

Van Manen, M. (1997). *Researching lived experience: Human science for an action sensitive pedagogy*. (2nd ed.) London, ON: The Althouse Press.

FROM FEELING OF CULTURAL LOSS TO NOSTALGIA TO AGENCY (PRAXIS) FOR SUSTAINING HOME AND PLACE

MIKE DEVINE

MAKING SENSE

Sustainability, Values, Practices and Transforming
the Communities We Want

Many grandparents play an important role in the lives of their grandchildren. While some may feel that grandparents are less involved in the lives of their grandchildren today than in the past, the literature suggests that grandparents are very involved and that the relationships are important to both (Even-Zohar, 2011, Ruiz & Silverstein, 2007, Taylor, Robila & Lee, 2005). This chapter analyzes the section of this book titled: Sense of Community and Community Profile: Grandparents and Grandparenting Styles for common themes related to community and grandparenting. This chapter uses a content analysis approach (Krippendorff, 2004) with these chapters to seek out common themes that emerge from the documents which may provide more insight into the lives and the roles of grandparents, past and present, including the concept of diaspora where children are living in other communities, whether in the province of Newfoundland and Labrador, in other provinces in Canada or globally. The content analysis approach is both qualitative and quantitative (Bryman, 2001). Frequencies of words or phrases are tabulated in the text. It is these frequencies that is the focus of the analysis to analyze common patterns or themes (Weber, 1990).

Seven main themes emerged from these papers and are identified and discussed below. The themes provide insight into the roles of grandparents, how they relate to grandchildren and some reflection on the meaning of these themes on grandparenting today and into the future. The seven themes include; (1) mutual support, (2) close knit community, (3) community care of children, (4) religious influences, (5) knowledge and skills transmission, (6) accepting change, and (7) grandparenting roles today.

Mutual Support is defined by Brown and Hannis (2012) as the informal network acting as a bridge between family and bureaucratic services by providing informal care and help in times of crises. One strong theme in the papers was mutual support or 'helping one another out' in time of need. Grandparents were identified as role models in the helping role (Amanda C), a role that is identified in the literature as being important to both grandchildren and to grandparents (Neikrug, 2000). They were the models in the community for when someone needed a hand they were there to help out in any way they could help. In another case, in a farming community, the notion of helping out was also verbalized in terms of the sharing of crops to individuals in the community (Heather S). Those who had extra crops shared with

A. Singh and M. Devine (Eds.), Rural Transformation and Newfoundland and Labrador Diaspora: Grandparents, Grandparenting, Community and School Relations, 375–382.

the less fortunate. Related to this theme was the sense of everyone being considered equal in the community (Jenine B); there was not a hierarchy. Everyone felt part of the community and all felt valued by others. Another grandparents viewed his community as being still 'close knit' today, even though people were more independent (Nadine V). Some communities have managed to stay 'connected' to one another, even if there is more of an individualist approach, being independent as opposed to being interdependent. Historically, the collectivist notion in community appears to be related to times when basic necessities were the focus for individuals, families, and communities. People needed each other. This need, this interdependence also translated into a strong sense of a close knit community. The fact that the province of Newfoundland and Labrador is an island province also contributes to this sense of community (Wilkinson, 2008). Being able to give to others and knowing that others were there for you should you need help created the true sense of community.

Close Knit Community Close communities are identified by their ability to relate to others and to draw meaning and identity from within community (Homan, 2011). Being close knit as a community was another theme related to mutual support. In some instances older people were referred to as 'Uncle' and 'Aunt' or as 'Mr' and 'Mrs' as a sign of respect and/or affection (Ann Marie F; Ashley C.). It was the recognition that, as elders, they had gained knowledge and wisdom that was valued by the community, not unlike many aboriginal communities (Brownlee, Nickoway, Delaney and Durst, 2010). One grandparent stated that "...strong family ties are critical to a meaningful life", suggesting the critical importance of family within community (Amanda C). This very insightful statement reflects the importance to all of us that we are fulfilled in our relationships with others. Others viewed loyalty to their ancestors and to the land as a way to be close knit as a community. Research states that the longer one resides in a particular community the stronger the ties to that community (Crowe, 2010). Land has traditionally been of great value to families in Newfoundland and Labrador. Passing land from one generation to the next is a symbolic way to ensure connections to family as well as connections to community. Given that some grandparents (and grandchildren) have several generations who occupied the same community and the same land, attachment to the land and to the people is strong. This grandparent also talked of the 'give and take' that is important in relationships (Crystal F.), a recognition of the need, in small communities, to 'get along' and the suggestion of the importance of relationships in our lives.

Being close knit in terms of extended family was exemplified through traditional meals each week with the Newfoundland "Jiggs dinner"; every Sunday the grandparents provided the meal and extended family, adult children and grandchildren, shared a meal (Heather S.). This tradition was not uncommon and is a tradition kept by families today. Also, sharing of a meal has some religious connotations for these Christian communities. It is a reminder that we are part of a greater community of God and that they should always be thankful for what they have. Another grandparent talked of the fact that the elderly were private and that there was no gossip or jealousy (Jenine B. and Jodi M.), the notion of respect for others in community (Patterson, Cromby, Brown, Gross & Locke, 2011). The practice of not gossiping or not being jealous of one's neighbour also has connotations of a Christian religious ethic – to 'love thy neighbour as thyself'. Some reflections on community today stated that 'families keep more to themselves today' (Jodi M). As communities moved from a more collectivist way of living (interdependence) to a more individualist way of living (independence), the 'need' for community changed. The change has been interpreted by the grandparents as communities not being as close. Related to this change is what other grandparents talked about in terms of relationships. As people became more individualistic in their lives the relationships changed and these changes included a loss as the relationships were no longer interdependent. The independence may be a concern for older people who are more likely to become socially isolated (Steward, Craig, MacPherson & Alexander, 2001). However, one grandparent talked about the fact that the community is still close knit today (Nadine V.). This view appears to be related to the fact that this grandparent is very involved in community and appears to be an informal leader. He has connections with many individuals and groups in the community; therefore, his experience of his community is one of connectedness or a feeling of being 'close knit'.

Community Care of Children Another aspect of being a close knit community was related by a number of grandparents to children in the community and the concept of the community caring for the children. In Western society today there is an emphasis and legislation that dictates minimum levels of care to children. This minimal standard is expressed under provincial jurisdictions in Canada with some differences between provinces. However, the common theme is that of the nuclear family being primarily, if not exclusively, responsible for the care of children. The concept of community care of children is not a focus. In grandparents discussing child care, they, as children, were often free to move about in their community without being under the watchful eye of their parents. However, there was an understanding that other adults in the community were part of the watchful eyes on children. For example, one grandparent stated that children were "...watched out for" in the community by adults and another grandparent stated that, if a child got in trouble in the community, "...the parents would know it before the child got home". This community responsibility provided a sense of security for the adults as well as the children; it was better to have all adults eyes on the children than only the eyes of the parents on the children. The collectivist approach to child care fit with other aspects of community where there is an interdependence in helping out and sharing in responsibilities for child care.

Religious Influence As referenced above, religion played an important part in the lives of people in community in the past. One grandparent expressed the sentiment, "Thank God for what we have", the belief in a higher power providing for and protecting her. This grandmother also connected the declining closeness in community to the decline in the place of religion in the community, a sense of loss in community and in religion (Ashley C. & Heather S.). Other grandparents stated that religion was "top priority" and acknowledged the importance of the "...higher power to protect". As well, it was stated that the church was "...the rock of the community" (Crystal F. & Natasha S.). In several cases the church played a central role in the community, people relied on the church and their religious beliefs to help them cope with life's challenges. Religion also provided meaning for individuals, families, and communities. One grandmother talked of the declining influence of the church and how she had stopped going to church a number of years ago due to a rude minister (Jenine B.). This example is dissimilar to other experiences as the grandmother may have had a strong faith but the institution of the church did not have to be tolerated, in her view. Still another grandmother's family was very involved in church as her mother worked for the local priest and she and her children still go to church today (Nadine V.). This is an example of a grandmother and her children continuing with their traditional way of being, in the religious sense – a continuity of relationships, past practices of ancestors and valuing that aspect of their lives.

Knowledge and Skill Transmission Historically children learned skills from their parents and grandparents; skills were handed down to children and grandchildren (Ann Marie F.). In the traditional community in the past, people had to be more independent as they often did not have the resources to pay someone else to do needed work. Also, work was often the same type of work that the parents and grandparents did – for example, men in the fishery taught fishing skills to the sons and grandsons. There was often a strict division of labour between men and women. Grandmothers taught skills to daughters and granddaughters such as sewing, knitting and cooking while grandfathers taught skills to sons and grandsons such as fishing skills, wood cutting, basic carpentry work, and so on. As one grandfather stated, their grandparents "...taught us how to survive" (Crystal F.) as means of livelihood such as the fishery was unpredictable at best and there was literally, the danger of not having enough food to 'put on the table'. There was also the belief as expressed by one grandparent that grandparents have a responsibility to "...pass on culture and traditions." (Crytstal F.). For grandparents they believed that they had a responsibility to pass on essential skills and knowledge in order to survive. Even as children, they had responsibilities with basic chores they were required to do as part of the collective of the family. Today as well as in the not too distant past, the focus on in higher education and, for rural communities, this means that youth, upon graduation, may not stay in their communities. This notion of getting a higher education suggests a more individualistic perspective on life and on living, a sense of being more independent within community and a realization that the geographical community one grew up in may not be the community in which their children will grow up.

Accepting Change Many of the grandparents have accepted that their communities have changed. Out migration is a factor in the change in community. Young people move out of the community and often out of the province. As well, older people are dying. There is a sense that the community values are being eroded. One grandmother added that it is not the number of people in a community that matters as much as it is the attitudes of those who stay in the community (Ashley C.). Another grandmother expressed the need for people to move to "...have a chance at life", the implication being that the youth need to make the best life they can for themselves, to reach their highest potential, which may not happen in a dying community. The same grandmother expressed a strong sense of resiliency when she said; "You can't hold us down". It is a spirit of community that still lives in her and her sense of place. Another grandmother and grandfather, in accepting that the community is dying, stated that it is better to have no community than to "...see the children suffer trying to make a living." (Crystal F.). Rural decline is not a new phonemon either in the province of Newfoundland and Labrador or internationally (Hardcastle, Powers & Wenocur, 2011). One of the outcomes of grandchildren not growing up in Newfoundland is that "...they don't have Newfoundland pride"; a sense of values and place that are considered by Newfoundlanders and Labradorians to be unique. One grandfather expressed his sense of identity with his community when he said, "...this place is in my soul", the concept of soul being that part of a person which is deepest within the individual and that never dies. The accepting of change can be related to the grieving process where one accepts the loss and moves on to live life in the 'new normal' way of being (Breen & O'Conner, 2010).

Grandparenting Roles Today. When grandchildren live nearby, in the same community or in a nearby community, there is usually regular contact with grandparents (Drew & Silverstein, 2007). One grandmother, for example, stated that her granddaughter sleeps over on a regular basis. Within the same family the adult daughter calls the neighbor "Aunt" as she slept over with the neighbor for two years after her husband died, providing concrete support to a community widow during her grieving process. A grandfather talked about the fact that, in the past, the grandparents taught the children and grandchildren how to survive whereas today the grandparents give a sense of security and love to the grandchildren; the notion of Maslow's hierachy of needs where previous needs were literally those for survival, while today higher level needs (love and security) are being met, in part by the grandparents (Maslow, 1954). The role of grandparents may have changed and this role continues to be very important to the development of the grandchildren. In another situation, a grandmother took advantage of the option to retire early in order to provide full time child care to her new granddaughter. The grandmother did not want a 'stranger' caring for her grandchild and was very aware of the need for the granddaughter to have the best possible start in life as well as to develop a relationship with this granddaughter. Another grandmother stated that she is particularly close to one grandchild but loves all the grandchildren the same. She has two grandchildren in another province whom she stated are 'spoiled' and don't know the value of hard work. This comment by the grandmother is reflective of the many changes in society that have occurred since the grandmother was a child and how different childhood can be today compared to when grandparents were children. Whereas today children and youth often have limited responsibilities and may live at home up to 25 years of age (particularly if attending a post-secondary institution), in the past grandparents had set duties and responsibilities at a very young age. As well grandparents 'became adults' at a much younger age. In the past it would not have been unusual for a youth at age 16 years to be working full time in the fishery or at secretarial or related job and to be married with children before the age of 20 years. Thus, for some grandparents today, it is difficult to see such great differences in the experiences of children and youth and these differences may result in barriers to relationship development between grandchildren and grandparents.

In one example the grandmother stated that she was affectionate with her grandchildren but had not been affectionate with her children, citing the fact that she had too many pressures as a mother. Given that this grandmother stated that she had taken on most of the responsibilities of parenting due to the fact that her husband was 'a drinker', she must have experienced high degrees of stress. The focus may have been on providing the necessities on a day to day basis with little time or inclination for affection for her children, her loving and caring may have been expressed in ensuring that the essentials were provided for her children. Another grandfather spends much time with his grandchildren, taking them for walks, taking them to church, visiting grandchildren in another province regularly as well as providing child care regularly. He stated that he misses the grandchildren in another province and said that "...it hurts when grandchildren hardly know you". In this case the grandparent is very involved in the daily lives of his grandchildren and is mindful of the differences with his grandchildren who are 'away'. His commitment to and wanting to have a deeper relationship with all grandchildren is obvious. In another case the grandmother was very close to and very involved with her grandchildren. At the time of the interview she had been caring for grandchildren full time for 5 months due to an abrupt illness of her daughter. This example demonstrated the critical role of grandparents in times of crises where grandparents 'step in' to provide full time, temporary care to their grandchildren.

Grandparents, in these case studies, provide high levels of care and often have high degrees of involvement in the lives of their grandchildren. As grandparents they were able to reflect on their own grandparents and the important roles they played in their lives. The current grandparents' sense of being as grandparents is influenced by their own experiences of their grandparents. With time comes change and grandparents were able to identify many changes and also to be able to identify their own important roles in the lives of their grandchildren, regardless of where their grandchildren live. While relationships with grandchildren in other parts of the province or outside the province are strong, there is a sense of loss in terms of the limited contact and, thus, different relationship with their grandchildren.

Communities and its members today are more independent and, thus, there is less interaction between community members, as stated by the grandparents. This sense of independence was expressed as a loss by grandparents, the loss being related to less interaction with community members but may also be a loss in terms of feeling more socially isolated. In rural communities in particular, older people are dying and younger people are moving out of the community. The result is often a sense that the community is not as close knit as it was in the past. Religion is not playing as central a role in the lives of communities today as it did in the past. For many grandparents this lesser role of religion is also experienced as a loss in community cohesion and within themselves. Grandparents also see themselves as having a responsibility to pass on the culture and traditions. However, passing on skills and knowledge is not viewed as being as important today, particularly where education is accepted as being very important for the youth to attain in order to build a good life for themselves. However, the reality is that the future of the community is bleak when youth move to larger centers to find work. Despite having children and grandchildren in other provinces and countries, grandparents are aware of the importance of providing love and a sense of security to their grandchildren, wherever they may live.

Grandparents today continue to play an important role in the lives of their grandchildren. The levels of commitment are sometimes quite high. One example above is where the grandmother retired early to provide care to her infant granddaughter. Wherever grandchildren live, grandparents are committed to having a relationship with them. For some, the reality of having grandchildren that 'hardly know them' is difficult. Grandparents may also provide very high levels of care such as the grandmother that was providing full time care for five months to her grandchildren when her daughter became ill. For some grandparents their sense of loss is great. If a grandparent lives in a rural community, s/he may experience the loss of the interdependence within community, the loss of colleagues who die, the loss of children and grandchildren who move 'away', the loss of the influence of religion and the loss of the community itself which may be dying. Despite these many losses grandparents show resiliency in accepting the many losses and keeping a focus on what can be done as opposed to what cannot be done in their life situations.

REFERENCES

Breen, L.J., & O'Conner, M. (2010). Acts of resistance: breaking the silence of grief following traffic crash fatalities. *Death studies, 34*, 30–53.

Brown, J.D., & Hannis, D. (2012). *Community development in Canada.* Toronto: Pearson Canada.

Brownlee, K., Neckoway, R., Delaney, R., & Durst, D. (2010). *Social work and aboriginal peoples: perspectives from Canada's rural and provincial norths.* Thunder Bay, Ontario: Center for Northern Studies, Lakehead University.

Bryman, A. (2001). *Social research methods.* New York: Oxford University Press.

Crowe, J. (2010). Community attachment and satisfaction: the role of a community's social network structure. *Journal of community psychology, 38*(5), 622–644.

Drew, L.M., & Silverstein, M. (2007). Grandparents' psychological well-being after loss of contact with their grandchildren. *Journal of family psychology, 21*(3), 372–379.

Even-Zohar, A. (2011). Intergenerational solidarity between adult grandchildren and their grandparents with different levels of functional ability. *Journal of intergenerational relationships, 9*(2), 128–145.

Hardcastle, D.A., Powers, P.R., & Wenocur, S. (2011). *Community practice: theories and skills for social workers.* New York: Oxford University Press.

Homan, M.S. (2011). *Promoting community change: making it happen in the real world* (5th Ed.). Belmont, USA: Brooks/Cole Cengage Learning.

Krippendorf, K. (2004). *Content analysis: an introduction to its methodology* (2nd Ed.). Thousand Oaks: California.

Maslow, A.H. (1954). *Motivation and Personality,* New York: Harper & Brothers.

Neirkrug, S.M. (2008). A new grandparenting. *Journal of gerontological social work, 33*(3), 103–117.

Patterson, A., Cromby, J., Brown, S.D., Gross, H., & Locke, A. (2011). 'It all boils down to respect doesn't it?': enacting a sense of community in a deprived inner-city area. *Journal of community and applied social psychology, 21*(4), 342–357.

Ruiz, S.A., & Silverstein, M. (2007). Relationships with grandparents and the emotional well-being of late adolescent and young adult grandchildren. *Journal of Social Issues, 63*(4), 793–808.

Steward, M., Craig, D., MacPherson, K., & Alexander, S. (2001). Promoting positive affect and diminishing loneliness of widowed seniors through support intervention. *Public health nursing, 18*(1), 54–63.

Taylor, A.C., Robila, M., & Lee, H.S. (2005). Distance, contact, and intergenerational relationships: grandparents and adult grandchildren from an international perspective. *Journal of adult development, 12*(1), 33–41.

Weber, R. (1990). *Basic content analysis.* Newbury Park, California: Sage Publications.

Wilkinson, D. (2008). Individual and community factors affecting psychological sense of community, attraction, and neighboring in rural communities. *Canadian review of sociology, 45*(4), 305–329.

AMARJIT SINGH & JOAN OLDFORD

FUTURE NEWFOUNDLAND GRANDPARENTS

"Imagine That"

ABSTRACT

In this concluding chapter in this book on Newfoundland and Labrador grandparents, we employ the colloquial expression 'Imagine That!' as a framework for envisioning a future for eventual grandparents in the province. Using a sample population drawn from students enrolled in Oldford's Education class, these potential future grandparents were challenged to write poems under the heading 'Where I Come From.' Their collective responses were symptomatic of a group with a social self, sense of belonging, and personal identity tied to a very specific and deliberate place; a place that incorporated childhood memories with accumulated knowledge and a past that helped mold them and come of age – a place (Newfoundland and Labrador) that could only be described as a 'home.'

Employing the concept of social self – specifically the 'I' and 'Me' components of the term as developed by theorist George Herbert Mead – we forward a version of our own to characterize future Newfoundland and Labrador grandparents; that is, an identity we refer to as the "Newfoundland and Labrador Global Cosmopolitan Social Self" (NL-GCSS). We believe the development of this social self, which balances the contesting and interactive forces of 'I' and 'Me,' is crucial for future grandparents in this province in dealing with the challenges and complexities of modern, everyday life in an increasingly globalized world. In forwarding such a notion, we first arrange the voices of our students into seven categories, and then present students' authentic voices to readers to make sense of those voices from readers' own perspectives. Here, the voices of the students through the use of extensive quotations give a rich, qualitative and "poetic" feel to the narrative presented in this chapter.

"In order of our version of things to stand," to borrow a quote from the text, we pose a series of challenging questions to address the problems facing future Newfoundland and Labrador grandparents and, by extension, the development of the NL-GCSS. In asking these questions, we lay forth the necessary but not sufficient social psychological, cultural, linguistic, and material conditions, needed in society for the development of this new social self to prosper and become an effective link between the local and the global forces. As such, we see the NL-GCSS as not only desirable but also wholly attainable and necessarily a best way to attain sustainable development of rural communities and lifestyles in the context of globalization.

A. Singh and M. Devine (Eds.), Rural Transformation and Newfoundland and Labrador Diaspora: Grandparents, Grandparenting, Community and School Relations, 383–434.

Future Newfoundland and Labrador grandparents can play a transformative role as "organic intellectuals" in the development of this type of social self by shaping the future direction of social, cultural and economic development of this province. They can do this by imagining a "good enough" and "in between" balance of life styles – a right mix of urban and rural life styles – and then practicing grand parenting directed toward achieving these imagined "good enough" life styles made possible by reality of emerging global "multiple modernities". Newfoundlanders and Labradorians often feel that rural communities and life styles those communities offer truly characterize Newfoundland and Labrador as place and home. They love this place and the life styles it offers, and so do not want to see them completely swept aside by the winds of global, but still Western oriented lop-sided modernity project, and the accompanying lust for "nation-building."

In Chapter three in this book Helen M. Buss (aka Margaret Clarke) alludes to the fact that,

> The Newfoundland and Labrador tourists book has adopted for its motto the phrase that is a typical reaction of their citizens to any new fact, fancy or phenomenon: 'Imagine That'. I can remember hearing the phrase constantly as a child. It seems to me now that it was a way adults could show both approval and disbelief at the same moment. Maybe they were just being noncommittal, maybe they were suspending disbelief, but I think it is a healthy reply to make to a child, who having meandered through some probably awkward and highly improbable description of events, half concocted, half actual, hears an adult say 'Imagine That!' Better than to have him tell you you're a liar, stupid or otherwise at fault. Better than having some patient parental unit of the present day try to be helpful about the difference between reality and fantasy. 'Imagine That!' had many tones and shades of meaning, from true amazement with a real exclamation mark to a slightly ironic twist with disbelief just below the surface. But whatever its tone, it always gives you the benefit of the doubt, allows your version of things to stand. (p. 63)

As well as for Buss, the phrase "Imagine That!" will give us the benefit of the doubt, will give us hope that our version of things in this chapter will stand.

In this chapter we[1] attempt to make our version of things stand as we imagine what future Newfoundland grandparents would be like. In order to do this we decided to revisit voices of young adult Newfoundlanders and Labradorians who were Joan Oldford's students. We (Joan) listened to their voices when they attended her classes. In this chapter the focus is on those students because we assume that one day these young adults would be grandparents. Later in the chapter we present their voices in detail, and also describe the context in which we listened to their voices in response to the question: "Where I Come From."

However, before doing that, we think a glimpse of what is entailed in their voices may be in order, because it enables us to initiate conversations with others about aspects of Newfoundland and Labrador's present and past history (see Chapter two), and encourages us to imagine an emergence of new cultural and social contexts in the future, in which these students will be living their daily lives as grandparents. What we see in most students' voices is deep attachment to Newfoundland and Labrador. For them Newfoundland and Labrador is a place and home for living and raising their children. They dearly love Newfoundland for various reasons, and most of them do not want to permanently leave this province in order to live somewhere else. For example, here is a quick view of voices of some students claiming deep attachment to their communities: Carrie says, "I am from a place where togetherness is known.... I come from a town where no one is a stranger....Where you can walk late at night without any danger....I come from a family with a sister and brother.... Who are all very close and protect each other." In Amanda's voice, "I come from a seaside town filled with friendly people." Would these young adults, whose voices we present herein, face similar situations, like many other young adults in Newfoundland and Labrador are facing today and have faced in the past -situations in which they are/were compelled to live in diaspora? (see Chapter one).

To be sure in the long history of Newfoundland and Labrador young and not too young adults have gone away to earn a living, willingly or unwillingly. However, in the context of recent changes brought by the forces of globalization we are once again witnessing the phenomena of "going away" repeating itself in rather accelerating ways, even at a time when several new initiatives are being taken to reverse or slow down this trend in the province (see Chapters one and two). This unwanted emigration on the part of many people in Newfoundland and Labrador appears to have created many challenges for those who want simultaneously to enjoy a multiple set of lifestyles: one set of lifestyle that Newfoundland and Labrador as a place and culture offers them, the second set that a global consumer society offers or promises to offer in the future, and the third one which is some form of combination between the first and the second. What forms of lifestyles are possible and sustainable now and in the future, and under what material, social-psychological and cultural conditions? Such is the nature of tension between social and cultural changes ushered by forces of globalization, and the concomitant deep desire of people to protect certain cherished local values and lifestyles (see endnote 5, in Chapter one), which makes Newfoundland and Labrador a unique place and home for living and raising a family, through various forms of resistance. For example, despite decades of decline in the rural economy, other odds, and perceived anti-rural development and social and economic policies in Newfoundland and Labrador, there are still many people who live in Newfoundland and Labrador in small rural communities (outports), while some of those who had gone away have managed to return to the province. This decision and action on the part of such people can be seen as their form of resistance to anti-rural forces (see Chapter one).

Our Version of Things to Stand

Our version of things, then, is that under certain conditions, future Newfoundland and Labrador grandparents, including the young adults whose voices we present in this chapter, would be able to carve out multiple forms of lifestyles that are "in between" the local and global life styles, and that they would also consider desirable and sustainable. Thus, in our view, in between life styles are those that are optimal mixtures of local cherished values and global consumer culture that individuals, families, and communities consciously choose in a given cultural and social context, and who also perceive that those life styles are sustainable and are "good enough" for their immediate daily gratification and overall happiness and well-being in the long run. In other words, they are relatively well aware of their actual needs, wants, and material conditions in which they live. We imagine one possible choice for future grandparents to attain such in between lifestyles is to develop a new social self, and we are here calling it the "NL local global cosmopolitan social self" (NL-LGCSS). We are imagining that this new social self will function as a useful intellectual and practical tool for them in negotiating those two (local & global) lifestyles in a creative, imaginative, and reflective manner – the result of which would be multiple forms of in – between lifestyles available to them that they would perceive as satisfactory, attainable and sustainable. This new self-concept would enable them to transform their communities and adapt to changing family structures in ways in which they could combine local and global resources in creative and imaginative ways. However, the development of this new self-concept may be possible only under certain conditions. These conditions pertain to bringing about changes in the areas of education and schooling, the way we think about modernity and globalization, the way we do research and produce new knowledge, and the way we act, re-learn, re-frame and reorganize our practices in various specific situations we face in our daily life. Later in the chapter we describe in detail these conditions in which it could be possible to develop NL-LGCSS. Here we are buying into an idea that conceives interdependence between social self and society. The general idea is that as societies change so do the social selves of individuals and vice-versa. Many people hold this perspective on the relationship between individual and society, and we will elaborate those ideas later in our discussion in this chapter in the section on agency.

The Context: Where I Come From

In order to imagine our version of things and to simplify the organization of the material in this chapter, we do the following things - (a) describe the context in which we have listened to the voices of those students, (b) describe the backgrounds of students who would be future Newfoundland and Labrador grandparents, (c) describe the larger context in which we imagine these grandparents would find themselves living either outside this province or away from their own communities in the province: this means they will be living in diaspora in both cases, (d) describe the meaning of living in diaspora, and the experience of becoming diasporic grandparents, (e) describe diasporic and non-diasporic grandparents, (f) describe how future Newfoundland

and Labrador grandparents might experience everyday life in the 21st century, (g) describe what legacy they could pass on to their grandchildren – diasporic, non-diasporic or cosmopolitan. We then categorize the voices of these future grandparents into seven categories. Following this we raise certain questions we imagine that these grandparents would face when they try to pass on certain aspects of their desired legacy to the grandchildren – for example, especially their desire to maintain local and global lifestyles, and their love for Newfoundland as 'home' where they live and raise their families. Finally we describe the conditions in which our version of things would have a "good enough" possibility to stand.

It may be worthwhile to note that many of these themes, ideas and the language we use to describe and imagine the orientation and action of future Newfoundland and Labrador grandparents in this chapter have been discussed in Chapter one in this book. The difference is that the discussion therein provides a broader global cultural context in which the roles of grandparents have acquired different significance in almost all countries in the world due the globalization process.

This chapter and the other chapters in this book describe the specific contexts and situations in which grandparents in Newfoundland and Labrador are adapting to global and local changes in creative, imaginative and local ways.

The above is an important point to keep in mind while reading this chapter and the others in this book. Specifically, the readers may note that in all these chapters in this book the contributors illuminate the actions of grandparents, their grand parenting styles, and sense-making orientations, while they live their daily lives in different communities with their own histories. The contributors have done this through listening to the voices of the grandparents and highlighting them.

In writing this chapter, like other contributors to this book, we have listened to the voices of young adults who would be future Newfoundland grandparents, and at the same time we have dared to make our version of things stand. "Imagine That!"

Who are Future Newfoundland and Labrador Grandparents?

In this chapter the future Newfoundland and Labrador grandparents are those students who attended Joan Oldford's classes during Fall Semester in Education 3312, a course for pre-service teachers of language arts, who, with Joan, engaged in writing poems and publishing them through a literacy practice of 'author's chair' (Ada and Campoy, 2004).)The poems were entitled, "Where I Come From..." and were written by three cohorts of students in their professional year of study.

One of the objectives accomplished by this activity was an exploration of the personal and imaginative purposes of language in primary/elementary classrooms. Although young children engage in using personal and imaginative language significantly in their everyday life outside of school, the classroom itself has offered little support for their language uses. A study by Pennell (1977) found only 5.5 precent of utterances in classrooms were of a personal or imaginative purpose. As children interact with teachers and peers their self-concept and attitudes toward expressing feelings develop. Kash and Borich (1978) observed that "each event in the educational experience has potential for self-concept change". Consequently, the classroom needs to provide a context where children "can be open, accepting, autonomous and explorative" so that they develop positive self-concepts.

Teachers seeking to teach writing must be concerned with students' feelings about themselves, school and writing. They need to communicate their genuine enthusiasm by inviting students to share their "voices". According to Graves (1997), "Kids don't write with good voices unless the teacher has one". Writing the poems, "Where I Come From"... was an opportunity for pre-service teachers to express their "voices" to one another in a classroom setting.

A second objective for writing the poem was the hope that sharing our poems would help establish community in our classroom. In using 'author's chair' we celebrated our creative accomplishments, while giving and receiving helpful feedback and response to our poems with our colleagues. Whenever the classroom can be perceived as such a community of writers/learners, students are more likely to persist in taking risks and, will thereby, achieve continuously. We will have more to say about the necessity of this way of classroom teaching when we discuss the role of education and schooling for our version of things to stand.

Voices of would- be Newfoundland and Labrador Grandparents and the Significance of the Social Self

In Oldford's class the pre-service teachers, as authors, were invited to visualize the places of their childhood and persons who had influenced them (significant others) to create a poem for sharing with the other students during 'author's chair'. A description of the process we followed in composing and publishing our poems is found in an excellent book, *Reading, Writing and Rising Up: Teaching about Social Justice and the Power of the Written Word by Linda Christiansen* (2000) and is also published in a teachers' newspaper, Rethinking Schools (2000). The poems written using the above framework reflect both the rich diversity and common experiences of students entering their professional year in the study of Primary/ Elementary education in our Faculty.[2] These poems constitute the voices of would-be grandparents that we categorize later.

Initially, as Joan Oldford explains, students made these responses to a question "Where I Come From". This question was raised to achieve certain pedagogical goals in the context of specific objectives of the course, but the scope of the question asked and the goal to create a safe space where students could register their imagination in their own voices was much broader. Thus, according to Oldford, the question was placed in a much broader framework that imagined that the classroom needs to provide a context where children "can be open, accepting, autonomous and explorative" so that they develop social self-concepts that are always emerging in imagined contexts.

Later in the chapter we will have more to say about the significance of the notion of the social self and how a specific form of social self could be developed in the classroom context as well as by exposing students to various non-formal and informal educational processes operating in the larger social and cultural context. This could be done by listening sympathetically to the responses (voices) of students to various questions. For example, for our purpose in this chapter, we listened to the responses of students to the topic, "Where I Come From".

For us the significance of the social self lies in the fact that types of changes in social self occur in relation to types of societal changes and vice-versa. We will specifically review aspects of discourses on the need to develop the "I" part of the social self, more so than the "Me" part of it in the context of the 21st century-discourses that are related to the seminal work of George Herbert Mead, and many others like him.[3]

Suffice here to mention that, according to Mead, the individual can have multiple social selves. The fact is that there is both conformity and individuality in the social self. The social self has two phases that are in constant disagreement/tension with each other: the "I" and "Me" part. "I" is the immediate, unpredictable, creative part of the social self, and the "Me" is the part which adapts to the expectations and perspectives of others leading to conformism. The "I" emerges in new ways in interactions with others, giving the individual some degree of freedom/agency. It allows the individual to reflect on past, present and future. It makes an individual conscious of her/his own biography (his/her own life circumstances) and the biography of society, and relation between the two. The "I" is the instant and creative response of the self to others. In Mead's view, "I" and "Me" are not things or structures of the self; both are processes that are part of the larger process that is the social self. Society controls us by emphasizing the "Me". We feel comfortable when we use the "Me" part of ourselves to live in the social world that surrounds us, and society gets enough conformity to allow it to achieve its goals. At the same time because the "I" is creative it makes it possible for society to change. The "I" provides a steady infusion of new ideas to society to prevent it from growing stagnant. Because of this mix of "I" and "Me", both individuals and society are able to function better.

As mentioned earlier, our version of things is that the future Newfoundland and Labrador grandparents will more likely be able to greatly balance the mix between the "I" and "Me" part of the social self. They will have what we label the "NL local global cosmopolitan social self" (NL-LGCSS). This form of social self will enable them to understand the complexity of everyday life experiences encountered everywhere in a globalized world, as well as make them more aware of the intricacies of living locally and globally in everyday life in the 21st century. "Imagine that!" if future Newfoundland and Labrador grandparents feel comfortable being both "CFA" (Come From Away) and at the same time enjoy the happiness, joy and inner satisfaction that they experience while living in beautiful small coves and in communities in which new forms of social relations seem to have emerged, where the families still have remained interconnected, albeit in various degrees of intimacies. "Imagine that!" if the future Newfoundland grandparents decided to pass on this legacy to their grandchildren. From the standpoint of normal life course processes, it is likely that most of these students, whose voices we present below, will be grandparents in the next thirty years or so.

We have created seven categories to group their voices. We have done so to highlight their relative and subjective tastes, desires, preferences, and sense of distinctions they make between Newfoundland and Labrador and other geographical, cultural, political and economic places and spaces. We have tried to create these categories on the basis of the meanings these students accord to various characteristics they like that constitutes Newfoundland and Labrador as a unique place and home.

The Larger Context: Newfoundland Diaspora, Diasporic Subjectivity, Living in Diaspora, Meaning of Living in Diaspora, Diasporic and Non-diasporic Grandparents, and Grand Parenting Passing Legacy in the 21st Century (d, e, f, and g).

The concepts of diaspora and diasporic subjectivity have several connotations. It is not our intention to address here the full theoretical intricacies of these terms.

One common experience most of Newfoundlanders and Labadorians have is aptly captured by the final report of the Newfoundland and Labrador Royal Commission on Renewing and Strengthening our Place in Canada (2003). It states that "with job losses in many parts of the province being so severe and without sufficient growth in employment opportunities elsewhere in the provincial economy, people have been forced to choose between unemployment and out-migration" (p. 35).

When people are forced to leave their communities for one reason or another to go away and live somewhere else, they are said to live in diaspora and have diasporic subjectivity and experiences. We get a taste of diasporic subjectivity by listening to the voice of Sylvia, a student in Joan's class. In her words, "where I come from family and friends are valued and loved"... "I come from a home that is filled with sounds of laughter and smells of homemade goodies." She loves her friends, family, and home so much. This realization on her part makes her say that "When I am away, I miss where I come from." Here Sylvia's feelings are personal and radiate a sense of intimacy. This is what we mean by diasporic subjectivity in this chapter.

There are many other connotations attached to the concepts of diaspora; these are insightfully discussed by Jennifer Bowering Deslisle in her paper "Newfoundland Diaspora: Moving through Ethnicity and Whiteness" (2008a).

Some of the key ideas associated with the term diaspora used by other authors include: victimization, mass trauma, the legacy of colonialism, experiences of adjustment and nostalgia for a distant, past homeland, a strong connection to home, and an intense desire to return to it during one's life time.

The more traditional meanings of the term 'diaspora' include: exile, loss, dislocation, powerlessness, painful and coercive displacement or plain pain.

People do not necessarily have to move out of this province. Delisle (2008a) points out that according to Helen Buss the term diaspora also includes migration of people from small outports (small communities) to St. John's. Buss calls this the "ultimate diaspora" of Newfoundland (p. 64).

Delisle states that "clearly Newfoundland out-migration is both statistically and culturally significant. But can Newfoundland out-migration, as a predominantly white, economically motivated movement that occurs mainly within Canada, legitimately be considered 'diasporic'?" In her paper she goes in detail to suggest "that diaspora does usefully describe the phenomenon of Newfoundland out-migration, because of the connotation that diaspora traditionally carries" (Delisle 2008a, pp. 64–65).

As far as grandparents are concerned, diaspora is a situation in which many grandparents in Newfoundland and Labrador are experiencing new relationship[s] with their grandchildren and families at a much faster rate. For example, some grandparents might find themselves in a situation in which their adult sons and daughters, along with their children, i.e., grandchildren, have moved from the province or are not living together, because one has to leave this province to earn a living in some other place, such as Alberta or Ontario. Therefore, diasporic grandparents are those grandparents whose adult children are gone away to find work outside this province or away from their communities, sometimes splitting their families into two halves. But many of these young sons and daughters have a strong and lingering desire to return to Newfoundland and Labrador (NL), their loved homeland. Similarly, the family of those young adults who stay back home never cease to say to them "Come Home B'ys [Boys]". Those who are unable to come back home see themselves as living in diaspora forever (See Chapters Two and Three).

On the other hand, non-diasporic grandparents are those grandparents whose adult children do not have to leave home or this province to find jobs somewhere else; these grandparents do not experience split family situation[s] in the same way as do the diasporic grandparents.

Given the possibility of becoming diasporic grandparents, how would future grandparents in Newfoundland experience their everyday lives in the 21st century? What legacy would they pass on to their grandchildren – diasporic or non-diasporic? "Imagine That!" In this section we try to do just that!

In every society and culture each generation passes on its legacy to the next generation. Each generation is interested in its family roots and in knowing how the previous generation grew up, what their childhood was like, what their first home-away-from-home was like, what their political and religious views are, what did happiness meant to them, what were the most important lesson they learned, what were their hopes for their children, and how much they loved their children. This by no means is an exhaustive list because today members of a household exhibit multiple arrangements under the impact of technological changes. As a result a variety of family structures exist, and these family structures and membership may further have multiple meanings of family, especially in the context of rapidly changing social media and its impact on social networking and social relations (Mitchell, 2009).

As the 21st century progresses, other changes in the organization of political, economic, religious, social, cultural and spiritual areas are more likely to change everyday life experiences of individuals at both local and global levels. These individual and social experiences are likely to be very different. How would people everywhere manage to live with differences? What meanings would people attribute to differences at both local and global levels? What are the different ways people everywhere can re-evaluate their family legacies? How will people relearn to set up new goals and aspirations for themselves? In this changing local and global context of 21st century, would the future Newfoundland and Labrador grandparents insist on passing on the legacy of their own parents and grandparents? Or would they become grandparents in a "come from away" (CFA) type of family household? "Imagine That!"

Categorizing the Voices of Future Newfoundland and Labrador Grandparents

We have already explained above the reasons for creating seven categories of attachment to represent the voices of these young students who one day will be parents and grandparents. These categories are: (1) attachment with the natural beauty of this province that surrounds them. It is expressed in the satisfaction they get when they experience the beauty of the vast ocean, small islands surrounded by ocean water, beaches covered with sand and pebbles, the ocean filled with sea shells, fish and cod and watching the sky above the land and the ocean covered with stars (2) attachment with the land, the farmland, that allows people to experience [the] enjoyment and satisfaction that comes with activities associated with farming; the land that produces a variety of berries – partridge berries, blueberries, bakeapples and allows people to savour the satisfaction and pleasure that is associated with picking berries (3) attachment with handmade things such as houses, knitted clothing, quilts, home-cooking, (4) attachment to a sense of family and community that allows people to enjoy slow, caring and primary relationships; a community in which everyone knows the name of others, no one is seen as a stranger, and where there are frequent family and communal gatherings, (5) attachment to preserving memories through photographs, stories and history that seems to arouse in them emotions, deep hidden feelings of pain and pleasure; such an attachment enables to them to define themselves as a proud resilient people, (6) attachment to values such as hard work, honesty, caregiving and family love, and (7) passing on family legacies. Here are the voices of future grandparents. Following Van Manen (1997) and Fook (2012), we plan to let the voices of all students speak for themselves to give a rich, qualitative feel to their narratives. Perhaps it is not out of place to add a personal (Oldford) reflection here. Having grown up in a rural community in the Province of Newfoundland and Labrador, and remembering my parents and grandparents working hard to make a living and contributing to building a caring community with others, I cannot avoid feeling the importance of their interaction in creating in myself a sense of humanity and community. Coupled with their values and living was the beautiful natural environment of ocean, islands and forest that contributed to my developing a spiritual sensitivity. Thus, from my perspective I am claiming that the sense of place that is Newfoundland and Labrador enriches both a personal and collective sense of self while instilling a sense of connectedness and transcendence, locally, globally and universally.

(1) *Attachment to the Landscape and Ocean*

The voices of these young students who one day will be parents and grandparents, as expressed in their poems, show a deep attachment to Newfoundland and Labrador as a place they love the most. Their poems attest to their feelings, love and sense of intimacy, soulfulness and attachment to natural elements present in the environment surrounding them while they were growing up in Newfoundland. In those poems they talk about wind, salty fresh air, sand, forest, lakes, flowers, ponds, beaches, grass, hills, valleys, stars, waves, rocks, fog, and the sensuality these natural elements provide. Their voices show attachment to walks in woods, the smell of forest and deep nuances of nature that brings in them feelings of Newfoundland as a special place in their hearts – a deep satisfaction and pleasure this place provides to them. Nadine says, "I come from....where the chill of the air blows from the sea...," and in Amanda's voice "I come from sprays of salt water carried by a strong wind on a sunny afternoon....I come from a fresh cut grass on a hazy summer evening when laziness rubs from head to the tips of my toes." In Holly's words "I come from the ocean; always remembering crashing waves and salty wind on my face." Tanya says, "I come from a place of beach rock and ocean ways, where the salt of the sea, stings your nose." Becky says, "...I come from a sandy shore beside the ocean...." In Sheri's voice, "I come from atop a high plateau beside a freshwater lake.... I come from an evergreen forest teeming with Black Spruce and Balsam Fir....," and Leanne voices her sensuality, "It is not a place that's on the edge of the sea, where fish is at the heart of everyone's glee.... We look to our green fields and they give us great pleasure." In Bridget words, "I come from a land surrounded by water; an adventurous beach lay beneath us, a playground of wonder." April says, "I come from a house with a dory to play in while catching stickle backs and frogs." In Melissa's words, "I come from hills and valleys where you can pick berries as colourful as a rainbow." In Carrie's voice, "I come from a place where the air is fresh and clean....And where nightly millions of stars can be reached." Dawn says, "I come from a big rock in an open field, where my imagination ran free."

(2) *Attachment with Activities Provided by Ocean, the Land, and the Farm Land*

The attachment to the ocean and the land by these would be grandparents goes beyond the scenic panorama offered by this form of natural beauty. It appears that it is the activities associated with the ocean and the land, especially the farmland, that change some form of spiritual bond between these young people and Newfoundland and Labrador as a place. These intricate and elaborate activities include fishing, berrypicking, carpentry, building boats, homes, churches, community halls, and many more artefacts needed for everyday survival. People rely on the ocean and the land for propagation of family and community and engage in activities such as vegetable gardening for household needs, raising sheep and cattle, and chickens for daily meals. In Krista's voice, "I come from fisherman and farmers." Krystal says, "I come from farmers and fishermen, carpenters, teachers as well....farming is what we are known for."

It may be interesting to note that none of the respondents made any reference to activities related to church, government institutions, politicians or school activities. Perhaps this indicates they are separating their feelings, consciously or unconsciously in the public spheres from how they experience their daily lives regulated by the state and its various organizations. In fact, their voices make us witness the experiences of engaging in activities associated with farming; and picking wild berries while savouring the satisfaction and pleasure that accompanies those activities. Further, it is clear from the voices of would be Newfoundland grandparents that attachment to the landscape, ocean, and farmland provides them with opportunities to engage in many activities.

(3) *Attachment with Handmade Products and Feeling of Intimacy and Pleasure Intimacy Provides*

The farmland is extended to an attachment with handmade products and activities of everyday life associated with producing those products such as home grown vegetables, homemade foods, preparation of favourite foods by families in their houses, cooking and preserving of foods from the land and sea such as capelin, moose, rabbit, and all kinds of berries and other wildlife animals and birds; constructions of houses; knitting, stitching, sewing, crocheting, and making of handmade quilts. These activities provide the context in which intimate socialization among family members, siblings and friends takes place. In Dawn's voice, "I come from homemade bread and molasses, and summers at the cabin with Nan and Pop." Jennifer says, "I come from fun annual family BBQs filled with barbecued capelin, steaks, hotdogs and Aunt Angie's great macaroni salad." In Melissa's words, "I come from vegetable soup and home grown veggies, and family drives to Gander." In Karla's words, "I come from pot roast and homemade bread, and from weekly visits that cease to exist now on special occasions." Julie says, "I come from chicken, mashed potatoes and gravy, dressing, salt meat and carrots every Sunday in Mammy's small living room." In Dawn's voice, "I come from homemade bread and molasses, made by my father." In Amanda's words, "I come from macaroni and cheese, homemade bread and toutons, all topped with partridgeberry jam." Jennifer voices, "I come from cooked Sunday dinners, with partridgeberry cheesecakes, or rhubarb pie," and Tanya says, "I come from homemade bread, fish, and jiggs dinner, where the great smell holds for hours." Pam says, "I come from pea soup, toutons and fresh homemade bread." In Amanda's words, "I come from the smell of fresh-baked bread, fried cod breeches, and my Ma's homemade partridgeberry tart."

Many references to cooking in these voices seem to indicate that love and care for cooking is appreciated by the future Newfoundland grandparents; meals prepared with caring are valued. Gloria says, "I come from the small waxed floors, molasses on warm homemade bread, and every kind of soup imaginable." There is appreciation of freshly prepared family meals made from scratch. In April's words, "I come from cooked meals and cookies made from scratch." Cindy says, "I come from Mom's trifle and Mrs. Theresa's raisin buns....I come from bakeapples picked on sweet-smelling marshes." Other handmade products are similarly appreciated. In Becky's voice, "I come from a house my Great-grandfather, Gideon, built," and Kara says, "I come from a house built with my dad's two hand[s], filled with childhood memories that will never be forgotten." In Katherine's voice, "I come from African violets and warm handmade quilts." In Carrie's voice, "I come from Sunday dinners and homemade bread.... And home-knit blankets to put on your bed." Through these voices their sense of pride, tradition, and culture comes to life.

The voices above appear to relish slow and quiet lifestyles filled with happy memories associated with things made by the loved members of one's family. Meals are prepared from scratch, using ingredients from land and sea, prepared by loved ones with care and love. In this life style[s] memories and storytelling, and keeping in touch with friends and family members are much appreciated and desired. A sense of satisfaction, rootedness, security, belonging and intimacy is deeply felt. Dianna says, "I come from old stories and quilts sewn by hand...and no matter how far away, I'll always love this land"

As with home-cooking, knitting and building homes as personal and social activities are another source of intimate feelings for these future Newfoundland grandparents. These deep feelings are also felt with one's pets. In Tina's words, "I come from homemade quilts, and my dog, Dougle, who usually slept at the foot of my bed." In Karla's voice, "I come from a house built with my dad's two hands, filled with childhood memories that will never be forgotten." Jennifer says, "I come from mom and dad, knitter and carpenter." In Dianna's words, "I come from a playhouse with home-made swings that holds childhood memories- such marvellous things" (See Helen Buss's chapter in this book for place of nostalgia and coloured memory).

(4) *Attachment with Sense of Family and Community*

This form of attachment allows people to enjoy slow, safe, caring and primary relationships; a community in which everyone knows each other's name, no one is seen as a stranger, and where there are frequent family and communal gatherings with lively social interactions, helping each other and feeling interdependent. Carrie says, "I am from a place where togetherness is known.... I come from a town where no one is a stranger....Where you can walk late at night without any danger....I come from a family with a sister and brother....Who are all very close and protect each other," " In April's words, "I come from playing cards on Sunday with laughter, family dinners and get-togethers.... I come from a special place of love....It's a home to me." In Amanda's voice, "I come from a seaside town filled with friendly people." Sylvia says, "Where I come from family and friends are valued and loved. I come from a home that is filled with sounds of laughter and smells of homemade goodies. When I am away, I miss where I come from." In Bridget's words, "I come from a large family, eleven children where loneliness was a foreign term." In Nadine's, voice "I come from a family that made me believe that to live life, you have to love life and also grieve. As a child with an older sister and brother we learned through the years to depend on each other." Ashley states, "I come from a place where nobody is a stranger.....where children can play without any danger....I come from a neighbourhood where everyone lends a hand....Whether cooking or cleaning we help all we can."

(5) *Attachment to Preserving and Creating Memories through Photographs, Stories and History*

There are stories and history that seems to arouse emotions, deep hidden feelings of pain and pleasure; such an attachment enables these future grandparents to define themselves as proud people who have and can survive all odds, while helping each other and using the resources of the land and sea. In Lesley's voice, "I come from a world spilling with multitudes of memories, hopes and dreams." In Todd's words, "I come from family trips and photos of everything. I come from memory books and family trees." Amanda's says, "I come from a bedroom of great memories written in my cherished diaries.... I come from the kitchen table discussing family history while sipping on Tetley Tea." Tanya states, "I come from precious memories held by a little purple box ....Where my past, present, and future are kept safe. In "Sheena's voice, "I come from a place that I'll never quite leave, from memories and dreams." In Jennifer's, words "I come from books filled with pictures and friends filled with memories, who won't let me forget." Carla says, "I come from secret childhood diaries and cherished family photo albums." In Elizabeth's words, "I come from an album full of yesterday ....I laugh at those pictures and sometimes I pray....I come from the memories of all those who are dear, they made the town a home for so many years." In Crystal's voice, "I come from the memories that reside....In the trunk in Mom's closet....And in each other." Tina say says, "I come from pictures that are littered in old photo albums tucked away, that hold the memories of a childhood I will always cherish and one that I will never forget!" In Nadine's words, "I come from a childhood where memories were made; many will stay in my heart forever, though others will fade." In Lisa's voice, "I come from 23 photo albums standing at attention on the shelf....I smell the sweet sea-side waves, the great outdoors and realize how lucky I am."

(6) Attachment to Values Such as Hard Work, Truth Telling, Taking Care of Others and Family Love

In Pam's voice, "I come from a home where honesty....is always the best policy....I come from a studious work ethic, always do your best." Carla says, "I come from strong family ties and solid moral beliefs." Amanda states, "I come from qualities like loyalty, honesty, and humour, part and parcel of my large, loving family." Christa voices, "I come from parents who taught me the value of hard work to gain rewards." In Valerie's words, "I come from the strength of God....Support of family and....determination of self." In Amanda's voice, "I come from strong work ethics embedded in me by Linda and Paul."

(7) Passing on Legacy to Their Grandchildren

Here are examples of typical voices of a few students who already have a vision of legacy that they would like to pass on to their families:

> In Jennifer's voice, "I come from a past which has created me, and at this present time I am working towards a future that will enable me to be the best that I can be, so that I can one day provide the support and guidance to my own family that my parents have given me, while helping mold me from a helpless child to a mature adult." In Amy, words, "I come from rainy days imagining the future". And Heidi says, "I come from dreams, goals and an endless imagination..." Christa says, "I come from the view that children are our future." In Elaina's voice, "I come from most precious words. You can be whatever you want to be." And Danielle says, "Where I come from...the vast universe has been perfectly crafted, working in harmony for the continuation of life. Where I come from..." In Kimberley words, "I come from a home that is warm and is my refuge from life's complexities and inequalities and frustrations."

From the voices of these students it appears that they can imagine now what they would like to do in future. But imagine how Jennifer and others like her would define that future in the context of contingencies offered by global/local dynamics and changes associated with this dynamic! How would she navigate different paths that would enable her to "one day provide the support and guidance to my [her] own family that my [her] parents have given me [her]? And what would be the context by in which she would be "...imagining the future" differently for her grandchildren?

Similarly, imagine how Amy, Heidi, Christa, Elaina, Danielle and Kimberly would be navigating a maze of changing situations to accomplish the visions that they have at this age? Jennifer C. says, "I come from a place that gave me the best it could to carry me wherever it is that I want to go." Would she be able to go wherever "I [she] want to go" when she is a grandmother? In Donna's voice, "I come from a fishery that ran out of fish. I come from tired, old people who no longer can wish. I come from roads and fields that are all overgrown. I come from a place that I no longer call home." Would the fishery return "...that ran out of fish...", and would the young people be able to stay with the old ones? Do the current grandparents have something to offer to the future grandparents about the re-organization and sustainability of fishery-related practices in rural Newfoundland, based on their experience, imagination and dreams? Would the future Newfoundland grandparents be interested in fishery-related policy issues?

Further, for our version of things to stand we ask: would today's young Newfoundlanders, who at the present love Newfoundland and Labrador as a place and home, become "diasporic" individuals and grandparents as they experience the reality of the 21st century? To be sure diaspora produces "diasporic grandparents"-grandparents who do grand parenting from "away". "Imagine That!" What types of grandparents would these young folks become, and what sorts of legacy would they pass on to their children if they themselves feel like "come from away" (CFA) when they visit Newfoundland and Labrador, the place they now love so much at this stage of their life. Helen Buss (1999) captures the meaning of CFA in Newfoundland and Labrador in her own way as she explains that "in Newfoundland 'away' is the word they use to explain the crass, the ignorant or the merely mysterious acts inevitable to the condition of being foreign to a place" (p. 10).

Within our version of things, we imagine that perhaps some of those young Newfoundlanders would become "diasporic grandparents", while others would remain in love with NL, even though they might live most of their lives in "diaspora", and would pass on their legacy of Newfoundland and Labrador as a place to their children. (See Chapters Two and Three). In our version of things this will happen under certain conditions, so below we turn to the discussion of those conditions.

Challenging Questions and Conditions for Our Version of Things to Stand

In this section we discuss some challenging questions and conditions for our version of things to stand.

Some Challenging Question

For our version of things to stand, we suggest that the questions posed above, and other similar questions raised below, can only be adequately answered by using the language of critical reflection, hope, and possibilities, examples of which we provide later in a different section of the chapter. In addition we will have more to say later about the critical way of thinking and imagining. In this connection we will review aspects of the role of human agency in the emergence of a new social self.

There are many problems that individuals and communities in Newfoundland and Labrador face at given moments and situations in everyday living. We will also point to the necessary role of the social self in framing, reconstructing and solving those problems, individually and collectively. For present struggles can only be meaningfully understood by relating past experiences to imagine new ways of living and making future plans of action to attain the corresponding future.

Even though students value their attachment to their community life, they are not unaware of the challenges of living there. To continue the focus: in Wendy's words, "The population is declining.... People have moved away...The place I just told you about." In Elaina's voice, "I come from a place that hurts me to see dwindle." Imagine what would their places be like for Donna, Wendy and Elaina when they become grandmothers? Would these places be different from what they are now? Would the sustainable population somehow increase in their communities in near future? (see Rob Greenwood's chapter in this book).

In Joan's voice, "I come from a home that I will soon have to leave....With my family behind me, I know I will achieve." Imagine if thirty years from now Joan comes back to her home! And Tiffany says, "I come from a home that is warm and is my refuge from life's complexities and inequalities and frustrations." Imagine what would happen to Tiffany if her home thirty years from now is no more a home "... that is warm and a refuge from...frustration"? Tiffany is unsure what the future will be but she is optimistic because of the love she had received in the past where she comes from. In her voice, "I come from a past of love, a present that is constantly shaping me, and a future that is unknown but optimistic....I come from behind a chair where imagination was everything and reality meant nothing."

In Joan's and Tiffany's voices above we can imagine glimpses of Newfoundlanders living in diaspora and all the fears, anxieties, and pleasures associated with diasporic experience. (See Helen Buss's chapter in this book)

Lisa admires her roots in small towns even though she has experienced life in bigger cities: "I come from small towns and even bigger cities where I admire my roots, appreciate my surroundings, and am thankful for all these wonderful childhood years." In Mary's words, "I come from.... a Family of Four ... A family that has very deep roots... And believes that we only need each other... We stick together through everything... And know there is always someone else to count on" Melissa says that "The globe is more than just a spinning entity, but a beautiful land where a variety of creatures coexist... Where I come from...The country is a melting pot of different nationalities, where freedom, peace and love are the ultimate goal." Kimberley's voice: "I come from a life of experiences and expectations that have inspired who I am and I would not change a thing".

In the above voices we detect both the devastating assaults of the present day capitalist form of modernity and modernization processes (historically conceived as a Western project) on small rural communities, and at the same time, presenting the possibility of the emergence of a cosmopolitan outlook resulting out of the local/global dynamics to which we have already alluded in Chapter One of this book. In this chapter we intend to expand on some of those earlier themes (desire by rural/outport people in Newfoundland to represent themselves in discussions surrounding issues such as causes of out-migration and return migration, sustainability of their communities, families, lifestyle choices, cultural values, and for their very survival in terms of being a distinct political, social and economic entity in the context of globalization).

There are more challenging questions, and these are: would these students as future Newfoundland and Labrador grandparents be able to develop a unique Newfoundland and Labrador local global cosmopolitan social self (NL-LGCSS)? How would they make use of their human agency to frame and solve current and future individual and social challenges in different situations and contexts? How would they make use of their agency and the emerging "I" part of their creative and imagining social self in relation to the dominating, deterministic, and conforming "Me" part of the social self?

We contextualize the above questions in the next section by way of discussing aspects of discourses in selected areas. These areas are: education and schooling; modernity and globalization; the functions of "academics", "intellectuals", and the ordinary citizenry in society and culture; the human social- psychological agency, and the colonization of knowledge and the decolonization of research methods and methodologies. We focus on the self-reflective language that interrogates and problematizes prevailing discourses in these areas from various perspectives, including the language of those people who are generally critical of certain aspects of the current form of capitalist modernity dominated by mostly North American neo-liberalism as economic ideology. In our view the "Me" part of the social self uncritically tends to conform to the expectations of this ideology. In many countries educational reforms have been initiated by the governments under the dictates of neo-liberalism. We will have more to say about this trend later in the education and schooling section.

Our Way of Making Sense

In our way of making sense, we imagine a need for increased familiarity with reflective and critical language on the part of the future Newfoundland and Labrador grandparents and its availability to them may enhance their engagement with the forces of global modernity in a creative manner. Further, such engagement may play a crucial role in the emergence of a creative and imaginative part of their social selves-the "I" part. This will be a long-term ongoing learning process. Here we are claiming that to the extent that these future grandparents learn to overcome the deterministic and controlling tendency seemingly inherent in the global modernization process, and to the extent they are able to deepen their understanding of how the globalization process has a negative impact on rural societies in Newfoundland and Labrador and other parts of the world, they may be successful in developing the new NL-LGCSS (Newfoundland and Labrador Local Global Cosmopolitan Social Self).[4]

Moreover, in addition to Mead's perspective of the "I" and "Me" relationship discussed herein, the life course perspectives in social gerontology are helpful here to make sense of the development of NL-LGCSS. Social gerontologists and cognitive psychologists study change in mental processes associated with social change. On this take "the mind not only coordinates but determines who we are as individuals [our self-concept] (Quadango, 2008, p.150–151)." Quandango reports that research on creativity and wisdom in these areas informs us that "whereas creativity is a measure of divergent thinking, meaning the production of alternative solutions to problem or situation, expert knowledge that people acquire in the fundamental pragmatics of life is what most people think of as wisdom... More precisely, wisdom is an ability to grasp paradoxes, reconcile contradictions, and accept compromises (p. 151, ibid.)." According to Ardelt (1997, p. 16) "wise people do not necessarily know more facts than other individuals, but they comprehend the deeper meaning of the generally known facts for themselves and others (cited in Quandango, p. 154)." We imagine that, equipped with NL-LGCSS, future Newfoundland grandparents will be in a good position to come up with alternative and balanced solutions to problems created by the local/global demands of social change as wise people. That is to claim that this social self (NL-LGCSS) could very well be the social self that would enable future Newfoundland grandparents to be both local, with deep roots in Newfoundland and Labrador as place and home, while at the same time being global and cosmopolitan, feeling comfortable enough to be both CFA (Come From Away, see Chapter 3) and at the same time committed to finding ways and means to sustain their homes and communities creatively and imaginatively. In other words, we imagine that these future grandparents would be able to creatively mix their diasporic and global experiences with their love for the land, ocean, landscape in Newfoundland and Labrador, and with their attachment to Newfoundland as their home and preferred place to live. They might do this by frequent visits, through acting upon their imagined plans to revitalize their small communities, and through making provisions to settle in Newfoundland permanently at some point in their life.

What are the necessary material conditions for our version of things to stand? We now turn to the discussion of those conditions in certain areas that are necessary for this to happen. As mentioned earlier these areas are: (1) education and schooling; (2) modernity and globalization; (3) the functions of academics, intellectuals, and the public in society and culture; (4) the human social-psychological agency, and, (5) the colonization of knowledge and the decolonization of research methods and methodologies.

Education and Schooling

We suggest that to develop the "I" part of the social self in general, and by implication the NL-LGCSS, we need to revisit the social processes and systems of education that are involved in socializing and civilizing us. That is, we need to look much deeper into the functions of three systems of education – formal, informal, and non-formal – prevalent in Newfoundland, and in other societies. For these systems of education globally are inextricably interdependent, and are intertwined in complex ways with economic, social, legal, religious and cultural aspects of societies everywhere. These systems are involved in socializing young and old alike in every society today. Education systems at elementary, secondary, and postsecondary levels produce, reproduce, and disseminate particular forms of knowledge involving every sphere of our lives in today's society. We use those forms of knowledge in daily practices. That is, we use them to manage, mediate, navigate, and negotiate to solve our daily personal and social problems through various activities and actions we engage in. From Mead's perspective, it can be said that it is the "Me" part of the social self that enables us to act this way. The "Me", generation after generation, enables individuals to behave and act by taking into account generalized values and beliefs of others in society and culture. Thus it helps us to live what is considered normal daily life by adapting to the commonly accepted cultural values, beliefs, and tastes of the larger society. In this sense the "Me" is considered conformist, conservative, and deterministic. We need also be aware of the emergence of the "I" part of the social self while acting within the framework of the "Me" part.

For example, educational systems in Newfoundland and Labrador have passed through roughly four phases of transformation: early colonial, non-formal and informal education systems; schools organized by churches in small and larger communities; education systems jointly organized by the government of Newfoundland and religious denominations, and the current system of government organized non-religious denominational education system. In the past, the denominational system exerted a significant influence on the socialization process of both the young and the old. Consequently, most people learned values held important by their respective religious denominations. In turn, they passed on those values to their children and grandchildren both at home, schools, churches and other places of social gatherings in the public spheres (play grounds, wedding ceremonies, and other such functions) and during interactions in social clubs as part of the regular socialization process. Those religious denominational values learned at all those places became a dominant part of their overall world view or social self. The voices of the future Newfoundland grandparents presented above reflect those dominant values. For example, values such as respect and caring attitudes for all people in the community; loving, intimate attachments with family members, concern for the physical environment of their communities were passed to them by generation after generation by their parents, grandparents and great-great-grandparents. It can be assumed that these values reflect the "Me" part of their social self.

However, at the same time the culture of Newfoundland and Labrador provided spaces for the development of the "I" part of the social self in relation to the "Me" part. In this historical process it created a new form of local "Me". In chapter one, we have already explored this relationship between global and local (see footnote). This new local "Me" can be seen as relatively more in tune to global forces that were transforming Newfoundland society and culture into a modern society. We will discuss the hallmark of Western capitalist modernity and globalization in the next section.

It is interesting to mention here that this historically developing local form of the "I" became instrumental in bringing about many social and cultural changes in Newfoundland and Labrador. To cite one example, it can be said that it was this local "Me" which was mostly the driving force behind the historic action taken by Newfoundlanders that dismantled the denominational system of education in Newfoundland and Labrador in 1998. This is seen as a fundamental historic change by many Newfoundlanders. (McKim, 1988; Galway and Dibbon, 2012; Sheppard, Brown and Dibbon, 2009).

However, as long term residents, participants/observers and observers of Newfoundland and Labrador society, culture, and educational systems; we notice a new form of "I" is emerging in reaction to the "old" form of the "Me" discussed above. This means that the social self of many Newfoundlanders and Labradorians is changing, and they are looking at the relationship between Newfoundland and Labrador society and culture, and educational systems in a different way. This new form of emerging "I" appears to be more aware of the thinking of certain critical observers of school and society worldwide. These observers include varieties of organic intellectuals, artists, writers, academics, experts, researchers, stakeholders, and citizen groups. We have already referred to discourses related to these categories in Chapter One (see endnotes 7 and 8), but will further elaborate on these social categories and conversations that surround their work in the later part of this paper. As an example, in Newfoundland and Labrador many individuals in these groups have been interested in the issue of ongoing migration from Newfoundland and Labrador, and have referred to this phenomenon of out-migration as a Newfoundland and Labrador diaspora. Delisle (2008, ii) states that "this exodus has become a significant part of Newfoundland culture." Delisle herself is interested in this topic and writes that in her work

> I examine several important literary works of the Newfoundland diaspora, including the poetry of E.J. Pratt and Carl Leggo, the drama of David French, the fiction of Donna Morrissey and Wayne Johnston, and the memories of Helen M. Buss/Margaret Clarke and David Macfarlane. These works also become the sites of a broader inquiry into several theoretical flashpoints, including diasporic authenticity, nostalgia, nationalism, race and whiteness, and ethnicity. I show that diasporic Newfoundlanders' identifications involve a complex, self-reflexive, postmodern negotiation between the sometimes contradictory conditions of white privilege, cultural marginalization, and national and regional appropriations. Through these negotiations they both construct, and problematize Newfoundland's place within Canadian culture and a globalized world (ii-iii).

In our reading, this phenomenon – the cultural production by these writers – engages the conventional "Me" part of Newfoundland and Labrador culture in light of the local/global dynamics in creative and imaginative ways. Thus, from our perspective in this chapter such work by people in Newfoundland and Labrador becomes the social context of ambitions that serves as the enabling condition for the development of the "I" part of the social self in which it becomes possible for Newfoundlanders and Labradorians to develop a specific form of self. In this book we have called this new emerging social self, the NL-LGCSS (Newfoundland and Labrador Local

Global Cosmopolitan Social Self). In addition, in remembering, retaining and sharing this theme of "exodus" and related issues, we want to point out that it also is abundantly expressed in the lyrics of the folk music of this province. Too numerous to list are songs in this category but several ever popular among people in rural areas include "Salt Water Joys" and "Grey Foggy Day".

Basically, many critical scholars (see endnotes, 4, 6, 9, 11, 14, and 16 in Chapter One) point out that today's educational systems are organized and function under the perspectival influence of neoliberal economic market ideology in the context of globalization. This way of organizing educational systems leaves very little room for the development of the "I" part of the social self as defined in this chapter. It can be observed that the current educational system in Newfoundland and Labrador is being transformed according to the dictates of market-oriented neoliberalism (McCann, 2000). According to many writers neoliberalism has become a destructive path to local and international education (Barlow and Robertson, 1994; Orelus, 2007; Portillo and Malot, 2008). That is to say, this orientation appears to have become a major part of the "Me" for researchers in Newfoundland and Labrador. All things considered, including the dialectic of the global and the local (Wilson and Dissanayake,1996), and educational systems (Arnove and Aleberto, 2007), we believe this new "Me" has become a major artificial barrier to the development of the NL-LGCSS and to its role in bringing about certain types of social and cultural changes as discussed in this chapter.

What should be done to effectively and creatively deal with this apparently unstoppable trend at this moment in Newfoundland and Labrador history? We are suggesting that a reflective and critical exploration of neoliberalism's influence on the development of education systems in Newfoundland and Labrador is necessary if people in Newfoundland and Labrador want to enjoy both local and global life styles. This we do below, and for the same reasons we also engage in reflective and critical exploration of other related topics such as modernity and globalization; intellectuals, academics, intelligentsia, and the public; social-psychological agency, and the colonization of knowledge and the decolonization of research methods.

This is not the place to talk in any detail about neoliberalism and education reforms undertaken by many governments in many countries in the context of globalization. A huge number of critical and reflective studies exist in this area. We will highlight only a few studies that show that globalization creates inequalities in all spheres of life for most people. Engaging with the issue of social inequalities is to understand how inequalities in social, political, economic, legal, racial, gender, ethnic, and cultural spheres are globally structured, as well as to find out ways and means to transform them to create a more socially just society. Thus, for example, from a social justice point of view, many people now believe that globalization has created inequalities in all spheres of life; that globalization dominated by neoliberalism did not bring a reduction in global poverty; that policies imposed by the International Monetary Fund on countries have been disastrous for the poor and the environment, and that the gap between the very rich and the very poor regions of the world keeps growing (Peet, 2003). Furthermore, much more needs to be done to reduce the digital divide in the area of new global technologies. Much has also been written to contest the legitimacy in many countries of government policy and its subordination to and participation in the neoliberal project of global capital. In discussing the growth of undemocratic (Un) accountability, Hill (2007, p. 116) points out that "within education and other public services, business values and interests are increasingly substituted for democratic accountability and the collective voice," and to the loss of critical thought, thereby documenting "the increasing subordination of education, including university education, and its commodification." (CFHE, 2003; Hill, 2001b, 2002b; Levidow, 2002). Ross and Gibson (2007, p.2) point out that "Neoliberalism is the prevailing political economic paradigm in the world today and has been described as a world 'monoculture', in that, when neoliberal policies are criticized, a common response is 'there is no alternative' (aka TINA)." Further, according to Martinez and Garcia, (2000, cited in Ross and Gibson, 2007, p. 3), "the main points of neoliberalism is that it insists on the elimination of the concept of 'the public good' or 'community' and replacing it with 'individual responsibility' and pressuring the poorest people to find solutions to their lack of education, health care, health, etc." Moreover, neoliberalism "is about policies and processes whereby a relative handful of private interests are permitted to control as much as possible of social life in order to maximize their personal profit." (McChesney, 1998, p. 7, cited in Ross and Gibson, 2007, p. 2) According to Ross and Gibson (2007, p. 2) "…neoliberalism is another term for global market liberalism and for free-trade policies."

According to Suarez-Orozco (2004, p. 3), as the 21st century evolves the role of education will become crucial. He states that "education's challenge will be to shape the cognitive skills, interpersonal sensibilities, and cultural sophistication of children and youth whose lives will be both engaged in local contexts and responsive to larger transnational processes. We claim that two domains in particular will present the greatest challenges to schooling worldwide: the domain of *difference* and the domain of *complexity*." This definition of 21st century interests us the most, because in this chapter and chapter one we have been suggesting that the development of a particular type of education system in Newfoundland and Labrador is necessary if people in this province want to come up with forms of life styles that are some type of mixture of modern consumer society and the local life styles they want to keep intact now and in the future. Suarez-Orozco explains the issue in this area succinctly:

> Globalization is experienced as unsettling in many parts of the world because it threatens deeply held cultural models and social practices. I suspect that the complex challenge of globalization may turn out to be managing to maintain the proactive feature of local culture—such as local worldviews, values, and morals, local religious beliefs and practices—while acquiring the instrumental skills and sensibilities needed to thrive in the global space (HGSN, April 1, p. 4).

Historically, most rural societies, at one point or the other, adopted "modern" educational and economic developmental models, which were indifferent if not inimical to rural development or even outright anti-rural. Has this been the case for Newfoundland? This question needs to be explored at this point in Newfoundland history with greater urgency in the age of neoliberalism.

In our view the system of education in Newfoundland and Labrador will be better off if it finds ways to balance the dictates of market oriented neoliberalism and the demands of social justice. In the Newfoundland and Labrador context it means engaging in dialogue in re-thinking of restructuring the educational systems. The goal of this effort should be to find ways to provide intellectual tools and associated language to K-12 students in schools and to students attending post-secondary educational institutions and the university –the intellectual tools and language that would encourage them to build on their desire to find alternative ways to develop and sustain rural and urban communities in this province in the context of on-going conversation about local/global changes that are occurring in every contemporary society. This way of thinking is based on the arguments presented by critical social and educational theorists, teachers, administrators, and other stakeholders in education, that there are substantial and qualitative differences between schooling and education, and between curriculum and pedagogical goals (Singh, 2001; Doyle and Singh 2006). We believe if these ideas become part of everyday conversation about issues related to rural/urban development in this province, the general public will also be in position in bringing about changes to the existing "informal" and "non-formal" educational systems in this province. This means that people in Newfoundland and Labrador together would be in better position to collectively come up with alternatives to changes ushered by global liberalism. Further, we have suggested in Chapter one and in this chapter that educational systems and cultures that encourage and expect people to produce their own local knowledge in relation to global trends provide a necessary but not sufficient condition for the development of NL-LGCSS.

In another classroom learning and teaching pedagogical situation I (Singh, 2007) asked my student interns to write down their response to the question: "What does local/global mean to you?" In analysing their voices I sensed that a good number of students agreed with the statement Mona, who was one of their peers, made. In Mona's words, "honestly, I do not know what being local and/or global means." Most student interns showed no use of "social justice language" as used by people critical of modern societies dominated by neoliberalism. Instead, the interns used the language of globalization of culture. According to Manfred Steger (2003), there are four dimensions to globalization: economic, political, cultural, and ideological. He points out that "cultural globalization refers to the intensification and expansion of cultural flows across the globe" (p. 69). Looking at interns' responses I noticed that there were ample voices affirming cultural identities. Cultural identity converses, among other things, about place, nationality, history and ethnicity. Cultural globalization in this area has created a feeling of global togetherness among people, having a global soul. Shelly seems to articulate this feeling well:

I think that in today's society, especially the society we live in, be local is to be global. I come from a small town of 500 people, yet already I have visited five different countries. I had to learn to fit into their cultures and societies. This is made easier at this time in history because of the exposure, through media, movies, schooling, etc., to learn about how these people live. Also, in living in such a small town, I keep in contact with people from all around the world through email, chat programs and telephone. So, to be local would mean that you're familiar with your immediate surroundings, friends and culture. But, you can also be familiar with many other cultures as well. Today, we are almost all connected together – globally."

In Jenny's words, "I consider global or a global village to consist of the people of the world to be related in aspects of human life and to be connected in some way, i.e., communication. It involves a relationship of beliefs or social attitudes between ethnic communities and nations. It involves societal effects on each other."

What did it mean to be local and global to most interns? It appears to us that for most it meant the ability to absorb, choose, and consume elements of different cultures that interns thought were more suitable to their tastes. The current education system socializes students to be consumers of "things" as we have pointed out in Chapter One in this book. If this trend continues, and if what we are suggesting here makes some sense, it is not hard to imagine that future Newfoundland grandparents, like most of people now, might only focus on the consumption of goods which are produced by people who are not treated fairly and justly (Steger, 2010). This uncritical desire to consume "things" by those future Newfoundland grandparents who see issues related to social justice in a different light may encourage them to live in diaspora – away from Newfoundland and Labrador, the place and home they love to their bones, as we have witnessed through the voices of two sets of students in this chapter.

Modernity and Globalization

According to many commentators, the way most people live their everyday lives is dominated by the process of modernity, and the modern view. Modernity is one aspect of globalization. Globally it is the expectations of the Western modernization project to which the "Me" part of the social self has become accustomed to conform to over the last two to three hundred years. From our perspective, in order to fully understand the meaning of this project and how it influences behaviour, actions, and the social selves of millions of people, it is necessary that we critically engage and grapple with the "conditions of modernity" and the "consequences of modernity". There exists an insurmountable amount of writing in this area. Given this fact, we only touch upon a very few points and themes that serve our purpose here. We want to assert that attaining an understanding of modernity creates conditions in which it becomes possible for us to develop the "I' part of the social self. Here we are assuming that the

"I" emerges through the critiquing of "Me" in right situations and contexts to create an imagined future. With this purpose in mind, below we present the viewpoints of those commentators who are part of the global anti-modern movement.

Griffin (1996, cited in Steve Odin, 1996, pp. x–xi) explains that this movement is "convinced that modernity can and must be transcended" by "constructive" or "revisionary" postmodernism and not by the "point of view of deconstructive postmodernists..." To be sure, anti-modern movements rose in the past, but they "failed to deflect or even retard the onslaught of modernity for various reasons." (p. xi) Those who advocate an anti-modern movement

> ...do not hold the naively utopian belief [held by many past anti-modern movements] that success of this movement would bring about a global society of universal and lasting peace, harmony, and happiness, in which all spiritual problems, social conflicts, ecological destruction, and hard choices would vanish... There is...after all.... the presence of a transcultural proclivity to evil deep within the human heart, which no new paradigm, combined with a new economic order, new child-rearing practices, or any other social arrangements, will suddenly eliminate (p. xii).

However, proclivity to evil does not deter advocates of present-day anti-modernist movement believers. In their view, "the human proclivity to evil in general, and to conflictual competition and ecological destruction in particular, can be greatly exacerbated by a world order and its worldview" (p xii). In their view "modernity exacerbates it [evil] about as much as imaginable. We can therefore envision, without being naively utopian, a far better world order, with a far less dangerous trajectory, than the one we now have" (p. xii). According to Griffin a constructive or revisionary postmodern world;

> will involve postmodern persons, with a postmodern spirituality, on the one hand, and a postmodern global order, on the other. Going beyond the modern world will involve transcending its individualism, anthropocentrism, patriarchy, mechanization, economism, consumerism, nationalism, and militarism. Constructive postmodern thought provides supports for the ecology, peace, feminist and other emancipatory movements of our time, while stressing that the inclusive emancipation must be from modernity itself. The term *postmodern*, however, by contrast with *premodern*, emphasizes that the modern world has produced unparalleled advances that must not be lost in a general revulsion against its negative features (in Odin, 1996, pp. x–xi).

Further, Griffin points out that "constructive or revisionary postmodernism involves a new unity of scientific, ethical, aesthetic, and religious intuitions. It rejects not science as such but only that scientism in which the data of the modern natural sciences are alone allowed to contribute to the construction of our worldviews, and that "revisionary postmodernism involves a creative synthesis of modern and pre-modern truths and values (Griffin, p. x and p. xi, ibid.)."

There are two points which we want to highlight on this take on modernity as described by Griffin. Firstly, going beyond the modern means dealing effectively, creatively, and imaginatively with issues surrounding social justice; it also means going beyond cultural globalism that encourages unbridled consumption of one's favourite cultural items in the global market. We have alluded to these points in the earlier section on education and globalization in this chapter and also in chapter one. Secondly, a creative modern and premodern synthesis of truth and values is a necessary condition for the development of NL-LGCSS.

But furthermore, imagine what would happen if future Newfoundland and Labrador grandparents become aware of the negative impact of globalization, if the educational systems get reorganized through rethinking and provided them the freedom to think critically about the local/global dynamic. Imagine if, as a distinct cultural group, they organize themselves, the defence against further exploitation in the changing labour process. Imagine, if they decide not to go away from Newfoundland and Labrador just to make more money in order to consume things just for the sake of consuming them. Imagine if future grandparents who occupy different positions in society get involved in the emancipatory politics of inequality. Imagine if the local concerns get highly politicized in the ongoing conversations about societal, economic and market issues. Imagine if in these conversations the politics of self-actualization (quality of life) come to emphasize elements of spirituality embedded in Newfoundland and Labrador culture. Among other ingredients of spirituality are such things as: morality, soulfulness, intellectualism, philosophy, and religion. Imagine if values oppositional to spirituality, such as unbridled materialism and consumerism, lose their power over future Newfoundland and Labrador grandparents. Imagine if they come up with practical ways of mixing materialist and consumerist desires with spirituality. Imagine if they figure out ways to simplify their lives. Imagine if they figure out satisfying ways to walk leisurely in the woods instead of having a frantic run to the shopping mall. Imagine if at some point in their careers they choose giving up promotions and raises to spend more time with families. Imagining past, present and future lifestyles in this way and choosing to mix things together would enable people to develop new forms of social selves. The "I" part of the social self plays a crucial role in this process.

To further elaborate on the concept of modernity and globalization, Lauzon (2011, p. 77) explains that "while modernity was in principle a totalizing [Western] project to be exported to and even, according to many, violently imposed on all human beings, modernity was in practice, from the eighteenth century onwards, conceived of in terms of nation-states." Further,

social theorists in the nineteenth and twentieth centuries also emphasized the emergence of certain other hallmarks of modernity, besides the nation-states, such as industrialization, urbanization, commoditization, bureaucratization, routinization, the split between the private and public spheres, the rise of capitalism, of constitutional democracy, of mass media, of public intellectuals and professional academic expertise, or of special techniques of surveillance, and discipline, as producing and shaping modern societies" (p. 77).

This has also been the case in Newfoundland and Labrador. Historically, most public intellectuals, professional academics and mass media have wanted to transform rural Newfoundland and Labrador society into a modern one. Brian Peckford served as a premier of Newfoundland and Labrador from 1979 to 1989. In his immortal words, Premier Brian Peckford claimed that "someday the sun will shine and have not will be no more" in Newfoundland and Labrador (Peckford, 2012). In 2012 some of the intellectuals, researchers, experts, and academics are claiming that they are involved in the nation-building project in Newfoundland and Labrador. Later we will have more to say about the consequences of the modernization process in Newfoundland and Labrador and the role of intellectuals, researchers, educators and experts in light of those consequences. In the Canadian context Newfoundland and Labrador has been seen as a poor and underdeveloped province. However, within the province itself, who has become "have" and who remains "have not" is an important question. "Imagine That!" if "have nots" are really vanished in Newfoundland and Labrador, or will be "no more" in near future.

Further, the Western modernity was conceived as a unilinear modernization project. On this take Western European cultural values were seen as superior to non-European and Eastern European cultural values. Thus some European societies were labelled as modern while all other non-European and Eastern European societies were labelled as traditional. It was assumed that one day all societies in the world would become modern if they followed step-by step the path taken by European societies in becoming modern. Lauzon points out that "…the investment by Westerners in minutely studying other societies gives the lie to the commonplace that the ideas, practices, and institutions associated with modernity were purely products of Western Europe and/or of North American" (2011, p. 80). To be sure, non-Europeans have also long ago criticized this interpretation of modernity that "traditional cultures and values are at best quaintly irrational signs of an unchanging immature society that should be radically transformed (Lauzon, 2011, p. 81)." Although, historically, people who have settled in Newfoundland and Labrador were of European ancestry, they also were perceived by Western European theorists of modernization as traditional and backward. Their cultural values, like the values of non-western societies, were seen as irrational (Kennedy, 1997). We elaborate on these points later while discussing the work of Linda Tuhiwai Smith (2002) and her associates on the subject of colonization and decolonization of research methodologies and the implications of these ideas to the social selves of future Newfoundland grandparents.

Thinking of modernization as a unilinear project has had the most damaging impact on the psychic of individuals, communities and societies that have been labelled as "traditional" in contrast to "modern". Traditional individuals and communities were and still are seen as backward, and their cultural values presumed to be irrational. They were and still are constantly subjected to policies of the nation-state to modernize them. Basically, modernization is a process in which people must shed their "traditional" values entirely to become modern. "Imagine That!"

As pointed out above, it is not only non-Western societies that were subjected to the project of unilinear modernization. This was also the case for Newfoundland and Labrador, even though the majority of its inhabitants were part of a European diaspora. The small communities (or outports) were studied using theories of modernization developed by European thinkers. For example, it was claimed that "classic ouport society epitomized Durkheim's concepts of mechanical solidarity. Communities were socially similar, egalitarian, relatively self-sufficient units..." (Kennedy, 1997, p. 305).

To be sure, all these qualities of Newfoundland and Labrador communities were and still are seen as negative aspects within the framework of modernization theory. If Newfoundlanders and Labradorians want to be a part of modern societies, it is claimed they have to get rid of these qualities. In this perspective Newfoundland and Labrador society is labelled traditional and Newfoundlanders and Labradorians are stereotypically called by some Canadians as stunned "Newfies". When powerful people put negative and humiliating labels on other people whom they perceive as different from them, the labelled persons must find ways to respond to those negative labels to protect their dignity and social selves as human beings. The well-known Newfoundlander, Bob Wakeham, in another context recently wrote in the local newspaper, *The Telegram*, that "Many of us have been subjected on occasion to the 'newfie thing' while travelling on the Mainland over the years, and reacted in our own way. In my case, I usually responded with a nasty spiel, invariably sprinkled with expletives" and "... these mindless caricatures of Newfoundlanders still exist. And they should never be ignored (nor, for that matter, should the patronizing routine of the 'good little friendly Newfs' with 'no price tags on his doors' be ignored (Sunday, November 5, 2011, p. A21)."

Newfoundlanders and Labradorians are no different from other people elsewhere when it comes to being negatively labelled. Most people feel wounded in these situations. So they express sentiments similar to Bob Wakeham. Derogatory words can wound (Matsuda, 1993). For example, like Bob Wakeham, many people in non-Western societies have been challenging the way they have been represented in stereotypic and derogative ways by those who have studied them and their communities using theories developed by modernization theorists. Kennedy writes "...the outport communities of today are very different from those [studied by researchers in 1960s]. Today, outport people interact more with the outside world and, indeed, many are leaving to join it... Outport people are more apt to have read some anthropology- perhaps on their own community-and they are beginning to be concerned about issues of representation and cultural appropriation [by 'experts'] (1997, p. 313)." As Kennedy states

I sense that outport Newfoundlanders now want to tell their own story [notice the title of Chapter One and the epigraph]... Outport people now publish their own local histories and recollections. For me, this is a very positive development. The plethora of these recent local publications codifies outport life differently than either the anthropologists of the 1960s and 1970s or any other more recent academic research. The Moratorium places many outport communities, and the academic study of them, at an uncertain crossroads (p. 313).

We have touched upon these concerns in Chapter one, when emphasizing the significance of producing local and common sense forms of knowledge.

In contrast to the unilinear perspective is a cosmopolitan perspective on modernization. Adherents to this perspective advocate a sensible mixing of traditional values with emerging modern values that characterize any changing society and culture. A merging of traditional and modern values does not necessarily mean destruction of traditional values. The multilinear outlook on modernization emphasizes the unique creative ability of humans and their capacity to mix modern and traditional values together in a manner that allows them to negotiate and reinterpret their new environment in the most appropriate ways. It is recognized that no culture or society is completely modern or traditional. That is, in each culture there are modern and traditional elements, depending upon the meanings people attach to these elements at any given time. The meaning of being modern and traditional acquires a more flexible and pragmatic definition. Individuals are expected and encouraged to learn new roles which make sense to them in terms of their own unique biographies or experiences in life. The relativity of morals and the range of appropriate roles are emphasized. Various lifestyles which are in tune with individuals' ecological systems are tolerated. Deviant behaviour is not necessarily seen as sick behaviour. Novelty in behaviour has been seen as healthy, leading to a cultural leap and the overcoming of cultural lag. (Gusfield, 1967; Rosenthal, 1983; Rudolph and Rudolph, 1984). This perspective on modernization is more likely to facilitate individuals in developing a mutable self, i.e., a reflective and cosmopolitan social self. Further, it is emphasized that people present a certain mode of self to negotiate with others in working out solutions to their everyday problems, and that people are actively involved in presenting their self to others in a manner that allows them to experience some control or power (Zurcher, 1977; Deegan and Hill, 1987; Blumer, 1969; Popkewitz, 2008; Barnes, 2002).

Some recent scholars of modernity "have begun to use the expression of "multiple modernities" and "alternative modernities" in ways that refuse modernity's conventional claim to universality (Lauzon, 2011, p. 82)." In S.N. Eisenstaedt's words,

the notion of multiple modernities...goes against the view of the 'classical' theories of modernization and of conversion of industrial societies prevalent in the 1950's, and indeed the classical sociological analyses of Marx, Durkheim, and even Weber, ...[who] all assumed, even if only implicitly, that the cultural program of modernity as it developed in Modern Europe and the basic institutional constellations that emerged there would ultimately take over in all modernizing and modern societies; with the expansion of modernity, they would prevail throughout the world (Cited in Lauzon, 2011, p. 82).

Many writers have discussed the idea of alternative modernities (Gaonkar, 2001), In talking about 'alternative modernities' Dalip Parmeshwar Gaonkar writes that "modernity today is global and multiple and no longer has a governing center and master-narratives to accompany it..." Further, "... In short, modernity is not one, but many." In addition to this "people (not just the elite) everywhere, at every national and cultural site, rise to meet [modernity], negotiate it, and appropriate it in their own fashion." According to Gaonkar, "...despite the conventional tendency to present it [modernity] as an abstraction, modernity, must be always historically embedded in every cultural site at which its elements are put together in a distinct way and in response to local circumstances" (Gaonkar, 1999, cited in Lauzon, 2011, p. 83).

Imagine what modernity would mean to future Newfoundland and Labrador grandparents, their children and grandchildren! One of the hallmarks of today's capitalist modernity is consumerism. As pointed out earlier, it appears that most would-be Newfoundland and Labrador grandparents are enjoying living in a consumer society at this moment. They seem to enjoy lifestyles offered by this type of society. Can we imagine that thirty or forty years from now these grandparents might have a different perspective on this consumption-oriented society? Would they be looking for "alternative modernities" or re-envisioning their relationship with Newfoundland and Labrador, the place and home they love so much, within the linguistic perspectives of "multiple modernities" now available to them? Given the material conditions in local circumstances, how would future Newfoundland and Labrador grandparents put together the elements of alternative modernity? Would they be able to combine local and global things together in the space that is available between the local and global poles? In our imagination the answer to the last question is "yes". Yes, they can by making use of (tapping into) the emerging new Newfoundland and Labrador local global cosmopolitan social self (the "I") and merging it with the "Me" part. This new "Me" would be the alternative "Me".

Finally, notwithstanding the negative aspect of modernity that we have presented in this section, one of the fundamental hallmarks of modernity is that one has freedom "to begin making oneself and the human world according to one's own plans. This principle of reflective self-determination is frequently cited as one of the fundamental hallmarks of modernity." (Lauzon, 2011, p. 73) This means that one can make oneself and the human world according to one's own imagination. What is the meaning of the terms freedom and self-determination? The way Newfoundlanders understand the meanings of these two terms would further allow us to imagine whether or not the future Newfoundland grandparent would have the above new form of social selves. To be sure the meaning of freedom, agency, self-determination, and other such terms have been defined by intellectuals, academics, intelligentsia, and the citizenry. We turn to discussion of these ideas below.

Intellectuals and Academics, Intelligentsia, and the Citizenry

(1) *Intellectuals and Academics*

In Chapter One we have discussed Gramsci's ideas in relationship to the importance of common sense and good sense knowledge and the role of organic intellectuals in producing good sense forms of knowledge in the self-image of their communities in which they function as intellectuals (Greaves, 2008). We have seen that Gramsci in his discussion of intellectuals points out that all men and [women] are intellectuals, but not all of them function in society as intellectuals. According to him, "Intellectuals educate and discipline the entire culture." In this sense, according to Antonio Gramsci (1971) intellectuals play a central role in the production and reproduction of social life, and have had a vital role in history (see the endnote, 8). We imagine that future Newfoundland and Labrador grandparents will function as organic intellectuals in their communities and bring about changes that correspond to the communities' self-images.

In this section we review on-going conversations about the social functions of a variety of intellectuals. Our particular interest lies in imagining, learning, reflecting on, and understanding the role of future Newfoundland grandparents in socializing their children and shaping current Newfoundland society and culture. We ask these questions: What function would educated people in Newfoundland and Labrador who would be grandparents thirty or forty years from now, choose to play in society? What sort of knowledge would they produce and pass on to their children? Who would benefit the most from the knowledge they produce? Who would fund their schooling and higher education? We are interested in asking these questions, because in our view answers to these questions would influence the development of their social selves and self-images, which, in turn, would be a strong input in shaping the future of Newfoundland and Labrador society socially, economically, politically, and culturally. We will later discuss the relationship between social self, self-image and human agency in shaping situations in which individuals experience relationships with others and live their daily lives.

Aronowitz and Giroux (1985) analyse the social function of educators as intellectuals by using four categories: (1) transformative intellectuals, (2) critical intellectuals, (3) accommodating intellectuals, and (4) hegemonic intellectuals. These, they claim, are ideal-typical categories. They (1985) explain that "Gramsci attempts to locate the political and social function of intellectuals through his analysis of the role of conservative and radical organic intellectuals" (p. 35). Whereas the conservative organic intellectuals prefer to be agents of the status quo, the radical organic intellectuals choose to provide the moral and intellectual leadership to a specific class, in their case the working class. But they could also perform similar functions for any other dominated group. These categories of intellectuals are not supposed to be too rigid.[5]

In light of the analysis offered by Aronowitz and Giroux (1985) we ask further questions: Would the forms of knowledge produced and disseminated by the current intellectuals in Newfoundland and Labrador, and consumed by the citizenry, and especially the young people in K-12 schooling and at institutions of higher education, provide the right conditions for the growth of NL-LGCSS? Will the future Newfoundland and Labrador grandparents function as organic intellectuals to provide the moral and intellectual leadership to a class of people who are interested in the sustainable development of rural communities and lifestyles in the context of global changes dominated by neoliberalism? "Imagine That!"

Many grandparents today in Newfoundland and Labrador have attained higher formal education as compared to their own grandparents. Similarly, it is not difficult to imagine that most would be Newfoundland and Labrador grandparents will relatively be more in tune with new technologies and new areas of academic studies and research. They will have relatively easy access to comparative and critical knowledge in all areas of human endeavours and at all levels of society: local, regional, national, and international. They will be the beneficiaries of an incessant and free flow of information in the postmodern world in which they grew up. In this sense they will be some sort of intellectuals. Therefore, it makes sense to us to ask such questions as: What sort of intellectuals would they be? What function are educated people, grandparents and not-grandparents, (as intellectual) playing in today's Newfoundland and Labrador society as its institutions and culture transform? One way to find answers to these questions is to carefully and reflectively read many reports and articles that have been written in the last four decades on reforming education, schools, economy, and social institutions in Newfoundland and Labrador. We have already discussed some of the issues related to these areas in section one and two above.

Historically, terms such as intellectuals, academics, intelligentsia, and citizenry have been defined differently in different cultures and societies. More recently there have been many formulations of the notion of intellectuals as a social category (Fuller, 2005), and their function in society by Karl Mannheim, Sartre, Henry Giroux, Edward Said, Elvin Gouldner, to name a few. Our focus is limited to the discussion of certain aspects of the function of "intellectuals", "intelligentsia", and "academics" as social categories undertaken by scholars of different ideological bent. Our interest also lies in understanding how the citizenry have to translate and learn to make sense of the ideas produced by the different social categories of intellectuals.

In response to Kellner's (2005) review of his book, Fuller says that it has been understood that "intellectuals are mainly in the business of promoting ideas. This means, among other things, that they must assume the existence of ideas. This is already a tall order in postmodern academia, which tends to regard ideas as annoying remnants of the dreaded 'metaphysics of presence'." In contrast to postmodern academia, Fuller says that "I do not deny the central role that academics continue to play in the certification, elaboration, and reproduction of the disciplinary discourses and techniques that carry the authority of "knowledge" in the wider society. However, a "knowledge worker,".... is not necessarily an intellectual".[6]

Further, in response to Kellner's review, Fuller mentions four general conditions "for the general fit for the existence of ideas." The number four condition is useful for our discussion here: that "ideas are shared in the strict sense, i.e., an idea does not spring full-blown from an original genius who then imprints it on the masses; rather an idea comes to be realized gradually as more people participate in its production." We are interested in condition number four because we believe that it is important for the public to realize that knowledge is not only produced by intellectuals, philosophers, and academics alone but also by many others in society who occupying different class positions.[7] For, according to Fuller, "even academics need to work to become intellectuals." Following this way of conversation, we believe that it is important for different groups of public in Newfoundland and Labrador to create for themselves safe spaces where they feel they have some possibility for getting involved in the production of knowledge (see Chapter one) for their own communities based on their own hope, desire, and imaginations. This way of producing knowledge, we maintain, has more potential to come up with language for people who are looking for finding the right mix of rural and modern living life styles, and sustainable rural development in Newfoundland and Labrador, and elsewhere. In this context, we view grandparents as being the major source of knowledge production in Newfoundland and Labrador society, especially at this time when rural communities are being forced to transform by government policies and the forces of globalization (see Chapter one).

(2) *Intelligentsia*

The term, 'intelligentsia' applies to a group of highly educated members of a population who undertake to lead the people. The drive for professional education in the context of the modernization process gave rise to intelligentsia. People belonging to this class became members of elite classes of intellectuals. The need for educated specialists created a new class of intelligentsia. The members of this group became available for hire as professionals: clerks, doctors, lawyers, researchers, and so on, and came to be considered as the backbone of the modern nation, and, thus, enjoyed high social status.

Some authors believe that members of the intelligentsia produce knowledge ordered and paid for by the dominant group or the ruling class in society. In this sense they are intellectuals who make their living by selling their labour and, therefore, in many cases, are exploited by the capital. For example, in the field of education and schooling many special interest groups hire specialists to produce knowledge from their perspectives in order to influence public policies related to education and schooling. Governments, institutions of higher education, funding agencies, and private foundations do the same thing. In the last four decades in Newfoundland and Labrador a number of reports have been produced advocating school and educational reform from particular perspectives. Reviews of some of these reports can be found in several recently published books (McKim, 1988; McCann, 2000; Sheppard, Brown & Dibbon, 2009; Galway & Dibbon, 2012). On the other hand, some writers use the term, 'intelligentsia' to refer to intellectuals and professionals belonging to a upper middle class, whose main task is to produce and distribute knowledge to people as public figures.

(3) *On Social Functions of Intellectuals*

In sections (1) and (2) we have alluded to the discussion of the functions of intellectuals at some length. In this section we want to highlight two particular points that Garmsci and Feuer make. Gramsci argues that "intellectuals view themselves as autonomous from the ruling class." They offer their knowledge on the market. However, his perspective is that every social class needs its own intelligentsia to shape its own ideology. Highly educated people as intellectuals must choose their social class. Some observers of intellectual life believe that every scientist or scholar is regarded as an intellectual only when she/he adheres to or seems to be searching for an ideology (Feuer, 1969, 1963). Are the educated people and intelligentsia in Newfoundland and Labrador aware of, consciously or unconsciously, for which class or social group they are working? What role do organizations and processes of learning and teaching play in the formation of certain form(s) of class consciousness among students in Newfoundland and Labrador education system? Will future Newfoundland grandparents as intellectuals be able to choose which class they should be working for? Will they be able to imagine new ways of sustaining their rural life styles while embracing modern living or vice-versa?

(4) *Ordinary Citizens, Sense Making and the Colonizing Nature of the Professional Knowledge*

How does the citizenry in Newfoundland learn to make sense of the ideas produced by academics, intellectuals, and intelligentsia? In order to answer this question we highlight and describe some additional points in relation to the work academics, intellectuals and intelligentsias carry out. As an example, let us focus on work carried out by some category of social scientists, such as by professional and career oriented social and behavioural scientists. These scientists conduct various studies. What should be kept in mind is that it is a costly and time-consuming enterprise for professional and career-oriented social and behavioural scientists who work at various institutions, occupying different positions and seemingly having multiple interests, to carry out their studies. Also, their studies are couched within the frameworks of on-going disciplinary (educational, economics, management and social sciences, etc.) discourses. Several questions related to the cost of studies should also be raised here such as: Who pays researchers to do research? What is the nature of the funding agencies? How are the findings of research written and conveyed to the audiences? Who are the primary audiences? Who provides the data? Who are the beneficiaries of the research findings? What are the purposes and goals of any given research endeavours? Under what conditions is money allocated to them? What sorts of constraints are put on researchers? How does a set of research studies fit into some scheme of larger social or organizational policy? What is this scheme and whose scheme is it?

Another related point that one needs to be aware of is that only the professionals who are well versed in conversing with each other, using the language of their disciplines, fully seem to understand the logic behind these studies. Therefore, many educated citizens, who are not members of those academic linguistic communities, find it difficult to understand the exact nature of the studies. This is where the challenge of producing local, experiential, and common sense knowledge lies, which we have discussed in Chapter one in this book.

The assumption here is that professional knowledge, produced by the experts, in particular academic disciplines, by itself, is colonizing in nature (see Chapter one), and is not sufficient for making policy decisions which have the potential to affect the lives of many citizens, their families and communities. This claim would most certainly apply to future grandparents. In addition to this, citizens living in their communities have to be aware of the official knowledge. This form of knowledge is produced by the government, schools boards, etc., and variously affects people's ways of thinking and their everyday living.

Problematic Nature of Translation of Professional Knowledge and Three Forms of Knowledge

The state is mainly engaged in enhancing the modernization process. So it is assumed here that a good policy-making process in various departments of the state, as well as in the public spheres, should take into account three forms of knowledge that we have alluded to above: local, experiential, and common sense knowledge.

In light of the above discussion, it seems necessary that people working and living in small communities in Newfoundland and Labrador need to cultivate certain sets of abilities and skills of their own to enable them to produce contextually specific translations of professional and official forms of knowledge, even though the translated knowledge may not be totally sufficient for making sense of one's local environment. To be sure, translation generates its own problems. But the point is that individuals should be able to produce local knowledge of their own by developing a new language set, allowing them to rearticulate any changing situations and the subtle nuances surrounding those situations. This new set of languages could be a more effective vehicle for expressing their concerns about what is happening in their communities and families, and schools than the professional or official languages. In our case we find examples of this new language in the voices of grandparents documented in this book.

Citizens' own experiences on the work sites in their communities could be a rich source of producing a new set of language. Through this learning process and with raised awareness, they could become organic researchers in their own right. In this newly created role of researcher, as familiar and focused participant observers of their own daily practices, they can describe their own experiences of living in their families and communities, and produce their own suitable narratives. In this way they can also overcome the problem of lack of financial support to conduct research. In order to achieve these goals, locally specific ways to meet challenges must be found. Witness the narratives of grandparents in this book. Through their narratives, diasporic and non-diasporic grandparents tell us how they take care of their grandchildren and other family members in various situations. In other settings, fishers or persons in Newfoundland and Labrador have produced their own local knowledge that is not always in agreement with knowledge produced by academic and government fishery scientists (Finlayson, 1994). Similarly, parents in various communities have their own specific narratives about how schools in this province work and should work. The knowledge produced by parents in many cases is very different from the official knowledge produced by academic and government educational researchers.

In light of the ideas presented above, imagine how present, highly educated parents, some of whom will be grandparents, would function as academics, intellectual, and intelligentsia! In our imagination we see many of them functioning as organic and transformative intellectuals, having developed a Newfoundland and Labrador local/global cosmopolitan social self. They will function as rural organic intellectuals simply because they love Newfoundland and Labrador as a place and home where they are committed to live and raise their children against all odds, barriers to free speech and communication and free from demands of the current educational system and modernization process dominated by neoliberalism. We also imagine these parents and future grandparents will support and engage in democratic principles such as, freedom, equality, justice, human rights, and social welfare policies. They will oppose anti-environmental and anti-rural policies as ushered by globalization by creating a social movement and increased political participation within the framework of a global civil society. (See, Endnote 7, in Chapter One).

In summarizing, what we have said above is well expressed by Young and Levin (2002, p. vii)

> …that knowledge is something people make for themselves, whether individually or, more often and more powerfully, in groups or social settings. Our sense of what the world is and how it is to be understood comes from the collision between each of us as a person — our ideas and experiences — and the events of our lives, many of which are beyond our control. People can and do disagree vehemently on what seems to be straightforward matters.

To that, we add that often it is hard to uncover the nature of the forces that inhibit and constrain our actions. But if we want to commit ourselves to changing those conditions, then there are certain forms of actions we need to pursue. Our colleague Clar Doyle (1993) often reminds us that transformation works alongside the hegemony, i.e. dominant viewpoint: "Transformation, which should be allowed to seep through our institutions and relationships, usually comes in small doses and usually happens over time. Transformation usually happens with gentle hands. Transformation usually happens through cultural production" (p. 130). This leads us to the discussion of the notion of agency and its relationship to the development of the "I" part of the social self.

Social-Psychological Agency

Many scholars and others have discussed the question of human agency, so for our purpose here it is not necessary to review a vast amount of writing that exists in this area. Roger Frie's (2008) book reviews the work of several scholars on the subject of human agency. George Herbert Mead developed his view of the reflexive self as socially constructed in 1934. John Fiscalini (2008, p. 158) states that "psychological agency, or one's view of it, is linked to one's implicit or explicit psychological concept of the 'I' and the 'Me'-the working theory of the nature of the self," as developed by George Herbert Mead.

Our interest in the development of the "I" part of the social self and its relation to the psychological agency originated from our desire to imagine the current and future agency of a number of individuals and groups of people such as: Newfoundland and Labrador grandparents, educators, researchers, and intellectuals. It is a desire that is based on our local, common, and good sense knowledge (see, endnotes 8 & 17 in Chapter one) and understanding of the society and culture of Newfoundland and Labrador, yet in its orientation open to consideration of professional knowledge produced by researchers from multiple perspectives on the nature of Newfoundland and Labrador society and human agency.

Therefore, in this section we selectively and briefly review the perspectives of a few contemporary academic and professional psychologists mainly included in Frie's (2008) book who borrow from the social psychology and theory of self-development as advanced many years ago by George Herbert Mead (1934, 1938, 2002); they have borrowed Mead's ideas concerning self and agency that emphasize his perspectival realism (Martin, 2008, p. 99).

Our particular focus in this section is on the contribution of these scholars in clarifying the abstract concepts of the "Me" and "I" parts of the social self as developed by George Herbert Mead and the relationship of "I" to psychological agency. We attempt to clarify the relationship between "Me" and the "I", and relationship between the "I" and agency by way of presenting statements by some of these psychologists that we hope to remember and hope that our readers may like to do the same. These statements provide us with some basic sensitizing ideas in approaching agency as a "central phenomenon that must be accounted for in any explanatory framework of human action" (Frie, p. vii).

It should be recalled that in this chpater we have endeavoured to imagine that future Newfoundland grandparents perhaps would more readily be able to develop the NL -LGCSS (Newfoundland Local Global Cosmopolitan Social Self). One of the major assumptions in this paper is that one's social self is a necessary but not a sufficient process integral to bringing about any kind of social and individual transformation. Herein we have imagined that the NL-LGSSC, especially the development of the "I" part of it, will enable future Newfoundland and Labrador grandparents to behave and act in ways that will enable them to create " in-between" spaces where they can maintain both the local and global life styles. We have alluded to this point in the First Chapter in some detail. Jenkins (2008, p. 196) states that "as people mobilize their agency, they master their difficulties, bring about 'adaptive transformation,' and even have an impact on the sociocultural context that ultimately sustains them." We now turn to the review of work of selected scholars.

Basically Frie (2008, p. 2) is interested in mapping "out a space of agency and self-experience that transcends the distinction between modernist certainty and postmodernist fragmentation." The contributors in his book "maintain that agency is not reducible to biophysical properties, or to depersonalized social and cultural forces. And in the wake of a widely held conception that equates agency with Western and gender-biased notions of individuality and autonomy, they argue that agency is not an isolated act of detached self-reflection and choice (p. 2)." Frie states that "the objective, rather, is to reconfigure agency as an emergent and developmental process that is fundamentally intersubjective and contextualized (p. 2)." His and the interest of the contributors' interest lie in promoting a version of agency that "is not based on rational self-mastery or cognitive certitude, but on the affective, embodied, and relational processing of human experiences (p. 1)." Again he states that "our contexts enable our agential capacity, yet our agency, however personal or private it may feel, can never occur outside of these contexts (p. 10)."

In relation to the self, Modell (2008, p. 45) states that it "has its origins in our body, in our relation to the other, and in our culture." Martin (2008, p. 106) in his discussion of "elaborating a neo-Meadian approach to the questions of agency" explains that for Mead (1934),

the 'Me' is socially organized set of perspectives of others that one takes. (Mead understands perspectives as orientations to situations and things that are related to possible conduct.) The I on the other hand, is the response that an individual makes to these perspectives. I am a 'Me' in that I make use of (actually or imaginatively) the words and actions of others within sequences of social interactions, but my 'I' is an emergent, creative response to the symbolized action sequences and structures of my 'Me'. Whereas the 'Me' is knowable and highly predictable, the 'I' is not an object of experience. Its trace may be detected in memory, but only as it appears ex post facto. I only can access my 'I' by remembering the responses it makes to my 'Me'. In temporal terms, the 'I' is the response to the 'Me' that occurs in an immediate, momentary, and the already passing present, with the aim of restructuring the 'Me' in the future. When the 'I' has acted, 'we can catch in our memory and place it in terms of that which we have done,' even though, within the newly emergent present, it already has passed into the restructured 'Me' ' (Mead 1934, p. 203, cited in in Jack Martin, p. 106).

Further,

the 'I' and the 'Me' coexist in a dynamic, temporal relation within which the 'I' responds unpredictably and freely to the 'Me' that arises through taking the perspectives of others and the broader society. For Mead, the self and its activity are conditioned, but not determined entirely by the social processes within which they emerge. Human agency is conditional but free (Martin, p. 106).

Moreover, unlike natural, noninteractive, natural kind, humankind are self-interpreting and self-reactive agents. For many developmental psychologists and scholars in other disciplines like Tomasello, Vygotsky, Gadmer, Heidegger, Taylor, George Herbert Mead (1934, 1938, 2002) and Ian Hacking "the goal has been to describe the emergence of an agentive form of human being-in-the-world that differs from the other forms of existence (Martin, 2008, p. 111)." Martin explains that "it does not matter to a rock or a cat if it is described as valuable or mean spirited" (p.111). However, "it matters to us if we are categorized by others as lazy, talented, ambitious, and so forth. Moreover, our reactions to such descriptions and classification are part of what constitutes us as the kinds of persons we are (p. 111)." Thus, the kind of persons we are is due to the fact that "we are constantly emergent as human agents because we are caught up in ongoing processes of self-interpretation and self-reactivity (Martin, 2008, p. 111)." As well, according to Martin, it is

...our participation in educational and other life contexts that provide us with more varied, complex, and multiperspectival tools of thought and action, we are immersed in an ever-widening horizon of sociocultural experience....This is a historical, cultural, and contemporary world populated by ideas, debates, problems, issues, and challenges that command attention, and that encourage and enable the cultivation of increasingly complex forms of understanding, acting, and being (Martin, 2008, p. 105).

Consistent with Martin's commentary here, in our discussion of education, modernization, intellectuals and psychological agency in this chapter, and in other chapters in this book, we have tried to provide readers multiperspectival tools we believe will enable future Newfoundland and Labrador grandparents to develop the Newfoundland Local Global Cosmopolitan Social Self.

To continue, Albert Jenkins' (2008) discussion of the contribution of an agency throws light on the work of social scientists and intellectuals in the twentieth century, who study the psychological situation of people of colour and multiculturalism in America. He states that "in the latter half of the twentieth century as the nation was forced to address racism more seriously...As a result the victims of individual and institutional racism in the white society were made responsible for their own plight" (p. 189) and "little attention was given to the role of white society in creating problems for ethnic minorities (p. 190)."

Further, according to Jenkins "equally as important as this tendency to blame the victims for their predicament, social scientists seemed to show an almost complete lack of understanding of the resilience and resourcefulness that people of color frequently showed in their efforts to survive and transcend oppressive conditions (p. 190)." He states that,

...while I affirm that people are in crucial ways constituted by culture, human experience and behavior also derive from the functioning of people's psychological agency, defined as the ability to conform to, add to, oppose, or disregard sociocultural and/or biological stimulation. I have particularly emphasized the human propensity to think dialectically; the capacity to imagine opposite or alternative possibilities in the presence of a given situation (p. 188).

He points to ethnic minority social scientists' critique of Western psychology, as they try to articulate new psychological frameworks for understanding ethnic and cultural diversity.

For Jenkins, psychological agency is a crucial concept for minorities. His description of psychological agency is explicitly or implicitly related to the "I" part of the social self. For critical transformation to take place, our participation in un-reading, opposing, and disregarding of those educational and other life contexts that imprint negative labels on us, is important (Martin, 2008).

When people are put in categories that impose negative labels on them, they want to resist the negative labels placed on them in the name of science. It is a global response by "local", "traditional", "marginalized", "ethnic", "indigenous", "radicalized", and "gendered" humankind to the processes of modernization, globalization, and modernity as articulated within the framework of Western social sciences, and social sciences of non-Western nations built on the theories and assumptions of Western, institutionalized social science enterprise (Singh, Hammnet, Poter & Kumar, 1984; Giddens, 1990,). In this context the others also want to self-represent themselves. They want to tell their own stories. They want to talk and want others, who have developed habits of not listening to them, to listen to them. They want to return their gaze to those who have historically gazed at them for a long period of time.

The people in large and small communities (outports) in Newfoundland and Labrador have ample taste of such treatment afforded to them by social science enterprise. We have alluded to this point in our earlier discussion of function of education, research enterprise, and production of knowledge by intellectuals and experts in Newfoundland and Labrador (Kennedy, 1977). Pat O'Flaherty (2012, p. 5) points "to the comments made in the national and international media that demean, or reflect a prejudice against, Newfoundlanders. Since its founding [in the 1990s] the Institute [The Bond Institute] has responded to, among others, Jeffery Simpson, Hugh Winsor, Margaret Wente, Joey Slinger, John Allemang, Daphne Gordon, Bill Lankhof, Norman Wester, the Calgary Herald, Globe and Mail, CBC Cross Country Check-Up (Producer), Montreal Gazett, Toronto Sun, New Stateman, Toronto Star, and EnRoute magazine."

Thus, resistance often surfaces in subtle and not so subtle ways. The rural people in Newfoundland and Labrador had resisted such negative labels in the past and are resisting it today in this way: "given discourses suggesting [rural people] are lazy and draining government coffers, and a political climate that support withdrawing support from rural communities at a time when [they are also threaten by] by environmental degradation….the very fact that they still live and work in their communities is an indicator of resistance (MacDoland, Neis & Grzetic, 2006, p. 207)."

Thus, we see the call for decolonization of social science research and methodology (see Chapter one, endnote 18) by many people globally as an important step in bringing about critical transformation. We also see it as an attempt to develop situated agency and the creation of new meanings. Roger Frie (2008, p. 1) is helpful here:

The current fascination with the biophysical and sociocultural origins of human action has lent new importance to the questions of agency. The capacity to be an agent, to act purposefully and reflectively, depends on the biological, social, and cultural contexts that inform and shape who we are. But agency is more than a mere effect of these contexts. Psychological agency also involves the capacity for imagining and creating potentially new and different ways of being and acting and, as such, cannot be explained purely in terms of its biological, social, or cultural determinants.

It is Frie's idea that psychological agency involves the capacity for imagining and creating potentially new and different ways of being and acting, and Jenkins idea that psychological agency is a crucial concept for minorities, and an attempt by many minority and other social scientists to develop situated agency and creation of new meaning outside the framework of Western social science that interest us the most. In Newfoundland and Labrador, Kelly and Yeoman (2010) document voices of a new generation of cultural workers, who imaginatively, creatively, and using their situated agency "offer their insights by way of inspiring and furthering the kind of dialogue that might lead to [desired] change through a heartfelt addressing of issues and dimensions of loss to this place we have all, at some point in our lives, called 'home'" (Kelly and Yeoman, 2010, p. 8).

Further, according to Frie (2008), a theory of situated agency "locates the origin of human action neither solely in the individual nor in the biophysical and sociocultural contexts. Rather, the potential for psychological agency and the creation of meaning is seen to exist within a web of intersecting biophysical, social, and cultural determinants in an ongoing generative and developmental process (p. 1)." And he states that "while many social-scientific approaches face the challenge of accounting for the lived experience of agency, traditional definitions of agency in terms of free will and autonomy fail to account for the very contexts that make action possible to begin with (p. 1)." Both Frie and Jenkins emphasize that human agency involves the capacity to imagine opposite or alternative possibilities in the presence of a given situation. We now turn below to the discussion of decolonizing social science research and methodology. It is one way to imagine alternative possibilities in the present production, dissemination, and consumption of knowledge dominated by neo-liberal ideology.

The Colonization of Knowledge and the Decolonization of Research Methods

In this section we present aspects of the work of Smith (2002). One of the major concerns of Smith et al. is with the decolonization of research methods. In Chapter One, we have already alluded to the prevalence of discourses on the colonization and McDonaldization of everyday life by experts and researchers of all pursuits. Smith writes "from the vantage point of the colonized, a position from which I write, and choose to privilege, the term 'research' is inextricably linked to European imperialism and colonialism. The word itself, 'research', is probably one of the dirtiest words in the indigenous world's vocabulary. When mentioned in many indigenous contexts, it stirs up silence, it conjures up bad memories, it raises a smile that is knowing and distrustful. It is so powerful that indigenous people even write poetry about research. The ways in which scientific research is implicated in the worst excesses of colonialism remains a powerful remembered history for many of the world's colonized peoples. It is a history that still offends the deepest sense of our humanity. Just knowing that someone measured our 'faculties' by filling the skull of our ancestors with millet seeds and compared the amount of millet seeds to the capacity for mental thought offends our sense of who and what we are." (Smith, 2002, p. 1)

Can we develop the "I" part of the social self in the context of the type of research perspective Smith et al. describe? How do we free those aspects of our daily lives experienced as seemingly overly determined by experts and researchers who function as intelligentsia in Newfoundland and Labrador, as well as, from those experts and researchers who are far away from here? Although Smith et al. write about the indigenous people, we believe their work is relevant to all those who are interested in the emancipation of their daily lives from knowledge produced by intelligentsia which is at times colonizing in nature (see Chapter one, endnote 23). As groups at all levels, teachers, students, social workers, cultural and community workers, health professionals, critical pedagogues, politicians, social policymakers live their everyday lives in relation to other people, so does an individual citizen. Each individual separately and as part of a group may find it useful to reflect on these questions: How could people in Newfoundland and Labrador learn and choose to function as organic intellectuals who desire to have lifestyles that are in between the local and global? Have their cake and eat it too? What direction would the transformation of Newfoundland society take if the change process is articulated from the perspective of those organic intellectuals? "Imagine That!"

Smith and her associates suggest a need for decolonizing research. Imagine if that really happens! In Newfoundland and Labrador! When organic intellectuals produce knowledge, it may be decolonized. At least there is hope. When that happens, we maintain the conditions are created in which it becomes possible to develop new forms of social selves. The "I" part of the social self emerges, we believe, when one is free to do research in a decolonized space. In this space one can investigate by imagining doing research with people in one's own communities, situational contexts, and environment by inventing novel alternative perspectives. Smith and her associates offer twenty five ways of doing this sort of research (Smith, 2002, pp.142–162). We have imagined and created Figure 1 based on our reading and understanding of Smith's and other scholars' work which we have discussed in this chapter and in chapter one. In Figure 1 below we list these twenty five ways in relation to the perspective of social self, specially the "I" part of it, as developed by George Herbert Mead in his seminal work and by others whose work we have discussed in this chapter.

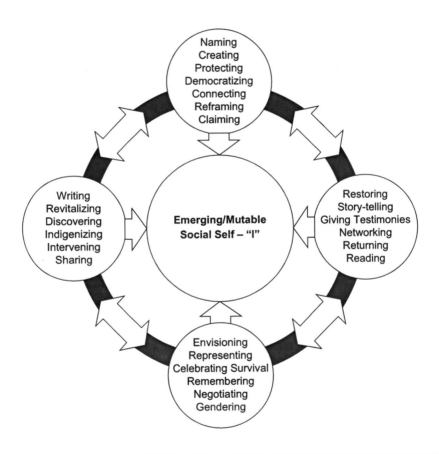

References: i Smith, Linda Tuhiwai (2002) 5th Impression. *Decolonizing methodologies: research and indigenous peoples*, New York: ZED Books LTD, Chapter 8, pp. 142–162; Louis A. Zurcher, Junior (1997). *The mutable self: a self-concept for social change*. Beverly Hill. Sage Publications; Odin, Steve (1996). *The social self in Zen and American pragmatism*. New York: State University of New York Press.

Figure 1. Decolonizing methodologies and the development of the social self "I".

Within the scope of this chapter it is not possible to discuss these twenty-five perspectives as articulated by Smith and her associates. Below we briefly describe our vision of how decolonized space makes it possible to have intimate conversations among grandparents, teachers, students, academics, intellectuals, intelligentsia, etc. so that we can create a safe space that is conducive to the development of "I" part of the collective social self.

Let us return to the question we posed above: how can cultural workers expand the development of the "I" part of the self- the creative, emergent, and imagining part? We suggest that twenty-five distinct research projects developed by Smith and her associates allow us to be creative and imaginative in providing us with a language that enables us to develop the "I" part of the social self. Imagining enables us to express the deep mystery of being a person and creativity tolerates multiple expressions affirming ourselves, our communities, and enlarge our perspectives. Smith (2002) explains,

> The projects are not claimed to be entirely indigenous or to have been created by indigenous people. Some approaches have arisen out of social science methodologics, which, in turn, have arisen out of methodological issues raised by research with various oppressed groups. Some projects invite multidisciplinary research approaches. Others have arisen more directly out of indigenous practices. (p. 142)

Further, Smith draws upon a distinction made by Sandra Harding (1987) "...between methodology and methods, that is, 'A research methodology is a theory and analysis of how research does or should proceed...' and, 'A research method is a technique for (or way of proceeding in) gathering evidence.' ...Indigenous methodologies are often a mix of existing methodological approaches and indigenous practices. The mix reflects the training of indigenous researchers which continues to be within the academy, and the parameters and common sense understanding of research which govern how indigenous communities and researchers define their activities" (p. 143).

From our critical pedagogical perspective and personal experiences and observations in the field, we believe that this "mixing of" formal training, and "the parameters and common sense understanding of research" opens the possibility for the development of safe spaces in which the "I" part of the social self can develop. Individuals and communities of interest groups need to learn the language, skills and practices required for doing this sort of mixing in their daily lives and produce nuanced local knowledge which will help all involved to make sense of their surroundings in meaningful ways. For example, it can be said that all sorts of interest groups in Newfoundland and Labrador were able to do the form of mixing of cultural values and everyday living practices to produce nuanced local knowledge that led to the decision to dismantle the denominational educational system in this province as we pointed out earlier. To be sure the debate involved the expression of multiple views on the issues involved. (see Chapter one)

For us, to voice our concerns about research and expert knowledge does not mean that we are speaking against the value of the research and work of experts in solving the problems we face in our daily lives. We are interested in encouraging people of all walks of life to produce local nuanced knowledge. Like many others, we believe it is better to combine at least three forms of knowledge to make sense of problems we face in our daily lives and their possible solutions. We name these three forms of knowledge: common sense knowledge, professional knowledge, and official or state knowledge. Production of common sense knowledge is based on individuals' perceptions of reality and experiences of daily life, professional knowledge is produced by professionally trained people in various academic disciplines, and official or state knowledge is produced by people who work for the state or government (see Chapter one, Endnote 14).

Let us focus on a few ways of decolonizing methodologies proposed by Smith (2002) such as reclaiming, remembering, negotiating, storytelling, sharing, celebrating, negotiating, etc. (See Fig. 1). For example, the contributors to this book reclaim the recorded voices of present day grandparents. They do so by recording their voices in informal, intimate, and safe spaces through conversations with them in the context of daily living in their own communities and homes. We can imagine that in this context these grandparents in Newfoundland and Labrador are engaged in developing the "I" part of their social self when they remember present and past roles in their families, and anticipate roles they will be playing in future. Similarly, they appear to be negotiating their grandparents' roles with their own children and their spouses in the context of their communities' prevailing traditional cultural values, norms, and customs. Doing this involves both the grandparents and contributors being creative, imaginative, and hopeful in dealing with their significant others (children, grandchildren, extended family, community and school officials, etc.) in achieving the most optimal, supportive, and interpersonal and intrapersonal relationship that enhances everyone's well-being (Martin and Jackson 2008).

In a similar vein, we are suggesting that networking, naming, storytelling, revisiting past and present circumstances, celebrating survival, etc. provide grandparents, communities and members of the family an opportunity to invent a new language of interaction that may enable them to expand the "I" part of their social self in specific situations and contexts in Newfoundland and Labrador. Would this type of informal, intimate, and safe space for conversation be available to future Newfoundland and Labrador grandparents? Would the technology and social media take over this form of intimate interaction? Would the intimate relations between grandparents and grandchildren living in diaspora be only possible from a distance and in an alienated form? What role does intimacy play in living the "good life"? Would most future Newfoundland and Labrador grandparents be doing grand-parenting only from a distance? Imagine that! That is the challenge organic intellectuals and researchers must face here and now in Newfoundland and Labrador. How to be, and how much to be, "local" and "global" at the same time? What is the right mix? How do persons create spaces where this mix can be found?

In this chapter we have imagined and dared to suggest how to create conditions in which a Newfoundland and Labrador Local Global Cosmopolitan Social Self may develop, and hoped that this new social self may enable all of us in this province to find that right mix. "Imagine That!"

NOTES

[1]   In this paper the word "we", "our" and "us" mostly refer to the two authors of this chapter. In other contexts these words refer to people as whole in a generalized fashion.

[2]   We have transformed the collection of poems into a book, with a cover illustrated by Christa Maher, a student from Section 4 of Education 3312, Language Arts in the Primary/Elementary Grades. The cover was selected for the book of poems, "Where I Come From. . ." by the participation of all students in the three sections of Education 3312 who participated in composing the poems. The poems from this collection are now being published in *The Morning Watch* by permission from our 'teacher authors'.

[3]   For an elaborate and critical discussion of the social self in George Herbert Mead and American philosophy, the social self and I-Me dialectic of G.H. Mead, see Steve Odin's book, *The social self in Zen and American pragmatism*, Albany: State University of New York, 1996, In this book he also discusses the social self in classical American philosophy and work of scholars such as Charles Sanders Peirce (1839–1914) in relationship to French poststructuralism, William James (1842–1910), Charles Horton Cooley (1864–1929), Josiah Royce (1855–1916), John Dewey (1859–1952), Alfred North Whitehead (1861–1948), and many others, including the work of many Japanese scholars on the social self in modern Japanese philosophy.

[4]   The assumption here is that the critical encounter with Western modernity will hopefully create moment of new flow of experiences in the process of conversations with others and one's own social self through recognizing and remembering the function of the emerging "I" part of the social self in opposing the uncritical conformity of the "Me" to the global reality as constructed, represented, and disseminated through the dominant narrative of capitalist modernity – the form of modernity that is mainly dominated at the present moment by a particular variety of North American neo-liberal economic ideology. This narrative is systematically disseminated by the nation-state through various mechanisms, because historically the nation-state has emerged as major organized social institution vested with the responsibility of accomplishing the goals of the European modern project.

[5]   Somewhere else I (Singh 2001) have written about the work of Aronowitz and Giroux (1985), who analyse the social function of educators as intellectuals by using four categories: (1) transformative intellectuals, (2) critical intellectuals, (3) accommodating intellectuals, and (4) hegemonic intellectuals. These, they claim, are ideal-typical categories. According to them, transformative intellectuals take seriously the relationship between power and knowledge. They believe that society consists of the dominant group and the dominated groups. The dominant group uses knowledge as power for dominating purposes. This domination creates an atmosphere of despair for citizens who lack the knowledge and civic courage to challenge the values and beliefs of the dominating group. The function of transformative intellectuals is to create conditions in society where new values and beliefs can be produced. This in turn will provide opportunities for students in schools and citizens in the larger society to become agents of civic courage who will not give up hope of changing the school and society. By making despair unconvincing, they will engage in activities which will make society more open, equal and just, and produce a democratic society which celebrates human dignity.

The next group is the accommodating intellectuals who firmly hold values and beliefs of the dominant society and openly act to support it and its ruling groups. In other words, they uncritically mediate ideas and practices that serve to reproduce the status quo. Some of these intellectuals disdain politics by proclaiming professionalism as a value system. In other words, they like to uphold the concept of scientific objectivity, which they believe is politically neutral.

While the critical and accommodating intellectuals self-consciously function as free-floating in their relationship to the rest of society, the last categories of intellectuals, the hegemonic intellectuals, are tied up in the preservation of the institutional structures in which they are located. They go beyond upholding the concept of scientific objectivity and prefer to function as moral crusaders. Their desire is to provide moral and intellectual leadership to various factions of dominant groups and classes, making these factions aware of their common economic, political and ethical functions.

Aronowitz and Giroux (1985) explain that "Gramsci attempts to locate the political and social function of intellectuals through his analysis of the role of conservative and radical organic intellectuals" (p. 35). Whereas the conservative organic intellectuals prefer to be agents of the status quo, the radical organic intellectuals choose to provide the moral and intellectual leadership to a specific class, in their case the working class. But they could also perform similar functions for any other dominated group. These categories of intellectuals are not supposed to be too rigid. Wright (1978) points out that many intellectuals, including educators, occupy contradictory class locations. The experience of various types of intellectuals must be analysed in terms of the objective antagonisms they face on site.

[6] Cited in *Canadian Journal of Sociology* Online September-October 2005, See Review Forum The Intellectual retrieved from http://www.cjsonline.ca/reviews/inteltual.html October 2005.

[7] Although, not from the perspective of Gramsci, there has been in Newfoundland, some conversation about the existence of social classes. See S.J.R. Noel (1971), *Politics in Newfoundland*. Toronto: University of Toronto Press. Most people shy away from the discussion of class.

REFERENCES

Ada, A.F., & Campoy, F. Isabel (2004). *Authors in the Classroom: A Transformative Education Process*. Boston, Pearson Education, Inc.

Ardelt, Monica (1977). "Wisdom and Life Satisfaction in Old Age." *Journal of Gerontology, 52B*, 15–27.

Arnove, Robert F., & Aleberto, C. (2007). *Comparative education: the dialectic of the global and the local*. New York: Roman and Littlefield.

Aronowitz,, Stanley & Giroux, Henry (1985). *Education under siege: the conservative, liberal and radical debates over schooling*. Massachusetts: Bergin and Garvey Publishers, Inc.

Barlow, M., & Robertson, H.J. (1994). *Class warfare: the assault on Canada's schools*. Toronto, ON: Key Porter.

Barnes, Stephen (2002). "The contemporary relevance of George Herbert Mead's social psychology and pedagogy," *Ohio Valley Philsophy of Education Society*, pp. 55–63.

Blumer, H. (1969). *Symbolic interactionism: perspective and method*. Englewood Cliff, N.J.: Prentice-Hall, Inc.

Buss, Helen M., & Clarke, Margaret (1999). *Memoirs from away: a Newfoundland girlhood*. Waterloo, Ontario: Wilfrid Laurier University Press.

Christiansen, L. (2000). *Reading, Writing and Rising up: Teaching about Social Justice and the Power of the Written Word*. Milwaukee, WI: Rethinking Schools.

Campaign for the Future of Higher Education (CFHE) (2003). Retrieved from http://www.cfhe.org.uk

Delisle, J.B. (2008a). "A Newfoundland Diaspora?: Moving through Ethnicity and Whiteness", *Canadian Literature, Issue, 196*, 64–81.

Delisle, J.B. (May, 2008). *The Newfoundland diaspora*. Vancouver: *A thesis submitted in partial fulfillment of the requirements for the degree of doctor of philosophy*.

Deegan, M.J., & Hill, M. (Eds.) (1987). *Women and symbolic interaction*. Winchester, MA: Allen and Unwin, Inc.

Doyle, Clar & Singh, A. (2006). *Reading and Teaching Henry Giroux*. New York: Peter Lang.

Doyle, Clar (1993). *Raising curtains on education*. Westport, CT: Bergin and Garvey.

Eisenstadt, S.N. (Winter 2000). "Multiple Modernities," *Daedalus, 129*(1), 1–29.

Feuer, Lewis (1969). *Marx and the Intellectuals: a set of post-ideological essays*. Garden City, N.Y., Anchor Books.

Feuer, Lewis (1963*). The Scientific Intellectual: the psychological and sociological origins of modern science*.

Fiscalini, John (2008). "Dimensions of Agency and the Process of Co-participant Inquiry," in Frie, Roger (Eds.) (2008), pp. 155–174. op. cit.

Fook, J. (2012). *Social work: A critical approach to practice* (2nd Edition) Thousand Oaks: California. Sage Publications.

Frie, Roger (Eds.) (2008). *Psychological Agency: Theory, Practice, and Culture*. Cambridge, Massachusetts: A Bradford Book. The MIT Press.

Fuller, Steve (2005). "Pro Machiavelli: Response to Kellner," *Canadian Journal of Sociology*, Online September-October 2005. Also see Fuller, Steve (2004). "Intellectuals: an endangered species in the 21st century?" *Economy and Society* 33: 463–83. Cited in Review Forum, The Intellectuals, *"ProMachiavelli: Response to Kellner,"* Ibid.

Gaonkar, Dalip P. (Ed.) (2001). *Alternative modernities*. Durham: Duke University Press.

Gaonkar, Dalip P. (1999). "On Alternative Modernities." *Public Cultures, 11*(1), 13, 15 and 17.

Galway, Gerald & Dibbon, David (Eds.) (2012). *Educational reform: from rhetoric to reality*. London, Ontario: The Althouse Press.

Giddens, A. (1990). *The consequences of modernity*. Cambridge: Polity Press.

Gramsci, Antonio (1971). *Selections from the prison notebooks*, (Ed. and Trans.) Q. Hoare and Smith. New York: International Press.

Graves, Donald H. (1997). "A Critical Look at the Relationship Between Reading and Writing." Whole Language Umbrella Conference, July, Bellevue, Washington.

Greaves, N.M. (2008). "Intellectuals and the Historical Construction of Knowledge and Identity: A Reappraisal of Gramsci's Ideas on Leadership". *Cultural Logic*, pp. 21–29. ISSN 1097-3087.

Griffin, David R. (1996). "Introduction to Sunny Series in Constructive Postmodern Thought," in Odin, Steve (1996), op. cit., pp. ix–xiii.

Gusfield, J. (1967). "Modernity and tradition: misplaced polarities in the study of social change", *American Journal of Sociology, 72*, 35 1–62.

Harding, Sandra (1987). *Feminism and methodology*. Bloomington: Indiana University Press.

Harvard Graduate School of Education News Letter (HGSE News), February 26, 2004. Interview with Suarez-Orozco by Carol P. Choy.

Hill, D. (2001b). "State theory and the neoliberal reconstruction of teacher education: A structuralist neo-marxist critique of postmodernists, quasi-postmodernist, and culturalist neo-marxit theory," *British Journal of Sociology of Education, 22*(1), 137–157.

Hill, D. (2002b). "The Radical Left and education policy: Education for economic and social justice." *Education and Social Justice, 4*(3), 41–51.

Hill, D. (2007). "Education Perversion and Global Neoliberalism", In Ross, Wayne E. and Gibson, Rich. (2007). (Eds.), pp. 107–144, op.cit.

Jenkins, Adelbert (2008). "Psychological Agency: A Necessary Human Concept," in Frie, Roger (Eds.) (2008), pp. 177–199.

Kash, M., & Borich, G. (1978). Teacher Behaviour and Pupil Self-Concept. Read, Mass: Addison-Wesley, 11.

Kelly, Ursula A., & Yeoman, Elizabeth (Ed.) (2010). *Despite this laoss: essays on culture, memory, and identity in Newfoundland and Labrador*. St. John's, NL: ISER (Institute of Social and Economic Studies) Books, Memorial University of Newfoundland.

Kellner, Douglas (2005). "The Intellectuals, Review Forum," *Canadian Journal of Sociology*, Online September-October 2005, review of Fuller, Steve (2005). *The intellectuals*. Icon Books. See Fuller's response to Kellner in here.

Kennedy, J.C. (August 1997). "At the Crossroads: Newfoundland and Labrador Communities in a Changing International Context." *The Canadian Review of Sociology, 34*(3), 297–317.

Lauzon, M. (2011). "Modernity". In Jerry H. Bentley (2011) (Ed.). *The Oxford Handbook of World History*. Ney York: Oxford University Press, pp. 72–88.

Levidow, L. (2002, January). "Marketing higher education: neoliberal strategies and counter-strategies," The Commner, 3. Retrieved from http:// www.commoner.org.uk/03levidow.pdf

Martin, Debbie & Jackson, Lois (2008). Young Women in Coastal Newfoundland and Labrador Talk About Their Social Relationships and Health, *Newfoundland and Labrador Studies, 23*(1).

Martin, Jack (2008). "Perspectival Selves and Agents: Agency within Sociality," In Frie, Roger (Eds.) (2008), pp. 97–116 op. cit..

Martinez, E., & Garcia, A. (2007, February 26). What is "neoliberalism?" A brief definition. In Ross, Wayne E. and Gibson, Rich (2007) (Eds.), op. cit.

Matsuda, Mari et. al. (1993). *Words that wound: Critical Race Theory, Assaultive Speech and the First Amendment.* Boulder: Westview Press.

McCann, P. (2000). "The background to the Royal Commission on Education". *The Morning Watch,* 29(3–4). St. John's, NL: Faculty of Education, Memorial University.

McChesney, R.W. (1998). Introduction. In N. Chomsky, *Profit over people: Neo-liberalism and the global order.* New York: Seven Stories Press, pp. 7–16.

MacDonald, M., Neis, B., & Grzetic, B. (2006). "Making a Living: The Struggle to Stay." In, P. Sinclair and R. Ommer (Eds.), *Power and Restructuring: Canada's Coastal Society and Environment* (187–208). St. John's: ISER., 2006 print, p. 207.

McKim, Williams A. (Ed.) (1988). *The vexed questions: denominational education in a secular age.* St. John's: Breakwater Books.

Mead, G.H. (1934). *Mind, self, and society from the perspective of a social behaviorist.* Chicago: University of Chicago Press.

Mead, G.H. (1938*). The philosophy of the act.* C.W. Morris (Ed.). Chicago: University of Chicago Press.

Mead, G.H. (2002). *The philosophy of the present.* Amherst, N.Y.: Prometheus (Original work publish 1932).

Mitchell, Barbara (2009). Family matters: An introduction to family sociology in Canada. Toronto: Canadian Scholars' Press Inc.

Modell, Arnold (2008). "The Agency of the Self and the Brain's Illusion." In Frie, Roger (Eds.) (2008). *Psychological Agency: Theory, Practice, and Culture.* Cambridge, Massachusetts: A Bradford Book. The MIT Press, pp. 33–49.

O'Flaherty, Patrick (2012). "The Humiliation of Sir Robert Bond." *The Newfoundlander*, September, 2012, Opinion, p. 5.

Odin, S. (1996). *The social self in Zen and American pragmatism.* Albany; State University of New York Press.

Orelus, Pierre (2007). *Education under occupation: the heavy price of living in a neocolonized and globalized world.* Rotterdam: Sense Publishers.

Peckford, Brian (2012). *Someday the sun will shine and have not will be no more.* St. John's: Flanker Press Limited.

Peet, Richard (2003). *Unholy Trinity: the IMF, World Bank and WTO.* New York: Zed Books.

Pennell, Gay Su (1977). "Language Functions of First Grade Students Observed in Informal Classroom Environment," cited in Donald H. Graves, "Research Update," Language Arts 54, 455.

Popkewitz, Thomas S. (Ed.) (2008). *Inventing the modern self and John Dewey: modernities and the traveling of pragmatism in education.* New York: Palgrave Macmillan, (1st. edition).

Protilio, Bradley & Malot, Curry (2008). *The destructive path of neolebralism: an international examination of education.* Rotterdam: Sense Publishers.

Quadagno, J. (2008) (2'1 Edition). *Aging and life course: an introduction to social gerontology.* Toronto: McGraw-Hill.

Rosenthal, C.J. (1983). "Aging, ethnicity and the family: beyond the modernizing theory thesis", *Canadian Ethnic Studies, XV*(3), 1–16.

Ross, Wayne E., & Gibson, Rich (Eds.) (2007). N*eoliberalism and education reform.* Cresskill, New Jersey: Hampton Press, Inc.

Royal Commission on Renewing and Strengthening our Place in Canada. *Our Place in Canada: Main Report.* St. John's: The Royal Commission, 2003. Print.

Rudolph & Rudolph (1984). *Modernity of tradition: political development in India.* Chicago: University of Chicago Press. Reprint edition.

Sheppard, B., Brown, J., & Dibbon, D. (2009). *School district leadership matters.* Dordrech, The Netherlands: Springer.

Singh, A. (2001). "Becoming a Reflective Educator by Problematizing Privileged Discourses: A Case Study. In Singh, A., Doyle, C., Rose, A,, and Ludlow, K. (Eds.) (2001). *Teacher Training: a reflective perspective.* New Delhi: Kanishka Publishers, pp.52–102.

Singh, Amarjit (2007). "Voices of the Teacher Interns: "Local/Global and Diversity and School Justice Issues and Teacher Education," *The Morning Watch,* Vol. 35, Nos. 3–4, winter, 2007.

Singh, A., Hamnett, Mike, Krishma Kumar & Doug Porter (1984). *Ethics, politics, and international social science research: from critique to praxis.* Honolulu: University of Hawaii Press.

Smith, L.T. (2002). *Decolonizing methodologies: research and indigenous peoples.* London: Zed Books Ltd.

Steger, Manfred B. (Ed.) (2010). *Globalization the greatest hits: a global studies reader.* Boulder: Paradigm Publisher.

Steger, Manfred (2003). Globalization: a very short introduction. New York: Oxford University Press.

Suarez-Orozco (February 26, 2004). Interview with Suarez-Orozco by Carol P. Choy. *Harvard Graduate School of Education News Letter* (HGSE News).

Suarez-Orozco, Marcelo (2004). *Globalization: Culture and Education in the New Millennium:* University of California Press and Ross Institute.

Van Manen, M. (1997). *Researching lived experience: Human science for an action sensitive pedagogy.* (2nd ed.) London, ON: The Althouse Press.

Wakeham, Bob. *The Telegram,* (Sunday, November 5, 2011, p. A21), St. John's, Newfoundland and Labrador.

Wilson, Rob & Dissanayake, Wimal & (Eds.) (1996). *Global/local: cultural production and the transnational imaginary.* Durham & London: Duke University Press.

Young, Jon & Levin, Benjamin (2002). (Third Edition). *Understanding Canadian Schools: an introduction to educational administration.* Scarborough, Ontario: Thomson/Nelson.

Zurcher, L.A. (1977). *The mutable self; a self-concept for social change.* Beverly Hills: Sage Publications.

APPENDIX

The themes listed below provide insight into the roles of grandparents, how they relate to grandchildren in the context of family, school and community. It is our hope that these themes will provide the reader with an ability to focus on each or several of these themes in more depth and to reflect on the meanings they may have for the grandparents in this book. As well, these reflections may shed some light on how other grandparents may be experiencing their roles and multiple tasks as grandparents within the local/global context of their lives.

[NOTE: the 40 themes listed below can be found throughout the textbook. These themes may be used for discussion purposes, in conjunction with the Reflection Questions at the end of each chapter, as a pedagogical tool to stimulate learning.]

Themes
1. Helping to care for the grandchildren
2. Spoiling the grandchildren
3. Sacrifices/challenges of grandparents
4. Grandparents with grandchildren living away
5. Joy of being grandparents
6. Talking with grandparents
7. How grandparents view their role with their grandchildren
8. Activities with grandchildren
9. Grandparents' memories of grandchildren
10. Negative opinions about being a grandparent
11. Grandparents dealing with broken families
12. Helping others/helping out around the community
13. Pride in the community
14. Chores – helping out at home
15. Grandparents talking about the past/family/hardships
16. Difference between then and now change in community rapport/relationship
17. Change in community structure
18. Change in the role of grandparents
19. Changes in the importance of religion/church
20. Changes in the 21st century
21. Changes in relationship with peers
22. Moving away for work
23. Work and the fishery
24. Work

A. Singh and M. Devine (Eds.), Rural Transformation and Newfoundland and Labrador Diaspora: Grandparents, Grandparenting, Community and School Relations, 435–436.
© *2013 Sense Publishers. All rights reserved.*

25. Grandparents and video games
26. Using technology to communicate with family
27. Negative impacts of technology
28. Religion
29. Outmigration
30. Values
31. Traditions
32. Education
33. Strong work ethics, high morals and financial sense
34. Time spent with family
35. Lost traditions
36. Heritage
37. Grandparents talking about their grandparents
38. Grandparents' past times as adults
39. Grandparents' past times as children
40. Voices of children about the contribution of their grandparents